Praise for Microsoft Office Project for Mere Mortals®

"This book stands out of the ordinary as it is the first one on Microsoft Project I know to be completely driven by Project Management methods. This makes it a powerful assistant to the mere mortals who not only want to 'know a software' but use the tool for its true purpose: to manage a project."

—*Jan De Messemaeker, Mr.Sc. El. Eng., Microsoft Project Most Valuable Professional*

"As an 'old' MS project hand, I found this book to be very useful as well as for the beginner. Jansen's step-by-step on how to enter data into Project is right on—doing it any other way is a recipe for disaster. The tips and tricks at the end of the book are worth the price as well as the insight into Project 2007."

—*Kaaren A. Walsh, PMP*

"Patti Jansen's practice sessions are a great way to become familiar with Microsoft Project and the step-by-step instructions make it easy."

—*Kimberly Amaris, PMP*

Microsoft Office Project
► for Mere
► Mortals®

Addison-Wesley presents the
For Mere Mortals® *Series*

Series Editor: Michael J. Hernandez

The goal of the *For Mere Mortals*® *Series* is to present you with information on important technology topics in an easily accessible, common-sense manner. The primary audience for *Mere Mortals* books is that of readers who have little or no background or formal training in the subject matter. Books in the Series avoid dwelling on the theoretical and instead take you right into the heart of the topic with a matter-of-fact, hands-on approach. The books are not designed to address all the intricacies of a given technology, but they do not avoid or gloss over complex, essential issues either. Instead, they focus on providing core, foundational knowledge in a way that is easy to understand and that will properly ground you in the topic. This practical approach provides you with a smooth learning curve and helps you to begin to solve your real-world problems immediately. It also prepares you for more advanced treatments of the subject matter, should you decide to pursue them, and even enables the books to serve as solid reference material for those of you with more experience. The software-independent approach taken in most books within the Series also teaches the concepts in such a way that they can be applied to whatever particular application or system you may need to use.

Titles in the Series:

Database Design for Mere Mortals®*, Second Edition:*
A Hands-On Guide to Relational Database Design
Michael J. Hernandez. ISBN: 0201752840

SQL Queries for Mere Mortals®*:*
A Hands-On Guide to Data Manipulation in SQL
Michael J. Hernandez and John L. Viescas. ISBN: 0201433362

UML for Mere Mortals®
Robert A. Maksimchuk and Eric J. Naiburg. ISBN: 0321246241

VSTO for Mere Mortals™
Kathleen McGrath and Paul Stubbs. ISBN: 0321426711

For more information, check out the series web site at
www.awprofessional.com/ForMereMortalsSeries.

Microsoft Office Project
▶ for Mere
▶ Mortals ®

Solving the Mysteries of Microsoft Office Project

Patti Jansen, PMP

✦✦Addison-Wesley

Boston ▪ San Francisco ▪ New York ▪ Toronto ▪ Montreal
London ▪ Munich ▪ Paris ▪ Madrid
Cape Town ▪ Sydney ▪ Tokyo ▪ Singapore ▪ Mexico City

The publisher offers excellent discounts on this book when ordered in quantity for bulk purchases or special sales, which may include electronic versions and/or custom covers and content particular to your business, training goals, marketing focus, and branding interests. For more information, please contact:

> U.S. Corporate and Government Sales
> (800) 382-3419
> corpsales@pearsontechgroup.com

For sales outside the United States please contact:

> International Sales
> international@pearsoned.com

This Book Is Safari Enabled

The Safari® Enabled icon on the cover of your favorite technology book means the book is available through Safari Bookshelf. When you buy this book, you get free access to the online edition for 45 days.

Safari Bookshelf is an electronic reference library that lets you easily search thousands of technical books, find code samples, download chapters, and access technical information whenever and wherever you need it.

To gain 45-day Safari Enabled access to this book:

- Go to http://www.awprofessional.com/safarienabled
- Complete the brief registration form
- Enter the coupon code QVDF-A6EE-4LD5-2BE7-F7AK

If you have difficulty registering on Safari Bookshelf or accessing the online edition, please e-mail customer-service@safaribooksonline.com.

Visit us on the Web: www.awprofessional.com

Library of Congress Cataloging-in-Publication Data:

Jansen, Patti.
  Microsoft Office Project for mere mortals : solving the mysteries of Microsoft Office Project / Patti Jansen.
     p. cm.
  ISBN 0-321-42342-9 (pbk. : alk. paper) 1. Microsoft Project. 2. Project management—Computer programs. I. Title.

  HD69.P75J36 2008
  658.4'04028553—dc22

                         2007013809

 Copyright © 2008 Pearson Education, Inc.

ISBN-13: 978-0-321-42342-9
ISBN-10: 0-321-42342-9
Text printed in the United States on recycled paper at Courier Stoughton, Inc., Stoughton, Massachusetts.
First printing, July 2007

Editor-in-Chief
Karen Gettman

Acquisitions Editor
Karen Gettman

Senior Development Editor
Chris Zahn

Development Editor
Susan Brown Zahn

Managing Editor
Gina Kanouse

Project Editor
Andy Beaster

Copy Editor
Teresa Horton

Indexer
Heather McNeill

Proofreader
Eileen Clark

Technical Reviewers
Jan De Messemaeker, MS,
   Microsoft Project MVP;
Kaaren A. Walsh, PMP;
Kimberly Amaris, PMP;
Edward W. LaHay;
Kevin McKenzie; Paula Lim

Multimedia Developer
Dan Scherf

Cover Designer
Chuti Prasertsith

Composition
Fastpages

Contents

Foreword

I own or have owned at least two books for every version of Microsoft Project Professional Standard Edition (Project) since I began my project management career. Every time I bought a book I would leaf through it looking for the handling on a particular topic. If I found something that was close to answering my question, I bought the book. I suppose that is why I own multiple copies of Project references. Each book provided an answer from its perspective. If my perspective changed, or I needed to find an answer from a different perspective, I needed a different book. The other difficulty that I've had over my career is finding a book that presented Project from a project manager's point of view. I'm a real project manager, and I realize that the tools I use help me be a good project manager. But I also realize that project management is more than just a software tool.

Since starting my project management career, I've since become a project manager instructor and consultant. I'm constantly asked by my clients to recommend a good MS Project reference book. I've never felt comfortable recommending a book until now. This is where *Microsoft Office Project for Mere Mortals* comes in. I finally have found one book that presents Microsoft Project from a conversational, no nonsense perspective. It speaks in my language of project management and provides the information that supports me in the use of the tool. I knew I had found the right book when I found it talking about project management practices that must be considered that are functions outside of the toolset. And then I opened Chapter 3 and discovered how to create a new calendar by copying an existing one! The hints and tips it provides are really time savers.

This book covers the different versions of Microsoft Project. I can now carry one reference book with me when I'm working at a client's facilities. It doesn't matter what version of Project the company is running, I have one book that provides all the information I need.

What I love about this book is that it's not limited to specific industries or professions. We project managers all follow the same types of processes so you'll find that no matter what industry you are in, this book will work for you.

Whether you're experienced at project management or not, experienced at Microsoft Project or not, you'll find a wealth of information in this book that will allow you to use Microsoft Project in a way that works best for you. Enjoy

Microsoft Office Project for Mere Mortals®, and good luck in your project management endeavors.

Claudia M. Baca, PMP

OPM3 Certified Assessor and Consultant

President, Claudia M. Baca Project Management Consulting Services and best-selling author

If you are a new user of Microsoft Office Project (referred to as Project throughout the rest of this book) or someone who may have been using it for some time but never had formal training, this book is for you. If you want to understand how to use Project practically, and learn just what you need to know to use it, this book is for you. If you want to know all the technical details and all the features and functions available in Project, this book is not for you. If you want to know why Project does what it does, this book will cover that. If you just want the facts of how to use the tool and nothing more, this book might be more than you want. But if you don't know why Project does what it does, I'm not sure just telling you what to do is enough. And if you are an individual trying to learn Project on your own for personal projects or using it for your organization's projects, this book will cover your needs.

After years of teaching Project to various individuals and organizations, I believe I can help you focus on what you need to know to use Project the way you want. I am a project manger first, and I do not want to be a master scheduler: just someone who can build schedules that are good enough to help me manage my projects. Hopefully, that's what this book helps you do as well. If you do want to become a master scheduler, this book can help you understand the basics of building and tracking a schedule so that it is useful and practical to others who would use it.

The book is not written as a reference, but more as guidance for a journey. It ties what you are doing on your project with how you build and use your schedule. When you use Project you are the path maker, not the map maker. The Project schedule is a roadmap you refer back to again and again while you follow the natural ebb and flow of the project work. You will change your path as you go, and Project should be used to help you look at your various paths so you can change course if need be.

Also, as I've been teaching, it's become clear to me that there are two kinds of very valid scheduling methods that Project supports:

- **Duration-based scheduling** is an approach in which the project manager does not manage or record the true effort it takes to complete tasks. Duration-based scheduling leaves understanding and management of the true effort in the hands of the manager ultimately responsible for the work. The project manager creates a schedule based on how long it will take to complete tasks and monitors whether the tasks are started, completed, how close to completion they are, and the overall timeline of the Project.

- **Effort-based scheduling** takes the approach that the project manager plans and records the full effort of the project, addressing the detailed hours and multiple resources it takes to get the work done. The project manager tracks not only progress towards completion but also the specific number of hours it takes to get the project work done. The project manager analyzes the information and makes mid-course corrections as needed. This form of scheduling is more rigorous and time-consuming, but it provides far richer, detailed information for future project improvements.

This book addresses both types of scheduling practices so that you can understand each and make decisions for yourself about what kind of scheduling you want to do.

Project is an amazing project scheduling tool that enables you to easily review and track the effort, dates, and dependencies of your project activities. It is flexible and designed for real project scheduling solutions. But Project can also be very complex—it has so many features and ways to look at your project schedule, you can become overwhelmed. This book is meant to demystify why the tool works as it does and help you understand how you build a practical, useable, and maintainable schedule by using best practices methodology. The book discourages you from building a project schedule as a glorified spreadsheet with tasks, start and end dates listed, and people's names next to the tasks. Continue to use a spreadsheet application if that's all you want to do. And if your bottom line is project success (which I hope it is!), this book will help you understand some of the things you can include in a schedule related to project management best practices.

The book's coverage will also include some discussion of project management principles along the way to help frame what you are doing in the schedule by what you should be doing as a project manager. Best practices and methods will rely heavily on the standards described in the *Project Management Body of Knowledge Guide* published by the Project Management Institute and my numerous years of experience in project and program management. I will include some of the project management processes you need to perform before you build or change your schedule. However, I will not go into great detail about the project management processes. If you are serious about learning more about project management or gaining some incredible tips and insight if you are an experienced project manager, I recommend you read Claudia Baca's *Project Management for Mere Mortals*. I highly recommend you read that book in conjunction with this book, and I will refer to it often in this book.

As this book is not for developers nor does it cover complex customization processes, this book will not cover the details of building and using macros, formatting the visual interface of Project (such as Gantt chart bar colors and formats), and VBA programming for Project. It will also not cover exporting and importing data from other systems and details on using the capabilities of custom fields and outline codes. Also, some more complex subjects such as using master projects and earned value will be introduced but not discussed in detail. Although both are important, most new or intermediate users should not be using those functions until they are more comfortable using Project for their scheduling solutions.

What this book does is provide context, practical examples, plenty of figures so you can see how and why scheduling features are performed, plenty of practice, and a running case study to simulate how you might use Project in a real-life situation. You will also receive plenty of sample projects on the CD to help you experiment with Project and to see results of practices and the case study exercises. This book is not only for reading about Project; it is for practicing Project.

When you are done reading and working your way through the practices in this book, you will be more proficient with Project. You should know how you want to use Project (for duration-based or effort-based scheduling) and you should know the steps you need to take in building and tracking a schedule properly. If you follow the sequence for using Project as described, you should be able to build a solid schedule consistently with the best results. You should know some of the short-cuts and the best tools to make your schedule building faster and more efficient. However, you must practice on several projects to truly become proficient.

Microsoft Project Versions and Products Covered in This Book

This book covers only the stand-alone, desktop version of Microsoft Office Project—called Standard—using the English (United States) version of the product. Users of the Enterprise Project Management Solution for Project—called Project Server—might find this book useful for understanding the basic functioning of the client scheduling engine application, called Microsoft Project Professional. However, none of the enterprise features will be covered.

Although this book uses the latest version (Microsoft Office Project Standard 2007) for illustrations and descriptions, this book provides examples that will work in any version you have from Microsoft Project 2002 through 2007, highlighting significant changes between versions. The underlying Project scheduling engine and data structure have not changed from version to version. Each version adds features, but rarely is a feature removed. The graphical icons in each version have changed slightly, but the meaning of the icons, menus and features have remained the same. So you could buy this book to understand Project 2003, and not have to buy another book if you are thinking of upgrading to Project 2007. This mixture of versions may seem disconcerting for some readers, but this book emphasizes the concepts and the most important techniques in using Project. If this is an issue for you, then this book may not be right for you. However, keep in mind that an emphasis on concepts will help you understand the important basics if you upgrade to a newer version of Project.

This book covers the following versions of Project:

- Microsoft Project Standard 2002 (and the non-enterprise features of Project Professional 2002)
- Microsoft Office Project Standard 2003 (and the non-enterprise features of Project Professional 2003)
- Microsoft Office Project Standard 2007 (and the non-enterprise features of Project Professional 2007)

One more note: Different versions of infrastructure (such as Windows), or application (such as Excel) software may cause minor different results when opening field windows or saving or exporting to different applications or file formats. This book was written using the various Project versions on Windows XP, using Windows XP style.

Prerequisites and Conventions

Although you do not need to have previous experience using Project before using the tool, you should have familiarity with Microsoft applications and experience with navigation, toolbar buttons, and the common conventions of how they work. This will help you use Project. If you are not familiar with Microsoft applications, this book might be a bit difficult to use until you have more experience. This book assumes that you know common Microsoft functions such as selecting and highlighting rows and columns, copy, paste, print, and the standard Microsoft edit and format toolbar functions. Sometimes, though, this book will describe common Microsoft functions that contribute to your knowledge of using Project. For instance, even though printing is the same in all Microsoft applications, there are some nuances of Project that make printing a well-formatted project schedule hard, so I will cover what can make it easier.

As a convention, this book will use Project rather than Microsoft Office Project Standard as the naming standard for the tool. When describing a function to be performed in Project, this book will cover some of the ways you can perform the procedure but not all. Microsoft applications provide several ways to perform the same function via menu bar selections, toolbar buttons, right-clicking, left-clicking, and shortcut keys.

How to Use this Book

This book emphasizes practicing what you have learned. After a concepts discussion in each chapter, there will be step-by-step instructions for using a feature. At the end of the chapter, I provide practices and a case study for the features described. The CD contains practice schedules (.mpp files) that are associated with each chapter. The book will identify what file you can open and use for practice or to review the case study results. The practices identify an initial project schedule you can open from the CD in a chapter directory. The answer project is also provided on the CD—sort of a "before" and "after" example of the practice. The case study doesn't provide step-by-step instructions. It provides you general instructions so you understand where in the project lifecycle you are updating the schedule, what you should do, and what values to enter into the schedule without focusing on keystrokes. The resulting schedule is provided on the CD for your review.

You may conceptually understand the instruction in this book, but until you practice using the tool, pressing the keys, and seeing for yourself how Project reacts, it just isn't as effective. So when a practice area is indicated—just practice.

The first two chapters lay the foundation for Project, providing concept discussion, and the succeeding chapters start you into the methodology of building and tracking the schedule. The last chapter provides some tips you might use as you continue to use Project. If you are a new user to Project, you probably should read all the chapters in order, but you might want to check out the last chapter early to see if there are any tips that you like. For more experienced users, you may want to read the first two chapters and the last chapter first, to see if they give you some insight to some of your issues with Project first, then read chapters 3 through 12 to understand the schedule-building methodology.

Chapter 1, "Introducing Microsoft Project," provides an overview of Project, why you should use it, and introduces the high-level schedule-building methodology. It also describes effort-based and duration-based scheduling and ends with the case study that will be used throughout the book.

Chapter 2, "Revealing the Secrets of Microsoft Project," describes overall concepts—such as important fields, formulas (calculations), and rules (settings), that Project's data structure contains. Although this chapter doesn't tell you where and how to set them all, by reviewing this chapter, you will be aware of them before you encounter them in subsequent chapters. If you are an experienced Project user, I recommend you read this chapter first. This chapter may give you some "ah-ha" moments.

Chapter 3, "Building Your Schedule: Scoping Your Project," starts you on the journey of creating a schedule. It describes the very first steps you should perform: Plan your scope, build a work breakdown structure, and build a task outline. It describes how to create, open, and save a project and how you add project information and calendars. It also describes building a project from a project template.

Chapter 4, "Understanding Task Information," dives into tasks—what information you need to know about them, and how you enter and use milestones, deadline dates, tasks calendars, and task types. In the schedule building methodology, it focuses on tasks first, before introducing and adding resources, and helps you enter the scope of your project into the schedule without being distracted by the elements of time estimates and resources.

Chapter 5, "Sequencing the Work: Creating the Critical Path," describes how you start creating the critical path of your schedule by establishing the relationships and sequencing the tasks in your schedule. You will be introduced to linking using predecessors and successors and to leads and lags which help you tighten your schedule.

Chapter 6, "Understanding Resources and their Effects on Tasks," focuses on resources and entering estimates into Project. Once you've built the schedule, you need to understand the types of resources available, how to add resources to the project team, and the effects of adding resources to tasks. The chapter also discusses the best methods for entering estimates to the schedule and finally readdresses the critical path. The chapter introduces the concept of sharing resources across projects in an organization as well.

Chapter 7, "Using Project to Enter Cost Estimates," deals with project costs—how you assign costs to resources and tasks, rates on resources, and your budget. If you or your organization do not include costs in your Project schedule, you could skip over this chapter.

Chapter 8, "Polishing your Schedule," introduces you to how you review and correct common schedule-building errors. After you have done all your planning, there are probably some mistakes or oversights in the schedule (no one's perfect!). You may have duplicate resources or poorly-named tasks. This chapter provides you with methods and checks for reviewing your project. It describes groups and filters and introduces an audit view to help you review your schedule.

Chapter 9, "Reviewing Work Overload and the Critical Path," details how you review your schedule to tighten the critical path and help reduce resource overallocation when resources are over-assigned. Wanting to find an effective way of managing resources so they are not assigned too much work is one of the most common reasons people want to use Project. This chapter describes how the tool can help you analyze overallocation situations and how you will need to adjust the schedule based on your analysis.

Chapter 10, "Baselining: the Key to Tracking Your Schedule," explains baselining—the component in Project that records your original estimates and helps you get better about estimating in the future. Baselining also helps you track your project for variance so that you can adjust the project during execution. This short chapter describes how you perform a baseline and how it contributes to your schedule-tracking process.

Chapter 11, "Tracking Your Schedule," describes the iterative process of tracking your schedule during execution of the project. You will need to gather status and actual cost data to input into the schedule to see how it affects the schedule. By monitoring the schedule, you get an idea how off or on-track your project is, and it helps you consider alternatives in order to avoid crises later in the project.

Chapter 12, "Closing Down Your Schedule — The End is Only the Beginning," although short, describes the importance of performing certain closing actions in Project when your project is finished. This essentially is the final step in the schedule building/tracking methodology and part of the lesson is for you to consider reflecting on and learning from your mistakes and successes.

Chapter 13, "Project Mysteries Resolved!" brings the focus back to the features of Project. Throughout the book some features were introduced, but not described in detail. Chapter 13 covers such things as tips and tricks of formatting, using the Project Guide, and understanding the settings in the Options dialog box that affect Project behavior. And finally, it provides the final list for the Project-building methodology and references for continued reading or help.

Acknowledgments

I would like to thank Claudia Baca for being a fabulous professional partner and a more fabulous friend. As she and I wrote our companion books, we gave each other ideas and advice, and laughed and sighed together about our predicament of trying to complete our books in lives already too complex and busy. Can we ever ask for anything more than a good friend to help us through our life's journey? I doubt it, and there can be neither a truer nor better friend as well as a more respected professional in my life than Claudia Baca.

I also want to thank my family. They saw me with my head down on many a weekend or evening as I typed, typed, typed, (and occasionally swore) away. And sometimes they didn't see me at all as I left to go to the library or another location to concentrate. The only reason I could do this book is because I have a family that supports everything I do. As I watched my family's life change and grow, I sometimes wondered why I would let a book take me away from them. But for some reason, it is just their being there that made me persevere. Thanks Bert, Lee, and Davis; you are the best.

And although I played a lot with Project on my own, I really learned most from others, both colleagues and clients. I would like to thank both colleagues and clients: Russ Young, Steve Drevon, Roy Poole, and Kevin McKenzie who shared so much with me. I also want to thank some clients who asked so many great questions that I had to get better: Pam Peet, Julianna May, and Jeanette Chang. I also want to thank my company, QuantumPM, for creating a training curriculum that made me finally understand Project and letting me use some of its lessons and put my own spin on it in a book for general consumption. Thanks Rose and Kris for all your support and understanding as I was whining about having too much work to do!

I can't thank the reviewers enough. As I re-read some my writing and their comments, I cringed at some of the incomplete thoughts and sentences, and silly mistakes I had originally made and wondered how they got through reading some of the material. Their comments highlighted and improved some poor organization and overly complex writing so I could fix it. Though criticism is hard to take, it is one of the ways we get better. When given with the sincere and kind desire to help improve, criticism is a pill I can take. My reviewers were: Jan De Messemaeker, Kaaren Walsh, Kimberly Amaris, Ed W. Lahay, Kevin McKenzie, and Paula Lim.

And I want to thank everyone at Addison-Wesley who put up with me, especially Kristin Weinberger, my Editor, who heard excuse after excuse as to why

I was late. Kristin was firm but always kind and understanding. Her patience and guidance were invaluable.

I have to thank Elizabeth Peterson for introducing me to Addison-Wesley in the first place and motivating me to create this book. Chris Zahn (Senior Development Editor) and Susan Brown Zahn (freelance Development Editor) reviewed my chapters to make sure I used the proper formatting, wording, and did everything else I was supposed to do after reading the author guidelines but which I obviously missed until they pointed it out. Not only did they provide encouragement, but they were completely professional and kind in their doling out the corrections and suggestions.

I want to thank Michael Hernandez, Series Editor, for letting me join in on the series and for creating a series called "For Mere Mortals®." It is the perfect title for a book series, and Project is a perfect addition to it, as anyone who first uses Project might think they need to live on Mount Olympus to use it.

Many thanks to Romny French (Editorial Assistant) for continued help and clarifications as she helped guide me as I finished the book, all the production folks including Andy Beaster (Project Editor), Mary Sudul (Project Coordinator), Teresa Horton (Copy Editor), Eileen Clark (Proofreader), and Heather McNeill (Indexer).

About the Author

Patti Jansen, PMP, OPM3® Certified Assessor/Consultant is a senior project manager consultant and trainer with QuantumPM with over 20 years experience in the Information Technologies industry and 12 years in project and program management. She has managed multi-million dollar, multi-system integration projects for telecommunications and Internet companies. Through QuantumPM, Patti has been consulting, assessing, and training on project management processes and practices and Project Server implementations for 5 years. Most recently she has been giving Microsoft Office Project Server 2007 webcasts to students throughout the world. She has a BA from Colorado State University, a Master's degree in Applied Communication, and a certificate in Program Management from the University of Denver.

Patti continues to write and edit as part of her professional endeavors. On staff at QuantumPM, she has written and edited numerous chapters of *Microsoft Office Project Server 2003 Unleashed* and *Special Edition Using Microsoft Office 2003*. Patti is writing and editing several chapters of the soon-to-be updated versions of those books. She has served as the technical editor for *The PMP Project Management Professional Study Guide*, *Project Management JumpStart*, and *Herding Chickens: Innovative Techniques for Project Management* published by Sybex International. She co-authored *PMP: Project Management Professional Study Guide, Deluxe Edition* by John Wiley Publishing. Her first work for Addison-Wesley is *Microsoft Office Project for Mere Mortals*®.

Other professional experiences include teaching project management classes at Colorado State University, Denver Center and making project management and Microsoft Project presentations throughout the country. Patti is currently leading an international team responsible for updating the Knowledge Foundation book as part of the overall update of the Project Management Institute's OPM3 standard (the organizational project management maturity model).

Introducing Microsoft Office Project

*I do not think much of a man who is
not wiser today than he was yesterday.*
—Abraham Lincoln

Topics Covered in This Chapter

Using Project Rather Than a Spreadsheet or Text File

Using Project Effectively

Project Management Processes Create Success

What Is Effort-Based Scheduling?

What Is Duration-Based Scheduling?

Summary

Case Study: Preparing for Virtually Nostalgia's Web Site and Catalog Launch
Event (VNLE)

So what do you need to know to use Microsoft Office Project™ (called Project throughout the rest of the book)? Perhaps you have never used it at all, used it casually, or had some training and didn't quite understand everything, especially when you got back to the office and it didn't behave exactly like you thought it was supposed to. This chapter introduces you to some general concepts before jumping straight into the tool. It provides an overview of why you want to use the scheduling features of Project rather than a spreadsheet or text file. It introduces the sequence for building and maintaining a project schedule using Project that the entire book follows. It also describes some of the main project management methods you should use in conjunction with Project or those that using just Project will not cover. The chapter suggests that you should consider including the project management methods in your schedule to recognize the activities of project management, not just the work required for your project. Finally, many people decide to use Project not realizing that it requires you select some configuration options to enter and track your project according to the scheduling style needed for your organization. This chapter thus introduces the concepts of two different scheduling styles: effort-based scheduling and duration-based scheduling.

Using Project Rather Than a Spreadsheet or Text File

Why would you want to use Project rather than a spreadsheet or a task list in text file? A spreadsheet or task list might be fine (and actually best) for very small projects, personal projects, informal projects, or projects you know and can manage easily. However, you will want to use Project if you need or want to do the following:

- Plan a schedule from beginning to end by creating task relationships to get the right tasks done in the right sequence at the right time. Very few projects, if any, have all tasks occurring all at once.
- Understand how a task's duration or work will change when you add or remove people who are working on the task or how many people you might need on a task to get it done within a set time frame.
- Create and analyze a critical path (the longest path on the schedule—if the task's dates in the critical path change, the end date of the project will change).
- Run what-if scenarios to optimize your schedule.
- Learn from past schedules so you improve creating projects in the future.

Project contains scheduling formulas that help you perform scheduling actions that a spreadsheet or text file does not. People can be frustrated by the formulas if they don't understand them, especially if they used spreadsheets or text files that behave exactly as expected. Project doesn't work as expected to the uninformed. Once you are informed, you will understand that Project's scheduling behavior is as it should be.

Using Project Effectively

You need to focus on performing the steps of building a good schedule in a certain order to be able to use Project effectively. You might have used Project a lot like I did, when I started using it without learning about its underlying scheduling engine: I would add each task and for the task I would enter the duration, add the resources who would do the work, then move to the next task and do the same. However, I learned that if I used Project as it was designed to be used, with true project scheduling techniques in mind, I would create a more effective structure, and Project would not behave like it had a mind of its own (which I believed it did for a while). The following activities of building and maintaining your project schedule illustrate the methodology you should use. The pictures associated with the activities will be used at the beginning of each chapter to illustrate the points in the process as you build and maintain your schedule.

Create and Enter the Project Scope

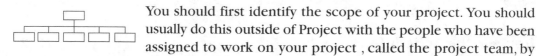 You should first identify the scope of your project. You should usually do this outside of Project with the people who have been assigned to work on your project , called the project team, by identifying the deliverables that define what you will and will not do to accomplish the project. In addition, you will build a work breakdown structure (WBS) to identify the hierarchical decomposition of activities you will perform on your project. You might have seen a WBS depicted visually as hierarchical boxes, almost like an organization chart. Your organization might already have a WBS, recommending the phases and repeatable tasks within each phase your projects should contain. For instance, in a decomposition of the higher level category or phase called Initiation, you might have tasks such as Write justification, Secure funding, Obtain approval, and Create project charter.

Define Key Task Attributes

 Indicate the attributes of each task in the schedule, such as deadlines or constraints (imposing date restrictions on the tasks) and what kind of work they represent, such as approval points or work that will be performed to accomplish an activity.

Define Task Relationships

 Indicate the task relationships effectively and realistically so you understand the sequence for performing the work in your schedule and the critical path of the schedule as a whole.

Add Resources and Estimate Their Work

Add resources and include how much time they can work on the task. In many cases, resources do not work 100% of their available time on your project. Because resources are constrained by other projects and overhead work within an organization, you should consider how much of their productive time they can work on your project. You would then add them on your project at the reduced amount of time (e.g., 50% or 25%).

Estimate the Cost of Tasks and the Project

Add rates to resources and use cost or budget resources to estimate the costs of the project. You might just track an overall budget, or you might have detailed costs per task.

Review the Schedule

Prior to finishing the initial project plan, review your schedule for any errors.

Optimize the Schedule

Fix your schedule to ensure that no resources are overallocated too much work. Attempt to create the shortest schedule possible by adjusting the critical path. The critical path is the longest path of associated tasks in your schedule, which, if any task changes end dates, will change the end date of your project.

Baseline

Baseline (set a plan of record) your schedule to help you track and report on your project and adjust to variance.

Track the Schedule

Monitor, analyze, and report progress on your schedule. Tracking is a periodic, recurring process designed to obtain and review status regularly throughout the execution of your project.

Close Down the Schedule

Close the schedule by completing all tasks and learn from your estimating mistakes.

If you use these steps to build and track your schedule, you will eventually create a network that shows you the activities, relationships, and timeline so that you can view and analyze your schedule through its completion. Figure 1.1 illustrates a very simple network you might create. You will be listing activities but also show what your project "looks like" to a project team and other stakeholders who need to understand the work of the project. Project has many views to allow you to review and analyze your schedule. Views are described in Chapter 2, "Revealing the Secrets of Microsoft Project."

Figure 1.1   *Illustration of a project schedule*

Project Management Processes Create Success

A schedule is not a project plan, and it does not ensure the success of the project. A project plan is a myriad of project documents that describe to others how you will manage your project. The start of a good project schedule is following good project management discipline and processes. Some people might expect Project to help them plan a perfect project, yet they ignore the other processes that are part of good project management. Some very talented people build a schedule, admire it, and expect the project team to use it, never talking to the project team as they build the schedule. Expecting the schedule to ensure project success or not talking to team members is a sure path to failure. The schedule only indicates what people need to do and when, but someone needs to help a team focus on the right activities and help members get their work done.

However, it can take a great deal of time for a project manager to manage a schedule in Project and manage the project's work. Some companies hire people who know a project scheduling tool well so that a project manager can focus on the processes of project management. Depending on the size of projects and the time it takes to build and track projects, your organization might wish to hire project schedulers supervised by the project manager so he or she can focus on the team, communication, and managing the work of the project. Once you learn what it takes to use Project correctly and provide you with the most value, you can decide to use Project yourself or hire someone else to build and manage schedules for you. Every project manager should understand the basics of a project scheduling tool, how to use it for analysis, and how to interpret the changes that adjustments to the schedule provide. As you think about how you will use Project to build and track a schedule, consider the following other items you will need to balance as you manage your project.

The most important functions you can perform to facilitate project success are these:

- **Defining project scope:** Understanding what you need to do and *only* what you need to do.
- **Identifying stakeholders and their needs:** Understanding who you have to make happy (or at least satisfy) on the project.

Neither of these two functions involves creating a project schedule. The work itself might be in a schedule and contribute to the activities that will be in the schedule, but without working on those two elements you might as well forget about a schedule. Understanding scope keeps you on track. For instance, if you bow to your software developers, who say you need the latest computer technology to develop your new software product, you will be managing the changes and costs the new technology will cause above and beyond the normal issues of your project. A better solution might be to develop the application first, then propose porting it to the new technology in a later project.

Understanding your stakeholders helps you meet their expectations. You need to understand the environment and politics in which you are managing your project. Although being on budget and on time are two important tenets of a successful project, there have been late and overbudget projects that have been successful because they satisfied the expectations of the stakeholders. For instance, Denver International Airport had its project problems (including a separate project for handling the baggage that initially did not meet one set of stakeholder expectations), but the airport layout (aesthetically and in terms of convenience for both passengers and pilots) was a great success, meeting the needs of two of the most important stakeholders.

Although scope definition and stakeholder analysis are two of the most important project management activities you can perform, there are other activities that will help you be successful. The following list describes these activities and how they might or might not be incorporated into how you use Project.

- **Risk management** is a technique that helps you identify the things that might go right or wrong on a project before they happen. The processes you use to perform risk management help identify risks so you can create contingencies or enhance opportunities. These contingencies or enhancements might be activities that you can put in a project schedule during the planning process.

  For example, you identify rain as a risk to your house-painting project. You will not use Project to identify your risk, but you might use it to pad your schedule with 5 more days, decide to work extra on the weekends, or decide to buy a giant tarp to protect the area of the house you are painting, which you will include as an activity and expense in the schedule. There is a large body of literature on risk management you can read, but remember that if you use this project management technique, you should figure out how to incorporate outcomes into your schedule.

- **Procurement management**, which is the process of acquiring from vendors anything your project won't be making or performing for yourselves, helps you determine what you need to do to manage vendors and what to expect of them on your project. You should include the activities you expect vendors to perform versus what you will perform, what hand-offs you expect them to make, what approval points you expect, and when payments should be made in a plan you create for managing the vendor. In your schedule you might include approval and hand-off milestones (a major event, deliverable, or achievement you want to recognize in your project), deliverables, or costs you expect to incur, and any vendor activities you need to monitor for progress. You might include vendor status meetings or an on-site walkthrough as part of your project schedule.

- **Project communications** establishes the methods and timing of project communication. Even if you present your Project schedule to stakeholders on your project, they probably won't understand the project. For instance, the project's objectives aren't described in the project schedule, nor is a description of how the team will accomplish the work included. It doesn't describe the quality expected, nor does it list the risks on the project. In fact, a project schedule might actually confuse most of your stakeholders. You will need to create a communications plan and decide what to communicate (e.g., status, budget, project course corrections, escalation), when to communicate (e.g., daily, weekly, or monthly), and how to communicate (e.g., via e-mail, face-to-face meetings, or phone calls). If the project manager does not have a plan to formally and informally communicate to the team, communication can get out of hand, and the team might start doing things based on rumors or assumptions rather than the objectives of the project.

  You might want to enter a task for creating and updating the plan, even if you don't add every detail of the communication plan or its continued activities in your project schedule. You might want to capture actual work you spend on communications and enter it into the task to understand how much time you spend on project communications.

- **Performance reporting** allows you and your stakeholders to see where your project progress stands and projections of the project finish date and costs. Project includes some of the capabilities that allow you to create reports for performance reporting. You might need to create some reports or documents using other Microsoft Office products such as Word, Visio, or Excel, so it's important to understand what you need out of a project schedule if you are required to report progress or status to management.

- **Team development and management** provides guidance about how you can help a team work together. The project manager must think through the skill sets of a team and facilitate the training, communication methods, and conflict resolution that can help a team become far more effective in completing its project activities. A project schedule might show how long an activity will take, but behind that listed activity are a lot of assumptions about the team, such as how many people will work on it, how they will work together, and the expertise of the resources on the task. The project manager must maximize the capability and motivation of the resources on the project tasks. When you build the schedule, you might be able to include team building exercises and project-relevant training. When you estimate tasks' work effort, you might need to consider the level of knowledge and dynamics of the team to help your estimate's accuracy. Once the project starts, you and your team should report on issues your project is having, which often identifies and deals with problems addressing activities you might need to modify on your schedule.

While using this book, you might want to refer to *Project Management for Mere Mortals* by Claudia Baca for a more thorough discussion concerning the project management framework for creating the Project schedule. It is not mandatory to purchase this book, but if you are not a seasoned project manager and need help in understanding the ins and outs of project management, you might find it worthwhile. The book describes project management practices centered around the following items and much more:

- Project charter, scope, work breakdown structure, and performance measurement
- Creating a project plan (which is the entire plan, not just a project schedule)
- Defining project activities and sequencing them
- Estimating tasks and resources, including costs
- Understanding and planning for quality
- Planning communication

- Managing risk
- Creating a schedule and a budget (manually, without using a tool)
- Understanding project execution and tracking
- Controlling change and closing a project

Throughout this book, I discuss these processes in a way that will help you think about what you will enter into the schedule for planning and executing your project schedule better. In some cases, that will include a description of items that will help your schedule but cannot be directly reflected in the schedule.

Besides the kinds of project management processes already listed, you also need to understand the culture and temperament of your organization, how project management is structured in your organization, and what authority you can expect to have. You might also want to use the five project management process groups described in *A Guide to the Project Management Body of Knowledge (PMBOK® Guide)* to help you structure the phases of your project. This book is generally structured based on the five processes: Building a schedule reflects some of the work you would undertake in Initiating and Planning. Tracking your project describes what you do during Executing and Monitoring and Controlling. Closing your project describes some of the activities you perform in the Closing process. When you build your project schedule consider including tasks that can help you address the following project processes:

- **Initiating:** Performing the processes and activities that authorize the project or a phase of your project. Some process activities you would perform in this project phase are to develop a project charter and preliminary project scope statement.
- **Planning:** Performing the processes and activities that help you plan the project, including developing a project plan, which is a textual document that describes how you will manage the project. Some of the numerous process activities in this group are scope planning, schedule development, cost budgeting, quality planning, human resource planning, communication planning, risk response planning, and contract planning (if you will be using vendors for your project).
- **Executing:** Performing the processes and activities to perform the work of your project. Although there are several project management

processes in this group—such as performing quality assurance, developing a project team, and selecting sellers (vendors)—this is usually where you perform the bulk of your project work. This is especially true with the activities within a project lifecycle according to your industry—such as designing, coding, or testing for a software project.

- **Monitoring and controlling:** Performing the processes and activities that help you report your project status and help you stay on track
  or get back on track if your plan goes astray. Some of the processes you might carry out are scope control, schedule control, and quality control.

- **Closing:** Performing the processes and activities that help you close down your project or a phase in the project. This might include activities such as lessons learned (also known as postmortem or post project review in some organizations) and processes such as contract closure.

Last but not least, if you are creating a schedule within a particular business application, industry, or market, or your company uses a particular methodology, you will have particular lifecycles you should follow. In the information technology field, the software development lifecycle phases might consist of Concept, Design, Program, Test, and Implement. You should build a schedule that combines the project management process group activities with the phases of your particular industry lifecycle. Often the industry lifecycle phases are accomplished during the project management Executing process group.

What Is Effort-Based Scheduling?

Now that I've introduced you to the concepts of the project management processes you should be performing during your project, you should understand a key concept about Project itself. It is designed for effort-based scheduling. Project is a dynamic tool, not a static spreadsheet that holds tasks exactly as you input them (although it might look like that initially). It is programmed to show what will change in a schedule based on the number of people you place on the task, the amount of effort (work in hours), and how long the task might take over time. Once you start tracking your schedule, it will show you how the schedule changes when you enter actual progress data. Without knowing some of the options and settings that you need to establish to plan your specific type of project and how the work is done in the project, you will almost certainly end up frustrated when your schedule does not do what you think it should. The following example introduces you to the concept of effort-based scheduling, so don't expect to follow along in Project. This book covers the actual steps to building a schedule starting in Chapter 3, "Building Your Schedule: Scoping Your Project."

You can (and should) define several things about a task to use the full capabilities of the tool. A house-painting project (which includes prep, priming, and painting) illustrates the capabilities. Project helps you think about the work a bit more precisely than you might without it. When you first enter the tasks into Project it looks like Figure 1.2 (if you use the Gantt Chart view, which is discussed later). Project also allows work to be scheduled on weekends, although by default it does not.

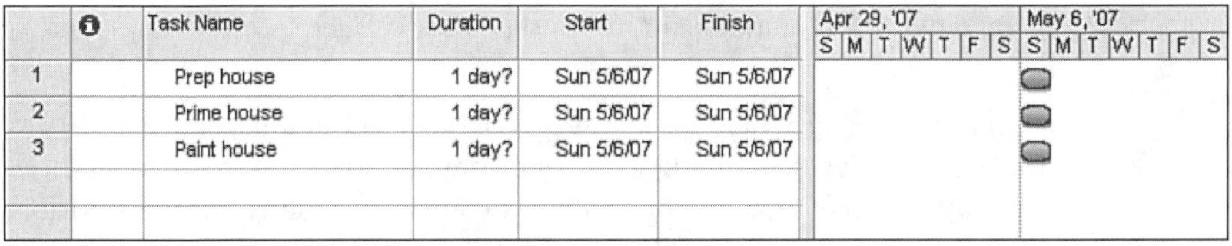

	❶	Task Name	Duration	Start	Finish	Apr 29, '07 S M T W T F S	May 6, '07 S M T W T F S
1		Prep house	1 day?	Sun 5/6/07	Sun 5/6/07		▭
2		Prime house	1 day?	Sun 5/6/07	Sun 5/6/07		▭
3		Paint house	1 day?	Sun 5/6/07	Sun 5/6/07		▭

Figure 1.2   *House-painting tasks.*

You—not the tool—have to do the thinking about each of these tasks and you have to plug in the thought processes. Of course in other projects, it might be your team members doing the thinking about the work. For instance, in prepping you need to scrape and sand off the old paint. You might need to replace some surface areas of the wood or plastic you are painting. This is a lot of hard work (the hardest part of painting a house). You could say that this will take you two weeks to complete, but you need to analyze what those two weeks consist of: Can you work 8 hours a day, 2 hours a day, or only on the weekends? Will you have help or not? Maybe some days you think you will get your child or spouse to help, but other days you won't. Maybe you just aren't motivated to do this painting. You hate this kind of job and you know it's hard for you to keep at it. Maybe you are motivated and will stay focused and get it done with lots of hard work, which you are willing to do. So it might take you a week to complete 8 hours of work, or it might take you 2 days to complete 8 hours of work based on conflicts in your schedule or your own motivation. Here are a couple of ways you might approach this:

- You can estimate the amount of work and how many people you have, then let the tool tell you how long it is going to take (which is the recommended way to use the tool). This is effort-based scheduling.
- You can how long you have to do the work (2 weeks) without respect to the number of people or work effort it will take. This is duration-based scheduling.

This section illustrates effort-based scheduling. I continue to use the house-painting schedule to show how the schedule ebbs and flows with your thought processes based on the work itself. Please note that I do not describe how to build this schedule in Project here; I do that in subsequent chapters. This section is an attempt to illustrate a concept without describing the steps you will use in the tool. In fact, the illustration violates how you should build an effort-based schedule. It goes out of process to attempt to illustrate how effort affects the tasks on your project.

So, for the prep house task, you decide it will probably take about 2 weeks, including weekends. You enter 14 days in the Duration field. Now your project looks like Figure 1.3.

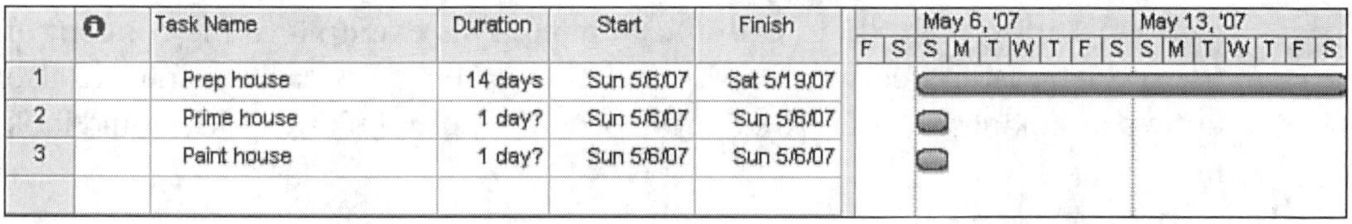

	ⓘ	Task Name	Duration	Start	Finish	May 6, '07 F S S M T W T F	May 13, '07 S S M T W T F S
1		Prep house	14 days	Sun 5/6/07	Sat 5/19/07		
2		Prime house	1 day?	Sun 5/6/07	Sun 5/6/07		
3		Paint house	1 day?	Sun 5/6/07	Sun 5/6/07		

Figure 1.3 *Duration entered on the prep house task*

You continue estimating the rest of the work. You think priming the house will take 1 week and painting the house about 1 week, which Figure 1.4 illustrates.

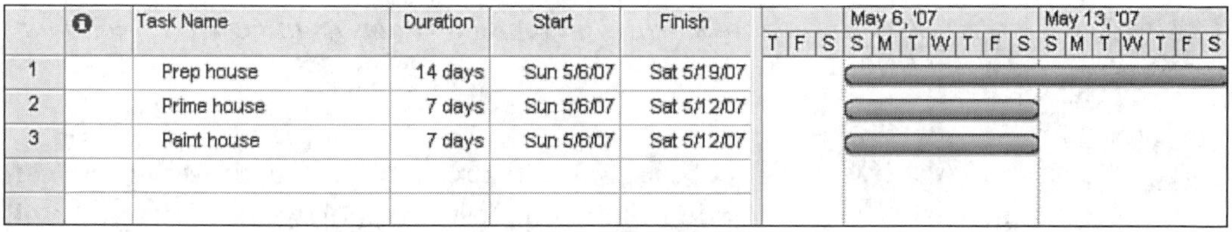

	ⓘ	Task Name	Duration	Start	Finish	May 6, '07 T F S S M T W T F	May 13, '07 S S M T W T F S
1		Prep house	14 days	Sun 5/6/07	Sat 5/19/07		
2		Prime house	7 days	Sun 5/6/07	Sat 5/12/07		
3		Paint house	7 days	Sun 5/6/07	Sat 5/12/07		

Figure 1.4 *Duration entered on prime and paint house tasks*

Next, you want to indicate when you can do the work. In this case, the work is sequential, so you can't do it at the same time. Many folks new to Project try to type a start and end date into the project to make this work. This creates constraints, and you are doing little more than creating a spreadsheet in the tool. The following Figure 1.5 illustrates this concept, which is not recommended.

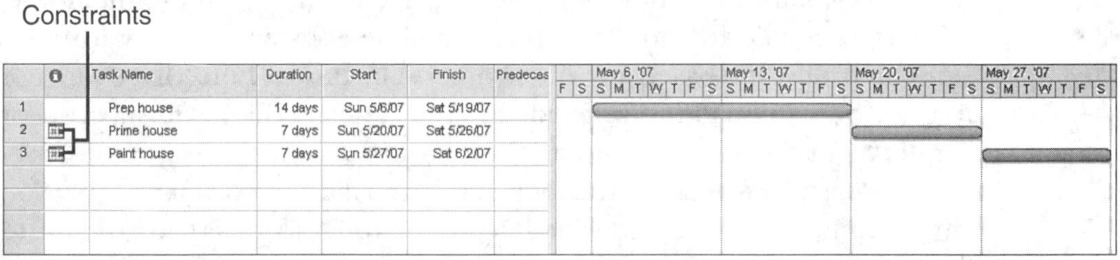

Constraints

Figure 1.5   *Constraints are not recommended to indicate start or finish dates of a task*

Instead, it is better to link tasks to show relationships between the tasks to define when you can get started on a task. In this case, you know that you can't start the priming until you are done with the prepping, and can't start on the painting until you are done with the priming. This exemplifies the concept of using relationships between tasks to define when tasks can get started, also known as linking tasks in Project. Your schedule, after linking tasks, would look like Figure 1.6.

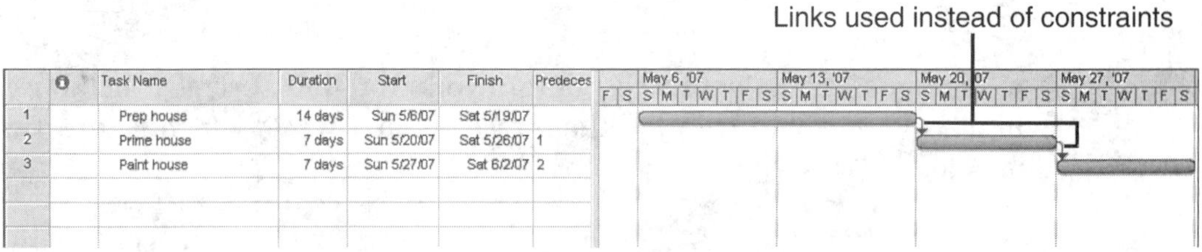

Links used instead of constraints

Figure 1.6   *Project tasks linked and starting on the same dates as in Figure 1.5 without constraints*

Figure 1.6 shows that because the tasks are now linked, the schedule can change easily based on the number of resources or work effort you will have for the tasks. It shows the same end date of June 2 in the Finish column for the Paint house task but instead of saying it is constrained by a specific date you typed in, it is actually constrained by the end date of the task that precedes it.

So let's see what happens as you start thinking more about the work itself for each task. For prepping the house, you start breaking down why you think it will take 2 weeks: You don't have full days from Monday through Friday because you have a full-time job and your family won't be available all the time either. You will only be able to work between 5 p.m. and 9 p.m. each day. You also want to limit your time on weekends. You are now thinking more about the work effort rather than the duration when you think about people's time and skills available for the work. You decide the prep job will take about 55 hours. You enter the work estimate into the schedule (notice a Work column has been added to the view; I'll discuss more about that later) as shown in Figure 1.7.

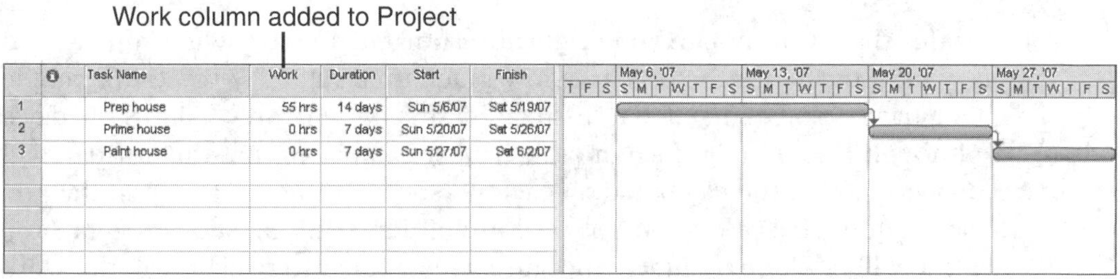

Work column added to Project

	ⓘ	Task Name	Work	Duration	Start	Finish	May 6, '07	May 13, '07	May 20, '07	May 27, '07
1		Prep house	55 hrs	14 days	Sun 5/6/07	Sat 5/19/07				
2		Prime house	0 hrs	7 days	Sun 5/20/07	Sat 5/26/07				
3		Paint house	0 hrs	7 days	Sun 5/27/07	Sat 6/2/07				

Figure 1.7   *Work (or effort) added to Prep house task*

Now, you are ready to add yourself and your family as resources into the picture. Although you allow a full 8 hours a day of work in a project calendar, you know that you will have limited time to work. So you estimate that you will be able to work 50% of the time each day (about 4 hours each day), your spouse about 10% each day, and your child about 25% each day. This isn't a precise estimate, but it's close enough. You will get a clear view of progress when you record the time as you actually perform the work. Enter the expected amount of time (see the Units field in Figure 1.8) you think each resource can work. Project then estimates the time each resource will work and adjusts the duration based on your input. Figure 1.8 shows, in a split window view, how each of these resources is added for the Prep house task.

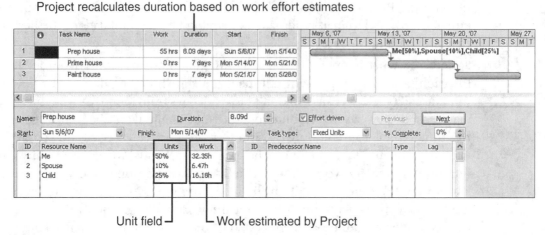

Project recalculates duration based on work effort estimates

Unit field — └ Work estimated by Project

Figure 1.8 *Units field indicates amount of time each resource is available to work on the task*

Notice that even though you originally estimated 14 days when you entered a work estimate for the task and how much time each day you think people will have, Project itself has estimated that it will only take 8.09 days. Although the .09 might seem odd, Project calculates that the last day will only take .09 of the day based on each person's effort on that day. In the previous figures, based on your original use of duration, you showed your project would be done by June 2. Because you decided to really break the work down by effort and how much each resource has to work each day, you have a more accurate schedule. If you think it is unrealistic for you to work 50% (4 hours a day), when you think about it a bit more, you could change your estimated availability to 25% rather than 50% and the duration of the task would expand. You won't do that right now but hopefully you understand why you might want Project to calculate the duration. Project uses specific pieces of information to give you a more precise estimate.

To keep this example simple, you won't complete the rest of the schedule with resources and work estimates. So let's assume you have started the Prep house work. You are now tracking actual work progress to see what your estimate will be for completing the entire project based on the current information.

Each day you have your family members report how much time they have worked and you enter the time. You and your family report your time as shown in Figure 1.9. The Resource Usage view allows you to enter actual work per day into the schedule and is discussed in more detail in Chapter 2.

	❶	Resource Name	Remaining Work	Actual Work	Details	May 6, '07							May 13, '07			
						S	M	T	W	T	F	S	S	M	T	W
1		⊟ Me	0 hrs	37 hrs	Act. W	5h	2h	3h	4h	3h	3h	6h	5h	2h	4h	
	🏃	Prep house	*0 hrs*	*37 hrs*	Act. W	5h	2h	3h	4h	3h	3h	6h	5h	2h	4h	
2		⊟ Spouse	0 hrs	9 hrs	Act. W	3h	0h	0h	0h	2h	2h	2h				
	🏃	Prep house	*0 hrs*	*9 hrs*	Act. W	3h	0h	0h	0h	2h	2h	2h				
3		⊟ Child	0 hrs	17 hrs	Act. W	3h	1h	0h	0h	2h	0h	3h	1h	3h	4h	
	🏃	Prep house	*0 hrs*	*17 hrs*	Act. W	3h	1h	0h	0h	2h	0h	3h	1h	3h	4h	
					Act. W											
					Act. W											
					Act. W											

Figure 1.9 *Entering actual work in a project schedule*

When you finish the Prep house task, it took more time to complete (63 hours) and it took 10 days rather than the original 8.09 expected as shown in Figure 1.10; not bad, only a little behind. Based on the actual work collected for this task, it looks like you need to nag your spouse to help out a bit more, and maybe get your child to put in a bit more work now and then. Now the end date of the project is 5/29, only 1 day late.

	❶	Task Name	Actual Work	Actual Duration	Duration	Start	Finish				
1	✓	Prep house	63 hrs	10 days	10 days	Sun 5/6/07	Tue 5/15/07	Me[75%],Spouse[38%],Child[50%]			
2		Prime house	0 hrs	0 days	7 days	Wed 5/16/07	Tue 5/22/07				
3		Paint house	0 hrs	0 days	7 days	Wed 5/23/07	Tue 5/29/07				

Figure 1.10 *Based on actual effort entered into Project, project completing 5/29 rather than 5/28*

This is the idea of effort-based scheduling and tracking. Rather than pasting in start and end dates, which are artificially created by the scheduler, you enter tasks, their relationships, and estimates based on how much people can really work on tasks. You let Project calculate the schedule, and as work actually occurs (which very rarely is as planned), let Project show you the changes that will occur to other tasks that rely on your task being completed. Just try and show this kind of ebb and flow of how work is planned and executed in a spreadsheet!

There are far more complexities to how work gets done than this simple example can show. For instance, you can start some tasks while you are in the middle of another. After you have prepped one side of the house, your spouse could start priming that side, while you and your child continue prepping the other three sides of the house. You also might have to wait between tasks sometimes. For instance, you might have to wait two weeks before the hue of paint you want arrives in stores, because you selected one of the latest and trendiest hues on the market. Maybe your child signed up for a trip to Europe you didn't know about and he or she will be gone throughout the time you are painting your house. All of these various nuances of the work itself can be reflected in Project to show how a project's timeline can change your schedule.

After looking at this example, you might say to yourself, "Well, I didn't want Project to calculate the duration and I don't know how much time I will really be working on the tasks. I just know it takes me about a week and that's all I ever need to know." If so, you might actually want to perform duration-based scheduling. This will still allow you to build what-if scenarios and see changes to the schedule if you enter actual progress using duration-based scheduling. However, it is not as accurate as effort-based scheduling, and you rarely learn exactly what it takes to complete an activity for a project. In other words, it's harder to get better because you are not estimating or tracking using a more discrete estimating method about tasks. Duration-based scheduling tends to hide all the elements of what it takes to get work done: You don't see how many units of a person's time is available (usually), and you don't know how much work a person really put into the task.

What Is Duration-Based Scheduling?

You might choose not to use effort-based scheduling. Some organizations simply do not need to estimate or track the hours spent on a task. You might not need to indicate how many units (or people) it takes to get the task completed. Whether it took 40 hours or 4 hours, you just care that it takes 2 weeks. Duration-based scheduling identifies one person responsible for the task or tasks and an estimate of the length of time (usually in days) it will take to accomplish the work, rather than understanding and capturing the effort it takes to get the work done. You might get an estimate from a vendor or a team lead of 3 weeks, and that's all you get. The vendor or team lead might have assigned 10 people full time to the work, or perhaps 1 person half time. You probably understand to some extent the effort the task requires, so you can judge if the duration is realistic, but it's the vendor or team lead's responsibility to get the task done in the time frame provided. For instance, you know that patching a stretch of road takes 2 days, whereas completely resurfacing it would take a week, but you leave it to the contractor responsible for the task to provide you with the estimate, and the contractor manages the effort and number of people on the task. On your project, you do not need to track effort, just whether or not the task is progressing as expected. There are important concepts you need to understand about Project to help make sure you do not accidentally change this kind of scheduling method if you add more people to the task. These concepts are not readily apparent in the tool. Chapter 4 "Understanding Task Information" covers this in detail, but for now, understand that although duration-based scheduling does not use the full power of Project, it does allow you to create and alter task dependencies, understand the critical path, and track progress. To understand this form of scheduling, let's go through the same house-painting scenario. Figure 1.11 shows the same schedule. In this case, you have decided to estimate that it will take the entire family 2 weeks to prep, 1 week to prime, and 1 week to paint the house. You are making certain calculations in your head, and the time frames are goals you have. This is all you need to enter in the schedule.

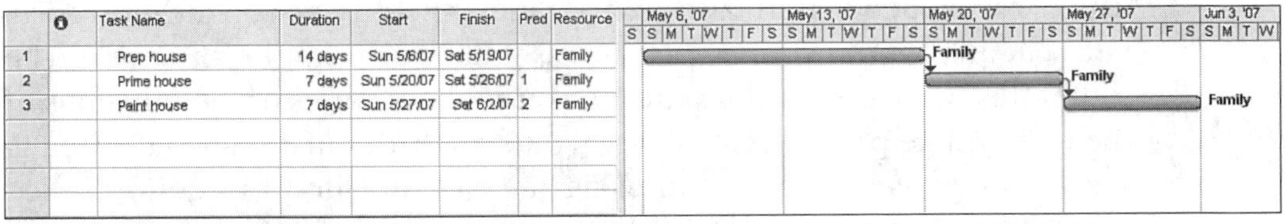
Task Name
Duration
Start
Finish
Pred
Resource
May 6, '07
May 13, '07
May 20, '07
May 27, '07
Jun 3, '07
1 Prep house 14 days Sun 5/6/07 Sat 5/19/07 Family
2 Prime house 7 days Sun 5/20/07 Sat 5/26/07 1 Family
3 Paint house 7 days Sun 5/27/07 Sat 6/2/07 2 Family
Family
Family
Family

Figure 1.11 *Duration-based scheduling showing one entity as responsible for the task*

You then track the schedule a different way. By the end of the first week of the prep work, you might make an overall assessment of how much you have completed (you could have done something similar for our first, effort-based example as well). You look at the prep work and decide your house is about 40% complete. You enter 40 in the % Complete column for the task as shown in Figure 1.12.

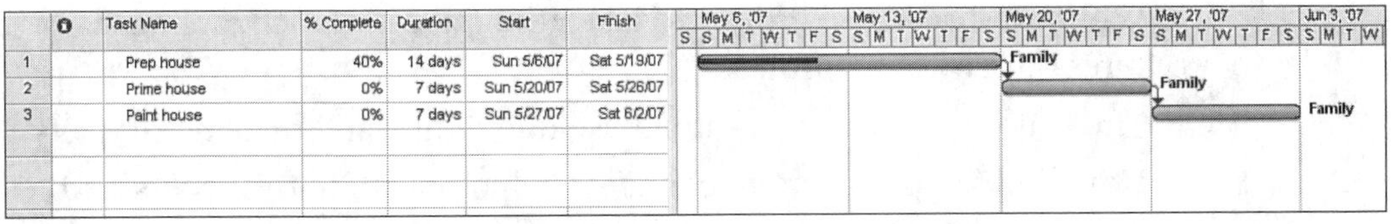
Task Name
% Complete
Duration
Start
Finish
May 6, '07
May 13, '07
May 20, '07
May 27, '07
Jun 3, '07
1 Prep house 40% 14 days Sun 5/6/07 Sat 5/19/07
2 Prime house 0% 7 days Sun 5/20/07 Sat 5/26/07
3 Paint house 0% 7 days Sun 5/27/07 Sat 6/2/07
Family
Family
Family

Figure 1.12 *Entering % Complete value for a duration-based schedule*

When you take a look at Figure 1.12, you can see you are a bit behind, as you expected to be 50% complete by now. This gives you a good indication of how you are doing, but you did not enter the actual hours of effort to perform the work, or the remaining hours you still have to complete the task. You might have worked 10 hours, or you might have worked 70 hours. You also do not see how much each family member actually worked on the task. Project still calculates hours in the background, and in fact, Project estimated the task would take 112 hours (14 days × the 8 hours total available each day). Because you entered only one resource, Project estimates the work for one resource at 8 hours a day. If you are using duration-based scheduling you should ignore the hours spent on the task.

After reviewing these concepts, you might wonder what kind of scheduling you want to do, effort-based or duration-based. There is no perfect answer and you might consider one more thought when deciding: How do you want to track progress? It takes a lot of effort to capture actual hours day-by-day and moderate effort to collect hours per week (or other time increments). You might just prefer to capture percent complete, or actual start and finish dates. I recommend effort-based scheduling, as it will give you the most accurate schedule, but in your particular case that might not be an option. The rest of this book, besides introducing you to the features of the functions of the tool, will help you decide. You might start with duration-based scheduling, and then as you mature in using the tool, decide to use effort-based scheduling. Or you might decide to jump right into effort-based scheduling. You are the best person to judge the nature of your project, your needs or the needs of your organization, and how comfortable you feel with the two types of scheduling.

Summary

This chapter introduced you to the following overarching topics of this book:

- Why you should use Project to take advantage of its scheduling features built into the product.
- The major sequence you should use in building and tracking projects.
- How project management concepts help contribute to success, and how you should build them into your schedule.
- The difference between effort-based and duration-based scheduling.

These topics are revisited in the rest of the book so you will understand how to use Project to build and maintain a Project schedule without having to know everything there is to know about Project. In the next chapter, I describe the Project data structure, formulas, interface, and views to ground you in the basics of Project before you jump into building a schedule.

Case Study: Preparing for Virtually Nostalgia's Web Site and Catalog Launch Event

A practice case study will help you understand various schedule building techniques and practice them. The case study appears at the end of each chapter, and addresses most of the instructions from the chapter to put them to use in the case study. The case study will be the same in each chapter, but you will build or adjust the schedule according to the new information you have learned. In real life, you understand your project more as you obtain more information from the project stakeholders. When you build your schedule, you will continue to update it as you can apply your new knowledge to your schedule. This iterative approach to schedule building is realistic, and the building of the schedule for the case study uses this iterative approach. You will simulate how you build, execute, and monitor the schedule through the lifecycle of your project.

Here's the scenario for the case study. Chris Williams has been charged with a new project: an event celebrating the launch of the Web site and catalog for Virtually Nostalgia, a company that sells products that hearken to the days of your or your parents' childhood. Chris started with the organization about six months ago, when the company started up as a subsidiary of a larger organization that wanted to exploit the retail nostalgia market. Virtually Nostalgia has built up its inventory of vendor products, and plans to publish its catalog and launch its Web site in about nine months.

Chris has successfully managed various small projects for the organization, and this is an excellent opportunity for her to demonstrate her capabilities to everyone in the organization. The event will introduce the new Web site and catalog to the world at an annual vendor event in Las Vegas. Not only will Virtually Nostalgia be introducing its Web site and catalog to potential customers, but it will also be presenting these materials to companies that might align with it and advertise its wares. The company also hopes to entice several industry analysts to review and promote its products. Several executives and key personnel from Virtually Nostalgia will use this event to promote the company and celebrate the launch.

Chris will work with many parts of the organization to plan and execute this launch event. She will create a project plan that accounts for the full scope of the project, budget, quality, procurement of vendor services (e.g., catering), project team development, and communication, and then execute and monitor the project based on the plan and schedule. In Chapter 3, you will see how Chris starts building the schedule based on understanding the expectations of those in the organization who are sponsoring the project and the scope of the activities that must be performed to successfully complete the project. She will apply the initial lessons from Chapter 3 to start the schedule.

Review Questions

1. Why would you want to use Project rather than a spreadsheet or text file to manage your project's schedule?
2. What is the overall methodology you should use for creating and maintaining a schedule in Project?
3. What are the most important functions that facilitate project success?
4. How is risk management incorporated into the project schedule?
5. What are the five project processes that contain tasks you should consider incorporating in your project schedule?
6. What is effort-based scheduling?
7. What is duration-based scheduling?

Revealing the Secrets of Microsoft Project

To know that one has a secret is to know half the secret itself.
—Henry Ward Beecher

Topics Covered in This Chapter

Recognizing the Underlying Rules of Project

Understanding the Project Data Structure

Using Primary Project Data Fields

Project Behavior and Definitions

Navigating Project and Some Quick Tips

The Major Project Views

What Are Project Tables?

Practice: Navigating and Using Project Views

Summary

This chapter reveals most of the secrets of Project. If you have tried using the tool and do not know its secrets, you might think it has a mind of its own. Perhaps you have been frustrated when it changes the duration when you added a resource on a task. You might have entered work hours on a task, then find that Project changed the number of units (the percentage of the resource's assignment) a person is working on a task. This chapter describes the secrets up front, which many books on Project neglect to do. If you learn about the secrets immediately, you might be more likely to accept the methodology suggested in this book, or at least know that when you added the resource to the task why it changes the duration.

To help reveal the secrets, I first describe the Project data structure, the most important fields in the data structure, some of the rules and formulas that exist in the data structure that affect how the schedule behaves, some tips for using the tool efficiently, and some of the views you can use to see the data in ways that allow you to understand Project's behaviors. The beginning of the chapter is designed to introduce concepts, and is not meant as a guide to get around in Project. I then introduce simple navigation concepts. The chapter ends with practices to give you a feel for using the features and interfaces, called views, that expose the Project data structure and allow you to look at the data in various ways. You will not have a case study, as this is more about the features in the tool than the methodology of building a schedule.

Recognizing the Underlying Rules of Project

As discussed in Chapter 1 "Introducing Microsoft Office Project" many people start using Project and expect it to act as a spreadsheet. They enter information on a task—such as a date in the Start field—which puts a constraint of "Start No Earlier Than" on the task as shown in Figure 2.1. The figure shows how a constraint is added as soon as a user typed in a date in the Start field (of 1/8/07). I define constraints in Chapter 4, "Understanding Task Information," but for now, understand that just by typing in the date, the user caused a behavior in Project that many people don't even notice until later when the schedule starts behaving in a way they don't expect. Just by entering a start date, Project assumes that you now want to make sure that this particular task cannot start prior to the date you filled in, even if you later find out you could start it earlier.

Project icon indicating that a constraint has been added to the task

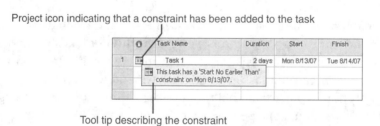

Tool tip describing the constraint

Figure 2.1   *Constraint set by Project when you enter a date in the Start field*

This behavior is part of the Microsoft Project scheduling engine, a very sophisticated set of rules about the way a schedule should behave, based on fundamental project management scheduling techniques. That's why the tool is complex: The rules are not apparent. Project is an application that someone has programmed, and if you don't understand some of the underlying programming, you might be dismayed by the tool's behavior. I tell students that no matter what they think, Project is behaving according to very logical and proper scheduling behavior even if it might not be what they want it to do. In using this tool, you need to understand its rules to either change some of the defaults that create the rules you don't want the tool to follow or to use the default rules to create a schedule as designed.

Understanding the Project Data Structure

Microsoft Project is an application with a specific data structure that has been designed with certain assumptions. What you see when you first open a project is the interface to help you input data into the Project data structure. In Figure 2.2 the interface you see is the Gantt Chart view. Notice the vertical strip on the far left side of the screen displaying Gantt Chart.

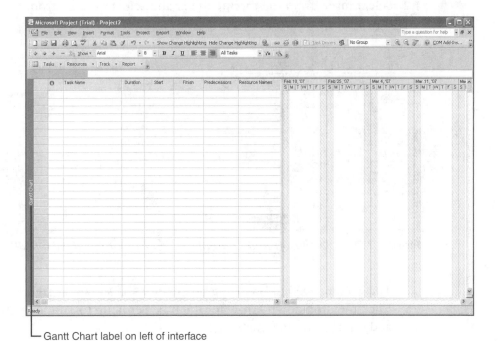

└ Gantt Chart label on left of interface

Figure 2.2 *Gantt Chart view*

The Gantt Chart view expects you to enter a task name, and if you do not enter anything specifically in the Duration, Start, and Finish fields of the row, Project will enter a duration of 1 day and the current date in the Start and

Finish date fields. Once you enter anything into a row (even a blank into the task name) in the view, you have created a row of data in the Project data structure for the task.

To understand that the row in the view contains more data than can be seen, you can expose more fields for the row than what is showing in the default Gantt Chart view. In Project, you will find the terms *column* and *field* used interchangeably. When you are inserting a column into any view, you are exposing a field from the Project data structure in the view you are displaying. For instance, to expose the % Complete field, you would perform the following steps:

1. Highlight a column (in this case, the Duration column). The column inserted will show up to the left of the column that you highlight.

2. Select Insert from the top menu bar and select Column from the drop-down list as shown in Figure 2.3.

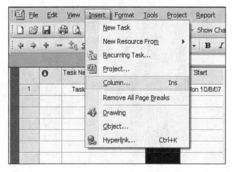

Figure 2.3 *Select Insert and Column to expose a data field for a task*

3. The Column Definition dialog box displays as shown in Figure 2.4. Click the drop-down arrow for the box. Scroll up to find % Complete and select it by clicking it.

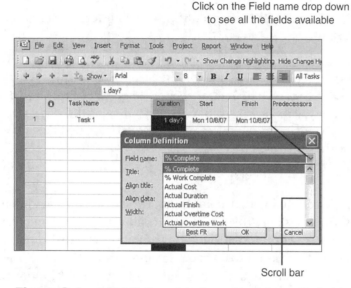

Figure 2.4   *Select % Complete from the Column Definition dialog box*

4. Press OK, and the % Complete column will display to the left of the Duration column as shown in Figure 2.5.

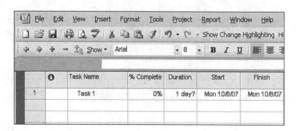

Figure 2.5   *% Complete field now exposed in Gantt Chart view.*

You can select a field by typing the first character or characters of its name

You can easily find a field in the Column Definition dialog box drop-down list by entering the first letter or character of its name. For instance, if you wanted to find the Work field quickly in the drop-down list, you can type "w" to take you to the beginning of all fields starting with "w." If you type "wo," Project will take you to the first field that begins with "wo," which is "Work."

You could insert column after column until you saw every field that is available to describe a task in Project. Figure 2.6 shows the % Complete, WBS, Priority, Actual Work, Work, Actual Duration, Actual Start, Actual Finish, Cost, and Actual Cost fields exposed for three tasks in the Gantt Chart. So when you are working with a task row, think about all of these fields, and many, many more actually existing in the task's data structure, and that they could possibly have data in them even if you don't see them in the view.

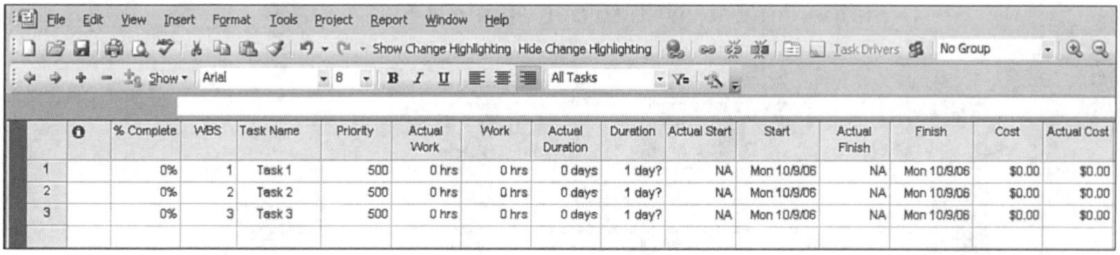

Figure 2.6   *Several fields exposed from the data structure in the Gantt Chart*

Notice that each task has been given a number on the far left side and there is data in the fields for each task. All the exposed fields have been populated with calculated or default data. There are hundreds of fields that are available to describe a task in Project. Some are fields just like you see in Figure 2.6, with defaults, formulas, or calculations. See "Using Primary Project Data Fields" later in this chapter to learn more about formulas or calculations in some of the most important fields of Project. Other fields are empty and you can customize how you will use them. In Figure 2.7, the field called Text1 in the Gantt Chart view allows you to enter any kind of text you would like to enter to describe the task.

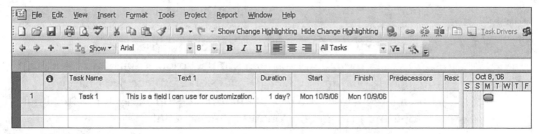

Figure 2.7   *Text1 field (column) added to view for customized data.*

As a general rule, don't copy rows into other schedules

As a general rule, unless you know exactly what you are doing, it is a not a good idea to copy a row or rows from one project schedule to another. Now that you know Project has more than 100 fields for each task, consider that you might unknowingly be copying data from one schedule to another. As an example, if you enter 50% Complete on a task, a value is entered into the Actual Duration field. If another user copies your task row with a series of other tasks that she wants to duplicate in her schedule, she has just copied the Actual Duration into her schedule.

If you want to remove the column (also known as hiding the column) you entered into a view, you can simply highlight the entire column by selecting the column header, and press Del on the keyboard. You aren't really deleting the field from the data structure—you are merely hiding the column from the view. If you highlight a column and right-click it, you will see a drop-down list as well and see (among others) two options that allow you to Insert column or Delete column.

Tasks, Resources, and Assignments in the Project Data Structure

There is another concept to understand about the Project data structure. The data, in general, is structured according to these categories: tasks, resources, and assignments.

- Tasks are the activities in the schedule. You must have tasks to build a schedule. See Chapter 3 "Building Your Schedule: Scoping Your Project" for more about creating and managing tasks in the schedule.

- Resources are the people, equipment, or materials available to you to perform the work on your project. Project 2007 has introduced two new kinds of resources to help you calculate costs: cost and budget resources. Although not resources in the strictest sense, they will help you include cost and budget estimates on a project. See Chapter 6 "Understanding Resources and Their Effects on Tasks" for more about creating and managing resources in the schedule.

- Assignments are specific resources assigned to specific tasks. See Chapter 6 for more about creating and managing assignments in the schedule.

Some of Project's most important views are designed based on the idea that each of these categories has particular kinds of data that are typically associated with it. For instance, tasks can have a duration but resources can't. You cannot add the Duration field in a view that is designed to describe resource information. An assignment is a resource or resources added on a task so assignment views will contain data about the resource's work on the task. Project also has settings that affect how each of these categories will behave. The following example illustrates how each category is associated with views in Project.

The Gantt Chart view is designed as an interface into the task data structure of the Project for you to enter information about the task. In Figure 2.8 you see a row for a task (Task 1) in the Gantt Chart view. If you hover over the Information icon (it looks like a file folder), a tool tip called Task Information appears.

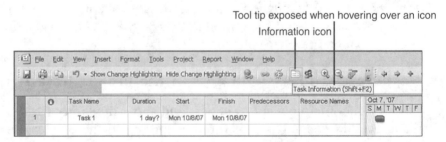

Figure 2.8   *Icon selected showing Task Information*

When you click on the icon, the Task Information dialog box displays, as shown in Figure 2.9. You can enter or review more information about a task than what is available in the Gantt Chart view. However, there are many more fields in the data structure relating to tasks. You could also insert any of the fields showing in the Task Information dialog box in the Gantt Chart view.

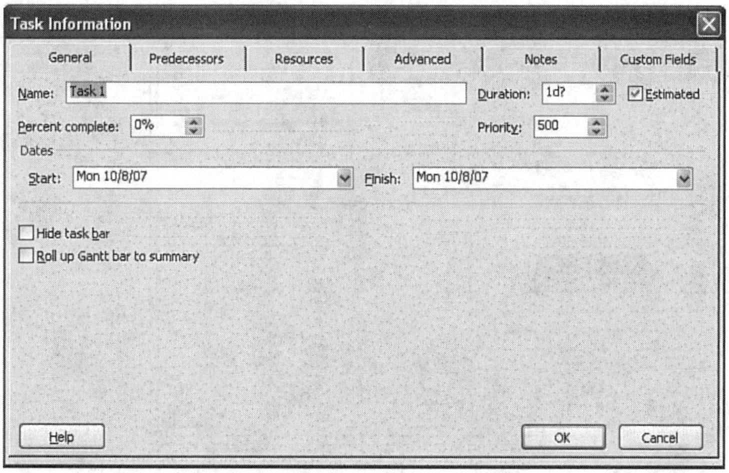

Figure 2.9   *Task Information dialog box*

The main view for entering information about resources is called the Resource Sheet. This view's main function is to describe the major attribute of the resources on your project. Notice that the exact same Information icon shown in Figure 2.9 is shown in this resource view. However, if you hover over the same icon, the tool tip displays Resource Information as shown in Figure 2.10.

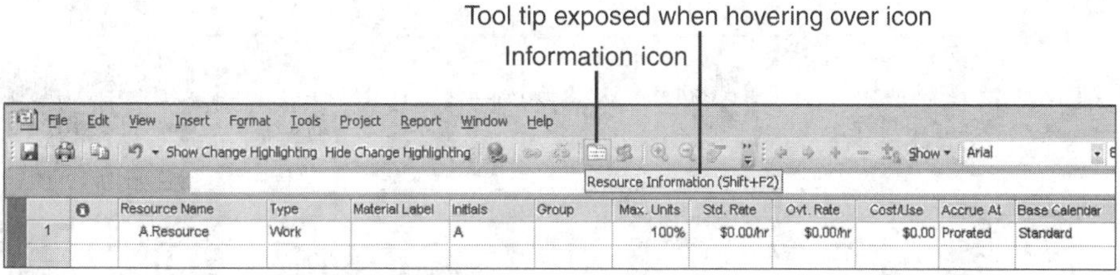

Figure 2.10   *Icon selected showing Resource Information*

If you click on the icon, you will see the Resource Information dialog box, as shown in Figure 2.11. This dialog box allows you to enter or review additional data about a resource that does not display in the Resource Sheet view.

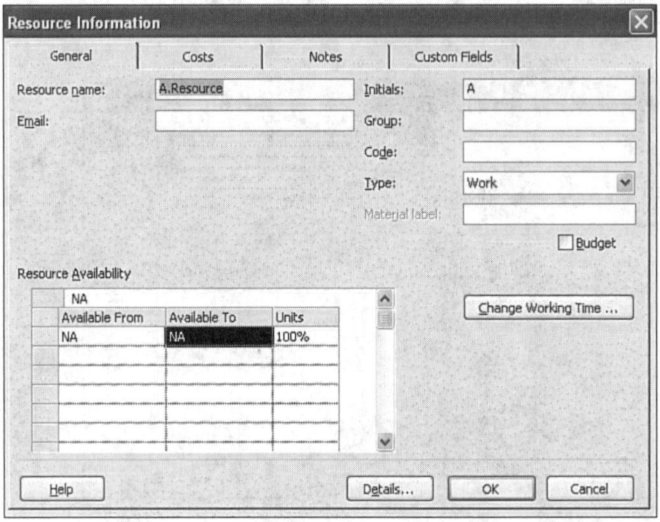

Figure 2.11 *Resource Information dialog box*

One of the major views for reviewing information about assignments is the Resource Usage view. This view's main function is to show how the work is assigned to the task once you have assigned a resource to the task. Once again, the Information icon looks the same as that used for tasks and resources, but it is associated with the assignment as shown in Figure 2.12.

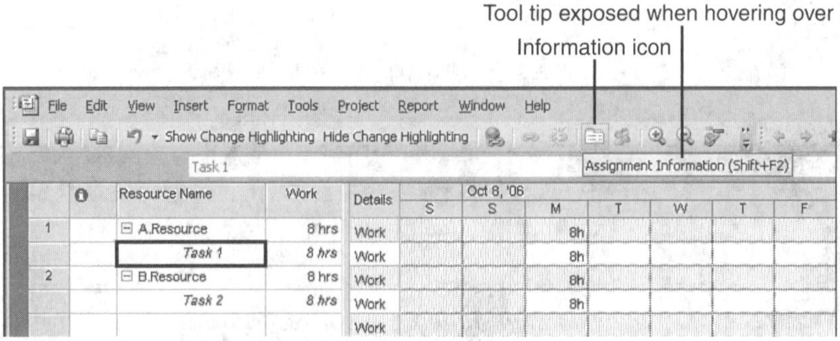

Figure 2.12 *Icon selected showing assignment information*

As you can see, when you click on the icon, the Assignment Information dialog box displays as shown in Figure 2.13. Once again, the Assignment Information dialog box displays much more information about the assignment than is shown in the Resource Usage view, but there is more data not displayed in that view as well.

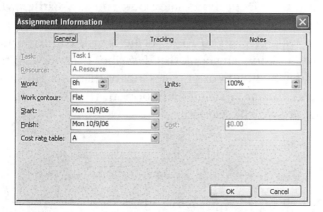

Figure 2.13   *Assignment Information dialog box*

In summary, Project is designed to capture and display information about tasks, resources, and assignments. Data is associated with each of these categories of data, and there are fields that describe these categories of data and settings that affect them.

Using Primary Project Data Fields

In the previous section, I described the categories the Project data structure uses, and in this section, I describe some of the most important fields and settings in Project. At times, you can have fields (e.g., Work) that are associated with each kind of category. For instance, Work can be associated with the following:

- A task to indicate the total number of hours expected for the effort of the task.
- A resource to indicate the total number of hours the resource will work on all tasks in a project.

- An assignment to indicate the total number of hours a particular resource will work on just his or her portion of the task on a project. For instance, the task's work might be 40 hours, but Resource A has an assignment for 20 work hours, and Resource B has an assignment for 20 work hours.

Remember that Column Definition dialog box you saw earlier when you inserted a column into a view? If you scrolled through it, you saw hundreds of fields that are available to you to describe a task (or a resource in a resource view). I don't know any book that describes every field. If this book did, it would probably be hundreds of pages longer than it is. However, there are fields in Project that are extremely important to scheduling and how Project works that are worth describing.

Use Project Help to learn more about the fields you see

When you don't understand a field you can use Project Help to understand what it means. You can hover your cursor over any column displaying. You will see the name of the field and a hyperlink for Help, as shown in Figure 2.14. Click the hyperlink to open the Project Help dialog box for the particular field as shown in Figure 2.15. You might want to insert a column to check help for it. The help information might be slightly different in each version of Project, but this feature works the same in all of them.

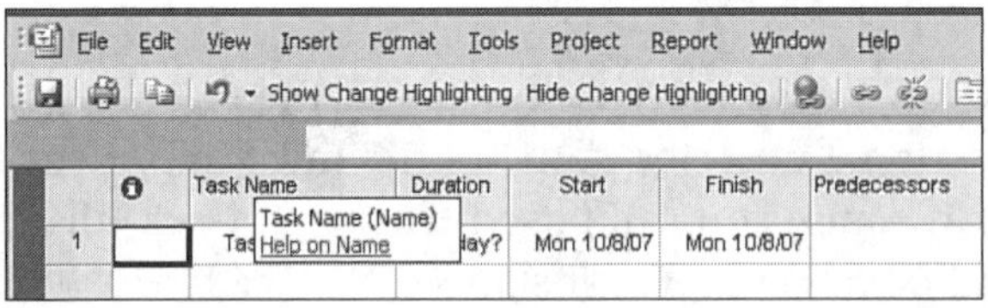

Figure 2.14   *Tool tip on Task Name that allows you to select help*

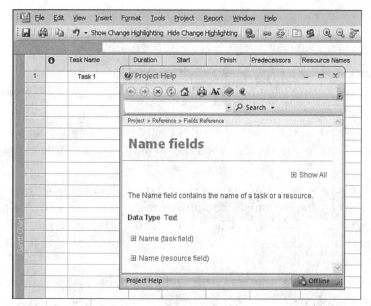

Figure 2.15   *Help dialog box in Project 2007 that describes the task Name field*

What fields are important to understand, as there are so many available? The following fields are important to scheduling and budget information produced by Project (the fields are exposed in Figure 2.16 so you can see how they look in a project).

- **Work:** The amount of time or effort scheduled on a task or for an assignment. In the following example, work is 80 hours for both Task 1 and Task 3.

- **Duration:** Total span of time to be expended on a task, from start to end date of the task. This differs from work significantly. For instance, a task might be scheduled to start on 10/8/07 and end on 10/19/07, for a total duration of 10 days. However, the amount of work or effort for someone to complete the task may only be 40 hours. In the following example, the duration is 10 days for both Task 1 and Task 3.

- **Cost:** Amount of dollars or other currency that might be expended in performing the task. Cost in the following example is $8,000 for both Task 1 and Task 3. This was calculated by Project, which calculated the per hour rate of the resources on the task. You can't see the rate in this view, but the resources have been assigned a rate of $100 per hour.

There are many interesting nuances about cost, especially actual cost. See Chapter 7 "Using Project to Enter Cost Estimates" for more information on costs.

- **Start:** Date the task and resource assignments for the task would begin. Start date for Task 1 in the following example is Monday, 10/8/07.

- **Finish:** Date the task and resource assignments for the task would end. The Finish date for Task 1 in the following example is Friday, 10/19/07.

- **Predecessors:** Task or tasks (shown by ID number) that come before a task can start or finish. The predecessor for Task 2 is Task 1 and the predecessor for Task 3 is Task 2 in the following example. Of course, the first task does not have any task coming before it, so it has no predecessor.

- **Successors:** Task or tasks (shown by ID number) that start or finish after a task starts or finishes. The successor for Task 1 is Task 2 and the successor for Task 2 is Task 3. Of course, the last task does not have any task coming after it, so it has no successor. See Chapter 5 "Sequencing the Work: Creating the Critical Path" to understand the many ways to set up relationships between tasks.

- **Units (amount available for a resource to be assigned to a task):** The percentage or amount of units a resource (or resources) is available to work on a task or tasks. In other words, if a resource is set to be able to work at 50% units, the resource can only expend half its capacity on the task. In the following example, for Task 1 in the Resource name field, Resource A is set at 50% units, and Resource B is also set at 50% units (shown in brackets after the resource name). On Task 3, the resource shows nothing after it, which means that Resource A is set at the default of 100% units on the task.

Field definitions vary based on what data field you are displaying

The definition of a field can differ depending on what portion of Project you are reviewing. For instance, Work in the Gantt Chart is the total amount of time (effort) it will take to complete the task. Work on the Resource Sheet for a project is the total amount of work the resource has been assigned on all tasks in the project.

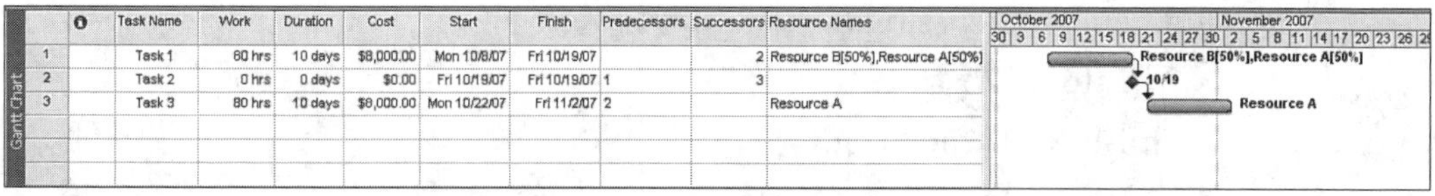

	0	Task Name	Work	Duration	Cost	Start	Finish	Predecessors	Successors	Resource Names
1		Task 1	60 hrs	10 days	$8,000.00	Mon 10/8/07	Fri 10/19/07		2	Resource B[50%],Resource A[50%]
2		Task 2	0 hrs	0 days	$0.00	Fri 10/19/07	Fri 10/19/07	1	3	
3		Task 3	80 hrs	10 days	$8,000.00	Mon 10/22/07	Fri 11/2/07	2		Resource A

Figure 2.16   *Important Project fields exposed*

Although there are numerous other fields in Project, the preceding fields are some of the most important in understanding the scheduling and cost calculations in the scheduling engine. There are other fields that set how the fields react. Although each of the following fields is described briefly here, each is also described in far more detail in later chapters. Some of the most important of these field settings are the following:

- **Effort-driven:** This setting drives the task duration when resources are added or removed from a task. If the effort-driven field is set to Yes, (which is the default setting), then when resources are added to a task, they will share the work assigned to that task. The Work field will stay at the present value, even if you continue to add resources to the task. For instance, let's say the Work field is set at 50 hours and the Duration is initially 10 days. If you assign 5 people to the task, Project will set each resource to work 10 hours (it assumes an even sharing of the work unless you tell it otherwise). The duration of that task will be reduced to 2 days because, in essence, the work is shared between the resources and will take only 1/5 as long in calendar days if one person were working on the task alone. If this is set to No, then no matter how many people are assigned to the task, the duration will not change because the work will not be shared among the resources.

- **Task Type:** There are three settings for this field: Fixed Units, Fixed Duration, and Fixed Work. This setting affects a calculation, Work equals Duration times Units, that sits in the scheduling engine. The data in one field might change based on a change in one of the other two fields. This is a very important setting that I discuss later in this chapter and in more detail in Chapters 4 and 6. The default Task type setting is Fixed Units. The Task Type and Effort-driven fields work together to affect how duration is affected on a task.

- **Constraint Type:** There are eight settings that define how constraints are set for dates in Project. The constraints describe how you want to constrain or set the start or finish dates for a task:

- As Soon As Possible
- As Late As Possible
- Finish No Earlier Than
- Finish No Later Than
- Must Start On
- Must Finish On
- Start No Earlier Than
- Start No Later Than

  If you select one of these settings and indicate a particular start or finish date, then the schedule will react accordingly. I discuss this more in Chapter 4 but for now think about this as telling the schedule exactly when you want the task to start or end.

- **Work Contour:** This is how work will be scheduled day-by-day. The default contour is Flat, which indicates you want Project to schedule work evenly over the duration of a task. See Figure 2.17, which shows how a resource is assigned to work on a 5-day, 40-hour task. Project applies the resource's time on a Flat contour, scheduling the resource at 8 hours a day. If the resource were assigned to work on a 5-day, 20-hour task, Project would schedule the resource at 4 hours a day. There are many alternative contours available, such as front- or back-loaded. but most people only use or need to use the Flat contour. In this book, I do not cover the alternative contours available.

ⓘ	Resource Name	Work	Details	Oct 7, '07 S	M	T	W	T	F	S
1	⊟ Resource A	40 hrs	Work		8h	8h	8h	8h	8h	
	Task 1	*40 hrs*	Work		8h	8h	8h	8h	8h	

Figure 2.17   *How Project scheduled time day-by-day using a Flat contour*

- **Timephased:** Data within Project can be shown in a timephased format. Project distributes the cost, allocation, and work information for tasks, resources, or assignments across time. Even though you might enter Duration as being 20 days, when a resource is added to the task, Project distributes the work to be performed over months, weeks, days, hours, and minutes, which is accessible in the Project data structure. Figures 2.18 through 2.23 illustrate this timephased distribution in the Project data structure in the Resource Usage view. The only thing that has changed in each view is the timescale so that the timephasing is exposed. Depending on the length of your project, you might find a week-by-week timephased view to be the right level of detail. However, some people use Project to schedule critical operational maintenance projects that requires an hour-by-hour or minute-by-minute schedule, and the detailed timephased view might be appropriate.

ⓘ	Resource Name	Work	Details	Qtr 4, 2007	
				Oct	Nov
1	⊟ Resource A	80 hrs	Work	80h	
			Cost	$8,000.00	
	Task	80 hrs	Work	80h	
			Cost	$8,000.00	

Figure 2.18 *Timephased data by month*

ⓘ	Resource Name	Work	Details	Oct '07			
				30	7	14	21
1	⊟ Resource A	80 hrs	Work		40h	40h	
			Cost		$4,000.00	$4,000.00	
	Task	80 hrs	Work		40h	40h	
			Cost		$4,000.00	$4,000.00	

Figure 2.19 *Timephased data by week*

ⓘ	Resource Name	Work	Details	M	T	W	T	F
1	⊟ Resource A	80 hrs	Work	8h	8h	8h	8h	8h
			Cost	$800.00	$800.00	$800.00	$800.00	$800.00
	Task	80 hrs	Work	8h	8h	8h	8h	8h
			Cost	$800.00	$800.00	$800.00	$800.00	$800.00

Figure 2.20 *Timephased data by day*

ⓘ	Resource Name	Work	Details	Mon Oct 8				Tue Oct 9		
				12 AM	6 AM	12 PM	6 PM	12 AM	6 AM	12 PM
1	⊟ Resource A	80 hrs	Work		4h	4h			4h	4h
			Cost		$400.00	$400.00			$400.00	$400.00
	Task	80 hrs	Work		4h	4h			4h	4h
			Cost		$400.00	$400.00			$400.00	$400.00

Figure 2.21 *Timephased data by hour (by half day)*

	❶	Resource Name	Work	Details	8 AM	10 AM	12 PM	2 PM	4 PM
1		⊟ Resource A	80 hrs	Work	2h	2h	1h	2h	1h
				Cost	$200.00	$200.00	$100.00	$200.00	$100.00
		Task	*80 hrs*	Work	2h	2h	1h	2h	1h
				Cost	$200.00	$200.00	$100.00	$200.00	$100.00

Figure 2.22   *Hourly timephased data (2-hour increments)*

	❶	Resource Name	Work	Details	Wed Oct 10, 6 AM				Wed Oct 10, 9 AM				Wed Oct 10, 10 AM	
					0	15	30	45	0	15	30	45	0	15
1		⊟ Resource A	80 hrs	Work	0.25h	0.25h	0.25h	0.25h	0.25h	0.25h	0.25h	0.25h	0.25h	0.25h
				Cost	$25.00	$25.00	$25.00	$25.00	$25.00	$25.00	$25.00	$25.00	$25.00	$25.00
		Task	*80 hrs*	Work	0.25h	0.25h	0.25h	0.25h	0.25h	0.25h	0.25h	0.25h	0.25h	0.25h
				Cost	$25.00	$25.00	$25.00	$25.00	$25.00	$25.00	$25.00	$25.00	$25.00	$25.00

Figure 2.23   *Timephased data by minutes.*

New users of Project are sometimes confused by what the Work, Duration, Start, Finish, and Cost fields really mean. As an example, the Work field is actually the current estimate for the work at completion. You might have originally estimated a task would take 40 hours, but as you enter progress during the execution of the project, the Work field might change to indicate that currently, the estimate is 50 hours (based on progress reported by the resource completing the task). The following terms can designate the Work, Duration, Start, Finish, and Cost fields:

- **Current:** The current value for the data element which indicates what will be accomplished at completion of the project. This term does not appear in front of the data fields. For instance, when you see the data in the Work, Duration, Start, Finish, or Cost fields, they contain values that indicate what will happen if the current course of action continues. The Baseline field is the real estimate, not one of the Work or Duration field. Once you start tracking, the fields contain the current estimated values, based on recording the Actual and Remaining field values.

- **Actual:** The data value based on what actually happens when you enter data to track your project progress. For instance, the planned Duration field might be 10 days, but when you ask the team members how long it really took to get the work done, they tell you 12 days. You would enter 12 in the Actual duration field. What is perplexing (until you know better) is that when you enter 12 in the Actual duration field, the current duration field will change to 12, too. This is because of a formula described in the next section of this chapter. If you use the baseline field described next, you don't have to worry about this phenomenon.

- **Baseline:** The data value in the field based on your recording of the planned fields at a point in time. When you are satisfied with the estimates in the planned Duration and Work fields, you can perform an action that baselines the schedule. This captures a record of those planned values. Then, when you enter actual values into a field, you can see the variance between your original planned estimates and the actual values. For instance, if your planned Duration is 10 and you baseline the schedule, Baseline Duration is entered with 10. Once you record an Actual Duration value of 12, the Duration field will change to 12, but the Baseline Duration field will remain at 10 so you know what your original estimate was.

- **Remaining:** This designation in front of a field indicates how much is remaining in the planned estimate when an actual value is applied. For instance, let's say you have a planned Duration of 10 days. You apply an Actual Duration of 2 days. That means the Remaining Duration is 8 days.

See Figure 2.24 to illustrate this concept. Your planned duration estimate for a task was 10 days. Let's say your team tells you they have completed 2 days on the task. You enter the information in the Actual Duration field as shown. Notice that the Remaining Duration field displays 8 days.

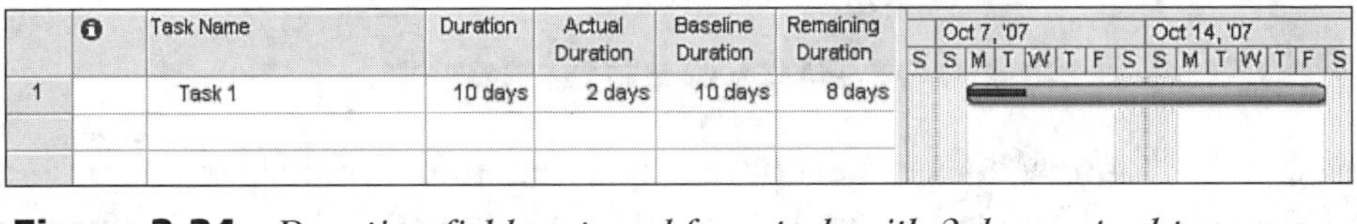

	❶	Task Name	Duration	Actual Duration	Baseline Duration	Remaining Duration	Oct 7, '07 S S M T W T F S	Oct 14, '07 S M T W T F S
1		Task 1	10 days	2 days	10 days	8 days		

Figure 2.24 *Duration fields exposed for a task with 2 days actual progress reported*

Then, 10 days later, the team tells you they are actually done, and it took a total of 12 days. Figure 2-25 shows what this would look like in the fields. Notice that the Duration field is 12 days, the Remaining Duration field is 0, and the Baseline Duration field is the only one that shows the original estimate of 10 days.

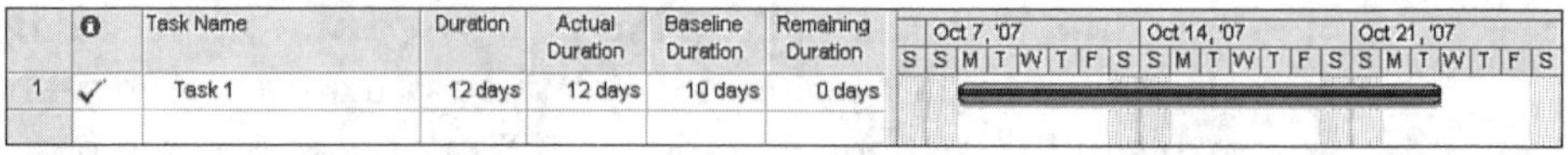

	❶	Task Name	Duration	Actual Duration	Baseline Duration	Remaining Duration	Oct 7, '07 S S M T W T F	Oct 14, '07 S S M T W T F	Oct 21, '07 S S M T W T F S
1	✓	Task 1	12 days	12 days	10 days	0 days			

Figure 2.25 *Duration fields reflecting values after actual progress is entered on the schedule*

Table 2.1 shows the various designations for schedule and budget fields.

Table 2.1 *Various Field Designations*

Current	Actual	Baseline	Remaining
Work	Actual work	Baseline work	Remaining work
Duration	Actual duration	Baseline duration	Remaining duration
Cost	Actual cost	Baseline cost	Remaining cost
Start	Actual start	Baseline start	Not applicable
Finish	Actual finish	Baseline finish	Not applicable

Keep these fields in mind as you schedule tasks and review actual progress for costs, work, and duration of tasks in the schedule.

Project Behavior and Definitions

Not only does Project have a data structure around task, resource, and assignment categories and fields that are core to the way project scheduling works, Project also uses formulas, calculations, and rules that affect scheduling behavior. You cannot see these formulas, calculations, and rules, except in the behavior of Project itself. In this section, I describe some of the behaviors, but this by no means is all-encompassing.

Scheduling

Project uses particular settings, fields, and formulas when scheduling based on the information you enter. First and foremost, the calculations occur to the schedule because by default Project is set to automatically calculate scheduling changes. This setting can be turned off by selecting Tools from the menu bar, then clicking Options and setting the Calculation mode to manual on the Calculation tab. Experienced schedulers, or those familiar with other scheduling systems, sometimes turn the setting off, but you should leave it on initially to learn how it works.

The most important calculation in Project is this:

Duration × Units = Work

also known as

Work/Units = Duration

or

Work/Duration = Units

The calculation and its result are easier to remember if you keep in mind that units refers to resources (1 resource at 100% allocation is 1 unit).

Figure 2.26 shows the result of this formula for a task in Project. Work has been inserted as a column in the Gantt Chart view and the columns have been moved to better reflect the formula.

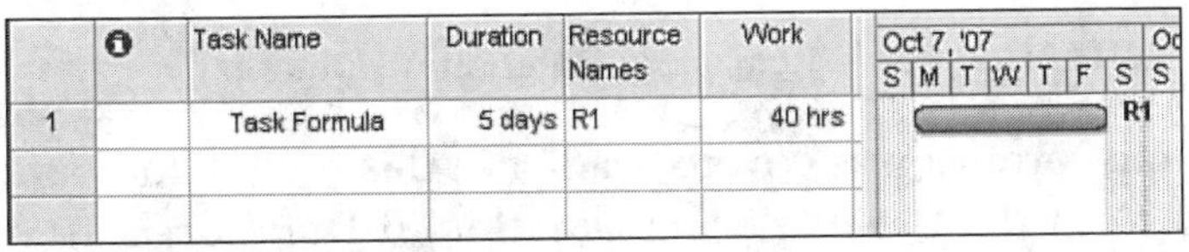

	ⓘ	Task Name	Duration	Resource Names	Work	Oct 7, '07 S M T W T F S S		Oc
1		Task Formula	5 days	R1	40 hrs		R1	

Figure 2.26   *Duration × Units = Work*

The task has a Duration value of 5 days (with a day being set at 8 hours). One resource (R1) is assigned at 100% (1 unit) on the task, meaning the resource is set to spend 100% of an 8-hour day on the task. If you assign another resource to the task, two units (200%) are assigned to work on the 40-hour task. The result is shown in Figure 2.27.

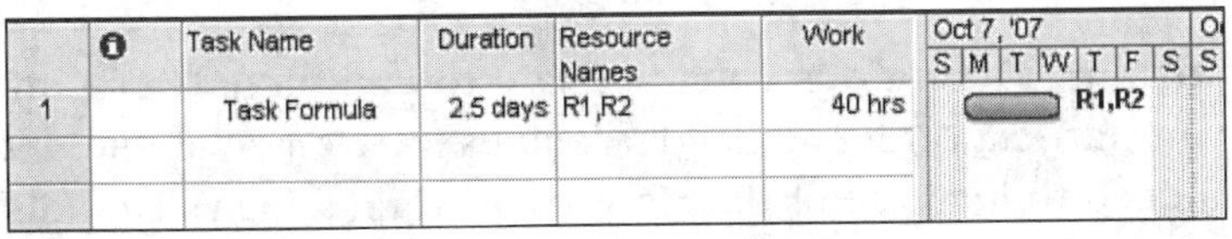

	ⓘ	Task Name	Duration	Resource Names	Work	Oct 7, '07 S M T W T F S S	O
1		Task Formula	2.5 days	R1,R2	40 hrs	R1,R2	

Figure 2.27   *Duration × Units = Work and another unit (resource) added*

Project assumes that the two resources will share the work. The best way to illustrate this is changing the formula around a bit.

Work/Units = Duration. 40/2 = 20 hours = 2.5 days duration

Project calculates based on fractional hours and minutes and converts the hours into duration. The calculations used are also based on project and resource calendars in Project (which you can customize). Chapters 4 and 6 describe the formula and how it uses calendars and other settings extensively. When you think you have set a duration, resources, and work, and you change the data in any one of those fields, the formula kicks in and most likely you will see Project calculate something new in one of the other fields that you didn't quite expect (unless you know about the formula and associated settings, such as the effort-driven flag and Task types as described in the earlier section "Using Primary Project Data Fields").

Remember planned (also known as current), remaining, and actual designations to the Work, and Duration fields? They are actually parameters in a formula:

Actual Work + Remaining Work = Work

and

Actual Duration + Remaining Duration = Duration

Although this formula was covered earlier in this section for work, let's take another look at the formula using Duration. If Duration is 10 days, and a resource worked 6 days, then the Remaining Duration is 4 days as shown in Figure 2.28.

	❶	Task Name	Duration	Actual Duration	Remaining Duration	Start	Finish	F	Jan 7, '07 S S M T W T F	Jan 14, '07 S S M T W T F S
1		Duration Task	10 days	6 days	4 days	Mon 1/8/07	Fri 1/19/07		▬▬▬▬▬▬▬▬▬	

Figure 2.28   *Duration = Actual Duration + Remaining Duration*

The Remaining Duration is your estimate to complete (ETC) information. When you start capturing actual data values for your schedule, and you find that you need to increase or decrease your original plan's Duration or Work values, it is best practice to change the Remaining duration or Work field, rather than changing the Duration or Work field. Let's say that after you enter the 6 actual days of duration, you ask the resource performing the work how much time is left to finish the work. She says 6 more days. It would be tempting to add the 6 days to the Duration field, but notice what happens, as shown in Figure 2.29.

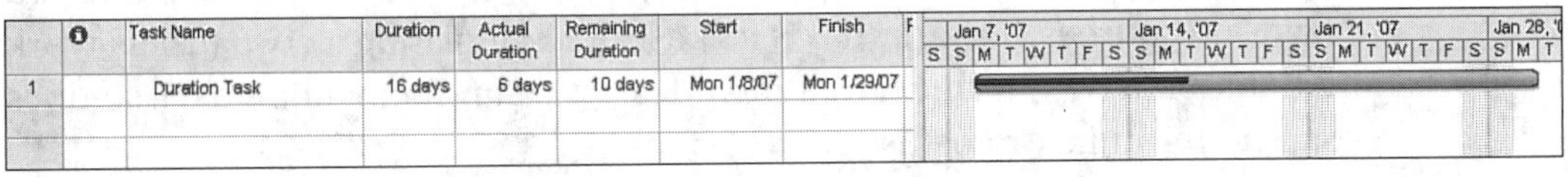

❶	Task Name	Duration	Actual Duration	Remaining Duration	Start	Finish	F	Jan 7, '07	Jan 14, '07	Jan 21, '07	Jan 28, '
1	Duration Task	16 days	6 days	10 days	Mon 1/8/07	Mon 1/29/07					

Figure 2.29 *Adding 6 days to the Duration field increases the estimate and shows Remaining Duration at 10 days.*

If you enter the remaining work of 6 days in Duration, Project increases the duration to 16 days, but what you really meant is that it is 6 days past the Actual Duration value of 6. To avoid this issue, it's best to use the Remaining Duration (or Work) field. If you enter 6 in the Remaining Duration field based on Figure 2.28, the Duration field is automatically adjusted as shown in Figure 2.30. Remember if you use Baseline Duration you'll always have the original estimate of 10 days available.

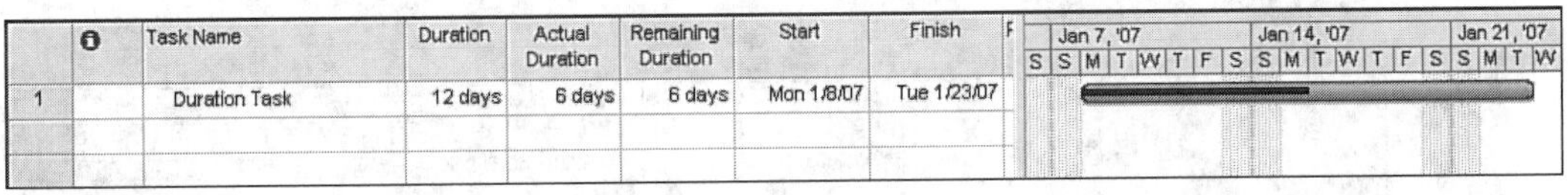

❶	Task Name	Duration	Actual Duration	Remaining Duration	Start	Finish	F	Jan 7, '07	Jan 14, '07	Jan 21, '07
1	Duration Task	12 days	6 days	6 days	Mon 1/8/07	Tue 1/23/07				

Figure 2.30 *Changing the Remaining Duration value to 6 days changes the Duration field for the proper new estimate*

Dates are also part of the scheduling engine. The following formula helps you understand how the finish or start dates are set when you enter a value in the Duration field, or how, while entering schedule progress, entering dates in the Actual Finish or Actual Start fields could affect the value in the Duration field. The formula is:

Finish date – Start date = Duration (not including the nonworking days in your calendar)

Duration is the number of working days between the two dates. If you change the duration of a task while you are working on your schedule, the start and finish dates could change.

Costs

Costs have certain rules, settings, and behaviors as well. By default, the Actual Cost field is calculated by Project, and you cannot enter data into that field directly, although you can change that setting. In general, Project expects you to have a resource on a task that is its basis for calculating a cost. Just as work and duration have a formula that includes actual and remaining data, so does cost. The formula for cost is:

Actual Cost + Remaining Cost = Cost

Let's take a look at this formula for costs. This example describes a nonlabor cost also known as a fixed cost. For this example, you might have budgeted for a server for your Information Technologies project. You have decided to use a line item (New Server Purchased) to estimate the cost and then record the actual cost when it comes in. You have been quoted $2,500. When you enter $2,500 in the Cost field, it immediately enters the same amount in the Remaining Cost field (and Actual Cost, of course, is 0). Now, let's say that you have to pay a down payment on the server about a month after you start the project. You enter 20% complete on the task to show that you have paid for some of the server as shown in Figure 2.31.

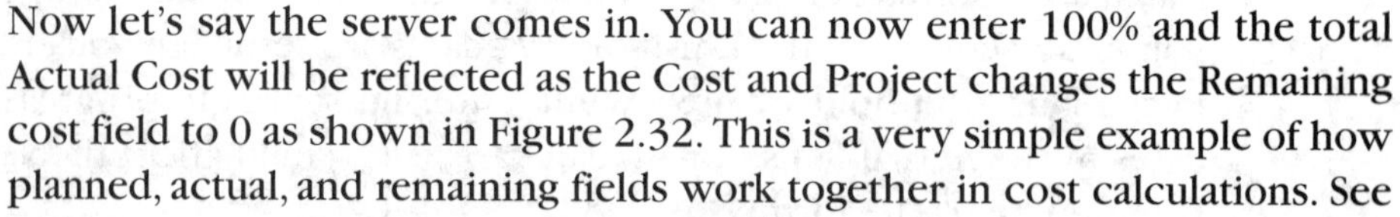

	❶	% Complete	Task Name	Fixed Cost	Cost	Actual Cost	Remaining Cost	Oct 7, '07	Oct 14, '07
								S M T W T F S	S M T W T F S
1		20%	New Server Purchased	$2,500.00	$2,500.00	$500.00	$2,000.00		

Figure 2.31 *Actual Cost + Remaining Cost = Cost*

Now let's say the server comes in. You can now enter 100% and the total Actual Cost will be reflected as the Cost and Project changes the Remaining cost field to 0 as shown in Figure 2.32. This is a very simple example of how planned, actual, and remaining fields work together in cost calculations. See Chapter 7 and Chapter 11 "Tracking Your Schedule" to understand more complex situations of entering and recording actual cost data into Project.

Click on the X to remove the side pane

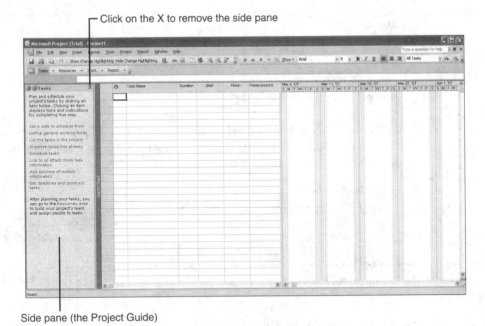

Side pane (the Project Guide)

Figure 2.32 *Remaining Cost set to 0 after line item is 100% complete*

Project 2007 has a new cost resource

Nonlabor costs have been problematic in past versions of Project although the Fixed cost field could be used to indicate a nonlabor cost. Project 2007 introduces a new resource type called a cost resource. You can assign a cost resource on a task and it will behave entirely independent of the labor cost calculations and the duration or work on a task. See Chapter 7 for more about cost resources.

When adding resources to a task, the additional complexities of cost can be reflected in the following calculation:

Standard rate of resource(s) assigned × Work hours = Cost of a task

As an example, Task 1 has an estimate of 50 hours of work. Resource A has been assigned to the task and Resource A's standard rate is $100. Figure 2.33 shows Resource A's Std. Rate value in the Resource Sheet.

	ⓘ	Resource Name	Type	Material Label	Initials	Group	Max. Units	Std. Rate	Ovt. Rate	Cost/Use	Accrue At	Base Calendar
1		Resource A	Work		R		100%	$100.00/hr	$0.00/hr	$0.00	Prorated	Standard

Figure 2.33 *Standard rate applied to a resource*

Then Resource A is added to the task in the Gantt Chart view as shown in Figure 2.34. Based on a standard rate of $100 × 50 hours, the cost of the task is $5,000.

	ⓘ	Task Name	Work	Duration	Cost	Start	Finish	Resource Names	Oct 7, '07 ... Oct 14, '07 ... Oc
1		Cost Task	50 hrs	6.25 days?	$5,000.00	Mon 10/8/07	Tue 10/16/07	Resource A	Resource A

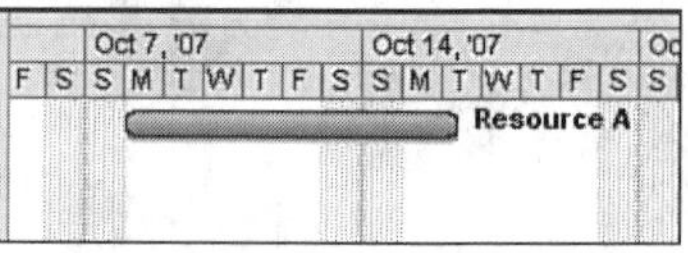

Figure 2.34 *Rate x Work = Cost of the task*

There are also calculations based on consumable resources, such as the price of gas per gallon, called material resources. See Chapter 7 for more information about material resources.

Resources

Resources are the people, equipment, or materials that can be assigned to a task that ensure the task gets completed. To understand resources, it is useful to understand a few key terms: Units, Availability, and Overallocation. Although Project 2007 has introduced two new resources called Cost and Budget resources, this section focuses on the type of resources that are assigned to perform the work on a task.

- **Units:** The amount of a resource's time that can be assigned to a task. Units can be expressed in percentages or decimals. If Resource A is assigned to work on a task at 75% units, he can work 75% on the task each day, calculated as 6.4 hours a day if his normal work day is set at 8 hours. 100% units would mean the resource could work full-time on the task.

- **Availability:** The amount of time a resource is available to work. Availability is a combination of a resource's calendar (the days she can work, and how many hours per day she can work), and how many units of the resource is available for the project and the task. For instance, a resource might be set to be available to work for 40 hours a day, 5 days a week. The resource is assigned to a specific task at 40%. In this case, the resource is available for only 3.2 hours per day to work on the task (8 hours × .40 = 3.2 hours).

- **Overallocation:** The amount of time a resource is set to work on projects beyond their availability. For instance, if a resource is available at 100% (and has a resource calendar set for 8-hour work days), but has been assigned two projects, the resource might be set to work 16 hours per day over the span of time during which the projects' tasks overlap. Project will show a resource as overallocated even if the scheduled work exceeds availability for only one minute. Also, Project will allow you to grossly overallocate resources because it doesn't know whether you are going to level the resources or not. Part of your job as a project manager is to level the work of the project so resources are not overallocated. See Chapter 9 "Reviewing Work Overload and the Critical Path" to learn more about overallocation.

Navigating Project and Some Quick Tips

Once you know that there are a lot of fields, calculations, and settings in Project that affect the behavior of Project, understanding the Project interface will increase your efficiency in using the tool. In this section, I describe how you can get around in Project, and what some of the best views are. The first view you always see when you open up Project is the Gantt Chart view, shown in Figure 2.35. There is nothing else you have to do, other than click on the Project application (after installation) to get this initial screen.

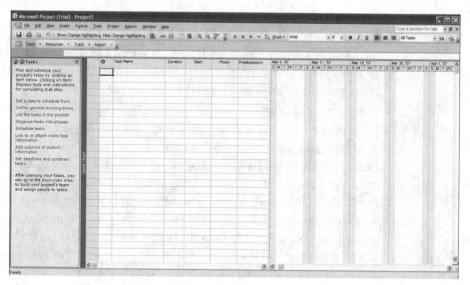

Figure 2.35   *The initial Gantt Chart view with the Project Guide side pane displaying*

Figure 2.35 might be slightly different than your initial interface. You might have some different defaults already loaded, or if you have used Project before, your interface might be displaying some different icons or toolbars. Other Project versions aren't too much different; just the shape and coloring of the icons have changed from previous versions to Project 2007. From Project 2002 through Project 2007, the features and functions have not changed much.

The pane on the left side is the Project Guide. It loads by default when you first open Project 2007. The Project Guide was a feature added in Project 2002 and provides a step-by-step instruction for using Project. You might want to use it once you understand the overall methodology for building and tracking a project schedule and it will help support what you learn in this book. To learn more about the Project Guide, see Chapter 13 "Project Mysteries Resolved!"

You can remove the Project Guide side pane by clicking the X in the upper right corner of the pane as shown in Figure 2.35. In past versions of Project, you would also see a task pane which you could also remove by clicking an X in the upper right corner of the pane. You could also display the task pane by selecting File on the menu bar, then clicking New. Although these side panes can be useful to step you through particular tasks you perform in Project, in this book I describe items on the interface with them removed, unless their functions are expressly used.

The menu bar, toolbars, and view bar that display on this view do not change as you move between views in Project. Figure 2.36 displays the standard navigation tools for Project.

Project Guide toolbar   Menu bar   Standard and Formatting toolbars on one line

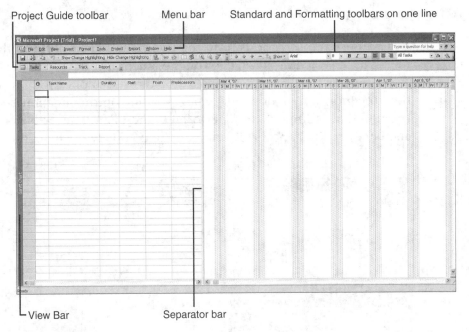

View Bar   Separator bar

Figure 2.36 *Gantt Chart view with more room for entering and viewing data*

The menu bar allows you to select most any function you want to perform. When you click a function in the menu bar, a drop-down list displays to select a particular function. The Standard and Formatting toolbars contain icons that allow you to perform the most common functions of Project more easily than using the menu bar. Although you might have removed the Project Guide side pane, the toolbar for using it is still visible. This allows you to bring the Project Guide back easily if you'd like to use it. The view bar is the vertical strip on the far left of the view.

Although not a part of navigation, the separator bar is a common element on several views, and on the Gantt Chart view it distinguishes the task entry sheet area on the left side from the Gantt Chart bars on the right side of the view. You enter the tasks in the entry sheet on the left, and can visually see the timescale on the right side to help with scheduling decisions. You can click and hold down the mouse on the separator bar and move it horizontally to display more task entry columns on the left side, or more Gantt Chart bars on the right side. You will see this separator bar on several views and you can move it on those views as well.

Using the Menu Bar

You will use the selections from the top menu bar to perform the major functions in Project. You can click on the function at the top of the bar, such as File, as shown in Figure 2.37, and a drop-down list appears. Click the selection to perform the function listed. Depending on the function, sometimes the function is immediately performed and sometimes a dialog box or another selection appears for you to use to complete the function.

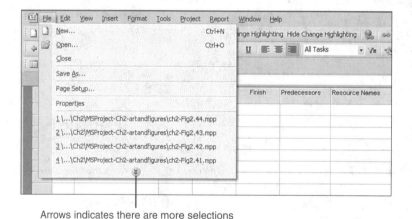

Arrows indicates there are more selections

Figure 2.37   *Drop-down list after selecting File on the menu bar*

In Figure 2.37 notice the double arrows at the bottom of the drop-down list. As with all Microsoft Office applications, the double arrows at the bottom of the drop-down list indicate that there are more selections. If you are like me, you find it annoying that you can't see all the selections unless you wait a moment or two, or unless you click on the arrows. This book shows full menus. In case you have not been introduced to how to change this behavior follow these steps:

1. Select Tools from the menu bar and click Customize.

2. Click Toolbars.

3. The Customize dialog box appears, as shown in Figure 2.38. Select the Options tab.

4. Select the Always show full menus check box and click Close in the dialog box. Now when you click File in the menu bar, the full drop-down list displays.

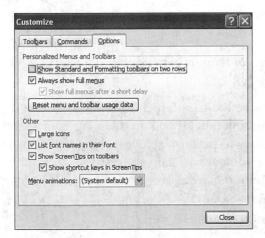

Figure 2.38   *Select the Always show full menus check box in the Customize dialog box*

This book does not cover each selection in the menu bar unless it is a common function needed in building or tracking your schedule. However, this book uses the functions from the menu bar to describe how to perform Project steps. As with all Microsoft products you can right-click in a field or double-click to be more efficient in performing the same function, some of which is introduced in the course of this book.

Using the Toolbars

The Formatting and Standard toolbars show by default and contain some of the most popular buttons (also called icons) for performing functions in Project. You also might not see all the possible buttons on the toolbars. In Figure 2.36, the majority of the buttons for the two toolbars show on one strip. You can see all the buttons or set the toolbars to two rows by selecting the Toolbar Options button at the very far right of the toolbar, shown in Figure 2.39.

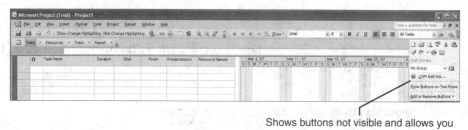

Shows buttons not visible and allows you
to choose to display all buttons on two rows

Figure 2.39   *Show hidden buttons or buttons on two rows*

You can also add and remove toolbars, which can be very useful depending what you are doing in the schedule. If you are tracking your schedule, you can add the Tracking toolbar to perform some tracking functions more easily. You can also remove toolbars to gain more room in your view. For instance, the Project Guide toolbar displays by default, and you might want to remove it if you do not use it often.

To add or remove toolbars, follow these steps:

1. Select View from the menu bar, then click Toolbars.
2. The resulting drop-down list shows all the toolbars available for you to remove or add as shown in Figure 2.40. Notice that all toolbars displaying have a check mark next to them. To remove a toolbar, click it on this list and it will be removed. To add a toolbar, click it on this list, and the toolbar will be added.

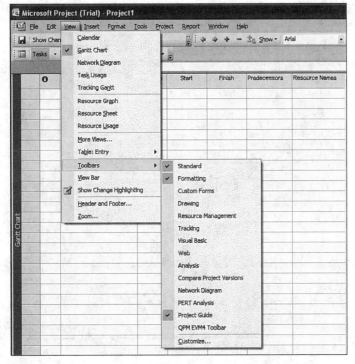

Figure 2.40 *Use the toolbar drop-down list to add or remove toolbars.*

Using the View Bar

You might have noticed the vertical strip on the left of the views of Project and sometimes people have that vertical strip set differently. When you first open your project schedule view, you might see a thin strip with Gantt Chart written vertically in it. You might also see a wider strip, with icons and view names listed in the strip, as shown in Figure 2.41. The View Bar displays the most popular views in Project.

To display the View Bar follow these steps:

1. Select View from the menu bar.

2. Near the bottom of the drop-down list, click View Bar. The View Bar will appear as shown in Figure 2.41.

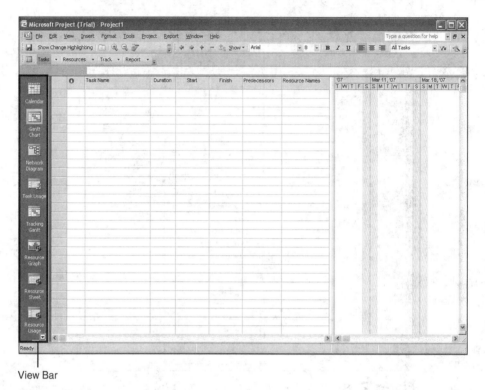

View Bar

Figure 2.41 *The view bar*

To remove the View Bar, perform the same steps. Because the View Bar is selected, when you click View Bar again, it clears the option.

Why would you use or not use the View Bar? It's based on personal preference. If you use it, it takes up a bit more space on your desktop but it is easy to click and scroll between the various views. When you use it, it's a little harder to tell what view you are on, as the icons are shadowed. When you don't use the View Bar, you can easily see the name of your view as shown in Figure 2.36, where Gantt Chart is easily displayed in the vertical strip. If you prefer to leave the View Bar off of your interface, you can select View from the menu bar and see the same selections in a drop-down list, or right-click the view name you see, and select from the list there as shown in Figure 2.42.

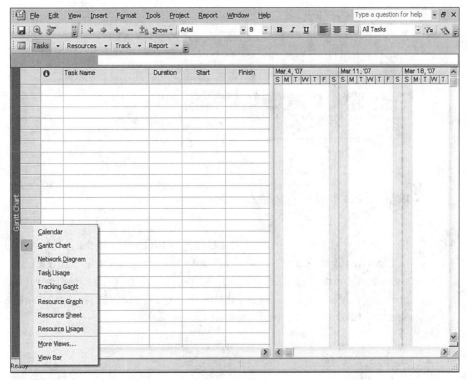

Figure 2.42   *Right click on the Gantt Chart view bar strip on the left to get a list of other views*

Once you have gained more experience with views and know what behavior to expect from each, you might wish to remove the View Bar for more room on your Project views.

Entering Data into Project

To enter task data into the Gantt Chart view, simply type the task name in the Task Name field and then click the next cell to enter data into the next field. You can enter task data into a task's row, but when you initially build your schedule, focus on entering the task names. In using the Gantt Chart view, some students get confused as to why they can't perform an action even though they did it before. It's possible that they have not gotten out of "entry mode" while entering data. To illustrate Figure 2.43 shows information in the Task name field in the Gantt Chart.

Entry mode area

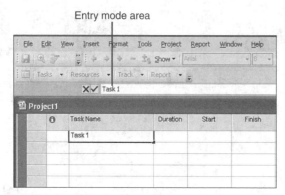

Figure 2.43   *Entry mode in Project*

Notice that the field still has a black highlight around it, and there is no data in the Duration, Start, or Finish fields. Also, you see an X and a check mark in the entry field above Task Name. If you were to go to the menu bar immediately to select a function from the File drop-down list, you would see something similar to what is shown in Figure 2.44.

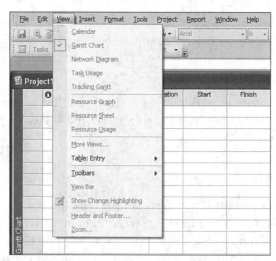

Figure 2.44   *Unavailable selections in gray while in entry mode.*

Most of the selections are unavailable in the drop down list. However, if you click out of the field into which you are entering data and into a new field, you will be able to select other functions in Project and the data you type will be entered. Also note that when you enter a task, Project displays the task number in the gray area to the left, whereas if you are in entry mode, the task will not have a number. You should be able to move your cursor around to any field to easily enter and get out of entry mode.

You can accidentally add rows of data

You can accidentally add rows of data to Project. You can press the spacebar without knowing it, and see a blank task show up in the schedule. I once saw thousands of rows for a blank resource added to the Resource Sheet that the Project user didn't even know she added. Although data showed in other fields in the row, blanks had been entered in the Resource name field. It didn't look like anything was in the rows, but Project recognized a blank and repeated it. The user might have hit a key that repeated the blank resource names over and over again. Figure 2.45 shows blank tasks added accidentally at the end of a project. Usually the mistake isn't quite this drastic but it is common enough for several rows to be added to Project without you knowing it.

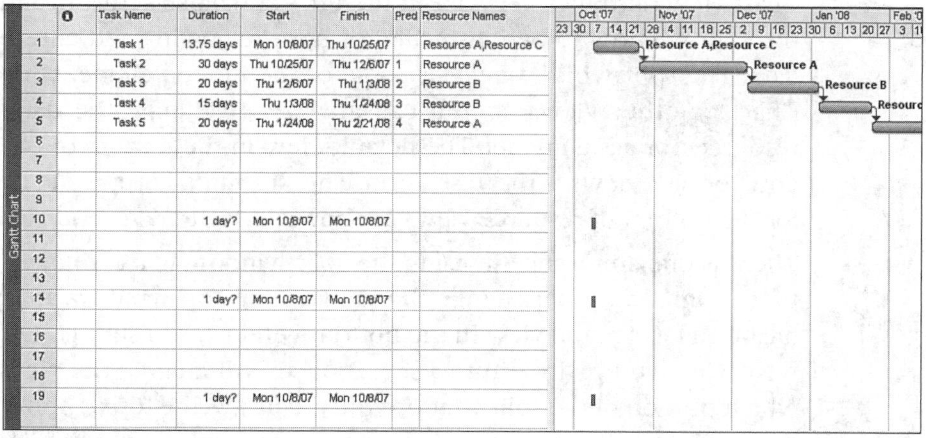

Figure 2.45 *Blank rows added to the file*

The Split Window

The Split Window function in Project is very useful in providing you with additional information about tasks or resources in whatever view you have chosen. Initially, it might confuse new Project users because it does not simulate the split window function of other Microsoft products. It introduces a completely different window with different information than what is in the top window, unlike other Microsoft applications that simply split the same application information in two. To see the Project split window, follow these steps:

1. On the menu bar, select Window.
2. Click Split. You'll see a view similar to that shown in Figure 2.46.

To remove the split window:

1. On the menu bar, select Window.
2. Click Remove Split. The split window will be removed.

Once you know the secrets of Project and understand that work and unit fields can be different for each resource and do not display on the Gantt Chart view (although they are in the Project data structure) you might find the split window to be invaluable for both reviewing and entering Project data. The split window reveals some of the hidden elements in the Gantt Chart or other views so you can analyze or change the data for tasks, resources, or assignments. The default view in the bottom of the split window for task views is the Task Form. The Resource Form is the default view for the bottom of resource views as shown in Figure 2.46 and Figure 2.47.

There is one annoyance in using the split window when you use it the first time: Sometimes you change the view in the top window, and you really meant to change the view in the bottom window. You start getting lost as to what view you really want to see. Project will change the view based on which portion of the split window you are in, i.e., the top or bottom portion. For novices, I recommend removing the split window when you want to change your views.

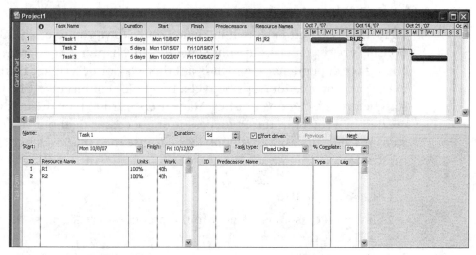

Figure 2.46   *Task Form split window for task views*

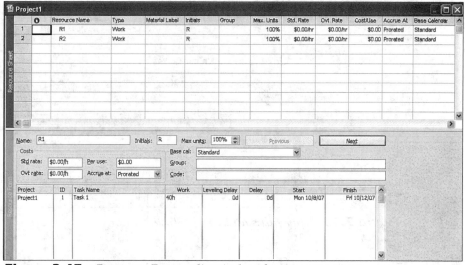

Figure 2.47   *Resource Form split window for resource views*

Using Common Buttons on the Toolbars

You might find some of the toolbar buttons easier than using the drop-down lists from the menu bar. In the following section, I describe some of the most useful toolbar functions in Project.

Link or Unlink Tasks

The Link Tasks button shown in Figure 2.48 allows you to easily create relationships between tasks in your schedule. In Chapter 1 you learned briefly about task dependences, which is another way of describing linking. Linking creates the relationships between two tasks. For instance, one task can't start before another one finishes. Many users learn to type the task identifier created by Project in the Predecessor or Successor field but the following steps provide an easy way to link tasks. To use the Link Tasks button, follow these steps:

1. Click on the first task.
2. If the successor task is next to the predecessor task, press the Shift key and click the second task.

    If the tasks are nonsequential in your task list, use the Ctrl key plus a left-click of your mouse to select the tasks.
3. Click the Link icon. The second task is now the successor of the first task selected.

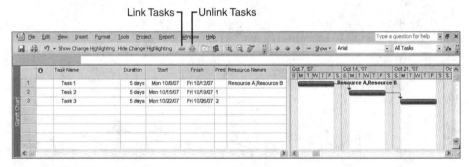

Figure 2.48   *Link Tasks and Unlink Tasks buttons*

You can also unlink tasks using the Unlink Tasks button. Click on the tasks you want to unlink and click the Unlink Tasks button as shown in Figure 2.48.

Information Button

The Information button provides more information about a task, resource, or assignment. You saw the Information button in Chapter 1. When you are in a particular view (task, resource, or assignment) and you click this button, as shown in Figure 2.49, you will see a dialog box that allows you to see or enter more information about the task, resource, or assignment than allowed by default in the view. Many people use the Information button to enter data rather than just using the view fields displayed.

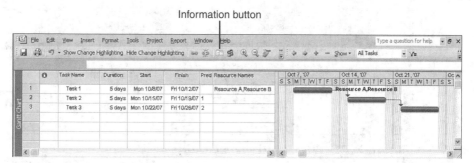

Figure 2.49 *Information button displays additional data on task, resource, and assignment views*

Zoom In and Zoom Out on Timescale

As shown in Figure 2.50 the Zoom In and Zoom Out buttons are convenient-to-display Gantt Chart bars in the timescale based on discrete time spans. By pressing the buttons once or several times in a row, you can change the timescale of the project.

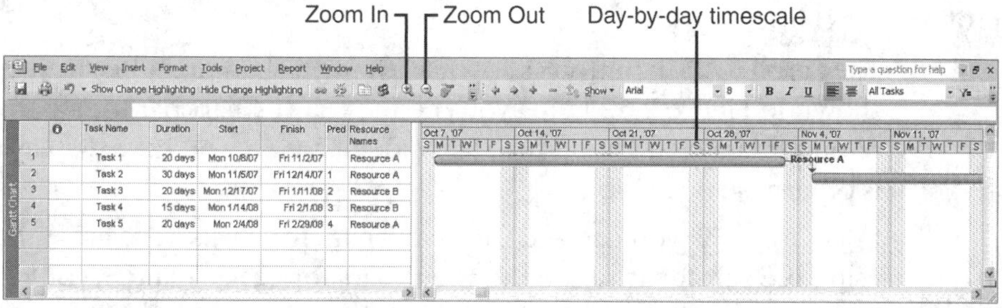

Figure 2.50 *Zoom In and Zoom Out buttons can be used to change the timescale quickly (the timescale is day-by-day)*

Let's spend a moment on the Zoom In and Zoom Out buttons, to show how they might be useful to you. Figure 2.50 shows a project as it would normally show using a daily timescale on the right side of the Gantt Chart. As you can see, the tasks are long, and you cannot see all of the Gantt Chart bars for each task to get a feel for the length of the project. Click on the Zoom Out button (the icon with the minus in it) twice to see a weekly view as shown in Figure 2.51.

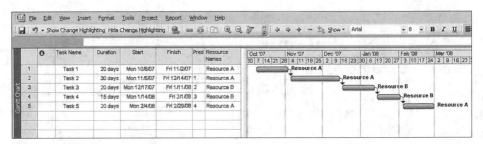

Figure 2.51   *Week-by-week timescale*

The week-by-week timescale displays a much better view. Viewing weekly rather than daily Gantt Charts allows you to see more of the project at once. To zoom in to see the day-by-day timescale again, click the Zoom In button (the icon with the plus sign in it) twice. Go ahead and click the Zoom In and Zoom Out icons to check out how they change the timescale on any Project view. You might end up using the Zoom In and Zoom Out buttons a lot. If you would like to practice using the Zoom In and Zoom Out buttons, open the project schedule called Ch2-Fig2.50-ForZoomIn-ZoomOutPractice.mpp on your CD.

Scroll to Task

The Scroll to Task button (known as Go to Task in previous Project versions) shown in Figure 2.52 helps you see the Gantt Chart bar for a particular task or other data element on the right side of a view you have displayed when it is otherwise not visible.

In Figure 2.52, you can see the Gantt bars for Tasks 1, 2, and 3. Rather than using the scroll bar to see the Gantt bars for Tasks 4 and 5, you can click on Task 4, then click the Scroll to Task button and you will see the bars as shown in Figure 2.53.

Using the scroll bar in the area below the timescale will do the same thing, but using the Scroll to Task button is much quicker, especially in a long schedule with a lot of tasks. The Scroll to Tasks button also works on the Resource and Task Usage views, which are assignment views. Figure 2.54

Scroll to Task

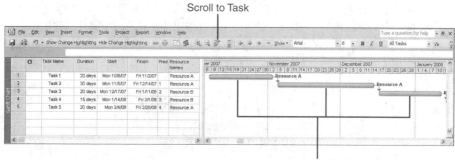

Gantt chart bars showing for Task 1, 2, and 3

Figure 2.52 *Scroll to Task button to display the Gantt Chart bar for any task you select*

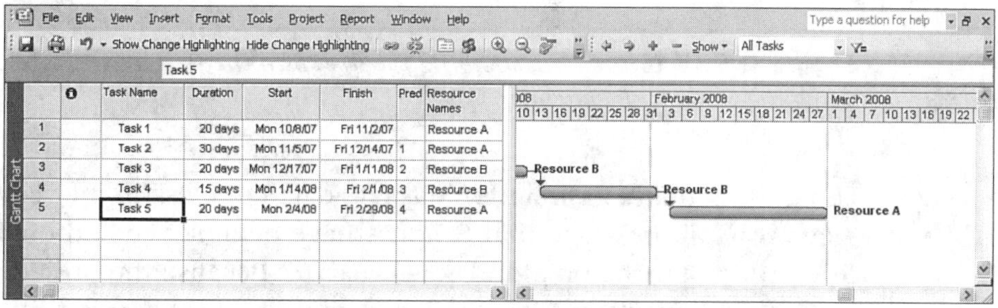

Figure 2.53 *Clicking on the Scroll to Task button for a selected task brings the task's Gantt bar into view*

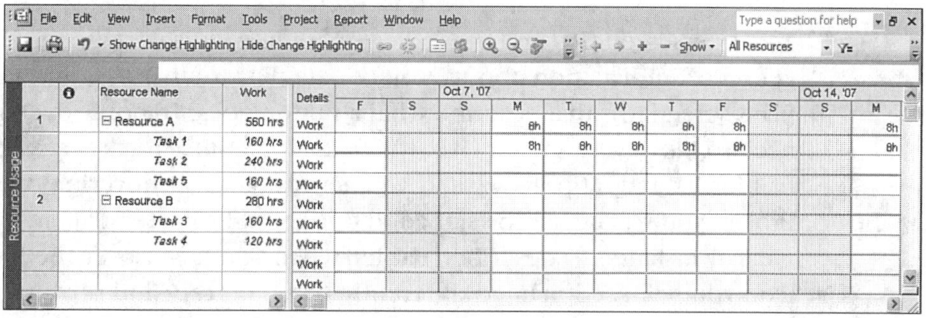

Figure 2.54 *Resource Usage view for five-task project showing only data for Task 1*

shows the Resource Usage view for the five-task project. Hours have been assigned to Resource A for Task 5, but they do not show in the timescale. If you select Task 5 and click the Scroll to Task icon you'll see the result shown in Figure 2.55.

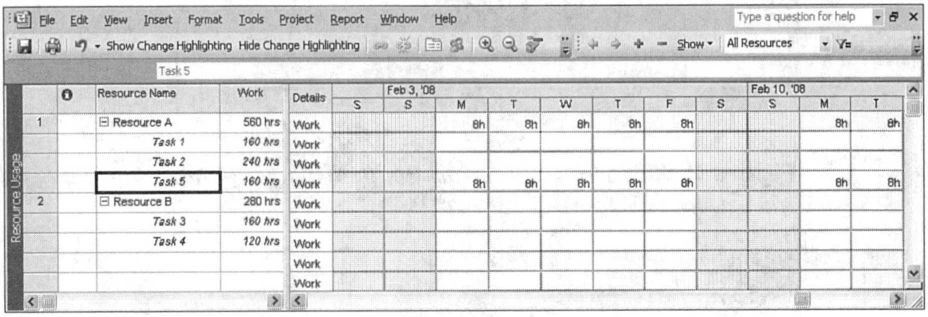

Figure 2.55 *Hours now showing for Task 5 in the Resource Usage view after using the Scroll to Task icon*

Using the Scroll to Task button displays data for a task in the right side of a view. You can now see that 8 hours have been scheduled on Task 5 for Resource A starting on Monday, February 4. Because the project begins in October, you would need to scroll a great deal to find the data for the task if you started scrolling from Task 1.

Hover over Fields to Obtain More Information

Tool tips, screen tips, and the Indicator column in Project are terrific ways to get more information about Project data. For toolbar buttons, Project displays screen tips that describe what a button does. To hover over a field, you need to move your cursor over the field (sometimes it takes a while to get a feel for it), and a tip displays. If you get real good at hovering over icons in Project you will get all sorts of good tips about Project or data in your schedule. For instance, as described earlier, when you hover over the Information icon you will see it named differently, based on the kind of view you are in (task, resource, or assignment). Figure 2.56 shows a screen tip that lets you know the Assign Resources button allows you to enter resources on tasks. It also displays the keyboard shortcut for displaying the Assign Resources dialog box.

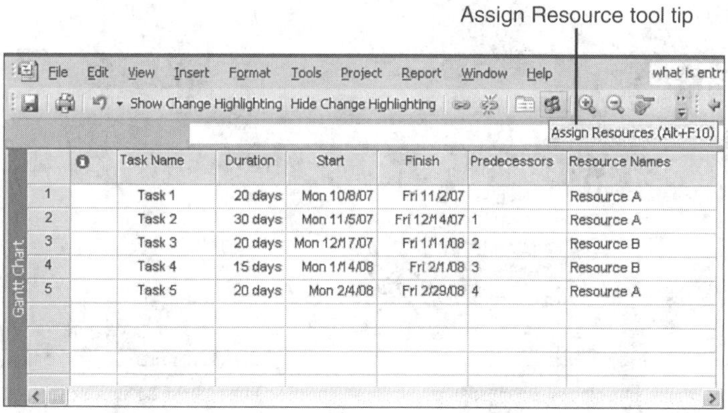

Assign Resource tool tip

Figure 2.56   *Screen tip for the Assign Resources button also shows keyboard shortcut*

You can also hover over column headers in fields to receive a tool tip that allows you to get more information about the field, as shown in Figure 2.57. In this example, the Cost/Use field tool tip also shows the full name of the field in parentheses (Cost per Use) as well as a hyperlink for receiving more information about the field.

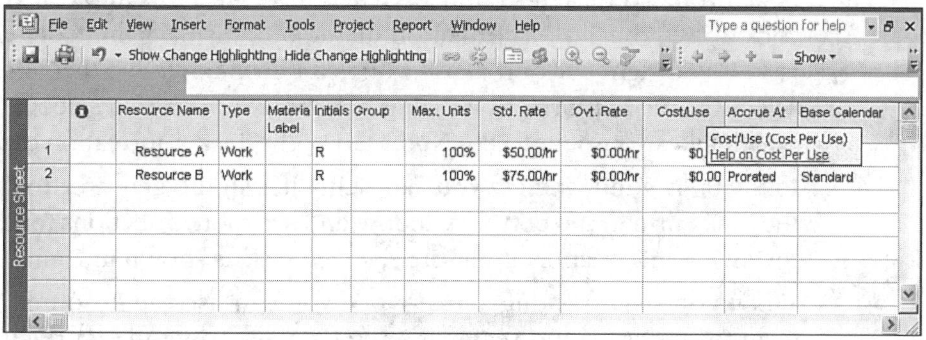

Figure 2.57   *Tool tip for the Cost/Use field.*

The Indicator column might display important information about a task. In Figure 2.58, the icon in the Indicator field indicates that a constraint is on the task. The constraint indicates the particular kind of constraint (Finish No Earlier Than) and the constraint date of 1/14/08. You could click the Task Information button in the toolbar, go to the Task Information dialog box, and click the Advanced tab to also find out what the constraint is, but using the Indicator field is more efficient.

Indicator column

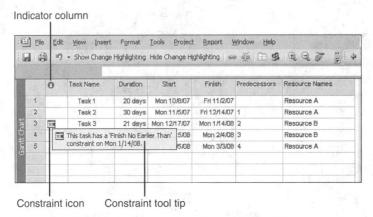

Constraint icon   Constraint tool tip

Figure 2.58   *Tool tip about a constraint.*

Right-Click, Double-Click, Click, Click, Click?

As in most Microsoft applications, you can right-click and double-click your mouse buttons to perform functions in Project. With Project, you'll learn that you could have performed a function with a mouse-click, rather than using five keystrokes. Sometimes a right-click or double-click provides dialog boxes you can't seem to find anywhere else. As an example, if you double-click a task, the Task Information dialog box displays immediately for that task. If you right-click on a task, you get a drop-down list that allows you to select the Task Information dialog box, but you can also select Task Notes, which takes you right to the Notes tab in the Task Information dialog box.

In the Split Window view, you can right-click in the gray area to the right of the Task Form in the bottom window, and see more selections for entering or reviewing information about the selected task as shown in Figure 2.59.

When you start tracking actual work, you can use the Resource Work task form for entering and reviewing the data as shown in Figure 2.60. Notice that you have the resource assignment information such as Work, Baseline, Actual, and Remaining work all in one place. If you remember the formula for Work described earlier, this can be very important to see when the data starts changing for your project schedule.

What you get when you right-click or double-click is different based on what part of the screen your cursor is sitting in. Just a fraction of an inch difference in where your cursor is can make a difference in what you see. As you

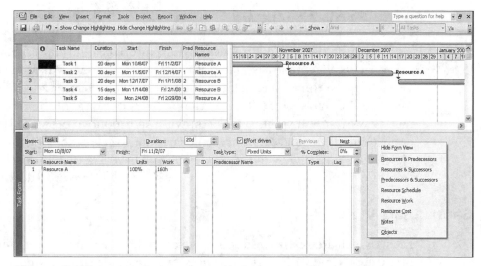

Figure 2.59 *Right-clicking in the Task Form brings up more views.*

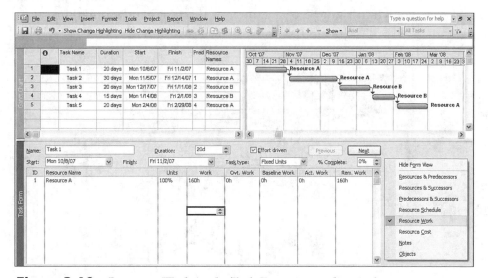

Figure 2.60 *Resource Work in the Task Form in a split window.*

use Project, hover, click icons, right-click, or double-click here and there and see what you get. You might be surprised and learn more about Project in the meantime.

The Major Project Views

As previously discussed, Project provides interfaces into its data structure called views. Views allow you to both enter data and review data in table and visual formats. You've seen a lot of the views in this chapter, and most views involved the Gantt Chart. This section focuses on some of the most important views you will want to use. You will want to move between the views easily to help you analyze Project information. To select any of the following views, click on the view in the view bar if you have it showing, or select View from the menu bar, and click on the view showing in the drop-down list.

Gantt Chart View

Let's say you are ready to start a new schedule. The Gantt Chart view is the first view to open, but it is also a great way to enter your task data. You can enter all of your tasks and quickly create relationships between the tasks in this view. You can essentially create an outline of your project in this view. As shown in Figure 2.61 I can enter the task names, durations, and resources, and see the relationships of the tasks easily in this view.

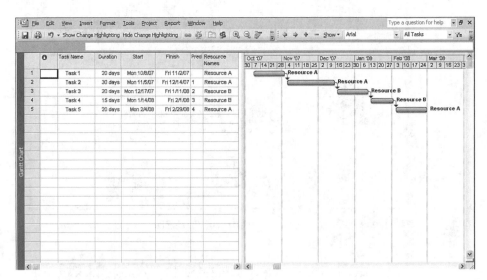

Figure 2.61   *Gantt Chart view: The left side helps you build task outline and right side helps you understand dependencies and the path of your project*

If you use the split window or the Task Information dialog box, you can add more data for each task as well. You might want to add the Work and Successor columns to this view to have just a bit more information when building the schedule. As you draft your schedule by adding and changing tasks and assigning resources, you can watch how the tasks change by looking at the right side bar chart. The bar chart especially helps you analyze the path of the work in your project schedule.

Resource Sheet

Before adding resources to your schedule, it's a good idea to build the team of people who can work on your project. The Resource Sheet is the main view for entering the resources available to work on your schedule and to enter data about them (e.g., their hourly rate or resource group). As shown in Figure 2.62 the Resource Sheet provides a table for entering major resource data.

		Resource Name	Type	Material Label	Initials	Group	Max. Units	Std. Rate	Ovt. Rate	Cost/Use	Accrue At	Base Calendar
1		Resource A	Work		R		100%	$50.00/hr	$0.00/hr	$0.00	Prorated	Standard
2		Resource B	Work		R		100%	$75.00/hr	$0.00/hr	$0.00	Prorated	Standard
3		Resource C	Work		R		100%	$0.00/hr	$0.00/hr	$0.00	Prorated	Standard
4		Resource D	Work		R		100%	$0.00/hr	$0.00/hr	$0.00	Prorated	Standard
5		Resource E	Work		R		100%	$0.00/hr	$0.00/hr	$0.00	Prorated	Standard
6		Equipment 1	Work		E		100%	$0.00/hr	$0.00/hr	$0.00	Prorated	Standard
7		Cost Resource 1	Cost		C						Prorated	
8		Material Resource 1	Material		M			$0.00		$0.00	Prorated	

Figure 2.62   *Resource Sheet for adding resource attributes*

You want to enter the resource names using some consistent naming format, and then add a rate (Std. Rate) to indicate their cost of doing work (if appropriate) and how much they will be available for the project (Max. Units). By opening the Resource Information button for the resources (by double-clicking on each resource name), you can change their calendar to indicate how many hours per day they are available to work, and if there are any days they cannot work, such as vacation days. This view is often ignored, because people add names in the Resource names field in the Gantt Chart view, but it is a good idea to review the Resource Sheet view frequently to see if you have duplicate resources (remember, Jim Moore and JimMoore are two different resources to Project) and to understand the attributes assigned to your resources to make sure they are assigned consistently.

Task Usage View

The Task Usage view, as shown in Figure 2.63 is best for looking at how the work is assigned to each resource on your schedule. Each task shows the resource individually listed under the task. In Figure 2.63 notice that Task 1 has two resources on it and the rest have only one. Resource A and Resource C each are working 40 hours for the week of the 7th and 14th. The total work for Task 1 is 80 hours a week for two weeks.

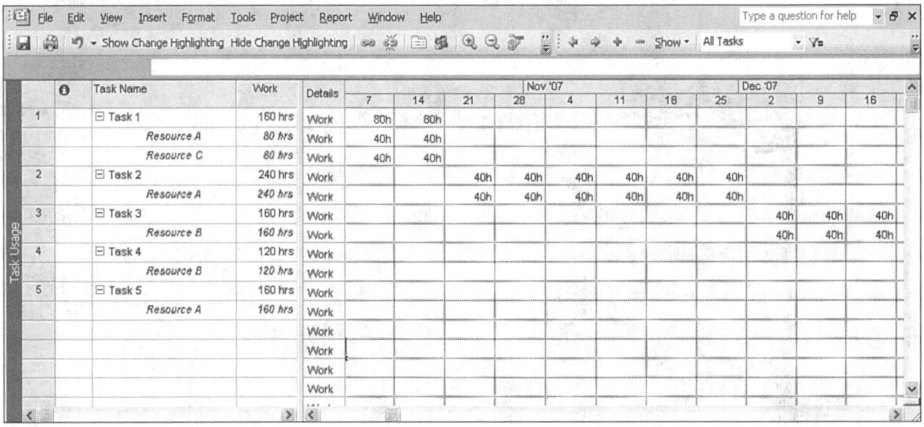

Figure 2.63 *Task Usage view to analyze how task resources are assigned to tasks on a timephased basis*

The Task Usage view is more of an analysis and troubleshooting view rather than an entry view although you can enter work amounts in the view. Once you enter work into this view, it sets the work and you will find it harder to adjust the work later. You can see how you assigned resources on a task on a day-by-day, week-by-week, or month-by-month basis. You may want to use this view to enter Actual Work on a day-by-day or week-by-week basis. See how to enter Actual Work data in this view under the Resource Usage view description.

Resource Usage View

In contrast to the Task Usage view which focuses on tasks, the Resource Usage view focuses on showing all the tasks each resource has been assigned. The Resource Usage view is the best view for showing if a resource has too much work, as each task the resource is assigned is listed under each resource. The Resource Usage view, shown in Figure 2.64, allows you to look at the tasks to which a resource is assigned. Notice that in this view, Resource A is assigned to three tasks, and is assigned to Task 1 and Task 2 at the same time. In this view, the overallocated resources are shown in red, with an icon next to them indicating this overallocation.

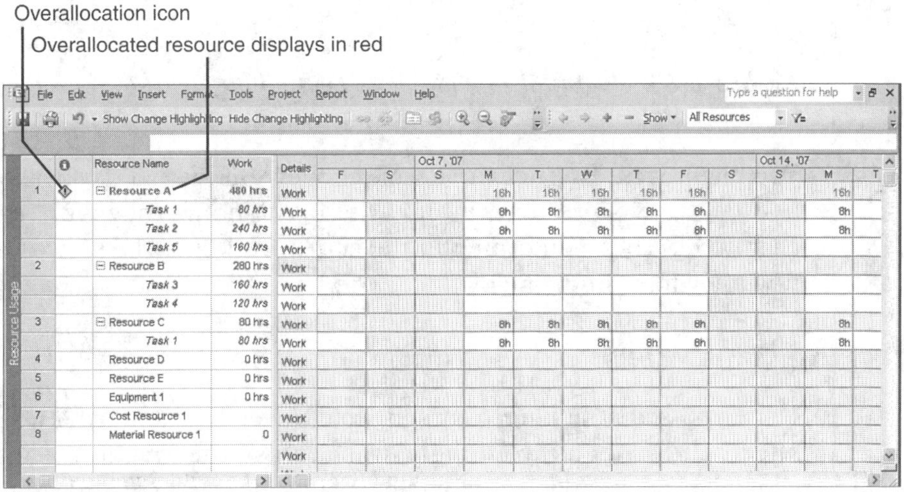

Figure 2.64   *Resource Usage view for analyzing tasks assigned to resources and overallocation of work*

This is extremely handy for analyzing how a resource is assigned to work on a day-by-day, week-by-week, or month-by-month basis.

You might want to use the Resource Usage and Task Usage views to enter actual work information. You can add fields to the right side of Usage views to help you enter or review other data. For instance, you want to enter actual work for Resource A for the weeks of October 7 and October 14. You could include the Actual Work field to enter the data as shown in Figure 2.65. To add the field, right-click in the right side of the view, which opens the Detail Styles dialog box for fields that can be added to the view. Click the Actual Work field that displays in the drop-down list and it will be added to the right side of the view.

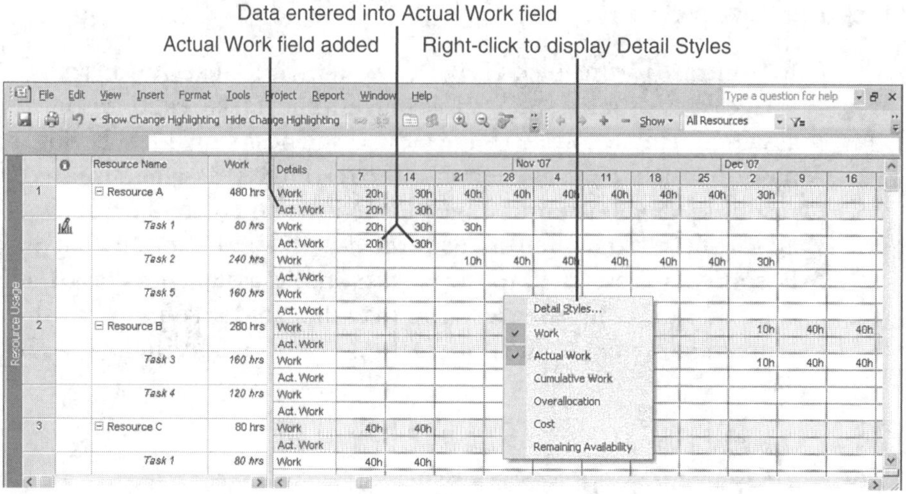

Data entered into Actual Work field

Actual Work field added   Right-click to display Detail Styles

Figure 2.65   *Right-click to add more fields to the right side of a Usage view.*

You might want to print the Resource View out with a day-by-day or week-by-week view so resources can write in the hours they work each day or each week. Then you can enter the actual work into the view directly from how they filled in the fields.

Tracking Gantt View

Once you start tracking your schedule to see how entering task progress affects the schedule you might want to use the Tracking Gantt view as shown in Figure 2.66. If you baseline your schedule to record your estimates, you can quickly see the difference between your original baseline estimates (the lower bar in Figure 2.66) and the actual work progress and the new date your work is estimated to complete (the top bar in Figure 2.66).

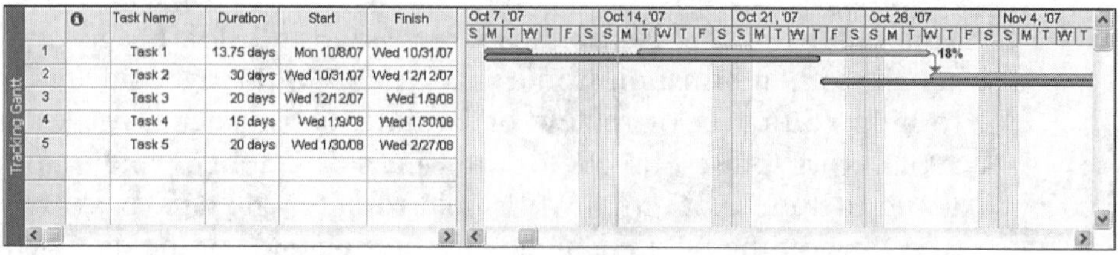

Figure 2.66   *Tracking Gantt view indicates the change in schedule based on entering task progress*

Notice that in Figure 2.66 the original estimate for completion was 10/25/07, but as Actual Work was recorded for the timeframe, the new Finish date is now 10/31/07. Based on reviewing the Tracking Gantt view, you can decide if you think you need to ask resources to work overtime or your project can tolerate the delay at the current pace.

More Views

Project contains 25 views that you can use for entering and analyzing your project data. The view bar shows only some of them. If you would like to see all the views available, select Views from the menu bar, and click More Views as shown in Figure 2.67.

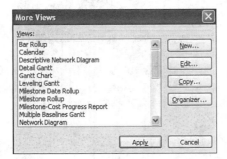

Figure 2.67   *A list of more views available in Project*

Take a look at some of the different views and how the data is different in each view. You can open the file called Ch2-Fig2.67-DifferentViewsPractice.mpp on your CD to practice switching between views and reviewing the practice. You can use any of the tips already described to manipulate the data in the views you review.

What Are Project Tables?

Tables are preset columns in Project that expose different fields in Project in sheet format, usually based on a particular function for schedule analysis or data entry. For instance, if you want to enter actual task progress information, such as percentage complete or actual duration, there is no obvious view to allow you to enter this data. However, Project has a table called Tracking that contains fields for entering actual values.

When you select Views and scan down the drop-down list, you will see a selection called Table: Entry as shown in Figure 2.68. By default, the sheet format table associated with the Gantt Chart is the Entry table. It's purpose is to allow you to enter data into the most common fields of Project. However, you could choose to display a different table on the left side of the separator bar, such as the Tracking view. Tables can display columns about tasks or about resources, depending on what kind of view you are displaying.

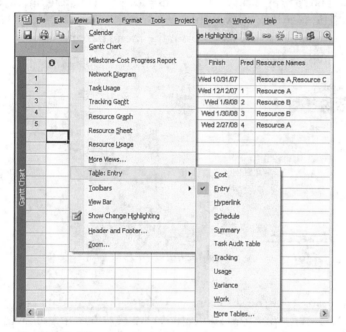

Figure 2.68 *Selecting a different table for the Gantt Chart view*

To see the Tracking table in the Gantt Chart view, select Views from the menu bar. Hover your mouse over the Table: Entry selection until you see another drop-down list, then click Tracking. Figure 2.69 shows several tracking fields available in Project that by default display in the Tracking table.

Sometimes you can get confused if you do not remember to return the table to the original view, so to display the Entry table again, select Views from the menu bar, then hover your cursor over Table: Tracking until you see the drop-down list, then click Entry.

Project allows you to build your own custom tables and views. As you start to understand Project better, you might find that you want to design your

Top bar indicates estimated to complete date for current progress

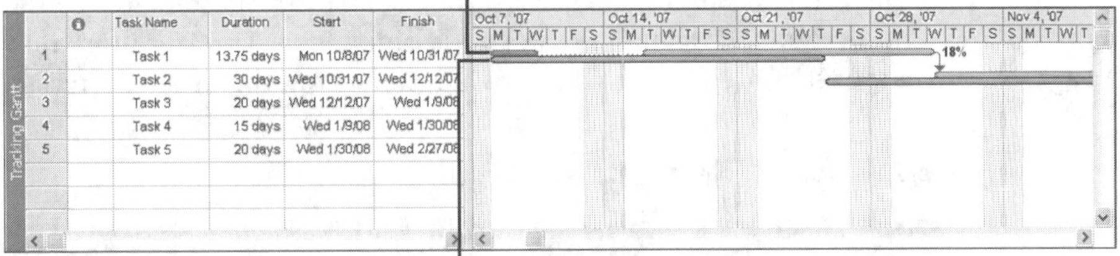

Bottom bar indicates original baseline estimates

Figure 2.69   *The Tracking table in the Gantt Chart view*

own data entry tables and views specific to you or your organization's needs. Chapter 11 describes how you can create your own custom tables and views.

Practice: Navigating and Using Project Views

Now that you've learned some of the basics of Project, it's time to practice them. The following practices allow you to get familiar with the Project interface by creating a new project, adding tasks, inserting columns, and learning to use various views and some of the tips presented so far in this book. This practice will contain some figures to help you make sure you are seeing what's expected, but eventually, practices will include just the steps you should perform.

Practice 2.1

Creating a Project and Using Views

This practice will help you to see the various fields available in the Project data structure. You will also practice adding columns to the Gantt Chart view, which is handy when you have a view up and want to see more information. Don't be surprised if some new tips are introduced—it's to keep you on your toes. However, if you don't perform the practice, the tips will be described in subsequent chapters.

1. Open Project. You should see the Gantt Chart view. You might have a side pane on the left of the interface that displays the task pane if you are using Project 2002 or Project 2003, or the Project Guide if you are using Project 2007.

2. Close the side panes by clicking the X showing in the upper right corner of
    the side panes until you see a screen similar to Figure 2.70. See the earlier sec-
    tion called "Navigating Project and Some Quick Tips" for more information
    about the side panes and removing them from the Project interface.

Project is named Project1 until it is saved

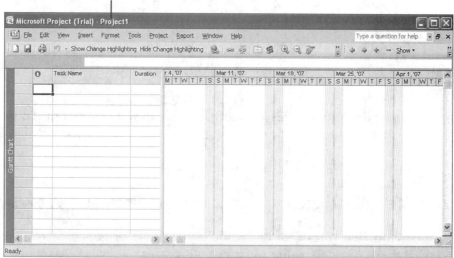

Figure 2.70   *Gantt Chart interface without a side pane showing*

Your view might not be the same

Please note that the view you see might be slightly different. Your toolbar
might display some different buttons, or you might see a View Bar on the
left side of your view based on previous selections made for using Project. The Project interface will not always be the same, depending on settings and options each user selects when using Project.

3. Notice that the project schedule's name is Project1. The project will keep
    this name until you save it. Every time you start a new project in a session,
    Project will assign the next sequential number to each temporary project.

    Enter Task 1 in the Task Name field and move the cursor to the Duration field
    by pressing the right arrow key on your keyboard or clicking your mouse in
    the Duration field. Project automatically enters 1 day in the Duration field,
    and today's date in the Start and Finish date fields (unless some rule has been
    set differently in your version of Project).

Notice that Project enters the number 1 in the gray area to the left of the task. This is the task ID that indicates the position of the task in the task list. Once you create a more comprehensive task list, Project will assign a new ID to the task if it is moved.

4.   To expose other fields in the Project data structure than those that appear in the Gantt Chart view by default, you can insert a field in any view. In the current Gantt Chart view, click the Duration field (you can click the Duration header to highlight the entire column, or in Duration field's cell if you like).

5.   Select Insert on the menu bar and click Column in the drop-down list.

6.   The Column Definition dialog box displays as you saw in Figure 2.3 and Figure 2.4.

7.   In Field name, click the drop-down arrow to the right of the field.

8.   Now scroll up and down the list of visible fields by clicking on the scroll bar. This illustrates the numerous fields available in Project for a view. In fact, each of these fields is actually in the data structure for each task. Data might already be in the field if you were to add it to the view (although the data might be a zero, an NA, or as in the Duration field, 1 day).

Find the Text1 field and scroll down some more. Note that there are 30 Text fields. These are fields in Project available for you to use or customize to further describe the task as you want. For instance, you might include a description of an issue associated with the task. Custom fields are discussed more in Chapter 4.

9.   Now, scroll up until you find Actual Duration and click OK.

Most dialog boxes have an OK button, but some don't

Note that most dialog boxes in Project have an OK button to enter the action you are performing, but a few pop-up boxes do not have an OK button. Double-check to make sure there is an OK button on the dialog box. If not, you can close the box and the change you made will be applied.

10.   You should now see the Actual Duration column after Task Name and before Duration.

When you choose to insert a column, it is inserted to the left of the column on which your cursor is positioned. You might practice adding several other columns, perhaps including Remaining Duration, using these same instructions to see the various fields you could add to the views you have.

11. Now, because you have added a column and exposed a field in the Project data structure in the Gantt Chart view, it might be useful to know how to get rid of it.

Click the Actual Duration column header so the column is highlighted. You can either press the Del key on your keyboard or you can right-click and select Hide Column in the drop-down box. You are not deleting the column, only removing exposure of it in the view you are using. You cannot actually remove a column or field from the Project data structure, so don't worry about hiding columns in any Project view.

12. To see another view of this task, select View from the menu bar and click Resource Sheet. Because you have not added any resources yet, this view is blank. If you decide to show the View Bar to the left of your Project interface, you can select the Resource Sheet from the View Bar if that is easier for you.

13. Enter R1 in the Resource name field. Notice that Project has entered data in the row for the resource. This resource's row of data is now added to the project (if you save the project). Also notice that the resource ID of 1 has been entered for the resource.

14. Select View from the menu bar, and click Gantt Chart again. On Task 1, click the Resource Name field (you might have to move the separator bar to the right to see the Resource Name field). Click on the arrow that displays after you click the Resource Name cell. R1 will display in the drop-down list. Selecting a resource this way is better than typing in the resource: R1 and R 1 are two different resources to Project. You should have a Gantt Chart similar to Figure 2.71 (although your Start and Finish dates might be different).

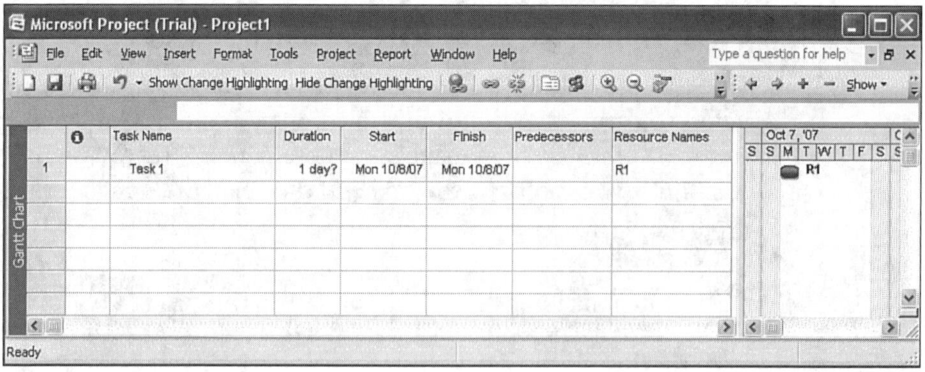

Figure 2.71   *Gantt Chart now shows Task 1 and R1 assigned to the task.*

15. Select View from the menu bar, and click Resource Usage as shown in Figure 2.72. You should see 8 hours on the Start date of the task. If you cannot see the 8 hours, click on Task 1, and then click the Scroll to Task button in the toolbar (see the earlier section "Navigating Project and Some Quick Tips" for more information about the Scroll to Task button).

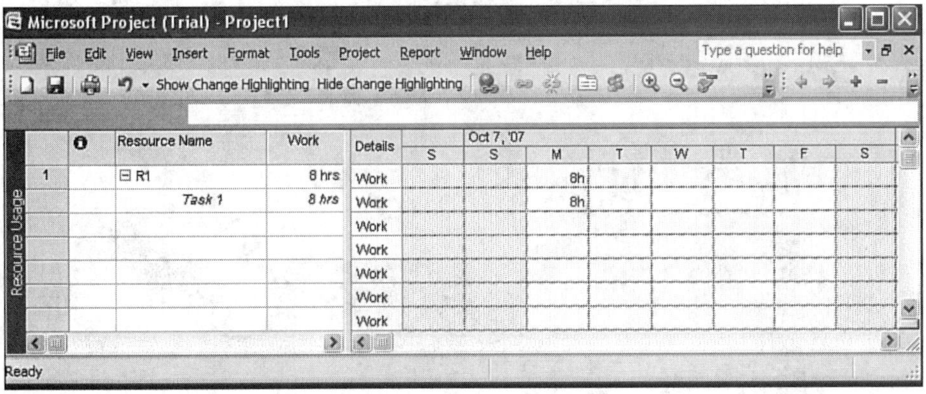

Figure 2.72 *Resource Usage view showing that R1 is assigned 8 hours of work for Task 1*

16. Because this is a simple practice, it's not worth saving this project. Select File from the menu bar and click Close in the drop-down list. Click No in the resulting dialog box. Project is still open but you have no active project in it.

So now you have inserted a column to expose more of the Project data structure and moved about to navigate in different views for a one-task project.

Practice 2.2

Creating a New Project and Using the Split Window

This practice helps you become familiar with using the Split Window function as the split window is used often in this book for practices and to explain concepts. The split window allows you to see hidden data fields that are not readily available in the default Gantt Chart view.

1. Start with all projects closed in Project (click Close after selecting File from the menu bar until Project is all gray). To create a new project, click the New project button, shown in Figure 2.73. If you do not see the New button, select Show buttons as also shown in Figure 2.73 and click the button.

2. If the task pane or Project Guide is showing, click on the X in the upper right corner of the pane.

3. If the view bar is showing on the far left of the Gantt Chart, select View from the menu bar, and click View Bar to remove it. Remember you can display or

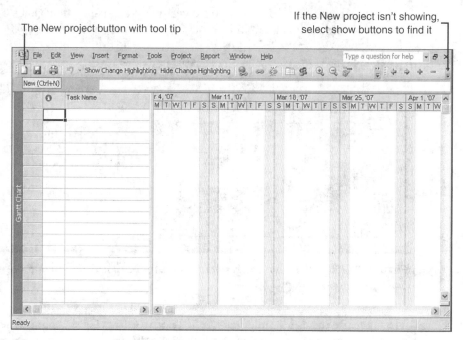

Figure 2.73   *Use the New Project button to create a new project*

not display the View Bar to the left. You can gain more room on your view if you remove it.

4.   Add a task name (e.g., Task 1) on the first line of the project and click the Duration field on the task.

5.   Select Window from the menu bar and click Split.

6.   The split window appears with the Task Form view in the bottom portion of the window. Make sure you click in the top Gantt Chart portion of the view. Notice that the Gantt Chart name is highlighted at the very left of the top window, and that Task Form name is dimmed in the bottom portion.

7.   Make sure your cursor is on the new task you created in the Gantt Chart.

8.   Now click in the bottom window. You can click in the field under Resource Name, for instance. Notice that the Task Form name on the right side is highlighted, and the Gantt Chart name now is faded out. You can easily click between the windows, and the active window is highlighted, whereas the inactive window's view name is dimmed.

Also notice that in the Task Form, not only can you see Resource Name, you can see Units and Work. Because the Work field is not shown by default, nor is it shown for each resource on the Gantt Chart view, you might find it useful to see resource work data.

9. Right-click the Task Form name in the horizontal strip in the bottom window. A drop-down list of available views displays. Click the Task Usage view. Only the line in the Task Usage view for the task you have in the upper window appears as shown in Figure 2.74. If you had not selected Task 1 in the upper window, you wouldn't even see the display as shown in Figure 2.74—there would be no line item showing.

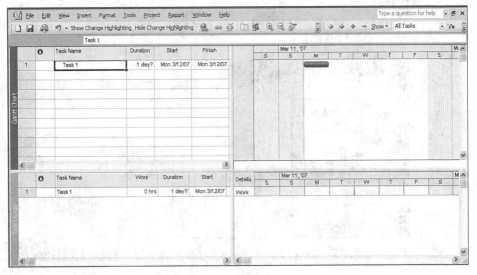

Figure 2.74   *Task Usage view in bottom window*

10. Let's say you want the Task Form back in the bottom window. Right-click again on the Task Usage name on the left of the bottom window. Where is it in the drop-down list? It's under More Views, as shown in Figure 2.75. Select More Views.

11. In the More Views dialog box, scroll down until you find the Task Form view, and then select it.

12. Click Apply. If you did anything to click out of the windows or off the task name as described here, you might be somewhat lost in the windows. As a general tip, if you use the split window and have the wrong view up in the top or lower window, remove the split and start over.

    If you followed these directions to the letter, you are back to the Gantt Chart showing at the top and the Task Form showing at the bottom.

13. To remove the split window, select Window from the menu bar.

14. Click Remove Split. For those of you who are back to the familiar Gantt Chart view, congratulations! For those of you who still don't see the Gantt Chart view you are used to, right-click on whatever view you see in the left area of

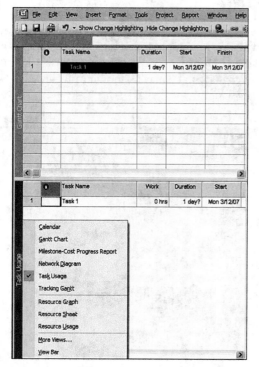

Figure 2.75   *Select More Views to get to the Task Form view again*

the view, and select Gantt Chart from the drop-down list. You might want to try this exercise again, just to practice with the split window to get used to it.

15. Close the project without saving by selecting File, then click Close and click No in the resulting dialog box.

Summary

Hopefully you learned some of the most important secrets of Project in this chapter. By learning the secrets now, you are armed with more information than many users have after using Project for years (including myself when I first took a simple class to get me started in Project a long, long time ago). In fact, I have taught classes in which I introduce these secrets immediately and a student nods and says, "So now I understand! I never knew why I felt Project had a mind of its own." You were introduced to the concept that Project is a data structure with hidden fields and rules for tasks, resources, and assignments and those rules affect the behavior.

Some primary Project data fields are Work, Duration, Cost, Start and Finish dates, Predecessors/Successors (task relationships), and Units (how many resources are assigned to complete a task). Also, by default, Project has flags set that affect how tasks behave (e.g., Effort-driven, Task Type, Constraint) or how resources are assigned work over time (Work Contour). One of the major behaviors in Project is that it designates assignment of work over time, called timephased work. Not only does Project assign work over a time span (e.g., daily, weekly, monthly), but you can select different timescales to see how a resource is assigned to work over that timescale.

In addition to major fields and flags, Project has different states for fields. For instance, Current work or Duration is the estimate for the value at completion, Baselined is a point-in-time estimate (usually the original or agreed-to value), and Actual is the actual value for work or duration of a task reported during execution and tracking. Remaining Work is the amount of time estimated to complete assigned work or duration after progress has been recorded. These common designations for fields in Project are also part of important formulas in Project. Some of these formulas are as follows:

$$\text{Duration} \times \text{Units} = \text{Work}$$

$$\text{Actual Work} + \text{Remaining Work} = \text{Work}$$

$$\text{Actual Duration} + \text{Remaining Duration} = \text{Duration}$$

$$\text{Actual Cost} + \text{Remaining Cost} = \text{Cost}$$

$$\text{Standard rate of resource(s) assigned} \times \text{Work hours} = \text{Cost of a task}$$

If you know that these formulas exist, and cannot be altered in Project, then you start to understand the behavior of Project.

By understanding that resources have availability based on their calendar of time available to work, and how much they can be assigned to a task (called units), you begin to understand that you could overallocate a resource by assigning more work than is possible for that resource to complete.

Hopefully, the navigation introduction helped you to get around in Project and you will try some of the tips while using the schedule-building methodology described in the rest of this book. You can use the major views—Gantt Chart, Resource Sheet, Resource and Task Usage, Tracking Gantt—and tables, such as the Entry and Tracking tables, to enter data and to review and change a schedule according to your specific requirements.

The next chapter starts you off on your schedule-building journey. Using a particular method and sequence of building your schedule, you can use Project as a tool to help you manage your project, rather than the obstacle it can feel like to the unenlightened.

Review Questions

1. When you do not see a field in a view you would like to see, how do you expose the field?

2. What are three categories of the project data structure?

3. Name five of the primary Project fields.

4. How can you see timephased data in Project?

5. What four designations are associated with the Work and Duration fields?

6. What is the most important formula to know in Project?

7. How is a resource's availability calculated in a project?

8. What is the View Bar?

9. What displays in the lower window of the Gantt view in Project when you select Split Window from the menu bar in Project?

10. Why would you want to use the Scroll to Task button?

11. Why would you use the Tracking table rather than the Entry table?

Building Your Schedule: Scoping Your Project

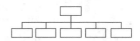

In every phenomenon the beginning remains
always the most notable moment.
—Thomas Carlyle

Topics Covered in This Chapter

The First Steps in Planning a Project Schedule

Building a Task List: Creating a Work Breakdown Structure Outside of the Tool

Naming and Saving Your Project

Set Project Information and the Calendar

Building the Work Breakdown Structure in the Tool: Outlining—Summary and Subtasks

Using Project Templates

The Project Schedule Building Methodology So Far

Practice: Setting up the Schedule

Summary

Case Study: Starting the Schedule

Now that you have learned some basics about the Project interface, you are ready to start building a schedule. Your first task in Project is to build a task list, but in the beginning of this chapter I discuss some of the first things you need to do, most of which you do without using Project. You have to plan your project to know what to put into Project. I cover building a task list based on a work breakdown structure (WBS), which is a hierarchical, deliverable-oriented decomposition of the work of your project. A WBS provides you with an understanding of your project scope and deliverables so you can build a truly usable schedule rather than a laundry list of things to do. After you know your major deliverables and associated activities, you will set up the Project schedule with a project start date and a calendar that includes any holidays or other days excluded for working. You also need to apply good project naming conventions when saving the schedule. You will learn how to format a good Project WBS from scratch and also how to use project templates to create a schedule based on a previously developed schedule. A template provides a prebuilt WBS based on the collective experience of others who came before you building similar projects. Finally, you will have exercises and a case study to practice what you have learned in this chapter.

The First Steps in Planning a Project Schedule

Project has two important functions in project management: providing a schedule for making sure your project tasks complete on time and helping build a budget. However, before you get to those two items, you have to figure out exactly what it is you have to schedule—you must understand and document all the work of your project. In fact, by simply documenting all the work of your project and making sure you only work on the tasks you document, you have achieved one of the most important aspects of your project: managing the scope of your project.

Project Charter

You need authorization to proceed on a project. Whether it is painting your house or starting a new project at work, you need others to agree that it is a necessary project. For house painting, you would probably have a discussion with your spouse about how long it will take, how much money you have to spend, and how you are going to accomplish the work. At work you would probably have an executive telling you to proceed and describing to you what your goal is and what resources you can use. This authorization to proceed on the project can be informal or formal, but it occurs in some way. In business, it should be written, and it should have information about the objectives, budget, and timeline of the project. It should also provide some indication about what it is you must deliver to achieve success: Is it a marketing plan, a review, and presentation to the board by September 10? Is it your house prepped, primed, and painted in a nice light blue paint that won't chip or scratch for 15 years? You get some verbal or written indication that helps you understand as much about the work as you can early in the project so you can plan for it. A project charter authorizes the work of the project. At work, this authorization should help you gain authority and recognition as project manager. A sponsor, manager, or someone who has high-level leadership authority in your organization should let your organization know you are in charge of the project and describe your authority over budget, resources, and the work of the project. The information of the project charter is input to the project plan, and ends up helping you understand what you need to include in the project schedule.

Some of the information you might have in a project charter includes the following:

- The reason for the project: What is the driver for it?
- Purpose of the project.
- The high-level business requirements for building and executing the product or service for the project.
- Important dates for major deliverables you should meet (e.g., when a design should be approved, or when you have to provide the marketing presentation).
- An estimated budget: How much do you think you will spend to complete the project to the satisfaction of the project requirements?
- General information about the factors that can influence the success of the project, such as the people who care and are part of the project (called stakeholders), and assumptions and constraints.

Read Chapter 2 of *Project Management for Mere Mortals*

Chapter 2 of *Project Management for Mere Mortals* will describe the project charter, the elements of obtaining project authorization, and understanding the Measure of Performance (MOP), which can help you understand the expectation for project success.

Defining Project Scope

After you have authorization to proceed with the work, you then need to become very clear about what the work is. What activities (the tasks) and categories of those activities (phases or summary activities) will you perform to get the project done? How much work will there be? What deliverables must be completed to get the project done? Defining the scope well and prior to building the schedule will help your project succeed better than if you start building your tasks lists in Project immediately. There are two elements to defining scope: a scope statement and the WBS. The scope statement is a written document that further describes some of the elements of the project charter. The WBS is a visual or outline representation of the activities in your project.

The scope statement is a very detailed document about many of the same elements you might have described briefly in the project charter. You might document items such as these:

- Description and objectives of the project. Also a description of what defines success for the project.
- Product or service requirements (in fact, you might develop a separate, detailed set of requirements specifications).
- Expected deliverables broken into further detail. For instance, one of your deliverables stated in the project charter might have been "Testing." In more detail, you might have such deliverables as:
  - Obtain test team
  - Create test plan
  - Obtain test plan approval
  - Test
  - Review test results
  - Complete test report
  - Obtain test report approval
- A high-level schedule for the milestones and deliverables.
- A description or listing of project risks (a listing of those things that might jeopardize or provide opportunity for the project), assumptions (those things assumed to be true and valid for the project), and constraints (those things that limit your project work).
- A listing of activities that are outside the scope of your project.
- People or resources involved in completing your project and how your project might be organized in using them. This might be a listing such as five engineers, one specification writer, two testers, and one testing facility.

- Estimated budget. Because you identified the previous items in your scope, you should be able to provide a more detailed budget for your project than in the project charter.

The scope statement helps define the boundaries of your project. If you or anyone on the project goes outside of these boundaries (or it looks like you will as you start executing your project), then you and your team would need to take action to bring the project back into the original scope as described in this statement, or you might start a change process to allow for the additional work for the project.

Again, for any project you are ready to begin, you should create this scope statement. For a simple project, it might be something quickly jotted down for each of the items just listed. Even for a personal project such as painting your house, you should look at the previous and be able to verbally describe each item for your project. On a project for work, you should create a document that describes each listed item in detail for your project. Make sure you check with your organization to see if it has a scope statement template, or you can search the Web for some nice scope statement templates if your organization doesn't have any.

> **Read Chapter 3 of *Project Management for Mere Mortals***
>
> Chapter 3 of *Project Management for Mere Mortals* describes defining scope, including how to build requirements for your project.

Building a Task List: Creating a Work Breakdown Structure Outside of the Tool

When you have completed the scope statement you are ready to create a WBS. This is the source of your project schedule and it helps you build the task list in Project. As mentioned before, a WBS is a task list in outline form or a visual chart of the project. Your main process for building a WBS is to understand and document the main categories, phases, or overall structure of your project. Then, you break down those overall categories into smaller activities that you could easily describe to someone fulfilling the task. For painting your house, the categories or phases of the work are prep, prime, and paint. Then as you think about the breakdown of activities, you might come up with a WBS that looks like Figure 3.1.

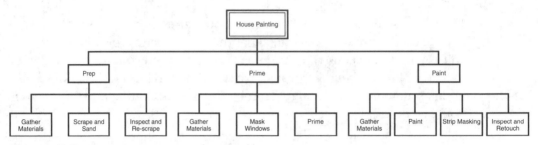

Figure 3.1   *WBS for house-painting project*

The outline form would look something like the following outline.

House Painting

1.0 Prep

        1.1 Gather materials

        1.2 Scrape and sand

        1.3 Inspect and re-scrape

2.0 Prime

        2.1 Gather materials

        2.2 Mask windows

        2.3 Prime

3.0 Paint

        3.1 Gather materials

        3.2 Paint

        3.3 Strip masking

        3.4 Inspect and retouch

You might actually find a preexisting WBS or outline of typical kinds of projects on the web. These project templates are available in various places, and I list some of these in the section called "Using Project Templates" later in this chapter.

It's worthwhile looking for project templates before you ever build your project. Why invent something new when you can use the thoughts of project managers and project teams before you?

However, if you are planning a project for which you cannot find a template, I recommend creating a visual, chart-like form of the WBS as shown in Figure 3.1. If you draft it using sticky notes, it is easier to move the activities around. For instance, you and your project team could get together and brainstorm all of the activities of your project based on your scope statement and the deliverables you have so far. You might use the sticky notes to write down all of the activities of the project. You could group the activities under broad categories, and move the activities around within or across the categories. If you created a visual WBS for the house-painting project, you may realize that you'd rather see the "Gather materials" task on the same level as Prep, Prime, and Paint because that will require going to the store and purchasing the materials, and is an activity that should stand on its own. If so, then your WBS might be changed to something like Figure 3.2.

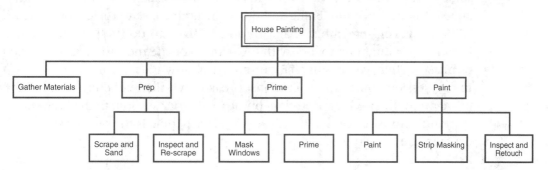

Figure 3.2 *WBS for house-painting project rearranged*

I recommend going through this exercise because although it's easy enough to change tasks around in Project, it is much easier to work with your team using a visual diagramming method to temporarily move and group your tasks. Because the Gantt Chart is a list method of creating your work, it is often hard to see all of the tasks at once for moving them about into their proper categories of similar or dependent work. If you have small projects, or ones that you have done many times, it might be easier to just put the tasks in Project rather than going through a visual diagramming process with your team. Use your judgment, but consider the WBS-building exercise as a great team-building exercise as well.

> **Refer to Chapter 3 of *Project Management for Mere Mortals***
>
> Chapter 3 of *Project Management for Mere Mortals* has a far more detailed description of building a WBS. If you are interested in building a WBS, I recommend reading more about the structure and process of building a WBS there.

Whatever method you use to build a WBS, make sure you build it or verify it with your project team. The project manager does not know most of the work itself; the team does. The team will help you understand what needs to be in the project that you alone might never think of. Even if you use a template, you need to review it with the team. They might recommend more detail or suggest you remove some tasks. They might not understand what some of the tasks are. As a team, you can work to clarify the tasks. This can appear to be an overwhelming and time-consuming task to review or build a WBS. However, remember that you do not have to do it all at once. For instance, you might first work with the team to create the various categories or phases. Then, you might analyze and break down just a particular phase. In one session you might elect to just break down the marketing phase and move on to the product prototype phase in another session. In the long run, working with your team to build the project schedule is the only way a project manager should proceed.

Naming and Saving Your Project

This section introduces how to create a new, open an existing, and save a Project file so you are prepared to start on your project schedule-building journey.

Creating a New Project File

Based on how you are starting out you will do one of the following to create a new Project file:

- If you have not opened the Project application yet, select the application. There are several methods for finding the application after it has been installed, and this book assumes that you have a shortcut or know how to get to the application. When you open the application, you will see Microsoft Project – Project1 in the title bar of the application window. You are ready to start adding tasks. You might want to remove the side pane as discussed in Chapter 2 "Revealing the Secrets of Microsoft Project," by clicking the X in the upper right corner of the Project Guide or task pane.

- If you already have Project open, click the New button on the toolbar as shown in Figure 3.3. You might want to remove the side pane from the view by clicking the X in the upper right corner of the Project Guide or task pane.

- If you already have Project open, you can also select File from the menu bar, and click New. The New Project side pane appears and you can select Blank Project from the side pane, create a new project based on an existing project, or build a new project from Templates as shown in Figure 3.3.

Notice that when you start a new project, Project names it Project1 (or Project2, or Project3, depending on if this is an additional project created during the current session).

New button for selecting a new Project

When creating a new Project, Project increments the new file's number

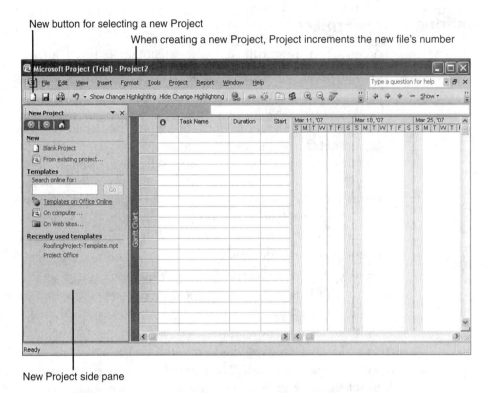

New Project side pane

Figure 3.3   *New Project side pane for creating a new project*

Saving a Project File

You can save your project at any time. If it is the first time you save, you will be required to name the project. If you have already named your project, Project will just save the current file in the last location it was saved. When you select File from the menu bar, then Save for the first time (or use the Save button on the toolbar), a Save As dialog box similar to that shown in Figure 3.4 will appear. If necessary, you can select another directory for saving the file, and enter the project name in the File name field. Click Save to save the file in the location you selected.

In Project 2007, you will see a new button in the lower left of the Save As dialog box. The button contains an option for mapping to a network drive and for password protecting the file under General Options. Some of the other options you see in the drop-down list are unavailable when you are saving.

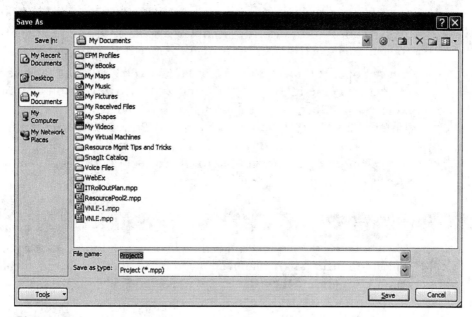

Figure 3.4   *Dialog box for saving your project*

Opening a Project File

To open an existing file you can click on the Open button on the toolbar (as in other Microsoft applications) or select File on the menu bar, then click Open. The Open dialog box displays documents from the My Documents folder (which is where Project saves your project files by default). Select the directory if different from the one showing, select the file, and click Open.

In Project 2007, before opening the file you can select the file and click the Tools button and perform various actions as shown in Figure 3.5.

Figure 3.5   *Tools button available in Project 2007*

If you want to open a recently used file, select File from the menu bar, and the last four Project files you used will display at the end of the File menu. You can then click on one of the files to open it.

You can open a Project 2002 file in Project 2003 and 2007. You can open a Project 2003 file in Project 2002 and 2007. However, you cannot open a Project 2007 file in Project 2003 and a converter will not be available to do this until late 2007. If you need to open a Project 2007 file, your only real solution is to have the originator of the file save it as a previous version. When you save a file, select Microsoft Project 2000 – 2003(*.mpp) in the Save as type field.

Naming Conventions

When you save your project, name it whatever is appropriate for your organization (it's nice to have naming conventions if files are shared in your organization) by entering the name in the File name field and clicking Save. Notice that the name of the project is now in the title bar on the file as shown in Figure 3.6. Do not use special characters, and if the name is more than one word, it is often a good idea to name it with an underscore or dash between the words, rather than a space because in some computer systems and older applications, the filename will show with a strange character between the words if you use a space (e.g., you might see some thing like Named%Project.mpp instead of Named Project.mpp).

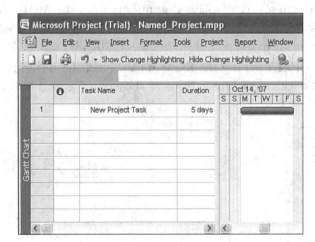

Figure 3.6 *Saved filename displays in the left of the application's title bar.*

When should you save changes to your Project file?

As you are working in your file, you might want to think about when you save your changes. Unlike other Microsoft applications that allow multiple undo steps, Project versions prior to 2007 only allow one undo step on a file. If you make several changes, and you realize you do not want to keep them, saving frequently will mean you have to retrace your steps to remove your changes because you cannot undo your work. However, if you do not save your file frequently, you could lose your changes if there is a computer glitch or your application freezes. As you work on your file, think more about the work itself and your confidence in the changes you made, rather than how long it has been since a save. If you make one change that you like, save it. If you are performing several changes, and you are not sure about the outcome of those changes, don't save until you are done and satisfied with the changes. An alternative is to save every hour or so and use a time convention in naming (Big_Project_July15_130). Then when you are confident in the very last version, you can delete the prior ones.

Project 2007 and later versions allow multiple undos, so this is less important if you have a later version of Project.

Project's Filenames

Project contains a couple of different kinds of file types, including these two, which you will usually use in Project:

- **mpp:** This is the default file extension name for a project schedule. Example: My_Project.mpp.
- **mpt:** This is the file extension for a project template. A template will preserve certain information that you can use over and over again. It is better to use a template than to copy other project schedules. You might preserve good project schedules that your organization would like to use again as a template. See "Using Project Templates" later in this chapter for more information.

You might notice there are also other file extensions, as shown in Figure 3.7. Most of these are used for exporting data to other applications or databases from Project. Figure 3.7 shows the Project 2007 file formats you can save.

Project 2002 and Project 2003 contain other file formats you can use such as a Project Database, Web Page, and Project 98. Describing the other file formats is outside the scope of the book, but if you are looking to open or save Project files in other applications you can explore what these files can do for you by typing File Formats in the Search field within Project Help. Look for the subject called "File formats supported by Microsoft Office Project."

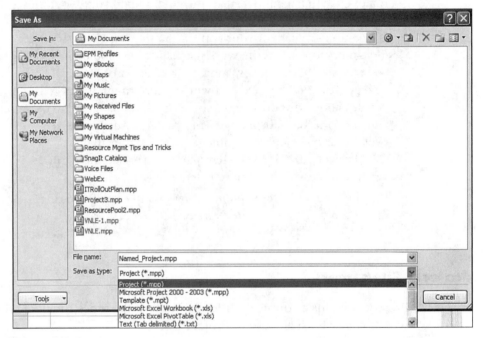

Figure 3.7   *Some file formats in Project*

Set Project Information and the Calendar

Let's get started on a project now that you know the various methods for creating, saving, and opening Project files. Whether you have a preexisting project template or are ready to build your WBS into the project, you need to set up your Project file with initial attributes. You will create a project calendar and indicate the start date of the project.

If you can get into the habit of performing these steps each time you create a new project, you will be building good habits and you will have fewer issues with Project down the road.

Create a Project Calendar

Creating a project calendar is an easy step to forget because you just want to start typing in your project tasks. However, if you forget as you are executing your tasks and reviewing the schedule, you might find that the work is several days behind compared to the date the schedule shows you should be done, perhaps because you forgot to account for a couple of holidays. Using the default standard calendar out of the box Project will allow you to schedule your resources during those days. If your organization has holidays (and I certainly hope it does), you will probably need to create a project calendar to account for them. If you have a personal project, and you know you cannot work on certain days during the project, you will want to have Project take those days into account. When you indicate nonworking days for your organization on the calendar, Project will make sure that no work is scheduled for that day and will adjust the end date of the work schedule accordingly. You can create as many customized calendars as you want to account for nonworking time on your project. Project ships with three calendars that can be used for various conditions:

- **Standard:** This is the main calendar you will work with and all projects are automatically assigned to this calendar. It is set to allow work from 8 a.m. to 5 p.m. each day Monday through Friday, with noon to 1 p.m. being nonworking time (assuming an hour for lunch). The hours are not associated with time zones. Using these times, the calendar assumes the work day to be 8 hours long. Project will schedule work within that time frame each day if you use the Standard calendar. It also indicates that Saturday and Sunday are nonworking days.

  Note that when you add holidays, you will not see them easily in the Gantt Chart view. In Figure 3.8 the calendar has been altered to indicate that Tuesday, December 25 and Tuesday, January 1 are nonworking days. Also, the weekends are nonworking days. Although it looks like the Gantt Chart has scheduled work throughout these days with the horizontal bar crossing the weekends and those holidays, if you notice the gray vertical columns for those days, they indicate the weekends and December 26 and January 2 are nonworking days.

  The Usage view as shown in Figure 3.9, clearly shows that time has not been scheduled during weekends and on December 26 and January 2.

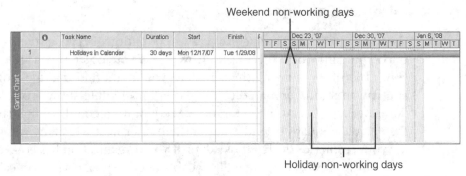

Figure 3.8   *Gray vertical lines indicate nonworking days in the schedule*

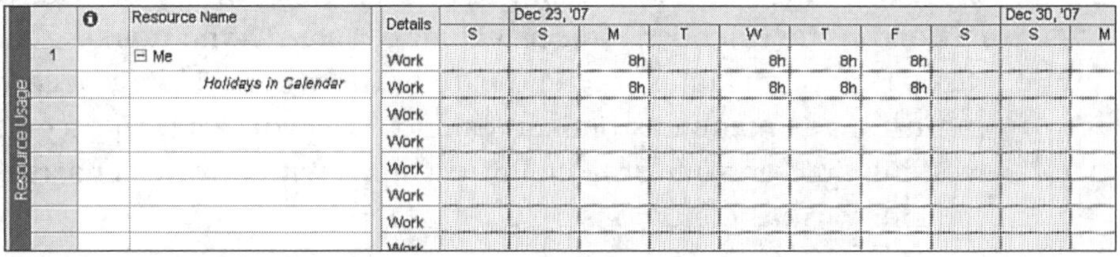

Figure 3.9   *The Resource Usage, which shows a timephased data view, clearly shows work is not scheduled for nonworking days*

Change the default Gantt Chart view for showing nonworking time

Although by default Project shows the Gantt chart with the Gantt Chart bar going through nonworking times, this is merely the way Project is visually displaying bars on the chart. You can change this by making non-working time stand out more on the Gantt Chart by selecting Format on the menu bar, then selecting Timescale. If you select the Nonworking Time tab in the Timescale dialog box that appears, and select the In front of task bars option, the nonworking time will show more prominently in the Gantt Chart view as shown in Figure 3.10.

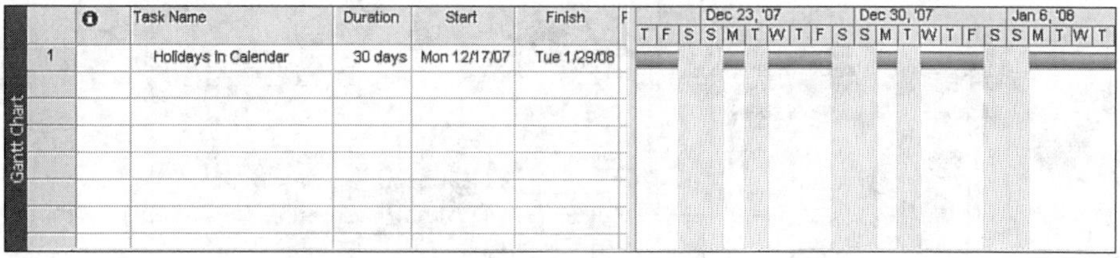

Figure 3.10   *Nonworking days showing prominently in Gantt Chart*

- **24 Hours:** This calendar allows for 24 working hours per day, every day of the week. You will probably not use this calendar for most of your projects, but Project provides this calendar for several special circumstances you might encounter. Some projects might use three shifts to accomplish the project's goal in a very short, concentrated time frame, such as highway improvement projects or critical power plant upgrades. You might also copy this 24-hour calendar and then alter it. For instance, you might need to show that you work 7 days a week, 8 hours each day. This might be the calendar you copy and change for that. You will see how to copy and alter a calendar later.

- **Night Shift:** This calendar is set for 8 hours of work from 11 p.m. to 8 a.m., 5 days a week. If you are interested in using this calendar, check out how the days are set by reviewing the calendar in Project.

Creating a Project Calendar for Project 2007

The interface in the Project calendar has changed in Project 2007 from previous versions. The next section provides instructions for Project 2002 and 2003. To set nonworking days in the project calendar, do the following:

1. After creating a new file or opening an existing project, select Tools from the menu bar.
2. Select Change Working Time from the drop-down list. You will see the Change Working Time dialog box shown in Figure 3.11.
3. Click on the day you want to make a nonworking day.
4. In the Exceptions tab, enter the name of the nonworking day (e.g., New Year's Day).
5. Continue forward and account for the other nonworking days in the calendar until all are entered.

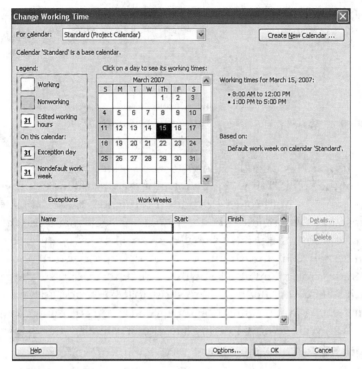

Figure 3.11   *Change Working Time dialog box*

If you would like to create nonworking days for recurring instances (perhaps creating a 5-year calendar to account for New Year's Day for the next 5 years), also click the Details button.

In the section called Recurrence pattern, shown in Figure 3.12, click the Yearly button, and select End after in the Range of recurrence section. You can enter 5 in the Occurrences field. Click OK.

6. Click OK when done with changing nonworking time.

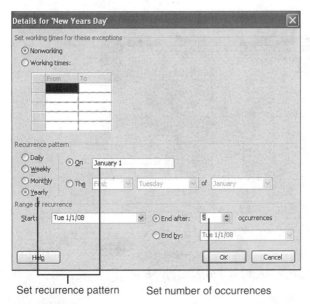

Set recurrence pattern   Set number of occurrences

Figure 3.12 *Set recurrence pattern for nonworking time*

Creating a Project Calendar for Project 2002 or Project 2003

Project 2002 and Project 2003 allow you to create nonworking days but do not allow for recurrences over several years—you have to set them for each year.

1. After creating a new file or opening an existing project, select Tools from the menu bar.
2. Select Change Working Time from the drop-down list. You will see the Change Working Time dialog box shown in Figure 3.13.
3. Click on the day you want to make a nonworking day.
4. Click the Nonworking time option in the upper right section of the dialog box.
5. Continue forward and account for the other nonworking days in the calendar until all are entered. Click OK.

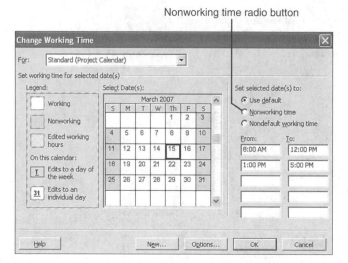

Nonworking time radio button

Figure 3.13   *Change Working Time dialog box*

Calendars are reset for each project

For all versions of Project, if you change the Standard calendar for one project and then create a new project, the changes you made are not automatically available to the new project. You need to copy the change you made into the Global.mpt, which is a file that makes items that are changed from the default settings available to all projects in your application. See "Making a Calendar Available for All Projects" later in the chapter to understand how you can reuse calendars that you have changed or created.

The following section describes various tips for changing calendars. You might need to change calendars to change working times, add nonworking time, or copy a calendar and use it for other projects besides the one you are on.

> **Calendars can also be assigned to resources and tasks**
>
> Calendars are by default associated with resources, and they can also be assigned to tasks. For instance, Mary might have a calendar assigned to her to indicate she is available for part-time work only 4 hours a day. A particular task might have a calendar assigned to indicate that the task (e.g., performing an application upgrade) can be performed over the weekend, whereas the rest of the tasks in the schedule should honor the weekends and holidays of the project. These three uses of calendars work together to indicate how work can be scheduled for a project. Task and resource calendars are discussed in more detail in Chapter 4 "Understanding Task Information" and Chapter 6 "Understanding Resources and Their Effects on Tasks" respectively.

Changing Working Time

In some cases, you might need to reduce or increase the default 8 hours available on a project by changing the working time in a project calendar. To do so, follow these steps:

1. Select Tools from the menu bar.

2. Select Change Working Time from the drop-down list. You will see the Change Working Time dialog box.

3. Click on the day or days for which you want to change the time. For Project 2007, click the Work Weeks tab first.

   In Project 2002 and Project 2003, if you want to change several days in a row, you can click the first day you want, then press and hold down the Shift key. Then click through the rest of the days up to the last day in the row or rows you want to change.

   If you want to change a column to make the change for the same day of the week, click on the day designation column (e.g., "M" for Monday), and the entire column will be highlighted as shown in Figure 3.14. The change you make will affect all days in the column before and after what you select. For instance, if you select all the Mondays in November, all Mondays in the calendar will be changed.

   In Project 2007, after selecting the Work Weeks tab, in the Details For dialog box, select the day of the week you would like to change as shown in Figure 3.15.

4. In Project 2002 or Project 2003, click the Nondefault working time option as shown in Figure 3.14 and in Project 2007 click Set day(s) to these specific working times as shown in Figure 3.15.

5. Change the times in the From: and To: fields as desired. For example, in Figures 3.14 and 3.15, the default 5:00 p.m. was changed to 6:00 p.m. This will change the available project hours on all Mondays to 6 hours.

6. Click OK. In Project 2007, click OK again to exit the calendar.

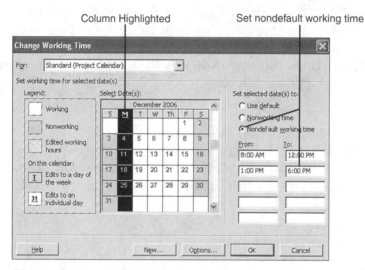

Figure 3.14   *Highlighting a column and changing working time in a calendar in Project 2002 or Project 2003*

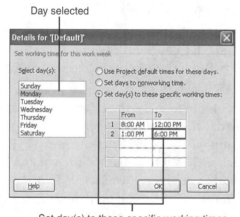

Figure 3.15   *Selecting a day and changing working time in a calendar in Project 2007*

When you change working time to anything different from 8 hours, you should also change a setting to ensure the duration field display reflects the same way in your project schedule. Select Tools from the menu bar, then click Options. On the Options dialog box, select the Calendar tab, and change hours per day to whatever you changed the hours to in the calendar. Notice on the tab you can also change the hours per week and days per month if appropriate for your organization.

Creating a New Calendar by Copying an Existing One

One of the best ways to create a new calendar is to copy one that already exists. For instance, you might want to create a special calendar for a project that indicates that people can only be scheduled to work on weekends. Maybe this is a house-painting project, and you can only get to the work on the weekends. You could create a new calendar called Weekend Calendar by performing the following steps:

1. Select Tools from the menu bar.
2. Select Change Working Time in the drop-down list. You will see the Change Working Time dialog box.
3. In Project 2007 click Create New Calendar, and in Project 2002 or Project 2003 click New. The Create New Base Calendar dialog box will display as shown in Figure 3.16.
4. Type the name of the calendar you are creating in the Name field. In the example, the calendar has been named Weekend Calendar.
5. Click the Make a copy of option and select the calendar you want to copy in the drop-down list.
6. Click OK and then click OK again.

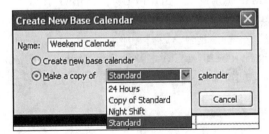

Figure 3.16 *Creating a new calendar by copying an existing one*

The new calendar is now available for the project you have displayed. You can make this new calendar active for the project in the Project Information dialog box, which is described in the later section "Setting the Attributes of the Project."

Making a Calendar Available for All Projects

For each new project you create, by default, the only calendars available to you are the three calendars shipped with Project. If you changed the Standard calendar to account for your organization's nonworking days or created a new calendar you would like to use for other projects, you need to copy those calendars to make them available for all projects. To do so, follow these steps:

1. Select Tools from the menu bar in the project that has the new calendar (you must be in the project that has the calendar you want to use for other projects).

2. Select Organizer from the drop-down list. The Organizer dialog box displays as shown in Figure 3.17. The Organizer allows you to copy fields, views, and other items you customize for availability to all of your projects.

3. Click the Calendars tab. Figure 3.17 shows the Weekend Calendar we created in the previous procedure. Notice that the three default calendars in the Global.mpt are on the left side of the screen. The calendars that are available in the current project are on the right side of the Organizer.

4. Click the new calendar on the right side in the current project.

5. Click Copy. Notice that the pointers next to Copy are now pointing toward the Global.mpt area on the left side of the display. This will move the new calendar from the current project into the Global.mpt, which will make the calendar available to all projects you create in the future.

6. Close the dialog box by clicking Close when you are done. You do not need to press OK to make this change effective.

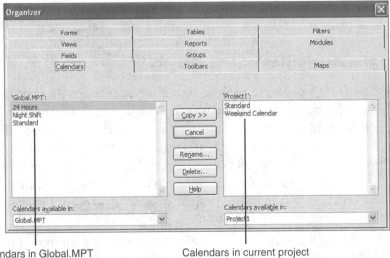

Calendars in Global.MPT   Calendars in current project

Figure 3.17   *Organizer dialog box*

Change the Standard calendar to your organization's calendar

For new projects you might forget to assign the project calendar to your project to indicate your organization's nonworking days. The Standard calendar is assigned by default. When you first start using Project, you might want to alter the Standard calendar to indicate the nonworking days for your organization for several years. Then, you would use the earlier instructions for making a calendar available for all projects to move the Standard calendar from your project to the Global.mpt. You would get a message asking if you want to copy over the existing Standard calendar in the Global.mpt, and you would want to do so.

Using someone else's calendar

At times, someone else might have created a calendar you would like to use. For instance, perhaps someone has set up a calendar for part-time work that allows for a 4-hour day. Rather than building that calendar yourself, you can just use theirs. To do so, have the creator send you a project that has the particular calendar. Open that project, and then use the earlier instructions for making a calendar available for all projects to move the particular calendar from the open project to the Global.mpt.

Once you have set up or made the calendar available for your project, you are ready to set up the start date and assign the calendar to your project.

Setting the Attributes of the Project

I recently looked at a project where the user typed the start date of the project into the first task of the project. This is one of the most typical ways people unfamiliar with Project show their project's start date. Rather than typing the date on the first task it's better to create a project start date. Let's say you want to start the project on October 8. However, the date you started building the project is October 1. For each project you create, after either creating or verifying you have the project calendar, you want to set the attributes of the project: the start date and the project calendar.

To set the start date and the project calendar in your new project, do the following:

1. Select Project on the menu bar.
2. Select Project Information. You will see the Project Information dialog box as shown in Figure 3.18.

Figure 3.18   *Project Information dialog box*

3. Type the date you want the project to actually start on in the Start date field. Now, rather than the project starting on 10/1, it will start on 10/8.
4. In the Calendar field, use the drop-down list to assign the appropriate project calendar. You can keep the Standard calendar assigned if you changed the Standard calendar to reflect your organization's nonworking time, as described earlier in the section "Making a Calendar Available for All Projects."
5. Click OK. Now your attributes are set, and you will be ready to build your schedule.

Although you do not need to use the other fields in this screen when you create your project, you might be curious about a few of them.

It is often very tempting for people to use the Finish date rather than the Start date for a project. As you create your project, your sponsor might say, "You must be done by April 30." In the Project Information dialog box, you might be tempted to select Project Finish Date in the Schedule from field and enter 4/30 in the Finish date field. Avoid the temptation. Build the schedule from the start and let the end fall where it may. If you do a good job of building a reliable schedule, you can compare your schedule end date with the date the sponsor says it must be completed. Sponsors typically want projects finished faster than can reasonably be accomplished. By developing a good schedule you can ask the sponsor, "You say the project must be complete by April 30, but the schedule the team and I developed shows that June 15 is a more likely date. Can you obtain additional resources to apply to the project to speed it up or is there some element of the scope that can be pared from the project?" You do not want to blindly build your schedule around a forced end date and have to try to deliver to a date that requires several miracles to achieve. However, if you are experienced and understand what can happen, you can schedule from the end date. To enter a date in either the Start date or Finish date field, you must first select which way you want to schedule by selecting the Schedule from date.

In the Project Information dialog box, the Current date value comes from the computer system and the Status date will be used when you start tracking the project as described in Chapter 11 "Tracking Your Schedule." The Priority field indicates the importance of the project and is used for leveling resources across several projects. Leveling is a process that helps indicate how you might resolve resource overallocations or conflicts if you have more than one project. Leveling is described in Chapter 9 "Polishing Your Schedule Part Deux: Overallocation."

The Options dialog box also sets some Project attributes

If you select Tools from the menu bar and click Options, you will see a dialog box with several tabs with fields that also set many attributes that affect your schedule's behavior. Other than choosing to display the Project Summary task as described later, you should not need to change any of the default settings. You should be aware of these settings, and they are described in greater detail in Chapter 13 "Project Mysteries Resolved!"

See the exercise at the end of this chapter to practice creating a calendar and setting the project start date and calendar.

Building the Work Breakdown Structure in the Tool: Outlining—Summary and Subtasks

Now that you have completed some very basic functions in setting project attributes and saving and naming the project file, you are ready to start building your schedule's task list. As you build your task list you do nothing more than enter and organize the tasks for your project. You will be tempted to add duration and resources on each task, but resist this urge. When I first started using Project (without much instruction), I added a task, then entered how long I thought it would take and the resource I thought it would need on it. I then did the same for the next task. I had all sorts of issues with Project (mostly because I didn't understand the scheduling algorithm in the tool), but as I have used the application more and more, I've learned that by simply getting the scope of the work into Project first, without worrying about the length of each task and who is going to perform the work, I am much less likely to have issues later on. By focusing on the scope, you won't let the other elements get in the way of your thinking at this stage. In the following section, I describe the best way to build your task list (WBS) into Project. I describe the functions you perform but remember—as pointed out earlier in the chapter—most of the work for understanding the scope and tasks of your project should have been done outside of the application first.

Adding the Project Summary Task

Before doing anything else, add the Project summary task to the Project file. A common mistake some students make is when they add their first task to represent an overall summary task for the project schedule as shown in Figure 3.19. This is not a good practice because Project itself provides this function using a zero task line. The zero summary line rolls up all the information for you about the project and displays the filename you used to name your project.

However, it is not obvious where you set the zero project summary task line in Project. Here is another mystery revealed. To show the Project summary task, do the following:

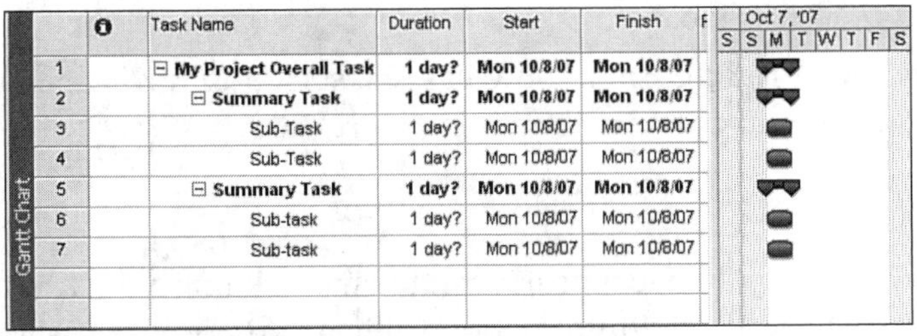

	❶	Task Name	Duration	Start	Finish	F	Oct 7, '07
							S S M T W T F S
1		⊟ **My Project Overall Task**	**1 day?**	**Mon 10/8/07**	**Mon 10/8/07**		
2		⊟ **Summary Task**	**1 day?**	**Mon 10/8/07**	**Mon 10/8/07**		
3		Sub-Task	1 day?	Mon 10/8/07	Mon 10/8/07		
4		Sub-Task	1 day?	Mon 10/8/07	Mon 10/8/07		
5		⊟ **Summary Task**	**1 day?**	**Mon 10/8/07**	**Mon 10/8/07**		
6		Sub-task	1 day?	Mon 10/8/07	Mon 10/8/07		
7		Sub-task	1 day?	Mon 10/8/07	Mon 10/8/07		

Figure 3.19 *Bad practice for creating a project summary task*

1. In the project you are building, select Tools on the menu bar and click Options.

2. You will see the Options dialog box, as shown in Figure 3.20.

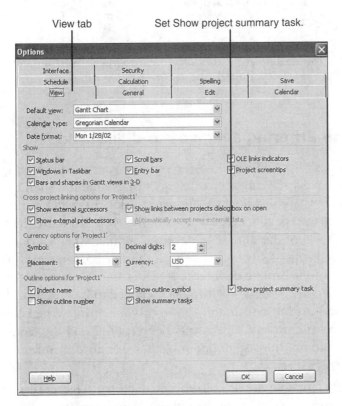

Figure 3.20 *Options dialog box*

3. Select the View tab.

4. In the lower right corner you will see a selection field called Show project summary task as shown in Figure 3.20.

5. Click OK.

Now your project will have a project summary task line, which is numbered zero, and it will display the information similar to the way it is shown in Figure 3.21.

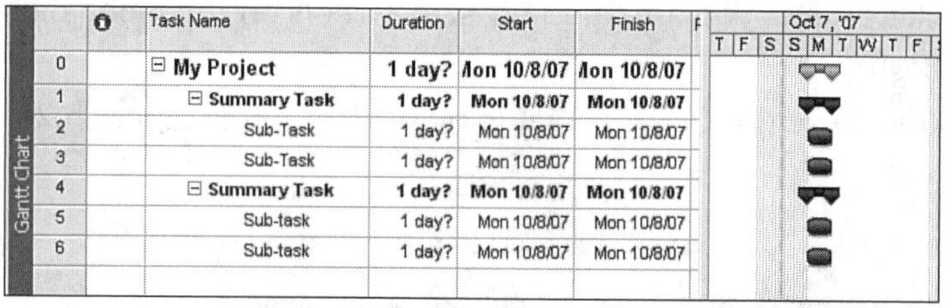

	❶	Task Name	Duration	Start	Finish	F	Oct 7, '07
							T	F	S	S	M	T	W	T	F
0		⊟ **My Project**	**1 day?**	Mon 10/8/07	Mon 10/8/07		
1		⊟ **Summary Task**	**1 day?**	Mon 10/8/07	Mon 10/8/07		
2		Sub-Task	1 day?	Mon 10/8/07	Mon 10/8/07		
3		Sub-Task	1 day?	Mon 10/8/07	Mon 10/8/07		
4		⊟ **Summary Task**	**1 day?**	Mon 10/8/07	Mon 10/8/07		
5		Sub-task	1 day?	Mon 10/8/07	Mon 10/8/07		
6		Sub-task	1 day?	Mon 10/8/07	Mon 10/8/07		

Figure 3.21   *The zero project summary line displays in your project Gantt Chart view*

Understanding and Entering Summary and Subtasks

Building your task list is like building an outline. Your WBS is built in such a way that you have your category or project phase names, such as Prep or Paint, which are the equivalent of summary tasks in Project at the outline level of 1. Then, the specific tasks, which are the work itself, are the subtasks at the second level of the outline under each summary task. If one of those tasks had several subtasks, they would be at the third outline level. The project can be an outline broken down into several summary tasks and subtasks, as deep as the outline takes you, although you need to be practical about the outlining based on the depth and scope of your work. When building a rocket, I suspect the project WBS is very deep (perhaps in the teens for outline levels), but in our house-painting project, we really only need two levels below the project level.

So for instance, for our house-painting project, we have determined the scope of the work and can show the outline as follows:

1.0 Gather materials

2.0 Prep

    2.1 Scrape and sand

    2.2 Inspect and rescrape

3.0 Prime

    3.1 Mask windows

    3.2 Prime

4.0 Paint

    4.1 Paint

    4.2 Strip masking

    4.3 Inspect and retouch

When we enter this into Project, it will look like Figure 3.22.

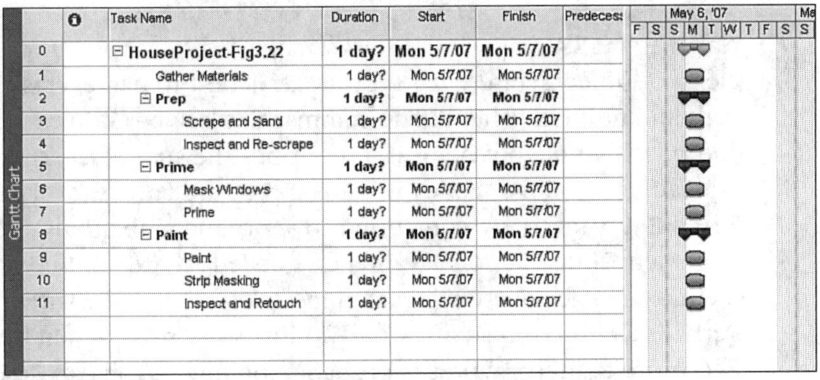

		Task Name	Duration	Start	Finish	Predeces:	May 6, '07 F S S M T W T F S	Ma S
0		⊟ HouseProject-Fig3.22	1 day?	Mon 5/7/07	Mon 5/7/07			
1		Gather Materials	1 day?	Mon 5/7/07	Mon 5/7/07			
2		⊟ Prep	1 day?	Mon 5/7/07	Mon 5/7/07			
3		Scrape and Sand	1 day?	Mon 5/7/07	Mon 5/7/07			
4		Inspect and Re-scrape	1 day?	Mon 5/7/07	Mon 5/7/07			
5		⊟ Prime	1 day?	Mon 5/7/07	Mon 5/7/07			
6		Mask Windows	1 day?	Mon 5/7/07	Mon 5/7/07			
7		Prime	1 day?	Mon 5/7/07	Mon 5/7/07			
8		⊟ Paint	1 day?	Mon 5/7/07	Mon 5/7/07			
9		Paint	1 day?	Mon 5/7/07	Mon 5/7/07			
10		Strip Masking	1 day?	Mon 5/7/07	Mon 5/7/07			
11		Inspect and Retouch	1 day?	Mon 5/7/07	Mon 5/7/07			

Figure 3.22   *The painting project entered into Project*

If you display the WBS column, the outline would look like Figure 3.23, which is exactly like the outline we created without using Project.

	❶	WBS	Task Name	Duration	Start	Finish	May 6, '07 S S M T W T F S S	Ma S
0		0	⊟ HouseProject-Fig3.23	1 day?	Mon 5/7/07	Mon 5/7/07	▼▼	
1		1	Gather Materials	1 day?	Mon 5/7/07	Mon 5/7/07	▬	
2		2	⊟ Prep	1 day?	Mon 5/7/07	Mon 5/7/07	▼▼	
3		2.1	Scape and Sand	1 day?	Mon 5/7/07	Mon 5/7/07	▬	
4		2.2	Inspect and Re-scrap	1 day?	Mon 5/7/07	Mon 5/7/07	▬	
5		3	⊟ Prime	1 day?	Mon 5/7/07	Mon 5/7/07	▼▼	
6		3.1	Mask Windows	1 day?	Mon 5/7/07	Mon 5/7/07	▬	
7		3.2	Prime	1 day?	Mon 5/7/07	Mon 5/7/07	▬	
8		4	⊟ Paint	1 day?	Mon 5/7/07	Mon 5/7/07	▼▼	
9		4.1	Paint	1 day?	Mon 5/7/07	Mon 5/7/07	▬	
10		4.2	Strip Masking	1 day?	Mon 5/7/07	Mon 5/7/07	▬	
11		4.3	Inspect and Retouch	1 day?	Mon 5/7/07	Mon 5/7/07	▬	

Figure 3.23   *The painting project with the WBS column added to the view*

Notice in this example that the Gather materials task is on the same level as the Prep, Prime, and Paint tasks. The only reason that Prep, Prime, and Paint are bold is because they have subtasks. This outlining is a basic structure in a schedule. How was this outline created?

You could just enter your tasks as you need and make tasks summary and subtask as you enter them. The following list describes some of the methods for entering project tasks.

- **Naming tasks:** As you enter tasks, make sure you name them so it is clear to someone else what they are. It is best to name a task with a verb and noun in general. The summary task does not have to be verb and noun, although it helps if it describes the sum of the subtasks beneath it. In all the names, it helps if they are fairly short and precise. You don't want to use something so short and ambiguous as "Write document," but you don't want a task called "Write Module 1482 document using specifications created in Task 68 and make sure it's edited." Perhaps a compromise of "Write Module 1482's document" would suffice. More than five words is probably too much. You can describe a task more fully in a Task Note. See the section "Using Task Notes Liberally" later in this chapter for more information on using task notes.

- **Enter tasks:** In the Task name field in the first row, enter a task name. This will automatically be added at the first level or take on the same outline level as the task before it. If you have just added a task at the second outline level, the next task you add will be at the same level. If you intend the next task to be at the first level, you need to outdent it as described later.

- **Indent a task:** To make a task a subtask to a previous task, click the task you want to demote in the outline, and then click the Indent button as shown in Figure 3.24. You can also select Project in the menu bar, then select Outline and then Indent in the drop-down lists.

- **Outdent a task:** To move a task up to a higher level, click on the task you want to promote, and then click the Outdent button, as shown in Figure 3.24. You can also select Project in the menu bar, then select Outline and then Outdent in the drop-down lists. Note, however, that if the task you are outdenting has subtasks to it, they will also be outdented.

Your Indent/Outdent buttons might be in a different location

You might find your outlining buttons in a different location on your toolbar, depending on if you have them on one or two rows, if you are showing them all, or how large your screen is.

Figure 3.24   *The Indent and Outdent buttons on the toolbar*

You have many handy tools available for expanding and collapsing this outline list to analyze your schedule. Select Project from the menu bar, click Outline, then select Show from the drop-down lists as shown in Figure 3.25. When you select Outline Level 1, you can show just the Level Tasks for the project as shown in Figure 3.26. For very large project schedules, by selecting various outline levels, you can analyze your project and view only certain sections rather than worrying about scrolling through the whole project.

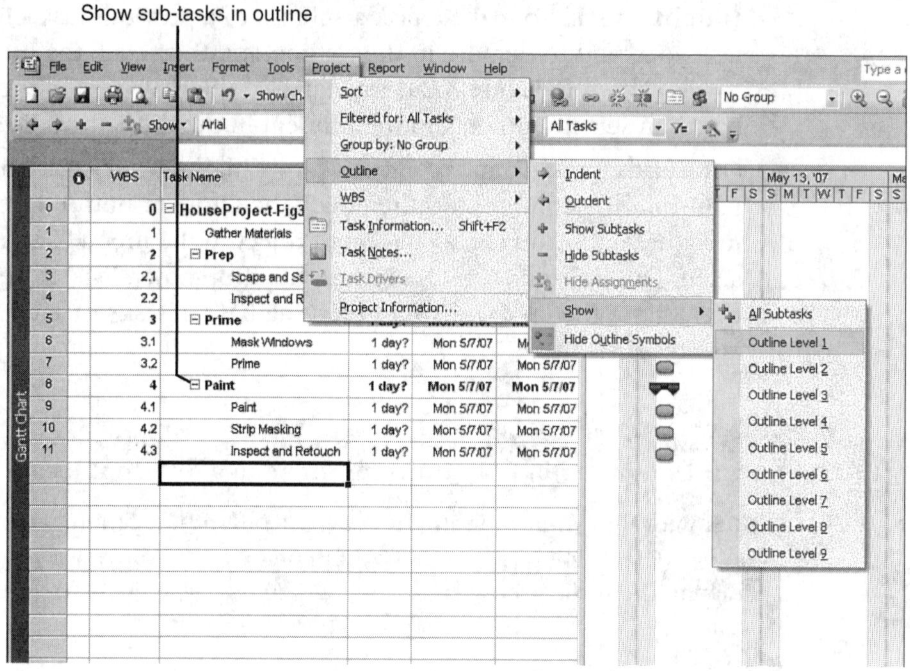

Show sub-tasks in outline

Figure 3.25   *Viewing outline levels in Project*

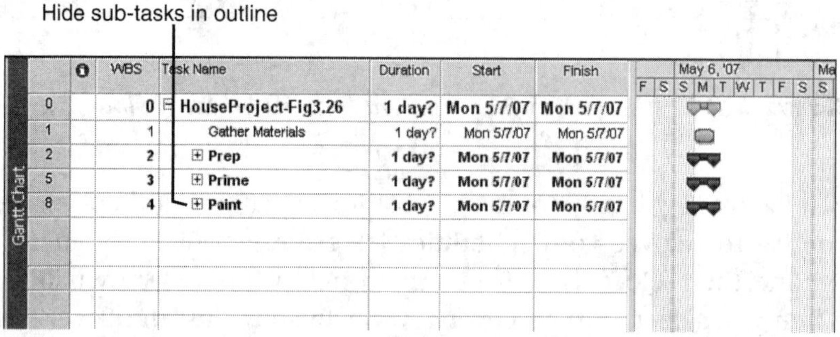

Hide sub-tasks in outline

Figure 3.26   *Showing only Outline level 1 in Project*

As shown in Figures 3.25 and 3.26, you have symbols in front of the tasks that look like a plus and minus symbol. By clicking these icons you can show (expand) or hide (collapse) your tasks easily as you review and adjust your schedule.

Sometimes the outlining doesn't seem to work. It is usually because you cannot demote or promote a task in the current outlining situation. A nice way to troubleshoot the outlining is to insert the WBS (if you have not defined the WBS code that would change the numbering schema) or the Outline number column to see how the outline is formatting. Also, you should avoid having a single task at a sublevel. When reviewing Figure 3.22 it might be tempting to include a subtask under task 1, Gather Materials, but it isn't necessary. Just as in an outline for an English composition paper, you should never have just one subject under a topic.

Using Task Notes Liberally

In addition to adding tasks and creating a WBS with outline characteristics, one other item can help you as you add tasks: using task notes. You can use them to remind you and your team members of the task completion details and help you keep the task names a bit shorter. To add a note to a task, just follow these steps:

1. Click on the task row for which you want to add a note.

2. Right-click so that you see the drop-down list in Figure 3.27, and select Task Notes in the list.

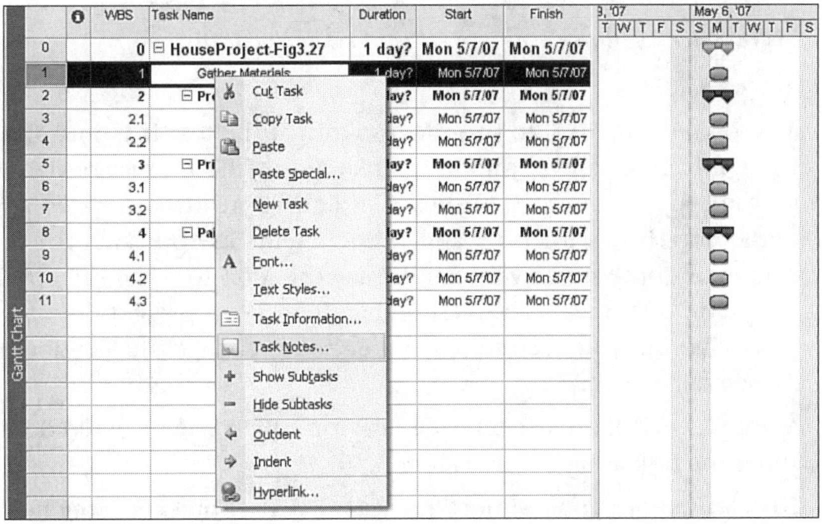

Figure 3.27 *Right-click on a task to see task options, including Task Notes, in the drop-down list*

3. The Task Information dialog box will display with the Notes tab selected. Here you can enter specific information about the task as shown in Figure 3.28.

4. Click OK.

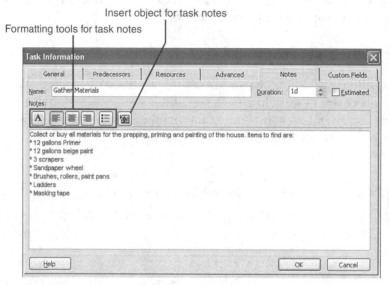

Figure 3.28 *Enter notes on a task to describe it further*

As shown in Figure 3.28 you can also format the text in a note. For instance, you could enter a hyperlink that links to the charter or a design document for the project. Figure 3.29 shows an Excel spreadsheet added as an object to the note. You can either attach documents as objects in the note to display their contents, or you can display the icon to open the application to get to the document. This can be handy to keep project documents easily accessible, but you need to remember not to change the location of the files to maintain the links.

A note icon will appear on each task for which you've entered information about the task as shown in Figure 3.30.

To delete a note, you just need to clear all text or objects in the notes area for a task.

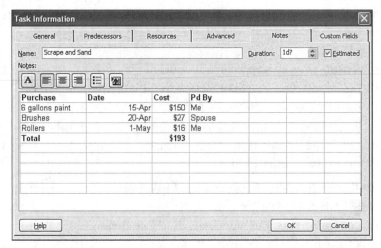

Figure 3.29   *A chart added to the Task Notes for a task*

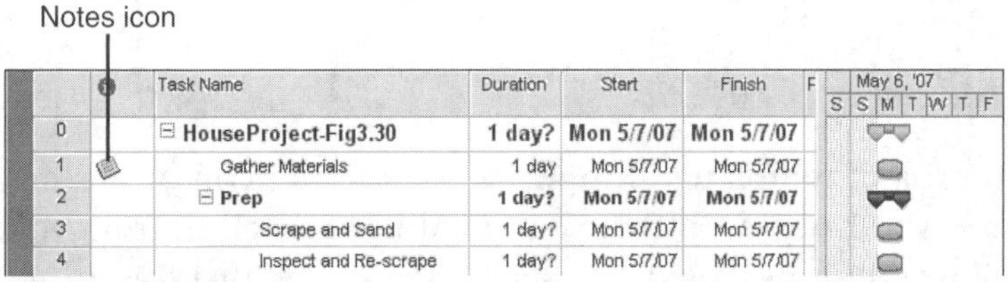

Figure 3.30   *Notes icon on the Gather materials task*

Using Project Templates

As suggested earlier, you might want to look into using preexisting WBSs. You can use these preexisting WBS templates for building your project rather than starting from scratch. Although you might think your project is totally unique, it is more likely that a similar project has been performed before. Check with others in your organization, surf the Web, or ask other project managers if they have performed a similar project before building a project from scratch. If you find a preexisting project file that is fairly well done (it is possible to find previous files that are illogical, poorly organized, or using poor project practices), you can take that file and use it as the basis for your project. You might even find a template in another application or just a listing of typical phases and tasks for a similar project. You can enter those tasks into your project file. Once you find a template or an example WBS for your project, you might want to save it as a template before working on your project. The following list gives some sources where you might find various templates or WBS examples.

- Microsoft provides typical WBS outlines on their Web site at http://office.microsoft.com/en-us/templates/default.aspx. Look for the Project link under Microsoft Office Programs.
- In your version of Project, you can find project templates if you installed the application using normal installation. I describe how you get to these templates later.
- Your organization or fellow project managers might also have templates you can use.
- Check out books and standards available through the Project Management Institute. The Project Management Institute provides a book called *Project Management Institute Practice Standard for Work Breakdown Structures*.

Finding Templates in Project

To find project templates shipped with your version of Project or to find templates you have saved that you might have received from your organization, follow the steps that are presented next. Note that this is one of the few items in Project that works differently for each version of Project.

To find the preexisting templates in Project 2002 do the following:

1. Select File from the menu bar.
2. Select New from the drop-down list, and you will see the New Project side pane. Do not click on the New button, as this will assume you are creating a project from scratch.
3. Click General Templates from the New from Template section of the side pane.
4. The Templates dialog box will appear. If you are selecting a template you or your organization has created, and you have saved the file as a template, use the General tab to use the template. If you would like to see the templates that Microsoft shipped with the application, select Project Templates.
5. To open the template, double-click the template, or select the template and click OK.

6. The project template file will be loaded.

7. You will want to review and change or add or remove the tasks you find in the template, but it's a great way to start. Then you will name and save your project as described in the section "Naming and Saving Your Project" earlier in the chapter. By default, when you save the project, it will be saved as an .mpp file.

To find the preexisting templates in Project 2003 or Project 2007 or to use templates you have previously saved in your application, follow these steps:

1. Select File from the menu bar.

2. Select New from the drop-down list, and you will see the panel shown in Figure 3.31. Do not use the New button if you are trying to use a project template, as you will not get this side pane.

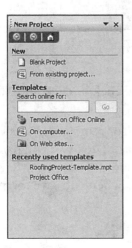

Figure 3.31 *Side pane for accesing templates in Project 2007 (almost identical in Project 2003)*

3. Select On computer (called On my computer in Project 2003) in this side pane.

4. The Templates dialog box will display. If you want to find templates you have saved previously, select the General tab. If you want to find the templates that Microsoft ships with Project, select the Project Templates tab, and you will see something similar to Figure 3.32.

Notice the button called Templates on Office Online. If you click this button, it will take you to the address where Microsoft provides free online templates.

Figure 3.32 *Templates available in Project*

5. Select the template you want and double-click or click OK. The template will open up in Project.

6. You will want to review and change, add, or remove the tasks you find in the template, but it's a great way to start. Then you will name and save your project as described in the section "Naming and Saving Your Project" earlier in the chapter. By default, when you save the project, it will default to an .mpp file.

Creating or Saving a Project Template

Creating and using templates is the way to go if you are a project manager. Learn from your past experience and your fellow project managers. If you want to save a project as a template or update a template that you have already saved, perform the following steps:

1. Create a new project or open a project that you want to use as a template. Select File from the menu bar.

2. Select Save As from the drop-down list.

3. Enter the template name in the File name field on the Save As dialog box.

4. Select Template (*.mpt) in the Save as type field.

5. You will see a Save As Template dialog box similar to that shown in Figure 3.33 (Project 2007 has some slight wording differences from Project 2002 and Project 2003). Best practice is to check all the items showing in the dialog box; this will make sure that any baseline or actual values are removed from the template and that any resource rates and fixed costs are also removed. This is especially important if you are using a project you copied from someone else.

6. Click Save. The file will now be available on the General tab as described earlier for selecting a template.

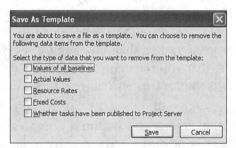

Figure 3.33   *Save As Template dialog box*

Set Project attributes before saving the template

One of the best reasons for using a template is that you can save the template with your organization's settings and views preset. For instance, you could create a 5-year project calendar with your organization's holidays on it, then go into Project Information for the template, and assign that calendar to the template. Always go to Tools, Options, and in the View tab, check the Show project summary task field. You could also add fields to special views your organization uses. Then, when you send the template to other people within your organization, you will have the same settings and views available for anyone using the template.

Please be aware that if you send the template to other people in your organization, when they open it and save it, they might accidentally save it as a file. Make sure everyone understands that they need to perform the steps listed earlier under "Creating or Saving a Project Template" to ensure they save the template as a template and not a project file.

You should not treat a template as a "dead" file. In other words, as you learn more about building projects, you should update a template to include new tasks that you have found should be included, or perhaps remove tasks that you thought were necessary, but are not appropriate for the kind of project the template represents. Or, you might find that you need to add new phases. In Chapter 12 "Closing Down Your Schedule: The End Is Only the Beginning" I discuss lessons learned, which is where you should review your project and with your project team, come up with ideas for making future projects better. If your team comes up with some ideas to make your project schedule better or some new tasks for the project, you should update the project template with the ideas from the team that apply to a schedule. This might take the form of notes on existing tasks rather than changing the tasks themselves. Your team might suggest that you rename some tasks or change particular characteristics of the tasks themselves, such as their task relationships or estimated duration.

To truly mature in project management and within an organization, you should consider using templates as one of the ways to move along the maturity path.

The Project Schedule Building Methodology So Far

In subsequent chapters, I continue building the list of the sequence in which you should build a project schedule. The following list describes the general steps for building a practical project schedule as discussed in this chapter.

- ☑ If you are using a template, select the appropriate template (you will probably want to change it based on the input of your project team). If you are building a project from scratch, build a WBS with your team, then move to the next step.
- ☑ Set up your project calendar if you do not have one available. Make sure you reflect your company's hours in Tools, Options, Calendar.
- ☑ In the Project Information dialog box, set your project start date and make sure your project calendar is assigned to the project.

☑ Start building (if your project is from scratch) or editing (if you are using a template) your task list. Make sure you indicate summary tasks and subtasks to help indicate the outline of your project schedule.

Practice: Setting up the Schedule

Practice 3.1

Setting up the Project Schedule

This practice will help you build an initial schedule, making sure you set up your file properly using the house-painting project to get you started. The rest of the book uses the house-painting project for practice. At the end of this practice you will be told where you can find the project file on your CD to see the practice results.

1. Open a blank project. If you see the Project Guide or task pane on the left side of the Gantt Chart view, click X in the upper right corner of the pane.

2. Select Tools, and then select Change Working Time from the drop-down list. The Change Working Calendar dialog box opens.

3. Scroll on the right scroll bar next to the calendar until you find January 2007.

4. You will ensure several holidays are marked as nonworking in the 2007 calendar.

   If you have Project 2007, click May 28 in 2007. On the Exceptions tab below the calendar, enter Memorial Day in the Name field. When you move to the Start field, the day should fill out, but if it does not, click in the field and select May 28, 2007 on the calendar. Move to the next Name row and enter Independence Day in the field. Click in the Start field next to the name you entered click the arrow and select July 4, 2007 in the resulting calendar. Click OK.

   If you have Project 2002 or Project 2003, click May 28, 2007 in the calendar, then click the Nonworking time option on the right side of the screen. Scroll through the calendar and make July 4 nonworking time as well. Click OK.

5. Now you will set the start date of the project. Select Project from the menu bar, and then select Project Information from the drop-down list. The Project Information dialog box will open.

6. For the house-painting project, enter May 7, 2007 in the Start date field. You will not need to assign a particular calendar to the project because you changed the Standard calendar to indicate nonworking time. Click OK.

7. Add the project summary task information line to the project by selecting Tools from the menu bar. Then select Options from the drop-down list. The Options dialog box will open.

8. Select the View tab and check the Show project summary task field in the lower right corner and press OK.

9. Now save the file. Select File from the menu bar, and then select Save from the drop-down list.

10. In the File name field, type House Painting Project and click Save. The name of the project should now display in the zero line of the project.

11. To close the file, select File from the menu bar, then click Close. The project is closed but the application itself is still available when you select Close.

Practice 3.2

Setting up the Task List

Now you will practice building a task list. You can use the schedule you just closed above, or you can use the one on your CD called, HousePainting-Practice-Chapter3-Practice2.

1. To use the file you just closed, select File from the menu bar and you should see the file at the bottom of the File menu. Select your file.

    If you use the file from the CD, select File from the menu bar and click Open. Select the directory for the CD and find the file on the CD and click on it.

2. You are ready to start building the project schedule task list with what you know now.

3. Enter the following tasks in the project. Don't forget to get out of entry mode when you are ready to perform a function on a task. (If you are in entry mode, the buttons on the toolbars will be unavailable and you cannot select them.):

    Gather materials.

    Prep. This will be a summary task.

    Scrape and sand. Click the Indent button to enter this as subtask of Prep.

    Inspect and rescrape. If you type this in immediately after the previous task, it will already be indented.

    Prime. If you type this in after the previous task, you need to make this a summary task by clicking the Outdent button.

    Mask windows. Click the Indent button to enter as this as a subtask of Prime.

    Prime. If you typed this in immediately after the previous task, it will already be indented.

Paint. If you typed this in after the previous task, you need to make this a summary task by clicking the Outdent button.

Paint. Click the Indent button to enter this as a subtask of Paint.

Strip masking. If you typed this in immediately after the previous task, it will already be indented.

Inspect and retouch. If you typed this in immediately after the previous task, it will already be indented.

4.　When you have entered your tasks, save your project by selecting Save from the menu bar, and clicking on Save.

If you would like to open a file to see or practice with the results of this exercise, open HousePainting-Practice-Chapter5.mpp.

Summary

In this chapter you learned that it's a good idea to build the scope and list of task activities outside of Project. This helps you be clearer and more efficient when you are ready to put the tasks into Project. You can still change them around, but the scoping exercise will help get the project team on the same page, and you will able to enter the tasks into the project easier. When you are ready to create a schedule, you need to do three things: Enter the project start date, include the calendar on the project to account for days off, and add the Project summary task as the top row of the schedule. If you do not have a calendar for your project, you might need to create one or change one that you have. As you build your project schedule, you will want to make the high-level tasks in your schedule summary tasks, and depending on your various WBS levels, include subtasks under them. This is a systematic pass on your schedule and might need to be completed in several passes to get the pieces right. One of the greatest benefits of Project is using templates, and using a schedule based on other project managers' experiences. You can find templates to use and modify on the Web, or you can use your own or your organization's past experience to build templates.

In the next chapter you will learn more about tasks in project, and how you can earmark important events in the project as milestones, and use deadline dates, task calendars, and task types in Project.

Case Study: Starting the Schedule

Chris Williams, the project manager for the Virtually Nostalgia Launch Event (VNLE), had worked to gain executive sponsorship from June Thompson, the Chief Operating Officer of Virtually Nostalgia. She had met with June to further understand the goals and budget for her project. Together, they agreed that getting a score for best of show greater than 125 for the event would warrant success for the project. June asked that the budget for the event be around $150,000. Chris started working on the project plan and a scope statement. She thought about the work itself and the departments and people who would be involved in the project and be on the project team. In thinking about the work, she decided she would be dealing with the following departments:

- **Sales Department:** Would probably staff the booth with salespeople and they should help craft some of the materials for the booth.
- **Marketing Department:** Would probably help create some of the materials needed for the event.
- **Logistics and Travel:** Setting up arrangements with the trade show, travel arrangements, and catering.
- **Operations:** Making sure the product inventory is ready to go, the catalog is created and printed, and the requirements for the online catalog have been sent to IT.
- **Business Development:** Would probably be involved in getting new vendors to partner on sales and advertising.
- **Information Technologies:** Working with them to make sure the Web site is ready and can handle the anticipated traffic from the launch.

Chris also thought about some of the deliverables for the project, things like the plan for the project, a prototype of the "event experience" (i.e., what the booth would look like), a prototype of a demo of the Web site, and the final deliverable, the event itself. She decided that the marketing plan for the event should probably be the first deliverable. She wondered if she could deliver that in about 3 months. From there she would create an event plan that would outline exactly what would be done for the event. She was hoping that she'd be able to complete the entire plan with specific details about a month or two after that. The final deliverable would be the event itself and the achievement of more than 125 points awarded.

Chris asked several people in your organization if they had seen a project template for a launch event, but no one was able to provide a template. Chris knew that she needed to get her core team together fairly quickly to lay out the WBS and verify the deliverables and the timing she was hoping to achieve. She decided to create a schedule using what she knew, even though she really needed to complete the WBS with the project team. She also realized that the best way to build a schedule was to add only the tasks and not worry about the timeline yet. So she sat down and opened Project to get started on the project.

So, as Chris Williams, to get started on your project, create a new project with the following information. If you need to remember how to perform any of these actions, review the relevant section in this chapter.

- Start the project on January 1, 2007.
- Make 1/1, 5/28, 7/4, and 9/3 nonworking days in the project calendar. If you are using Project 2007, create them as exceptions and enter names for the holidays.
- Add the Project Summary task.
- Save the schedule with the name VNLE-Chapter3.
- Add the following tasks. Try to add them in a verb and noun format:
  - Booth and materials.
  - Marketing materials.
  - Logistics for travel and catering. Include two subtasks under the summary task called Logistics of travel and Catering.
  - Verifying the inventory, the catalog, and Web site are ready to go for the launch.
  - Lining up new vendors.
  - Project plan.
  - Event experience prototype.
  - Prototype demo.
  - Execution of event itself.

When you are done entering tasks, save and name your project as the VNLE project. Open VNLE-Chapter3.mpp on your CD to see an example of Chris's initial work creating a project schedule.

Note

To get more background about this case study, read the Case Study background in Chapters 2 and 3 of *Project Management for Mere Mortals*.

Starting the Schedule

If you can, try to find a template before building your schedule. If you don't find one, work with your project team to build the WBS, which you can enter as summary tasks and subtasks into your schedule. Start your schedule simply:

1. Enter the start date.
2. Enter nonworking days in the project calendar.
3. Work on entering the scope of your project by entering the tasks and don't worry about estimates and resources yet.

If you get in the habit of setting up your schedule properly, when you start adding estimates and resources later your schedule will be more accurate, more realistic, and easier to work with.

Review Questions

1. What does a project charter do?
2. What is a scope statement?
3. What is a work breakdown structure (WBS)?
4. Can you create a work breakdown structure in Project?
5. After working in Project sometimes you see several filenames, such as Project1, Project2, and Project3 in the application. Why?
6. What is the file format extension for a Project file and Project template, respectively?
7. Where do you enter the project's start date?
8. Why do you select a project calendar associated with your project file?
9. Do you have to create a new calendar for every project?

10. What is the Project Summary task?

11. How do you create a subtask of a summary task?

12. Can you put a graph in a note on a project?

13. Why would you want to use a project template?

14. How can you share templates with other people in your organization?

Understanding Task Information

Success is the sum of details.
—Harvey S. Firestone

Topics Covered in This Chapter

Reviewing Task Information

Important Task Information

Understanding Duration and Work Fields on Tasks

What Are Task Types and Why Should I Care?

The Project Schedule Building Methodology So Far

Summary

Practice: Entering Milestones, Deadline Dates, Task Calendars, and Task Types in Your Schedule

Case Study: Continue Building the Schedule

Tasks are much more than just their name and an outline structure. When you build your WBS, you will also be thinking about other task information such as the following:

- Should it start or finish on or before a certain date (constraint)?
- What is the work effort (work) and how long in calendar days will the task take to complete (duration)?
- Is the task an approval point or deliverable (milestone) task?
- Does it need to have a special calendar (task calendar) or should it be governed by the project calendar?

This chapter describes the task information that you can create and view for your project. I describe milestones, constraints, deadline dates, and task calendars. You will want to use milestones to indicate major events or deliverables in your schedule, using them liberally to indicate the end of phases or completion of categories or summary tasks for a schedule. Constraints indicate when you need to constrain a task by a finish or start date. The various Project constraints will be defined so you know when you would enter them in the schedule, and why you would postpone entering them until the end of building the schedule. You will also learn how to enter deadline dates to indicate when a task must be completed, and how to add special calendars to tasks when a task must be governed by different working hours than the project calendar. This chapter also introduces how work and duration describe the effort and timeline for completing your task, although you will not enter that information yet. Nevertheless, you need to understand it to help you make decisions about how you will enter the information on the task. There is so much more information than just those elements available to describe a task, but this chapter introduces how and why you set this initial task information when building your schedule. I continue describing the recommended methodology for creating a project schedule and explore using that methodology with a practice exercise and the case study for Virtual Nostalgia.

Reviewing Task Information

In Chapter 2 "Revealing the Secrets of Microsoft Project," you learned that tasks contain many fields. Each task has data associated with it as columns, also called fields, in Project. You can add field after field in the Gantt Chart to see data associated with each task, or you can use the Task Information dialog box to see the most important fields available to describe tasks. In the following section, I describe some of the ways to understand the fields available for tasks.

Methods for Seeing Task Information

This section describes various ways you can see task information. The traditional way is to use the Task Information dialog box, which you saw in Chapter 2. There are several ways to display this dialog box. While your cursor is on a task in the Gantt Chart view, or any other kind of task view, you can:

- Click the Task Information icon to open the dialog box immediately.
- Double-click to open the dialog box immediately.

- Right-click and select Task Information in the drop-down list.
- Click Project in the menu bar and select Task Information in the drop-down list.
- Set your cursor on the blue Gantt Chart bar, right-click, and select Task Information in the drop-down list.

After you do any of these, the Task Information dialog box displays as shown in Figure 4.1.

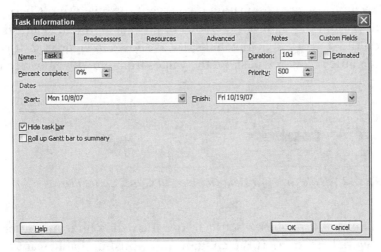

Figure 4.1 *Task Information dialog box*

Notice the six tabs on the dialog box. Each tab has a different set of data fields (although there is some data, such as Task Name, Duration, and Estimated, which is the same on each of them). If you use this dialog box during viewing of tasks, the last tab you looked at will show up as the first tab set. For instance, if you used the Advanced tab the last time you looked at the Task Information dialog box, its data will display the next time you bring up the Task Information dialog box.

Another way to see task information for a task is to insert a column. You already learned about inserting columns in Chapter 2 and Chapter 3 "Building Your Schedule: Scoping Your Project." All the columns you see in the Task Information dialog box can be shown in the Gantt Chart or other task views. For instance, in the dialog box shown in Figure 4.1 you see the Hide task bar field in the middle of the dialog box to the left. If you select the

Hide task bar field, Project actually removes the task's Gantt bar from the view.

To display that field (or any field on the Task Information dialog box) in the Gantt Chart view as shown in Figure 4.2 you would do the following:

1. Select Insert from the menu bar and click Column from the drop-down menu.

2. Select Hide Bar from the Column Definition dialog box and click OK.

3. For this particular field (which is what I call a designation field because you are designating if you want the blue Gantt Chart bar to display on the right or not), you would click in the field and an arrow on the side of the field will display as shown in Figure 4.2. If you click the little arrow, it will show the values from which you can select.

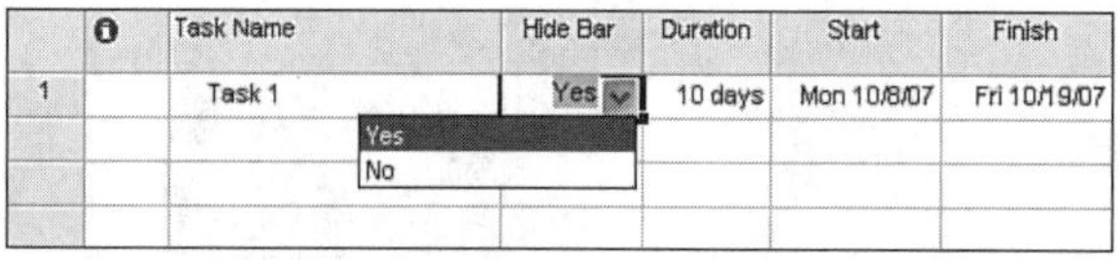

0	Task Name	Hide Bar	Duration	Start	Finish
1	Task 1	Yes ⌄	10 days	Mon 10/8/07	Fri 10/19/07
	Yes				
	No				

Figure 4.2   *Hide task bar field inserted in Gantt Chart view*

In some cases, it might be better to use the dialog box, and other times it might work best to insert the column. You would probably want to insert a column when you want to leave the information in the view you are using to easily enter or change fields that you use frequently. You might insert a column to see data easily for each task. For instance, if you want to see what Task Type each task has, you could insert the Type (notice the field is not named Task Type, but Type) column as shown in Figure 4.3. If you used the dialog box, you would have to click each task individually to see the same information. The dialog box might be useful when you have occasional settings or if you want to see a lot of information for each task.

Another form of viewing task information is via views or tables based on the kind of data you want to see. Select View from the menu bar, then select Table or More Views to see the various ways you can see task data. For instance, if you want to see cost information for tasks, follow these steps:

1. Select View from the menu bar.

2. Click Table, then click Cost from the drop-down list. The resulting cost table, and the specific data for costs will display as shown in Figure 4.4.

ⓘ	Task Name	Type	Duration	May 6, '07 S S M T W T F	S S May 13, '07 M T W
0	⊟ HousePainting-Figure4.3	**Fixed Duration**	**1 day?**		
1	Gather Materials	Fixed Units	1 day?		
2	⊟ Prep	**Fixed Duration**	**1 day?**		
3	Scrape and Sand	Fixed Work	1 day?		
4	Inspect and Re-scrape	Fixed Duration	1 day?		
5	⊟ Prime	**Fixed Duration**	**1 day?**		
6	Mask Windows	Fixed Units	1 day?		
7	Prime	Fixed Units	1 day?		
8	⊟ Paint	**Fixed Duration**	**1 day?**		
9	Paint	Fixed Units	1 day?		
10	Strip Masking	Fixed Duration	1 day?		
11	Inspect and Re-touch	Fixed Units	1 day?		

Figure 4.3   *Task Type column inserted showing differences for each task*

	Task Name	Fixed Cost	Fixed Cost Accrual	Total Cost	Baseline	Variance	Actual	Remaining	May 6, '07 S S M T W T F S
0	⊟ HousePainting-Figu	$0.00	Prorated	$9,650.00	$0.00	$9,650.00	$0.00	$9,650.00	
1	Gather Materials	$250.00	Prorated	$250.00	$0.00	$250.00	$0.00	$250.00	
2	⊟ Prep	$0.00	Prorated	$2,400.00	$0.00	$2,400.00	$0.00	$2,400.00	
3	Scrape and San	$2,000.00	Prorated	$2,000.00	$0.00	$2,000.00	$0.00	$2,000.00	
4	Inspect and Re-s	$400.00	Prorated	$400.00	$0.00	$400.00	$0.00	$400.00	
5	⊟ Prime	$0.00	Prorated	$3,000.00	$0.00	$3,000.00	$0.00	$3,000.00	
6	Mask Windows	$1,500.00	Prorated	$1,500.00	$0.00	$1,500.00	$0.00	$1,500.00	
7	Prime	$1,500.00	Prorated	$1,500.00	$0.00	$1,500.00	$0.00	$1,500.00	
8	⊟ Paint	$0.00	Prorated	$4,000.00	$0.00	$4,000.00	$0.00	$4,000.00	
9	Paint	$2,000.00	Prorated	$2,000.00	$0.00	$2,000.00	$0.00	$2,000.00	
10	Strip Masking	$1,500.00	Prorated	$1,500.00	$0.00	$1,500.00	$0.00	$1,500.00	
11	Inspect and Re-t	$500.00	Prorated	$500.00	$0.00	$500.00	$0.00	$500.00	

Figure 4.4   *Cost table showing various cost data for each task*

3. To return to the previous Gantt Chart view you are used to, select View from the menu bar.

4. Click Table, then click Entry from the drop-down list (which is the default table that the Gantt Chart view uses).

Because you don't know offhand what the various kinds of tables and views are that are available, you might want to create a project (or use the House-Painting practice project file you completed in Chapter 3) and click on each of the views and tables to see the various task data views. Don't forget some of these views focus on resource information, and in some cases, you might not actually have data entered yet that provides any valuable information in the table or view you select.

Multiple Task Information: Changing Task Data All at Once

One other item that the Task Information dialog box provides is the ability to change the data for several fields at the same time. For instance, in Figure 4.5 the Type column (Task Type) shows that all of the tasks (except summary tasks, which are always set to Fixed Duration) are set to Fixed Units, the default task type. Perhaps you want to change the task type to Fixed Duration for all of those fields. To do so take the following steps:

1. You can highlight all the fields, then click on the Task Information icon in the toolbar (or select Project in the menu bar and select Task Information from the drop-down list).

2. The Multiple Task Information dialog box displays as shown in Figure 4.5.

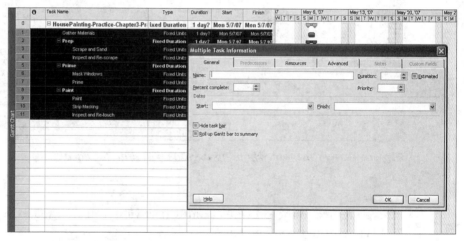

Figure 4.5   *Multiple Task Information dialog box*

3. Click the Advanced tab (if it's not already displayed).

4. Select Fixed Duration from the Task type drop-down list and click OK as shown in Figure 4.6.

Now that you know the various methods for finding task data, the next section describes what kind of task data is the most important to use while building your schedule.

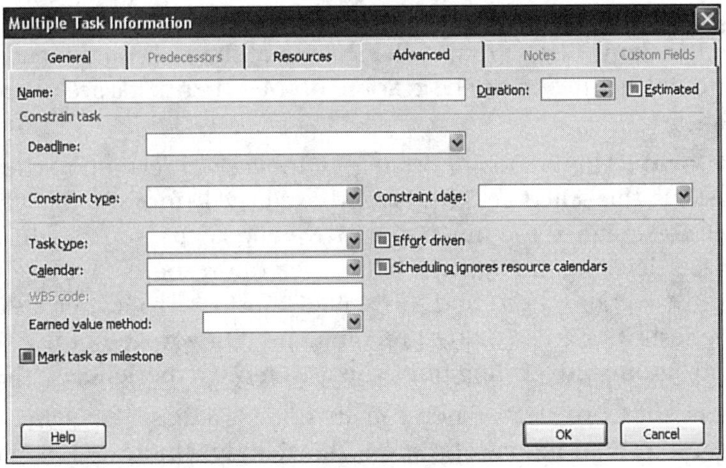

Figure 4.6   *Selecting Fixed Duration from the Task type drop-down list*

Important Task Information

With almost 300 fields of data available about a task (I actually counted them in Project 2002, and more might be available in later versions of Project), it's useful to know what data is most important to building a good schedule. Also, some fields are used in support of how Project is used rather than providing real data about the task. For instance, Duration and Work are important fields about tasks, whereas the Hide task bar field is about how the tasks show in the Gantt Chart, which is not really important unless you are trying to visually express something on your view. This section describes some of the most important information you need to know for understanding tasks. When you click each tab in the Task Information dialog box, the Task Name, Duration, and Estimated fields show up in each tab area. For more on duration, see the section "Understanding Duration and Work Fields on Tasks" later in this chapter. The Estimated field is what causes the question mark to show up after the number of days in the Duration field. Take a look at the Duration column in Figure 4.3 to see the question mark after 1 day. This question mark is merely a visual cue for you to indicate whether you are satisfied with your estimate (clear the field), or if you need to finish working on a better estimate (leave the field checked). The following list describes each of the Task Information tabs.

- **General:** As shown in Figure 4.1, most of the data fields on this tab are in the Gantt Chart view, such as name of the task, duration, and start and finish dates of the task. Some of the other fields are described in this list.

- **Priority:** This is the importance of the task in relation to the other tasks in the schedule. This is used exclusively for leveling, when people are assigned too much work (overallocated). You use the automated leveling tool (which helps even out resource work so they aren't overallocated), and this will give priority to higher tasks (the highest priority is 1,000). I recommend that you do not use this field and automated leveling until you gain more experience with Project.

- **Percent Complete:** Once you are done building your schedule and you start entering task progress, this field will indicate how far along you are in completing the work for the task.

- The **Hide task bar** and **Roll up Gantt bar to summary:** Indicates how the bars will display on the Gantt Chart. If you click Hide task bar then the blue bar will not show up on the Gantt Chart. If you click Roll up Gantt bar to summary, the blue task bars will show up on the summary bar. This is probably not a field you need to remember, but after you gain more experience with Project, you might want to experiment using these fields for displaying your Gantt Chart view differently.

- **Predecessors:** As shown in Figure 4.7, the fields on the Predecessors tab provide information about the relationships of the tasks that have been linked to it, or what task needs to precede the current task before it can start or finish. All the fields in this dialog box will be covered in Chapter 5, "Sequencing the Work: Creating the Critical Path." You might also prefer using the Split Window or the Gantt Chart bar for viewing or creating task relationships.

- **Resources:** As shown in Figure 4.8, the fields in the Resources tab show the resource(s) assigned to the task and how much of their available time (units) has been assigned to the task. By default, 100% of the resource's available time is assigned to the task. Chapter 6 "Understanding Resources and Their Effects on Tasks" describes resource information in more detail, including how you name resources and the best way to assign them to tasks.

- **Advanced:** The Advanced tab, shown in Figure 4.9, includes the most information about a task, and the purpose for many of the fields is not obvious. However some of the fields designate how the task behaves in the schedule. The rest of this section describes all the fields related to this tab.

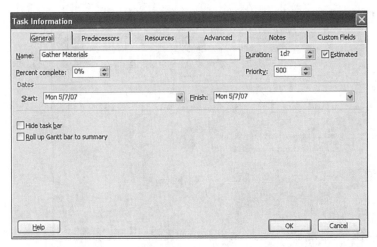

Figure 4.7 *The Predecessors tab describes task relationships*

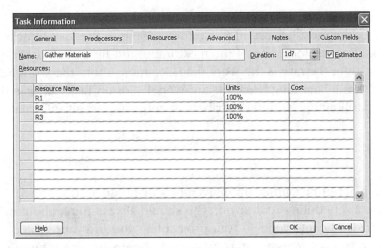

Figure 4.8 *The Resources tab describes resource information for a task*

- **Notes:** The Notes tab allows you to enter almost any information about a task. Notes were described in Chapter 3.

- **Custom Fields:** You can create custom fields to enter data about tasks that Project does not provide. For instance, for each task, you might want to indicate an account code for the accounts to which each task should be allocated for accounting programs. Creating custom fields is covered later in this section.

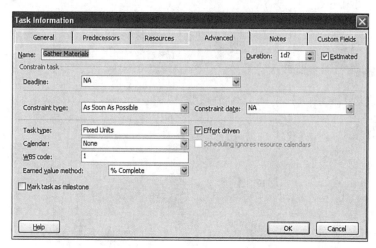

Figure 4.9 *The Advanced tab has many fields for designating scheduling behavior for the task*

Not all of the most important task information is in the Task Information dialog box. For instance, one of the most important fields that describes information about the task is the Work field. See more about the Work field in the section "Understanding Duration and Work Fields on Tasks" later in this chapter. The following section describes the most important information about tasks.

Milestones

Milestones can be significant deliverables or points in the project. Whether you use a scheduling tool or not, you should always think about milestones to mark significant events in your project that you and your project team use to gauge your progress. Just as on a trip, where you notice significant locations along your route and measure your progress accordingly, milestones do the same for a project. For instance, on a trip from Denver to San Francisco, milestones might be reaching Salt Lake City, reaching Las Vegas, and then finally reaching your particular destination in San Francisco. The milestones you identify along the way from the beginning to the end help you gauge where you are and how far you have to go. Those milestones also might help you understand how well you are doing along the way. If in Salt Lake City, your radiator starts leaking, you might surmise that your car will have problems and getting to San Francisco in fine shape and on time is in jeopardy. Milestones are critical for you to include in a project schedule. Usually, a milestone does not have duration attributed to it. Instead, it is like a marker that does not have effort associated with it, it's just a point in time.

For the house-painting project, you might decide that good milestones are tasks such as "half the house is prepped" and "entire house is prepped." Once you have completed prepping half the house, you can tell if you are ahead of or behind what you expected. You might also inspect the quality of the prepping at that first milestone to see if there are improvements or course corrections you must make for the rest of the prepping. In Project, to indicate a milestone, you can enter zero in the Duration field for a task. In the following house-painting project I entered the new tasks called 1/2 House prepped and House prepped and entered zero in the Duration field for each (see Figure 4.10). Notice that the symbol for a milestone is a diamond. Also note that the task is named as it has been achieved. By naming the task in noun–verb format (rather than verb–noun for regular tasks) you are indicating that something has been achieved, rather than something to be executed. When you start entering actual completion information, you can tell if the project is on track. The milestone markers help you think about where your project is at and how you are doing. After you've built a WBS, start entering milestones (or verify and add new ones if you are using a template that already has them). You should also use milestones to mark the end of a group of summary tasks or phases as well.

		Task Name	Duration	Start	Finish
0		⊟ HousePainting-Figure4.10	**1 day?**	**Sun 5/6/07**	**Mon 5/7/07**
1		Gather Materials	1 day	Mon 5/7/07	Mon 5/7/07
2		⊟ **Prep**	**1 day?**	**Sun 5/6/07**	**Mon 5/7/07**
3		Scrape and Sand	1 day?	Mon 5/7/07	Mon 5/7/07
4		1/2 House Prepped	0 days	Sun 5/6/07	Sun 5/6/07
5		Continue Scraping and Sand	1 day?	Mon 5/7/07	Mon 5/7/07
6		Inspect and Re-scrape	1 day?	Mon 5/7/07	Mon 5/7/07
7		House Prepped	0 days	Sun 5/6/07	Sun 5/6/07
8		⊟ **Prime**	**1 day?**	**Mon 5/7/07**	**Mon 5/7/07**
9		Mask Windows	1 day?	Mon 5/7/07	Mon 5/7/07
10		Prime	1 day?	Mon 5/7/07	Mon 5/7/07
11		⊟ **Paint**	**1 day?**	**Mon 5/7/07**	**Mon 5/7/07**
12		Paint	1 day?	Mon 5/7/07	Mon 5/7/07
13		Strip Masking	1 day?	Mon 5/7/07	Mon 5/7/07
14		Inspect and Retouch	1 day?	Mon 5/7/07	Mon 5/7/07

Figure 4.10   *Milestone tasks 1/2 House prepped and House prepped*

In Project, you can also mark a milestone by double-clicking the task, which brings up the Task Information dialog box. If you click the Advanced tab, you will see the field, Mark task as milestone, in the lower left corner of the Advanced tab. This feature allows you to mark a milestone that might have duration. For instance, one of your milestones might be prepping approved by spouse, and you think that might take 2 days (your spouse is very particular about prepping). Use milestones with duration sparingly and for good reason. Usually, when you create task relationships (which are discussed in Chapter 5), you would have some task with effort leading up to the milestone rather than putting emphasis on the milestone. So for the house-painting project, it would be better to have a task called Inspect prepped house, which you will assign your spouse. Then the next task linked immediately following that task is Prepping approved, which is a milestone task with no duration.

Use milestones liberally and judiciously

Milestones are incredibly useful. They help you see where your important dates for accomplishment are in your schedule. You can create filtered views that allow you to see just your milestones—which keeps you focused on the important events of your project—rather than the long efforts you have to achieve them. Good project scheduling uses milestones liberally, and makes them meaningful to indicate project success.

Deadlines

It's very common for new Project users to enter a date in the Finish field on the Gantt Chart to indicate when work on a task should be completed. While you build your schedule, rather than entering a Finish date, enter a deadline date on the tasks to indicate a date by which they must be complete. If you enter a date in the Finish date field, you will automatically create a constraint, and you might start getting warning messages about constraints that you might not understand. See the section on constraints later in this chapter to understand why you probably will want to use deadline dates rather than typing in a Finish date. To add a deadline, do the following:

1. Select a task and double-click it.
2. Click the Advanced tab if it isn't already showing. Use the drop-down list in the Deadline field as shown in Figure 4.11, and select the date

the task must be completed (or simply enter the date directly in the field).

3. Click OK.

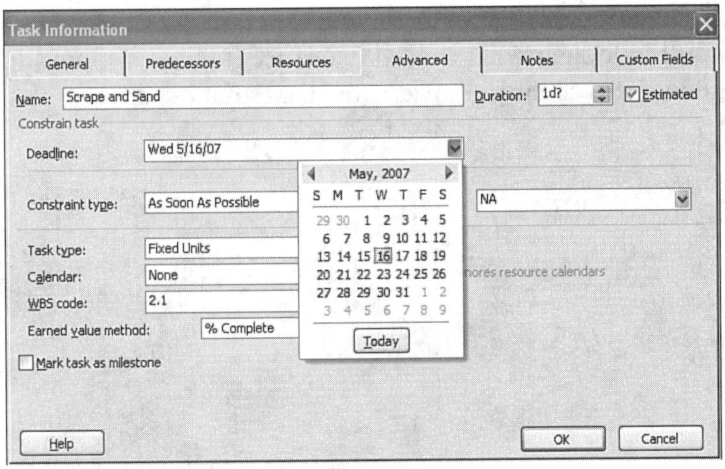

Figure 4.11 *Entering a deadline date*

A deadline marker appears on the right side of the Gantt Chart as shown in Figure 4.12. You can also insert the Deadline column to see the date of the deadline.

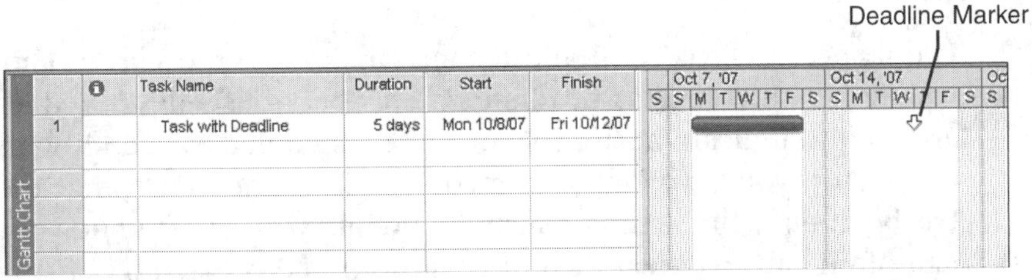

Figure 4.12 *Deadline marker showing in Gantt Chart area*

If you use the Deadline field a lot, you might want to add a Deadline column (shown in Figure 4.13) to your Gantt Chart view regularly so that you can easily see your task deadlines since the deadline marker is not easy to see on a long schedule. Deadlines are useful because unlike constraints, they do not force certain behaviors in the schedule. For instance, if you choose a constraint to end a task on a certain date, then the task is constrained to end on only that date, even if the other tasks previous to it can get done sooner and you could get the task done earlier. The deadline date will allow the task to end according to the flow of the work. As you build the schedule, and something you do changes the schedule so that you would miss the deadline, a marker will appear on the schedule as shown in Figure 4.13. Then, you can look at what caused it and see if there is some adjustment to the schedule you can make to actually make that deadline.

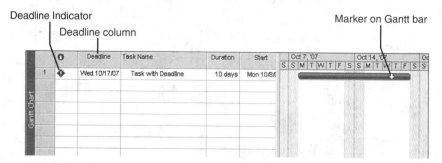

Figure 4.13 *Deadline indicator shows when deadline date will be missed*

The Deadline field does affect critical path (the tasks that form the longest path on your schedule and affect the end date of your project) calculations. Critical path and the deadline date's effect on it are described in Chapter 5.

Constraints

People new to Project often use constraints to set the start or end date for a task rather than using a deadline date as previously described. Constraints are used to indicate how a task must be scheduled to keep it within certain parameters you have for your schedule. This is fine to use once the schedule has been built, but setting constraints while you are building your schedule can often cause a great deal of frustration. Let's discuss constraints, what they are, when they should be used, and why you should avoid them unless you are clear about how to use them and what they do to your schedule.

A constraint restricts or prescribes the bounds of your task. A constraint affects the task relationships of the other tasks that have dependencies with the constrained task as well. Many people enter a constraint based on an artificial date prescribed by management, when the real constraint is the work itself, when tasks that must be done before or after it can get started, and how many resources can help accomplish it. For instance, let's say management says, "Get the design done by June 9. It's May 15 and with the resources you've been given and the work your experts have estimated, the design will take 25 days. If you start on May 15, you have 19 working days until June 9. If you constrain the date by setting an end date for June 9, and you enter the work estimates, Project will show a pop-up message essentially saying you have to start the project earlier than May 15 (the start date of the project) to get the work done, which is impossible. That message will keep popping up if you keep things the way they are as you keep working on the schedule. What you really need to do is set the deadline date, then see if you can add more resources, add work on weekends, or reduce the scope of the work to make the date (or show your sponsor a realistic schedule and hope you can get more time). It's easier to experiment with these options if you have a deadline date rather than a constraint that keeps making this pop-up message display as you adjust the schedule with various options. Create your schedule entering duration or work estimates and task relationships, which lets Project show you what your dates are, rather than you forcing dates through constraints. After you have finished the iterative work of adjusting the schedule you can put the constraint on the task (although a deadline date might still be better).

Project has a set of eight constraints. Some are flexible, allowing the constraints of the relationships of the work itself determine what happens to the task. Some are less flexible, so if a task relating to it changes, the constraint you prescribe will stick. Many times a task prior to a constrained task will get done early, and you will show a gap in your schedule while you have to wait to start the next task. The constraint As Soon As Possible is set by default for every task. Figure 4.14 shows the available constraints that you can prescribe in Project.

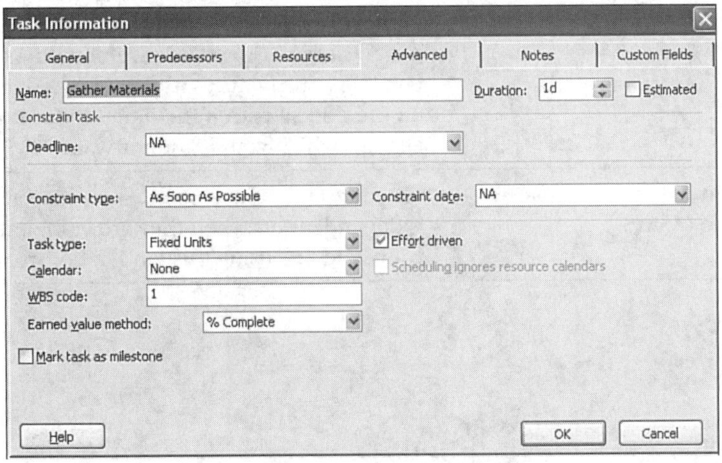

Figure 4.14 *Available constraints in Project*

Task Relationships

Before discussing constraints any further, it's worth a moment to discuss task relationships, which were briefly introduced in Chapter 1 "Introducing Microsoft Office Project" and which I describe in more detail in Chapter 5. The best method for creating a schedule is to show relationships or dependencies between tasks. For instance, before you can paint the house you should prep the house. You show that dependency by creating a relationship between the tasks by linking them as shown in Figure 1.6 in Chapter 1. Constraints can affect the task dependency dates. In the examples described following Table 4.1, linking will indicate task relationships to help you understand what constraints do.

Table 4.1 describes these constraints and assumes you are building your schedule from a project start date, as this book recommends.

Table 4.1 *Constraints, Flexibility and What They Do to the Task*

Constraint Name	Flexibility	What the Constraint Does to a Task
As Late As Possible (ALAP)	Flexible	Based on other task dependencies, schedules the task as late as possible but not delaying tasks coming after it if its duration does not change. This constraint can be quite useful to use when you want a task to finish just before the next task but not get started too soon. This constraint is sometimes used in construction to indicate when a piece of machinery should be delivered, so that it isn't delivered too soon. Otherwise you spend money paying for the machine to sit prior to the next task requiring it. Be careful with As Late As Possible constraints as it could postpone events on the critical path if the duration for it should change, which you might not want.
As Soon As Possible (ASAP)	Flexible	Schedules the task as soon as possible after tasks it is dependent on when they are complete. Build your schedule using this kind of constraint.

Constraint Name	Flexibility	What the Constraint Does to a Task
Finish No Earlier Than (FNET)	Somewhat flexible	Based on task dependencies, restricts the task to completing on or after the finish date entered. When you type a date in the Finish field for a task, this is the constraint that is set. In most cases you do not want to actually constrain your schedule to this, because if the task is done early it will apply this constraint, and the schedule indicates that you cannot start your next task until the constraint date occurs. If you actually have this condition, use a Deadline date. However, if indeed you cannot start the next task until a particular date, use this constraint. You can set a lag (a delay in starting the next task) or even use the resource calendar (to set some days the resource will not work) to set this type of constraint, both of which are more flexible than using this constraint.
Finish No Later Than (FNLT)	Somewhat Flexible	Schedules the task so that it must finish on or before the date indicated. In most cases, this is the constraint people really want when they type an end date in the Finish field because it does allow a task to complete early, but again I recommend you do not use this constraint unless you have a very specific reason to do so. To use this constraint, you will have to use the Advanced tab in the Task Information dialog box and set the constraint and date or insert the Constraint type and Date fields in the Gantt Chart. You cannot make this constraint occur by typing a date in the Finish field.
Must Finish On (MFO)	Inflexible	Schedules the end date of the task on the Finish date you enter, and does not allow for finishing before or after that date. This fixes that date in the schedule and all tasks have to respect this end date restriction. If the work on this task gets done early for some reason, you cannot start the next task until the date in the Finish field. This might be very necessary for fixed events that you simply cannot change. To use this constraint, you will have to use the dialog box and set the constraint and date or insert the Constraint type and Date fields in the Gantt Chart. You cannot make this constraint occur by typing a date in the Finish field.

(continues)

Table 4.1 *Continued*

Constraint Name	Flexibility	What the Constraint Does to a Task
Must Start On (MSO)	Inflexible	Schedules the start date of the task on the Start Start date you enter, and does not allow you to start before or after that date. This fixes that date in the schedule, and all tasks have to respect this start date restriction. If previous tasks get done early for some reason, you cannot start this task until the date in the Start field. This might be very necessary for fixed events that you simply cannot change. To use this constraint, you will have to use the Advanced tab in the Task Information dialog box and set the constraint and date or insert the Constraint type and Date fields in the Gantt Chart. You cannot make this constraint occur by typing a date in the Start field.
Start No Earlier Than (SNET)	Somewhat flexible	Based on task dependencies, restricts the task to starting on or after the start date entered. When you type a date in the Start field for a task, this is the constraint that is set. In most cases you do not want to actually constrain your schedule to the date because if the previous task is done early, you will probably want to allow it to start. However, if indeed you cannot start the next task until a particular date use this constraint. For instance, you will use it to tell Project that a task that could be started before today but that has not been started yet can only start tomorrow at the earliest.
Start No Later Than (SNLT)	Somewhat flexible	Schedules the task so that it must start on or before the date indicated. In most cases, this is the constraint people really want when they type a start date in the Start field, but again I recommend you do not use this constraint unless you have a very specific reason to do so. To use this constraint you will have to use the Advanced tab in the Task Information dialog box and set the constraint and date or insert the Constraint type and Date fields in the Gantt Chart. You cannot make this constraint occur by typing a date in the Start field.

Examples of Constraints

The following examples describe the constraints and how you might use them. Always create your schedule with the flexible constraints. Later, as you refine your schedule by adding resources, duration, and work, and make the tasks' relationships as logical as possible, then you can add constraints (sparingly).

- **As Late As Possible:** At times you might want to set this constraint on a task to make the task start and finish as close to the next task as possible. Let's say you are gutting a house to completely remodel it. You have to obtain a permit, hire a crew, and have a large trash bin delivered to throw out the trash from the house. Figure 4.15 shows the schedule, its constraints shown in a column, and its linked tasks for the work of the project.

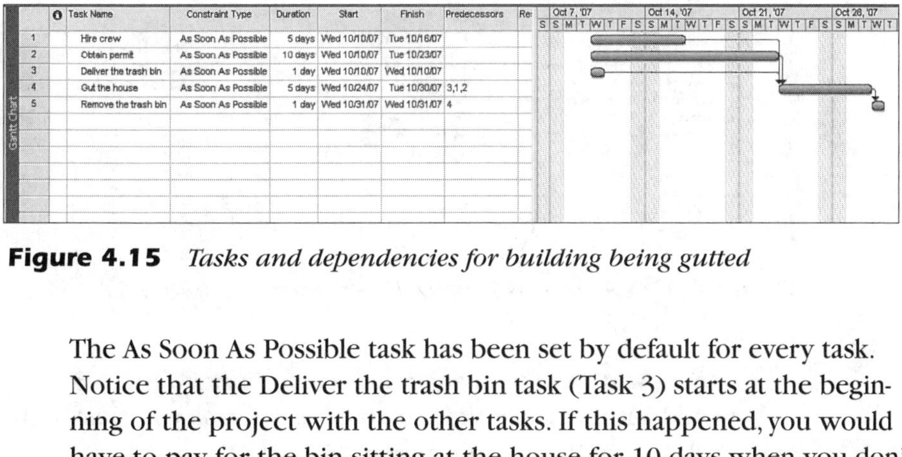

		Task Name	Constraint Type	Duration	Start	Finish	Predecessors	Re
1		Hire crew	As Soon As Possible	5 days	Wed 10/10/07	Tue 10/16/07		
2		Obtain permit	As Soon As Possible	10 days	Wed 10/10/07	Tue 10/23/07		
3		Deliver the trash bin	As Soon As Possible	1 day	Wed 10/10/07	Wed 10/10/07		
4		Gut the house	As Soon As Possible	5 days	Wed 10/24/07	Tue 10/30/07	3,1,2	
5		Remove the trash bin	As Soon As Possible	1 day	Wed 10/31/07	Wed 10/31/07	4	

Figure 4.15 *Tasks and dependencies for building being gutted*

The As Soon As Possible task has been set by default for every task. Notice that the Deliver the trash bin task (Task 3) starts at the beginning of the project with the other tasks. If this happened, you would have to pay for the bin sitting at the house for 10 days when you don't need it. You could force a constraint and enter 10/23 in the Start date field on Task 3, but what if the project actually gets started 2 weeks later than this? Or, as you work with this schedule, you might find it only takes 5 days to obtain the permit (yes, I know that even 10 days is absurdly quick for obtaining a permit). With a forced constraint of 10/23 and the permit taking 5 days less, then the schedule will change as shown in Figure 4.16.

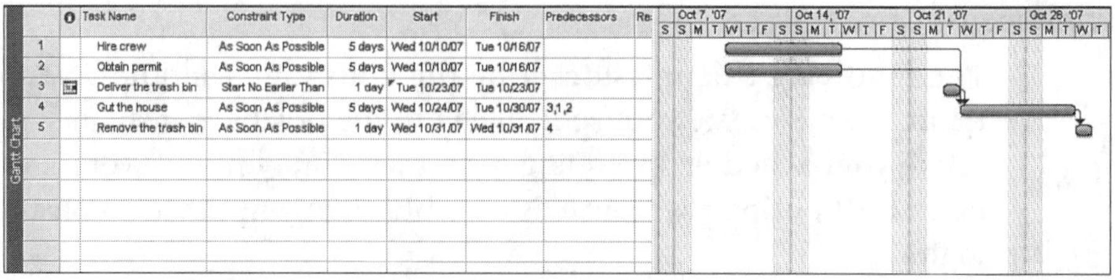

Figure 4.16   *Forcing a start date for the Deliver trash bin task and showing delay of starting work, waiting on the trash bin to be delivered*

You can change the start date of Task 3, but setting the constraint to As Late As Possible allows for the same manual changes and will ebb and flow with any changes as you change items in the schedule. In Figure 4.17, the original project (shown in Figure 4.15) now has an As Late As Possible constraint on Task 3.

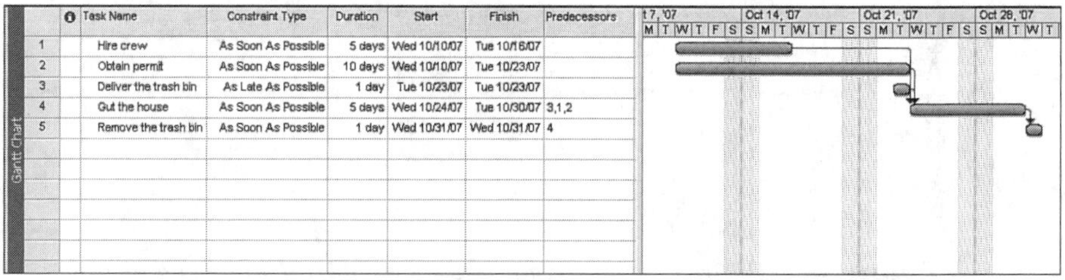

Figure 4.17   *As Late As Possible task constraint on Task 3*

Now, if you were to change the Obtain permit task to 5 days, Task 3 would automatically slide to 10/16 as soon as you change the duration on Task 2, as shown in Figure 4.18.

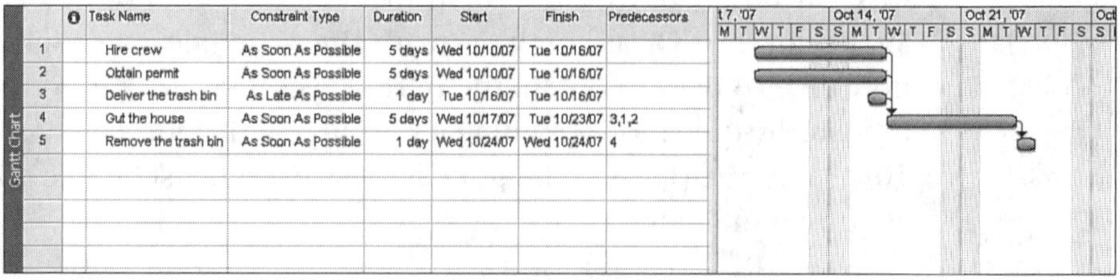

Figure 4.18   *Task 3 changes automatically when Task 2 changes to start on 10/16*

If you have decided to schedule the project from the project end date, then the As Late As Possible constraint is the default task constraint type.

- **As Soon As Possible:** This constraint type is automatically applied to every task by default if you are scheduling your project from the project start date. This will start the task as soon as possible based on any task relationships for the task. Notice in Figure 4.15 that Task 4—the work to gut the house—is scheduled as soon as possible after the permit is obtained. It can't start any sooner, because you must have the permit before you can start the work or you will be violating city and county laws. You should leave all of your tasks to this default constraint while you are building your schedule, unless you have identified a task that warrants an As Late As Possible constraint.

- **Finish No Earlier Than:** This constraint type is set when you type a date in the Finish field to indicate that you cannot complete the task before the date you entered. Let's say you are redoing your patio and you are laying a special tile that is extremely sturdy, just right for outside use. However, you must lay the tile within a day after laying a stabilizing foundation into which you will glue the tile. The special glue needed for laying the tile on the foundation will not be available until 8/15 or later, so you enter the date of 8/15 in the Finish date field for the Lay special foundation task, which constrains the task to completing no earlier than that day. Figure 4.19 shows an example of a Finish No Earlier Than constraint on the task.

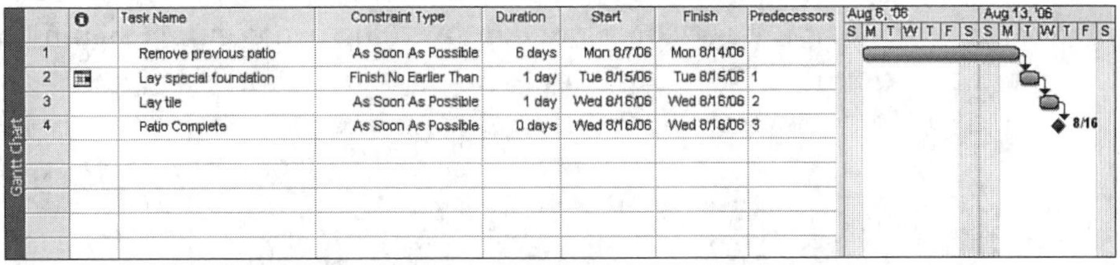

	❶	Task Name	Constraint Type	Duration	Start	Finish	Predecessors
1		Remove previous patio	As Soon As Possible	6 days	Mon 8/7/06	Mon 8/14/06	
2	📅	Lay special foundation	Finish No Earlier Than	1 day	Tue 8/15/06	Tue 8/15/06	1
3		Lay tile	As Soon As Possible	1 day	Wed 8/16/06	Wed 8/16/06	2
4		Patio Complete	As Soon As Possible	0 days	Wed 8/16/06	Wed 8/16/06	3

Figure 4.19   *Finish No Earlier Than constraint on task*

If for some reason the removal of the previous patio takes 4 days rather than the originally estimated 6, the new schedule would display as shown in Figure 4.20. You'd have to wait to start Task 2.

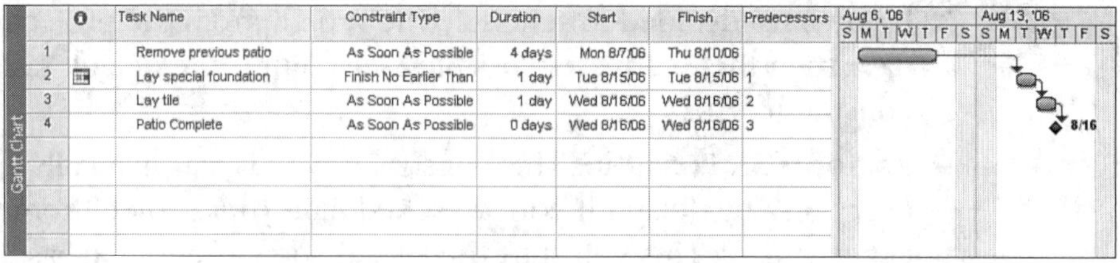

Figure 4.20   *Previous task is shortened, but Finish date stays the same on Task 2*

However, if the first task takes 8 days the Task 2 end date will slide 2 days past the original end date. You will complete the task a couple of days later (see Figure 4.21).

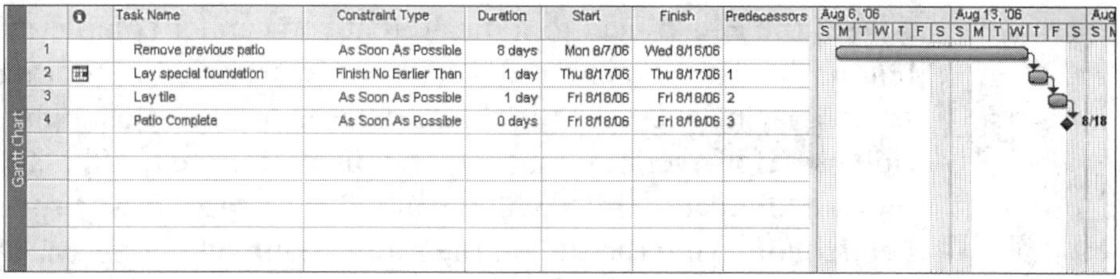

Figure 4.21   *The date on Task 2 is allowed to slide out later than 8/15*

- **Finish No Later Than:** This constraint type restricts the task to finishing on or before the date you set as the Finish date. Let's say you are buying a house. You need to start moving in on 11/6. With that in mind, you must complete the financing and contract signing on or prior to 11/3. So in Figure 4.22 you can see the constraints set for 11/3. If for some reason Task 1 or 2 complete prior to 11/3 there is no issue.

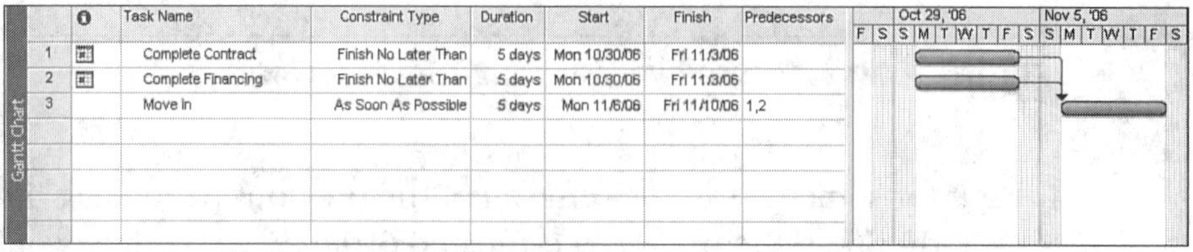

Figure 4.22   *Tasks 1 and 2 are set with a Finish No Later Than constraint of 11/3*

However, if the task for some reason would take longer than the end date constraint, you would get a message indicating that you simply can't make the task go any longer. You would have to start the task prior to the project start date (see Figure 4.23). If you have that luxury, you could make your project start earlier and be able to deal with the issue, but if you can't, this alert lets you know that you will have to do something else to ensure you complete the task by the time you need it.

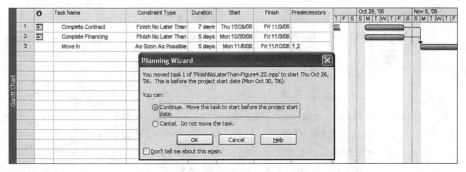

Figure 4.23   *Message when scheduling causes constraint to behave according to Finish No Later Than constraint*

- **Must Finish On:** This constraint type means that the task has to finish exactly on the Finish date and cannot finish earlier or later than that date. A good example might be a store grand opening. You have advertised the date and, no matter what, this task must finish on the advertised date. This particular setup is shown in Figure 4.24.

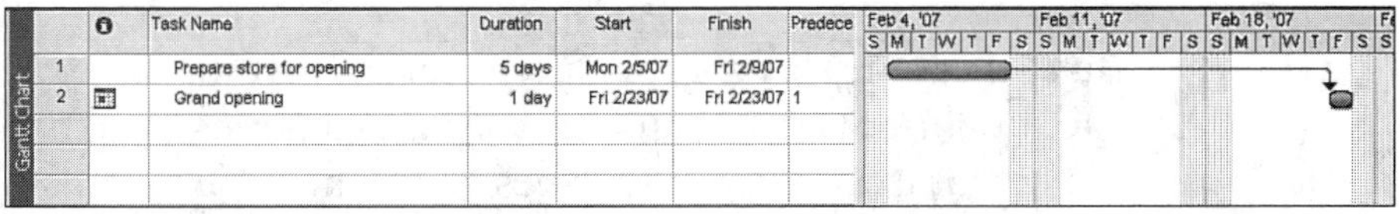

	❶	Task Name	Duration	Start	Finish	Predece
1		Prepare store for opening	5 days	Mon 2/5/07	Fri 2/9/07	
2		Grand opening	1 day	Fri 2/23/07	Fri 2/23/07	1

Figure 4.24   *Grand opening task with 2/23 Must Finish On constraint*

This works fine if you put in enough contingency (some extra time to account for all those unanticipated problems that occur on projects), but let's say, after more work you realize that the preparation will take longer than planned—in this case 5 days extra. You would get a scheduling message such as the one shown in Figure 4.25.

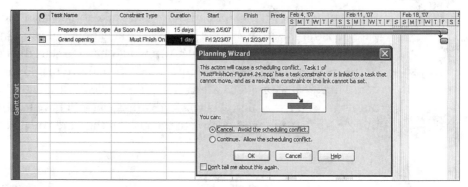

Figure 4.25   *Message when Must Finish On constraint will cause a scheduling issue*

If you allow the scheduling conflict, you will get the problem shown in Figure 4.26. The work of the previous task actually continues through the day the store was supposed to open. If this is work that needs to be done prior to the grand opening, the work will be done while customers are in the store.

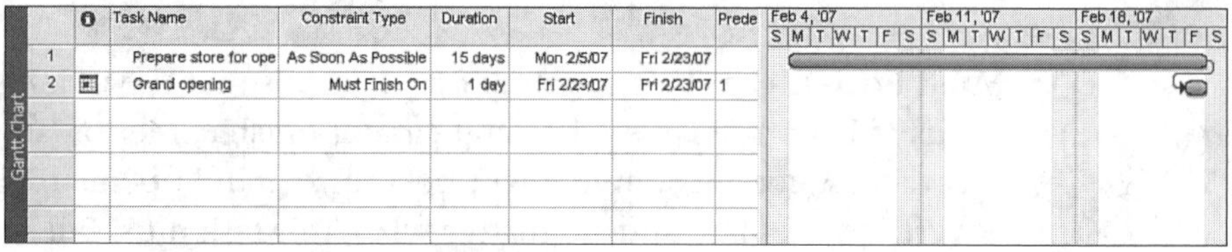

	❶	Task Name	Constraint Type	Duration	Start	Finish	Prede
1		Prepare store for ope	As Soon As Possible	15 days	Mon 2/5/07	Fri 2/23/07	
2	▥	Grand opening	Must Finish On	1 day	Fri 2/23/07	Fri 2/23/07	1

Figure 4.26   *Grand opening ends while previous preparation task continues at the same time*

- **Must Start On:** This constraint type means that the task has to start exactly on the Start date and cannot start earlier or later than that date. In this example, you have designed a new computer system for a state agency and it will be implemented on the same day the old system is retired. The system changeover must start on a particular date, as everyone will be trained and the changeover has been heralded in the press. The rather shortened schedule might look something like that shown in Figure 4.27.

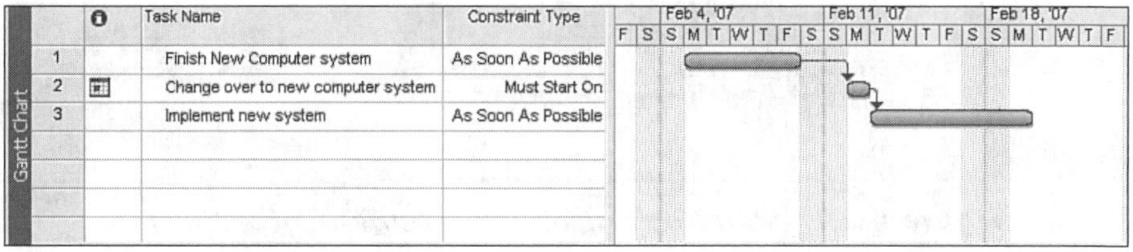

Figure 4.27   *Must Start On constraint on the Change over to new computer system task*

If for some reason your estimate was wrong, and you were to change the schedule to one day longer for Task 1 and you allowed the scheduling conflict message you receive, the schedule would result as shown in Figure 4.28.

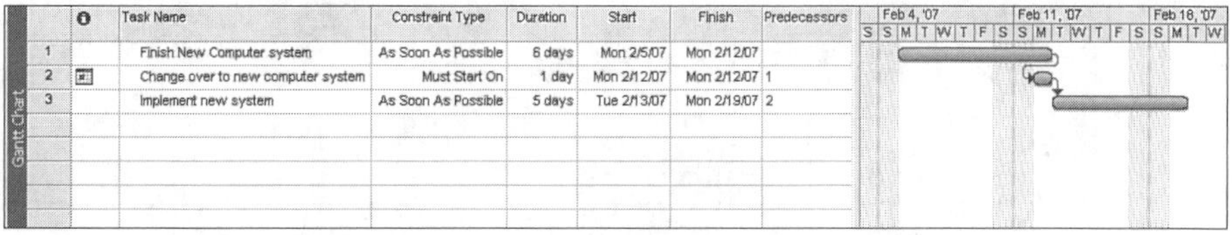

Figure 4.28   *Scheduling conflict with Must Start On date if previous task takes longer*

If you are able to complete the new computer system and get started on the changeover simultaneously, this would work, but it's unlikely. Again, you would need to work on an alternate plan (isn't it always working the weekend?) if this occurred.

- **Start No Earlier Than:** This constraint type will prevent a task from starting sooner than the date you enter in the Start field. For example, you have found out that you cannot get any resources to test two software modules prior to December 15. You can schedule the coding according to your estimates, but indicate that testing of them will have to start on 12/15 and no earlier, when you will actually have resources to test. As you can see in Figure 4.29, there is a 2-day lag (delay) between the end of coding Module 2 and testing the modules. Even if you change Task 2 to show it will be done even sooner, the gap between starting Task 3 and Task 2 will remain. You will have to use it to tell Project that a task that could be started before today but that has not been started yet can only start on the date indicated at the earliest.

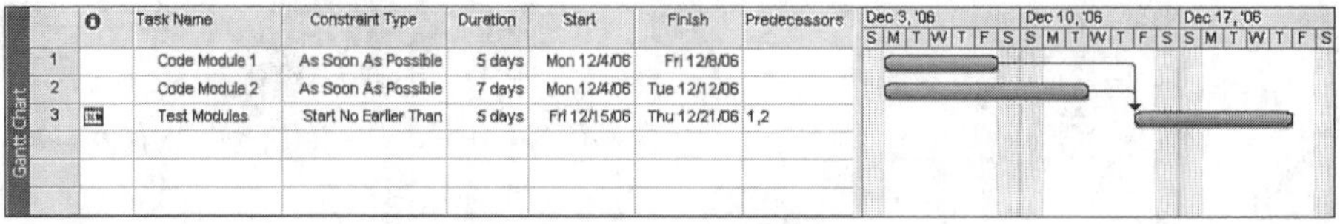

Figure 4.29 *Start No Earlier Than constraint for testing task*

- **Start No Later Than:** This constraint type ensures a task starts on or before the date entered in the Start field. This is a project that many people have gone through—having a baby. The doctor has said that the birth will be induced on 2/19 if the baby is not born prior to that and you need to get the baby's room ready. In Figure 4.30, this constraint is shown.

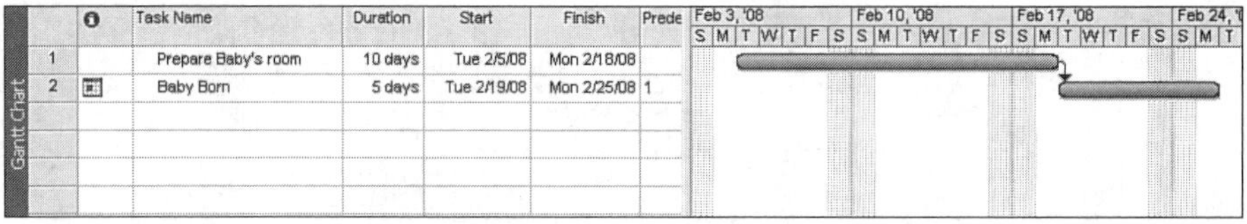

Figure 4.30 *Start No Later Than constraint on Task 2*

The work on the room preparation can continue for several days past the 10 days originally estimated but if the estimate takes any longer than the due date and you accept the scheduling conflict message you will see, you would see a schedule similar to the one in Figure 4.31.

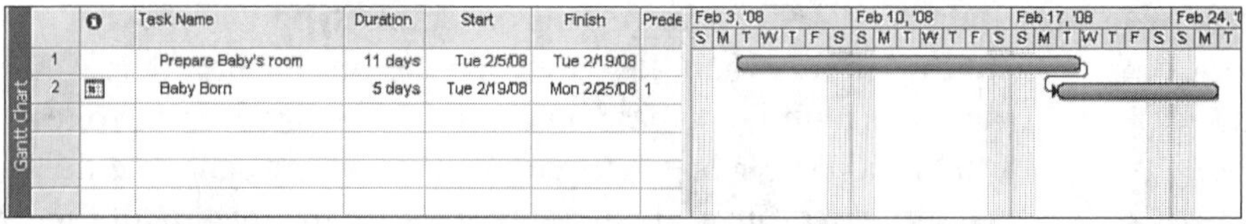

Figure 4.31 *Schedule issue if constraint is ignored on Task 2*

It might make logical sense to use constraints when you are very sure of the behavior you are trying to obtain with a constraint. They can be very useful to tell you via a scheduling message that you are not going to be able to make your date. However, if you use constraints as you are building your schedule, before you understand the basis of the work, the task relationships, your work effort, and how many resources will help get the work done, you might have so many scheduling messages that you start cursing Project. The real issue is that you might be putting constraints on the tasks when they really just aren't appropriate to the nature of the work itself. I say this one more time: Don't type in start or finish dates or apply constraints until you have as much of the scope of your task in your schedule as possible and you've iterated through the building process several times.

Task Calendars

You were introduced to using project calendars in Chapter 3 to account for days that your organization or the project might not be working—such as holidays. You will learn more about resource calendars in Chapter 6, which helps account for time resources are not available to work, but what if you have a situation where a task or two have special conditions in which you need to show less or more time available for working on the task? For instance, let's say the entire project should be on the company calendar that includes holidays and weekends as nonworking days, but you have a task that requires work on the weekends. You can create a calendar and attach it only to that task to schedule work to override the project calendar and the resource calendar if you choose. To do so, follow these steps:

1. Create the calendar as described in Chapter 3 in the section "Creating a New Calendar by Copying an Existing One."
2. Select the task for which you want a special calendar and double-click it.
3. Click the Advanced tab if it isn't already showing. Select the calendar from the drop-down list in the Calendar field as shown in Figure 4.32.
4. Press OK.

An icon will display next to the task as shown in Figure 4.33 to let you know you have a calendar attached to the task.

You have another selection to consider when you select this task calendar. Notice that the field next to the Calendar field called Scheduling ignores the resource calendars flag shown in Figure 4.32. Resource calendars take precedence over all other kinds of calendars unless you select the flag. If a resource calendar is set for a resource to be off on Saturday and Sunday, Project will not let you assign work to the resource on either of those days.

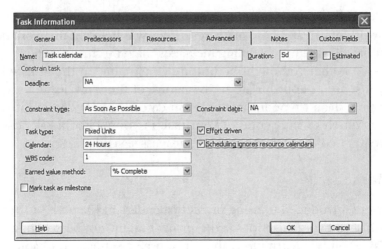

Figure 4.32 *Select a task calendar in the Advanced tab*

	❶	Task Name	Duration	Oct 7, '07							Oct 14, '07							Oct 21, '0
				S	S	M	T	W	T	F	S	S	M	T	W	T	F	S	S	M	T
1		Task calendar	5 days																		

Figure 4.33 *Task calendar icon*

However, if a task has a task calendar attached that includes weekends as working days and the Scheduling ignores resource calendars check box for a resource is selected, when the resource is assigned to the task, Project overrides the resource calendar and allows the resource to be assigned to work over the weekends. To ensure resources you assign to the task are scheduled to work for the weekend (if that is what you need), then you need to select the Scheduling ignores resource calendars check box. You might rarely use task calendars, but it is great way to solve many scheduling issues for some tasks.

Custom Fields

Although you've seen several fields that can describe a task, sometimes you want to include your own specific information about a task. You can insert specific columns to further describe information about the field than what shows by default in the Gantt Chart. For instance, the Work field can be inserted to show the work effort estimated for a task. You can also create

custom fields for tasks to describe task information beyond the programmed fields that Project expects you need for project scheduling. You
can enter important information your organization cares about in relation
to a task. For instance, let's say for your project you also want to note status
information for each task. Figure 4.34 shows the status of tasks in the house-
painting project.

	ⓘ	Task Name	Task Status	Start	Finish
0		⊟ **HousePainting**		**Sun 5/6/07**	**Mon 5/7/07**
1	📝	Gather Materials	Done	Mon 5/7/07	Mon 5/7/07
2		⊟ **Prep**		**Sun 5/6/07**	**Mon 5/7/07**
3		Scrape and Sand	Son still working on his section-3/4 done	Mon 5/7/07	Mon 5/7/07
4		Inspect and Re-scrape	Inspection complete on 3/4	Mon 5/7/07	Mon 5/7/07
5		House Prepped		Sun 5/6/07	Sun 5/6/07
6		⊟ **Prime**		**Mon 5/7/07**	**Mon 5/7/07**
7		Mask Windows		Mon 5/7/07	Mon 5/7/07
8		Prime		Mon 5/7/07	Mon 5/7/07
9		⊟ **Paint**		**Mon 5/7/07**	**Mon 5/7/07**
10		Paint		Mon 5/7/07	Mon 5/7/07
11		Strip Masking		Mon 5/7/07	Mon 5/7/07
12		Inspect and Retouch		Mon 5/7/07	Mon 5/7/07

Figure 4.34   *Custom field Task status inserted into project.*

To create this Task status field, you would do the following:

1. Select Tools from the Menu bar.

2. Select Customize from the drop-down list. You will see the Custom
   Fields dialog box shown in Figure 4.35. In Project 2002 and Project
   2003, the dialog box is called Customize Fields and also contains a
   Custom Outline Codes tab that allows you to create tables and field
   values. In Project 2007 the outline code is now a selection in the Type
   field for custom fields. In this case you are just creating a text field via
   the Custom Fields dialog box.

3. Select Text from the drop-down list in the Type field. Text fields will
   now display in the list on the left of the dialog box.

4. Select the Text 1 field and click Rename as shown in Figure 4.35.

5. The Rename Field dialog box will display as shown in Figure 4.36.
   Type the new name of the field in the area showing and click OK. In
   this case, type "Task Status" in the field.

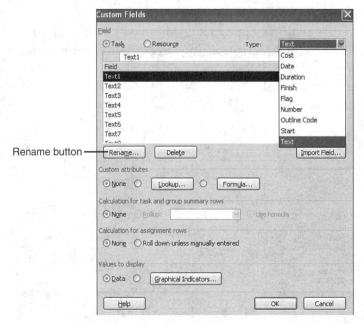

Rename button

Figure 4.35 *Custom Fields dialog box*

Figure 4.36 *Rename Field dialog box*

6. Notice in Figure 4.37 that the new name now shows in the Customize Fields dialog box. Click OK.

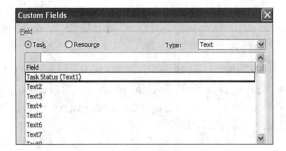

Figure 4.37 *Text field 1 now shows the new name*

7. You have now created the field, but as with any field not already show-ing in your views, you need to insert the column. To do so, double-click the column before which you would like the new column to display. You will see the Column Definition dialog box as shown in Figure 4.38.

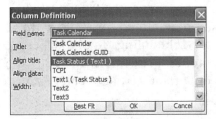

Figure 4.38   *Column Definition dialog box showing field name*

Notice that the default name of the field is showing, but the name you cre-ated for it is also displayed. The field also shows as both Text1 (Task Status) and Task Status (Text1).

8. Press OK and you will see the column inserted (refer to Figure 4.34).

This section of the book is just introducing you to custom fields so you can add your own data to describe tasks as part of task information. As you get more familiar with Project, and you find you want to perform calculations on fields or enter your own information, explore custom fields to help you accomplish this. However, make sure you check to see if Project already has a field you think you need before creating a custom one.

Look for Project fields before creating your own

I was once teaching a class where I inserted the Baseline work field, which displays your original estimate for a task (because the Work field changes as you add actuals or make changes; see Chapter 2). One of the students mentioned that he created a custom field called Original esti-mate to deal with the fact that the Work field changed. This was a very clever way to resolve his issues, but the tool already had the solution in it. He simply hadn't discovered it.

Understanding Duration and Work Fields on Tasks

Chapter 1 introduced the concept of effort-based scheduling. Chapter 2 introduced the Work and Duration fields, as well as other important fields that can describe project tasks. Let's dig a little deeper into work and duration in relation to tasks, as this book revisits the fields a lot. Not only do these fields have specific behaviors as programmed for Project, they also have important meanings and uses for scheduling. In the schedule-building process, you will be tempted to enter estimate information into the fields for a task as you add the task, but it's important to wait to enter estimates later in the schedule-building process.

Many people consider duration to be the only way to estimate a task. The immediate thought is, "It will take 2 weeks to paint the house." But what does that 2 weeks consist of? Is it one person working 5 hours each day, two people working 3 hours each day, or someone working a few hours here and there each of those days? As a project manager you might work for organizations where a resource or functional manager tells you that testing the new television model your project team will be designing will take 5 weeks. He will assign the workers and do what it takes to get the TV tested in those 5 weeks. You do not know how much work it will take, nor does your organization expect you to provide that information in the schedule. This is duration-based scheduling, where the project manager has no authority over the work of the people assigned to a task. Many organizations successfully use this kind of scheduling. If you use this kind of scheduling, you might not care very much about the Work field. In fact, the information the tool provides you about work is probably inaccurate. The test team might be using five people and will expend 950 hours to do testing. However, you will only put the resource manager's name on the task and when Project calculates the task it will say the work is 200 hours. However, you don't really care if they spend 200 hours or more than 950 hours; you just expect the testers to get the work done in 5 weeks to ensure your schedule is met. Notice some implications about this, however: You are probably not responsible for the cost of the work on the task or the project budget. If you were, the amount of work would be important because the resources' rates times the hours expended would relate to the cost of the task. You'll see more about costs in Chapter 7, "Using Project to Enter Cost Estimates."

As soon as you add a resource in the Resource names field on the Gantt Chart (or in any other view), Project populates work effort information about tasks for effort-based scheduling. Project assumes that most organizations want to schedule and understand work effort for each task. Project managers who perform effort-based scheduling are more likely to have authority over the work of the people on the project. By using both duration and work to describe the task, you can achieve more accurate estimates and better historical data about what it takes to get the tasks of a project done. Organizations that want to understand how resources are being used and project managers who want to understand their tasks in more detail will use this method for building schedules.

Throughout this book, think about the kinds of project schedules you are building or how you will be entering estimate information on each task: Are you getting only duration information about the tasks, or are you getting work and duration information? In some cases, you might be getting both: You are receiving duration estimates for tasks from other functional areas, but for your own tasks, you are able to estimate both work and duration. There are issues and advantages for both kinds of task estimates.

Ask estimators both how much effort will it take and how long will it take

If you are relying on other people to provide you estimates, start asking them two questions about each task: How long will it take and how many hours will it take to complete? They might say 2 weeks. Then, when they say it will take 60 hours, you know they will not be working full-time on your task in that 2 weeks. This might indicate that it will be hard to get the work done, as they are probably assigned other tasks not related to your project and that might vie for their time.

Let's illustrate the Work and Duration fields for the house painting. In Figure 4.39, let's say you've given each task a duration. You already created task relationships by linking the tasks. We'll talk more about task relationships in the next chapter.

You have not added resources yet, so zero displays in the Work field. As described in Chapter 1, Project automatically creates an estimate for the Work field when you add a resource in the Resource Name field. Project calculates the resource working 8 hours each day for the duration entered. If you enter a resource on Task 1—Gather Materials—the Work field will be filled with 24 hours (3 days × 8 hours). Figure 4.40 illustrates this behavior.

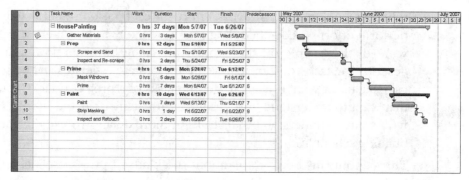

Figure 4.39 *Duration entered for each task and work is zero*

	❶	Task Name	Work	Duration	Start	Finish	Predecessors	Resource Names
0		⊟ HousePainting 4.42	296 hrs	37 days	Mon 5/7/07	Tue 6/26/07		
1	✎	Gather Materials	24 hrs	3 days	Mon 5/7/07	Wed 5/9/07		R1
2		⊟ Prep	96 hrs	12 days	Thu 5/10/07	Fri 5/25/07		
3		Scape and Sand	80 hrs	10 days	Thu 5/10/07	Wed 5/23/07	1	R1
4		Inspect and Re-scrape	16 hrs	2 days	Thu 5/24/07	Fri 5/25/07	3	R1
5		⊟ Prime	96 hrs	12 days	Mon 5/28/07	Tue 6/12/07		
6		Mask Windows	40 hrs	5 days	Mon 5/28/07	Fri 6/1/07	4	R1
7		Prime	56 hrs	7 days	Mon 6/4/07	Tue 6/12/07	6	R1
8		⊟ Paint	80 hrs	10 days	Wed 6/13/07	Tue 6/26/07		
9		Paint	56 hrs	7 days	Wed 6/13/07	Thu 6/21/07	7	R1
10		Strip Masking	8 hrs	1 day	Fri 6/22/07	Fri 6/22/07	9	R1
11		Inspect and Retouch	16 hrs	2 days	Mon 6/25/07	Tue 6/26/07	10	R1

Figure 4.40 *Work calculated when resource is added to a task*

If you were to add another resource to one of the tasks showing, then the duration would change because (using the default settings) Project assumes you want the work on the task to be shared. For instance, if you add another resource to the Gather materials task it would change to 1.5 days in duration. The section "What Are Task Types and Why Should I Care?" later in this chapter describes the default settings further.

You can also enter the work estimate directly into the Work field. Figure 4.41 shows the same estimated durations as the previous examples, but you will also see the work estimated for each task in the Work field. Notice that there are no resources on the tasks.

Now, when you enter a resource in the Resource Name field, Project calculates how much each day the resource will be working. The resource will work a percentage of the time in an 8-hour day. Figure 4.42 shows the percentage of time the resource will work, if they work for the duration indicated, and the duration provided. The formula discussed in Chapter 2

$$\text{Work} = \text{Duration} \times \text{Units}$$

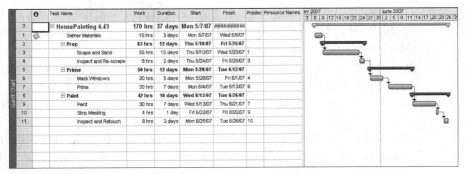

Figure 4.41   *Work and Duration values entered for each task*

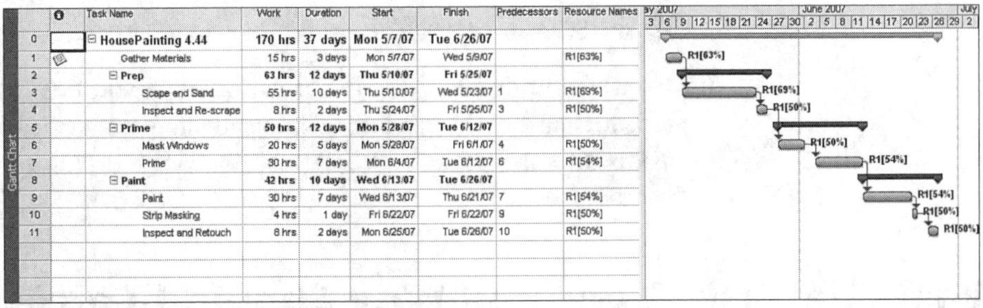

		Task Name	Work	Duration	Start	Finish	Predecessors	Resource Names
0		⊟ HousePainting 4.44	170 hrs	37 days	Mon 5/7/07	Tue 6/26/07		
1		Gather Materials	15 hrs	3 days	Mon 5/7/07	Wed 5/9/07		R1[63%]
2		⊟ Prep	63 hrs	12 days	Thu 5/10/07	Fri 5/25/07		
3		Scape and Sand	55 hrs	10 days	Thu 5/10/07	Wed 5/23/07	1	R1[69%]
4		Inspect and Re-scrape	8 hrs	2 days	Thu 5/24/07	Fri 5/25/07	3	R1[50%]
5		⊟ Prime	50 hrs	12 days	Mon 5/28/07	Tue 6/12/07		
6		Mask Windows	20 hrs	5 days	Mon 5/28/07	Fri 6/1/07	4	R1[50%]
7		Prime	30 hrs	7 days	Mon 6/4/07	Tue 6/12/07	6	R1[54%]
8		⊟ Paint	42 hrs	10 days	Wed 6/13/07	Tue 6/26/07		
9		Paint	30 hrs	7 days	Wed 6/13/07	Thu 6/21/07	7	R1[54%]
10		Strip Masking	4 hrs	1 day	Fri 6/22/07	Fri 6/22/07	9	R1[50%]
11		Inspect and Retouch	8 hrs	2 days	Mon 6/25/07	Tue 6/26/07	10	R1[50%]

Figure 4.42   *Work and Duration entered for each task with resources entered*

kicks in and Project calculates the amount of a resource's time. This gives you far more information about each task than you would have if you just entered duration.

So, what does understanding Work and Duration fields have to do with task information needed to build your schedule? First, although the Duration is a data field displayed by default in the Gantt Chart, Work is just as important (if you are doing effort-based scheduling). Second, you need to understand that Duration is all you need for duration-based schedules. Finally, it illustrates the amount of information that can distract you from thinking about each task itself and the relationships between each task when you initially build your schedule. For instance, if you focus on the estimates and the resources on the tasks, you might miss the fact that you could actually start the Inspect and Rescrape task earlier (e.g., as each side of the house is done), rather than waiting for the whole house to be completed, which this relationship illustrates.

Just as Project provides you the Start and Finish fields in the schedule (which you should not use while building your schedule because they create constraints), do not enter anything into the Duration (or Work) field until after you have added most of the tasks and created relationships between each of them. Even though the order of the fields on the Gantt Chart looks like you should be entering them in the order of Task Name, Duration, Start, Finish, Predecessors (task relationships), and Resource Names, first just enter Task Name for all tasks in your schedule. Worry about estimates and resources after you build the scope of your project in the WBS and after you create your task relationships.

> **Read Chapter 4 of *Project Management for Mere Mortals***
>
> To get a head start on understanding task relationships and how to get more accurate information about your tasks, read Chapter 4 of *Project Management for Mere Mortals.*

What Are Task Types and Why Should I Care?

There is one more piece of task information that contributes to your understanding of task data. Two fields are programmed into Project that greatly affect the behavior of your project schedule, but they are related to the intrinsic purpose of the task: Task types and Effort-driven. These two fields are on the Advanced tab of the Task Information dialog box, as shown in Figure 4.43, and also show up if you insert the columns Type and Effort Driven, as shown in Figure 4.44, or use the split screen as shown in Figure 4.45.

Remember the formula,

Work = Duration × Unit [where Unit is the amount of a resource or resources]

that sits in Project (yes, I mention it a lot)? Task types define which element in the formula should remain constant, no matter which of the other two operands of the formula might change. Effort-driven describes how tasks will react when you add a resource to a task that already has a resource on it, or remove a resource if there are two or more resources on a task. There are three task types:

Task type　　　　　Effort driven

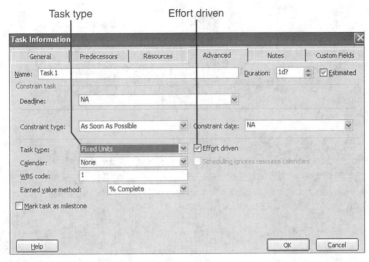

Figure 4.43　*Task type field and Effort-driven fields in the Advanced tab*

	❶	Task Name	Type	Effort Driven	Duration
0		⊟ HousePainting	**Fixed Duration**	**No**	**37 days**
1	🖉	Gather Materials	Fixed Units	Yes	3 days
2		⊟ **Prep**	**Fixed Duration**	**No**	**12 days**
3		Scape and Sand	Fixed Units	Yes	10 days
4		Inspect and Re-scrape	Fixed Units	Yes	2 days
5		⊟ **Prime**	**Fixed Duration**	**No**	**12 days**
6		Mask Windows	Fixed Units	Yes	5 days
7		Prime	Fixed Units	Yes	7 days
8		⊟ **Paint**	**Fixed Duration**	**No**	**10 days**
9		Paint	Fixed Units	Yes	7 days
10		Strip Masking	Fixed Units	Yes	1 day
11		Inspect and Retouch	Fixed Units	Yes	2 days

Figure 4.44　*Task type (called Type) and Effort driven fields inserted into the Gantt Chart*

- **Fixed Units (the default):** The amount of resources is fixed, so if you change the Duration or Work, Project will not change the amount of resources.

- **Fixed Duration:** The time span the task will take is fixed, so if you change the Work or Units, Project will not change the Duration.

- **Fixed Work:** The effort of the work is fixed, so if you change the Duration or Units, Project will not change the Work.

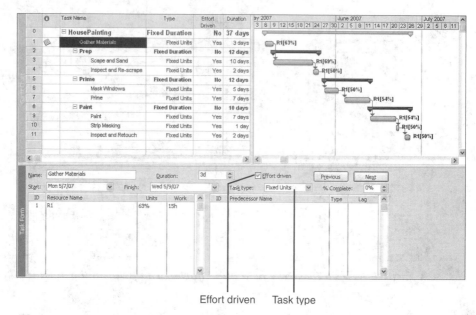

Effort driven   Task type

Figure 4.45 *Task type and Effort driven fields in the Task Form view when using a split window*

Once you learn more about Task Types, you might decide to change the Fixed Units default by selecting Tools from the menu bar, then clicking Options and changing the Default task type field on the Schedule tab. Effort-driven is a toggle: It's either on or not, Yes or No.

The term *fixed* describes exactly what it says: If you select Fixed Duration and you type 10 in the Duration field and you increase or decrease the Work field or add or remove resources (units), then the Duration field will stay fixed at 10. If you didn't change the Task Type field from the default Fixed Units, and you increase or decrease the Work field, then the Duration field would change. This implies that you actually need to decide which kind of task type you want to use based on how you want the task estimate calculations to behave. The best way to understand this is to show changes in Project itself based on task type. Let's take a look at the behavior of the first task type, Fixed Units.

In Figure 4.46 the task is 5 days long, 20 hours worth of work, and has the resource units fixed at 50% meaning the resource can only work 4 hours a day.

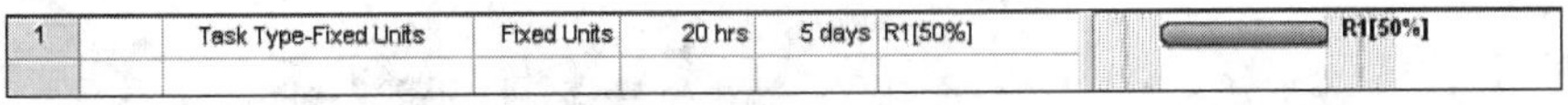

| 1 | | Task Type-Fixed Units | Fixed Units | 20 hrs | 5 days | R1[50%] | | | R1[50%] |

Figure 4.46 *Tasks with Fixed Units of 50%*

If you change the work to 40 hours, the Duration increases to 10 days as shown in Figure 4.47, because the Resource Units are fixed.

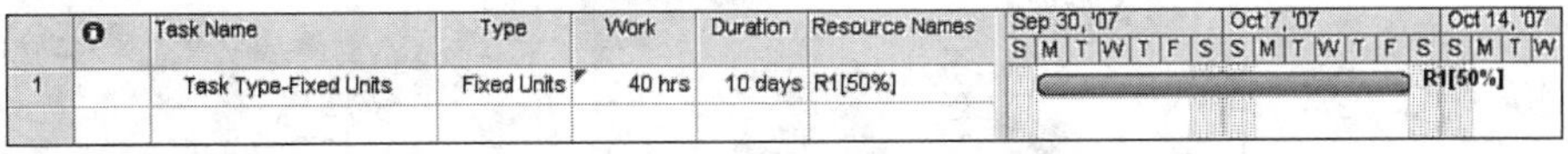

	❶	Task Name	Type	Work	Duration	Resource Names	Sep 30, '07 S M T W T F S	Oct 7, '07 S M T W T F S	Oct 14, '07 S M T W
1		Task Type-Fixed Units	Fixed Units	40 hrs	10 days	R1[50%]			R1[50%]

Figure 4.47 *On Fixed Units task, on changing Work, Duration changed*

Based on the original situation in Figure 4.46, changing the Duration to 15 days increases the Work to 60 hours as shown in Figure 4.48 again because the resource is fixed at 50%.

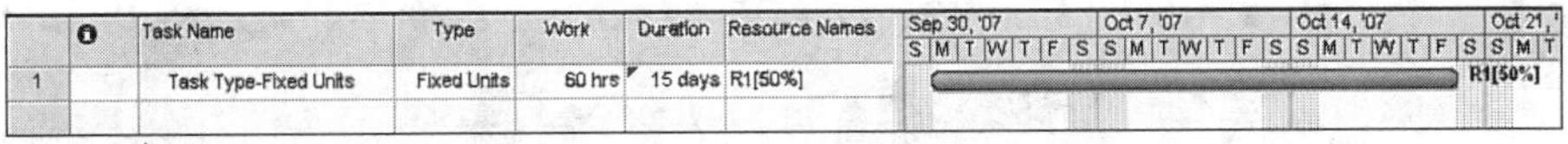

	❶	Task Name	Type	Work	Duration	Resource Names	Sep 30, '07 S M T W T F S	Oct 7, '07 S M T W T F S	Oct 14, '07 S M T W T F S	Oct 21, S M T
1		Task Type-Fixed Units	Fixed Units	60 hrs	15 days	R1[50%]				R1[50%]

Figure 4.48 *On Fixed Units task, on changing Duration, Work changed*

Now, using the original task set up from Figure 4.46, changing the Units to 100% changes the Duration to 2.5 days and Work remains the same as shown in Figure 4.49. For any fixed task type, if you change the item that is fixed, one of the other operands of the work formula will change based on preset rules in Project. Project prefers to make changes to Duration before it will change Work.

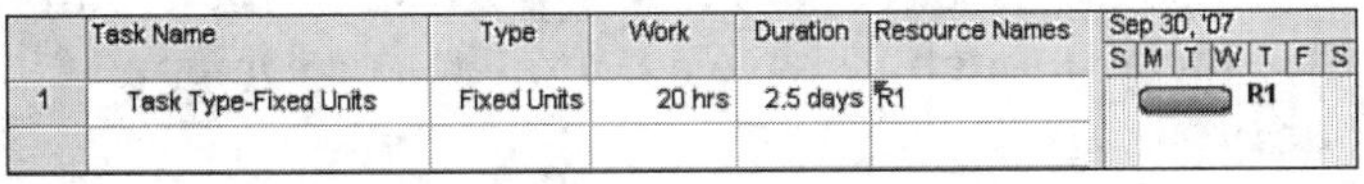

	Task Name	Type	Work	Duration	Resource Names	Sep 30, '07 S M T W T F S
1	Task Type-Fixed Units	Fixed Units	20 hrs	2.5 days	R1	R1

Figure 4.49 *On Fixed units task, if Units is changed, Duration changes*

Project 2002 and later versions have Smart Tags

Project 2002 and later versions have a feature called Smart Tags. Because the behavior based on task type is not apparent in the tool, Microsoft programmers added this help function. You will see a green triangle in the upper corner of a field and if you hover over it, you will see a symbol with an arrow next to it. If you click the arrow, it will provide options and text that describe the various behaviors that are possible for the work formula. You can select what you want Project to do. Figure 4.50 shows an example of the Smart Tag.

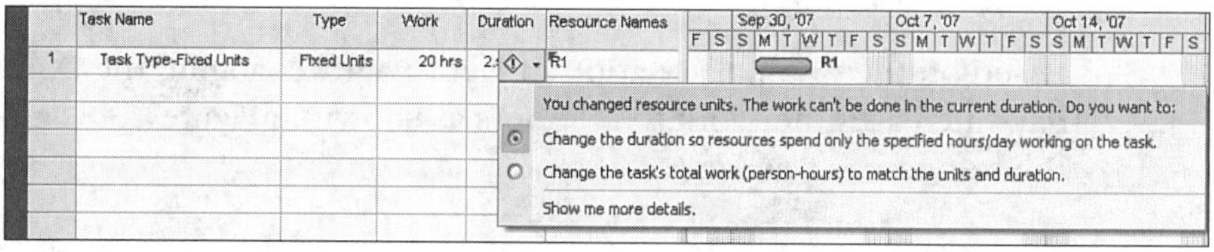

Figure 4.50   *Smart Tags let you decide the behavior you want for the Work formula*

This is a nice intellectual exercise to see how this formula works, but why is this important? In some cases, you will have tasks where the functional manager told you, "I can only give you Jose 4 hours a day," or she might say, "Jose is working on another project at the same time so he can only work for you half time." You would want to make sure that you add Jose to the schedule at 50% units and his dedication to your project needs to stay that way. Project assumes that the availability of a person to do your work is the most common situation for your projects so the default task type is Fixed Units. In most cases, if you have someone working for you, they have a lot of other obligations and you only have them for a portion of their time every day, unless you are lucky enough to have a contractor or someone entirely dedicated to your project.

Now, let's take a look at a Fixed Duration task type in the same way. All of these changes are based on the setup in Figure 4.46 but the task type is Fixed Duration. In Figure 4.51 I have changed Work to 40 hours. Because Duration is fixed, the Units changed to 100% (remember that if you see no brackets on the resource, it means 100%).

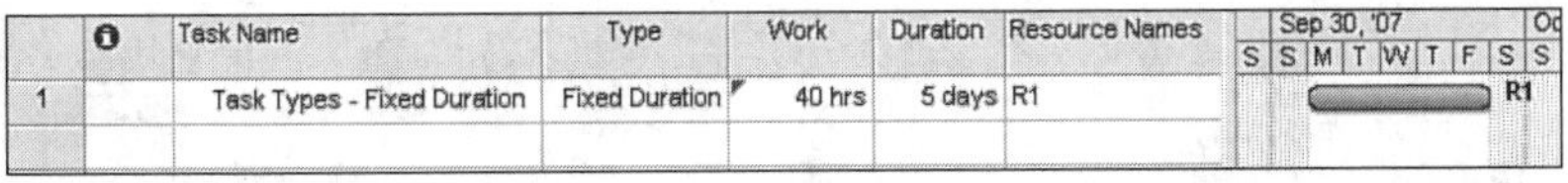

	❶	Task Name	Type	Work	Duration	Resource Names	Sep 30, '07 S S M T W T F S S	Oc
1		Task Types - Fixed Duration	Fixed Duration	40 hrs	5 days	R1		R1

Figure 4.51   *On Fixed Duration task, on changing Work, Units change*

If you change Duration to 15 days, Project changes Work before Units based on Project's calculation preferences. So in this case, Work will change to 60 hours as shown in Figure 4.52.

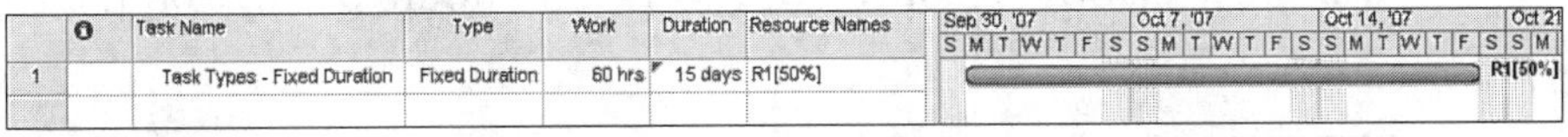

	❶	Task Name	Type	Work	Duration	Resource Names	Sep 30, '07 S M T W T F S	Oct 7, '07 S M T W T F S	Oct 14, '07 S M T W T F S S M	Oct 21
1		Task Types - Fixed Duration	Fixed Duration	60 hrs	15 days	R1[50%]				R1[50%]

Figure 4.52   *On Fixed Duration task, on changing Duration, Work changes*

When you change Units to 100%, Work changes to 40 hours as shown in Figure 4.53.

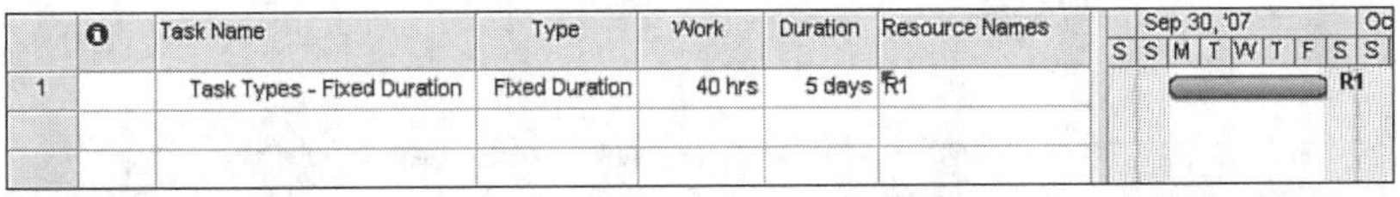

	❶	Task Name	Type	Work	Duration	Resource Names	Sep 30, '07 S S M T W T F S S	Oc
1		Task Types - Fixed Duration	Fixed Duration	40 hrs	5 days	R1		R1

Figure 4.53   *On Fixed Duration task, on changing Units, Work changes*

So why would you want to designate a task Fixed Duration? You might have tasks that have been designated to take a certain amount of time, no matter what. Perhaps your organization takes 5 weeks to test a product. If more or less people are put on the task, it doesn't matter; the formula needs to ensure that the task remains at the duration you entered.

Last, let's take a look at the Fixed Work task type. Again, you will base this on the situation set up in Figure 4.46, but the task type is changed to Fixed Work. As with the previous examples, you would change Work to 40. Remember Project's order of preference of changes. Will Project change the Duration or the Units field? As shown in Figure 4.54, Project changes Duration to 10 days.

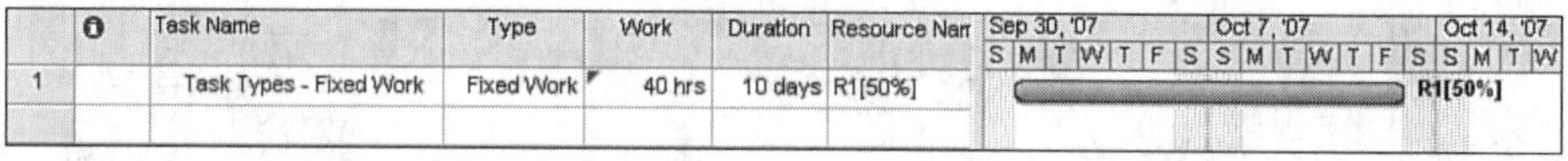

❶	Task Name	Type	Work	Duration	Resource Nam	Sep 30, '07		Oct 7, '07		Oct 14, '07
						S M T W T F S	S M T W T F S	S M T W
1	Task Types - Fixed Work	Fixed Work	40 hrs	10 days	R1[50%]					R1[50%]

Figure 4.54   *On Fixed Work task, on changing Work, Duration changes*

Now, you will change Duration to 15 days. This is an interesting change: It changes Units to 17%. If the resource is going to have 20 hours to work on the task in 15 days, that translates to working on the task at 17% per day, as shown in Figure 4.55. If you were to look at how Project allocates the time per day, it will show that the resource will work 1.33 hours per day on the task.

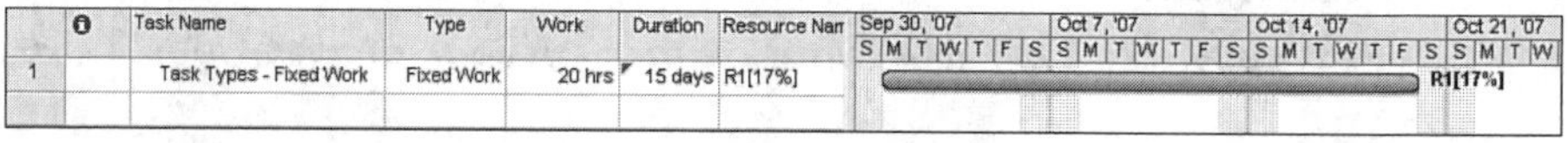

❶	Task Name	Type	Work	Duration	Resource Nam	Sep 30, '07		Oct 7, '07		Oct 14, '07		Oct 21, '07
						S M T W T F S	S M T W T F S	S M T W T F S	S M T W
1	Task Types - Fixed Work	Fixed Work	20 hrs	15 days	R1[17%]							R1[17%]

Figure 4.55   *On Fixed Work task, on changing Duration, Units changes*

Finally, when you change Units to 100% (as in Figure 4.56), the Duration changes to 2.5 days.

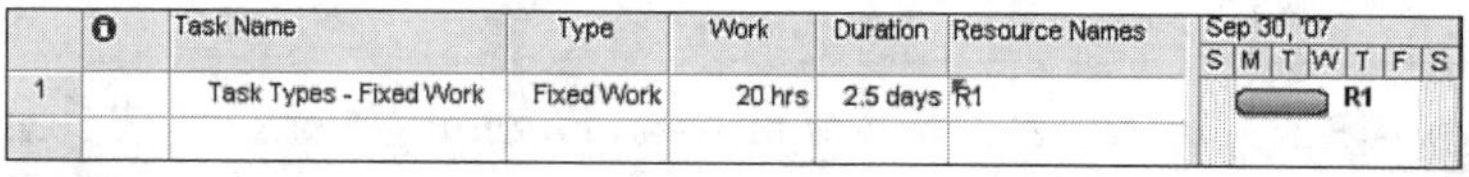

❶	Task Name	Type	Work	Duration	Resource Names	Sep 30, '07
						S M T W T F S
1	Task Types - Fixed Work	Fixed Work	20 hrs	2.5 days	R1	R1

Figure 4.56   *On Fixed Work task, on changing Units, Duration changes*

Now why would you want to make a task type Fixed Work? Let's say the estimate you received for the task was 50 hours. If you don't make the task fixed and the manager tells you that Jose can now only work 30% of his time on the task and you change the units to 30% in the schedule, then the work estimate might change when you didn't intend it.

If this isn't difficult enough to understand, you have one more item to add to the equation: the effort-driven designation on tasks. Effort driven designates that resources assigned to tasks will share the work. Work is affected by adding a resource to a task that already has a resource or resources on it, or removing a resource from a task that has two or more resources on it. To explain this conceptually, if you want a task to be effort driven, you want its duration to vary according to how many people work on it. If the task is estimated to take 40 hours, and one person works on it, it will take 5 days, but if two people work on it, it will take 2.5 days. If you have an 80-hour task that is taking 10 days and you have two people working on it, and you remove one person from work on the task, it will now take 20 days to complete. If you take off the effort-driven designation on a task, then the duration of it will not change based on how many people are put on it. Let's take a look at what this means using the same sort of setup used in our previous examples. Let's look at a Fixed Units, Effort-Driven task, which is the default task designation. Figure 4.57 shows the initial setup.

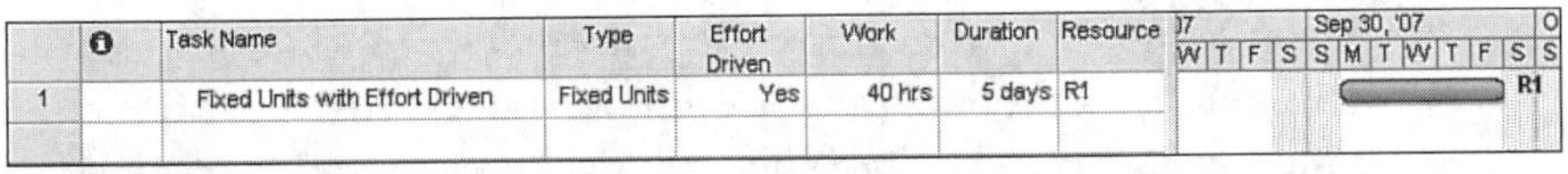

	❶	Task Name	Type	Effort Driven	Work	Duration	Resource	J7 W|T|F|S	Sep 30, '07 S|M|T|W|T|F|S|S	O S
1		Fixed Units with Effort Driven	Fixed Units	Yes	40 hrs	5 days	R1			R1

Figure 4.57 *Fixed Units, Effort-Driven task*

When another resource is added to this task, the work remains at 40 hours, but Project assumes the work is shared equally, and it shortens the duration to 2.5 days as shown in Figure 4.58.

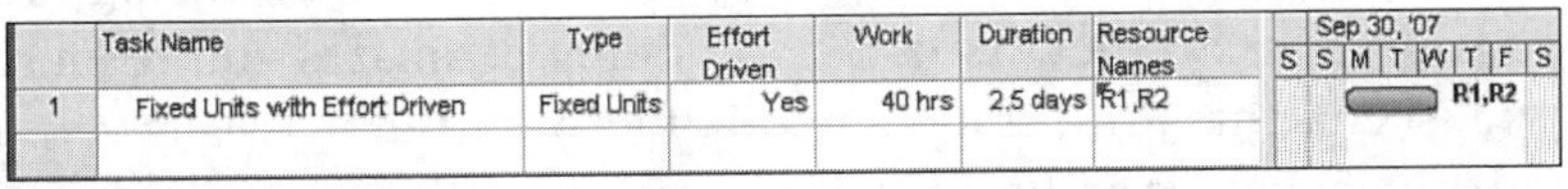

	Task Name	Type	Effort Driven	Work	Duration	Resource Names	Sep 30, '07 S|S|M|T|W|T|F|S
1	Fixed Units with Effort Driven	Fixed Units	Yes	40 hrs	2.5 days	R1,R2	R1,R2

Figure 4.58 *Duration is reduced when another person is added to the task*

Now let's see what happens when you remove the effort-driven designation in Figure 4.59. Work increases because the effort is no longer supposed to be shared. Each resource is assigned 40 hours to work on the task.

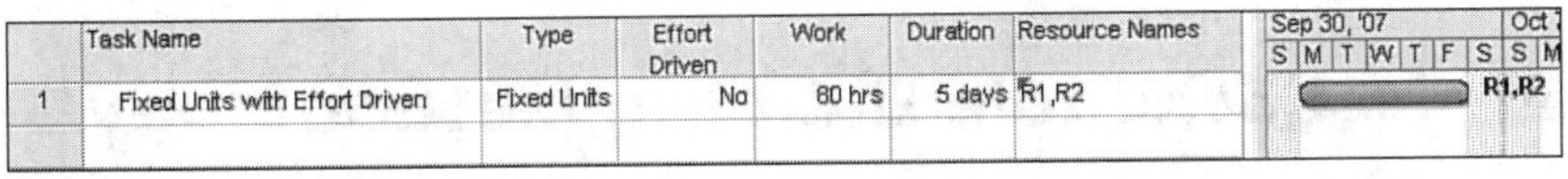

	Task Name	Type	Effort Driven	Work	Duration	Resource Names	Sep 30, '07 S|M|T|W|T|F|S|S	Oct S|M
1	Fixed Units with Effort Driven	Fixed Units	No	80 hrs	5 days	R1,R2		R1,R2

Figure 4.59 *Work increases and duration remains the same*

Worry about this effort-driven designation only when you have two or more resources assigned on a task. Project wants you to tell its scheduling engine if you want it to calculate a shortening of duration if several people share the work on the task, or if you really want it to just add people to a task at the same amount of work effort, and thus not reduce the time it takes to get the work done. Keep in mind that sometimes you have several people on the task and you want them to all work at different amounts. In other words, Jose needs to work 50 hours and Rose needs to work 80. To add people at different rates, add them using the split window. With the split window you can add people at different units and with different work amounts.

> **Assign one person to a task**
>
> If you do not like what this effort-driven designation does, clear it, or consider creating one task for each person assigned to the task. Sometimes it's just easier to use the tool if you assign each person separately to the task. This can get unwieldy on some projects, but in many cases it can be the best way for you to analyze and manage the individual work of people.

Here's one last item to think about when setting the task type and effort-driven designation for building your schedule. You are telling Project how you want a task to act. As you start adding estimates and resources to the task it seems that Project has a mind of its own, but it's really your mind that guides its behavior by designating its task type and effort-driven calculation. Project's behaviors are completely programmatic and logical according to its formulaic parameters. Keeping this in mind, you will need to continue considering task types throughout the project scheduling lifecycle, including when you start tracking progress on your tasks. Sometimes you want to change the task type. Just because you set it once doesn't mean you might not want to change it later.

The Project Schedule Building Methodology So Far

Based on what you have learned, the following steps and sequence describe the best methods for building your schedule. The items emphasized in this chapter are indicated in italics.

The steps for building a project schedule so far:

☑ If you are using a template, select the appropriate template (you will probably want to change it based on the input of your project team). If you are building a project from scratch, build a WBS with your team, then move to the next step.

☑ Set up your project calendar if you do not have one available. Make sure you reflect your company's hours in Tools, Options, and Calendar, if different than the defaults.

☑ In the Project Information dialog box, set your project start date and make sure your project calendar is assigned to the project.

☑ Start building (if your project is from scratch) or editing (if you are using a template) your task list. Make sure you indicate summary tasks and subtasks to help indicate the outline of your project schedule.

☑ *Add milestone tasks to indicate significant events, deliverables, or approval points in your project.*

☑ *Enter deadline dates for appropriate tasks. This is a better way of indicating dates when tasks need to be completed rather than typing in a finish date on a task.*

☑ *Add task calendars to tasks to indicate exceptions to the project calendar if needed. You will probably not need these kinds of calendars often.*

☑ *Review all tasks. Decide what kind of tasks they are for the schedule-building process. Change the Task type and Effort-Driven fields if appropriate.*

Although constraints were discussed in this chapter, I strongly suggest you avoid using them during this schedule-building process. Add them later when you finalize your schedule, if necessary.

Read Chapter 2 of *Project Management for Mere Mortals*

Chapter 2 of *Project Management for Mere Mortals* briefly discusses milestones and constraints.

Summary

While entering tasks into your schedule to build your project scope, you also need to consider the information or designations you want to include on tasks to tell Project how you want the schedule to behave. First, Project provides several ways for viewing and entering task data: the Task Information dialog box and adding columns to views. Because Project contains hundreds of fields of information about tasks, you might want to focus on the most important ones that are available on the Gantt Chart and Task Information dialog box.

Understand how milestones can help you build a more viewable schedule focusing on only the key events of the project, and how deadline dates are a great way to see if your estimates and resource limitations will make you miss the deadline. You learned that you should not enter constraints when you first build your schedule. Although fine for indicating dates you would like the tasks to meet, you should enter constraints once you are done with building the schedule rather than while you are building it. Attaching task calendars to specific tasks provides you the flexibility to override the working times designated for the schedule or resources when you need to schedule work outside the bounds of your normal working hours. You learned that if you or your organization need to enter any data about tasks that Project does not provide, you can use custom fields to do so.

Finally, you learned more about the Work and Duration fields and how they work together in a schedule. You found out more about how people might estimate tasks from either a work or duration perspective and how that information can be entered into Project. Task types and Effort-Driven task information affects the behavior of Project's scheduling engine. By designating if a task is Fixed Duration, Work, or Units, and if the task is Effort Driven, you will affect how the Work = Duration × Units formula calculates for each task.

The next chapter covers task relationships, one more piece of information about a task. Each task in your schedule is related, with another task needing to be completed or started before it. Building task relationships builds the critical path, the shortest path through the schedule that determines the end date of your project.

Practice: Entering Milestones, Deadline Dates, Task Calendars, and Task Types in Your Schedule

As already described, the next steps in building a schedule are to enter milestones, enter deadline dates, create task calendars, and designate task types. In this practice, you will practice using some of the features discussed in this chapter. Use the file called HousePainting-Practice-Chapter4.mpp file to begin the practice.

Practice 4.1

Using Milestones

After selecting Open from the File menu in the menu bar and selecting HousePainting-Practice-Chapter4.mpp, follow these steps:

1. Click the entire Task 5 (Prime) row so that it is highlighted.

2. Right-click so that you see a drop-down list and a selection on it called New Task, and click the New Task selection. Note that if you click on just a section of the task, you will not get the same drop-down list to allow you to insert a new task.

3. Type "Prepping Complete" in the Task name field and type zero in the Duration field.

4. Click the entire Task 9 (Paint) row so that it is entirely highlighted (click on the far left of the row to highlight it all).

5. Right-click so that you see a drop-down list and a selection on it called New Task, and click on the New Task selection.

6. Type "Priming Complete" in the Task Name field and type zero in the Duration field.

7. Click the Task Name field of the row after Task 13, which should be entirely blank, and type "Painting Complete."

8. Type zero in the Duration field.

9. Select File from the menu bar and click Save As in the drop-down list. The Save As dialog box will appear. Type a filename that you prefer in the File name field and click Save to save to the file location you prefer.

You should have a file that is similar to the file on the CD called HousePainting-Practice-Chapter4-Practice1-Result.mpp. Note that we entered a milestone at the end of each phase of the project. This is good practice to indicate key events in your project, and it also helps you when you start building task relationships. Of course, you can enter more milestones than these, which I recommend for large projects and to break up tasks that might be very long so that you can create checkpoints or approval points for your project. Later you will create some views to see just milestones to easily analyze how you are doing on important dates in your project.

Practice 4.2

Using Deadlines

In this practice you can continue using the file you saved or use the file on the CD called HousePainting-Practice-Chapter4-Practice1-Result.mpp to start with.

After selecting Open from the File menu in the menu bar and selecting the file you want to use, follow these steps:

1. Double-click on the milestone task called Prepping Complete. The Task Information dialog box will appear. You will put a deadline date on this task, because you know you will have help from your child through May 25, and after that you may not get his help as he may be going on a school trip to Europe.

2. Click on the Advanced tab, and enter 5/25/2007 in the Deadline field and press OK. You can type the date in, or you can click on the arrow next to the field and use the pop-up calendar. Click on the arrows to get to the right month and year and click on 5/25/07. Make sure you get the date right. If you are practicing this exercise in a year other than 2007, it is very common to accidentally select the wrong year.

3. Let's create one more deadline date—the date you want the entire project to be completed. Double-click on the milestone task called Painting Complete. The Advanced tab should already by selected since that's the tab you last used while you were in this project.

4. Enter 6/30/2007 in the Deadline field and press OK. You can type the date in, or you can click on the arrow next to the field and use the pop-up calendar. You want to have the painting done by June 30, as you will be going on vacation shortly after that.

5. View the deadline marker and dates to make sure they are set correctly. To do so, scroll in the bar chart area of the Gantt Chart until you see the green markers on the two dates. Sometimes, if you enter the date wrong, it won't be easy to find the deadline marker on the Gantt Chart. To make it easier to see deadline dates, right-click on the Task Name field and select Insert Column from the drop-down list. The Column Definition should appear.

6. Click on the down arrow next to the Field name field and press D on your keyboard to scroll through the field names until you find Deadline. Click on Deadline and press OK.

7. The Deadline field will display prior to the Task Name field in the Gantt Chart view and you can double-check the deadline dates here. If they are not

5/25/07 for Prepping Complete and 6/30/07 for Painting Complete, then you can correct the dates. You can type the dates in, or you can click in the field and see the arrow and select to see the calendar date picker.

8. Remove the Deadline column by clicking on the column and pressing the delete key (Del) on your keyboard. This hides the column in the view again.

9. Select File from the menu bar and click on Save As in the drop-down list. The Save As dialog box will appear. Type a file name that you prefer in the File Name field and press Save to the file location you prefer.

You should have a file that is similar to the file on the CD called HousePainting-Practice-Chapter4-Practice2-Result.mpp. Entering deadline dates is a better way to indicate dates you must meet rather than typing a date in the Finish date for a task.

Practice 4.3

Using Task Calendars

In this practice you may continue using the file you saved, or use the file on the CD called HousePainting-Practice-Chapter4-Practice2-Result.mpp to start with.

1. Select Open from the File menu in the menu bar and select the file you want to use.

2. Currently, the House Painting project is set up to work week days only. You really want to work this project during the week so you can have fun on the weekends. However, you want to have the opportunity to do the Scrape and Sand task during the weekends since it is a grueling task. So first you have to create a task calendar called Weekend Calendar to allow for weekends during the time you will scrape and sand.

3. Select Tools, and then select Change Working Time from the drop-down list. The Change Working Calendar dialog box will display.

4. Click Create New Calendar (in Project 2002 and 2003, it's the New button), and the Create New Base Calendar dialog box will display.

5. Type the name of the calendar you are creating in the Name field. In this case, type Weekend Calendar.

6. Click on the Make a copy of radio button and select Standard from the drop-down list.

7. Click OK.

8. Scroll on the right scroll bar next to the calendar until you find May 2007.

9. If you are using Project 2007, click on the Work Weeks tab and click the Details button. Select Sunday and Saturday by holding down the control key (Ctrl) and click your mouse on each day. Click on Set day(s) to these specific

work times, and enter 9:00 AM in the From field and 5:00 PM in the To field. Click out of the fields and click OK. Click OK one more time to close the Change Working Time dialog box.

If you are using Project 2002 or 2003, click on the column header with the S representing Sunday, and the entire column should be highlighted. Press the Ctrl key on your keyboard, and click on the column header with the S representing Saturday. The entire column should be highlighted. Click on the radio button next to Nondefault working time in the upper right section of the dialog box. The times of 8 a.m. to noon and 1 p.m. to 5 p.m. will show up in the From and To fields. Press OK.

10. The Weekend Calendar has been created and you now want to attach the calendar to the Scrape and Sand task so weekends will be included. Double-click on the Scrape and Sand task. The Task Information dialog box displays.

11. Click on the Advanced tab if it is not showing. Click on the arrow in the Calendar field and choose Weekend Calendar in the drop-down list. Notice the field called Scheduling ignores resource calendars. Chapter 6 details more about resource calendars but remember that resource calendars take precedence over project or task calendars: This field allows the task calendar to take precedence on this task only.

12. Check the Scheduling ignores resource calendars field and press OK. The task calendar icon will display in the Indicator column next to the task.

13. Select File from the menu bar and click on Save As in the drop-down list. The Save As dialog box will appear. Type a file name that you prefer in the File Name field, and press Save to the file location you prefer.

You should have a file that is similar to the file on the CD called HousePainting-Practice-Chapter4-Practice3-Result.mpp. Task calendars allow you to override the working times pre-set for the project and resources. Although not used often, they can help you solve some scheduling issues for some of your task working time exceptions.

Practice 4.4

Setting a Task Type

In this practice you may continue using the file you saved or use the file on the CD called HousePainting-Practice-Chapter4-Practice3-Result.mpp to start with.

1. Select Open from the File menu in the menu bar, and select the file you want to use.

2. Although you believe you can use the default task type of Fixed Units and Effort-Driven designation for most of your tasks, you have decided that the Gather Materials task should be Fixed Duration, not Effort Driven, because

you have a set time frame in which you can gather the materials prior to starting on the house. To set this, double-click the Gather Materials task. The Task Information dialog box will appear.

3. Select the Advanced tab if it is not already showing. Select Fixed Duration from the drop-down list in the Task Type field. Also, clear the Effort Driven check box and click OK.

4. To insert the Task Type column in the Gantt Chart view, select the Duration field and right-click. Select Insert Column from the drop-down menu and in the Column Definition dialog box, click the arrow to the right of Field name and find the Type field (you can type "ty," which will take you to the field immediately). Click OK.

5. To insert the Effort-Driven column in the Gantt Chart view, select the Duration field and right-click. Select Insert Column from the drop-down menu and in the Column Definition dialog box, click the arrow to the right of Field name and find the Effort Driven field (you can type "ef," which will take you to the field immediately). Click OK.

6. Select File from the menu bar and click Save As in the drop-down list. The Save As dialog box will appear. Type a filename that you prefer in the File name field and click Save to save the file to the location you prefer.

You should have a file that is similar to the file on the CD called HousePainting-Practice-Chapter4-Practice4-Result.mpp. Task types determine how Project will calculate and schedule a task when estimates and resources are added to tasks. It helps if you identify which designation you want to use while building your task list so that you consider the nature of the work early on, rather than when you enter your estimates and resources.

Case Study: Continue Building the Schedule

On the VNLE project, as you might remember, Chris started her schedule earlier but realized she really needed to talk to her project team to understand the scope of the work. She also took a class in Microsoft Project and realized she had been building schedules in a less than efficient way. So she decided to start over on her project schedule. First, she had her meeting with her project team and they created a WBS that she could use to describe the work of her project. She will create the initial WBS in Project based on the visual WBS provided in Figure 4.60. You can practice more by making the changes described or by just reviewing the resulting files on the CD.

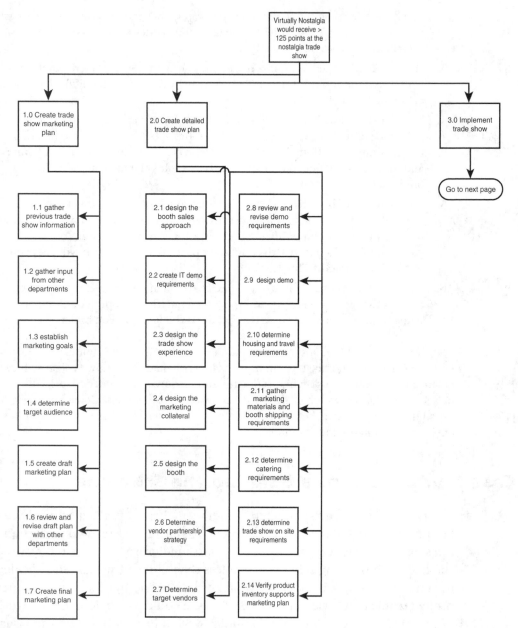

Figure 4.60 *WBS created by VNLE team.*

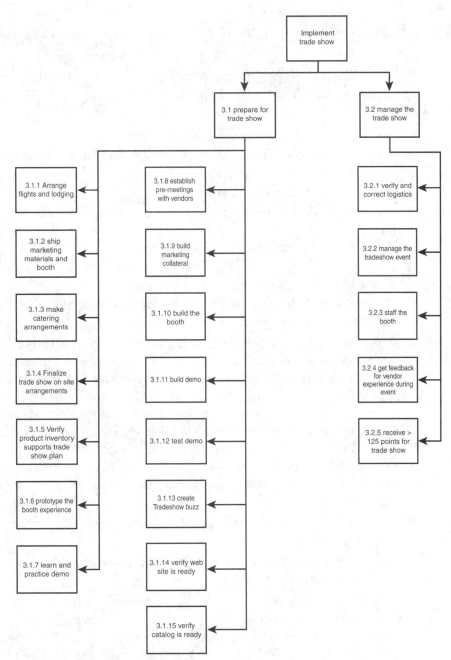

Figure 4.60   *WBS created by VNLE team.*

Read the case study in Chapter 4 of *Project Management for Mere Mortals*

The case study in Chapter 4 of *Project Management for Mere Mortals* describes in more detail how this WBS was built.

1. Start with the schedule file on the CD called VNLE-Chapter4-Start-CaseStudy.mpp. This contains all the basic information provided for the project calendar.

2. Type in the tasks according to what you see in the WBS into the schedule. Enter the Level 1 items as summary tasks and Level 2 (3.1 and 3.2) items as other summary tasks below the first level.

3. Once you have completed that, open the file called VNLE-Chapter4-FirstWBS.mpp. This file is based on the WBS. Some names might have changed slightly from the WBS, but you can use your file or this file to continue building your project.

4. One of the things Chris learned in her Microsoft Project class is that it is a good idea to include tasks for all of her activities as a project manager. This is especially important because she wants to get historical data about how much time it takes to perform project management activities. She will be able to include them in lessons learned and help her company understand the time it takes to manage projects. She decides to add one more WBS deliverable: Project management activities. See the file on the CD called VNLE-Chapter4-SecondWBS.mpp to see the activities she adds. This changes the numbering from the original WBS.

5. Now you should enter milestones. The following list describes the items you should add.

    - Enter a milestone at the end of each phase and name it to show completion of the phase.

    - Review the work and decide to enter approval points for some of the activities, such as: Receive trade show marketing plan approval, obtain booth and demo design approval, and receive completed booth and demo approval. You might think of more approvals or deliverables than these. When you are done, you can use VNLE-Chaper4-Milestones to start the next step or use your own file.

Notice that adding milestones to this schedule has changed the numbering of the WBS. If you have a specific WBS, it is better to create a custom field and enter the WBS numbers rather than using the Project WBS field, or you can type the specific WBS numbers in the WBS field. You can also define a WBS code and sequence by selecting Project from the menu bar and clicking on WBS.

6. Now you need to review the list to see if there are any specific deadlines to enter. Chris had a rough plan for completing specific tasks, and she puts deadlines on them as follows (you might want to insert the deadline column to easily enter the deadlines):

   • Marketing Plan complete on 3/30/07

   • Detailed Plan complete on 6/1/07

   • Event taking place on 9/24/07 (the task is Manage trade show events)

   • Event ends 9/28/07 (this is the Project Complete task)

   The result of this work is on your CD as VNLE-Chapter4-Deadlines.mpp.

7. Last, Chris looked through her tasks to think about what kind of task types they should be. In most cases, the tasks are effort based. The team members will be loaned to her from other departments at a certain percentage of their time as they will not be full time, but she will be managing their tasks and work effort.

   Chris realizes that the easiest way to do this is to insert the Type and Effort Driven columns and review each task to think about the tasks and how she wants them to behave. You might want to do so, too. On completion of this exercise she changes the following tasks from the default Fixed Units, Effort Driven.

   • **Perform project activities:** She will be performing these activities throughout the project. She makes this task Fixed Duration, Effort Driven.

   • **Manage trade show events:** The trade show is a week long, and the length cannot be changed. She makes this task Fixed Duration, not Effort Driven.

   • **Staff the booth:** This corresponds to the week of the trade show, and the length cannot be changed. She makes this task Fixed Duration, not Effort Driven.

If you would like to see the final result of these changes, see the file called VNLE-Chapter4-TaskType.mpp on the CD.

Chris is ready to move on to the next steps of building a schedule: creating task relationships and understanding the critical path of her project. We'll review those techniques in Chapter 5 and continue the case study there.

Adding More Task Information to the Schedule

Building your project schedule is a methodical process: first entering the scope of your project via the WBS, then reviewing it to add more task information. Once you enter your tasks (grouped in summary and sub-tasks according to the WBS categories) you will want to do the following:

- Enter milestones
- Enter deadline dates
- Change the Task type and Effort driven designations for tasks if appropriate

If you iterate through the steps of building your schedule, reviewing your methods as steps, it will help you build a better schedule.

Review Questions

1. What are at least three methods for viewing task information that is not showing in the Gantt Chart?
2. What does the Multiple Task Information dialog box do?
3. What are the main tabs on the Task Information dialog box?
4. What are custom fields?
5. Why should you use milestones?
6. What is a deadline date and how do you set it in Project?
7. What are the eight constraint types and which ones should you use when building your schedule?
8. How can task calendars supplement resource and project calendars?

9. If you obtain duration estimates for tasks from a manager, and do not know how many resources are working on the task, are you building a duration-based or effort-based schedule?

10. When you enter a duration estimate on a task, and no resources have been assigned, what is calculated for the Work field? Why?

11. What are the three task types?

12. Let's say you have a task type of Fixed Duration for a 2-week task, and your original work estimate was 40, with a resource (R1) working on the task at 50%. You change your work estimate to 60. What will change in Project?

13. What does the Effort-Driven designation do on a task?

Sequencing the Work:
Creating the Critical Path

A straight path never leads anywhere except to the objective.
—Andre Gide

Topics Covered in This Chapter

Now you know all about working with tasks, except for one of the most critical items: linking your tasks to describe relationships (dependencies) between tasks. Creating dependencies between tasks is the first step to creating the critical path, or the sequence of tasks in your project that determines when your project will end. The tasks on the critical path must be completed on time for the project to complete on time. You might have seen various project schedules: some that do not show linked tasks, some that have a few but not all tasks linked, or tasks linked sequentially, which is not how we usually work (unless we have only one project team member). In this chapter you learn about the different kinds of task relationships that initiate the building of the critical path in Project: All tasks have dependencies on other tasks, even if we'd rather not take the time to identify them. If you have any tasks in your project that are not related to another task (even if it's the last task in the project), you might question if that task is really necessary. In this chapter, I cover the different methods for linking tasks in Project by understanding task predecessors and successors. I also discuss lags and leads as useful ways to more accurately characterize the task relationships and visit the network diagram, which is one of the ways to build and view task relationships. The lessons from this chapter are added to our steps in the project schedule building methodology. Last, you practice using task relationships and use our case study to demonstrate task relationships.

> **Read Chapter 4 of *Project Management for Mere Mortals***
>
> To understand the background of creating task relationships and sequencing the work of your project, see "Sequencing the Work" in Chapter 4.

Linking Tasks

In the following section, I describe the various methods of linking tasks in Project to create task relationships. You can choose the method you like the best.

Using the Link Tasks Button

You might find an advantage to linking tasks by using the Link Tasks button in the toolbar, because you can use it to methodically work through the relationships of all the tasks in your project. You would select one task, then use the Link Tasks button to click on the next task (and subsequently on any other succeeding tasks) you think should follow in your schedule. This method makes you deliberately think about the relationships between pairs of tasks one at a time.

To order tasks in the schedule sequentially, follow these steps:

1. Highlight the first task (the predecessor), and then select the next task (the successor or successors) or all subsequent tasks, as shown in Figure 5.1.

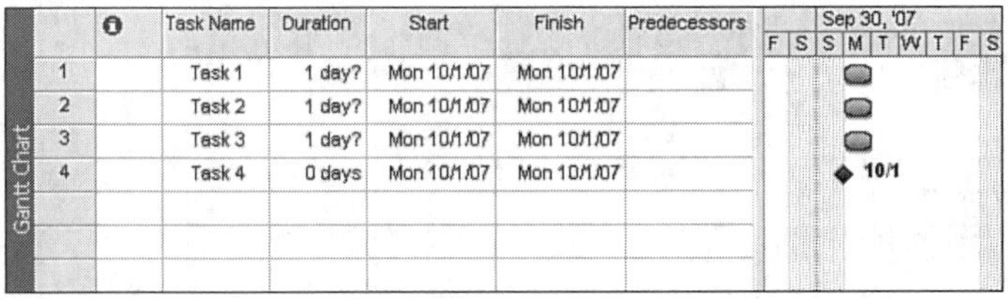

	Task Name	Duration	Start	Finish	Predecessors
1	Task 1	1 day?	Mon 10/1/07	Mon 10/1/07	
2	Task 2	1 day?	Mon 10/1/07	Mon 10/1/07	
3	Task 3	1 day?	Mon 10/1/07	Mon 10/1/07	
4	Task 4	0 days	Mon 10/1/07	Mon 10/1/07	

Figure 5.1 *Linking tasks sequentially*

2. Click on the Link Tasks button. Figure 5.2 shows the result.

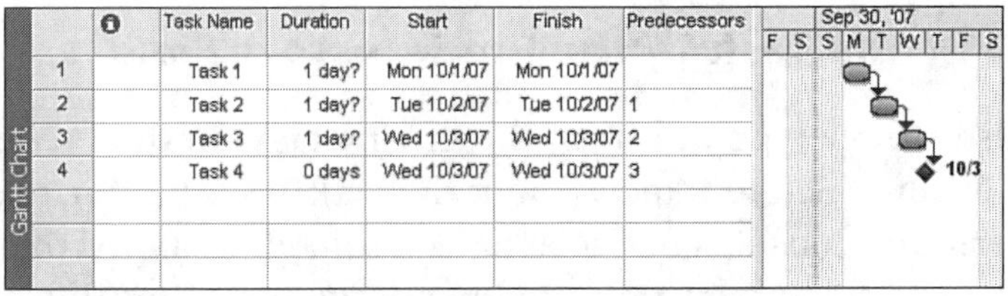

	Task Name	Duration	Start	Finish	Predecessors
1	Task 1	1 day?	Mon 10/1/07	Mon 10/1/07	
2	Task 2	1 day?	Tue 10/2/07	Tue 10/2/07	1
3	Task 3	1 day?	Wed 10/3/07	Wed 10/3/07	2
4	Task 4	0 days	Wed 10/3/07	Wed 10/3/07	3

Figure 5.2 *Linking tasks sequentially*

This method, however, doesn't work if you are trying to link several parallel tasks. For instance, let's say you want to link Task 1, Task 2, and Task 3 individually to Task 4. You would have to link Task 1 to Task 4, then Task 2 to Task 4, then Task 3 to Task 4.

To link two or more tasks that are not sequential, follow these steps:

1. Highlight the first task you want to link. Press and hold down Ctrl, and then click the other task. Figure 5.3 illustrates the result of the action.

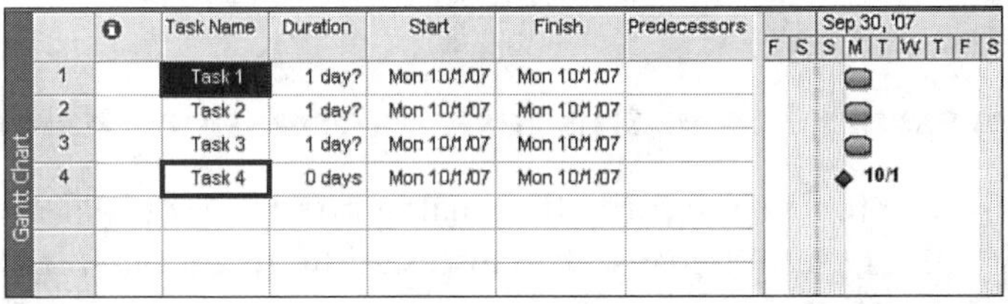

	Task Name	Duration	Start	Finish	Predecessors
1	Task 1	1 day?	Mon 10/1/07	Mon 10/1/07	
2	Task 2	1 day?	Mon 10/1/07	Mon 10/1/07	
3	Task 3	1 day?	Mon 10/1/07	Mon 10/1/07	
4	Task 4	0 days	Mon 10/1/07	Mon 10/1/07	

Figure 5.3 *Linking tasks that are not sequential*

2. Click the Link Tasks button. Figure 5.4 shows the result.

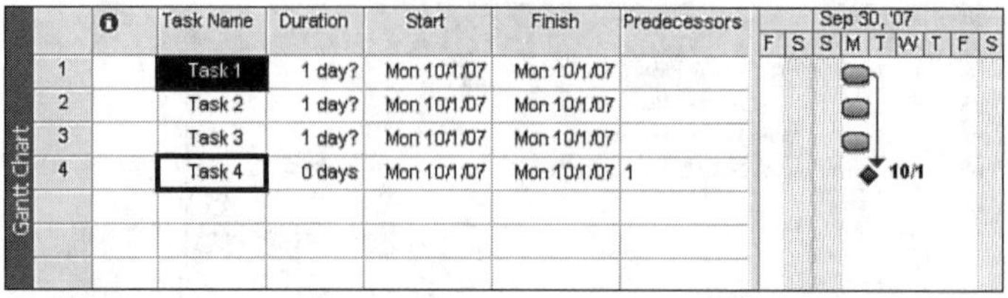

		Task Name	Duration	Start	Finish	Predecessors
1		Task 1	1 day?	Mon 10/1/07	Mon 10/1/07	
2		Task 2	1 day?	Mon 10/1/07	Mon 10/1/07	
3		Task 3	1 day?	Mon 10/1/07	Mon 10/1/07	
4		Task 4	0 days	Mon 10/1/07	Mon 10/1/07	1

Figure 5.4 *Tasks that are not sequential being linked*

You might find this method a bit laborious as you link most of the tasks one at a time, but it makes you think through each task relationship individually.

Typing in the ID of the Task in the Predecessors Field

You can also simply type the ID of the linking tasks in the Predecessor or Successor column. Before I knew about the Link Tasks button, this is how I used to create relationships between tasks. I sometimes typed the wrong ID number in the field and improperly linked two tasks, but this can be the most efficient way to create parallel task relationships. To add links via a Predecessor column, type the number of the task or tasks that come before the current task in the Predecessor column as shown in Figure 5.5. If you are entering multiple ID numbers, type a comma in between each one.

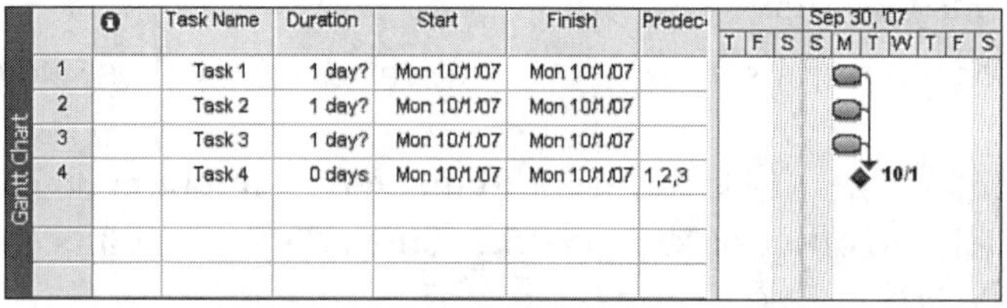

		Task Name	Duration	Start	Finish	Predec
1		Task 1	1 day?	Mon 10/1/07	Mon 10/1/07	
2		Task 2	1 day?	Mon 10/1/07	Mon 10/1/07	
3		Task 3	1 day?	Mon 10/1/07	Mon 10/1/07	
4		Task 4	0 days	Mon 10/1/07	Mon 10/1/07	1,2,3

Figure 5.5 *Typing task ID numbers in the Predecessor field*

Using the Predecessors Tab in the Task Information Dialog Box

You can also use the Task Information dialog box to link tasks, as shown in Figure 5.6. This is useful because you also see the relationship type (Finish-to-Start) and the Lag information field (see the section "Using Leads and Lags to Reflect Realistic Scheduling Situations" later in this chapter for more information about what these additional relationship attributes mean). The window is large and blocks the total view of the schedule, although you can move it around on the screen to make it easier to use.

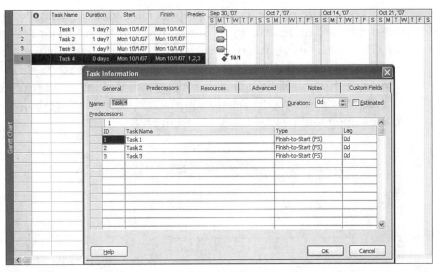

Figure 5.6   *Indicating task relationships via the Task Information dialog box, Predecessors tab*

Split Window

Another method is the split window as described in Chapter 2, "Revealing the Secrets of Microsoft Project," for creating relationship links. This is a great method to see the Gantt Chart view and still see more of the other relationship attributes such as Finish-to-Start and Lag. This way of linking tasks is shown in Figure 5.7.

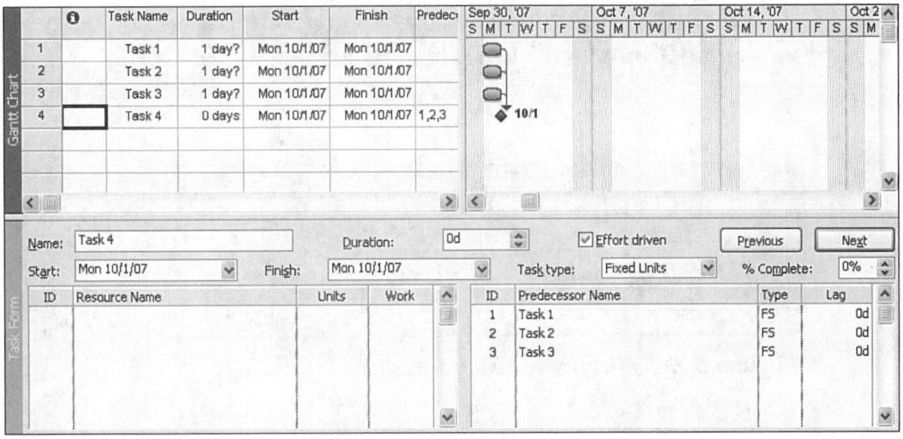

Figure 5.7   *Indicating task relationships via the Split Window feature*

Here is one more tip for those of you who are adept at using the mouse and those who are more visually oriented. You can create task relationships via the Gantt Chart itself. To do so, click on the Gantt chart bar and pull it down to the task you want to relate it with. This can be extremely effective in thinking through relationships—as instead of looking at a list of task names you are truly showing the relationship of tasks explicitly by dragging the link to the dependent task, as shown in Figure 5.8.

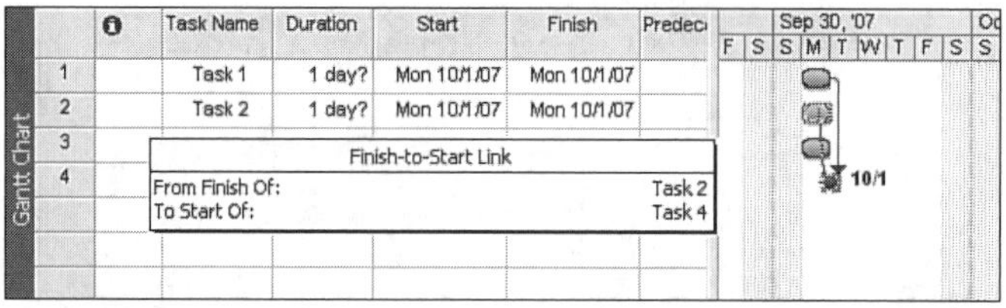

Figure 5.8 *Indicating task relationships via dragging the task link to another task*

Do not link backward unless it is intended

In the preceding example, linking was performed by linking from a task at the beginning of the task list to a task lower in the list such as Task 1 to Task 4 and so on. This indicated that Task 4 comes after Task 1. If you link backward—for instance clicking on Task 4 and using the Link Tasks button to link to Task 1—that means Task 1 should occur after Task 4. The result is shown in Figure 5.9 and it might not be what you really wanted. At times you will want this kind of relationship. Just be aware of the order in which you are linking tasks.

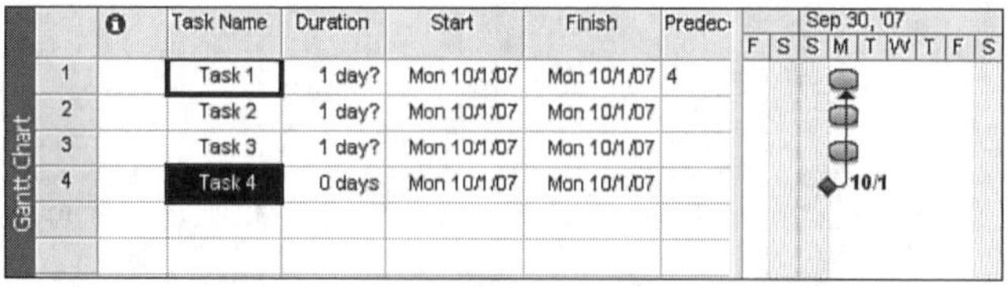

Figure 5.9 *Linking a task backward*

Project provides you many methods to indicate the relationships between tasks. Although this is a standard feature (providing many methods for doing something) of much of Microsoft's software, it is something that allows you to develop your own style.

Using Task Relationships and Linking to Sequence the Work

After you build the WBS as completely as possible and define task types and any other information for each task, create task relationships to show the dependencies between the tasks in your project. There are two elements about task dependencies: what the sequence is for tasks and what kinds of relationships they are (finish-to-start, start-to-start, finish-to-finish, or start-to-finish). Some tasks must be sequenced one after the other, e.g., you have to prep before you prime, and you have to prime before you paint, as these are sequential tasks done one after the other in a project. Some tasks can be done at the same time; that is, for a roofing project, you could obtain the permit and at the same time hire the crew to do the roofing. In another case, a task that must be done after another might be able to get started a little early. For instance, in a roofing project, you don't have to wait to finish removing the previous roof before laying the new roofing. Part of the crew could start laying the new roofing on a portion of the house that already has the old roof removed while another part of the crew removes the roofing on the other side of the house. Although you can do things that make the work occur simultaneously, everything should be linked to create these relationships. Even if a task starts at the beginning of the project and continues throughout the length of the project (e.g., project management activities), it should at least link to the last task in the project.

So, as you define relationships and analyze each task, you will define what tasks come before the task and what tasks come after the task. These are defined as follows:

- **Predecessors:** Tasks that should be worked on before a particular task.
- **Successors:** Tasks that should be worked on after a particular task.

In Project, there are many ways to see and indicate predecessor and successor tasks; two are by ID number of dependent tasks and by visually looking at and maneuvering tasks on charts. In the Gantt Chart view, you automatically see the Predecessor column, but it's important to keep in mind the Successor column. Figure 5.10 shows the House Painting project tasks linked sequentially and the Successors column inserted.

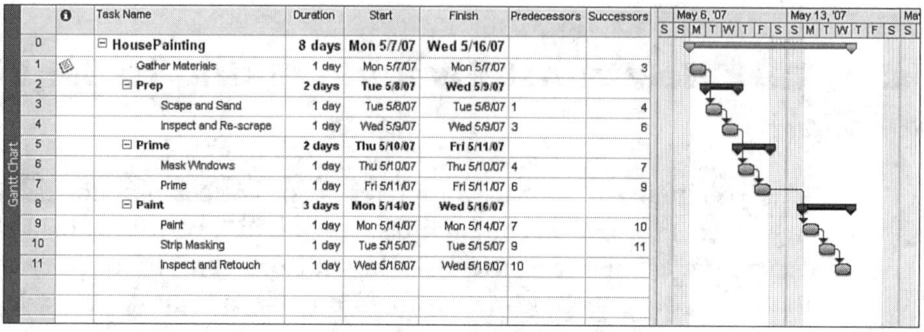

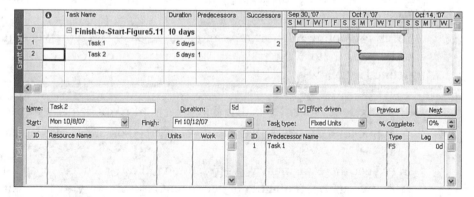

	❶	Task Name	Duration	Start	Finish	Predecessors	Successors
0		⊟ HousePainting	8 days	Mon 5/7/07	Wed 5/16/07		
1	🖉	Gather Materials	1 day	Mon 5/7/07	Mon 5/7/07		3
2		⊟ Prep	2 days	Tue 5/8/07	Wed 5/9/07		
3		Scape and Sand	1 day	Tue 5/8/07	Tue 5/8/07	1	4
4		Inspect and Re-scrape	1 day	Wed 5/9/07	Wed 5/9/07	3	6
5		⊟ Prime	2 days	Thu 5/10/07	Fri 5/11/07		
6		Mask Windows	1 day	Thu 5/10/07	Thu 5/10/07	4	7
7		Prime	1 day	Fri 5/11/07	Fri 5/11/07	6	9
8		⊟ Paint	3 days	Mon 5/14/07	Wed 5/16/07		
9		Paint	1 day	Mon 5/14/07	Mon 5/14/07	7	10
10		Strip Masking	1 day	Tue 5/15/07	Tue 5/15/07	9	11
11		Inspect and Retouch	1 day	Wed 5/16/07	Wed 5/16/07	10	

Figure 5.10 *Predecessors and Successors columns*

On the right side of the chart you can see how the tasks are linked. You can also see the relationships by using the split window.

As you define which tasks are dependent on which, you also can decide what kind of relationships they have. Project allows you to define four kinds of relationships as follows:

- **Finish-to-Start (FS):** A task must finish before another can start as shown in Figure 5.11. In other words, the successor task cannot start until the predecessor task finishes. An example in house painting is that you must prep before you can prime the house. Project always sets this as the default relationship when you link two tasks.

Figure 5.11 *Finish-to-Start relationship; FS displays in Type field*

- **Start-to-Start (SS):** Two tasks can start at the same time as shown in Figure 5.12, but the successor cannot start until the predecessor is started. An example of this is having two tasks that need to start at the same time, such as writing requirements and creating testing procedures for the new software application.

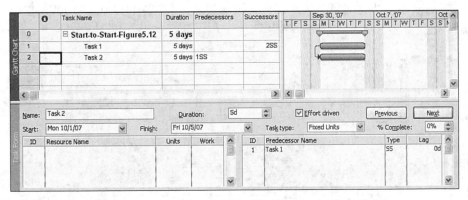

Figure 5.12 *Start-to-Start relationship; SS displays in Type field*

- **Finish-to-Finish (FF):** Two dependent tasks should finish at the same time as shown in Figure 5.13. The successor cannot finish until the predecessor has finished. An example of this is in the completion of a building—the electrical work and environmental systems should be finished at the same time.

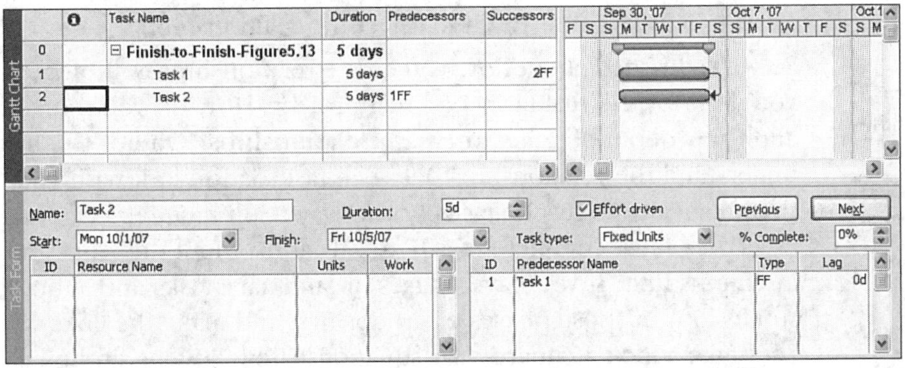

Figure 5.13 *Finish-to-Finish relationship; FF displays in Type field*

- **Start-to-Finish (SF):** The dependent task cannot finish until the previous task starts. The successor cannot finish until the predecessor starts as shown in Figure 5.14. Let's say you are producing a new car. Although you have done the marketing research, this task is dependent on some of the cars being shipped and looked at by customers to complete the marketing process. Therefore, the marketing can't be complete until the cars have started shipping and the marketing group gets some feedback. This kind of task relationship is rarely used in project schedules.

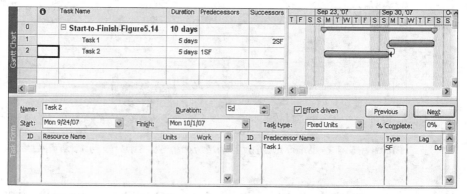

Figure 5.14   *Start-to-Finish relationship; SF displays in Type field*

Notice that by showing the split window, you can easily change the task relationship of the tasks by using the drop-down list in the Type field next to the Predecessor name field in the Task Form. When you click on that field you will see FS (Finish-to-Start), SS (Start-to-Start), FF (Finish-to-Finish), and SF (Start-to-Finish) from which to select the relationship.

So we've learned about how you create relationships in Project, but how do you do it for the real tasks of a real project? How do you think about tasks and their dependencies to create relationships? One of the best ways to understand the relationships between tasks is to work with your team and think logically about the tasks or the way team members can complete the tasks they must complete. It is better to think about the work and sequence in chunks first: If you have phases or summary tasks and subtasks or milestones look at those phases or groups first and make the links within them. Let's take a look at a particular situation. The following grouping of tasks in a project to reduce the time it takes to train customer representatives needs to be sequenced. The following tasks have been identified:

1.1   Interview CSR supervisors

1.2   Determine current customer complaints

1.3   Determine current training time

1.4   Investigate what is currently trained

1.5   Create current state document

2.1   Create approach document

2.2   Determine whether to rewrite or start over

2.3   Create learning objectives

2.4   Determine whether to use a new technology

In the project schedule with summary tasks and milestones added, the WBS would appear as shown in Figure 5.15.

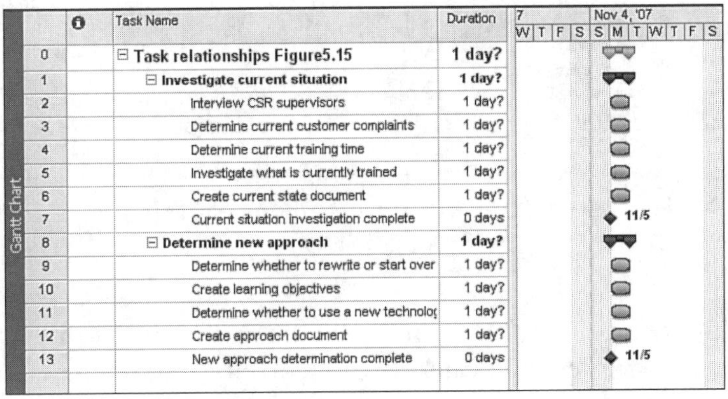

	❶	Task Name	Duration	7 WTFS	Nov 4, '07 SMTWTFS
0		⊟ **Task relationships Figure5.15**	**1 day?**		
1		⊟ **Investigate current situation**	**1 day?**		
2		Interview CSR supervisors	1 day?		
3		Determine current customer complaints	1 day?		
4		Determine current training time	1 day?		
5		Investigate what is currently trained	1 day?		
6		Create current state document	1 day?		
7		Current situation investigation complete	0 days		◆ 11/5
8		⊟ **Determine new approach**	**1 day?**		
9		Determine whether to rewrite or start over	1 day?		
10		Create learning objectives	1 day?		
11		Determine whether to use a new technolog	1 day?		
12		Create approach document	1 day?		
13		New approach determination complete	0 days		◆ 11/5

Figure 5.15   *WBS to create relationships*

When you create relationships between tasks, it is generally a good approach not to link summary tasks, although it is not strictly prohibited except in situations where logic dictates they should not be. Some people find linking summary tasks for Finish-to-Start relationships quite efficient. However, summary tasks are simply a nomenclature for grouped tasks and represent a summary of the tasks, not the real work itself. Because you might insert tasks, or lose track of individual tasks in your critical path, you might consider always linking subtasks or milestones rather than summary tasks. This book discourages linking summary tasks, so all examples exclude linking of summary tasks.

When you look at Task ID 2 through Task ID 5, you realize all of these can be started at the same time because there are no dependencies between them (leaving resource availability out of the picture). You could relate these as Start-to-Start tasks, but because it is the beginning of the project, you can have them all start at the start date of the project. To link these tasks, select Task 2 and select Task 6 (using the Ctrl key), then click the Link Tasks button. Then link the rest of the parallel tasks for a resulting schedule, as shown in Figure 5.16.

	🛈	Task Name	Duration	Predecessors	Successors	Nov 4, '07 F S S M T W T F S S
0		⊟ Task relationships Figure5.16	2 days?			
1		⊟ Investigate current situation	2 days?			
2		Interview CSR supervisors	1 day?		6	
3		Determine current customer complaints	1 day?		6	
4		Determine current training time	1 day?		6	
5		Investigate what is currently trained	1 day?		6	
6		Create current state document	1 day?	2,3,4,5	7	
7		Current situation investigation complete	0 days	6		11/6
8		⊟ Determine new approach	1 day?			
9		Determine whether to rewrite or start over	1 day?			
10		Create learning objectives	1 day?			
11		Determine whether to use a new technolog	1 day?			
12		Create approach document	1 day?			
13		New approach determination complete	0 days			11/5

Figure 5.16 *Tasks 2 through 5 are linked to Task 6 in a finish-to-start relationship*

Now, you need to link this work to the last milestone: Current situation investigation complete. Because Create current state document is the last item completed, you can link it to Create current state document, also shown in Figure 5.16.

You are now ready to create the task relationships in the next section of the project: Determine new approach. You will think about the tasks the same way, as you realize that the three tasks building up to creating an approach document can be worked on at the same time. So you create a structure similar to the previous grouping as shown in Figure 5.17.

Now that you have linked within the group of tasks themselves, you can look at the linking between groups. You really don't want to determine the new approach until you've assessed the current situation, so you can link the milestone that completes the investigation into the current situation to the first task of the new approach as shown in Figure 5.18. In this case, because these tasks do not begin at the start of the project like the previous group's

	ⓘ	Task Name	Duration	Predecessors	Successors	Nov 4, '07
						F S S M T W T F S
0		⊟ **Task relationships Figure5.17**	2 days?			
1		⊟ **Investigate current situation**	2 days?			
2		Interview CSR supervisors	1 day?		6	
3		Determine current customer complaints	1 day?		6	
4		Determine current training time	1 day?		6	
5		Investigate what is currently trained	1 day?		6	
6		Create current state document	1 day?	2,3,4,5	7	
7		Current situation investigation complete	0 days	6		11/6
8		⊟ **Determine new approach**	2 days?			
9		Determine whether to rewrite or start over	1 day?		12	
10		Create learning objectives	1 day?		12	
11		Determine whether to use a new technolog	1 day?		12	
12		Create approach document	1 day?	9,10,11	13	
13		New approach determination complete	0 days	12		11/6

Figure 5.17 *Linking of the next set of tasks*

	ⓘ	Task Name	Duration	Predecessors	Successors	Nov 4, '07	Nov 11, '07
						F S S M T W T F S	S M T W
0		⊟ **Task relationships Figure5.18**	4 days?				
1		⊟ **Investigate current situation**	2 days?				
2		Interview CSR supervisors	1 day?		6		
3		Determine current customer complaints	1 day?		6		
4		Determine current training time	1 day?		6		
5		Investigate what is currently trained	1 day?		6		
6		Create current state document	1 day?	2,3,4,5	7		
7		Current situation investigation complete	0 days	6	9,10,11	11/6	
8		⊟ **Determine new approach**	2 days?				
9		Determine whether to rewrite or start over	1 day?	7	12		
10		Create learning objectives	1 day?	7	12		
11		Determine whether to use a new technolog	1 day?	7	12		
12		Create approach document	1 day?	9,10,11	13		
13		New approach determination complete	0 days	12		11/8	

Figure 5.18 *Linking of the next set of tasks with the previous set and using the Start-to-Start relationship*

parallel tasks, you realize you need to start them at the same time somehow. You could either make all of them start-to-start relationships, then link the Current situation investigation complete milestone to the first task, or you could link the Current situation investigation complete milestone to each of the three tasks. A clean approach is to link the previous milestone to each of the three tasks, and Figure 5.18 shows the result of this linking.

Hopefully, this helps you understand the way you think about how you use linking in Project to establish the logical sequence of how work is done. Sometimes (and perhaps most often) it is not a step-by-step sequence: It is parallel tasks. However, this sequencing is actually based on thinking about the tasks themselves without reference with external factors such as resources in the first few iterations of building your schedule. It is key that you and your team adjust the task relationships based on the content of the work and how it must be performed.

A good methodology for building a schedule separates the work that needs to be done from the sequence in which it needs to be done. Forget about the resources; think about the work itself as you use Project to build your schedule. Later when you add the resources, you can adjust the schedule for who you have. For instance, you might have two parallel tasks but only one person who can work on them, and a resource can't get several full-time tasks done at the same time. In the beginning, however, this process makes you understand the relationships and constraints of the work itself.

The next section introduces the network diagram, which also allows you to sequence your tasks. Project has the capability to allow you and your team to use Project to build the relationships graphically (using the network diagram) or in a list (in the task list of the Gantt Chart view), and which method you choose to create task relationships illustrates how Microsoft has designed a method just for you. Try different ways for thinking through task relationships and use the best method for your style to create them using Project.

Network Diagrams in Project

Building relationships in the Gantt Chart view might not be the most natural or easy way for you and your team to understand and build the task dependencies of your project. As described in Chapter 3, "Building Your Schedule: Scoping Your Project," laying out the WBS using sticky notes is similar to how you could build a network diagram. You could lay out the relationships of the tasks in your WBS using sticky notes and use the network diagram in Project itself to show the relationships of your schedule's tasks. You and your team can put up the tasks on a large wall and sequence the work by drawing lines between tasks to show the relationships. With the sticky notes you can easily move tasks around as you make changes to the relationships.

> **Read Chapter 4 of *Project Management for Mere Mortals***
>
> To understand how to build a network diagram using the sticky note method, see "Sequencing the Work" in Chapter 4.

Some Project users like to use the visual aspect of the network diagram to build relationships, but there are some limitations to the view, such as limited screen size for viewing the entire network at once. However, if you can learn to work with it, you can see the tasks across pages and paste them up to see the network of task relationships. Let's see how you might build a network diagram through Project using the training project described earlier. Take a look at Figure 5.15 as a review. From the Gantt Chart, select View, then Network Diagram. Figure 5.19 shows the training project in a Network Diagram view.

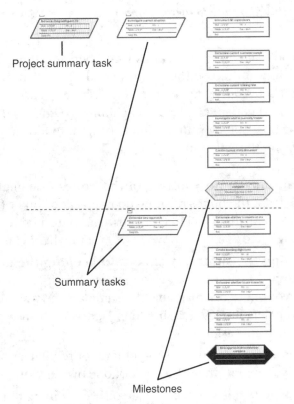

Figure 5.19 *Network diagram for customer service representative training*

With this view, you can put your cursor on a task and drag your cursor to the dependent task to link them. Figure 5.20 shows the tasks now linked in the network diagram (without the project summary task showing). You could have also clicked each task and used the Link Tasks button to create the task relationships.

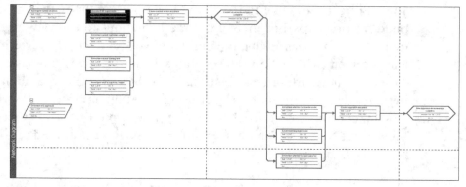

Figure 5.20   *Tasks linked on the network diagram*

If you decide you would like to try using this view, there are some things to keep in mind. You will want to use the Zoom In and Zoom Out buttons as described in Chapter 2 to help you see the view better. Right-click in the white area of the box to get special layout capabilities. Figure 5.21 shows you the Layout dialog box. Some options you might want to look at for using the network diagram are the following:

- **Turn off the automatic positioning of the boxes:** You might want to do this if you want the boxes to show up in positions other than what is shown. You might also find that you want to turn on the automatic positioning once you have moved one task to where you want it.

- **Turn off showing the summary tasks and keeping the tasks with the summary tasks:** These selections can be especially useful when building your network diagram. The summary tasks sit all by themselves in the default view (as shown in Figure 5.19) and can take up room and cause confusion.

- **Link style:** This allows you to use straight lines or rectilinear lines to show links and you might prefer the look of one over the other.

- **Showing the page breaks:** Select this if you are planning to print out the view. You will get a feel for how the network diagram will print and how much space it really takes up.

Practice using the network diagram and see if it suits your style. Due to the page layout considerations, though, many people return to using the Gantt Chart, which allows you to see the network of tasks a bit easier. You might also be tempted to build your project's WBS using the network diagram, but

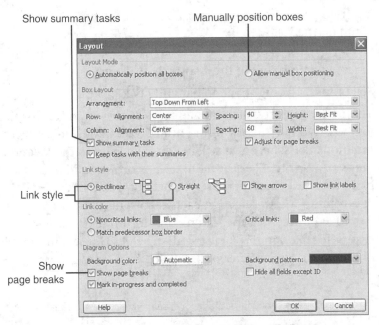

Figure 5.21 *Layout box for network diagram*

you might want to build the WBS on the Gantt Chart view, then use the network diagram to perform the task sequencing.

Task Dependencies Between Projects

You can also link tasks between projects. Let's say you are doing major home improvement projects and you decide to install a new roof as well as paint your house around the same time. Perhaps you want to wait to start painting until after the roofing is complete (although you are okay with prepping and priming while the roofing is occurring). You could link the Perform roofing task in your Roofing project with the Paint task in the House Painting project. This way, if the Perform roofing task dates change, you will see the impact of the date change on your House Painting project. There are a couple of ways to do this, but one of the best ways is creating a master project and linking the tasks from the two projects within this one master project. Creating a master project is an advanced topic, but it is worth discussing as an introduction to show how you might use it for interproject dependencies. In this example, you have created the Roofing and House Painting projects separately. Note that if you would like to practice using a master project, you have two projects on your CD as noted at the end of this section. Then, you would do the following:

1. Open a new project in the Gantt Chart view.
2. Select Insert from the menu bar and click Project.
3. The Insert Project dialog box appears as shown in Figure 5.22 (the dialog box layout is slightly different in Project 2002 and Project 2003 but functions the same). You will need to navigate to the location of the files you want to insert into the master project and they will need to be in the same directory. Use your Ctrl key and click on both projects you want to insert, selecting each according to the order in which you would like them to appear in the master project. For instance, in this case, select RoofingProject first, then select HousePainting. Click Insert in the lower right corner of the dialog box.

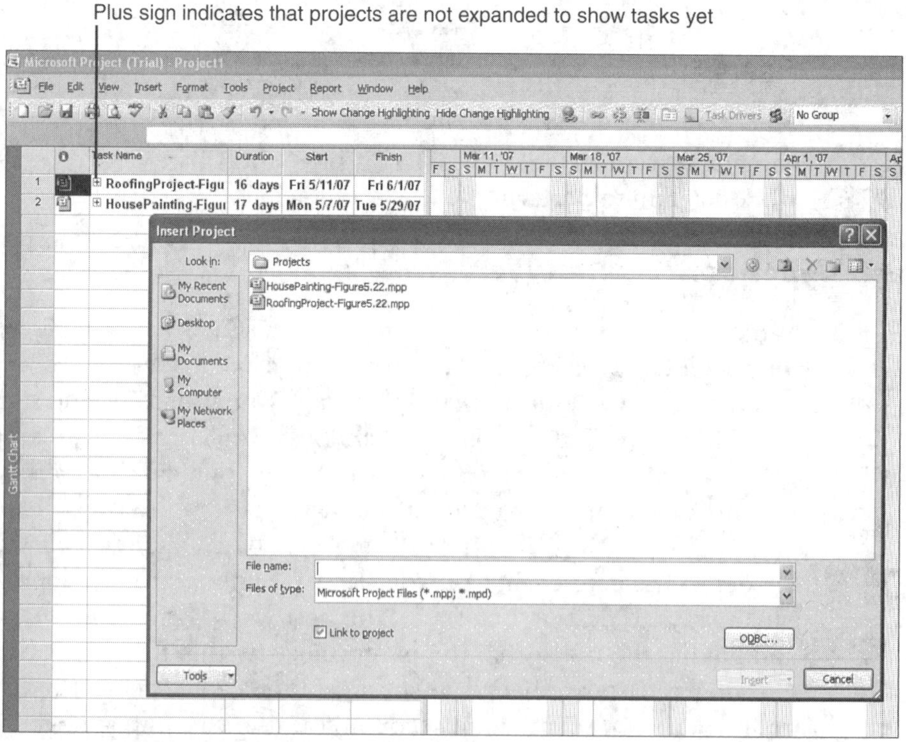

Figure 5.22 *Insert Project dialog box and master project with Roofing and House Painting projects inserted*

4. The projects will display in the master project with icons next to each and all of their tasks will be hidden. Click the expand icon next to each project (the plus sign), and you will see all the tasks in the project as shown in Figure 5.23. Note that you can press the Scroll to Tasks button and the Zoom Out button on your toolbar so you can see the entire task network for each task.

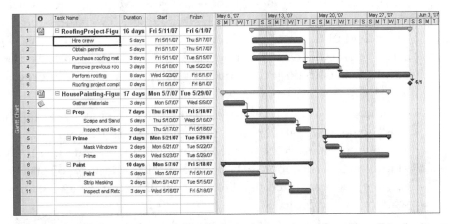

Figure 5.23   *Roofing and House Painting projects showing all tasks in a master project*

5. Next, select the Roofing project complete task, hold down the Ctrl key, and select the Paint task in the Paint project. Click the Link Tasks button and the two tasks will be linked as shown in Figure 5.24.

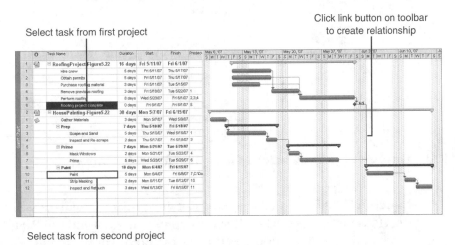

Figure 5.24   *Two tasks linked from separate projects*

In Figure 5.24, the Perform roofing task ends on 6/1, so the Paint task is delayed a few days longer than would otherwise occur based on the Prime task being completed by 5/29.

Now you either save this entire project as a master project or simply save the changes to the Roofing and House Painting projects separately. To start, select File from the menu bar and click Close. This allows you to save the master project to a named file or not. If you save the master project, name it clearly as a master file in its name and make sure it is in the same directory as the individual files. Once you decide to save or not save the master project, a series of Save dialog boxes appears so you can decide to save the changes you made to each project. If you want the links between projects to be established, you need to save the individual files.

What makes master projects a problem is that the link in the individual files now includes the full directory, filename, and task ID from the other project as shown in Figure 5.25. If you do not keep the separate project files in the same directory location, the link can be broken. Master projects and the projects they have inserted need to be carefully managed and shared by those working on the projects.

Linked task showing grayed out in project

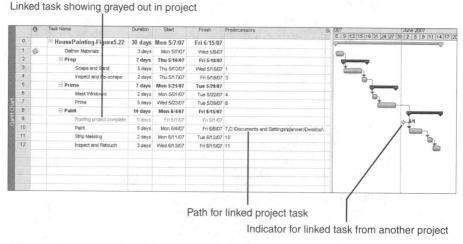

Path for linked project task

Indicator for linked task from another project

Figure 5.25   *Path for linked tasks from a different project*

Notice in Figure 5.25 that the other Roofing project's task is now showing in the House Painting project. It shows up in light gray, and the Paint task will show up in the Roofing project, again, in gray. If you would like to create a master project or link tasks within two projects, use the following files on the CD:

- RoofingProject-Figure5.22.mpp
- HousePainting-Figure5.22.mpp

> **Once established, a master project will stay updated**
>
> If you establish a master project, changes in the subprojects of the master project will be updated in the master project the next time you open a master project. Also, if a date changes in one project that has a link to a second project, the second project will be changed as well.

Using Leads and Lags to Reflect Realistic Scheduling Situations

Besides creating the relationships between tasks, you can include an additional characteristic of dependencies: whether they have a lead or lag applied. Even though one task needs to start after the previous task, it is possible that the next task can start a bit earlier than right after the finish of the task before it. In essence the next task in sequence can get a head start, which is called a *lead*. There are also times that a successor task can't start immediately after the previous task is complete. This delay in starting the next task is called a *lag*. Leads and lags are usually applied to finish-to-start relationships and are defined as follows:

- **Lead:** When a successor task can start before the finish of the predecessor task, in essence creating a head start for the successor task. Figure 5.26 shows how a lead on the Strip masking task allows you to start the task a few days before the house-painting task is complete. In such a case, your spouse could start stripping the masking off the windows of one side of the house that has been painted while you continue painting another side of the house.

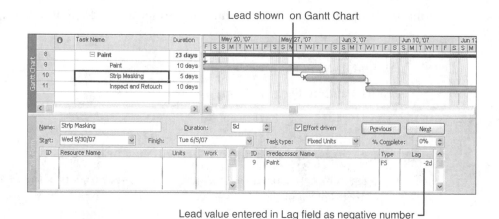

Lead shown on Gantt Chart

Lead value entered in Lag field as negative number

Figure 5.26   *Lead of Strip masking starting 2 days early*

Notice in Figure 5.26 that the lead is entered into the Split Form view (via the split window) in the Lag field. I entered –2 to indicate the amount of the lead. You can also enter a percentage in this field, such as –30%, to indicate the successor task can start at a percentage of the predecessor task's duration, as shown in Figure 5.27.

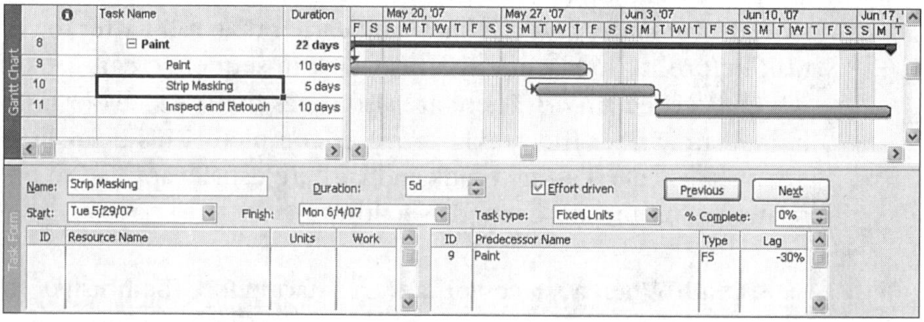

Figure 5.27   *Lead of Strip masking entered as percentage of the previous task's duration*

- **Lag:** When a successor task should be delayed after the finish of the predecessor task, creating a delay for the successor task. Figure 5.28 shows how the painting task is delayed 3 days after finishing the priming task. The lag could be due to needing some time off or maybe a delay in getting the paint color you actually wanted.

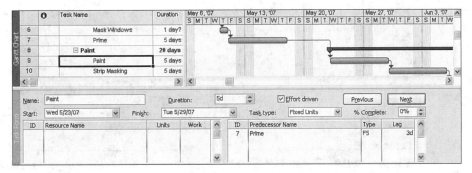

Figure 5.28 *Delay of the painting to start 3 days after the priming is done*

As before, you can also enter a percentage of the duration of the predecessor task to indicate the lag amount. You can use lags to indicate a delay between a task being complete and approval being obtained. In many organizations today, it can take weeks to obtain approval signatures and you might not be able to move on to other parts of the project before that approval is obtained, so this is useful for that situation.

Generally, you would enter leads and lags later in the schedule-building process, but you need to understand how they are part of task relationships. Once you have durations and effort on the tasks and people assigned, you need to think through whether you can use leads to shorten your schedule or lags to delay it based on the nature of the work. For instance, you wouldn't want to use a lead if the same person is on both the successor task and is working full time on the tasks.

Using the Predecessors and Successors Columns Effectively

The default Project Gantt Chart interface is often all you need when building a schedule, but just as it doesn't have the Work column showing by default, it also doesn't have the Successors column showing, which can be an important column when creating task relationships. As Predecessors shows all the tasks that need to occur prior to the task you have the cursor on in the Gantt Chart, Successors are the tasks that come after it. This can be very important in very long project schedules. Figure 5.29 demonstrates a situation that could be typical in your project schedule: As you are linking tasks, thinking about predecessors, you realize that Task 1, Task 2, and Task 4 don't need any predecessors, as they will start off the project's start date.

	❶	Task Name	Duration	Start	Finish	Predecessors	Successors	Oct 7, '07 S S M T W T F S S	Oc
0		⊟ Predecessor-Successor-Figure5.29	3 days?	Mon 10/8/07	Wed 10/10/07				
1		⊟ Summary Task	2 days?	Mon 10/8/07	Tue 10/9/07				
2		Task 1	1 day?	Mon 10/8/07	Mon 10/8/07				
3		Task 2	1 day?	Mon 10/8/07	Mon 10/8/07		4		
4		Task 3	1 day?	Tue 10/9/07	Tue 10/9/07	3	5		
5		End Milestone	0 days	Tue 10/9/07	Tue 10/9/07	4		◆ 10/9	
6		⊟ Summary Task	3 days?	Mon 10/8/07	Wed 10/10/07				
7		Task 4	1 day?	Mon 10/8/07	Mon 10/8/07		8,10		
8		Task 5	1 day?	Tue 10/9/07	Tue 10/9/07	7	9		
9		Task 6	1 day?	Wed 10/10/07	Wed 10/10/07	8			
10		End Milestone	0 days	Mon 10/8/07	Mon 10/8/07	7		◆ 10/8	

Figure 5.29 *Predecessor and Successor columns indicating relationships*

You complete all the linking using the Predecessor column. At first glance, the relationships look good, and you might think you've linked your schedule completely. However, a glance at the Gantt Chart and at the Successor column shows you there is something not quite right. Task 1 doesn't have a successor, for one. In fact, a lot of the tasks don't have successors. There are two very general guidelines about linking tasks (other than summary tasks which should not be linked):

1. Every task should have a predecessor, except for tasks that start at the beginning of your project.
2. Every task should have a successor, except for the last task.

A good rule of thumb is that when you have finished linking all your tasks, insert the Successor column in your view and see if any tasks are missing successors. Even if there is not a perfect task to link to, it could be linked to the last task of the project or the last milestone in a phase. To complete the schedule above, the Successors would be entered as shown in Figure 5.30.

	❶	Task Name	Duration	Start	Finish	Predecessors	Successors	Oct 7, '07 S S M T W T F S S	Oct 14, '07 S M T W T
0		⊟ Predecessor-Successor-Figure5.30	3 days?	Mon 10/8/07	Wed 10/10/07				
1		⊟ Summary Task	2 days?	Mon 10/8/07	Tue 10/9/07				
2		Task 1	1 day?	Mon 10/8/07	Mon 10/8/07		5		
3		Task 2	1 day?	Mon 10/8/07	Mon 10/8/07		4		
4		Task 3	1 day?	Tue 10/9/07	Tue 10/9/07	3	5		
5		End Milestone	0 days	Tue 10/9/07	Tue 10/9/07	4,2	10	◆ 10/9	
6		⊟ Summary Task	3 days?	Mon 10/8/07	Wed 10/10/07				
7		Task 4	1 day?	Mon 10/8/07	Mon 10/8/07		8,10		
8		Task 5	1 day?	Tue 10/9/07	Tue 10/9/07	7	9		
9		Task 6	1 day?	Wed 10/10/07	Wed 10/10/07	8	10		
10		End Milestone	0 days	Wed 10/10/07	Wed 10/10/07	7,5,9		◆ 10/10	

Figure 5.30 *Tasks in Successor column are added to complete the critical path*

Using Task Relationships to Develop the Critical Path

The critical path is the sequence of dependent tasks that define the longest path in your schedule. When each of your project's tasks is given an estimated duration, the sum of the durations of the tasks on the critical path dictate your project's finish date. Some tasks must be done in a certain order, and that's all there is to it, based on the intrinsic nature of the work or the people on the job. If a task in the critical path gets completed sooner or later than estimated, the project end date will shift. Let's take an example using the Roofing project shown in Figure 5.31. No durations are assigned on the tasks yet, but it does show the possible critical path.

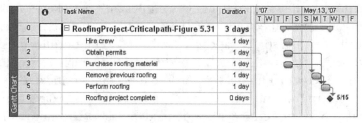

Figure 5.31 *Tasks in the critical path*

The following tasks are on the critical path:

- Hire crew
- Remove previous roofing
- Perform roofing

> **Critical path can be displayed as tasks in red on the Gantt Chart**
>
> Although this book is not printed in color, the critical path tasks on the figures are shown in red on the Gantt Chart. To see the critical path, you can use the Gantt Chart Wizard by selecting Format in the menu bar to format the Gantt Chart bars to show the critical path tasks. When you are looking at these charts, note the length of the tasks to see the critical path.

Once estimated durations are added to the schedule, it becomes even clearer that the same tasks are on the critical path, as shown in Figure 5.32.

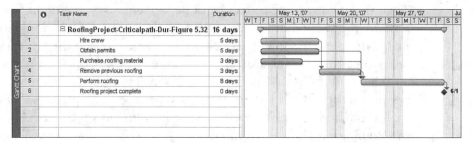

Figure 5.32   *Durations added to a project showing the critical path*

The Purchase roofing material and Obtain permits tasks have slack; that is, the materials do not need to be purchased until just before you are ready to perform the roofing, so the task has some slack. The permits must also be obtained before the roofing can be performed. The Purchase roofing material task has 5 days that it could slip before it becomes critical to its dependent task, Perform roofing. The Obtain permits task has 3 days that it could slip before it becomes critical to its dependent task, Perform roofing.

If the Obtain permits task was estimated at 9 days as shown in Figure 5.33, then it becomes one of the tasks on the critical path and the Hire crew and Remove roofing tasks are no longer critical path tasks.

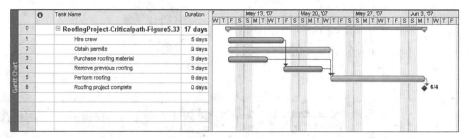

Figure 5.33   *Critical path changes when Obtain permits task increases in duration*

If the tasks in this project were done sequentially, the length of the project would have been much longer: It finishes on 6/13, and every task is on the critical path, as shown in Figure 5.34.

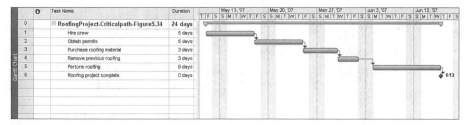

Figure 5.34 *All tasks are on the critical path*

If you built the project without linking, the critical path consists only of the longest task, as shown in Figure 5.35. This, of course, is not a very realistic schedule as it would be very difficult to get this work done all at the same time and it does not show the work effort realistically. However, this illustrates why it is important to link tasks and think about the dependencies of the work itself.

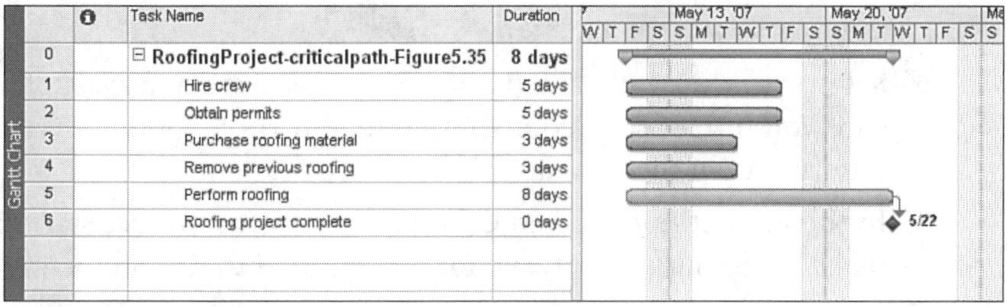

Figure 5.35 *Longest task is the critical path*

Chapter 6, "Understanding Resources and Their Effects on Tasks," and Chapter 9, "Reviewing Work Overload and the Critical Path," address the critical path again after you add work effort and duration to the schedule and you are ready to try and tighten up the schedule. The practical application of the critical path for a project manager is that it tells you what tasks you need to focus on. Once you start executing the project, and one of the tasks on the critical path takes longer than your estimate, then your project's end date will move out if you don't take action. It would be nice to only pay attention to critical path tasks, but there are times when a task not on the critical path can become a critical path task. As illustrated in Figure 5.33, when a non-critical path task takes longer than expected, such as the Obtain permits task, the task becomes a task on the critical path.

> **Read Chapter 9 of *Project Management for Mere Mortals***
>
> To understand the critical path and see how it is built "manually," review Chapter 9 in *Project Management for Mere Mortals*.

The Project Schedule Building Methodology So Far

Based on what you have learned, the following steps and sequence describe the best methods for building your schedule. The items emphasized in this chapter are indicated in italics.

The steps for building a project schedule so far are as follows:

☑ If you are using a template, select the appropriate template (you will probably want to change it based on the input of your project team). If you are building a project from scratch, build a WBS with your team, then move to the next step.

☑ Set up your project calendar if you do not have one available. Make sure you reflect your company's hours in Tools, Options, Calendar, if different than the defaults.

☑ In the Project Information dialog box, set your project start date and make sure your project calendar is assigned to the project.

☑ Start building (if your project is from scratch) or editing (if you are using a template) your task list. Make sure you indicate summary tasks and subtasks to help indicate the outline of your project schedule.

☑ Add milestone tasks to indicate significant events, deliverables, or approval points in your project.

☑ Enter deadline dates for appropriate tasks. This is a better way of indicating dates when tasks need to be completed rather than typing in a Finish date on a task.

☑ Add task calendars to tasks to indicate exceptions to the project calendar if needed. You will probably not need these kinds of calendars often.

☑ Review all tasks. Decide what kind of tasks they are for the schedule-building process. Change the Task type and Effort-driven fields if appropriate.

   ☑ *Link all tasks in the schedule, determining if they are Finish-to-Start,*
   Start-to-Start, Finish-to-Finish or Start-to-Finish relationships. Link
   among phases or task groupings first, then link between phases or
   groupings. Use the Predecessor and Successor columns to help you
   see if all tasks are linked.

As a rule of thumb, all tasks in a project schedule should show task relationships, although it is good practice to avoid linking summary tasks because they are categories of subtasks and do not represent the real work of the project.

Summary

This chapter emphasized one of the most significant steps in building a schedule: completing the sequence of activities in the project. All projects have a flow about them: You can't test until you have the product, or you can't train until you have the service developed. Project is designed to help you think about the flow of a project by indicating work activity relationships through the linking of tasks. Project provides many methods for linking tasks, and one of the easiest is to use the Link Tasks button on the Standard toolbar. You can create relationships of finish to start (the most used relationship), and start to start, finish to finish, and start to finish (the least used task relationship). You can also use leads (a head start on a task) and lags (a delay on a task) to create some flexibility in how tasks will be scheduled. Once you create your task relationships, you have the beginnings of the critical path, the longest path of tasks that indicate when your project will end.

The network diagram is a view that many people use to see task relationships. You can see it by selecting Views from the menu bar and clicking Network Diagram. It visually shows you the outline and path of your project, and also allows you to link tasks using your mouse. You can use a master project to link tasks between two projects if they have dependencies. If you create or use a master project, make sure you keep the files in the same directory so that the links are easily found and updated. With this chapter, the description of concepts and methods for building tasks comes to an end. In the next chapter, I start explaining resources, their information, and how assigning them to tasks further affects the schedule.

Practice: Linking Tasks, Using Leads and Lags, and Using the Network Diagram

This practice focuses on linking tasks and using task relationships as discussed in this chapter. Start with the file called HousePainting-Practice-Chapter5.mpp on the CD.

Practice 5.1

Creating Task Relationships

Once the WBS is built, a best practice is to first link the tasks within the phases of the project, then link between the phases of a project. To link your tasks, after selecting Open from the File menu in the menu bar and selecting HousePainting-Practice-Chapter5.mpp, do the following:

1. To make the linking easier to review, make sure the Gantt Chart is showing (select the first task and click the Scroll to Task button on the Standard toolbar). Then insert the Successors column after the Predecessors column. To do so, select Insert from the menu bar and click Column.

2. Select Successors in the Field name drop-down list and click OK.

3. The first task is Gather Materials. Because it begins at the start of the project, you will simply need to link it to the task or tasks that should come after it. In this case, you will link Gather Materials to the Scrape and Sand task in the first phase. To do so, click Gather Materials, hold down the Ctrl key and click Scrape and Sand. Release the Ctrl key and click the Link Tasks button.

4. Now take a look at the Prep phase of the project. Because all tasks in this phase are sequential, click Scrape and Sand, Inspect and Rescrape, and Prepping Complete while holding down the Shift key. When all tasks are highlighted, release the Shift key and click the Link Tasks button. What is the task relationship of these tasks? By default they are all Finish-to-Start (FS) relationships.

5. Scan the Prime phase of the project. Because all tasks in this phase are also sequential, click Mask Windows, Prime, and Priming Complete while holding down the Shift key. When all tasks are highlighted, release the Shift key and click the Link Tasks button. As before, these tasks reflect a Finish-to-Start relationship.

6. Last, take a look at the Paint phase. Let's say you believe that the two tasks Inspect and Retouch and Paint Trim must finish at the same time. First simply sequentially link all the tasks, then change the task relationship to make this easy. Hold down the Shift key and select Paint, Strip Masking, Inspect and Retouch, Paint Trim, and Painting Complete. Release the Shift key and click the Link Tasks button.

7. To change the relationship to Finish-to-Finish for the Inspect and Retouch and Paint Trim tasks, use the Split Window. Select Window from the menu bar, and click Split. The Task Form will display in the lower window. Make sure you can see the Paint Trim task by moving the lower window down if you need to.

8. Select the Paint Trim task in the upper window (the Gantt Chart view). In the lower window (the Task Form), the Inspect and Retouch predecessor task should be showing. Next to the field, you will see the Type field with FS in the field. Click in the field, select FF from the drop-down list and click OK in the Task Form window.

9. Look at the Gantt Chart: You should see the visual representation of a Finish-to-Finish relationship.

10. Now link between the phases. Select the Prepping Complete task, hold down the Ctrl key, and select Mask Windows. Release the Ctrl key, and click the Link Tasks button.

11. Select the Priming Complete task, hold down the Ctrl key and select the Paint task. Release the Ctrl key and click the Link Tasks button.

12. Inspect the Predecessor and Successor fields. The general rule is that every task should have a predecessor (except tasks that can start at the beginning of the project) and a successor (except the last task). Summary tasks should never be linked or have anything in the Predecessor or Successor columns.

If you would like to see the results of this practice, see HousePainting-Practice-Chapter5-1Result.mpp on the CD.

Practice 5.2

Creating Leads and Lags

Next, practice using leads and lags. You will use the file called HousePainting-Practice-Chapter5-Practice2.mpp on the CD for this practice.

Once you have added durations to a project, you can add leads and lags. Although you would do this later in the schedule-building process, it is useful to understand the concept now. To use leads and lags with your tasks, select File from the menu bar and click Open. Select HousePainting-Practice-Chapter5-Practice2.mpp from the CD.

1. First, you should have the split window showing in this view. If you do not, display the split window by selecting Window from the menu bar and clicking Split. Now review your tasks and the schedule and the tasks. Because you have a crew working on the painting project, many tasks can be worked in parallel. For instance, you could get a head start on the Inspect and Rescrape task. You could start it 2 days before the finish of the 7-day Scrape and Sand

task. To do this, click the Inspect and Rescrape task in the upper window. In the lower window (Task Form), in the Lag field, type -2d and press OK.

2. You also realize you could start priming the house shortly after you start masking the windows. Select the Prime task, and in the Lag field, type -3d and press OK.

3. Although you could probably find more cases to do something similar in the Paint phase, you decide to leave the tasks sequential. However, you realize that approval from your spouse usually does not occur immediately. It takes several days for your spouse to decide on the quality of anything. Therefore, before the project is complete, you decide to show a delay of a couple days. To do so, click Painting Complete, then type 2 in the Lag field and click OK.

If you would like to see the result of this practice, see HousePainting-Practice-Chapter5-Practice2-Result.mpp on your CD.

Practice 5.3

Use a Network Diagram

You can also practice building a network diagram. This is a little harder to do via step-by-step directions, because it is easy to drag a link to the wrong box or click on a box and create a new linked task. However, it's worth practicing if you are interested in using the network diagram to sequence your tasks. You will use the file HousePainting-Practice-Chapter5.mpp for this practice.

To sequence tasks using the network diagram, after selecting Open from the File menu in the menu bar and selecting HousePainting-Practice-Chapter5.mpp, follow these steps:

1. Select View on the menu bar, and select Network Diagram.

2. Notice that you cannot see all of the task. First, remove the summary tasks from this view to help. To do so, right-click in the white area of the view and click Layout. The Layout dialog box will appear.

3. In the Box Layout area of the dialog box, clear the Show summary tasks check box (the Keep tasks with their summaries check box should also be cleared) and click OK. This removes the summary task so the view will be easier to work with.

4. The view is still too big to see on the screen, so click the Zoom Out button on the Standard toolbar (the magnifying glass with a minus sign in it). You can probably only click it once so you can still read the boxes. If you click a second time, it will be hard to read the tasks in the box.

5. Now start the sequencing. Scrape and Sand will be performed after Gather Materials, so place you cursor on the Gather Materials box and hold down the left mouse button and drag it to the Scrape and Sand task. You should see a

little link icon show up, and when you release the mouse button, you should see that the two tasks are linked.

6. Click the Scrape and Sand box, hold down the left mouse button, and drag it to the Inspect and Rescrape task.

7. Now click the Inspect and Rescrape task, hold down the left mouse button, and drag it to the Prepping Complete milestone task.

8. To make this a little more interesting, let's say you've decided you have the resources to do the Mask Windows and Prime tasks at the same time after the prep task is complete. To do so, click the Prepping complete milestone, hold down the left mouse button, and drag it to the Mask windows task. Do the same with the Prime task: Click the Prepping Complete milestone, hold down the left mouse button, and drag it to the Prime task.

9. Then we have to link the Mask Windows and Prime tasks to the Priming Complete task. To do so, click Mask Windows, hold down the left mouse button, and drag it to the Priming Complete milestone task. Then click the Prime task, hold down the left mouse button, and drag it to the Priming Complete milestone task.

10. At this point, it is a bit harder to see the whole screen. To continue seeing the tasks, link all the Painting tasks together first. To do so, click the Paint task, hold down the left mouse button, and drag it to the Strip Masking task. Then, click the Strip Masking task, hold down the left mouse button, and drag it to the Inspect and Retouch task. Click the Inspect and Retouch task, hold down the left mouse button, and drag it to the Paint Trim task. Last, click the Paint Trim task, hold down the left mouse button, and drag it to the Painting Complete task.

11. Now, to link the last milestone in the Prime phase to the Painting phase, click Priming Complete, hold down the left mouse button, and drag it to the Paint task.

12. To see the whole diagram, click the Zoom Out button twice more. As you can see, it is impossible to read. Many people print out the network diagram to get the full effect. To understand how the printout will look, right-click in the white space of the diagram to open the Layout dialog box. Select the Show page breaks check box in the lower portion of the dialog box and click OK. You will see where the page breaks will appear.

To see the results of this practice, see HousePainting-Practice-Chapter5-Practic3-Result.mpp on the CD.

Case Study: Creating Task Relationships

On the VNLE project, Chris completed the WBS with her team, and entered the WBS into Project. She made sure the schedule had milestones to end each phase, added deadlines to important tasks, and changed the default task type for a few of the tasks. She then worked with her team to understand the sequencing of the work and made sure it was reflected in the project schedule. You can practice more by trying the changes described yourself, linking according to how you think the project should be sequenced, or just reviewing the resulting files on the CD.

Open the file VNLE-Chapter5-BeginCaseStudy.mpp to work on this case study.

1. To sequence the work, Chris remembered that it is easiest to do so within each group of tasks (within each summary task grouping), rather than trying to sequence all of the work at once. She also adds the Successors column to the Gantt Chart.

2. First Chris looks at the Project management activities grouping. She decides most of these activities are management activities that happen throughout the life of the project, but a few are done somewhere within the project activities. For instance, Create and document project scope must occur before most of the rest of the project can be planned and executed. Document lessons learned will be one of the last tasks to be performed. However, all of these tasks can be linked in some way. To link this section of the schedule she decides to link the following tasks:

   - Create and document project scope to Develop to the following three tasks individually: Develop and execute communication plan, Create and maintain project plan, and Project management activities complete.

   - Develop and execute communication plan to Project management activities complete.

   - Create and maintain project plan to Project management activities complete.

   - Perform project activities to Project management activities complete.

   - Document lessons learned to Project management activities complete.

3. Chris then decides to move on to the Create trade show marketing plan task. She worked with the marketing team and her team discussed this pretty thoroughly and agreed on the following:

   - Gather previous trade show information, Gather input from other departments, Establish marketing goals, and Determine target audience could all be done in parallel as input to the Create draft marketing plan task. Chris can link the first four tasks separately to the Create draft marketing plan task.

   - Create draft marketing plan and the rest of the tasks can be linked sequentially together.

4. Chris started getting the hang of this in Project: If she just linked items in each phase or group of tasks first, it was a lot easier than thinking she had to link everything all at once. Now she was ready to sequence the work for Create detailed trade show plan, a much longer grouping of tasks. The team worked on it and decided on the following sequencing:

   - Link Design booth sales approach to Design booth.

   - Link Create IT demo requirements to Review and revise demo requirements, which in turn is linked to Design demo.

   - Link Design the trade show experience to Design marketing collateral.

   - Link Design booth and Design demo to Obtain booth and demo design approval.

   - Link Design the trade show experience to Determine house and travel requirements.

   - Link Design marketing collateral and Obtain booth and demo design approval to Gather marketing materials and booth shipping requirements separately.

   - Link Design the trade show experience to Determine catering requirements.

   - Link Design the trade show experience, Determine vendor partnership strategy, Obtain booth and demo design approval, and Determine catering requirements separately to Determine trade show on-site requirements.

   - Link Verify project inventory supports marketing plan to Detailed trade show plan complete.

- Chris notices that several other tasks do not have predecessors, but she thinks that is okay for now: She thinks they will start based on the previous phase completing and will work on them after she finishes linking within the phase.

5. That was tough, but the team did a good job of thinking through the sequencing. When Chris looks at the project schedule so far, though, there are a lot of items in this grouping that aren't complete. Chris takes a closer look and thinks about the tasks again. She looks at the successors and determines that the following:

- Determine target vendors can be linked to Detailed trade show plan complete.

- Determine housing and travel requirements can be linked to Detailed trade show plan complete.

- Gather marketing materials and booth shipping requirements can be linked to Detailed trade show plan complete.

- Determine trade show on-site requirements can be linked to Detailed trade show plan complete.

6. Chris can move on to the linking of the next phase, Implement the trade show. It is broken down into two groups, Prepare for tradeshow and Manage the trade show, which the team can sequence separately. For Prepare for trade show, she decides to do the following:

- Link Arrange flights and lodging to Trade show preparation complete.

- She notices that Ship marketing materials and booth is in an awkward area on the WBS: She decides to move it after Receive completed booth and demo approval. (Select the task, select Edit from the menu bar, and click Cut Task. Then move the cursor to Create trade show buzz, select Edit from the menu bar, and click Paste.). Now the linking will look a bit better.

- Link Make catering arrangements to Trade show preparation complete.

- Link Finalize trade show on-site arrangements to Trade show preparation complete.

- Link Verify product inventory supports trade show plans to Trade show preparation complete.

- Link Verify product inventory supports trade show plans to Trade show preparation complete.

- Link Prototype booth experience to Build booth.
- Again, Chris sees another task that might link better if it were moved. She moves Learn and practice demo to after Test demo.
- Link Establish premeetings with vendors to Trade show preparation complete.
- Link Build marketing collateral to Trade show preparation complete.
- Link Build booth to Receive completed booth and demo approval.
- Sequentially link Build demo, Test demo, Receive completed booth and demo approval, and Learn and practice demo.
- Link Receive completed booth and demo approval to Ship marketing materials and booth.
- Link Ship marketing materials and booth to Trade show preparation complete.
- Link Create trade show buzz to Trade show preparation complete.
- Link Verify Web site is ready to Trade show preparation complete.
- Link Verify the catalog is ready to Trade show preparation complete.

7. At this point, Chris takes a look at the Predecessors and Successors columns to see what else she can do within the group she is looking at. It looks like Learn and practice demo needs a successor. Chris links it to Trade show preparation complete.

8. The last group now needs linking. Chris does the following for Manage the trade show:

    - Links Verify and correct logistics to Manage trade show events.
    - Links Manage trade show events to Receive best in show > 125.
    - Links Staff the booth to Receive best in show > 125.
    - Links Get feedback for vendor experience during event to Receive best in show > 125.
    - Links Receive best in show > 125 to Project complete.

If you would like to see or use the results of these changes so far, see the file called VNLE-Chapter5-CaseStudy-Middle.mpp on the CD.

9. Now Chris is ready to finalize the linking. She reviews each section separately again. Now she looks at all tasks that do not have a predecessor and determines how they should be linked. She also adds the Successors column to help review the linking. For the first section, Project management activities, she does the following:

   - Links Create and document project scope to Gather previous trade show information. This task can start when the project starts, so she leaves the Predecessors column blank. She also leaves the Predecessors column blank for the Perform project activities task because it also starts at the beginning of the project.

   - She then has to deal with Document lessons learned. She goes to the bottom of the schedule and finds Receive best in show > 125 and links that to the Document lessons learned task. Chris is done linking that section.

10. For the Create trade show marketing plan section, Chris links Gather previous trade show information, Gather input from other departments, Establish marketing goals, and Determine target audience sequentially. Then she changes these tasks to a Start-to-Start relationship because they can all start at the same time. Chris uses the split window, and makes the last three tasks in the sequence Start-to-Start relationships.

11. For the Create detailed trade show plan, Chris looks at all the tasks that do not have predecessors and links Trade show marketing plan complete to Design booth sales approach, Create IT demo requirements, Design the trade show experience, Determine vendor partnership strategy, and Verify product inventory supports marketing plan separately. This, in essence, starts all of these tasks as parallel tasks after the Trade show marketing plan is complete, which provides input into all of these tasks.

12. For the Create detailed trade show plan Chris links Trade show marketing plan complete to Design booth sales approach, Create IT demo requirements, Design the trade show experience, Determine vendor partnership strategy, and Verify product inventory supports marketing plan separately. This, in essence, starts all of these tasks as parallel tasks after the Trade show marketing plan is complete, which provides input into all of these tasks.

13. For the Prepare for trade show section of the project, Chris notes that a lot of tasks have predecessors missing. She will be looking at the Create detailed trade show plan phase tasks as possible predecessors. Chris does the following:

    - Links Determine housing and travel requirements to Arrange flights and lodging.

    - Links Determine catering requirements to Make catering arrangements.

    - Links Determine trade show on-site requirements to Finalize trade show on-site arrangements.

    - Links Detailed trade show plan complete to Verify product inventory supports trade show plans.

    - Links Design booth to Prototype booth experience.

    - Links Determine target vendors to Establish premeetings with vendors.

    - Links Design marketing collateral to Build marketing collateral.

    - Links Obtain booth and demo design approval to Build demo.

    - Links Detailed trade show plan complete to Create trade show buzz, Verify Web site is ready, and Verify the catalog is ready.

14. Finally Chris tackles the last section, Manage the trade show. She links Trade show preparation complete to Verify and correct logistics, Manage trade show events, Staff booth, and Get feedback for vendor experience during event.

15. Chris takes a look at the sequencing and thinks it looks pretty good but notices that the Project management activities complete milestone does not have a successor. She links it to the last task in the project, Project complete, because the project activities last until the end of the project.

You can review the results of this process in the file VNLE-Chapter5-EndCaseStudy.mpp on the CD. Chris is done with the sequencing. She realizes there might be a few mistakes, tasks, or relationships the team might have overlooked, but she knows that building a schedule is an iterative process and plans to review the schedule sequencing frequently as she continues working on it. Chris is ready to move on to the next steps of building a schedule: adding resources and work estimates. We review those techniques in Chapter 6 and continue the case study there.

Creating Task Relationships in the Schedule

Sequencing the tasks in your project is a methodical process in which you think through your tasks and what must happen to build a network of task relationships. It can be a hard job, but it becomes much easier if you chunk your work and establish relationships within summary task groupings first. To establish relationships you will want to do the following:

- Link tasks within summary task groupings first, including establishing any other relationships besides finish-to-start.
- Establish relationships for subtasks between summary tasks.
- Insert your Successor column and review all tasks to make sure they have both a predecessor (unless the tasks start at the beginning of the project) and a successor (unless it is the last task in the project).

You might not have all of the relationships established perfectly, but you will continue iterating through the steps of building your schedule and you might change some task relationships as you enter resources or estimates.

Review Questions

1. What are two methods for linking tasks?
2. What are predecessors and successors?
3. What are the four task relationships and which one is the least used?
4. What is the best method for linking tasks in a large schedule?
5. What are some advantages and disadvantages of using the network diagram to sequence tasks?
6. How would you use a master project to link tasks from two different projects?
7. What is a lead and when would you use it?
8. What is a lag and when would you use it?
9. Why do you want to insert the Successor column into your Gantt Chart when you are linking your tasks?
10. What is the critical path? Once you establish a critical path, can it change easily?

Understanding Resources and Their Effects on Tasks

The greatest achievement of the human spirit is to live up to one's opportunities and make the most of one's resources.
—*Marquis De Vauvenargues*

Topics Covered in This Chapter

So far in the book, I have focused on building the WBS to break down and decompose the deliverables and work of the project to manageable pieces of work, ensuring you account for the scope of the project. You also include any information about the tasks in Project, including the relationships between dependent tasks. If you use the schedule-building methodology properly, you've totally ignored both the resources and the estimates for getting the work done. This helps you focus on the work itself first, before thinking about the people or the issues of how long it really takes to get work done. However, you can't get work done without resources and you also need to estimate how long it will take to get the work done with the resources you have. The next step in completing the WBS is to create more definition of the work by assigning estimates and resources to complete the scheduling of the work. In this chapter I introduce adding resources and estimates to tasks. In Chapter 7, "Using Project to Enter Cost Estimates," I discuss the costs of resources, so I won't talk about that in this chapter.

It might seem obvious, but resources affect tasks, and the way resources are added to tasks can dramatically change the results of your schedule in Project. Users new to Project often add the resources at 100% of their capacity and they add duration to indicate how long it will take the task to complete. The new user enters percent complete to indicate task progress. In general, this is using Project to perform duration-based scheduling only and the user doesn't understand that the default settings in Project support effort-based scheduling. So, when the new users add more resources to the task, they don't understand why the task's length or work changes.

The process of using a good schedule-building methodology can help you understand and think so much more about the task, and how effort, work, or the resources on it affect the work itself. By understanding how much time a resource or resources can work on a task (few resources can actually work 100% of their time), and how much work effort it takes to complete a task, you can more closely match reality of work effort over time in the schedule. When you start being more realistic about how much a person can actually work on a task, you are starting to include resource management in the project schedule. Consider which you want to do: duration-based scheduling, which usually focuses on assigning responsibility for a task, or effort-based scheduling, which usually focuses more on assigning work based on how much a person can actually work per day. Both forms of scheduling are valid, and different projects or different situations in an organization could require use of one or the other but both require different setup, estimate gathering, resource assignments, and eventually tracking methods.

This chapter introduces you to what resources are, how to review their information, and the resource calendar and its affect on resource availability. It will also describe resource units, or how the amount of resources you add on a task will affect the task estimates. Although Chapter 4, "Understanding Task Information," discussed duration and work effort, I revisit the concepts again here to see how resources fit into the work formula equation. This is a lot of concept information before going into how you will assign resources. Then I describe the various methods for adding estimates to the tasks, and describe how leads and lags can help make the schedule more flexible. Although Chapter 5, "Sequencing the Work: Creating the Critical Path," introduced the critical path, once resources and estimates are added to the tasks, the critical path becomes much more meaningful—so I revisit it here.

> **Read Chapter 5 of *Project Management for Mere Mortals***
>
> Chapter 5 of *Project Management for Mere Mortals* provides information on resources and estimating. The chapter describes work and duration estimates, provides details on various estimating techniques, and emphasizes how estimates are a team or subject matter expert responsibility.

Reviewing Resource Information

When you create your WBS and get to the work package level you can start creating a resource plan, which indicates the kinds and numbers of resources you need. Usually you do not plan using named resources, but types of resources, such as trainer, service representative, or business analyst based on the kind of work you will be performing. When you are ready to actually enter the resource information in the schedule, you should know what kinds of resources you need.

In most cases, we think of a resource as being a person (or persons) available to be assigned to work on a task. The person might be a real person such as George, or might be a generic resource such as a business analyst. Many organizations schedule only people resources. However, resources can be anything that supports getting the work of the project completed, such as equipment or facilities (e.g., a training room), and can also be consumable (e.g., gas, pipes, or concrete). Project 2007 introduces two new kinds of resources: the cost resource, which allows you to enter costs on a task separate from other kinds of resources, and a budget resource, to indicate the overall budget on a project. The budget and cost resources are discussed briefly in this chapter, but they fit better in Chapter 7, which discusses costs and budget. In this book, I focus on people resources and briefly discuss the other kinds of resources.

Creating the Resources for a Project

Just as there are different methods for seeing task information as described in Chapter 4, there are different methods for entering and reviewing resource information. The Gantt Chart is a view for seeing task information. The main view for seeing resource information is the Resource Sheet. The Resource Sheet view lists and describes information for everyone or everything you have assigned or plan to assign in your schedule. The Resource Sheet is the pool of resources you can draw from when assigning people to tasks.

It's good practice to add resources in the Resource Sheet first to create your pool of resources, rather than typing them in as you assign them to tasks. You name your project team prior to assigning tasks. Many people enter resources by typing them in the Resource Names column in the Gantt Chart as they assign them to the task. Then later they are surprised when they go to the Resource Sheet view and see a resource listed several times with the same or similar names. If this happens, any analysis you would do for resource allocation will be skewed. To really understand resource assignments and allocation, you need to have one resource from your project's resource pool assigned to the multiple tasks he or she might need to perform in a schedule, not the same resource spelled five different ways. By adding them once to the Resource Sheet you can use a pull-down menu or dialog box to add resources to tasks to avoid having too many instances of a resource.

Set Project to warn you about adding ad hoc resources

Project contains a setting that will show a pop-up message if you try to assign a resource that is not on the project's Resource Sheet. Select Tools from the menu bar, then click Options. In the resulting Options dialog box, select the General tab. By default, the Automatically add new resources and tasks check box is selected. If you clear the check box, and you try and type a resource that is not in the project's Resource Sheet, you will get a pop-up message that says the resource you type in is not in the resource pool (added to the Resource Sheet). You can then select to add them to the Resource Sheet, or you could cancel the action and add them from the drop-down list instead. Using this setting is a great way to remind you of a good habit.

To add a resource to the project, follow these steps:

1. Select View > Resource Sheet view from the Menu bar. The view displays as shown in Figure 6.1. Some of the most common fields are called out in Figure 6.1.

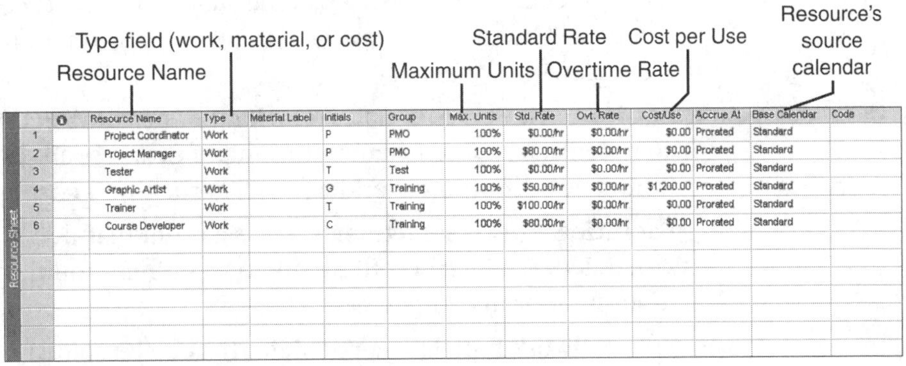

	❶	Resource Name	Type	Material Label	Initials	Group	Max. Units	Std. Rate	Ovt. Rate	Cost/Use	Accrue At	Base Calendar	Code
1		Project Coordinator	Work		P	PMO	100%	$0.00/hr	$0.00/hr	$0.00	Prorated	Standard	
2		Project Manager	Work		P	PMO	100%	$80.00/hr	$0.00/hr	$0.00	Prorated	Standard	
3		Tester	Work		T	Test	100%	$0.00/hr	$0.00/hr	$0.00	Prorated	Standard	
4		Graphic Artist	Work		G	Training	100%	$50.00/hr	$0.00/hr	$1,200.00	Prorated	Standard	
5		Trainer	Work		T	Training	100%	$100.00/hr	$0.00/hr	$0.00	Prorated	Standard	
6		Course Developer	Work		C	Training	100%	$80.00/hr	$0.00/hr	$0.00	Prorated	Standard	

Figure 6.1 *The Resource Sheet view*

2. Then type each resource into the Resource Sheet in the Resource Name field. As with naming tasks, it's important to name resources in a consistent, clear manner if you are sharing your schedule with other people in your organization. You might want to type the first name, enter a space, then enter the last name. You cannot enter last name, comma, then first name when entering names: A comma is a special delimiter not allowed in Project. If you need to enter resource names as last name, then first name, you could use a space or a period. If you are using the schedule informally, typing just first names or last names or even abbreviations is acceptable.

3. Enter other information about the resource in the Resource Sheet as needed.

The following list describes the kinds of resources you might designate in Project and why you might use them. The resource type is set by selecting a value in the drop-down list in the Type field, which you can see in the Resource Sheet view as shown in Figure 6.1, or in the General tab of the Resource Information dialog box when you double-click a resource in the Resource Sheet.

- **Work:** These are resources that perform some kind of work to complete a task. All resources, by default, are set to Work in the Type field. In general, you will use this resource designation for the following kinds of resources:

    - **People:** This can be a generic resource or a named person. If you are sharing or reporting on projects across an organization, it is good practice to establish a naming standard so that resource names will be the same and not prone to interpretations if others are reviewing your schedule.

    - **Equipment:** This is usually some kind of machine that helps complete a task. For instance, this might be a resource such as a front loader, computer, forklift, welder, truck, or a corporate jet.

    - **Facilities:** This is something such as a room that needs to be scheduled. For instance, this could be a training room, meeting room, auditorium, or garage.

    The resource work type uses a rate field that can be standard (Std. Rate field) or overtime (Ovt. Rate field). These rates will calculate costs for a task based on the number of units of the resource applied to the task × the number of hours (or days, depending on your setup for the calculations on the task). A rate can also be a cost per use (Cost/use or Per use cost field) rate that calculates a total cost when you assign a resource to a task. There is a lot more to rate information than what's described here, so read Chapter 7 for more detail. If you do not use costs, it does not really matter if you set the Type field or not when designating resources.

- **Material:** These are resources that are consumed based on a unit of measure that you can indicate in the Material label field. For instance, a material resource might be gas (measured in gallons or liters), cable (measured in feet or meters), or lumber (measured in running feet).

    The Material resource uses the Std. Rate field or Cost/use field to indicate the material resource. If you use the Std. Rate field, it will calculate the cost times the number of material resources you use.

In Project 2007, there is an additional resource type called Cost, and a new resource indicator called Budget. These are discussed in more detail in Chapter 7, which focuses on costs and budgeting.

- **Cost:** This type of resource is available in Project 2007 only. Cost resources allow you to assign costs to a task and will not affect the work or duration fields like a work resource. You can assign costs such as travel or lodging on a task.

- **Budget:** The Budget resource designation is only available in Project 2007. You can assign a Budget resource to the project summary task to indicate the overall work or cost budget of the project. You can use this to compare original work or cost budget to actual work or costs.

Generic Resources

When you initially build a project schedule, sometimes you don't know who will actually perform the work, but you know the skill set or position you need for the tasks. A generic resource is a name of the skill set or position that you can add to the schedule to help generate task information without using a person's name. For instance, you can build schedules using resources called project manager or trainer. Then, when you know who will be performing the task, you can substitute the name of the person for the generic resource. Figure 6.1 shows generic resources.

Build initial schedules with generic resources

When you use a template, you can build it assigning generic resources to tasks. Then later you can replace the generic resource with a real person who has been assigned to the task. This allows you to build a schedule knowing the kind of resources you need without knowing exactly who will perform the work.

Project Professional has a grayed out generic indicator

If you are using the Professional version of Project, rather than the Standard version, you will see an indicator on the General tab of the Resource Information dialog box with the label called Generic. The indicator is used only with the Project Server version of the product so you will not be able to indicate that a resource is generic using it. You do not have to mark the resource as generic to use a generic resource.

Methods for Seeing and Changing Resource Information

In the following section, I describe various ways you can see resource information on the Resource Sheet. The traditional way is to use the Resource Information dialog box. There are several ways to display the dialog box. While your cursor is on a resource in the Resource Sheet view, or any other kind of resource view (e.g., the Resource Graph, Resource Usage view or Task Form in the split window), you can do the following:

- Click the Resource Information button to display the dialog box.
- Double-click to display the dialog box.
- Right-click and select Resource Information in the drop-down list (this will not work in the Task Form view in a split window).
- Select Project from the menu bar and click Resource Information in the drop-down list.

Remember, you must have the cursor on the resource before performing these methods to get the Resource Information dialog box. After you use one of these methods, the Resource Information dialog box displays, as shown in Figure 6.2.

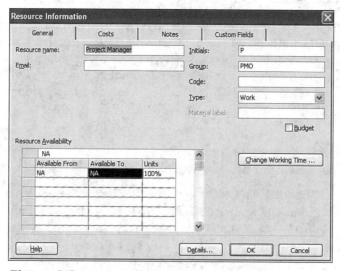

Figure 6.2   *Resource Information dialog box*

Notice the four tabs on the dialog box. Project 2002 and Project 2003 have another tab called Working Time, whereas Project 2007 has the same function accessed via a button called Change Working Time on the General tab. Each tab has a different set of data fields. If you use this dialog box to view resource information, the last tab you looked at will be displayed first. For instance, if you used the Cost tab the last time you looked at Resource Information, its data will display the next time you bring up resource information.

Another way to see resource information is to insert a column in the Resource Sheet. Chapter 2, "Revealing the Secrets of Microsoft Project," and Chapter 3, "Building Your Schedule: Scoping Your Project," describe inserting columns, but the columns you see on the Resource Information dialog box can be shown in the Resource Sheet or any other tabular resource information views (e.g., the Resource Usage view) and you might need to expose other resource fields not available in the Resource Information dialog box.

To display a field in the Resource Sheet view, you would follow these steps:

1. Select Insert from the menu bar and click Column from the drop-down menu.

2. In this example, use the Can Level field (used to indicate if a resource can be leveled during automatic leveling as described in Chapter 9, "Reviewing Work Overload and the Critical Path"). Select Can Level from the Column Definition dialog box and click OK.

3. For this particular field, you click in the field and an arrow on the side of the field displays, as shown in Figure 6.3. If you click the little arrow, it shows the values from which you can select.

	ⓘ	Resource Name	Can Level	Type	Material Label	Initials
1		Project Coordinator	Yes	Work		P
2		Project Manager	Yes	Work		P
3		Tester	Yes	Work		T
4		Graphic	No	Work		G
5		Trainer	Yes	Work		T
6		Course Developer	Yes	Work		C

Figure 6.3 *After inserting the Can level column in Resource Sheet, select value from drop-down list*

You can also view resource information via views or tables based on the kind of data you want to see. Select View from the menu bar and then select Table or More Views to see the various ways you can see resource data.

Some very useful views are the Resource Usage and Resource Graph views. One view you might select is the Resource Form, which provides resource and task information together. You can also access the Resource Form by splitting the window in the Resource Sheet. To do so, follow these steps:

1. Select a resource in the Resource Sheet.

2. Select Window from the menu bar and click Split.

3. You will see the Resource Form, as shown in Figure 6.4, in the lower portion of the screen. You can move from resource to resource to see the various tasks each resource is assigned.

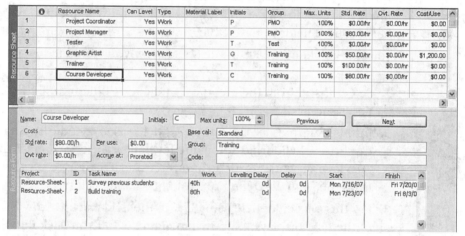

Figure 6.4   *Resource Form in Resource Sheet split window*

Don't forget some of the tables or views focus on task information, and in some cases, you might not actually have data entered yet that provides you any valuable information in the table or view you select.

Multiple Resource Information: Changing Resource Data All at Once

Just as you can select several tasks at the same time to get the Multiple Task Information dialog box, you can do the same for resources. However, there is not much data that you can actually change using this method, as a lot of information about a resource is specific to the resource. In Figure 6.5, when clicking on several resources, I have access to change fields for only the

General tab, and only fields that might have common characteristics for resources are available. To select multiple resource information, follow these steps:

1. Highlight all the resources to which you want to make common changes, and then click the Resource Information button in the toolbar (or select Project in the menu bar and select Resource Information from the drop-down list).

2. The Multiple Resource Information dialog box will display as shown in Figure 6.5.

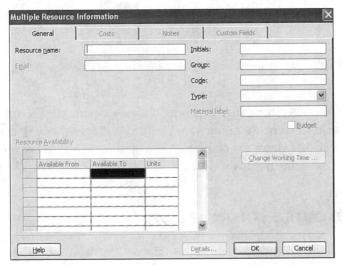

Figure 6.5 *Multiple Resource Information dialog box*

Note that most of the tabs are unavailable. Perhaps a more useful way to change fields so they are the same for several resources is to use the fill down capability to change all the values to the same value. Let's say you want to use the Group field so you can easily identify where each resource in your project works in your organization. Let's say you have several people from the training group and a couple from the project management office (PMO).

1. Select the Resource Sheet view.

2. In the Group field for the first resource you have in the Resource Sheet, type Training and move your cursor to the lower right corner

of the field. When you see a slim plus sign (not a thick one), pull it down until the value is entered for all resources as shown in Figure 6.6. This Fill Down capability can be used in most tables in Microsoft applications.

- You can perform the same function by entering Training in the first field in the column. Then highlight the rest of the rows of the column down to the last row you want to be filled with the same value. Select Edit, click Fill, and then select Down.

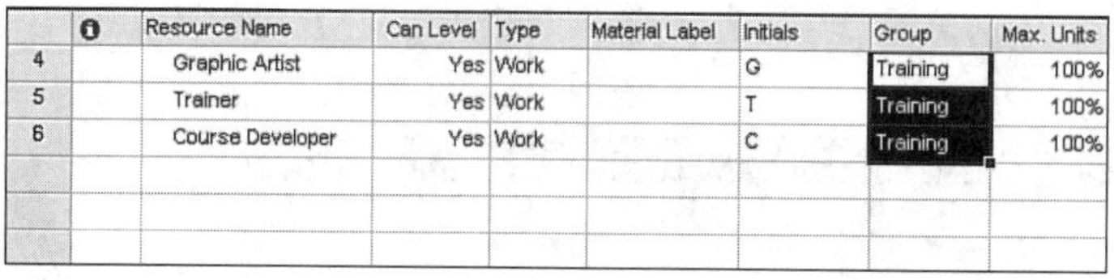

	ⓘ	Resource Name	Can Level	Type	Material Label	Initials	Group	Max. Units
4		Graphic Artist	Yes	Work		G	Training	100%
5		Trainer	Yes	Work		T	Training	100%
6		Course Developer	Yes	Work		C	Training	100%

Figure 6.6   *Entered value for all fields using the Fill Down capability*

Many organizations like using the group, code, or custom fields to help identify similar resource characteristics for resource analysis. Now that we know how to see various views for resource information, let's discuss some of the most important data about resources.

Important Resource Information

With all the fields of data available about a resource, it's useful to know what data might be the most important. In this section, I describe some of the most important information you need to know for understanding resources and their effects on tasks. The following list describes each of the Resource Information tabs or selections.

General Tab

As shown in Figure 6.2, most of the data showing on the General tab is in the Resource Sheet view. Some of the more important fields are described here. You can always click Help in the dialog box to learn more about fields not described here.

- **Resource name:** This is the name of the resource. It can be a proper name, a generic name, a first name, a last name, or any way you want to indicate the resource. When you enter a name, make sure that if other people see the schedule, they would know who you are talking about (e.g., Lee Neely, rather than just Lee, or Project Manager rather than PM). If you share schedules with other people in your organization, it's a good idea to come up with a naming standard.

- **Group:** Used to indicate the group or department to which a resource belongs. You can type in a general title for a group—such as Analyst, or for a department—such as Engineering. You will then be able to group or filter resources by this name. It will be important to enter the group name or department exactly the same each time you use this field for the best reporting results. See Chapter 8, "Polishing Your Schedule," for more information on grouping and filtering to help you analyze your data.

- **Code:** Used for any code associated with resources. For instance, you might have an account or cost center code (note that Project 2007 has added a Cost Center field) that you would enter here associated with resources. You will then be able to group or filter resources by this code. It will be important to enter the code exactly the same each time you use this field for the best reporting results. See Chapter 8 for more information on grouping and filtering to help you analyze your data.

- **Type:** Used to indicate the type of resource, which can change how the rate information will be calculated for a resource. The available resource types are as follows:
  - **Work:** Resources that perform some kind of work on a task, such as people, equipment, or facilities. See "What are Resources in Project" above for more detailed information about this resource type.
  - **Material:** Resources that are consumed and associated with a unit of measure, such as cable that is measured in feet. See "Reviewing Resource Information" earlier in this chapter for more detailed information about this resource type.
  - **Cost (available in Project 2007 only):** Resources associated with costs, such as travel.

  Project 2007 provides an additional designator, Budget, that is explained in more detail in Chapter 7.

- **Resource Availability:** As shown in Figure 6.2, there is a table in the Resource Information dialog box about resource availability. You can use this area to assign resources during the life of a project at different units. For instance, from April to June you can indicate a resource is available only 50% of the time, and then after June 1, is available 75% of the time. This would schedule the resource to work only 4 hours per day from April to June and then 6 hours per day after June 1 once the resource is assigned a specific task.

Workgroup is no longer used in Project

In Project 2002 and Project 2003 there is a Workgroup field in the General tab. This field was used to manage communication between groups prior to the Project Server product. This feature has been removed in Project 2007.

Working Time Tab or Change Working Time Button: The Resource Calendar

The Change Working Time dialog box shown in Figure 6.7 (or in Project 2002 and Project 2003, the Working Time tab) represents the resource's calendar. Resource calendars are extremely important to calculations when resources are assigned to a task. Three things affect assignment on the task: the project calendar, the resource calendar, and the number of units someone is assigned to the task. Notice that the calendar looks like the project calendar described in Chapter 3. It functions the same way, although you are affecting only resource information.

Every resource you assign in your project has a resource calendar. Resource calendars are initially based on the default Standard calendar (5 days a week, 8 hour days, no weekend work) but can be changed to indicate specific work availability for a resource. Initially, when you start your project, everyone has the same calendar. You can change every resource's calendar if you need to. For instance, some people might be working 4 days a week at 10 hours a day, and other resources might work 5 days a week at 4 hours a day. You might also want to indicate extended vacations or time off so that a person cannot be scheduled on a task during that time. The resource calendar is essentially the one true location where you can set detailed resource availability information (although there can be an exception if you choose to ignore a resource calendar if you apply a task calendar to a task as described in Chapter 4).

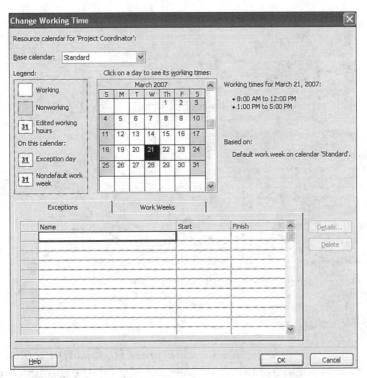

Figure 6.7 *Change Working Time dialog box in Project 2007, selected from the Change Working Time button on the General tab*

As a further example, let's say you want your family to work on the house-painting project throughout May and June. To indicate that your spouse is unavailable for the project during the week of May 20, you would indicate nonworking days on the resource calendar from May 20 through May 26. If your daughter can only work after school, you could create a calendar that shows her available to work only from 3 p.m. to 8 p.m. each weekday. This will ensure the work gets scheduled appropriately. See Chapter 3 to understand how to change the working time on a calendar.

Costs

This tab (shown in Figure 6.8) allows you to see the main rate and set a schedule of rates for the resource. This allows you to set effective dates for rates and to apply different rates for different tasks. Costs and using the fields displayed is described more in Chapter 7.

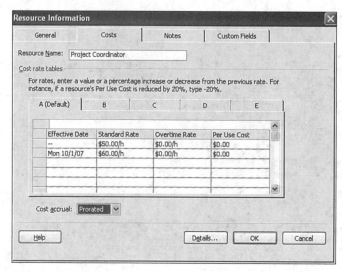

Figure 6.8 *Costs tab of the Resource Information dialog box*

Notes Tab for Resources

This tab provides a free space for entering text, object, or linked resource information. You can use this to include notes about the resource's expected days off, skill set, or other items you want to record about the resource.

Custom Fields Tab

This tab displays fields that you created for entering custom resource information.

You can also create custom fields for resources to describe resource information beyond the programmed fields in Project to describe resource characteristics. You can enter important information your organization cares about in relation to a resource. For instance, let's say for your project, you also want to note employment status (full time, part time, or contractor).

To create the example custom employment status field, you would do the following:

1. Select Tools from the menu bar.
2. Select Customize from the drop-down list. You will see the Custom Fields dialog box. In Project 2002 and Project 2003, the dialog box is called Customize Fields and also contains a Custom Outline Codes tab that allows you to create tables and field values. In Project 2007, the

outline code is now a selection in the Type field for custom fields. In this case you are creating a custom field showing a value.

3. Select Text from the drop-down list in the Type field. Text fields now display in the list on the left of the dialog box.

4. Select the Text 1 field and click the Rename button. Enter a new name in the field, such as Emp Status.

5. Project 2007 differs from Project 2002 and Project 2003 slightly for entering field values. These are the differences:

   For Project 2007, click the Lookup button as shown in Figure 6.9. The Lookup Table displays. Enter the values you would like in each row and click Close when you are done.

   For Project 2002 and Project 2003, click the Value List button and the Value List dialog box displays. You can type in the values you would like for the custom field. When you are finished, click OK.

6. Click OK. You can then insert the Emp Status column in the Resource Sheet and group or filter by the values in the field.

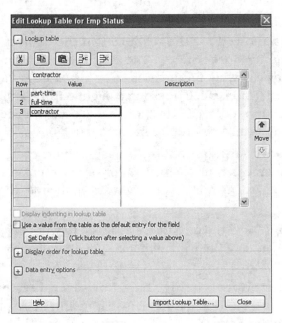

Figure 6.9   *Add values in the Lookup table list for a customized resource field*

See Chapter 4 for another description of building custom fields.

Assigning Resources to the Project and to Tasks

Perhaps the most misunderstood function in Project is assigning resources to tasks. As soon as it happens, it invokes a calculation, based on several variables. We've discussed a lot of these already: task types, calendars, and the scheduling algorithm using duration, work, and units in a preprogrammed formula. It's important to thoroughly understand how assignments are calculated on a task, what assignment units are, and how they affect your schedule.

You need to consider the following factors when assigning resources to tasks:

- **Resource calendar:** The amount of time a resource can work per day, per week, and per month.

- Resource Availability as indicated on the General tab of the Resource Information dialog box. As discussed in the previous section, the Resource Availability table allows you to indicate how much the resource is available for various times during the life of the project. By default, a resource is available 100%.

- **Maximum units allowed for the resource on the project (assigned on the Resource Sheet):** The amount of the resources' available time they can work for the project, or how much of a resource is needed. For instance, a resource might only be available to the project for 4 hours a day (50% maximum units), or you might need two business analysts on a task (200% maximum units).

- **Amount of resource assignment units assigned on each task:** Although the resource is available for 50% to your project, on a particular task, during a particular time, you might assign them to the task at 25% units.

- **Work contouring:** How the resource is assigned to work in a timephased manner, all of the work being assigned evenly over a time span (flat contour).

- **If the task's work effort is being shared by several resources (effort driven) or not:** If the resource is sharing the work, the time frame or duration the resource works on the task might be shortened or lengthened.

I provide an example of how these items affect the way a task is scheduled.

Duration-Based Scheduling Versus Effort-Based Scheduling

As described in previous chapters, you should determine what kind of scheduling you want to perform. You might be using duration-based scheduling: You are assigning a person to a task, but you really don't care about the work effort. You designate the length of the task to complete and monitor if you are completing the task effectively in the time allotted. Often, you only have one person assigned to the task and that is the person responsible for it, although others might work on the task. Your estimate is provided to you without concern about work effort and how much in a day the resource(s) will work on the task. The person providing the estimate has already—or should have—estimated how long the task is taking based on all the work the resource(s) will have on other projects, administrative work, and operational work. If you have received an estimate of 2 weeks, there can be 20 people or 2 people working on the task: All you care about is if the task is going to be completed in the time frame of the estimate provided.

In effort-based scheduling, you probably care not only about how long it will take, but also how much effort it will take to get the work done. You might have been told the work will take 40 hours, but that it will take 2 weeks. This means the resource is working on something else during the 2 weeks that also will take 40 hours of his or her time. Or you might have been told that the work will take 80 hours, but the resource can only work on it about 25% of the time. If you plug this information into Project, you will find that it will take 40 days to complete. If you have a task that takes 40 hours and you have two people work on the task, that means it can get done in 2-1/2 days, rather than 5 days if only one person were working on it. Effort-based scheduling assumes you have much more information about the task, and you care about all variables of the work formula (Work = Duration × Units).

Duration-based scheduling is less concerned with resource units

When you are scheduling based on duration estimates you receive, you usually really don't care how many people are on the task. Someone has given you an estimate based on the time frame (the Duration), and the effort it takes to finish the task should be embedded in the estimate. You don't care about the Work field in Project and how many hours it takes to get the work done. You will want to make the task type Fixed Duration and not Effort-Driven. You probably do not care about the Units assigned to the resource. If this is the case, the discussion about Units is irrelevant to you.

Resource Units

You often see the term *units* when describing resources. You will see it on the Resource Sheet attached to the resource indicating the amount of total available time the resource can work on your project. You will also see it when you assign the resource to a task: It is the amount of time the resource can work on a particular task. Units just means the amount of capacity a resource can work on a task or project. You can indicate units as either a percentage or a decimal proportion when you assign resources on a project. Most organizations leave the assignment units as percentage, basically indicating that a resource is assigned a percentage of its full capacity. For instance, if you indicate that a resource is working 100% on a task, this would mean either 10 people working 8 hours per day (or whatever their daily capacity is), or one person working 80 hours a day! If you indicate that a resource is working 50% on a task, this would mean the resource is working at 50% of an 8-hour day (if that is his or her capacity per day), or 4 hours. When using decimal to indicate assignment units, 10 would mean 10 people are needed for the task, or if you indicate .5, it would mean you would need half the capacity of the resource for the day, meaning essentially the same thing as using percentage. The terminology is all that is changing when you use percentage versus decimal proportions.

Changing the default assignment units

You can change the default for assignment units from percentage to decimals by selecting Tools, then Options. Select the Schedule tab, and select your preference—Percentage or Decimal—in the Show assignment units as field. If you click OK, you will change how the assignment units are displayed for just the current project. If you click Set as Default, and then click OK, the assignment units will be set to display what you selected for all projects.

Let's take a look at assignment units and how they affect your schedule with the combination of settings. In the following examples, I use percentage to display the assigned units and show all items that affect how a resource is assigned on a project. First, I have set up a schedule with four tasks estimated at 5 days each without resources so you can see how each resource is affected by different settings, as shown in Figure 6.10.

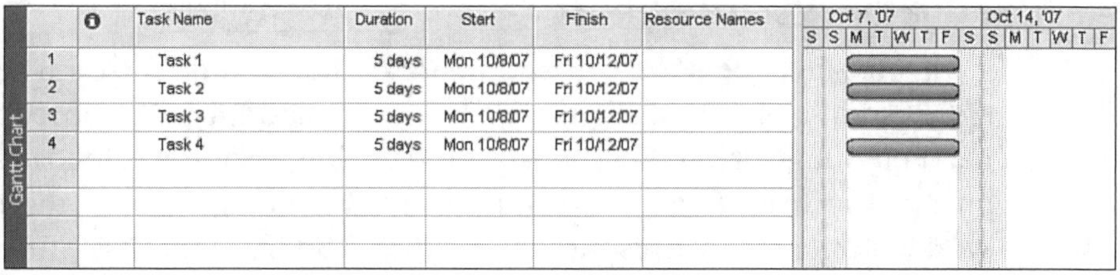

	❶	Task Name	Duration	Start	Finish	Resource Names	Oct 7, '07		Oct 14, '07	
							S S M T W T F	S	S M T W T F	
1		Task 1	5 days	Mon 10/8/07	Fri 10/12/07					
2		Task 2	5 days	Mon 10/8/07	Fri 10/12/07					
3		Task 3	5 days	Mon 10/8/07	Fri 10/12/07					
4		Task 4	5 days	Mon 10/8/07	Fri 10/12/07					

Figure 6.10   *Four tasks that are the same*

Four resources (R1–R4) are on the Resource Sheet as well. First, consider the resource calendar for each. This is what sets each resource's overall availability per day.

Resource Calendar

In this example, each resource is set up with an 8-hour day availability, except Resource 3, who works 4 hours a day (a part-time resource). The R3 calendar shown in Figure 6.11 displays both the Calendar and Details dialog boxes from Project 2007. See the section "Working Time Tab or Change Working Time Button: The Resource Calendar" earlier in the chapter for more information about setting a resource calendar.

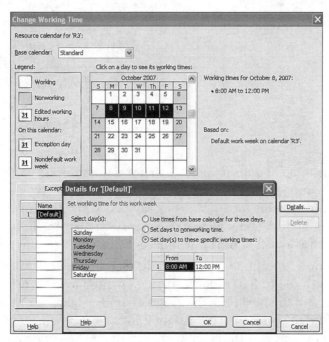

Figure 6.11   *Resource 3 works 4 hours per day (shown as 8:00 a.m. to noon)*

Maximum Units in Resource Sheet

Next, consider the Max. Units value (Maximum Units) for each resource in the Resource Sheet. In Figure 6.12, only R3 and R4 have the default 100% maximum units. Note that because the default resource calendar for R3 has changed to work for 4 hours a day as shown in Figure 6.11, the maximum working time for that resource per day is 4 hours (although you can't see it in this view).

Notice that the Base Calendar says Standard for R3. You could create a calendar specifically for resources that work the same part-time workday. If you have other resources that might have the same situation, you could create a part-time calendar. See the instructions for creating a new calendar in Chapter 3. You could name the calendar something like 4Hr Part-Time to indicate the kind of resource calendar it is. Then you would simply need to select it from the pull-down menu when you click in the Base calendar field for each resource that is working part-time.

	❶	Resource Name	Type	Group	Max. Units	Std. Rate	Ovt. Rate	Cost/Use	Accrue At	Base Calendar
1		R1	Work		50%	$0.00/hr	$0.00/hr	$0.00	Prorated	Standard
2		R2	Work		25%	$0.00/hr	$0.00/hr	$0.00	Prorated	Standard
3		R3	Work		100%	$0.00/hr	$0.00/hr	$0.00	Prorated	Standard
4		R4	Work		100%	$0.00/hr	$0.00/hr	$0.00	Prorated	Standard

Figure 6.12   *Resource Max. Units set to 50% for R1, 25% for R2, and default of 100% for R3 and R4*

Assignment Units

Besides using maximum units to indicate that you want resources assigned to tasks at a lower amount than 100% of their capacity, you can also assign someone at a specific amount on a task. Let's say you know that on a task the resources can only work about 50% of their capacity: They might be assigned other tasks on the project at the same time, or be assigned to other projects.

Add each resource to each task at 50% units. See the section "Methods for Assigning Resources to Tasks" later in this chapter for the methods for assigning tasks and the best ones for assigning units. Figure 6.13 shows you how each resource appears to be assigned in the Gantt Chart view. However, this tells you only half the story. If we review the Resource Usage view, we see in detail how each resource was assigned each day (Project uses the term *timephased* to describe this day-by-day scheduling) as shown in Figure 6.14. Each resource was assigned at 50% and 20 hours, and because R2 was set at 25% Max units in the Resource Sheet, the resource is now overallocated. If the resource were just assigned without setting the number of units on the task assignment itself, R2 would have been set at 25% with no resulting overallocation.

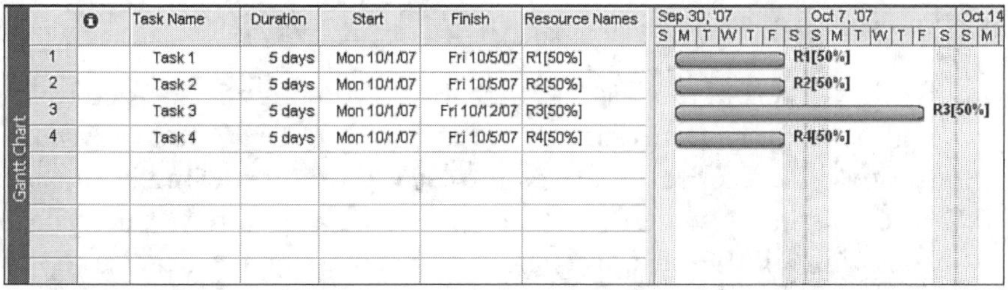

Figure 6.13 *Assignments at 50% for each task and resource*

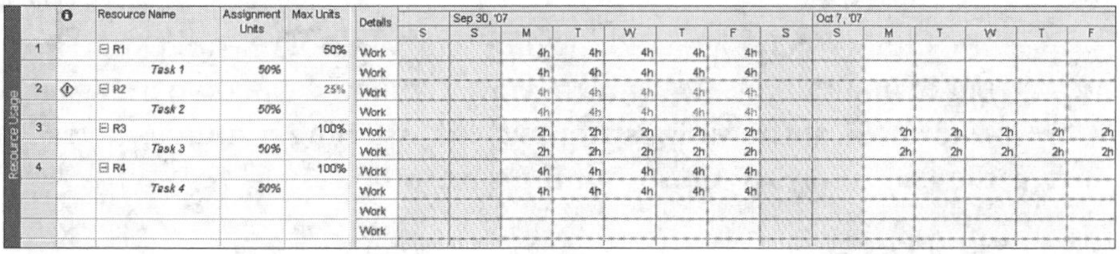

Figure 6.14 *Resource Usage view with Assignment Units and Max. Units columns added*

If you are doing effort-based scheduling, a good practice is to consider assigning resources at less than the default 100% to a task so you get a more accurate view of how much time they are spending on a task. An easy way to do this is to change the Max. Units value to how much they will probably be working on tasks on your project, such as 50% or 40%. When you assign resources to a particular task they will be assigned at that rate automatically. For instance, because R2 is set to 25% Max. Units in Figure 6.13, when you assign the resource to a task you do not need to indicate the percentage to be added; the resource will be added to the task automatically at 25%. Or you can directly add resources to tasks at a particular percentage, but this is more time consuming. See the section "Methods for Assigning Resources to Tasks" later in this chapter for specific ways to add resources to a task.

> **An alternative: Factor productivity into the estimate or change the resource calendar**
>
> Some project managers would rather just factor productivity into the estimate, rather than figuring out the units a resource can or should be assigned on a project. Others set up resource calendars allowing for 5 to 6 hours on workdays rather than the organization's standard 8-hour calendar.

Besides entering units at less than 100%, you might also need to indicate that you need more than one unit of a resource. For instance, you might need three service representatives to test the new ordering application, so you would assign Service rep at 300%. As long as you have entered 300% in the Max. Units of the Resource Sheet, you can assign the Service rep to tasks and not show overallocation if you do not assign the resources over that amount.

Methods for Assigning Resources to Tasks

Hopefully you understand the different kinds of resources and how the number of units affects how much work a resource can do per day on a task. Let's take a look at the various methods for assigning resources to tasks. These are the major ways to do so, but there are others.

Assign Resources

If you select Tools from the menu bar or click the Assign Resources button on the toolbar, you can use the Assign Resources dialog box to assign resources to tasks as shown in Figure 6.15. Please be aware that the icons in different versions of Project look slightly different, but you should still see an icon with the two heads that represent resource assignments.

The Assign Resources dialog box, shown in Figure 6.16, is an easy way to add resources. All the resources you added in the Resource Sheet view will show in the box, and you can assign several resources at different units per task, or you can add one resource to several tasks at the same time. You can also move the box around on the Gantt Chart view by clicking the header of the dialog box and dragging it where you want it to show, as shown in Figure 6.17.

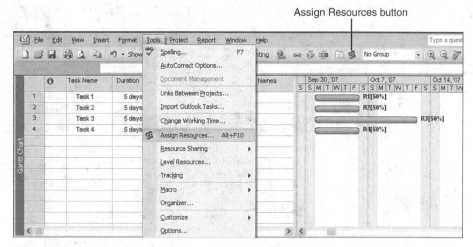

Figure 6.15 *Assign Resources selection or Assign Resources button on the toolbar*

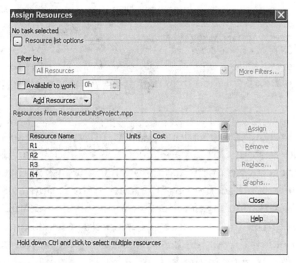

Figure 6.16 *Assign Resources dialog box showing resources previously set up in Resource Sheet view*

For instance, to assign R1 at 50% units to Task 1 through Task 4, you just need to highlight each task, enter 50% units, and either move the cursor off the resource selection or click the Assign button. Then the resource is added as shown in Figure 6.17.

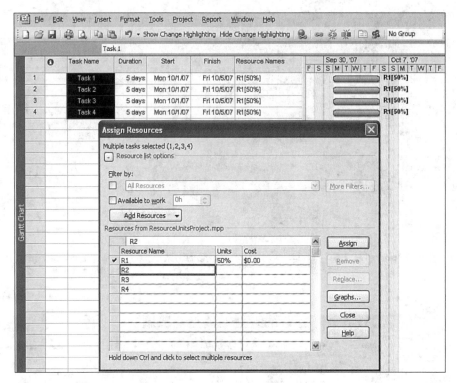

Figure 6.17 *Using the Assign Resources dialog box to assign a resource to all tasks*

You can also add all resources to various tasks at different units as shown in Figure 6.18. Hold down your Ctrl key to select Tasks 1 and 3, and then enter the various units for each resource to assign them to the task at that capacity. Remember, if a resource had been set to 50% units in the Resource Sheet, you would not have to set the units specifically on the task. The units set on a task by default are set from the Resource Sheet, unless you set something different in the Units field of the Assign Resource dialog box or you have more than 100% Max. Units assigned in the Resource Sheet. If you have more than 100% Max. Units assigned to a resource in the Resource Sheet, Project will assign 100% by default.

The Assign Resources dialog box also allows you to replace resources, so if you had entered generic resources such as project manager, you can click all the tasks the generic resource is assigned. Then you would use the Assign Resources box, click the resource, and click Replace. The Replace Resource dialog box appears with resources from which to select. Select the resource that should replace the generic on the tasks selected and click OK.

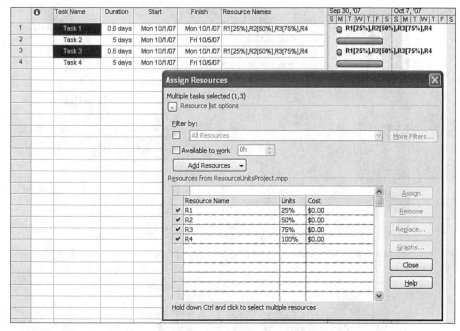

Figure 6.18 *Assigning resources at different units to tasks*

Split Window

Although the Assign Resources dialog box is easy to use, it has an important limit: If you are trying to assign specific hours to each resource on a task, you can't. The best way to do that is to use the split window. Select Window from the menu bar, and click Split to use the split window. When you are first learning Project, the split window really helps you understand how resources are assigned to tasks. In Figure 6.19 you can see how units and hours can be assigned to a task.

The problem with this resource assignment method is that you have to use it separately for each task. In most cases when you build a schedule you do not want to have to assign resources at this detailed level unless you need to create precise estimates with differences in work effort per person, you have a short schedule, or you are only scheduling in phases so that you don't have to schedule everything all at once. If you must assign each resource individually for different units and hours for large schedules, you could always add resources at their units and durations and let Project calculate the hours, then iterate through the schedule to adjust the time more precisely for each resource.

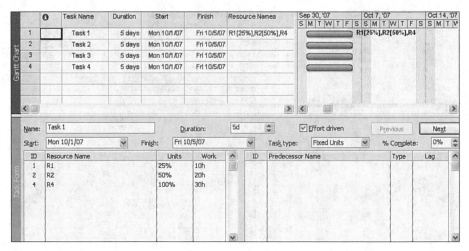

Figure 6.19   *Split window showing different units and different hours for each resource*

Consider hiring a project scheduler

If you use such a precise method for scheduling (which is truly effort-based) in your organization, you might consider hiring project schedulers. Project schedulers are dedicated to creating and updating schedules for project managers. It is close to a full-time job trying to obtain good estimates and keep the schedule up-to-date with task progress.

Task Information: Resources

Another method for assigning resources is similar to the Assign Resources function. You can select a single task and add resources or select several rows and select the Task Information button, and then click the Resources tab as shown in Figure 6.20.

Resource Name Field on the Gantt Chart

One of the most common methods of adding resources is simply adding a resource via the Resource Names column in the Gantt Chart view. You might want to avoid this method only because it is prone to error, as you usually don't want to add a resource at the default of 100% to a task. Or if you type in the name, rather than using a resource from the drop-down menu, you

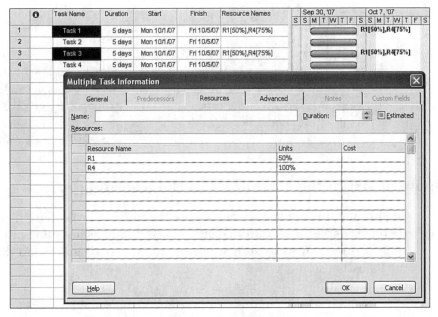

Figure 6.20 *Resources tab from the Multiple Task Information dialog box*

might have several instances of the same resource in your project schedule. If you are adding just one resource and it's okay to add the resource at 100% (or their Max. Units as you entered in the Resource Sheet), then make sure you click the drop-down box as shown in Figure 6.21. This method of adding a resource is excellent, though, if you are doing duration-based scheduling.

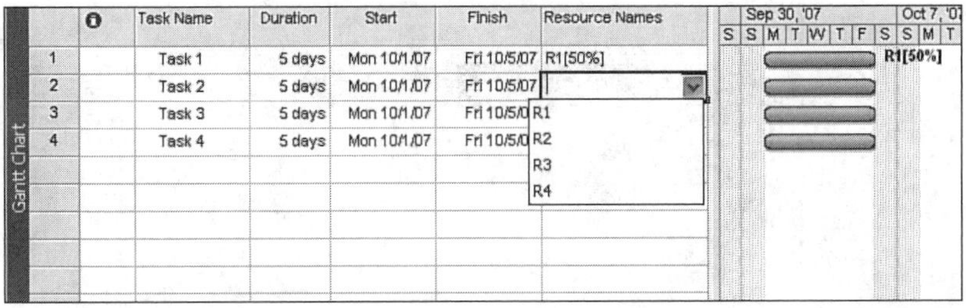

Figure 6.21 *Using the Resource Names field in the Gantt Chart for adding a resource*

You might prefer other ways of adding resources, but these are some of the most convenient methods.

Always think about units when assigning resources

As a general rule for effort-based scheduling, consider how much of the resources' time can truly be assigned to a task or tasks. Your schedule will be far more accurate if you consider whether a person is truly available to your project half the time (or any other capacity less than 100%) versus all of the time.

Example of Assigning Resources in the Roofing Project

To illustrate this process so far, let's use the Roofing project. In the last chapter the example left off after creating the WBS and establishing task relationships for the project, as shown in Figure 5.31. To assign resources perform the following steps:

- Assign resources in the Resource Sheet and set Max. Units for each resource.

  First add four resources to the Resource Sheet: Chief, Wilson, Jose, and Lila, as shown in Figure 6.22. Wilson, Jose, and Lila are the roofing crew. The schedule is based on all the work being performed by the roofing company rather than this being a home project. In this case, all resources are added at 100% Max. Units except for the Chief, who has three other roofing projects to manage at the same time. He is allocated at 25%. This means that whenever he is added to a task without changing his units, he will be added at 25%.

	❶	Resource Name	Type	Material Label	Initials	Group	Max. Units	Std. Rate	Ovt. Rate	Cost/Use	Accrue At	Base Calendar
1		Chief	Work		C		25%	$0.00/hr	$0.00/hr	$0.00	Prorated	Standard
2		Wilson	Work		W		100%	$0.00/hr	$0.00/hr	$0.00	Prorated	Standard
3		Jose	Work		J		100%	$0.00/hr	$0.00/hr	$0.00	Prorated	Standard
4		Lila	Work		L		100%	$0.00/hr	$0.00/hr	$0.00	Prorated	Standard

Figure 6.22   *Add resources in Resource Sheet view first*

- Assign resources to each task.

  Then add the resources to each task of the Roofing project. Not everyone will be available 100% of the time for the tasks, so you could assign them to the tasks appropriately as shown in Figure 6.23. To assign the Chief on the Hire crew and Obtain permits tasks, use the drop-down list in the Resource names field on the Gantt Chart to assign him his default Max. Units. For the other tasks, use the Assign Resources dialog box.

	❶	Task Name	Duration	Start	Finish	Pred	Resource Names	May 13, '07	May 20, '0
0		⊟ RoofingProject-ch6-Fig6.23	3 days	Fri 5/11/07	Tue 5/15/07				
1		Hire crew	1 day	Fri 5/11/07	Fri 5/11/07		Chief[25%]	Chief[25%]	
2		Obtain permits	1 day	Fri 5/11/07	Fri 5/11/07		Chief[25%]	Chief[25%]	
3		Purchase roofing material	0.33 days	Fri 5/11/07	Fri 5/11/07		Chief[25%],Lila[50%]	Chief[25%],Lila[50%]	
4		Remove previous roofing	1 day	Mon 5/14/07	Mon 5/14/07	1	Wilson,Jose[50%],Lila	Wilson,Jose[50%],Lila	
5		Perform roofing	1 day	Tue 5/15/07	Tue 5/15/07	2,3,4	Wilson,Jose	Wilson,Jose	
6		Roofing project complete	0 days	Tue 5/15/07	Tue 5/15/07	5		5/15	

Figure 6.23 *Resources assigned to actual tasks*

Notice that on the task of purchasing the roofing material, the Chief will supervise and Lila will do most of the work, and on the removal of the previous roofing, Jose is available for only half the time.

Following the recommended methodology, a team of people who can work on the schedule have been added and the people have now been assigned to tasks at an appropriate percentage of their time. You don't see estimates yet: The schedule just indicates a person's capacity on the particular task. Once more, you do not have to do this—especially when you are doing duration-based estimates—but it is a good way to start thinking about how much people are truly available to perform the work on your project. Next, we consider how you add estimates to tasks.

Entering Estimates in Your Schedule

Although the previous example illustrated adding the resource to a schedule first, you can get estimates and obtain resource assignments at the same time. You might also get estimates first, then find out who will be doing the work later. You should get an estimate from a subject matter expert or the resource's manager, and you need to get permission to use a resource. Often you get an estimate from others in your organization based on their expertise, historical data, or best guess, and the generic skill set or knowing what kind of position or positions are needed to perform the work. It is often later that you find out exactly who will work on the task unless you are in a smaller organization.

Of course, every organization is different. In the construction industry, you might see very accurate estimates published in industry papers based on similar work being completed on many projects. The general contractor might be hiring subcontractors, so the subcontractor will not need to assign specific resources to the tasks: The subcontractor simply has to get the work done according to the estimated duration on the schedule according to the subcontractor bid.

After you build a schedule using the generic resources and estimates you received from somewhere else or someone else, revisit every estimate when you are ready to add real resources to the tasks. When you build the schedule with generics, you might assume they are available to you full time, whereas a real person might only be available to you half time.

As long as you understand how Project reacts to your putting resources on tasks when you have entered estimates (using Task types, the effort-driven designator, and understanding the formula, Work = Duration × Units), it doesn't matter if you put resources on first, estimates on first, or both together for each task. Consider trying to hold off on entering the estimates or work effort to the schedule until you add the resources to the tasks though, because it forces a rigor of thought process concerning each task as to who will do the work prior to you entering how long it will take to do the work. If you are doing duration-based estimates only, it really doesn't matter if you enter the resources first, the estimates first, or both together: The preceding work formula does not come into play.

See Chapter 5 of *Project Management for Mere Mortals* to understand estimating techniques

Although many people no longer use a manual method of creating the WBS and estimating tasks described, there is an art to estimating as described in *Project Management for Mere Mortals*. Estimating is one of the most difficult and, usually, the most inaccurate processes in many organizations. Your organization should spend time discussing how estimates are gathered and provided to the project scheduler or project manager.

Much of the following section is based on your understanding of the Work formula:

$$Work = Duration \times Units$$

To help you understand the following section about entering estimates, it might be useful to review the section "What Are Task Types and Why Should I Care?" in Chapter 4 to review the formula and how it affects scheduling. Remember that when one variable in the formula changes, it usually changes another variable. Resources and their capacity for work on the task are the Units portion of the formula, and the Duration and Work fields in the Gantt Chart are the other variables in the formula.

Entering Duration-Based Estimates

Entering only duration estimates on a schedule is one of the most common methods for entering estimates if you are new to Project or project scheduling. It might also be the method of choice in mature scheduling organizations as well; it just depends on what the project is and the expertise of the people who are providing information for the schedule. However, duration-only estimates can be one of the least accurate methods. In many organizations, the estimates provided for duration-based scheduling have work effort embedded into the estimate without it being obvious. You might have a duration of 5 days for pouring concrete for a task, but you do not gather work or resource units information (i.e., you don't gather how many resources and their assigned capacity for each task), because a subcontractor has provided a duration estimate, and your organization simply needs to plan for that time frame. When executing the work, status is if the task is completing on time or not. The schedule itself does not need to hold the information about work effort or number of people it will take to do the job, as that is up to the sub-contractor to manage.

If you use duration only as an estimating method, you will never really know the original effort estimate for the work and cannot use it historically or compare actual work to the estimate later. Even though a manager or subject matter expert tells you it takes 6 weeks to design a widget, how will you really know what that estimate consists of? Will there by 5 people working 30 hours each week or 2 people working 20 hours each week during that time frame? If your organization is not trying to capture the actual effort it takes to do the work and you just want to know how long it will take, then it really doesn't matter what the work effort is. It is also difficult to understand how to shorten a schedule if you only have duration-based estimating.

You might have some tasks on your schedule that are duration-based, whereas other tasks might be effort-based. For instance, you might have a task called Testing the widget. You might receive an estimate from the testing group manager that it will take 3 weeks. You do not know who will do the work, but you expect certain deliverables, and you put the testing manager down as the resource. However, the testing manager delegates the work. You don't care how much time it takes; you just want to see the deliverables and the work completed on time. The duration-based scheduling works for this task. However, in the same project, you might also have a task called Design solution. You might have been given direct authority over an architect, two engineers, and a specifications writer to help you fulfill this work. You might decide to get a proper estimate that you need to perform effort-based scheduling on this task where you ascertain and estimate how much capacity they have for your task based on other obligations and how many hours the work takes for each resource. Then you can use Project to estimate how long the task will really take. This process would be a form of effort-based scheduling, which is described later.

In essence, which kind of estimate you receive from your team or others in your organization might be associated with your authority as a project manager. If you do not have authority over who is assigned to work and how many resources are assigned, then the estimates you receive are probably duration based.

In duration-based scheduling, use the Fixed Duration task type and the Non-Effort-Driven designation for the tasks. You will want to change the defaults in Project, and you might want to set this for all your projects.

So let's take a look at a few nuances of entering durations only. The examples include the Work column only to illustrate that it is still being affected in the data structure, but it probably isn't accurate, whether you want it to be or not.

Duration estimates should have work effort embedded in them

If you are using duration-based scheduling, where you are not concerned with the detailed effort estimates of the resources, then the work estimate is generally embedded in the knowledge and experience of whoever is providing the estimate and that is often not the project manager. Some organizations use this estimation process thinking that they are getting accurate work effort information. However, they purchase Project because they really want to know more about how resources are spending their time and if they are over- or underutilized. If that is so, the organization should consider effort-based scheduling.

Let's consider the Roofing project using duration estimates only. In the first example, as shown in Figure 6.24, all resources are added to the Resource Sheet at 100% capacity. Table 6.1 shows the estimates for the tasks.

Table 6.1 *Duration Estimates*

Task	Duration Estimate
Hire crew	5 days
Obtain permits	5 days
Purchase roofing material	3 days
Remove previous roofing	3 days
Perform roofing	8 days

You would first want to change the task type to Fixed Duration, Non-Effort-Driven. Once you enter the durations, the amount of work hours scheduled is based on full utilization of each resource each day. The chief might still have three other roofing projects to manage, Lila is only helping part time on the purchasing of the roofing materials, and Jose still can only work part time on removing the roofing material, but it doesn't matter. You are just trying to show how long it will take to get the work done.

Figure 6.24 *Resources assigned via duration-based scheduling without capacity (units) estimates*

The reason users sometimes get frustrated with Project is because they are trying to perform duration-based scheduling and they use the default task type of Fixed Units, Effort-Driven. Under these circumstances, when you first add the resources and the estimates at the same time, the estimates might be entered exactly as they were entered for Fixed Duration, Non-Effort-Driven, so on the surface everything looks fine.

However, if you start adjusting the schedule or forget to put a resource on the schedule and put it on later, the duration will change and you will be confused as to why. The default task type uses whatever is entered in Units or Work to calculate and adjust the schedule when you make a change. So if you forgot to put Jose on the Remove previous roofing task, realize your mistake and add Jose to the schedule. The result is shown in Figure 6.25. The duration is now shown at 2 days, because Project is performing Effort-Based scheduling as defined by the task type, Fixed Units, Effort-Based.

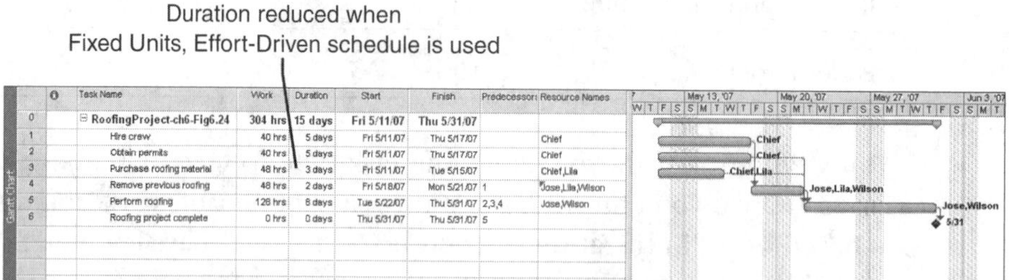

Duration reduced when
Fixed Units, Effort-Driven schedule is used

Figure 6.25 *Duration-based scheduling with the default task type and a resource added after initial schedule creation*

> ### Change the default task type if you are doing duration-based scheduling
>
> Although you can often get away with creating the schedule when you want to use duration estimates with the default task type, it is probably best to change the task type to Fixed Duration, Non-Effort-Driven. This way, if you add resources to a task or change resource units on a task, the duration estimate will stay the same as you originally estimated and intend. You might also decide to use the task type of Fixed Units, Non-Effort-Driven.

Tracking with Duration-Based Estimates

If you are using duration-based estimates and scheduling, you will want to use % Complete or Actual Start/Actual Finish dates to track the execution of your work. You could also enter Actual Duration to track your schedule status. You will be tracking either how far along you are or if you are done or not. It does not make sense that you would track day by day, or Actual work for this kind of estimating method. See Chapter 11, "Tracking Your Schedule," for the various methods you can use to track the status of your schedule when you are using duration-based scheduling.

Entering Work-Based Estimates

Many organizations are not satisfied with duration-based scheduling because they are worried about overallocating resources on a day-by-day basis. They want to achieve more accuracy in their estimates, or need effort information to understand hourly work rather than thinking about the schedule based on the span of time it takes to complete a task. The most accurate method to use for scheduling is that of effort-based scheduling. However, it's important to know that it takes more time and effort to estimate and track according to effort-based scheduling, so you need to consider that as a trade-off for the greater accuracy.

Also, just because you get duration estimates does not mean you are doing duration-based scheduling. If you receive a duration estimate, and also receive either how much capacity (Units) the resource(s) has to work on your project, or the amount of work it will take, you are performing effort-based scheduling.

Most people think of effort-based scheduling using work hours as the best form of estimating. To take estimates to a more granular level, estimates can be for the entire task or for each person on the task. For instance, you might estimate that the Remove previous roofing task is 60 hours, or you might estimate that Lila will expend 20 hours, Jose will expend 10 hours, and Wilson will expend 30 hours. Usually you choose how to provide the estimate based on the kind of work being performed.

Effort-based estimates are usually owned by the project manager

If you are using effort -based scheduling, the project manager usually has more authority over the project team. You might still get estimates from the functional or resource manager, but it usually entails both effort and duration (understanding work effort as well as how long it will take). Effort-based estimates can help an organization obtain more accurate and historic estimates for similar projects in the future.

With effort-based scheduling, you are managing all the variables of the Work formula: Work = Duration × Units. In doing so, you need to obtain estimates for at least two variables of the formula. The three possibilities for the two variables are the following:

- How much time it will take (Work or hours the task will take) and the capacity for work each resource has (Units). With these two estimates or variables of the formula, Project will estimate the Duration. For this kind of estimate, you should select Fixed Units, Effort-Driven or Fixed Work task types depending on which part of the formula variable you want to ensure stays fixed.
- Work and Duration. With these two estimates, Project will estimate the Units. For this kind of estimate, you should select Fixed Duration, Effort-Driven or Fixed Work task types depending on which part of the formula variable you want to ensure stays fixed.
- Duration and Units. With these two estimates, Project will estimate the Work. For this kind of estimate, you should select Fixed Duration, Effort-Driven. This is a great way to enter estimates when you want to get some kind of an idea of the work-effort but don't have good work estimates yet with historical data. This is the least accurate, however.

Your organization can decide how you want to get your estimates, and you need to ask for the estimates based on your task type. Let's look at the Roofing project using effort estimates now.

For the first kind of estimate method you receive an estimate of effort (hours) and capacity (units) for resources. Let's look at Table 6.2, which contains two estimates for each task: Work and Units.

Table 6.2 *Effort and Units Estimates*

Task	Work Estimate	Resource Units Estimate
Hire crew	10 hours	25%
Obtain permits	4 hours	25%
Purchase roofing material	6 hours	25% Chief – 2 hours 50% Lila – 4 hours
Remove previous roofing	60 hours	100% Wilson – 30 hours 100% Lila –20 hours 50% Jose – 10 hours
Perform roofing	120 hours	100% Wilson 100% Jose

As we think about the work, based on the tasks themselves, we are being more precise about the work effort.

For obtaining the permits, it really only takes 4 hours for the paperwork, submitting the permit, and follow-up. You realize what really takes so long is waiting for the permit to be approved. You could consider putting lag (see Lead and Lags below) on the task to represent the wait time, rather than attribute work effort to the task but in the example, you will just enter the estimate.

Purchasing the materials is shared between the chief and Lila, but the work between the two is different. The chief will be doing a lot of the calculations, and then Lila will actually purchase the materials. In this case, it will take the chief a couple of hours to do the calculations to complete the order. Then it will take Lila about 4 hours to get all the materials. Use the split window to enter the different units and work for each resource.

For Removing the previous roofing task you can estimate the effort it will take each resource to do the job based on speed and skill set. Use the split window to enter the Work and Units for each resource. Chief estimated

Roofing the house at 60 hours each for Jose and Wilson, who will be working full time. Figure 6.26 shows the schedule based on the estimates in Table 6.2 and entered into the schedule using the default task type of Fixed Units, Effort-Driven.

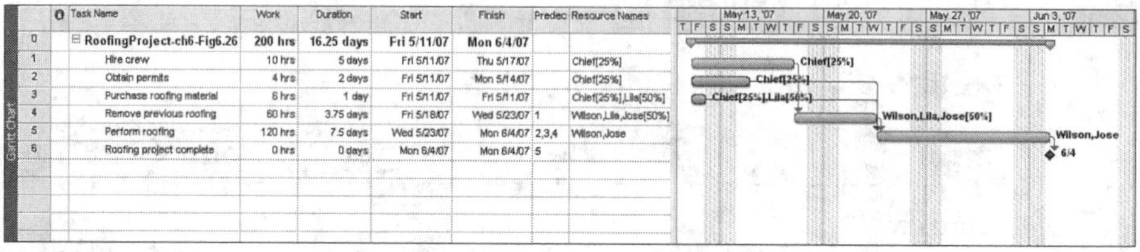

Figure 6.26 *Effort-based scheduling using Work (hours) and Units estimates*

Notice that Project has calculated the duration estimates based on Work and Units. An interesting point is that it will take 3.75 days for removing the roof because Wilson's work takes 30 hours. Included in the estimate is the knowledge that he performs a special function in roof removal that Lila and Jose can't help with, so his work takes a bit longer. In this case, although the work takes 60 hours, the work is not equally distributed.

This kind of estimating is useful if you are paying an hourly rate or you want to think about adjusting the schedule by working overtime. By looking at work effort, you can accurately decide to ask a resource to work 2 hours more each day to tighten the schedule. Notice that this schedule also shows the work will be done by 6/4 rather than 6/1 as shown in the duration-based schedule (only because of .25 days more in the estimate, which warns you that someone needs to perform a little overtime to be done by 6/1)). Because the estimates are more detailed, you are accounting for risks, skill sets, and how much time people really have to spend on the work. Effort-based scheduling often reveals that it really will take longer to get the project done. It is better to be realistic and accurate rather than figuring out a date that you will not make anyway. Note that if you use the Fixed Work task type, you will receive the same results when building your schedule.

If we obtain the work effort and duration for each task Project will calculate the units it will take to complete the work. Table 6.3 now contains the Work and Duration estimates without knowing the resource's capacity, and Figure 6.27 shows the results of the estimate entries.

Table 6.3 *Effort and Duration Estimates*

Task	Work Estimate	Duration estimate
Hire crew	10 hours	5 days
Obtain permits	4 hours	5 days
Purchase roofing material	6 hours	3 days
Remove previous roofing	60 hours	3 days
Perform roofing	120 hours	8 days

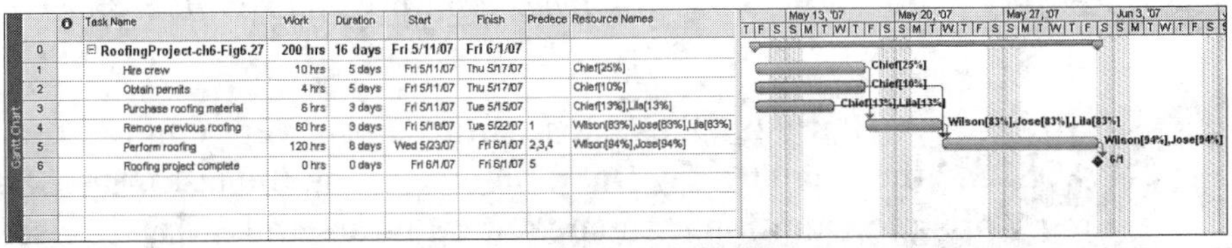

Figure 6.27 *Effort-based scheduling using Work and Duration estimates*

These results will occur if you use Fixed Work, or Fixed Duration, Effort-Driven only if you add resources first and then enter the Work and Duration estimates.

The order and method in which you add resources and estimates affect the schedule results

Project results can be different based on the order in which you add resources and estimates and the task type you select.

A word of caution—you can get different results when entering estimates based on how you enter them. To illustrate this, you could add estimates and resources in a different order on a roofing project task for a Fixed Work task type. In Figure 6.28, Work (at 60 hours) and Duration (at 3 days) estimates were entered. Then Lila, Jose, and Wilson were entered as resources. Notice that the duration changed to 2.5, and the resources were added at 100% units. This is because Project uses the 60 hours Fixed Work to calculate the task, then evenly distributes the task among the three resources.

	❶	Task Name	Work	Duration	Start	Finish	Predece	Resource Names	
0		⊟ RoofingProject-ch6-Fig6.30	60 hrs	4.5 days	Fri 5/11/07	Thu 5/17/07			
1		Hire crew	0 hrs	1 day	Fri 5/11/07	Fri 5/11/07			
2		Obtain permits	0 hrs	1 day	Fri 5/11/07	Fri 5/11/07			
3		Purchase roofing material	0 hrs	1 day	Fri 5/11/07	Fri 5/11/07			
4		Remove previous roofing	60 hrs	2.5 days	Mon 5/14/07	Wed 5/16/07	1	Jose,Lila,Wilson	
5		Perform roofing	0 hrs	1 day	Wed 5/16/07	Thu 5/17/07	2,3,4		
6		Roofing project complete	0 hrs	0 days	Thu 5/17/07	Thu 5/17/07	5		

Name: Remove previous roofing   Duration: 2.5d   ☑ Effort driven   Previous   Next
Start: Mon 5/14/07   Finish: Wed 5/16/07   Task type: Fixed Work   % Complete: 0%

ID	Resource Name	Units	Work		ID	Predecessor Name	Type	Lag
3	Jose	100%	20h		1	Hire crew	FS	0d
4	Lila	100%	20h					
2	Wilson	100%	20h					

Figure 6.28 *Fixed Work task type with Work and Duration entered first*

However, in Figure 6.29, Lila, Jose, and Wilson were entered first (with no Work and the default 1 day Duration entered on the task). Later, after receiving Work and Duration estimates of 60 hours and 3 days, those estimates were entered into the Work and Duration fields. You might see this phenomenon based on how you add your estimates. Just be aware this is caused by how Project is processing the work formula based on the order in which you entered the variables.

	Task Name	Work	Duration	Start	Finish	Predece	Resource Names	
1	Hire crew	0 hrs	1 day	Fri 5/11/07	Fri 5/11/07			
2	Obtain permits	0 hrs	1 day	Fri 5/11/07	Fri 5/11/07			
3	Purchase roofing material	0 hrs	1 day	Fri 5/11/07	Fri 5/11/07			
4	Remove previous roofing	60 hrs	3 days	Mon 5/14/07	Wed 5/16/07	1	Jose[83%],Lila[83%],Wilson[83%]	
5	Perform roofing	0 hrs	1 day	Thu 5/17/07	Thu 5/17/07	2,3,4		
6	Roofing project complete	0 hrs	0 days	Thu 5/17/07	Thu 5/17/07	5		

Name: Remove previous roofing   Duration: 3d   ☑ Effort driven   Previous   Next
Start: Mon 5/14/07   Finish: Wed 5/16/07   Task type: Fixed Work   % Complete: 0%

ID	Resource Name	Units	Work		ID	Predecessor Name	Type	Lag
3	Jose	83%	20h		1	Hire crew	FS	0d
4	Lila	83%	20h					
2	Wilson	83%	20h					

Figure 6.29 *Fixed Work Task type with resources entered first*

Finally, you can enter Duration and Units as estimates in Effort-Based scheduling. In such a case, Project is determining the work effort for you, which is a less accurate estimate than obtaining Work estimates. Table 6.4 shows the estimates received in this case.

Table 6.4 *Duration and Units Estimates*

Task	Duration Estimate	Unit Estimate
Hire crew	5 days	Chief – 25%
Obtain permits	5 days	Chief – 25%
Purchase roofing material	3 days	Lila – 50%, Chief – 25%
Remove previous roofing	3 days	Jose – 50%, Lila and Wilson both 100%
Perform roofing	8 days	Wilson and Jose both 100%

In Figure 6.30, you can see that the effort is actually being estimated based on the Duration estimates. Compare the Work estimates with Figures 6.26 and 6.27. You might not have gotten as accurate estimates, but with duration and amount of time the resources can work, you are getting close.

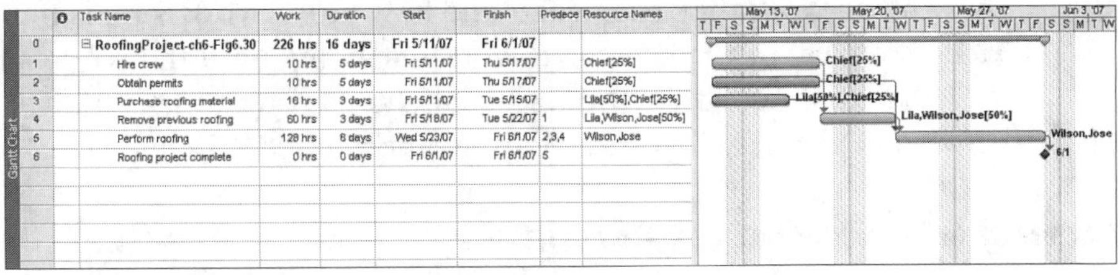

Figure 6.30 *Effort-based scheduling using Duration and Units estimates*

Many organizations use Duration and Units initially

Because it can be difficult to understand how to enter estimates, many organizations enter Duration and Units using Fixed Duration, not Effort-Driven set on all tasks initially. You might want to consider experimenting to see what method you prefer in entering estimates and resources.

What are those question marks I sometimes see in the Duration column?

The question mark shows up in the Duration field as a visual cue to indicate whether you are satisfied with your estimate. The question marks are set to display by default. You can remove these once you are satisfied with the estimates you've entered into the schedule. You can remove the question mark if you double-click a task, and then clear the Estimated check box on the General tab of the Task Information dialog box.

Tracking with Effort-Based Estimates

If you are using effort-based estimates and scheduling, you will want to use Actual Work data to track the execution of your work. You will ask resources how much work they have done, and how much work is remaining to get an accurate view of the estimated work remaining until the work is done on a task. See Chapter 11 for the various methods you can use to track the status of your schedule when you are using effort-based scheduling.

Entering a Work Budget Estimate

You can assign budget work resources in Project 2007 that allows you to set up the overall project work budget on the project summary task (zero) then you can track actual work to compare with the original budgeted work estimate.

To use a budget work resource, do the following:

1. In the Resource Sheet, add a resource name indicating it is a budget work resource. You might enter a resource such as "Labor."
2. Make sure the default value of Work is selected in the Type field.

3. Double-click the resource. You will see the Resource Information dialog box. Select the General tab and click on the Budget indicator on the right side of the dialog box and click OK.

4. Select View from the menu bar and click Gantt Chart.

5. Since you need to display the project summary task to assign budget resources, select Tools on the menu bar and click Options (if you do not already have the project summary task already showing). On the General tab, select the Show project summary task indicator and press OK.

6. Select the project summary task and use your favorite method of assigning resources. You might click the Assign Resources button on the toolbar. In the Assign Resources dialog box select the budget work resource you created and click Assign.

7. Next you need to enter the total work budget value. You can only enter the value in either the Task Usage or Resource Usage views. Select View from the menu bar and click Task Usage.

8. To enter the budget work, you must first add the Budget Work field. Select Insert from the menu bar and click Column. Select Budget Work from the Column Definition dialog box and click OK.

9. In the Budget Work field, enter the hours for the budget resource you have assigned to the project summary task. You can only enter a value on the resource row, not the top project row.

You may have several budget resources

You may use more than one budget work resource if you would like to indicate total work budget. For instance, you could have a work budget for contractors, and a work budget for full-time employees. When you create budget resources, you will want to make sure you name them clearly for each kind of work resources you are entering for each work budget you want to use.

Putting Estimating All Together

You can decide which type of estimates are best for you or your organization based on the time you have, your strategy for project schedules, and your need for preciseness. Just make sure that for whatever form of estimates you are using, you sync them up with the proper task type, and you get at least two of the variables to complete the work formula of Work = Duration × Units if you are doing Effort-Based estimating.

Leads and Lags

After adding resources and adding estimates, you can now see how leads and lags affect the end dates in your schedule. In Chapter 5 you saw how leads and lags can make your schedule more practical. As a reminder, here's the definitions of leads and lags:

- **Lead:** When a successor task can start before the finish of the predecessor task, in essence, creating a head start for the successor task.
- **Lag:** When a successor task should be delayed after the finish of the predecessor task, creating a delay for the successor task.

If you have someone on a task and you have estimates, you can better see how long a task might take or when tasks can start based on the resources assigned and the work itself. Let's take the schedule in Figure 6.26 to think about more realistic lead and lag examples. For example, it usually takes 4 days after the permit is submitted for it to be approved, so the Obtain permit task has had a 4-day lag added to it as shown in Figure 6.31. If for some reason, the permit gets submitted later than originally scheduled, the roofing task can't really start until after the approval, and the start date of the Perform roofing task will slide to a later date, as shown in Figure 6.32.

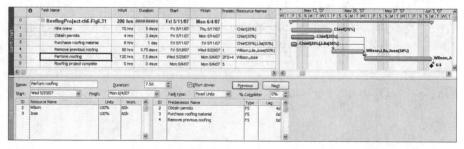

Figure 6.31 *Lag on Obtain permits prior to Perform roofing task*

Actual Start date moves task out

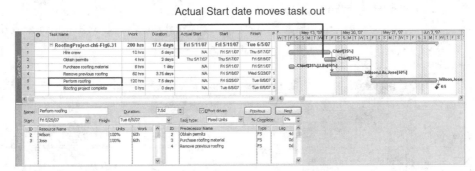

Figure 6.32 *Lag affects critical path if Obtain permit task does not start on time*

You could get a head start on the Perform roofing task if the work and resources allowed it. Let's say you have a large roof and the roofing has been completely removed on the west wing while you continue removing the roofing on the east wing. If you have obtained your permit and Jose has completed his work on the Remove previous roofing job, he could start performing the roofing on the west wing with the result as shown in Figure 6.33.

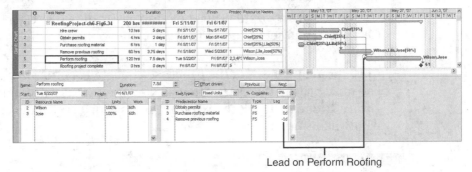

Lead on Perform Roofing

Figure 6.33 *Perform roofing contains lead for performing the roofing one day early*

Reviewing the Critical Path

Now that you have added resources and estimates, the critical path becomes more evident. You can also start making decisions about how you can change things so that you can shorten some tasks on the critical path to make your project complete sooner. To review the critical path, select View from the menu bar and click Tracking Gantt from the View menu bar. The result is shown in Figure 6.34 (the critical path tasks will show in red in your version of Project).

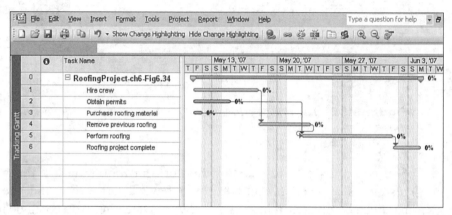

Figure 6.34   *Tracking Gantt chart showing critical path*

You can also format a critical path on the Gantt Chart by doing the following:

1. Select Format from the menu bar, then click Gantt Chart Wizard.
2. The Gantt Chart Wizard dialog box displays as shown in Figure 6.35. Click Next, and select the Critical path radio option on the second panel.
3. Click through the rest of the panels, selecting what else you would like to display on the chart. After clicking through all selections, click Format It, and then exit the wizard. The tasks that are on the critical path will display in red.

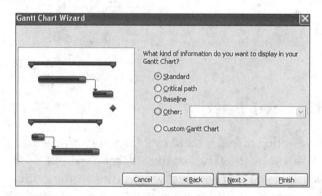

Figure 6.35   *The Gantt Chart Wizard*

Based on this you could consider bringing more people in to perform the roofing, or maybe try to escalate the hiring process if you want to see the project completed sooner.

> **Deadline dates can affect the view of the critical path**
>
> When you set Deadline Dates on the end of the project, your critical path will no longer display in red. The Deadline date sets the late finish for a task so a task with a deadline date later than its finish date has slack.

Sharing Resources Between Projects or Creating a Resource Pool

Although using a shared resource pool is an advanced function, it is worth introducing in this chapter in case your organization is interested in using one. Your organization can use a pool of resources that everyone can pull from using the Standard edition of Project. This can help you maintain your resource names consistently, and enables you to create calendars and resource information (e.g., rates) once rather than for each project. You can also see issues with overall resource allocation for your organization's projects. Then someone building a schedule can pull from the resource pool to build the Resource Sheet for his or her project. This resource pool is different than the resource pool in the Project Server edition. The shared resource pool allows you to mimic an enterprise resource pool, although it doesn't allow for the rigor of the Enterprise edition.

You can use this resource sharing pool for several projects. You might have several projects that will use the same or most of the same resources.

To use a resource pool you first need to build one. To do so, follow these steps:

1. Create a new project by selecting the New button on the toolbar.
2. Select View, then click Resource Sheet.
3. Enter the resource names and other information about each resource you would like to add to the pool.
4. Select File from the menu bar and click Save.

5. Name the project something obvious for your organization such as OurResourcePool and click Save. You do not *need* to add any tasks to the project, but you *can* create a project associated with this file.

Then, to use the pool, do the following:

1. Create a new project or use an existing project.

2. Open the resource pool project file containing the resources you want to share.

3. In the project you are updating (make sure you are not in the resource pool), select Tools from the menu bar, and click Resource sharing as shown in Figure 6.36.

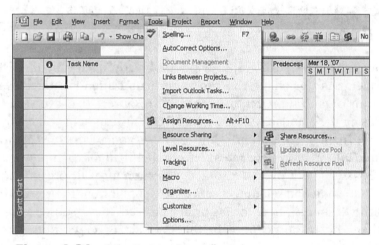

Figure 6.36 *Selecting to share resources*

4. Click Share resources. A screen like the one shown in Figure 6.37 displays.

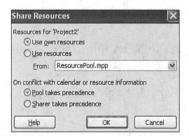

Figure 6.37 *Adding a selected resource pool to the project*

5. Click Use Resources and press OK, and the resources from the resource pool file will display in the project's Resource Sheet. Save your file.

When you open projects that have been previously linked to the resource pool, you will receive a message asking if you want to link to the resource pool again. If you have opened the resource pool file itself, you will be asked if you want to open read-only or read-write so that you can make modifications to the resources (which will lock others from making changes in the file although they can use it), or read-write in a new master file (which will also open the projects associated to the resource pool in one file) so you and others can make changes in the resource pool file. If you open the pool read-write, then the file will be locked from other users until the pool is saved and closed.

Maintaining a resource pool

It's important that someone maintains the resource pool and that you leave it in a place where the entire organization can find and use it. If you use shared network drives, you need to have rules to ensure the file does not get inadvertently moved so that users cannot find it.

If you are interested in using the resource pool, you will want to use the Help function in Project to get more information than this introduction provides.

The Project Schedule Building Methodology So Far

Based on what you have learned, the following steps and sequence describe the best methods for building your schedule. The items emphasized in this chapter are indicated in italics.

The steps for building a project schedule so far are as follows:

☑ If you are using a template, select the appropriate template (you will probably want to change it based on the input of your project team). If you are building a project from scratch, build a WBS with your team, then move to the next step.

☑ Set up your project calendar if you do not have one available. Make sure you reflect your company's hours in Tools, Options, Calendar, if different than the defaults.

☑ In the Project Information dialog box, set your project Start date and make sure your project calendar is assigned to the project.

☑ Start building (if your project is from scratch) or editing (if you are using a template) your task list. Make sure you indicate summary tasks and subtasks to help indicate the outline of your project schedule.

☑ Add milestone tasks to indicate significant events, deliverables, or approval points in your project.

☑ Enter deadline dates for appropriate tasks. This is a better way of indicating dates when tasks need to be completed rather than typing in a Finish date on a task.

☑ Add task calendars to tasks to indicate exceptions to the project calendar if needed. You will probably not need these kinds of calendars often.

☑ Review all tasks. Decide what kind of tasks they are for the schedule-building process. Change the Task type and Effort-Driven fields if appropriate.

☑ Link all tasks in the schedule, determining if they are Finish-to-Start, Start-to-Start, Finish-to-Finish, or Start-to-Finish relationships. Link among phases or task groupings first, then link between phases or groupings. Use the Predecessor and Successor columns to help you see if all tasks are linked.

☑ *Build the project team. Add all resources that might work on the project to the Resource Sheet for the project. If you are performing effort-based scheduling, enter the Maximum Units each resource can work on the project. You can use generic or real resources, but when you know who will do the work, you should replace generic resources with real resources.*

☑ *Assign the resources to each task. If you are performing Effort-Based scheduling, you might need to change the percentage of allocation a resource is assigned to individual tasks in some cases.*

☑ *Enter estimates to project tasks. For effort-based scheduling, enter two of the three variables in the Work formula: Work = Duration × Units.*

☑ *Review the schedule and enter leads and lags on tasks if appropriate.*

☑ *Review the critical path and adjust tasks if appropriate.*

Prior to building your schedule, you will need to decide if you are performing effort- or duration-based scheduling. That will help you decide how you enter resources and estimates on your tasks.

Summary

This chapter focused on resources and estimates. It's a lot for one chapter, but it's pretty important to think of resources and estimates together as you finish entering the work package-level information for your WBS. You first need to build the project team by entering resources in the Resource Sheet. Project contains different types of resources: work, material, and cost. You can also enter generic as well as named resources. Resources can have their own calendars to indicate their working time, and can have rates and custom data associated with them.

Once you have resources added to your project, you can assign the resources and estimates to tasks. When you assign resources, you can assign one or several to tasks. You can assign them at a particular percentage of their capacity, or at 100%. You can enter Work or Duration estimates. Whatever way you enter estimates, you need to consider if you will perform duration-based scheduling or effort-based scheduling. If you perform duration-based scheduling, you will enter your estimate in Duration and you do not care how many resources are working on your tasks—select the Fixed Duration Task type and designate them as Non-Effort-Driven. If you perform Effort-Based scheduling, make sure you obtain estimates for two of the three variables in the work formula: Work = Duration × Units. You can then enter any two variables on the task, and Project will calculate the third variable for you. Usually, you would obtain Work estimates for Effort-Based scheduling. You can use the Assign Resources dialog box to assign resources to tasks and enter estimates directly into the Work or Duration fields on the tasks, or Work in the split window if you have estimates for individual resources.

When you enter resources and estimates to tasks, you will want to see if there are some leads and lags you need to include to make your schedule more accurate. You should also review the critical path to see if it looks reasonable, or if you can shorten some tasks on it. In the next chapter, I discuss the money side of building a schedule. Although you entered resources here, if you entered rates on the resources, you also have costs associated with your project.

Practice: Adding Resources and Estimates to the Schedule

The following practices help you add resources and estimates to the schedule. The practices will use the house-painting project and have you assign you, your spouse, and your child to the schedule, then you will enter estimates for completing the work. Finally, you will review the schedule to see if you need to adjust it with leads and lags.

Practice 6.1

House-Painting Project: Assignments

The first thing you want to do after adding the tasks and sequencing them is add the resources to be used on the Resource Sheet. Use HousePainting-Practice-Chapter6-Practice1.mpp to start this practice.

1. After opening HousePainting-Practice-Chapter6-Practice1.mpp, select View and click Resource Sheet. The Resource Sheet view appears so you can enter your resources. To enter the resources, consider that you and your child might be able to work on the painting project at 100% Max. Units. This means that you may be able to work 100% of an 8-hour day, but when assigned to an actual task, you could be assigned at a different percentage. Your spouse only has 25% capacity to do any work during an 8-hour day.

2. Type Me, Spouse, and Child as resources in the Resource Sheet. Enter 25% in the Max. Units field for Spouse. Remember, this is to help ensure you create the team, and when you actually select resources, they are selected from drop-down lists, rather than having to type a resource in and possibly naming them wrong.

3. Return to the Gantt Chart by selecting View from the menu bar and clicking Gantt Chart. Now you are ready to assign resources to tasks. In this case, you are using the default task type and you are going to think about how much time each resource will really have to work on each task.

4. Click the Assign Resources button from the toolbar or select Tools from the menu bar and click Assign Resources. This will open the Assign Resources dialog box. Click the Gather Materials task, then select Me in the Assign Resource dialog box. Enter 25% in the Units field and click Assign.

   Click the second task, Scrape and Sand. For Units, enter 25% for Me and for Child. Your spouse has told you that he or she will be very busy starting in May, so you figure you will only get about 10% out of him or her, so enter 10 in the Units field for Spouse.

5. Enter the rest of the units according to Table 6.5 using the Assign Resources dialog box. Throughout this process, you really don't care what is in the Duration column for each task. You will add estimates next.

Table 6.5 *Task Assignments*

Task	Resource	Assignment Amount
Gather materials	Me	25%
Scrape and sand	Me	25%
	Child	25%
	Spouse	10%
Inspect and rescrape	Me	25%
	Spouse	25%
Mask windows	Child	25%
	Me	25%
Prime	Child	25%
	Me	25%
	Spouse	25%
Paint	Child	10%
	Me	25%
	Spouse	25%
Strip masking	Me	50%
Inspect and retouch	Spouse	25%
	Me	25%

The results of this practice are shown in HousePainting-Practice-Chapter6-Practice1-Result.mpp on the CD.

Practice 6.2

House Painting Adding Estimates

Now you will add estimates. You've decided to use work estimates.

1. Either use the file you just created, or use HousePainting-Practice-Chapter6-Practice2.mpp.

2. Insert the Work column. Enter the amount of work for each task presented in Table 6.6 into the Work column.

Table 6.6 *Hours of Work for Each Task*

Task	Hours
Gather materials	5
Scrape and sand	40
Inspect and rescrape	15
Mask windows	25
Prime	30
Paint	30
Strip masking	5
Inspect and retouch	10

3. In the case of the Paint task, we have specific areas of the house that each person will paint, so the work for each person is distributed differently, although the amount of time a person can work will stay the same.

   To enter different work estimates for different people it's best to use the split window. Select Window from the menu bar, and click Split. Click the Paint task in the upper window, then move your cursor to the lower window and enter 5 hours for Child, 20 hours for Me, and 4 hours for Spouse, and click OK.

Notice in your results that you have missed your deadline dates for finishing the prepping and the end date. This is okay for now, as we will continue to iterate through the schedule to make sure it's as tight and realistic as possible. Also notice that the durations that Project calculated based on resource units and work are not whole days. Project uses a precise calculation based on hours and minutes within an 8-hour day for all resources to come up with those durations. Because we care more about work than duration in this practice, the duration estimates are fine.

The results of this practice are given in the HousePainting-Practice-Chapter6-Practice2-Result.mpp file on the CD.

Practice 6.3

House Painting Lead and Lag

Now, you want to review the schedule to see if you can delay or get a head start on any tasks.

1. Either use the file you just created or use HousePainting-Practice-Chapter6-Practice3.mpp.

2. When you review the schedule, there are a lot of tasks you could start while the other ones are finishing. For instance, you could inspect and scrape the west wing after it's done and while the east wing is still being scraped and sanded. However, one of the issues with getting a head start on this task is that the same resources are doing both tasks. You doubt the resources can do both at the same time. However, you do notice that because you are doing the Strip Masking task, and your spouse is doing the Inspect and Retouch task, that job could start earlier. You will put a lead on the Inspect and Retouch task.

   Select Window on the menu bar, and click Split if you do not already have a split window open.

3. Click the Inspect and Retouch task. In the lower Task Form window enter –4h in the Lag field. Notice this also removed the Deadline warning marker on the last milestone of Painting complete.

4. Remove the split window by selecting Window on the menu bar and clicking Remove Split.

5. To review the critical path, select View from the menu bar and click Tracking Gantt. Inspect the critical path. Right now, the only task not on the critical path is Priming. Although this schedule might not look achievable right now (because resources are supposed to work on some tasks at the same time), that's okay. Schedule building is an iterative process and you will smooth out the schedule later. I explore analyzing and adjusting the schedule in Chapters 9 and 10.

If you would like to see the results of this practice, see the HousePainting-Practice-Chapter6-Practice3-Result.mpp file on the CD.

Case Study: Adding Resources to the Schedule

On the VNLE project, Chris added the tasks and linked them in Chapter 5. Now Chris is ready to add resources and estimates to the project schedule. To get the best understanding of resources and estimates, it's best if the project team meets to discuss the project's work activities. The VNLE project team worked with Chris to create the schedule and to decide on the generic resources and estimates as described in the case study in Chapter 6 of *Project Management for Mere Mortals*. In this exercise, Chris is going to add effort information and resources according to the estimates from Chris's team. You might choose to try this case study for more practice.

> **Read Chapter 5 of *Project Management for Mere Mortals***
>
> Chapter 5 of *Project Management for Mere Mortals* details the process for the team to gather resource assignments and task estimates.

Open the file VNLE-Chapter6-Begin-CaseStudy.mpp to work on this case study.

1. First Chris will add resources to the Resource Sheet according to Table 6.7. When Chris sees 6 core team members, she will enter Max. Units of 600% to indicate that the resource has 6 units of that generic position for the project tasks. The result of this work is in the VNLE-Chapter6-Middle-1-CaseStudy.mpp file.

Table 6.7 *Resources Needed*

Resource Needed	How Many Available?
Project manager	1
Executive sponsor	1
Core team	6
Sales team	4
VP Sales	1
Marketing team	2
VP Marketing	1
Business development team	1
VP Business development	1

Resource Needed	How Many Available?
COO	1
CIO	1
IT team	1
Logistics team	1
Marketing materials vendor	1
Booth construction subcontractor	1
VN Web project manager	1
Catalog department team	1

2. Then Chris adds the resources to each task according to the units required as shown in Table 6.8. Note that this also contains estimates for Work and Duration, which she could also add at the same time, but Chris decides to enter just the resources first—which is also an acceptable method in building Project schedules. She tries different methods for adding the resources, including the Assign resources button and the Resources tab of the Task Information dialog box. In this case, most everyone is being added at the default—100% units—unless the task requires more of them. The result of this work is in the VNLE-Chapter6-Middle-2-CaseStudy.mpp file.

3. Once Chris has added resources to the tasks, she's ready to add the estimates. Her team came up with two estimates and variables: Work and Duration (as shown in Table 6.8). Although we added most of the resources at 100%, they really won't be working like that. Some of the effort will be 2 hours over 1 day, so their units are really much less than 100%. However, because we left most of the tasks using the default task type (Fixed Units) the schedule will try and fix the units entered because of the work formula. Chris realizes that she needs to change all tasks to Fixed Work except for those few tasks that have already been designated as Fixed duration. She inserts the Type column and changes all tasks that are Fixed Units to Fixed Work (but she doesn't change milestones because they really don't matter). Chris uses the Fill down capability to change the Task type quickly.

4. Once Chris changed the Task types, she inserted the Work column and used the Split Window function to help enter the estimates. She enters the work estimates (for Fixed Work tasks) in the split window, then enters the duration estimates in the Duration field for each task. The result of this work is in the VNLE-Chapter6-End-CaseStudy.mpp file.

For the few tasks that are Fixed duration, Chris entered the duration given and the work effort, and let Project figure out the work effort. Notice that for the Manage trade show event task with the duration of 4 days, and 40 hours effort, it shows that the resources will be working 125%. During the trade show, Chris knows she'll be working overtime.

Table 6.8   *Case Study Resources and Assignments*

Task	Resource Estimate	Work Effort Estimate	Duration Estimate
Create and document project scope	Project manager at 50% Core team member	20 hours 30 hours	5 days 5 days
Develop and execute communication plan	Project manager at 50% Core team member	20 hours 20 hours	5 days 5 days
Create and maintain project plan	Project manager	To be determined	To be determined
Perform project activities	Project manager and 1 core team	To be determined	To be determined
Document lessons learned	Project manager and 1 core team	16 hours	2 days
Gather previous trade show information	Business development person 1 project manager 6 core team	16 hours 4 hours 4 hours each	5 days
Gather input from other departments	6 core team 1 project manager 1 VP Sales 1 VP Marketing 1 VP Business development 1 COO 1 CIO	4 hours each 4 hours 2 hours 2 hours 2 hours 2 hour 2 hours	3 days

Task	Resource Estimate	Work Effort Estimate	Duration Estimate
Establish marketing goals	1 core team 1 VP Marketing	4 hours 2 hours	1 day
Determine target audience	1 core team 1 VP Marketing	4 hours 2 hours	1 day
Create draft marketing plan	1 core team	8 hours	3 days
Review and revise draft plan with other departments	6 core team 1 project manager 1 VP Sales 1 VP Marketing 1 VP Business development 1 COO 1 CIO	4 hours each 4 hours 1 hour 1 hour 1 hour 1 hour 1 hour	2 days
Create final marketing plan	1 core team member 1 marketing person 1 VP Marketing 1 project manager	2 hours 2 hours 1 hour 1 hour	1 day
Design the booth sales approach	1 core team member 1 sales person 1 VP Sales	4 hours 8 hours 1 hour	2 days
Create IT demo requirements	6 core team 1 project manager	4 hours each 4 hours	1 day
Design the trade show experience	6 core team 1 marketing person 1 sales person 1 VP Sales 1 VP Marketing	8 hours each 8 hours 8 hours 1 hour 1 hour	5 days
Design the marketing collateral	1 core team member 1 marketing person 1 VP Marketing	8 hours 8 hours 1 hour	3 days
Design the booth	1 core team member 1 marketing person 1 VP Marketing	8 hours 8 hours 1 hour	3 days

(continues)

Table 6.8 *Continued*

Task	Resource Estimate	Work Effort Estimate	Duration Estimate
Determine vendor partnership strategy	1 core team member 1 business development person 1 VP Business development	4 hours 4 hours 1 hour	2 days
Determine target vendors	1 core team member 1 business development person 1 VP Business development	16 hours 16 hours 2 hours	5 days
Review and revise demo requirements	6 core team 1 IT person 1 project manager	2 hours each 2 hours 1 hour	1 day
Design the demo	6 core team 1 IT person 1 project manager	4 hours each 4 hours 4 hours	2 days
Determine housing and travel requirements	6 core team 1 project manager	2 hours each 2 hours	1 day
Gather marketing materials and booth shipping requirements	6 core team 1 project manager	2 hours each 2 hours	1 day
Determine catering requirements	6 core team 1 project manager	2 hours each 2 hours	1 day
Determine trade show on site requirements	1 core team member 1 logistics person	8 hours 8 hours	3 days
Verify product inventory supports the marketing plan	1 project manager 1 catalog department person	1 hour 1 hour	1/2 day
Arrange flights and lodging	1 logistics person	8 hours	5 days
Make catering arrangements	1 logistics person	2 hours	1 days

Task	Resource Estimate	Work Effort Estimate	Duration Estimate
Finalize trade show on site arrangements	6 core team	2 hours each	1 day
Verify product inventory supports the trade show plan	1 catalog department person	1 hour	1/2 day
Prototype the booth experience	1 core team member 1 marketing person 1 VP Marketing	4 hours 4 hours 1 hour	2 days
Establish premeetings with vendors	1 business development person	4 hours	3 days
Build marketing collateral	1 marketing person Materials vendor	8 hours 80 hours (to be revisited)	10 days
Build the booth	1 logistics person Booth construction subcontractor	8 hours 80 hours (to be revisited)	10 days
Build the demo	1 IT person 1 core team	16 hours 8 hours	5 days
Test the demo	1 IT person 1 core team	16 hours 8 hours	5 days
Learn and practice the demo	4 sales team	8 hours each	5 days
Ship marketing material and booth	1 logistics person 1 project manager 1 project manager	2 hours 2 hours 1 hour	1 day
Create trade show buzz	2 marketing team	40 hours	30 days
Verify the Web site is ready	1 project manager 1 VN Web project manager	1 hour 1 hour	1 day
Verify the catalog is ready	1 core team 1 project manager	1 hour 1 hours	1 day

(continues)

Table 6.8   *Continued*

Task	Resource Estimate	Work Effort Estimate	Duration Estimate
Verify and correct logistics	1 core team 1 logistics person	4 hours 4 hours	1 day
Manage the trade show event	1 project manager 1 core team	40 hours 40 hours	4 days
Staff the booth	4 sales team	32 hours each	4 days
Get feedback for vendor experience during event	1 business development person 1 project manager	8 hours 1 hour	4 days 1 day

Review the schedule. As you can see, Chris's project shows the team is going to get the work done months before the actual trade show, so there's still a lot more to do to adjust the schedule. After we review costs and budget in the next chapter, we will see how Chris continues to adjust the schedule for her project.

If you decide to practice this case study, and your schedule does not end up exactly like the final case study file, you might have done something different with the task types or entering the estimates or resources out of the recommended order. Remember, you can always refine your schedule. It is not important that it is perfect, and some of the issues might simply be typos. If this were one of your real projects, you would be more knowledgeable about all the data you are entering and less likely make the typos.

Entering Resources and Estimates

Entering resources and their information and estimates is the final piece in detailing the work packages of your project's WBS:

- Enter all the resources for your project in the Resource Sheet.

- Assign resources and enter estimates for each task. Obtain two variables in the Work formula (Work = Duration × Units) for the best estimates.

After you enter the resources and the estimates, you might find some mistakes. Don't worry about it: Just review the schedule and make corrections as you see them. Iterating to fix issues and continue planning through schedule building should be a habit, not a problem.

Review Questions

1. Where do you enter resources that might be assigned to tasks in your project?

2. Besides using the Multiple Resource Information dialog box to enter the same value for multiple selected resources, what other method can you use?

3. What are the two types of resources available in Project 2002 and Project 2003 and the additional resource type available in Project 2007?

4. Where do you change the calendar for a resource to indicate the resource can work other than the default standard 8 hours, 5 days a week?

5. Why would you create and use a custom field for resources?

6. What affects the resources availability in Project?

7. What is duration-based scheduling?

8. What is effort-based scheduling?

9. What are two methods for assigning resources to tasks?

10. How would you enter duration-based task estimates?

11. How would you enter effort-based task estimates?

12. Why do you revisit adding leads and lags and the critical path after adding resources and estimates?

13. What is a resource pool and why would you use it?

7

Using Project to Enter Cost Estimates

$

Beware of little expenses; a small leak will sink a great ship.
—Benjamin Franklin

Topics Covered in This Chapter

Introducing Project Cost Concepts

Assigning Costs to Resources and Tasks

Assigning Different Rates to a Resource

Your Project Budget

Tips and Recommendations for Dealing with Costs

The Project Schedule Building Methodology So Far

Summary

Practice: Adding Costs to the House-Painting Project

Case Study: Adding Costs to the Schedule

The estimated cost of project activities and other project expenses are the project budget. It is usually based on the estimate of the cost of the human resources spending time on your project activities and the nonhuman expenses (e.g., use of equipment, travel, software purchases, etc.) you need to complete your project. The estimates are based on the hourly, daily, or monthly rates of the human resources (which can include direct and indirect costs) and your estimates for the other expenses that you usually receive from others. At one organization I worked for, the finance department provided me the full-time equivalent cost for the job positions I had on my project team, and I could get other costs from my purchasing department contacts to provide prices for items our project planned to lease or purchase. How you decide to show project costs, and ultimately the project budget for your project, will vary according the requirements of your organization. You might only need to manage to an overall budget. Some organizations use the schedule to track actual hours, but the actual costs are applied by another system. In many organizations, the project manager might not even be responsible for including costs or budget in a project schedule.

> **Read Chapter 5 and Chapter 10 of *Project Management for Mere Mortals***
>
> Chapter 5 and Chapter 10 of *Project Management for Mere Mortals* describe estimating project costs and budget in more detail. Project calculates budget for you, but it's important to understand the underlying methods for estimating costs to make the best decisions for your project.

If you are responsible for including cost estimates as part of your project planning, you can use Project to help create and confirm cost and budget estimates. If you create the scope of the work fairly accurately, and you apply either real or generic resources to tasks with your organization's established rates, it is easier to have Project calculate the total budget than to take out the calculator and do it manually. In this book's companion book, *Project Management for Mere Mortals*, the calculations for the effort and costs of tasks for the case study are shown manually in a grid, whereas in this book I simply had to get the initial information and then enter the resource rates into Project. Project automatically calculated the entire project budget. If you do provide costs for a project, use Project for the calculations, rather than manual means.

The way to enter and understand project costs is not apparent in Project. The major views in the system do not show you costs, so you either have to add the cost fields that exist in Project or you need to know which views or tables to use to help you look at project costs. Also, the behavior of project costs can be as mystifying as how duration changes when you add resources, because there are hidden formulas and settings that affect cost. Hopefully, in this chapter I can demystify costs in Project. Project 2007 has come a long way to provide more and easier options for dealing with project costs and budget and with the new feature—cost resources—has really made adding nonlabor costs to tasks easy and sensible.

Project 2007 and some changes for resources

For Project 2007 users, all of the concepts described in this chapter are relevant. However, because of some of the enhancements in Project 2007 you will see a few items differently. For instance, when you view the selections in the Resource Type view, you will also see Cost, whereas users of previous versions will see Work and Material only. You will also have a Budget indicator in the Resource Information dialog box.

In this chapter, I focus on the various methods you can use to show cost estimates, including using resource rates applied to resources, per use costs, and fixed costs. I illuminate why you will definitely want to use effort-based estimates if you use hourly rates for resources and how you would show costs if you are creating duration-based schedules. Although I focus on building costs in your schedule in this chapter, and I discuss tracking in Chapter 11, "Tracking Your Schedule," I also introduce some things to think about for entering and tracking actual costs here. When you start tracking actual costs, Project's calculations and methods might surprise you, so it's important that you consider how you set up costs in the first place so Project helps you see actual costs as you expect.

Skip this chapter if you do not include costs in your project schedule

If you do not need to include budget or costs in your project, you could skip this chapter.

Introducing Project Cost Concepts

Project managers use one or more of the combination of three basic methods for estimating costs as described in the following list. Project provides equivalent types of methods for entering estimates for these three methods.

- **Top-down estimating (also called analogous estimating):** This usually involves creating an overall budget based on similar projects with recorded cost data. Once you get this overall cost information, you might enter a Fixed cost on the project summary task (the project's zero line), or in Project 2007 you could use a Budget resource on the project summary task. Often, project managers are provided this budget without having input into it, and they have to figure out how to plan and execute a project that will meet that budget. If possible, use Project to help you create your project schedule via bottom-up cost estimating (explained later) even if you don't have exact resource rates or expense costs from your organization. You will then see what you will be up against to meet your project budget goals.

- **Bottom-up estimating:** Each task's cost is estimated separately, usually based on the number of resources needed for the length or effort of the task and any expenses estimated for the task or project. This is usually the most accurate method for estimating project costs and calculating the project budget. In Project, this is equivalent to adding rates to resources and using the effort estimated for the tasks to calculate the task's costs. You would also add Fixed cost or the new Cost resource in Project 2007 to any tasks that have nonlabor cost estimates.

- **Parametric estimating:** This method of estimating uses a unit of measurement (e.g., gallons or feet) that can be multiplied by the number of units needed to complete the task. In Project, a form of this kind of cost estimating is using a material resource and assigning a rate to the unit of measurement.

Also, costs involve monetary value. One more element to costs is the currency you use in Project. This chapter focuses on dollars, but you can use Project with other currencies.

You can view different currencies in project costs

You generally need to use the same currency (e.g., euros or dollars) in your project. If you have different currencies in two projects that you want to consolidate, you must choose one currency. However, Project 2003 contains a wizard that allows you to view different currencies—in essence, a currency converter—although you need to provide the exchange rate. Select View from the menu bar, click Toolbars, and select the Euro currency converter. Project 2007 has removed this capability, and a suggested practice is to use the Cost rate tables on the Costs tab of the Resource Information dialog box to indicate various currencies.

Calculating Costs in Project

It's important to understand the elements that make up the costs in Project that contribute to these methods. Figure 7.1 shows many of the fields important to cost calculations. To create a similar view, you could use the Gantt Chart and insert the particular cost fields, as well as select the Resource Sheet in the lower portion of a split window.

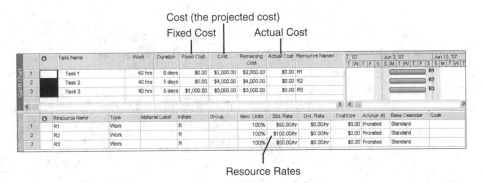

Figure 7.1   *Gantt Chart showing various cost fields*

The Cost field is the sum of all the other cost fields (Overtime Cost, Fixed Cost, and Cost) and reflects the projected costs of the project. The Cost field also includes the calculation of the number of hours (or whatever unit you measure work effort in, such as days) × the resource's rate. So in the preceding example, R1 is assigned to Task 1 for 40 hours and his Std. Rate is $50. So the cost of the task is the work effort × the rate, which is $2,000. Notice that the cost of Task 2 is different even though the hours are the same because the resource has a rate of $100. For the third task, both a resource and a Fixed Cost (a nonresource cost) are on the task. This means that the Cost for the task is the resource's effort (40 hours) × his or her rate ($100) plus the Fixed Cost of $1,000, so the Cost field is actually a total cost field. In many views in Project you will see a column named Total Cost; it is the same as the Cost field.

Overtime costs are part of all cost equations

Be aware that in all calculations for costs, planned, actual, and remaining overtime costs are included in any formula. To make the formulas and discussions simple, they will not be included. But if you are planning or recording any overtime, make sure you consider them in any of your cost analysis.

As with Project's work calculations, costs are applied at the assignment (resource applied to a task) and are summed at the task level. As shown in Figure 7.1, one resource is assigned a task. If more than one resource is assigned a task , then each assignment's costs are summed up in the Cost field as shown in Figure 7.2, which has the Resource Cost view in the upper window and the Task Form in the lower window. Each resource's cost is summed to the Cost field of Task 1.

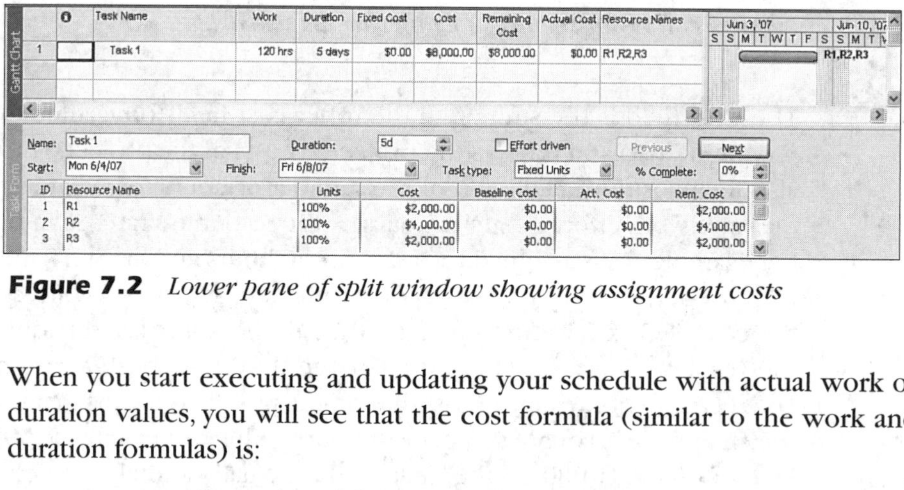

Figure 7.2 *Lower pane of split window showing assignment costs*

When you start executing and updating your schedule with actual work or duration values, you will see that the cost formula (similar to the work and duration formulas) is:

$$\text{Cost} = \text{Actual Cost} + \text{Remaining Cost}$$

The Cost field will always hold the calculation of work × the rates of the resources on a task. But what do you do with the other costs, such as nonlabor expenses estimated for a task? You can use the Fixed Cost field for nonlabor expenses. If you don't put resources on your project tasks, or you are performing duration-based scheduling and are not using the Work field to indicate effort, you could also use the Cost or Fixed Cost field to indicate the cost of the task.

Project, by default, calculates Actual Cost based on actual tracking

Project automatically calculates Actual Cost as actual work is entered on a task. You cannot type an amount directly into the Actual Cost field. You can change the default setting of Project automatically calculating Actual Cost by selecting Tools on the menu bar, clicking Options, and clearing the Actual Costs are always calculated by Microsoft Office Project check box on the Calculation tab.

Tracking costs is tricky based on not being able to enter incurred costs in the Actual Cost field. It's natural to want to, just as you can enter Actual Work if you want. If it's important to enter the Actual Costs, then turn off the setting that has Project automatically calculating the costs, but you will need to remember to enter them on the tasks. You cannot edit the Remaining Cost field at all, even if you deselect the automatic calculation.

Cost Accrual Methods

As you are building your schedule you might also want to consider what kind of accrual method you will use to indicate at what point in the task's schedule you want costs applied. You can designate that you want to incur costs at the beginning or end of the task or that you want the costs evenly distributed and incurred over the length of the task. These accrual methods are respectively labeled Start, End, and Prorated in Project. Prorated is the default setting. As you set the costs in the schedule-building phase, the costs will display according the method you select. See the section "Overtime Costs and Setting Accrual Method on the Resource Sheet" later in this chapter for more information about accrual methods.

Methods for Entering Costs

Project provides various methods of assigning costs to tasks, and the following list describes them. Each method is described individually, but you can include several methods on one task. For instance, you could have resources with resource rates on a task, and also have a Fixed Cost on the task to indicate a travel expense. The following list describes the most used methods:

- For Labor costs, indicates the cost of labor on a project. Please note that you could use Standard Rate and Per use Cost for equipment as well, which are work resources in Project.

   Standard Rates: Use resource rates and assign the resource to a task. To calculate costs using rates, assign rates to each resource in the Resource Sheet (Std. Rate and Ovt. Rate fields) and resources to each task. Project calculates each task's costs based on the hours assigned to each resource on the task. Project expects you to use this method to calculate labor costs. This supports the bottom-up method of estimating.

   Per use Costs: Use a Per use Cost to assign the resource to a task. To calculate a cost each time a resource is used, assign a Per use Cost in the Resource Sheet (the Cost/Use field) to charge a cost each time the resource is assigned to a task. A per use cost does not vary with the time the resource is used. The duration of the task can be 5 weeks or 5 days, but the cost is charged only once. Note that when the resource is assigned, Project uses the resource's assignment units in the calculation. This supports the bottom-up method of estimating.

   Please note that you could use this field for nonlabor costs to indicate a cost per use of a piece of equipment, which is still a work resource.

- For nonlabor costs, indicates the costs not related to labor (e.g., travel, services, machine or hardware purchases).

   Fixed cost: To calculate costs for nonlabor costs, enter a cost directly into the Fixed Cost field (e.g., $1,500 for travel or vendor services). This might often be combined with your assigning resources with rates to tasks. The total cost of the task will be a combination of the two costs. This supports the bottom-up method of estimating.

   Cost resource: In Project 2007, create a cost resource and assign the resource to an individual task. When you assign the cost resource, you can enter the projected cost as well. This supports the bottom-up method of estimating.

   Material cost: Use material resource rates and assign the resource to a task. To calculate costs using materials, assign material resources with a rate in the Std. Rate field. The rate is used for each measurable unit applied to the task. For instance, you have a task that will require you to rent a bus, and you will have to pay for the gas separately. You would assign a unit of measure (gallon) and a rate ($3.50) and estimate the amount of gallons it will take to complete the task. If you estimate

100 gallons, the cost of the task for the consumption of the gas will be $350. This supports the parametric method of estimating.

The following describe the various methods to indicate overall project budget costs:

- Use a Fixed Cost on the project summary task. Enter a total project budget amount in the Fixed Cost field of the project summary task. Note that you cannot use the Cost field to enter an overall budget amount on the project summary task. If you use Project 2007, use the budget resource rather than this method. This supports the top-down method of estimating. If you use this method, note that the rolled-up Cost field will include the Actual Cost plus the Fixed Cost in the summary project task line.

- In Project 2007, use a budget resource (applied to a cost resource) on the project summary task and assign the resource on the project summary task to contribute to an overall project budget. Note that you could have several budget costs (e.g., direct or indirect budget costs). This supports the top-down method of estimating.

> **You can enter a cost amount directly into the Cost field**
>
> You can enter a value into the Cost field directly to indicate the cost of a task. However, it is hard to track what the cost represents, although you could indicate what it represents in a Task Note. If you have an entry in the Cost field and enter another cost over it, Project will put the difference between the new Cost value and the previous cost value into the Fixed Cost field.

Examples of Entering Costs

To illustrate the various methods of assigning costs take a look at Figure 7.3. The Resource Sheet view for resources has various rates for calculating costs when the resources are placed on tasks. This focuses on using costs in versions of Project prior to Project 2007. You can review the additional Project 2007 cost methods in the section "Costs in Project 2007" later in this chapter.

	Resource Name	Type	Material Label	Initials	Group	Max. Units	Std. Rate	Ovt. Rate	Cost/Use	Accrue At	Base Calendar
1	R1	Work		R		100%	$100.00/hr	$0.00/hr	$0.00	Prorated	Standard
2	R2	Work		R		100%	$0.00/hr	$0.00/hr	$500.00	Prorated	Standard
3	M1	Material	Gallon of gas	M			$3.50		$0.00	Prorated	
4	R3	Work		R		100%	$0.00/hr	$0.00/hr	$0.00	Prorated	Standard
5	R4	Work		R		100%	$100.00/hr	$0.00/hr	$50.00	Prorated	Standard

Figure 7.3 *Resource Sheet setup for various cost situations*

Each resource has the following setup:

- R1 has a standard rate of $100.

- R2 has a cost per use rate of $500.

- M1 has been set up as a material resource with a gallon unit of measure. The cost assigned to that unit is $3.50.

- R3 has no rate assigned. If you put R3 on a task, there will be no cost automatically calculated for the task.

- R4 has both a standard rate ($100) and a cost per use rate ($50).

For each of the various tasks shown in Figure 7.4, you can see how Project calculated the Cost field based on various cost entry methods.

	ⓘ	Task Name	Resource Names	Cost	Fixed Cost	Work	Duration
0		⊟ Cost Calcuations		$16,900.00	$0.00	200 hrs	5 days
1		Resource with Rate	R1	$4,000.00	$0.00	40 hrs	5 days
2		Fixed Cost	R3	$1,000.00	$1,000.00	40 hrs	5 days
3		Cost In Cost Field		$2,000.00	$2,000.00	0 hrs	5 days
4		Per Use Cost	R2	$500.00	$0.00	40 hrs	5 days
5		Material Resource	M1[100 Gallons of gas]	$350.00	$0.00	0 hrs	5 days
6		Rate and Fixed Cost	R1	$5,000.00	$1,000.00	40 hrs	5 days
7		Rate and Per Use Costs	R4	$4,050.00	$0.00	40 hrs	5 days

Figure 7.4 *Various tasks showing how costs are calculated*

- The first task, Resource with rate, shows R1 assigned to the task with a $100 rate. Project multiplies the 40 hours in the Work field by R1's standard resource rate of $100 to equal a total Cost of $4,000.

- The second task, Fixed Cost, shows R3 with no rates and $1,000 entered directly into the Fixed Cost field. Project automatically enters the Fixed Cost amount in the Cost field, too, to show the total cost on the task. Because the R3 resource has no rates, Project does not use the hours to calculate cost.

- The third task, Cost in Cost field, doesn't have a resource on it and $2,000 entered directly in the Cost field. Notice that Project also automatically entered the cost in the Fixed Cost field.

- The fourth task, Per use Cost, shows R2 assigned to a task with a per use rate of $500. The value of 40 hours in the Work field is not used to calculate the cost at all.

- The fifth task, Material Resource, shows how a material resource shows the Cost based on the number of units (notice the 100 in brackets) × the material rate, $3.50 in this case.

- The sixth task, Rate and Fixed Cost, shows a task can have a resource (R1) with a rate assigned (100 × 40 hours = $4,000) and a Fixed Cost ($1,000). The value of $5,000 in the Cost field is the total of both.

- The seventh and last task, Rate and Per use Cost, shows that you can also have a resource with a rate, and a Per use Cost at the same time. R4's assignment is calculated as Standard Rate (100) × work (40 hours) + a Per use Cost ($50) for a Total Cost of $4,050.

Also note that Fixed Cost does not show a rolled-up total on the project summary task.

To understand how each of these cost entry methods distributes costs over time using a prorated accrual method, take a look at the Task Usage view shown in Figure 7.5. Notice that the per use cost is applied at the beginning and all other costs are spread evenly across the timeframe.

	O	Task Name	Work	Details	Sep 9, '07 S	M	T	W	T	F	S
0		⊟ Cost Calcuations	200 hrs	Work		40h	40h	40h	40h	40h	
				Cost		$3,820.00	$3,270.00	$3,270.00	$3,270.00	$3,270.00	
1		⊟ Resource with Rate	40 hrs	Work		8h	8h	8h	8h	8h	
				Cost		$800.00	$800.00	$800.00	$800.00	$800.00	
		R1	40 hrs	Work		8h	8h	8h	8h	8h	
				Cost		$800.00	$800.00	$800.00	$800.00	$800.00	
2		⊟ Fixed Cost	40 hrs	Work		8h	8h	8h	8h	8h	
				Cost		$200.00	$200.00	$200.00	$200.00	$200.00	
		R3	40 hrs	Work		8h	8h	8h	8h	8h	
				Cost		$0.00	$0.00	$0.00	$0.00	$0.00	
3		Cost in Cost Field	0 hrs	Work							
				Cost		$400.00	$400.00	$400.00	$400.00	$400.00	
4		⊟ Per Use Cost	40 hrs	Work		8h	8h	8h	8h	8h	
				Cost		$500.00	$0.00	$0.00	$0.00	$0.00	
		R2	40 hrs	Work		8h	8h	8h	8h	8h	
				Cost		$500.00	$0.00	$0.00	$0.00	$0.00	
5		⊟ Material Resource	0 hrs	Work							
				Cost		$70.00	$70.00	$70.00	$70.00	$70.00	
		M1	100 Gallons of gas	Work (		20	20	20	20	20	
				Cost		$70.00	$70.00	$70.00	$70.00	$70.00	
6		⊟ Rate and Fixed Cost	40 hrs	Work		8h	8h	8h	8h	8h	
				Cost		$1,000.00	$1,000.00	$1,000.00	$1,000.00	$1,000.00	
		R1	40 hrs	Work		8h	8h	8h	8h	8h	
				Cost		$800.00	$800.00	$800.00	$800.00	$800.00	
7		⊟ Rate and Per Use Cos	40 hrs	Work		8h	8h	8h	8h	8h	
				Cost		$850.00	$800.00	$800.00	$800.00	$800.00	
		R4	40 hrs	Work		8h	8h	8h	8h	8h	
				Cost		$850.00	$800.00	$800.00	$800.00	$800.00	

Figure 7.5   *Task Usage view showing distribution of costs over a week*

Costs in Project 2007

Two new capabilities in Project 2007 will help you manage costs better than previous versions: the Cost resource and the Budget resource. The Cost resource allows you to add a resource to a task and enter costs. The Budget resource allows you to designate cost resources as budget resources so they can be used to compare the project budget to actual costs for variance reporting.

Cost Resource

Perhaps one of the most flexible additions in Project 2007 is the Cost resource. You could create a resource called Travel and assign the resource to tasks as well as assign varying costs for travel on each task. The Cost resource functions similarly to the Fixed Cost field, but because you can name the resource, you can assign one or multiple Cost resources to a task. The Cost resource is not dictated by the Work, Duration, and Units fields as all other kinds of resources are.

To enter costs using Cost resources, you will create all the Cost resources in the Resource Sheet. Then, you can enter a specific cost for the cost resource as you're assigning it to the task as shown in Figure 7.6. You can then assign the same resource to the next task at a completely different cost.

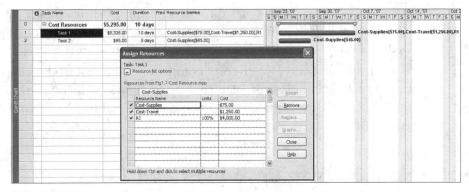

Figure 7.6 *Cost resources contributing to the cost of a task*

Budget Resource

You can assign a Budget resource in Project 2007 that allows you to set up the overall project budget on the project summary task (zero level). Then you can track actual costs to compare with the original budgeted costs. This is similar to using the Fixed Cost field on the project summary task in previous versions of Project, although you can create and assign more than one Budget resource. Figure 7.7 shows two Cost resources (Labor and Non-labor), designated as Budget resources, assigned to the project summary task with the total budget for each.

	🛈	Task Name	Budget Cost	Details	M	T	W	T	F	S	Sep 30, '07 S
0		⊟ BudgetCost	$225,000.00	Cost							
				Budget	$22,500.00	$22,500.00	$22,500.00	$22,500.00	$22,500.00		
		Labor Budget	$150,000.00	Cost							
				Budget	$15,000.00	$15,000.00	$15,000.00	$15,000.00	$15,000.00		
		Non-labor Budget	$75,000.00	Cost							
				Budget	$7,500.00	$7,500.00	$7,500.00	$7,500.00	$7,500.00		
1		Task 1		Cost							
				Budget							
2		Task 2		Cost							
				Budget							

Figure 7.7 *Adding Budget resource to project summary task in Task Usage view*

Which Costs Do You Use?

With all of the choices for entering costs, you will need to think through how you want to plan for and track costs. Use the Rates field for resources if you are doing effort-based scheduling, and Fixed Costs for nonlabor costs (or if you have Project 2007, the Cost resource). If you are using duration-based scheduling, enter costs directly into the Cost or Fixed Cost field for each task. If you do not need to track costs at a task level, you can add the budget amount in Fixed Cost, or use the Budget resource in Project 2007.

With this basic overview of costs complete, in the rest of the chapter I discuss how Project helps you plan your project budget and enter your planned cost. The next few sections in the book describe how you actually use the cost methods just described.

Assigning Costs to Resources and Tasks

Chapter 6, "Understanding Resources and Their Effects on Tasks," focused on assigning resources to tasks to indicate the work they need to perform. It also focused on some of the attributes that describe characteristics of a resource, such as their work type (work or material). Rates assigned to resources are another kind of attribute that describes the resource. In this section, I describe in detail how you assign resource and task costs in Project. I also discuss some of the issues you might have in tracking your costs once you start updating your project with actual work or costs.

Viewing Costs on a Project

Before going into entering costs, you might be interested in various views that can help you enter and view cost information. To view costs while in the Gantt Chart view, use the Split Window function, because you can see each resource's specific information easily, as shown in Figure 7.8:

1. Select Window from the menu bar and click Split.
2. As usual, the Task Form displays, but to see the cost information you need to right-click in the gray area next to the lower window and select the Resource Cost view for the Task Form.
3. In the upper Gantt Chart view, make sure your cursor is on the task for which you want to review resource cost information.
4. Remove the split by selecting Window from the menu bar and then clicking Remove Split.

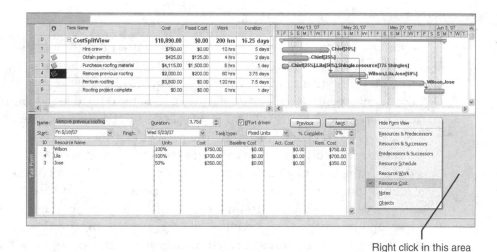

Right click in this area

Figure 7.8 *Select Resource Cost view in the Task Form by right-clicking in the gray area*

You can also see cost information by using the preestablished Cost Table as shown in Figure 7.9.

1. From the Gantt Chart view, select View from the menu bar.

2. Click Table: Cost. Although this table contains the major cost fields, Work, Duration, and Resources are not in the table, although you can see the Gantt Chart to the right to understand what contributes to the cost calculations. You might prefer to just insert the Cost, Fixed Cost, and Actual Cost columns in the Gantt Chart, and use the Cost Table only when you want to analyze cost variances.

3. To return to the Gantt Chart view select View from the menu bar and click Table: Entry.

	Task Name	Fixed Cost	Fixed Cost Accrual	Total Cost	Baseline	Variance	Actual	Remaining
0	⊟ CostTable	$0.00	Prorated	$10,890.00	$0.00	$10,890.00	$300.00	$10,590.00
1	Hire crew	$0.00	Prorated	$750.00	$0.00	$750.00	$300.00	$450.00
2	Obtain permits	$125.00	Prorated	$425.00	$0.00	$425.00	$0.00	$425.00
3	Purchase roofing mat	$1,500.00	Prorated	$4,115.00	$0.00	$4,115.00	$0.00	$4,115.00
4	Remove previous roo	$200.00	Prorated	$2,000.00	$0.00	$2,000.00	$0.00	$2,000.00
5	Perform roofing	$0.00	Prorated	$3,600.00	$0.00	$3,600.00	$0.00	$3,600.00
6	Roofing project compl	$0.00	Prorated	$0.00	$0.00	$0.00	$0.00	$0.00

Figure 7.9 *Cost Table view*

Entering Labor Costs for Tasks

To enter costs for labor you might decide to use rates for a resource. You would assign each team member a rate that then multiplies the hours assigned to the team member per task to calculate costs accurately. However, many organizations decide they do not want to include individual rates for resources because they feel this reveals resources' salaries to people who can access the schedule, including the project manager. Before your organization dismisses using rates to calculate costs to your project schedules, consider creating generic rates that are representative of the value of the various skilled positions in an organization. This generic rate is not based on salary and everyone would need to understand that. The rate often contains both direct and indirect costs, as well as an averaged rate for people in the position. For instance, a business analyst might have a rate of $30, and a financial analyst might have a rate of $25. If your organization is not comfortable with putting rates on the project schedule, you might want to just include overall budget amounts for labor and nonlabor costs on the project summary task.

Consulting firms like to indicate a billing rate to help understand what they should bill the customer, but the billing rate is usually different than the costs of the resource. Billing rates usually contain some kind of profit margin (hopefully). The billing rate can also be entered via the Rate field. In the next section, you can learn how you could show both your costs and your billing rates in one project using a Cost Rate table with both rates.

There is no out-of-the box solution for hiding costs on a project

Many organizations would like to include costs on a project, but restrict access and viewing to only certain people, especially when they are connected to resource rates. Unfortunately, Project has no out-of-the-box solution for hiding costs if you obtain the project file (of course, you can hide the information in printouts). If you would like this capability, you would need to customize the solution through a technical development effort. Although this might seem apparent, you can't just "Hide" the Cost columns either; anyone who knows how to use Project can find all the fields that describe the project's costs.

Entering Hourly Rates for Resources

If you choose to show estimated costs for tasks by assigning rates to resources, do the following:

1. Select View from the menu bar and click Resource Sheet.

2. Enter an amount in the Std. Rate field for the resource, as shown in Figure 7.10. As this is an attribute of the resource, you might find it much easier to enter this when you are first adding all of the resources to the Resource Sheet as described in Chapter 6.

Rates Assigned

		Resource Name	Type	Max. Units	Std. Rate	Ovt. Rate	Cost/Use	Accrue At	Base Calendar	Code
1		R1	Work	100%	$50.00/hr	$0.00/hr	$0.00	Prorated	Standard	
2		R2	Work	100%	$100.00/hr	$0.00/hr	$0.00	Prorated	Standard	

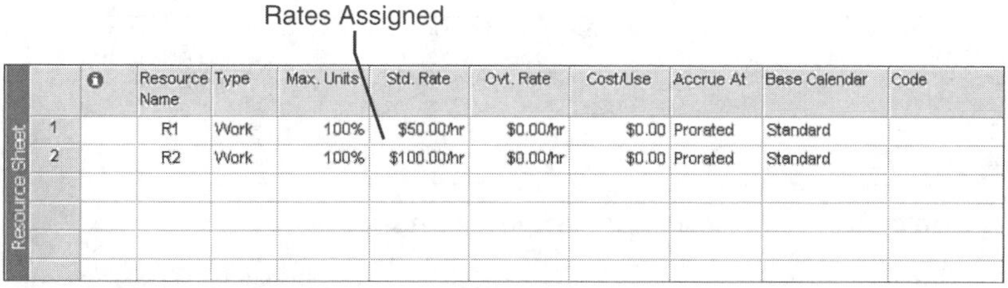

Figure 7.10   *Standard Rate assigned to two resources*

3. Assign the resource to the task as described in Chapter 6.

4. Enter the Duration or Work estimates in the Gantt Chart or some other task entry view and the cost is automatically estimated by an hourly rate based on the hours in the day and will be added to the Cost field for the task.

If you would like to use a daily rate, simply enter the amount (such as $100), and enter a "d" after the slash in the Std. Rate field to replace the hr in the field. You could even set a rate at per minute (min) or month (mon).

Entering Per Use Cost for Resources

If you want to enter a one-time cost for each time a resource is used, enter an amount in the Cost/Use field for a resource. Per use costs are useful when the amount of time you use the resource does not affect its cost. A per use cost is like a fixed fee for a resource. Perhaps you would like to indicate that a vendor is charging $500 for a task. You do not care whether the vendor works on the task for 50 hours or for 5 hours; the charge of the vendor on the task is $500. To use the Cost/Use, follow these steps:

1. Select View from the menu bar and click Resource Sheet.

2. In the Cost/Use field, enter the amount you want to be assigned for the one-time use of the resource.

3. Assign the resource to the task. The per use cost will added to the Cost field of the task.

Figure 7.11 shows the assignment of a per use cost versus a rate assigned to a resource.

Per use rate

	❶	Resource Name	Type	Max. Units	Std. Rate	Ovt. Rate	Cost/Use	Accrue At
1		R1-per use	Work	100%	$0.00/hr	$0.00/hr	$100.00	Prorated
2		R2-rates	Work	100%	$100.00/hr	$0.00/hr	$0.00	Prorated

Figure 7.11   *Per use cost assigned to resource*

In Figure 7.12, the Task Usage view shows how the cost is assigned in a cost per use in a time-phased view (the Task Usage view). Even though both resources are set to a Prorated accrual method, the first resource (cost/use) has the cost assigned on the first day, whereas the second resource, who has a standard rate applied, is distributed over the time he is assigned to the task. You might want to change the Accrue At field to End if you would like to incur the cost at the end of a per use cost on a task. Remember that this will be charged for each use of the resource, so this is best used on vendor tasks, travel, or other kinds of resources for which you don't mind incurring the costs at the beginning of the task.

	❶	Task Name	Work	Details	Sep 23, '07					
					S	M	T	W	T	F
1		⊟ Per-use cost	40 hrs	Work		8h	8h	8h	8h	8h
				Cost		$100.00	$0.00	$0.00	$0.00	$0.00
				Act. Cost						
		R1-per use	40 hrs	Work		8h	8h	8h	8h	8h
				Cost		$100.00	$0.00	$0.00	$0.00	$0.00
				Act. Cost						
2		⊟ rate cost	40 hrs	Work		8h	8h	8h	8h	8h
				Cost		$800.00	$800.00	$800.00	$800.00	$800.00
				Act. Cost						
		R2-rates	40 hrs	Work		8h	8h	8h	8h	8h
				Cost		$800.00	$800.00	$800.00	$800.00	$800.00
				Act. Cost						

Figure 7.12   *Per use cost assigned to resource on the first day, Standard rate distributed over time*

Entering Nonlabor Costs

Entering Costs for Material Resources

You can use material resources to help you estimate cost for items such as construction materials (number of boards per house), transportation fuel (gallons needed to transport your product across country), or laying cable (feet needed for laying cable for a computer room). You can create material costs following this procedure:

1. On the Resource Sheet, enter a resource name (e.g., Cable) and select Material in the Type field as shown in Figure 7.13. In this case the cost estimate for the resource is based on the number of feet of cable that is needed on a task.

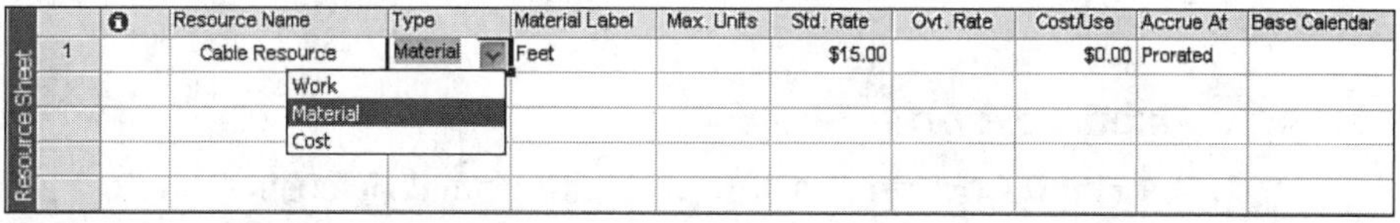

	ⓘ	Resource Name	Type	Material Label	Max. Units	Std. Rate	Ovt. Rate	Cost/Use	Accrue At	Base Calendar
1		Cable Resource	Material ▾	Feet		$15.00		$0.00	Prorated	
			Work							
			Material							
			Cost							

Figure 7.13 *Selecting material to indicate a material resource*

2. Enter a per unit rate for the material resource in the Std. Rate field.
3. Select View and click Gantt Chart.
4. Use your favorite method for adding the resource to a task. It's best to use a method in which the Units field displays so you can change it to the number of material units you will need for the task. You might use the Assign resources button, and change the Units as shown in Figure 7.14. The total cost of the task will be increased by the rate on the material resource multiplied by the amount of material (units) needed.

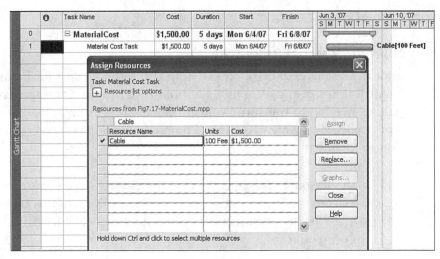

Figure 7.14 *Material resource assigned to a task*

Entering a Fixed Cost on a Task

Use a Fixed Cost on a task to indicate nonlabor costs. To enter a Fixed Cost, follow these steps:

1. Insert the Fixed Cost column by selecting Insert from the menu bar and clicking Column. Select Fixed Cost from the Column Definition dialog box and click OK.

2. In the Fixed Cost field, enter the amount of the Fixed Cost for the task.

3. Double-click on the task and select the Notes tab on the Task Information dialog box, enter a note that describes the Fixed Cost, and click OK.

Entering Cost Resource on a Task (Project 2007 Only)

To use a Cost resource (available only in Project 2007), you first need to indicate that a resource is a cost, not a work or material resource. To use a Cost resource, do the following:

1. On the Resource Sheet, enter a resource name (e.g., Travel) and select Cost in the Type field as shown in Figure 7.15. Notice that after you select Cost, you can no longer enter costs in the Std. Rate or Cost/Use fields.

	ⓘ	Resource Name	Type	Material Label	Initials	Group	Max. Units	Std. Rate	Ovt. Rate	Cost/Use
1		Cost-Travel	Cost		C					
2		Cost-Supplies	Cost ▾		C					
			Work							
			Material							
			Cost							

Figure 7.15   *Selecting Cost type to indicate a cost resource*

2. Select View from the menu bar and click Gantt Chart. You will need a dialog box that also includes the Cost field in it. On the task to which you want to assign a cost resource, select either the Assign Resources button (or select Tools from the menu bar and click Assign Resources) or use the Resources tab after double-clicking the task. Both of these dialog boxes contain the Cost field where you can enter the amount for the cost on the resource cost.

3. In the dialog box, select the Cost resource you want to assign, enter the amount of the cost in the Cost field as shown in Figure 7.16, and select Assign.

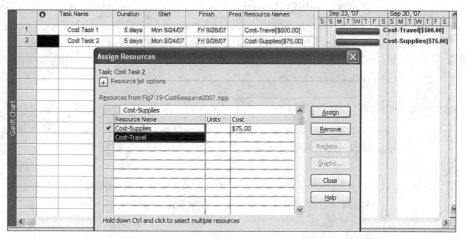

Figure 7.16   *Use the Assign Resources dialog box to assign cost to cost resource*

The Task Usage view, shown in Figure 7.17, shows that duration is still included, work is not, and the costs are distributed evenly over the week. The Cost resource can be added to tasks with work resources on them, and can be named specifically, such as vendor, travel, fees, supplies, or whatever particular cost you are indicating.

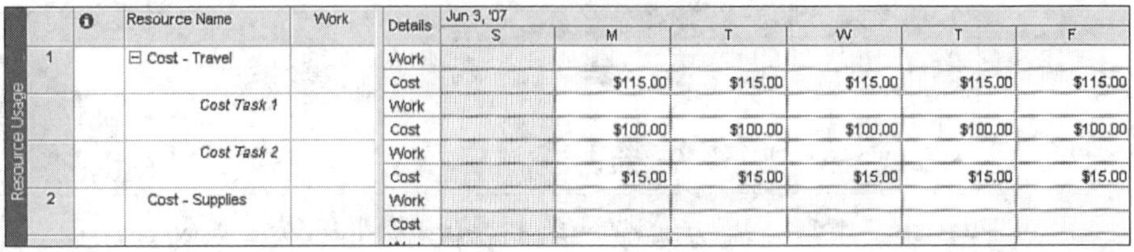

	❶	Resource Name	Work	Details	Jun 3, '07					
					S	M	T	W	T	F
1		⊟ Cost - Travel		Work						
				Cost		$115.00	$115.00	$115.00	$115.00	$115.00
		Cost Task 1		Work						
				Cost		$100.00	$100.00	$100.00	$100.00	$100.00
		Cost Task 2		Work						
				Cost		$15.00	$15.00	$15.00	$15.00	$15.00
2		Cost - Supplies		Work						
				Cost						

Figure 7.17   *Task Usage view showing resource costs distributed over time*

Custom Cost Fields

You can create your own special custom cost fields to indicate particular costs you need to show for your project. Select Insert from the menu bar, and click Column. Scroll down to the cost fields to see custom fields Cost 1 through 10. You can use the fields to directly enter special cost information for your project.

Entering Budget

In some cases, you might want to just include the overall budget in a project rather than detailed costs or you might want to hold the budget and be able to compare to it as you start recording actual costs. In Project 2002 and Project 2003 you can enter a Fixed Cost on the project summary task to indicate a budget, and in Project 2007 you have a new capability to enter budget using a Budget resource.

Entering Budget Using Fixed Cost

If you want to enter and monitor your original project budget using a single number, do the following:

1. If you do not have a project summary task showing, in the project file, select Tools from the menu bar and click Options. The Options dialog box opens. Select the View tab, and in the bottom right corner, select the Show project summary task check box and click OK.

2. Once the project summary task is displaying, insert the Fixed Cost column by selecting Insert from the menu bar and clicking Column. Select Fixed Cost from the Column Definition dialog box and click OK.

3. On the zero project summary task line, enter the budget amount in the Fixed Cost field. Because Fixed Costs do not roll up to summary tasks, the Fixed Cost field is ideal for holding the overall budget number.

Once you enter all of your costs, you can compare your projected costs (showing in the project summary task Cost field) and the budget amount in the Fixed Cost field. As you start entering actual progress information, you can compare Actual Cost to the Fixed Cost field.

Entering Budget Resources in Project 2007

If you want to enter and monitor your original project budget, you can use the new budget resource in Project 2007. A budget resource should be assigned to the project summary task. To use a budget resource, do the following:

1. In the Resource Sheet, add a resource name indicating it is a budget resource.

2. Click the Type field, and select Cost as the resource type. Note that for budget costs, you must use a cost resource.

3. Double-click the resource. You will see the Resource Information dialog box, similar to Figure 7.18. Most selections are unavailable because you have already made the resource a cost resource. Select the General tab, click the Budget indicator on the right side of the dialog box, and then click OK. Rate fields are disabled on the Resource Sheet.

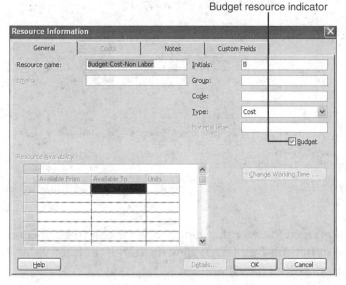

Figure 7.18 *Budget resource setup*

4. Select View from the menu bar and click Gantt Chart.

5. Because you need to display the project summary task to assign budget resources, select Tools on the menu bar and click Options (if you do not already have the project summary task showing). On the General tab, select the Show project summary task indicator and click OK.

6. Select the project summary task and use your favorite method of assigning resources. You might click the Assign Resources button on the toolbar. In the Assign Resources dialog box, select the budget resource or resources you want to assign and click Assign. You will see the budget resources assigned similar to what is shown in Figure 7.19, which is showing assignments already. You can enter budget information at any time during the schedule-building process.

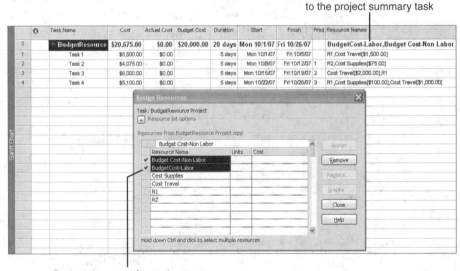

Budget resources assigned to the project summary task

Budget resources for assignment

Figure 7.19   *Budget resources assigned to the project summary task*

7. Next you need to enter the budget cost values. You can enter them only in either the Task Usage view or Resource Usage view. Select View from the menu bar and click Task Usage.

8. To enter the budget costs, you must first add the Budget cost field. Select Insert from the menu bar and click Column. Select Budget cost from the Column Definition dialog box and click OK.

9. In the Budget Cost field, enter the budget amounts for all budget resources you have assigned to the project summary task (see Figure 7.20). You can only enter a value on the resource lines for the project summary task.

Only entry fields of costs for budget resources

	❶	Task Name	Budget Cost	Cost	Actual Cost	Details	W	T	F	S	Mar 18, S
0		⊟ BudgetResource Project	$20,000.00	$20,675.00	$0.00	Work					
		Budget Cost-Non Labor	$8,000.00			Work					
		BudgetCost-Labor	$12,000.00			Work					
1		⊟ Task 1		$5,500.00	$0.00	Work					
		R1		$4,000.00	$0.00	Work					
		Cost Travel		$1,500.00	$0.00	Work					
2		⊟ Task 2		$4,075.00	$0.00	Work					
		R2		$4,000.00	$0.00	Work					
		Cost Supplies		$75.00	$0.00	Work					
3		⊟ Task 3		$6,000.00	$0.00	Work					
		R1		$4,000.00	$0.00	Work					
		Cost Travel		$2,000.00	$0.00	Work					
4		⊟ Task 4		$5,100.00	$0.00	Work					
		R1		$4,000.00	$0.00	Work					
		Cost Travel		$1,000.00	$0.00	Work					
		Cost Supplies		$100.00	$0.00	Work					

Figure 7.20 *Budget entered on budget resources in Task Usage view*

Notice that other costs have been entered into the project and show in the Cost field on the Task Usage view and in Figure 7.19 on the Gantt Chart. As you can see, the Budget Cost was supposed to be $20,000 and the plan shows $20,675. This is pretty close, but you'd have to take a closer look. In reviewing the Resource Usage view, you would see that the project is over-budget on the labor costs by $4,000. In the schedule-building process during planning, you might be able to make some adjustments by reviewing the budget and the costs in views. Alternately, now that you've actually built a more detailed plan and it has provided a more realistic budget, you might go back to the sponsor and ask for your planned costs to supersede the old budget figures.

Overtime Costs and Setting Accrual Method on the Resource Sheet

There are two more considerations for setting up how costs resource assignments will calculate: overtime and the accrual method. Both of these factors need to be considered during planning, but they matter most during execution of the project (unless you plan for overtime, which I hope you don't). If you do have situations where a resource has a different rate for overtime (some people get paid time and a half), enter the rate in the Ovt. Rate field. When you enter time in the Actual Overtime work field during project execution, then the Ovt. Rate will be used to calculate the actual costs for the tasks. Also, these overtime rates and costs are part of the total Cost calculation.

Many organizations have rules about when the costs are to be "put on the books." The financial rules of an organization often determine when costs should be recognized for accounting purposes. If you want the actual costs to be accrued differently than the default prorated method in the Accrue At field as shown in Figure 7.21, select Start or End.

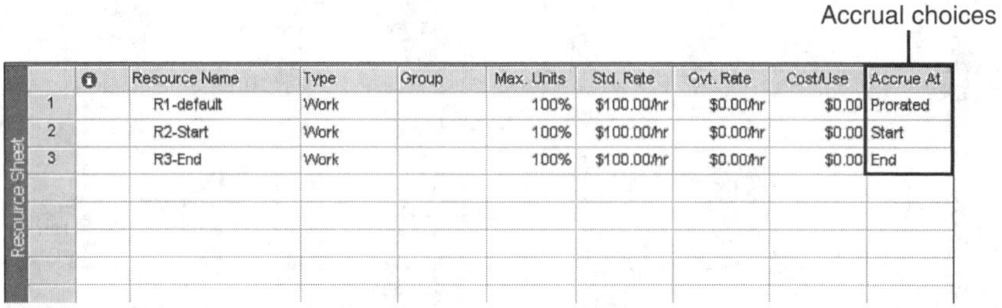

	Resource Name	Type	Group	Max. Units	Std. Rate	Ovt. Rate	Cost/Use	Accrue At
1	R1-default	Work		100%	$100.00/hr	$0.00/hr	$0.00	Prorated
2	R2-Start	Work		100%	$100.00/hr	$0.00/hr	$0.00	Start
3	R3-End	Work		100%	$100.00/hr	$0.00/hr	$0.00	End

Figure 7.21 *Accrue at field with selections of Start, Prorated, and End*

In the Task Usage view (shown in Figure 7.22) work is evenly distributed over the week. However, the costs are distributed according to the following methods:

- **Prorated:** Costs are distributed evenly over the task's duration and will be incurred on the dates shown.
- **Start:** The entire cost is incurred as soon as the task starts.
- **End:** The entire cost is incurred as soon as the task ends.

You can also change how Fixed costs will be accrued for all tasks by selecting Tool from the menu bar and clicking Options. On the Calculation tab you can select the accrual method in the Default Fixed Costs Accrual field.

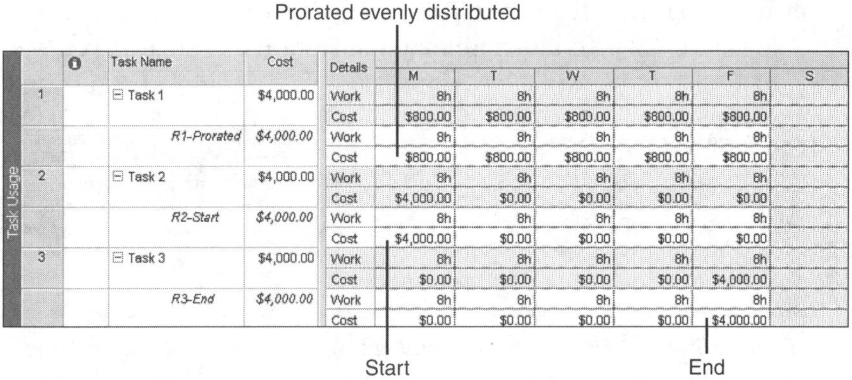

Prorated evenly distributed

	❶	Task Name	Cost	Details	M	T	W	T	F	S
1		⊟ Task 1	$4,000.00	Work	8h	8h	8h	8h	8h	
				Cost	$800.00	$800.00	$800.00	$800.00	$800.00	
		R1-Prorated	*$4,000.00*	Work	8h	8h	8h	8h	8h	
				Cost	$800.00	$800.00	$800.00	$800.00	$800.00	
2		⊟ Task 2	$4,000.00	Work	8h	8h	8h	8h	8h	
				Cost	$4,000.00	$0.00	$0.00	$0.00	$0.00	
		R2-Start	*$4,000.00*	Work	8h	8h	8h	8h	8h	
				Cost	$4,000.00	$0.00	$0.00	$0.00	$0.00	
3		⊟ Task 3	$4,000.00	Work	8h	8h	8h	8h	8h	
				Cost	$0.00	$0.00	$0.00	$0.00	$4,000.00	
		R3-End	*$4,000.00*	Work	8h	8h	8h	8h	8h	
				Cost	$0.00	$0.00	$0.00	$0.00	$4,000.00	

Start   End

Figure 7.22 *Three accrual methods shown in one Task View*

Using the Roofing Example to Enter Costs

To further understand the best methods for entering costs, it might be easier to use the roofing project as an example. In the last chapter, the roofing project ended with resources, duration, and effort added. Now the example will include rates and fixed costs to show how the project costs and budget are calculated. Table 7.1 shows the rates of the resources and some special costs for tasks.

Table 7.1 *Rates for Roofing Project*

Resource	Hourly Rate or Fixed Cost
Chief	75
Wilson	25
Jose	35
Lila	35
Permit	$125
Shingles	$5 per shingle
Roofing supplies	$1,500
Removal trash bin	$200

After entering rates in the Resource Sheet for the project, it would look like Figure 7.23. To illustrate material resource estimates, you see shingles.

	Resource Name	Type	Material	Initials	Group	Max. Units	Std. Rate	Ovt. Rate	Cost/Use	Accrue At	Base Calendar
1	Chief	Work		C		25%	$75.00/hr	$0.00/hr	$0.00	Prorated	Standard
2	Wilson	Work		W		100%	$25.00/hr	$0.00/hr	$0.00	Prorated	Standard
3	Jose	Work		J		100%	$35.00/hr	$0.00/hr	$0.00	Prorated	Standard
4	Lila	Work		L		100%	$35.00/hr	$0.00/hr	$0.00	Prorated	Standard
5	Shingles	Material	Shingle	S			$5.00		$0.00	Prorated	

Figure 7.23 *Rates and material resource added to Resource Sheet*

Then, you would return to the Gantt Chart. Once the rates are assigned to the resources, Project starts calculating the budget. To include other costs you would do the following:

- Add $125 for a fixed cost of a permit on Obtain permits. Add a note explaining that the Fixed Cost on the task is for the permit.
- Enter the shingle material resource on the task Purchase roofing material and for the estimated 775 shingles Lila and the Chief would have to purchase.
- Add a fixed cost of $1,500 for the other roofing supplies. Add a note to the task indicating that the Fixed Cost is for roofing supplies.
- Include a Fixed Cost for the Remove previous roofing task and add a note explaining the cost is for the trash bin rental.

The result is shown in Figure 7.24. The total budget for the first iteration of the project plan is $12,440. The total project Cost is rolled up in the project summary task (zero line). Also notice that the Fixed Costs do not roll up to the top line and that the Cost field is actually a combination of the Fixed Cost and the cost of the resource rates based on the resource's hours of work on the task. The lower pane of the split window shows the cost of each resource for the Purchase roofing material task.

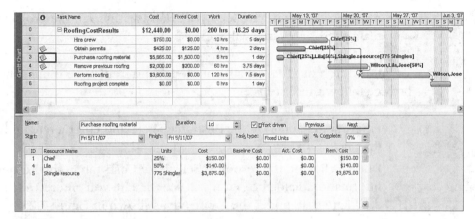

Figure 7.24   *Result of adding rates and other costs to the project*

Add notes if you are using Fixed Costs

Add notes to tasks if you are using Fixed Costs to identify the fixed costs. You might have a resource on a task when using Fixed Costs, so you need to make sure it's obvious what the fixed cost is.

The cost entry methods just described are probably the best methods for entering project costs, but you might also need to consider your organization's needs and how you are going to track tasks to decide how you will add costs to your project. If you are using Project 2007, you will probably start using Cost resources instead of Fixed Costs.

Assigning Different Rates to a Resource

Project has a nice feature that a lot of people don't know about or use, but it can help with many cost situations if you are using rates. You can use a rate table to indicate five different rates for a resource or have different rates for different time frames. A couple of examples for using this rate table might be the following:

- Your organization has a billing rate that you will charge the customer, and an internal costs rate, which will be your project's costs. You can then see the margin of profit you are expecting from your project.

- A project will continue for a year. Halfway through the project, your team's resource rates will increase.

To enter different rates on a resource for different time frames during the project, follow these steps:

1. Enter the resource on the Resource Sheet and enter a rate in the Std. Rate field.

2. Double-click on the resource. Select the Costs tab in the Resource Information dialog box. You will see the rate you entered in the Standard Rate field under the A rate tab as shown in Figure 7.25.

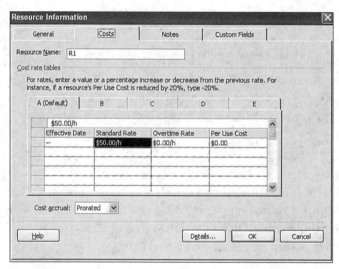

Figure 7.25 *Cost Rate Table showing Standard rate entered*

3. In the line just below the first line (for the same A tab), enter an Effective Date and a new rate as shown in Figure 7.26 and click OK.

As you can see, the rate change is from $50 to $100 on 6/10. You could also change the Overtime Rate, Per use Cost, and Accrual method on this tab. To continue the example, Figure 7.27 shows a 2-week task during the rate change time frame. The effective date of the rate change is the second week of the task. As you can see on the Task Usage view in Figure 7.27, the rate increases and each day's cost changes from $400 to $800.

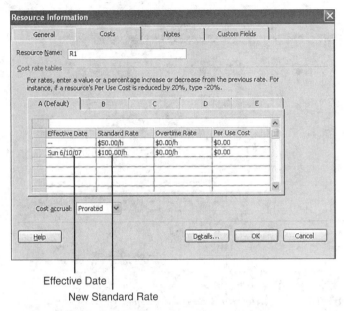

Effective Date
New Standard Rate

Figure 7.26 *New effective rate setting*

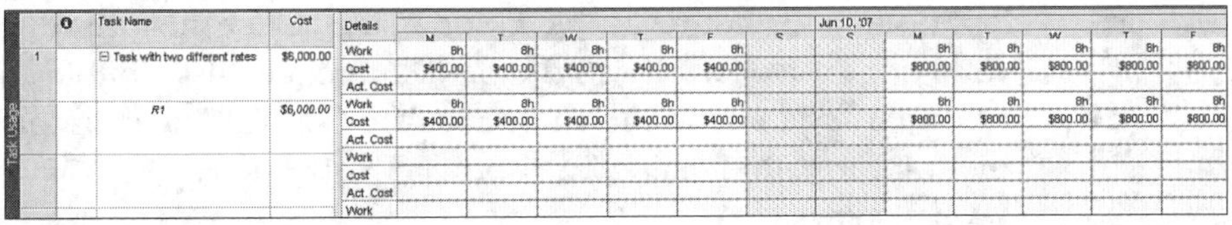

Figure 7.27 *Rate changes starting on effective date for new rate*

If you would like to have different rates in a schedule, you can use the A through E rate tabs. You will also have to indicate which rate to use when you are viewing the schedule. To set different rates in the same schedule, do the following:

1. Enter the resource on the Resource Sheet and enter the main rate you want to normally see in the Std. Rate field.

2. Double-click the resource. Select the Costs tab. You will see the rate you entered in the Standard Rate field under the A tab.

3. Click a different tab (in this example, the B tab), enter a rate in the Standard Rate field as shown in Figure 7.28 and click OK. In this example, the Standard rate for A is $50, and the B rate is $100.

Rate "B" selected

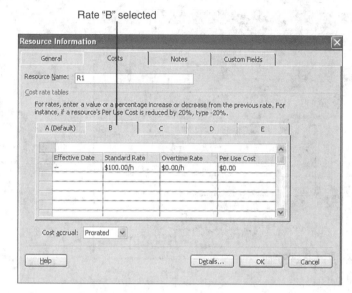

Figure 7.28 *Different rate (Rate B) on a project*

4. To view the change of costs for Rate B, select the Task Usage view. You can insert the Cost rate table column and select the rate you want from the drop-down list in the field. You could also double-click the resource assignment line and select the Cost rate table in the Assignment Information dialog box and click OK. See Figure 7.29 showing both displays.

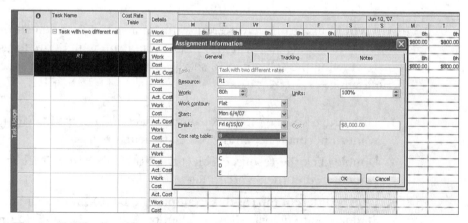

Figure 7.29 *Rate B assigned to resource*

Although Rate A was assigned as $50, the cost is now calculated as $100 because Rate B is used on the assignment. When you start tracking actual costs, you can toggle between rates to see the differences for the project based on the rates. Because you can't label the rate tabs, you will have to remember which tab is what rate or include this information in a note in the resource information.

Your Project Budget

In the preceding section, you saw how you can show budget for your project by entering a Fixed Cost or a budget cost resource (in Project 2007 only) on the zero line (project summary task) of your project. However, if you enter costs on tasks (directly or using rates on resources), then you are using the bottom-up cost estimating method. You can view the project budget based on the roll-up of the Cost field. You may have actually been provided a "budget" by your organization, but this is far more accurate, based on detailed planning of your team and you creating the schedule. There are several ways you can view your rolled up budget such as:

- In the Gantt Chart, make sure you show the project summary task line (zero line) from the View tab after selecting Tools and clicking Options. Then, insert the Cost column. The amount on the top line is the Project's estimated budget.

- Select Project from the menu bar, then click Project Information. Click the Statistics button in the lower left of the Project Information dialog box. The Project Statistics dialog box displays as shown in Figure 7.30. The estimated cost for the project based on your latest plans will be in the Current Cost field. Once you have finished iterating through planning your project, you will be using the Baseline Cost as your project budget.

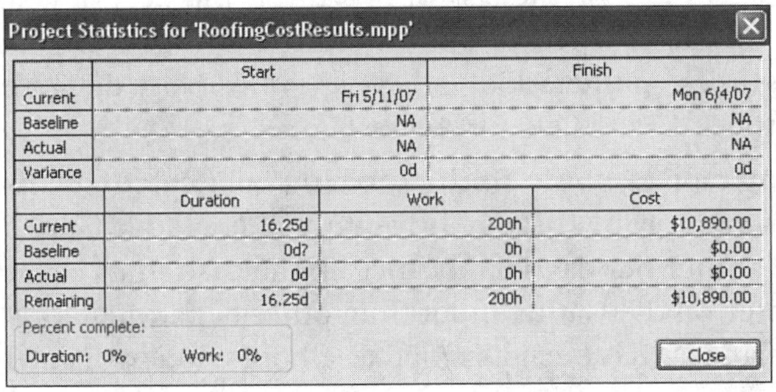

Project Statistics for 'RoofingCostResults.mpp'

	Start		Finish
Current		Fri 5/11/07		Mon 6/4/07
Baseline		NA		NA
Actual		NA		NA
Variance		0d		0d

	Duration	Work	Cost
Current	16.25d	200h	$10,890.00
Baseline	0d?	0h	$0.00
Actual	0d	0h	$0.00
Remaining	16.25d	200h	$10,890.00

Percent complete:
Duration: 0%   Work: 0%   Close

Figure 7.30 *Project budget showing in the Current Cost field.*

You might consider going back to your sponsor and showing him your project schedule with the Costs included and ask that the planned costs be considered as the true budget for your project.

Tips and Recommendations for Dealing with Costs

Although I've talked about all of the various methods for entering cost estimates in Project, you might still be wondering, "What's the best way?" The following list is a summation of some recommendations and some nuances about costs when you use Project to estimate costs and the project budget. It also contains a few things to think about when you start tracking costs, based on the cost entry method you chose. Hopefully, this will help you make decisions about how you will enter and track costs in Project.

- **For effort-based scheduling, use rates and let Project calculate your costs and actual costs**. Project will use the following formula (abbreviated by removing overtime costs) to calculate costs:

  Resource rate × Total hours on the task + Fixed costs = Cost

  Resource rate × Actual hours on the task + Actual fixed costs = Actual cost

  Please note the formula is based on the kind of measurement applied to the rate (e.g., hours or days). Don't forget that Cost is the projected cost and will change if your actual costs increase or decrease from your original cost estimate (usually based on the actual work increasing or decreasing).

- **For duration-based scheduling, use the Cost or Fixed Cost field to enter costs directly for tasks**. You will want to do this whether you have resources on the task or not. Insert the Cost or Fixed Cost columns into your schedule, and enter the costs for each task. If you have resources on the task to indicate responsibility, do not enter anything in the Std. Rate field for the resources.

- **Rounding causes some funky-looking cost calculations**. Because Project is multiplying by an hourly rate, you might have tasks that are less than 1 hour per day. For instance, in the case study at the end of this chapter, on the Gather input from other departments task, the project manager has been assigned to 4 hours total work at 17% over 3 days. This is 1.33 hours per day. If you were to continue to show the breakdown of costs on an hourly basis, the cost would become even stranger. So when the hourly costs multiplied by the hourly rate are added up, Project calculates the cost of the project manager's assignment to be $400.01, essentially caused by a rounding calculation. In some cases, the rounding can be quite annoying, but it is not more than a few cents per task.

- **Use the Rate field and Per use Cost fields together**. In some cases, you might have a rate on a resource, but each time that resource is used, there is an extra fee for using the resource. You can use the Per use field in the Resource Sheet to indicate this. If you do, not only will the Hours × Rate be calculated, but the per use fee will be added to the cost of the task. The last task in Figure 7.4 illustrated this possibility on Task 7: The resource had a Standard Rate, and a $50 Cost per Use rate.

- **You cannot edit actual costs by default**. Project will always calculate the actual costs when you enter percentage complete task progress information, or enter actual Work or Duration values in your schedule.

  You might want to enter costs directly into the Actual Cost field. You can set up your project schedule at the beginning to allow you to do this. However, you will have to remember to manually enter the costs according to how they are incurred and this is an all-or-nothing setting: It affects the entire schedule, so if you have some costs you want to enter manually, and others you want Project to calculate, you need to consider alternatives (discussed later).

  To manually enter all actual costs in your project, select Tools from the menu bar, and then click Options. On the Calculation tab, clear the Actual costs are always calculated by Microsoft Office Project check box as shown in Figure 7.31.

- **You can edit actual cost after a task is marked complete**. Although you cannot edit actual costs based on the default that has Project calculate the Actual costs for you, you can leave that selection on, and edit costs once a task has been marked 100% complete. In Figure 7.32, the task is marked 100% complete, and Project shows the Actual cost according to its calculation of Rate × Hours. It has evenly distributed the Actual costs.

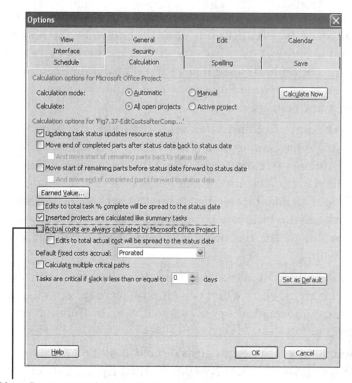

Manually enter costs by removing the checkmark

Figure 7.31 *Actual costs are always calculated by Microsoft Office Project check box is cleared*

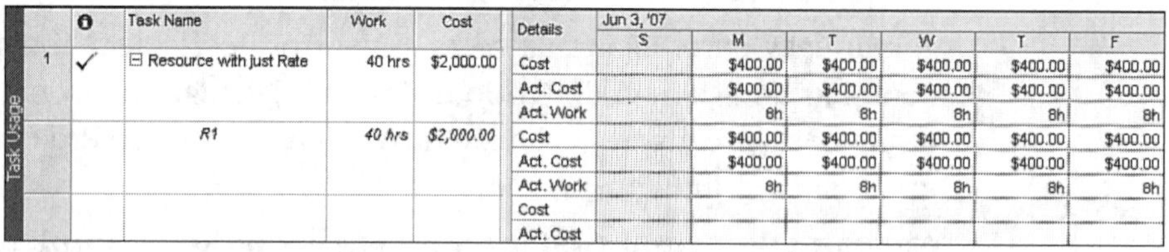

	❶	Task Name	Work	Cost	Details	Jun 3, '07					
						S	M	T	W	T	F
1	✓	⊟ Resource with just Rate	40 hrs	$2,000.00	Cost		$400.00	$400.00	$400.00	$400.00	$400.00
					Act. Cost		$400.00	$400.00	$400.00	$400.00	$400.00
					Act. Work		8h	8h	8h	8h	8h
		R1	40 hrs	$2,000.00	Cost		$400.00	$400.00	$400.00	$400.00	$400.00
					Act. Cost		$400.00	$400.00	$400.00	$400.00	$400.00
					Act. Work		8h	8h	8h	8h	8h
					Cost						
					Act. Cost						

Figure 7.32 *Actual cost calculated by Project according to plan when task is marked complete*

However, if you want to show exact dates of costs incurred rather than use Project's distribution, zero out the cost Project enters and enter the amount you want to show and on the date you want. You can also enter costs to indicate you exceeded planned costs. Figure 7.33 shows the situation of entering costs on the specific days you want to incur the costs and entering an actual cost that is over plan. The planned cost for the task was $2,000, which Project calculated. You can enter $1,000 on Tuesday and the final full cost on Friday. Because the actual cost was $200 more than the original cost, you can enter $1,200 on Friday. In case it worries you that you have lost what the original planned cost was, you will read about why you should use a baseline in Chapter 10, "Baselining: The Key to Tracking Your Schedule."

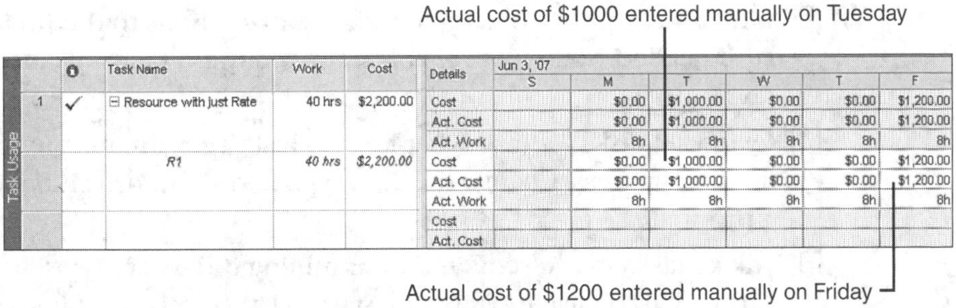

Actual cost of $1000 entered manually on Tuesday

Actual cost of $1200 entered manually on Friday

Figure 7.33 *Edited Actual Cost after task marked complete*

The Project Schedule Building Methodology So Far

Based on what you have learned, the following steps and sequence describe the best methods for building your schedule. The items emphasized in this chapter are indicated in italics. Because many organizations do not enter costs, I have also added a new "optional" indicator in this list.

The steps for building a project schedule so far are as follows:

☑ If you are using a template, select the appropriate template (you will probably want to change it based on the input of your project team). If you are building a project from scratch, build a WBS with your team, then move to the next step.

☑ Set up your project calendar if you do not have one available. Make sure you reflect your company's hours in Tools, Options, Calendar, if different than the defaults.

☑ In the Project Information dialog box, set your project Start date and make sure your project calendar is assigned to the project.

☑ Start building (if your project is from scratch) or editing (if you are using a template) your task list. Make sure you indicate summary tasks and subtasks to help indicate the outline of your project schedule.

☑ Add milestone tasks to indicate significant events, deliverables, or approval points in your project.

☑ Enter deadline dates for appropriate tasks. This is a better way of indicating dates when tasks need to be completed rather than typing in a Finish date on a task.

☑ Add task calendars to tasks to indicate exceptions to the project calendar if needed. You will probably not need these kinds of calendars often.

☑ Review all tasks. Decide what kind of tasks they are for the schedule building process. Change the Task type and Effort-driven fields if appropriate.

☑ Link all tasks in the schedule, determining if they are Finish-to-Start, Start-to-Start, Finish-to-Finish, or Start-to-Finish relationships. Link among phases or task groupings first, then link between phases or groupings. Use the Predecessor and Successor columns to help you see if all tasks are linked.

☑ Build the project team. Add all resources that might work on the project to the Resource Sheet for the project. If you are performing effort-based scheduling, enter the Maximum Units each resource can work on the project. You can use generic or real resources, but when you know who will do the work, you should replace generic resources with real resources.

☑ Assign the resources to each task. If you are performing Effort-based scheduling, you might need to change the percentage of allocation a resource is assigned to individual tasks in some cases.

☑ Enter estimates to project tasks. For effort-based scheduling, enter two of the three variables in the Work formula: Work = Duration × Units.

☑ Review the schedule and enter leads and lags on tasks if appropriate.

☑ Review the critical path and adjust tasks if appropriate.

☑ *[Optional] Set your cost default cost calculation methods: Have Project automatically calculate Actual Costs and decide on and set up your Cost Accrual method for the entire project.*

☑ *[Optional] Set up any other kinds of resources, such as material resources (set up cost and budget resources if you are using Project*

2007) if you want to include costs other than labor or equipment work costs in your project.

☑ *[Optional] Insert the Cost and Fixed Cost fields in the Gantt Chart view (or use the Table: Cost view). Enter Rates on resources, enter Fixed costs on tasks, or enter Total budget on the project summary task line depending on how your organization has decided to enter cost.*

Adding costs to the schedule can be very revealing. Managing a schedule is one thing, but seeing what a project actually costs based on the resources and other expenses of a project can make you a little more appreciative of staying on schedule.

Summary

Entering costs for your project helps you understand your project even more than just scheduling. Project managers, or anyone managing project work, have a lot of money in their hands. We often work for organizations that set project budgets prior to the project manager being assigned. Once the project manager is assigned, and the team scopes the project and creates the first blush of the schedule, it's possible that assigning costs can quickly show that someone greatly underestimated the budget for the project. If you do not consider the costs of the project, you are tackling only part of what it takes to do project management. It is possible that your organization deals with costs in other systems, which is fine. But there is a linkage between the schedule and the budget, and often it is hard to see the linkage if you do not have integrated systems or show the costs in the schedule. If you have the chance to enter costs for your projects (and, yes, it will create more work for you), then you should have all the underlying questions answered so you know how to enter your costs.

- Will your organization have you plan for and enter costs at all?
- Will you have rates you can assign resources or will you enter costs per task?
- Will you just need to enter the overall budget in the schedule and manage to that?
- What kind of accrual method do you need to use?

- Will you be tracking overtime costs?
- Do you want Project to calculate actual costs, or do you want to enter them directly?
- Are you managing just human resources, or do you need to include nonlabor expenses such as supplies, hardware and software purchases, travel, or fees?

Once you have answers to these questions, reading this chapter should have helped you understand how you will enter your costs to meet your needs. Once you are done entering the costs of your project, you are ready to move on to the next step: making sure you are ready to set the baseline to take a snapshot of your project's schedule and cost estimates prior to execution of the work.

Practice: Adding Costs to the House-Painting Project

The following practice exercises will help you practice adding resources rate and fixed costs to see how costs are calculated in projects. If you have Project 2007, you can practice using cost and budget resources as well.

Practice 7.1

Adding Resource Rates

Although the house-painting project is not a project that requires costing of tasks for the household doing the tasks, you might want to see what you will save by painting the house yourself, using typical rates a professional house-painting service might charge. In this practice, you will add rates to the house-painting project so you can see what it really might cost to have the project completed by professionals. To start, use the project called HousePainting-Practice-Chapter7-Practice1.mpp on your CD (or use a project you completed).

1. Because you have estimated the work effort and duration for the project, you are ready to enter the rates for the work on the project. After opening the project schedule, select View on the menu bar and click the Resource Sheet view.

2. Enter the rates as shown in Table 7.1 in the Std. Rate field for each resource.

Table 7.2   *Practice: Resource Rates*

Resource	Hourly Rate
Me	20
Spouse	25
Child	15

3. Return to the Gantt Chart view by selecting View on the menu bar, then click the Gantt Chart view.

4. Highlight the Work field (click on the column) and select Insert from the menu bar. The Column Definition dialog box opens. Select the Cost field from the Field name drop-down list and click OK.

5. View the total project budget so far on the project summary task Cost field. You realize you have supplies and other costs that have not yet been included in the estimate, so you will do so in the next practice. If you want to see the result, see the HousePainting-Practice-Chapter7-Practice1-Result.mpp file on the CD.

Practice 7.2

Practice Adding Fixed Costs

Use the file HousePainting-Practice-Chapter7-Practice2 on your CD for the following practice.

1. After opening the project schedule, highlight the Work field (click the column), then select Insert from the menu bar to open the Column Definition dialog box. Select the Fixed Cost field from the Field Name drop-down list and click OK.

2. On the Gather materials task, enter $125 as a Fixed Cost. What is the budget for the project so far? The Cost field on the project summary task line shows the budget.

3. Select View from the menu bar and click the Task Usage view. Click the first task, and click the Scroll to Task button in the Standard toolbar. (You could also press Ctrl + Shift + F5 to do the same thing.) Depending on when you are viewing the schedule, the work information might not be showing in the grid for the project. The Go to Selected Task function will bring up the first occurrence of work for the task.

4. Right-click on the right side of the view (where the grid is) and in the box that displays, click the Cost field. You will see the costs for the tasks and resources appear in the day-by-day grid. When you review the information,

you can see how the costs are evenly distributed over the time frame because you used the default accrual method of Prorated.

5. To see the Fixed Cost field in this view, right-click in the grid again. Click Detail Styles. In the Available fields list on the left, scroll down to the Fixed Cost field and click Show. When the field is entered on the right side, click OK. The Fixed Cost field will display on the grid as well, and you will see the amount distributed across the 3 days of the Gather materials task. Also, review all of the costs for the Child resource. Notice how the costs are distributed based on the daily hours scheduled for work.

6. Now, let's see how you can change the accrual method. Select View from the menu bar and click the Resource Sheet view. On the Child resource, select Start on the Accrue at drop-down list.

7. Select View from the menu bar and click the Task Usage view. Now review all the tasks for the Child and notice that the entire cost is shown on the first day of the task. If you would like to see the view after all of these changes, see HousePainting-Practice-Chapter7-Practice2-Result.mpp on the CD.

Practice 7.3

Practice Using Cost Resource in Project 2007

In this practice, you will create and assign a couple of cost resources to a task on the house-painting project. You can use the file HousePainting-Practice-Chapter7-Practice3-P2007.mpp for this exercise. Note that you can only open this file if you have Project 2007 until Microsoft finishes the converter program in late 2007.

1. After opening the project schedule, select View from the menu bar and click the Resource Sheet view. After the Child resource, enter Paint and then enter another resource called Brushes and other tools on the line after that.

2. For both resources, in the Type field, select Cost from the drop-down list.

3. Select View from the menu bar, and click the Gantt Chart view. For the Gather materials task, clear the amount in the Fixed Cost field by clicking on the cell. Press Del on your keyboard.

4. Select the Gather materials task. Select Tools from the menu bar and click Assign Resources. In the Assign Resources dialog box, assign $50 to the Brushes and other tools resource and $100 to the Paint resource, assign the resources to the task, and close the dialog box. If you would like to see the view after all of these changes, see HousePainting-Practice-Chapter7-Practice3-Result.mpp on the CD.

Practice 7.4

Practice Using a Budget Resource in Project 2007

In this practice, you will create and assign a budget resource for the house-painting project. You can use the file HousePainting-Practice-Chapter7-Practice4-P2007.mpp for this exercise. Note that you can only open this file if you have Project 2007 until Microsoft finishes the converter program in late 2007.

1. After opening the project schedule, select View from the menu bar and click the Resource Sheet view. After the Brushes and other tools line, enter Budget as a resource.

2. Click the Type field, and select Cost as the resource type. For budget costs, you must use a cost resource.

3. Double-click the resource. Select the General tab in the Resource Information dialog box, click the Budget indicator on the right side of the dialog box, and click OK.

4. Select View from the menu bar and click Gantt Chart.

5. To assign the budget resource to the project summary task line, highlight the top zero line and click the Assign resources button on the toolbar. In the Assign Resources dialog box select the budget resource and click Assign. You will see the budget resources assigned in the Resource names field for the project summary task.

6. Next you need to enter the budget cost value. You can only enter it in either the Task Usage or Resource Usage view. Select View from the menu bar and click Task Usage.

7. To enter the budget costs, you must first add the Budget cost field. Click on the Work column on the left side of the separator bar. Select Insert from the menu bar and click Column. Select Budget cost from the Column Definition dialog box and click OK.

8. In the Budget Cost field after the budget resource (not the top line), enter $4,000. You can only enter a value on the resource lines for the project summary task.

9. Select View from the menu bar and click Gantt Chart. Highlight the Cost column, select Insert from the menu bar, and click Column. Select Budget cost from the Column Definition dialog box and click OK. You can compare the Budget cost you had in mind with the projected Cost field that reflects your current costs if everything goes as planned in the schedule. It looks like you are doing fine. If you would like to see the view after all of these changes, see the HousePainting-Practice-Chapter7-Practice4-Result.mpp file on the CD.

Case Study: Adding Costs to the Schedule

On the VNLE project, Chris added Work and Duration estimates to the project schedule based on input from the project team. Now Chris will add the planned costs on the project. Chris decides she will use rates per hour, and she gets rates from the human resource department based on actual averaged rates, not on salaries. A few tasks where vendors are involved will be fixed price. The rates are included in Table 7.2.

Table 7.3 *Case Study Resource Rates*

Resource	Hourly Rate
Project manager	100
Executive sponsor	300
Core team	50 each
VP Sales	200
VP Marketing	200
VP Business development	200
COO	250
CIO	250
Business development person	50
Marketing person	50
Sales person	40
IT person	40
Logistics person	25
Marketing materials vendor	Fixed fee price of $1,000
Booth construction subcontractor	Fixed Fee price of $5,000
VN Web project manager	100
Catalog department person	25

Now, in some organizations, you would not see executive's time included in the costs of a project, but Chris feels that they are making significant contributions to the project, so she decides to include them. Also, because she did have the initial budget figure from June Thompson of $150,000, she can use that for the budget.

Open the file VNLE-Chapter7-Begin-CaseStudy.mpp to work on this case study and practice using costs in Chris's role.

1. First add rates to the resources on the Resource Sheet according to Table 7.2.

2. Also add a budget resource (if you have Project 2007) of $150,000 to the schedule. If you do not have Project 2007, enter the budget in the Fixed cost field of the project summary task. When you are done you can review the result of this work in VNLE-Chapter7-Result-CaseStudy.mpp.

3. What is the total budget based on the costs for resources so far for the project? See the Cost field on the project summary task to see the projected cost of the project.

Chris knows there a lot of other expenses that still need to be entered, such as travel, lodging, and all the handouts and giveaways, so she will have to go through another iteration of updating the project to add those in. After that, she will still need to fine-tune and make corrections. After Chris completes entering the other costs, she realizes that the next step is to analyze the schedule. Chris realizes that just because she has finished applying the best method for building a schedule, she isn't done. It is not perfect the first time it's built and she has made sure she has plenty of time to refine the schedule before she presents it to management.

Entering Budget and Costs

The costs of your schedule help you confirm your budget. When you build a schedule and add the labor and nonlabor costs based on a more detailed plan, you build the real budget for your project. When entering costs:

- Enter rates for resources to understand resource costs.
- Use Fixed Cost or a cost resource (in Project 2007) to include nonlabor costs to your project.
- Compare your initial budget to the costs your project schedule provides; you might find you need to revisit the initial budget.

Although not all organizations include costs in schedules, you might want to consider entering them to help you understand the kind of money each of your projects will cost to meet its goals.

Review Questions

1. What are the three cost estimating methods?

2. What are two Cost formulas?

3. How can you stop Project from calculating Actual Costs automatically?

4. What are the three accrual methods in Project?

5. How are standard rates used for calculating costs for a task?

6. What are Per use Costs?

7. What is a Fixed Cost?

8. What is a Cost resource in Project 2007? A Budget cost resource?

9. How are material costs calculated?

10. What are some methods for viewing costs?

11. Where do you enter the Budget cost for your project?

12. Where can you add different rates for one resource?

13. How can you compare the original project budget with the one that Project calculates when you have assigned costs to all your project tasks?

8

Polishing Your Schedule

Well done is better than well said.
—Benjamin Franklin

Topics Covered in This Chapter

What Errors Will You Look For?

The Various Methods for Reviewing Your Schedule

Checks to Review Your Schedule

Adding to or Changing the Schedule

The Project Schedule Building Methodology So Far

Summary

Practice: Looking for Errors

Case Study: Review the Schedule

Whew! The schedule is done. You've used the proper schedule-building methodology to create a decent schedule. You've included the scope of your work, work and cost estimates, how you will resource each task, and your task relationships. You also did as recommended and ignored worrying about it being perfect, so it's not really quite done. Is the first time you write a paragraph for a formal report the last time you look at it before sending it to a customer? If you are wise, you review it again with a gap in time between when you first wrote it and when you review it again so you can see your own errors. Just as you should edit your own writing, you should also edit your schedule. You need to take the time to step back and critically review it to look for logic or scheduling flaws. Chapter 10, "Baselining: The Key to Tracking Your Schedule," discusses setting the baseline, and before you baseline the schedule you really need to make sure it's in good shape.

In this chapter, I focus on the various methods you can use to critically review your schedule. First, I provide a checklist of schedule components to review. It focuses on easy-to-identify and fixable schedule issues. Next, the chapter describes methods, such as filters, groupings, views, and other features built into Project for reviewing the items described in the checklist. I focus on things like ensuring dates, resources, predecessors and successors, and other scheduling errors are fixed. Eventually you will be able to review the schedule in a very quick, methodical way. The next chapter focuses on the second part of reviewing your schedule: resource overallocation.

Checking your schedule

Some Microsoft Project vendors have created tools or custom filters for you to review your schedule. This book provides a Project view that allows you to audit your schedule. You might also look at tools, such as QuantumPM's QSA (QuantumPM Schedule Auditor), a Web-based auditing tool that allows you to set up some auditing rules for reviewing your project. Go to www.quantumpm.com for more information about QSA.

What Errors Will You Look For?

When you initially review your schedule, you can edit it for the those kinds of things that are more equivalent to checking your grammar in your writing; that is, are you creating a schedule with good structure and following the rules of building a schedule? Schedule building is both an art and precise technique that integrates with project management elements of communicating, considering risk, and obtaining well-justified estimates. Sometimes the schedule exposes issues that you need to take care of in managing your project—especially in execution—as you find out how good the initial planning was. The error checking described in this chapter probably will not help you in exposing missing elements for the way the project work is put together. That intellectual work is why you and your team are paid the big bucks. The following checklist helps with a structure and logic review. It's very important to remove the errors that can be distracting to you, your team, and anyone who looks at the schedule. For each of the possible audit review areas described, you can take two approaches:

- If the schedule is short enough, you can look at each error and eyeball your schedule.
- If it is a long schedule, you might use Project itself to help perform a more automated and systematic review.

To review your schedule, use the following checklist. Each item in the task list is described after the list. See the next section, "The Various Methods for Reviewing Your Schedule," for the various ways you can check these items using Project itself.

- Spelling and style
- Project preferences (Tools > Options selections in Project)
- Project attributes
- Task calendars
- Tasks and summary tasks (Outlining)
- Milestones
- Task relationships
- Task types
- Task constraints
- Work and Duration
- Resources and their attributes
- Resource calendars
- Costs
- Critical path
- Workloads

Spelling

Is your spelling in each task correct? This might seem minor, but if you choose to use your schedule in a meeting with executives and "task" is spelled "tsk," it can be a big deal. You have a spell checker capability in Project to help you find spelling errors. Make sure you select Tools from the menu bar and click Spelling to run a spelling check on the schedule after your first iteration, and as you add or change tasks in your schedule. In the Spelling tab of the Options dialog box, you can see the fields that will be checked for spelling errors in Project. Unfortunately, unlike other Microsoft applications, Project does not highlight the misspelled word in the field. You will need to do a little bit of investigation to find the word that is identified in the spelling check. If the error is not obvious when you run the spell checking tool, you can select Edit in the menu bar and click Find to look for words that show up in the spell checking tool.

For style checks you might look for the following:

- Verb–noun format for tasks
- Noun–verb past tense format for milestones
- Your organization's naming conventions
- Consistent abbreviations

Project doesn't provide for any automated form to look for style issues, but you can keep the checklist in mind when reviewing the schedule.

Project Preferences

Project preferences are the overall settings that determine the way some of your data displays or how calculations are made in Project. Check to make sure the preferences you select are what you really want for your project going forward. Select Tools from the menu bar and click Options. You should review all the selections on each tab to make sure that's how you want Project to behave as you continue to work on the project throughout the planning and executing lifecycle. Project preferences are described in more detail in Chapter 13, "Project Mysteries Resolved!" Some of the most important tabs to look at are these:

- **Schedule tab:** This tab shows you the defaults that will be used when you add or change tasks and reflect their work and assignment for the schedule.
- **Calculation tab:** This tab shows how Project will make calculations. The default for Calculation mode is Automatic and although you could change it, this book assumes you will leave the default setting. I have seen some cases where a Project user inadvertently changes the mode. The method for calculating actual costs is also on this tab as described in Chapter 7, "Using Project to Enter Cost Estimates."
- **Calendar tab:** This tab contains the settings for how Project will calculate information in the project. The settings on this tab will make

default formulas calculate and display data differently in the schedule. For instance, you could set your hours per day to 6 hours within this dialog box even if you indicate that the resource can work 8 hours a day on the project and resource calendar. When you assign a resource to work 40 hours on a task, you will see the duration of the task calculated as 6.67 days. Notice that if you set the days differently, the Gantt Chart bar stays the same. Make sure you sync up the settings in project calendars, resource calendars, and this Calendar tab as described in Chapter 3, "Building Your Schedule: Scoping Your Project."

Project Attributes

Check to make sure the start date for the project is accurate and that the project calendar is set. Your real project start date could be different than what's in the schedule if you created the schedule and the project was delayed. Also check to make sure the project calendar takes holidays or non-working days into account for your project.

Task Calendars

Check to make sure you have task calendars set appropriately for your tasks. If you have task calendars on tasks, make sure they are the right calendar, and that they are doing what you want them to do. Task calendars can be created in Change Working Time from the Tools menu and you attach them to the task by double-clicking the task and selecting the Advanced tab. You can select any calendar in the drop-down list. You might also have a task calendar that you don't mean to have on a task. An icon displays in the information field for the task showing that a task calendar is on a task if you have one.

Tasks and Summary Tasks

Make sure the tasks and summary tasks in your project make sense and are logically appropriate in the task outline of the project. You might consider checking the top-level tasks to ensure they are consistent and at the appropriate level for reporting status. Make sure the tasks are worded so they make sense: Most tasks should be in verb–noun format. In general, summary tasks should not have resources assigned on them.

Milestones

Make sure all the tasks that should be milestones are, and that all the tasks assigned as milestones should be milestones. You might check to see if the milestones are set with zero duration, if appropriate for your schedule. In general, you should not have resources on milestones (although you could use them to show responsibility—as long as you make a conscious decision to do so). You might also name your milestones in a noun–verb format such as Requirements Completed to help distinguish milestones from other kinds of tasks.

Task Relationships

Make sure you have task relationships for your tasks. If you don't have a predecessor or successor for a task (except for initial tasks and the last task and summary tasks), you might not really need to include the task in your schedule. Make sure your predecessors and successors describing the relationships of the tasks are appropriate. The relationships should be based on how you need to get work done on your project. Sometimes, on review, you realize you can perform the work more efficiently, or you might decide quality depends on creating some relationships you didn't first think were necessary. You should not have predecessors or successors on summary tasks.

Task Types

Ensure all your task types are appropriate for the tasks on your project. For instance, if you have decided to perform duration-based scheduling and you have not changed the default from Fixed Units, Effort-driven, you might find that tasks you have added are set incorrectly. If you have tasks that are effort-based and the settings set as Duration, Non-Effort-driven, they will not calculate as expected. I describe some methods later to help you review task types.

Task Constraints and Deadlines

Check to see if you have task constraints and deadlines and if they are appropriate for the tasks they are on. In the schedule-building process, it's good to avoid constraints. But once you have completely built your project, you might actually add some constraints to faithfully indicate how your tasks should behave as you track the work, or consider setting deadlines rather than constraints. Remove any constraints you should not have and set some constraints you believe are appropriate. If you have deadlines, review the deadlines to ensure they still make sense for what you know about your schedule presently.

> **Add constraints if appropriate**
>
> After you have built your schedule, you might want to add constraints (such as Must Start On, or Start No Later Than). While building the schedule, it's best to avoid constraints, but once the schedule is built, you might want to add them when you review your schedule.

Work and Duration

Review the Work fields and Duration fields to make sure they have values, and think about if they logically make sense. If you see a question mark (?) in the Duration field, verify that the task is your best estimate or still needs to be estimated. If it is your best estimate, remove the question mark by double-clicking the task and clearing the Estimated field check box in the Task Information dialog box.

Resources

Check resources to make sure you do not have any inappropriate generic resources on tasks (especially if you can really indicate a real resource name). Make sure you have the appropriate resources for each task, and ensure you do not have duplicate resources. For instance, check that you don't have two different spellings of the same resource and have assigned each to various tasks. You will also want to review resource attributes, such as their rates and resource types.

Resource Calendars

Review the resource calendars for each resource. You can do this in the Resource Sheet by double-clicking the resource. First, make sure the resource has the correct base calendar. Most resources will have the Standard calendar. You might need to make sure some resources have special calendars, such as for 4 × 10 work or part-time work to have their work calculated correctly in the schedule.

Costs

Review the cost fields and make sure the costs look reasonable and have been calculated correctly. If costs are not appropriate, review fixed costs and resource rates for the resources assigned to the tasks and how many hours they are assigned to the work.

Critical Path

You want to review the critical path to make sure the longest path of tasks to complete the project makes sense. If any task on this path is shortened or lengthened, the end date of the project will change. It's important to review this to make sure you have not misjudged any task relationships or durations or the slack (amount of time the task can be delayed before it affects a successor task) of any tasks not on the noncritical paths. Reviewing the critical path is an important final step to revising your schedule. In Chapter 9, "Reviewing Work Overload and the Critical Path," I discuss how you review the critical path in more detail.

Workloads

Ensure the resources are allocated correctly and equitably for the work they are assigned to on the project. There is a good possibility that resources on your project can be overallocated by being double-booked or your not taking into account other projects or work they have been assigned to within the organization. I discuss overallocation in more detail in Chapter 9.

The Various Methods for Reviewing Your Schedule

You will probably do a lot of editing as you see errors when you are building your schedule. When you add a resource to a task, you might see that an estimate is inaccurate due to a change in the task's work or duration calculation, for instance. The previous checklist provides you a systemized way of looking at your schedule. The various methods described later help you review your schedule based on using the schedule review checklist. For each of the following methods for the review described later, you will want to pay close attention to how you return to a normal view of the project. Many students get frustrated with Project because the review method's grouping, view, or filter stays the same if they do not reset the view or turn the grouping or filter off.

The following list provides you with some of the methods you can use to review your schedule. I will explain how you should set them up in Project and use them for reviewing the project in more detail later.

- **Formatting text:** You can change the color (e.g., use green for milestones, or blue for summary tasks), text, or other formatting style on tasks in the Gantt Chart. This way you can easily review your tasks in the Gantt Chart.

- **Sorting:** Sorting allows you to sort the schedule by particular fields such as Start date, Finish date, Resource names, or Cost. Perhaps you want to see all your tasks that cost the most: You can sort by the Cost field and see your most costly tasks first.

- **Grouping:** This allows you to group like fields. For instance, you could group items by critical and noncritical tasks.

- **Filtering:** Filtering allows you to show all tasks (or resources) that have a certain value. Let's say Joe is a resource you have assigned to tasks. You can sort by Joe, and review all the tasks he is on. If you looked at the Gantt Chart bars for the resource it might help you to see if Joe is overallocated and what critical tasks he is on. Perhaps Joe is in quality assurance, but he's been assigned to a requirements definition task. Reviewing just his assignments in the Gantt Chart would help make those kinds of mismatches more apparent.

- **Adding columns and using different views or tables:** Looking at your data in different ways is a great way to review your schedule. For instance, you could insert the Task types column and quickly review if the task types are correct and appropriate for the tasks. You could also change the table to a Schedule table, and review the late start and finish and slack you have for your tasks, to make sure that it looks reasonable.

- **Using graphs and viewing or printing reports:** Project has some interesting reports you can use to see information about your project. Most of the available views in Project are also available as printed reports. You could print out the Resource Usage view for each week, examine it manually, and then make the changes as necessary. In Project 2002 and Project 2003, you can export usage data to Excel and graph it to show trends for resource usage throughout the life of your project. In Project 2007, you can use a new feature called Visual Reports. You can use the Baseline Cost Report and see a graph of the costs for each task of the project. By comparing the costs graphically, you might see a task that seems out of kilter compared to the other tasks' costs.

- **Reviewing the schedule manually:** This is not so much using Project to review as just having your team review the schedule. You can print out portions or the entire schedule and confirm the reasonableness of the assignments and time frames with your team.

- **Using task drivers (Project 2007 only):** Project 2007 has a new feature that allows you to click on each task and see what's driving how it is being scheduled. Drivers include such things as the task's resources and their calendars, a constraint, the project start date, or a predecessor relationship.

- **Using Change highlighting and Undo (Project 2007 only):** Change highlighting is a new feature that will highlight all fields that change based on one change on a task. For instance, by increasing the hours on one task by 5 hours, you might see a change in Total Cost, Hours, and Duration, as well as the Start date and Finish date of all dependent tasks and the End date of the project (perhaps getting done 1 day later due to the small change). When you are making corrections to the errors you can use Change highlighting to get out of a correction that changed your schedule in a way you did not want it to.

Now let's take a look at each method and how you might use it to help you review the schedule and find errors in detail.

Formatting Text

Project has a built-in capability to change the text formatting for certain kinds of tasks it recognizes, such as summary tasks, milestones, and critical tasks. You can change the font, font style, color, and size to help you review the differences between tasks in the Gantt Chart. The Roofing project will illustrate this capability. Once you set these format changes for the text, you can keep them on the schedule and it will help you as you track your project.

To use the Format text capability for particular kinds of tasks, follow these steps:

1. In a project, select Format from the menu bar and click Text styles.

2. Select the kind of task from the drop-down list in the Item to Change field. Select a different text style from the Font, Font style, Size, or Color field.

3. Click OK. In Figure 8.1, the critical path has been changed to show 10-point bold italic font and red color.

4. You'll need to go through the same process for each kind of task (e.g., milestones or summary tasks) you want to change.

5. If you want to remove the text styles you selected, you will have to go through the exact same process and change the styles back to their original formatting.

When you use this method to review the schedule in the Gantt Chart, change the critical tasks, summary tasks, and milestones; too much formatting can be distracting for a viewer. Note that if you change to another view (e.g., Tracking Gantt) it will not have the formatting you selected. Also, if you do not like what you did, you will have to reselect the original settings. If you have Project 2007, you will need to perform the Undo function.

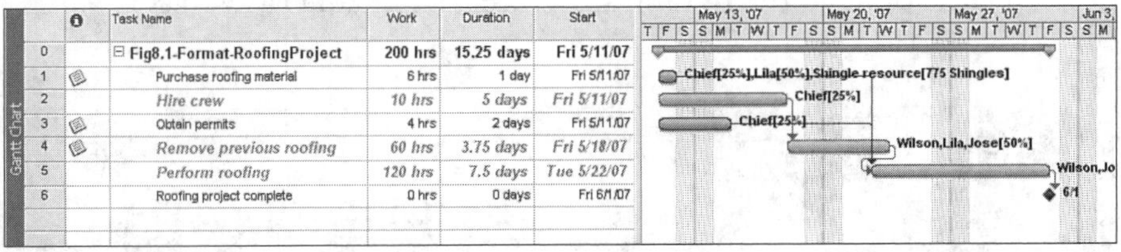

Figure 8.1 *Text style of critical path tasks changed to 10-point bold italic font and red color*

Change bar styles, too

You can also change the bar styles in the Gantt Chart if you want. Usually, Project's default settings are good enough, but you or your organization might have different styles you'd rather use.

Sorting

You can use sorting to review particular tasks by highest to lowest and vice versa. You might want to sort by costs to review your most "expensive" tasks first in a schedule. To use the sort feature, do the following:

1. In an open project, select Project from the menu bar and click Sort.

2. Select the particular sort you would like to use from the default list, or select Sort by for more options.

3. The display will automatically re-sort by the particular field you have selected. Figure 8.2 shows the Roofing project re-sorted by cost. It's interesting to review the project this way to see when the costs will occur and it might help you plan to ensure you have more money in the bank at the beginning or end of the project.

4. To return to the original sort in the Gantt Chart view, perform the same steps but select by ID from the available selections.

When you select the other options for sorting, the function is similar to Excel or other Microsoft products: You not only have a selection of most of the fields available in the Gantt Chart view, but you also can have the capability to sort on three fields and sort by ascending and descending order. Options at the bottom left of the Sort dialog box allow you to permanently renumber tasks or keep the outline structure (the default) as you sort.

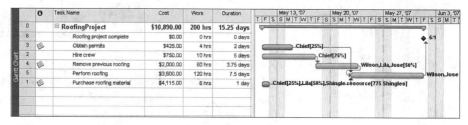

Figure 8.2 *Roofing project sorted by Cost field*

Grouping

Grouping provides you with a report format to group together all like tasks, resources, or assignments by your selection. If you wanted to see all tasks grouped together that have specific durations, you can do so using grouping. For another example, you could group together all resources based on like resource rates. This method might help you double-check rates for all your resources. To use grouping, follow these steps:

1. In an open project, select Project from the menu bar and click Group by.

2. Select the particular group you would like to use from the default list. Note that you can create your own custom groups. In Chapter 11, "Tracking Your Schedule," I describe creating custom groups in more detail.

3. The display will automatically be grouped by the particular selection. Figure 8.3 shows the Roofing project grouped in the Resource Sheet view by Rate. As noted earlier, you might want to review rates to ensure you have indicated the proper rate for each resource.

4. To return to the original view, select Project from the menu bar, click Group, and then click No Group.

Grouping is a wonderful reporting process, as well as a review process. Besides grouping rates in the Resource Sheet, you might want to group Constraint type, Critical tasks, Milestones, Duration, and, if you use the Priority field, by Priority.

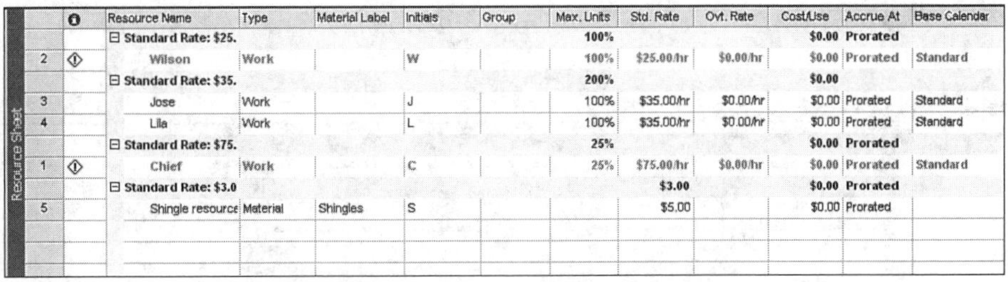

	🛈	Resource Name	Type	Material Label	Initials	Group	Max. Units	Std. Rate	Ovt. Rate	Cost/Use	Accrue At	Base Calendar
		⊟ Standard Rate: $25.					100%			$0.00	Prorated	
2	◈	Wilson	Work		W		100%	$25.00/hr	$0.00/hr	$0.00	Prorated	Standard
		⊟ Standard Rate: $35.					200%			$0.00		
3		Jose	Work		J		100%	$35.00/hr	$0.00/hr	$0.00	Prorated	Standard
4		Lila	Work		L		100%	$35.00/hr	$0.00/hr	$0.00	Prorated	Standard
		⊟ Standard Rate: $75.					25%			$0.00	Prorated	
1	◈	Chief	Work		C		25%	$75.00/hr	$0.00/hr	$0.00	Prorated	Standard
		⊟ Standard Rate: $3.0						$3.00		$0.00	Prorated	
5		Shingle resource	Material	Shingles	S			$5.00		$0.00	Prorated	

Figure 8.3   *Roofing project resources grouped by Rate*

If you select Project from the menu bar, Group by, and then Customize group by, you can also group by any field available in the drop-down list. For instance, as shown in Figure 8.4, you might want to group by the Estimated indicator. This would show you all tasks that still have the question mark on them and allow you to change the fields quickly by highlighting them all and doing a multiple task change. You might need to get a better estimate if the question marks seem to indicate you still need more confident estimates.

You can use the Group by capability on the toolbar to group and ungroup easily, as shown in Figure 8.5. Make sure you have the Formatting toolbar showing (View, Toolbars, Formatting) to see the Grouping capability on the toolbar.

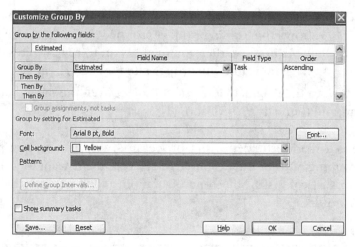

Figure 8.4   *Use grouping to group any fields available on a view*

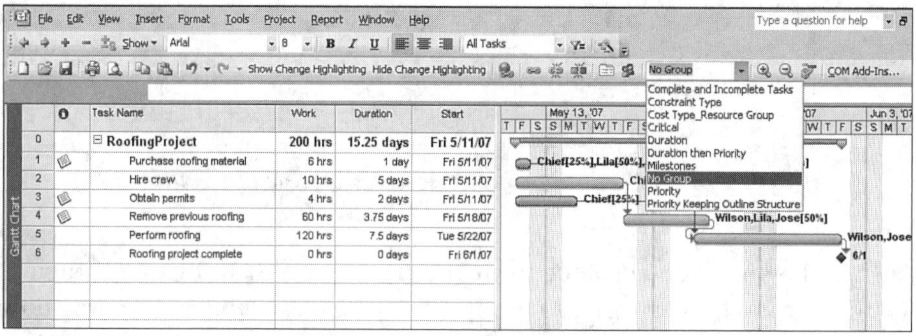

Figure 8.5   *Use the grouping function on the toolbar*

Filtering

Filtering, as with grouping, can be useful for systematically reviewing your schedule. Whereas grouping will divide all like tasks, resources, or assignments into different groups within the entire schedule, you can use filtering to see only the tasks, resources, or assignments specified by your filter criteria and eliminate any tasks not meeting those criteria. To use filtering, follow these steps:

1. In an open project, select Project from the menu bar and click Filter for.

2. Select the particular filter you would like to use from the default list. Note that you can create your own filters and use those as well. In Chapter 11, I describe creating custom filters.

3. In some cases, you will receive another dialog box so you can enter specifically what you want to filter on. For instance, if you select Filter for: Using Resource, a dialog box appears asking you for a resource name. If you select Filter for: Milestones, Project applies the filter directly on the file. Figure 8.6 shows the filtering selection from the Project selection, and the Roofing project filtered by all tasks with Jose as a resource.

4. To return to the original view, select Project from the menu bar, click Filter for, then select All tasks (or All resources, depending on what view you are on).

It can sometimes get confusing when you filter, if you forget you have done so. Remember to remove the filter, unless you intend to keep using the filtering for reviewing the schedule.

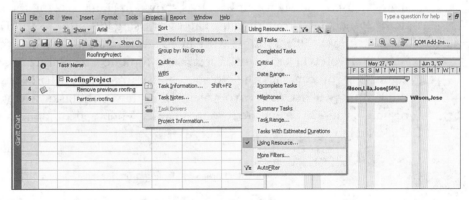

Figure 8.6 *Use filtering to see just the tasks a certain resource is assigned*

Note that you can see more filters than what you see in the default drop-down list (shown in Figure 8.6) by selecting More filters (shown in Figure 8.7). In the schedule review checklist described earlier, some of the items to review were deadlines, task calendars, estimated durations, and summary tasks; you can review them using selections in the More Filters dialog box. When you use the More Filters dialog box, you can also elect to highlight the filter instead, which will just change the color of the item selected. Thus, you will see the entire schedule rather than displaying only the tasks that meet the filter criteria.

Highlight will leave all tasks on project but highlight the filtered row

Figure 8.7 *More filters enable you to review various tasks or resources*

Another variation of filtering is autofiltering. You know what autofiltering is if you've used it in Microsoft Excel. As shown in Figure 8.6, the last selection in the Project tab drop-down list Filter for: Using Resource is AutoFilter (the icon for it looks like a funnel with an equals sign after it). When you select AutoFilter, you will see a small caret at the top of each column. As shown in Figure 8.8, you can click the tab and choose to filter by whatever shows in the drop-down list. When you want to review only tasks with a certain resource, you can select the resource name. When you are done reviewing, click the tab again, and then select All.

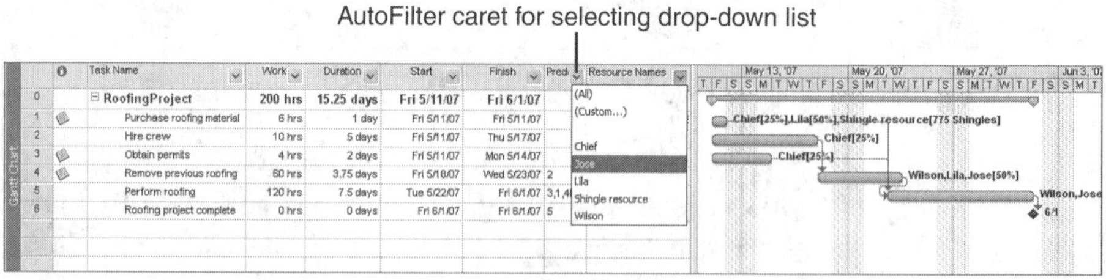

AutoFilter caret for selecting drop-down list

Figure 8.8 *Filtering for a resource allows you to see tasks for a particular resource only*

When you select Custom in the drop-down list of the AutoFilter, you can filter by several values at once as shown in Figure 8.9.

Figure 8.9 *Filtering for more than one value*

Notice the Save button in Figure 8.9. This allows you to actually save a filter, name it, and reuse the filter. When you select Save, you will have the opportunity to name and perform more customization options on the filter.

As with grouping, you can use buttons in the toolbar to more easily use filters. Figure 8.10 shows you the icons for filtering and autofiltering. When you use the Filtering button, you can see the filter that has been applied and it contains the complete list of out-of-the-box filtering values. The AutoFilter button can be used to easily toggle filtering on and off.

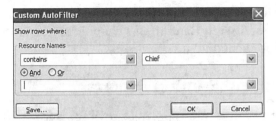

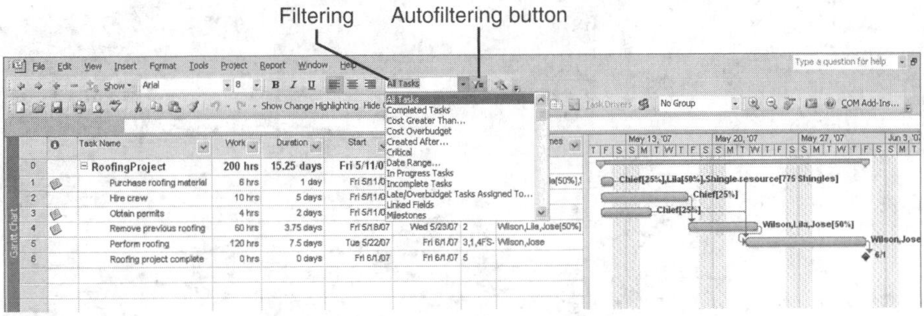

Figure 8.10 *Buttons for filtering and autofiltering*

Adding Columns and Using Different Views or Tables

One of the easiest forms of reviewing your schedule is inserting important columns in the Gantt Chart, Resource Sheet, or a usage view. Then, you can use the grouping or filtering capabilities in combination or alone to review the schedule. For instance, you might want to insert the Constraint type column to see what constraints you have added, and then sort or group on the various constraints and dates to ensure they make sense. You can create a new custom table and view to create reports that act as audit reports. See the section "Using a Special Audit View" later in this chapter to learn more about creating a custom view for schedule review.

Using Graphs and Viewing and Printing Reports

You might want to print graphs and reports to review your schedule. You have several options for doing so. As an illustration, Figure 8.11 almost speaks for itself. It shows the project's resource usage over time. It helps to analyze the peaks and valleys of the workload. This report allows you to think about the work of the project, and if, indeed, as it shows in this graph, there will be several weeks with no work, decide whether it is reasonable for the time frame shown. You can also look at this in a grid format or use the Resource Usage view to see the same thing in numbers, but this kind of chart gives you a great visual cue. You can also use the new feature in Project 2007 called Visual Reports.

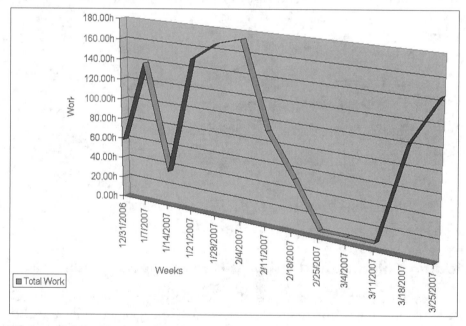

Figure 8.11   *Review of work over time*

Exporting and Graphing in Excel in Project 2002 and Project 2003

This section illustrates the graphing capability shown in Figure 8.11 available in Project 2002 and Project 2003. It describes how you can create a graph by exporting data to Excel.

To use the graphing function (as long as you have Excel with graphing capabilities on your desktop), do the following:

1. In the Project you want to graph or review in Excel, select View from the menu bar and click Toolbars, Analysis. (It is possible that the Analysis toolbar was not loaded if you customized your installation of Project and did not include the Analysis toolbar.)

2. The Analysis toolbar will display as shown in Figure 8.12. If you want to graph just certain tasks, select them; otherwise, click Analyze timescaled data in Excel.

Figure 8.12 *Use Analyze timescaled data in Excel to graph timephased data from Project*

Export to Excel

3. A five-step wizard will appear. Select the whole project or selected tasks in the Step 1 of 5 dialog box. Click Next.

4. Select the kind of data you want to show in the Excel spreadsheet and graph in the Step 2 of 5 dialog box, as shown in Figure 8.13, and click Next. The fields are limited. Many fields are perfect for reviewing the project after you start executing the project to review variances and earned value.

5. Select the From and To dates for the data you want to export and the Units you would like to see, such as Hours, Days, Weeks, Months, Quarters, and Years, and click Next in the Step 3 of 5 dialog box. Unless your project is extremely short or long or you are just trying to show portions of the project, Weeks or Months might be the best selection.

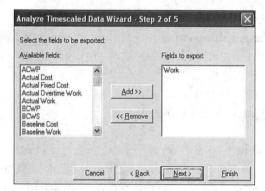

Figure 8.13   *Select the kind of data you want to export to Excel*

6. Select whether you want to graph the data or not and click Next in the Step 4 of 5 dialog box.

7. Finally, click Export Data to create the graph or spreadsheet. Excel will open if you have it on your desktop and show a graph as shown in Figure 8.11. If you do not have Excel or if you have a version that does not allow graphing, you will receive an error message.

8. You can close the file without saving or save the file for future reviews.

Using Visual Reports in Project 2007

In Project 2007 the Export to Excel function is no longer available but you can use a new feature called Visual Reports on the new Reports tab. You can use a similar capability to graph data as well and it is much more flexible with more fields for you to choose from. Figure 8.14 shows a graph similar to the one showing work over time.

To show a chart in Project 2007, do the following:

1. In your Project, select Report from the menu bar and click Visual Reports. (You might be prompted to add the Visual Reports capability if it has not been set up; you will need to make sure your machine has .NET 2.0 to use the feature.) A screen similar to Figure 8.15 will display.

2. Select one of the reports showing and click View. You can also click Save Data and select other views and fields in the resulting dialog box. After you click View, the chart you selected will display.

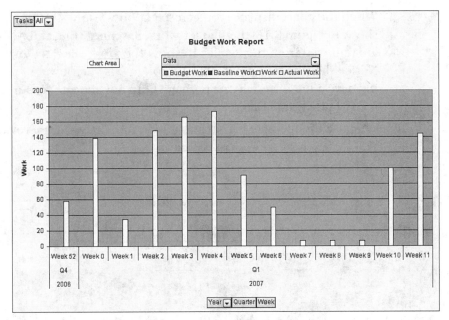

Figure 8.14 *Budget Work Report by week in Project 2007*

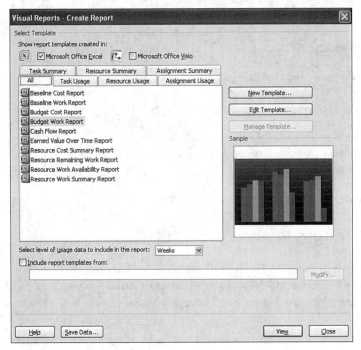

Figure 8.15 *Visual Reports - Create Report dialog box*

3. When the chart displays, you can select how you want the report to show. In Figure 8.16, the Budget work, Baseline work, and Actual work are removed from the display to show the work allocated over time. Notice that the work in Weeks 7 through 9 is very low, so I might simply have a lull in activity, or perhaps I did not allocate resources correctly in that time frame.

You can close the file without saving or save the file for future reviews.

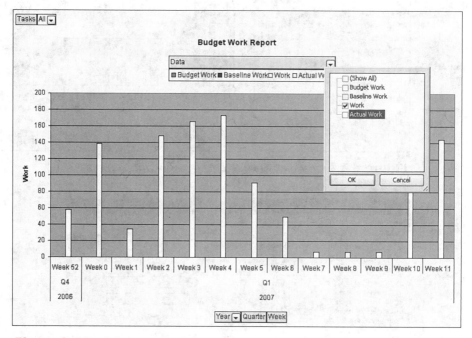

Figure 8.16 *Selecting the fields for viewing on the visual report*

See Chapter 11 for more about Visual Reports.

Viewing and Printing Reports

Use views and reports to help analyze the schedule as well. The following views might be useful to review your schedule. To use any of the views, select View from the menu bar and click More views.

- **Calendar view:** You can see how tasks stack up in a monthly calendar view. This can be very useful to review the logical positioning of tasks.

- **Resource Usage view:** Use this view to take a look at overallocation of resources. You can use the Zoom In and Zoom Out buttons to show the time scale as weekly or monthly. You can see the tasks listed under each resource and decide if the work tasks and hours assigned are right by reviewing each resource individually. As shown in Figure 8.17, you can see that during the week of May 20, Wilson is working 48 hours, rather than 40. Also notice that Wilson and Jose are working on the same tasks.

0	Resource Name	Work	Details	6	13	20	27	Jun '07 3
	⊟ Unassigned	0 hrs	Work					
	Roofing project complete	0 hrs	Work					
1 ◇	⊟ Chief	16 hrs	Work	6h	10h			
	Purchase roofing material	2 hrs	Work	2h				
	Hire crew	10 hrs	Work	2h	8h			
	Obtain permits	4 hrs	Work	2h	2h			
2 ◇	⊟ Wilson	90 hrs	Work		8h	48h	34h	
	Remove previous roofing	30 hrs	Work		8h	22h		
	Perform roofing	60 hrs	Work			26h	34h	
3	⊟ Jose	70 hrs	Work		4h	32h	34h	
	Remove previous roofing	10 hrs	Work		4h	6h		
	Perform roofing	60 hrs	Work			26h	34h	
4	⊟ Lila	24 hrs	Work	4h	8h	12h		
	Purchase roofing material	4 hrs	Work	4h				
	Remove previous roofing	20 hrs	Work		8h	12h		
5	⊟ Shingle resource	775 Shingles	Work (Shingles)	775				
	Purchase roofing material	775 Shingles	Work (Shingles)	775				

Figure 8.17 *Resource Usage helps you analyze tasks and work assigned to each resource per week*

- **Resource Allocation view:** This view is useful to review overallocation. You can see a graph that shows if a resource is overallocated over time. In Chapter 9, I review this capability in more detail.

For each view, you can also consider using the split window and combine views for great ways to analyze your schedule. For instance, in Figure 8.18 the Gantt Chart view is in the top window and the Resource Usage view is in the bottom window. You can see exactly how each resource is scheduled. It appears that Wilson is probably overallocated because Perform roofing can start before the Remove previous roofing task ends. So you might decide that the overallocation of Wilson might not be a problem: Perhaps it is actually Lila who will spend the last day removing the old roofing, while Jose and Wilson start laying down the new roofing.

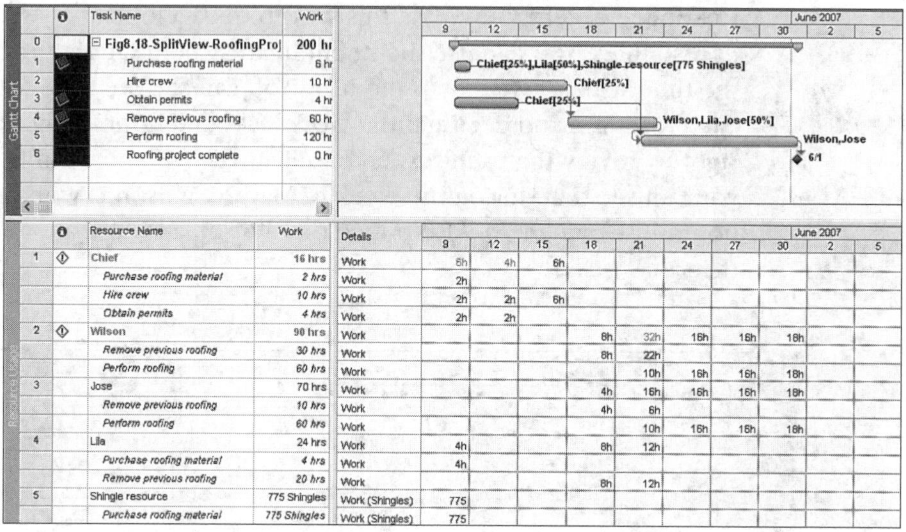

Figure 8.18   *Gantt Chart and Resource Usage in split window view*

You might use the cost and schedule tables for reviewing the schedule prior to finalizing it: Select View from the menu bar and click Table and select one of the following from the drop-down list. Again, you can use a split window to help see numerous data values at once.

- **Cost:** The table shows almost all of the cost fields at once.
- **Schedule:** The table shows slack and late start and finish to help you understand critical versus noncritical tasks. Chapter 9 provides additional review of this capability.

Project has many default reports that you can also use. For instance, you can print out the Task Usage and Resource Usage views according to the time frames you want. In Project 2002 and Project 2003, you can view the reports by selecting View from the menu bar, and then clicking Reports. In Project 2007, this function has moved under the Reports selection on the menu bar. As described earlier, you could also use Visual Reports in Project 2007 to analyze your schedule.

Reviewing the Schedule

One of the best ways to review the schedule is reviewing it with your team. You might consider printing out a network diagram view as shown in Figure

8.19. Printing out a large project can be quite intensive if you do it sheet by sheet (yes, many people do so and then tape the various pages together), but if you have access to a plotter, it can be very useful for the team to review. You could also print the Gantt Chart. To see a network diagram, Gantt Chart, or any other view that might take several pages, select the view you want to see, and then select File and Print Preview. Select the Multiple pages icon or press Alt + 3 as shown in Figure 8.19 to see what the pages would look like. Some organizations print this out and keep track of where they are in the schedule on a meeting or war room wall.

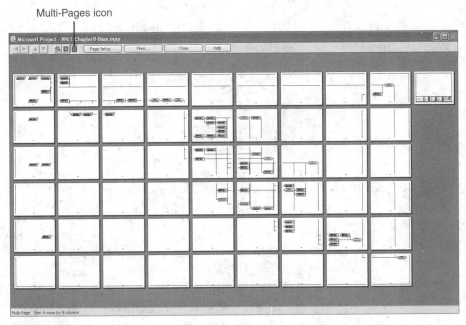

Figure 8.19　*View for VNLE project in network diagram*

Using Task Drivers (Project 2007)

Task drivers are available only in Project 2007 and show what influences the start date of a task in the schedule: the resources, constraints, predecessor tasks, lag, relationships, and so on. You might review each task of the whole project or sections of your project using this capability. To use task drivers to review your schedule, follow these steps:

1. Select a task. Select Project from the menu bar and click Task drivers. A screen similar to Figure 8.20 displays. You can also access the feature via the Project Guide (View, Toolbars, Project Guide) and on the Track tab, select See to determine what is driving the start date of a task.

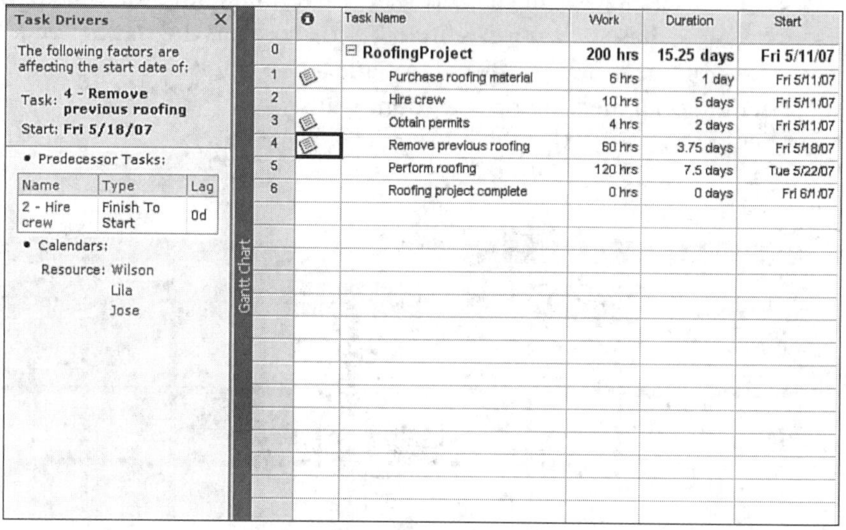

Figure 8.20 *Task drivers for reviewing a schedule*

2. You can click items showing in the Task driver pane to review why they are affecting the task. In Figure 8.20, if you click Resource: Wilson, Project will display Wilson's calendar. The calendar will display any nonworking days for the resource. When you click on the predecessor task showing in the pane (Hire crew in this example), you can then see what is driving that task (in this case, the project start date).

3. Once you have selected Task driver, you can click through each task to make sure what you are seeing makes sense for each task.

Using Change Highlighting and Undo (for Project 2007)

Perhaps one of the best methods for reviewing your schedule is using the Change highlighting and multiple Undo functions in Project 2007. As you review your schedule using the various capabilities described, you can actually make changes, review how the changes affect the schedule, and if the change affects your schedule differently than you expected, undo the change or changes. To use change highlighting, select View from the menu bar and click Show change highlighting or click the Show change highlighting button in the toolbar as shown in Figure 8.21.

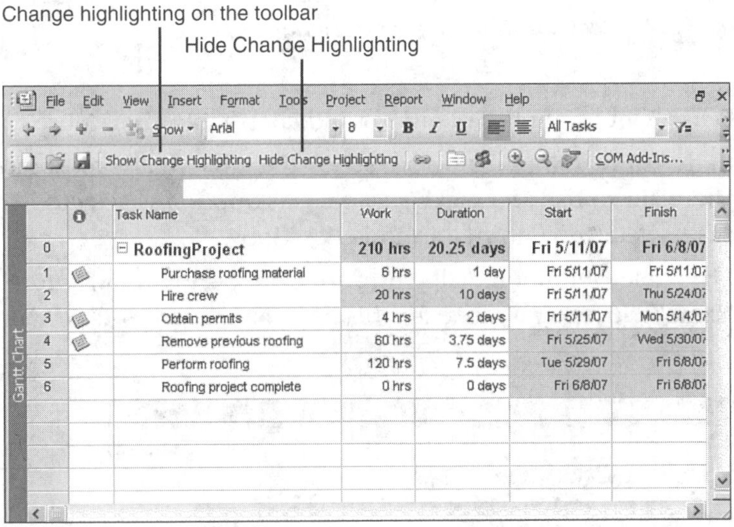

Change highlighting on the toolbar

Hide Change Highlighting

Figure 8.21   *Change highlighting shows task data that has changed when duration increased on the Hire crew task*

Using a Special Audit View

Perhaps the best method for performing a project review is to create a special view or views combining several of the methods already described. The following describes setting up a special audit table and how you might use it.

Task Audit Table

If you take my advice to review your schedule (and it's a temptation not to), you could actually take the time to create a view that helps you check your most important items in the schedule. If you are in an organization of project managers that like to share views or reports, you could share it. The following steps describe how I set up Figure 8.22. The initial steps are how you create a special view. Notice that I recommend copying an existing table or view. If you use a current one, you actually alter the table or view and you will not be able to use it again for other projects, so it's best to create a special view you can continue to use.

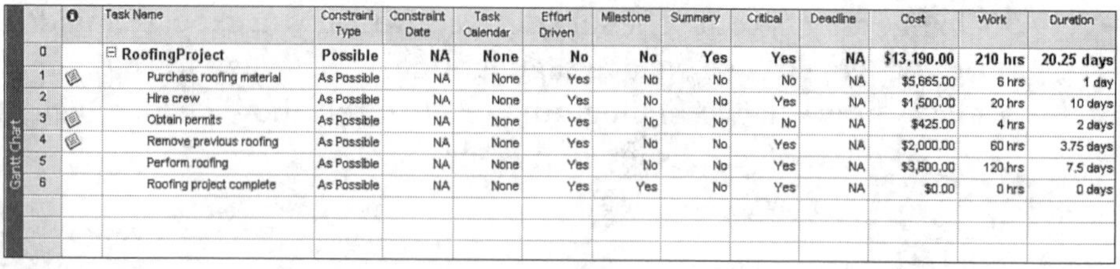

	❶	Task Name	Constraint Type	Constraint Date	Task Calendar	Effort Driven	Milestone	Summary	Critical	Deadline	Cost	Work	Duration
0		⊟ RoofingProject	Possible	NA	None	No	No	Yes	Yes	NA	$13,190.00	210 hrs	20.25 days
1	🗊	Purchase roofing material	As Possible	NA	None	Yes	No	No	No	NA	$5,665.00	6 hrs	1 day
2		Hire crew	As Possible	NA	None	Yes	No	No	Yes	NA	$1,500.00	20 hrs	10 days
3	🗊	Obtain permits	As Possible	NA	None	Yes	No	No	No	NA	$425.00	4 hrs	2 days
4	🗊	Remove previous roofing	As Possible	NA	None	Yes	No	No	Yes	NA	$2,000.00	60 hrs	3.75 days
5		Perform roofing	As Possible	NA	None	Yes	No	No	Yes	NA	$3,600.00	120 hrs	7.5 days
6		Roofing project complete	As Possible	NA	None	Yes	Yes	No	Yes	NA	$0.00	0 hrs	0 days

Figure 8.22 *Task audit table for reviewing your schedule*

1. Select View from the menu bar and click Table, then More tables.
2. In the More Tables dialog box, click the table that is most like what you want to use and make sure the Task option is selected. In this case, select the Entry table and click Copy.
3. The Table Definition dialog box appears as shown in Figure 8.23. In the Name field, enter a name for this new table, such as Task Audit Table.

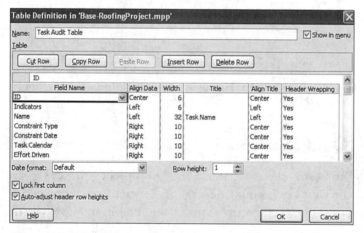

Figure 8.23 *Table definition for Audit table*

4. You can add columns easily in this table by inserting the column as a row in the Table Definition dialog box. Click the field row you want to insert a column in front of and then click Insert Row. You can select the specific column from the drop-down list in Field name. Insert the following rows prior to the Duration field: Constraint type, Constraint date, Type (task type), Effort driven, Milestone, Summary, Critical, Task calendar, Deadline, Cost, Work, and the Successor field

prior to the Predecessor field. Click the field called Show in the menu in the upper right corner of the dialog box so it shows in the table drop-down list so you will see the new table when you select View from the menu bar. Click OK.

5. If you would like to use this table, it is in a file on your CD called Task-Audit-Table-Project.mpp. You can copy this file to use on your projects by following the next steps. If you create your own table, you could follow the same steps.

6. Open Task-Audit-Table-Project.mpp in your version of Project. Select Organizer from the drop-down list to open the Organizer dialog box. The Organizer allows you to copy fields, views, and other items you customize for availability to all of your projects.

7. Click the Tables tab. On the left side of the screen are the default or other tables that are available in your Global.mpt template. On the right side of the Organizer are the tables that are available in the current project. The Task Audit table (or whatever table you created) will be on the right side.

8. Click Task Audit table on the right side of the project and click Copy.

9. Notice that the carets next to Copy are now pointing toward the Global.mpt area on the left side of the display. This will move the new table from the current project into the Global.mpt, which will make the calendar available to all projects you create in the future.

10. Close the dialog box by clicking Close when you are done. You do not need to click OK to make this effective.

See Chapter 11 for more on creating customized tables and views.

When you are ready to use this table after creating it and moving it to the Global.mpt template, you can use it to review any project. To do so, follow these steps:

1. In the project you want to review, make sure you are on a task or table view, such as the Gantt Chart. Select View, and then click Table.

2. In the drop-down list, select the Task Audit table (or the table you created) and the table will be applied to the view.

3. When you are done with your review, select View, click Table, and return to the table you would like to view.

Final Thoughts on Reviewing Your Schedule

As stated earlier, there is an art to scheduling, especially when it comes to understanding workloads. Some of what you decide about the schedule is based on your understanding of the nuances of what your organization and your resources tolerate. Pragmatically, as you review your schedule, there are some things you don't have to worry about. For instance, if resources are overallocated several days in a week, but not every day in the week, they might not be overallocated. If someone is allocated for 10 hours on one day and 6 hours on the next day, then the work can get done. In your organization, the situation might indicate that a resource is overallocated; in another, it might not be.

If your schedule is long, you might actually estimate order of magnitude on later phases of the project. You might try to perform more precise estimating for the early phases, such as planning and design, but you might have high-level estimates on testing and production until you are done with the early phases of the project. You might leave generic resources on the later tasks, so some of the tips about reviewing your schedule would not apply to later portions of the schedule. Some organizations might require schedules that have real resources on the schedule in later phases, because of their cultural need for more preciseness. Again, you have to adjust to your organization with the art of understand what it needs.

Although you want to try and be accurate, your plan will not be perfect. The true art of being a project manager is adjusting to real life, your organization's tolerances, and the changes that occur as your project progresses. The next step after building your schedule is to track what is really happening to the project and making adjustments as you go along. You should return to the schedule weekly to review. Execution tells the truth about a project, but planning is a form of trying to get it right by an accurate prediction. Good project managers know that they will need to adjust their schedules, and if they say it was on time and within budget, it is probably not because the project followed the plan perfectly, but because the project manager monitored and continued to review and adjust the work reflected in the schedule.

Checks to Review Your Schedule

Now that you know about the various methods of reviewing your schedule, here are the steps you should take for reviewing your schedule.

1. Create and save a special audit table or view for reviewing your schedule as described earlier.

2. Open your project.

3. Check spelling and style; think about who will be reviewing your schedule.

4. Check your project's settings on at least the Schedule, Calculation, and Calendar tabs in Tools, Options from the menu bar.

5. Check the project start date and project calendar in Project, Project Information.

6. Then, in the task audit table, check the following:
   - Task calendars
   - Deadlines
   - The task outline, making sure it makes sense
   - Milestones
   - Task relationships
   - Task types
   - Task constraints
   - Work and Duration
   - Resources on tasks (no duplicates) and generics
   - Costs

7. Change to the Resource Sheet view and check resources, rates, and their calendars.

8. Finally, check the critical path and overallocation of resources. In Chapter 9 I describe critical path and overallocation in more detail.

As you review the schedule, if you make a change, make sure you are careful about the changes, because you cannot undo the changes easily (unless you have Project 2007, where you can use Change highlighting and multiple Undo). In versions prior to Project 2007, don't hesitate to save a file with another filename before making changes that you are not sure about. Your disk space is cheap compared to your time. Both Multiple Undos and saving files are method to also try "what-if" scenarios if you need to try and adjust your schedule.

Adding to or Changing the Schedule

After you build your schedule, you will still make changes. In the following section I describe some items you might need to change or add and how you might use them and the consequences of changing them.

Notes

After you have published the schedule, if original estimates or expectations have changed on a task, it is a good idea to add notes to your schedule. The documentation provides information for you or others viewing the schedule to detail the changes made. To add notes, double-click any task or right-click a task and click Task Notes.

References to Project Documents

You can also indicate where project documents should be stored for each task. For instance, you might have a task called Approve marketing plan and you want to indicate where the approved marketing plan is stored. There are a couple of ways you could do this. You could use the notes for the task and indicate the network path for the document; or you could create a hyperlink for it, click the tasks, and right-click the task and select Hyperlink in the drop-down list. It's important to understand that the path or hyperlink has to be maintained if you use these methods.

No matter what method you have for storing project documents (and Project provides plenty of methods), it will not work as a central repository until everyone buys into it. It could take a while, but if you take the lead and find others who will help, you can create a habit so that all project documents are stored consistently and in one location. As soon as you hear someone asking another project manager, "Did you store it in the central network location (whatever the standard is you are trying to create)?" and others nod, the method will start working.

Adding or Changing Tasks

As you polish your schedule, you might find you need to add, remove, or change tasks. It's important to review all aspects of your schedule if you do this.

- **Adding (inserting) a task:** You use the same methodology for building the schedule when you add a task, but in a shortened format. You will decide where the task belongs in the WBS, which task type it is, how it should be linked (this is very important but easy to overlook—check the predecessors and successors of the task), and as you add estimates, you review how duration, work, and resources are being added to the task to reflect it accurately. Your schedule can be set to autolink inserted tasks (this is set by default via selecting Tools from the menu bar, clicking Options, and selecting the Schedule tab and selecting or clearing the Autolink inserted or moved tasks check box). You need to make sure the linking that occurs is really what you want. When you add the task, it usually changes the end date of the project or any successor tasks unless you made it a parallel task, and it almost always adds to work and increases budget.

- **Changing tasks:** Changing tasks might mean changing the name to something more meaningful or changing the attributes, resources, or estimates on the task. If you need to change the linking (predecessors or successors), you need to review the entire schedule to make sure you didn't create some other kind of strange looping or linking you didn't expect. If you are using Project 2007, make sure Change highlighting is enabled when you start changing tasks. It will help you analyze quickly what issues you might have with the change.

Links sometimes get "stuck"

Now and then, no matter what you do, the links between tasks create error or warning messages you cannot easily troubleshoot. Often, this is because you violate the best practice schedule-building methodology, or because of typos. Although it might seem frustrating to you, it can sometimes be better just to remove the links on a task and start over again. Every now and then, it's because of some logic that is not readily apparent to you and redoing the logic points out the issues. Sometimes you need to reexamine the full path of links to understand what is causing the issue. Again, if you have Project 2007, the multiple Undo and Change highlighting features will help you troubleshoot the issues.

- **Removing tasks:** If you remove tasks, sometimes you can orphan another task that was relying on it as a successor or predecessor. Before removing a task, make sure you see all the tasks that were relying on it and make plans to deal with any changes the removal causes.

Essentially, as you add, remove, or change tasks, you are extending the planning process for your schedule. You need to think through the same processes you thought through for building the schedule in the first place. Sometimes the changes mean that you are adding or removing work, which invokes change control. Although you might see issues in Project due to changing tasks (once the schedule is well developed), it might be a sign that you have made a change you need to bring to the attention of your sponsor or clients, because it adds to the scope of your project.

Changing Resources

As you change resources, make sure you consider the number of units, work, and duration. Changing resource is another form of art. Although you might change a named resource, it is often not just a name; you might have issues with skill set, training, or personality that can make changing a resource more complicated than a schedule implies. Based on your knowledge of the real people involved, you might need to change units, work, and duration to account for a person resource.

Reserves or Contingency

Often, you might want to include reserves, contingency, extra costs, or extra time that help defer risk in a Project schedule. You might also have a method to include contingency outside of the schedule itself; your manager or program might plan contingency as well. There are several ways to do this, and the following list provides you with just a few:

- Add a reserve percentage. You could just add extra days to your tasks and thus some reserve amount to both schedule and the resources on costs. If you have duration-based schedules, you might add a calculated amount to the Fixed Cost estimate for each task as well.
- You might also add extra days to the project by setting a deadline beyond the earliest finish date. Leave the tasks as they are but manage total slack (which now is your time contingency) on the final tasks (or on any task if you like).

- Add a small extra cost in the Fixed Cost field for each task. If you are already using the Fixed Cost field, this might not be the best solution.

- Add a line item or tasks for each phase or group of tasks with a cost indicating a reserve or contingency.

- Use the Program, Evaluation, and Review Technique (PERT) method for estimating task and use a weighted or pessimistic estimate to calculate contingency. Although it is beyond the scope of this book to describe this in detail, you can use an estimating method where subject matter experts provide you with optimistic (best case), pessimistic (worst case), and average (expected) estimates for a task. Project has a wonderful capability to allow you to enter these estimates and calculate your schedule from them.

  To use Project's PERT capability, select View from the menu bar and click PERT analysis from the drop-down list. You can use the button on the toolbar to guide you through entering each kind of estimate (best, worst, and expected) for tasks. You can use a weighted average calculation that provides the PERT estimate as the duration estimate you use in your schedule. Be aware that just getting the optimistic, pessimistic, and expected estimates from your project team or other experts can be a lot of work, so the risk needs to be worth the time you take.

You need to be very careful with contingencies. People will question why you are adding them and you should have some kind of rational and objective reasoning for adding a contingency.

Justifying contingency

To understand how to build and justify contingency, read Chapters 5, 9, and 10 in *Project Management for Mere Mortals*.

The Project Schedule Building Methodology So Far

Based on what you have learned, the following steps and sequence describe the best methods for building your schedule. The items emphasized in this chapter are indicated in italics. Because many organizations do not enter costs, I have also added an "optional" indicator in this list.

The steps for building a project schedule so far are as follows:

☑ If you are using a template, select the appropriate template (you will probably want to change it based on the input of your project team). If you are building a project from scratch, build a WBS with your team, then move to the next step.

☑ Set up your project calendar if you do not have one available. Make sure you reflect your company's hours in Tools, Options, Calendar, if different than the defaults.

☑ In the Project Information dialog box, set your project Start date and make sure your project calendar is assigned to the project.

☑ Start building (if your project is from scratch) or editing (if you are using a template) your task list. Make sure you indicate summary tasks and subtasks to help indicate the outline of your project schedule.

☑ Add milestone tasks to indicate significant events, deliverables, or approval points in your project.

☑ Enter deadline dates for appropriate tasks. This is a better way of indicating dates when tasks need to be completed rather than typing in a Finish date on a task.

☑ Add task calendars to tasks to indicate exceptions to the project calendar if needed. You will probably not need these kinds of calendars often.

☑ Review all tasks. Decide what kind of tasks they are for the schedule-building process. Change the Task type and Effort-driven fields if appropriate.

☑ Link all tasks in the schedule, determining if they are Finish-to-Start, Start-to-Start, Finish-to-Finish, or Start-to-Finish relationships. Link among phases or task groupings first, then link between phases or groupings. Use the Predecessor and Successor columns to help you see if all tasks are linked.

☑ Build the project team. Add all resources that might work on the project to the Resource Sheet for the project. If you are performing effort-based scheduling, enter the Maximum Units each resource can work on the project. You can use generic or real resources but when you know who will do the work, you should replace generic resources with real resources.

☑ Assign the resources to each task. If you are performing effort-based scheduling, you might need to change the percentage of allocation a resource is assigned to individual tasks in some cases.

☑ Enter estimates for project tasks. For Effort-based scheduling, enter two of the three variables in the Work formula: Work = Duration × Units.

☑ Review the schedule and enter leads and lags on tasks if appropriate.

☑ Review the critical path and adjust tasks if appropriate.

☑ [Optional] Set your cost default cost calculation methods: Have Project automatically calculate Actual Costs and decide on and set up your Cost Accrual method for the entire project.

☑ [Optional] Set up any other kinds of resources, such as material resources (set up cost and budget resources if you are using Project 2007) if you want to include costs other than labor or equipment work costs in your project.

☑ [Optional] Insert the Cost and Fixed Cost fields in the Gantt Chart view (or use the Table: Cost view). Enter rates on resources, enter Fixed Costs on tasks, or enter Total budget on the project summary task line, depending on how your organization has decided to enter cost.

☑ *Check your schedule for logic and scheduling errors using a special audit view or reviewing the errors using methods described in this chapter.*

Summary

After you have created your schedule and are ready to put the final touches on it, it's a good idea to review it, just as you would review any work you produce for others to see. The reviewing process of your schedule involves looking at all the areas of your schedule including the following:

- Review task names, task hierarchy (the WBS), relationships between tasks, and milestones.

- Review estimates on task timing, including duration, work, constraints, and deadlines. Review the entire schedule for reasonableness of duration and work.

- Review resources on the tasks and attributes about the resources (e.g., rates and calendars).

- Review the reasonableness and accuracy of costs for tasks and the entire schedule.

In the next chapter schedule review continues. You will see how you deal with overallocation and adjusting the critical path.

Practice: Looking for Errors

The following practice exercises have you check for errors using the Group and Filter capability in Project. Although these are excellent features for reporting, they can also help you check your project schedule for scheduling and logic errors.

Practice 8.1

Checking for Errors Using Grouping

To start, use the project called HousePainting-Practice-Chapter8-Practice1.mpp on your CD. This project will have a few issues for you to find while reviewing the schedule.

1. Before performing some grouping exercises, check your task's spelling. Select Tools from the menu bar, and then click Spelling. There should be one word misspelled. Correct the misspelled word.

2. Check to make sure your settings in the Options dialog box are appropriate. You want to make sure all new tasks that you add to the project are Fixed Units, Effort-driven. To make sure that happens, select Tools from the menu bar, and then click Options. Select the Schedule tab, and select the Default task type on the screen check box. Change the selection to Fixed Units if it is not Fixed Units, and click OK.

3. A task calendar is on Task 11, Paint. To remove the calendar, click twice on the Paint task, and on the Advanced tab of the Task Information dialog box, change the selection in the Calendar field to None, then click OK.

4. Review some of the items on the schedule using Grouping. First, review the constraints. You do not want any constraints on your project. To group, select Project from the menu bar, click Group by, and select Constraint type.

5. Double-click the task that shows in the Constraint type group, and on the Advanced tab of the Task Information dialog box. select As Soon as Possible in the Constraint type field. Click OK.

6. Remove the grouping by selecting Project from the menu bar, and select Group by. In the drop-down menu, select No Group.

7. Next, review the milestones. Do you have all the right milestones? To check them out, select Project from the menu bar, click Group by, and select Milestones. In this project, you probably have all the right milestones. This is a great way to review the milestone dates to see if they make sense and to see if you have accidentally entered resources on tasks and if the predecessors make sense. In this example, the Priming complete task has two predecessors. Does that make sense? In this case, it does because the masking of the windows and the priming will take place at the same time.

8. Remove the grouping by selecting Project from the menu bar and select Group by. In the drop-down list, select No Group.

9. Don't forget to inspect resources. Select View from the menu bar and click Resource Sheet. Select Project from the menu bar, click Group by and select Resource type. Depending on if you are using Project 2003 or Project 2007, you will either see Work and Material (Project 2000 through Project 2003) or Work and Cost (Project 2007).

10. Remove the grouping by selecting Project from the menu bar and select Group by. In the drop-down list, select No Group.

There is no result file for this exercise.

Practice 8.2

Checking for Errors Using Filtering

To start, use the project called HousePainting-Practice-Chapter8-Practice2.mpp on your CD.

1. Before performing some filtering exercises, check to see if your deadlines are set correctly. To review Deadlines easily, highlight the Task name field and select Insert from the menu bar. Click Column.

2. In the Column Definition dialog box, select Deadline in the Field name drop-down list, and click OK.

3. On the Prepping complete task, your deadline is 5/28, not 5/25. Click in the Deadline field on the Prepping complete task, click on the arrow in the field, and select 5/28/07 from the calendar.

4. Check all the successors and predecessors to make sure you have all your tasks linked. To include successors in your review, highlight the Predecessor field and select Successor from the menu bar. Click Column.

5. Notice that the Paint task is missing a successor. The Strip masking task comes after the Paint task. Enter 12 in the Successor field.

6. To check if any tasks are missing resources, select Project from the menu bar and click Autofilter from the bottom of the drop-down list. Arrows will appear on each column. Click on the arrow in the Resource names field. Names that are in the field for each task, and a blank line, appear in the list. To check out all of the tasks with no resources assigned, select the blank line.

7. You will see all the tasks with no resources. Summary tasks and milestones should not have resources, so they should be blank. However, the Strip masking task also lacks a resource. You can assign a resource to the task. The resource Me should be assigned at 50% allocation.

8. To remove the filter to get all the tasks back, click the arrow and select (All) at the top of the drop-down list.

9. To remove the Autofilter, select Project from the menu bar and click Filtered for. Click Autofilter at the bottom of the drop-down list to toggle the Autofilter off.

10. Some of the standard filters available are useful for reviewing the project. To filter for summary tasks, select Project from the menu bar and click Filtered for. Click Summary tasks from the drop-down list and click Apply. You can review the fields for each summary task as a sanity check to make sure they seem to make sense.

11. To remove the summary task filter, select Project from the menu bar and click Filtered for. Click All tasks from the drop-down list.

12. To filter for estimated tasks (those that still have the question mark in the Duration field), select Project from the menu bar, and click Filtered for. Click More filters. In the More Filters dialog box, select Tasks with estimated durations from the drop-down list and then click Apply.

13. You can review the fields for all the tasks that still have question marks. If you are using the question mark in that field to indicate that the task is still estimated and not confirmed with more solid estimates, you can remove the estimated designation. Double-click the tasks and any tab in the Task Information dialog box, clear the Estimated field and click OK.

14. To remove the filter, select Project from the menu bar, and click Filtered for. Click All tasks from the drop-down list.

15. This exercise has helped you understand how filtering can help you inspect your schedule.

There is no result file for this exercise.

Case Study: Reviewing the Schedule

Chris added other costs to finish off the first draft of the schedule. She included expenses for travel and lodging, building the booth, the registration fee, and other expenses. She entered them in the Fixed Cost field for the related tasks. She also met with June to discuss the budget and they both decided it was a good idea to add some contingency, reserves, and team award money for the project. Chris entered the cost contingency, reserves, and award money in the summary line of the Project management activities task. She is now ready to review the schedule to make sure it's as good as she can make it before setting the project plan baseline. Her first take is to review some of the common errors, using an audit table she created. She will use this audit table for all of her projects, and has already shared the table with Davis, a fellow project manager, so he can review his projects.

Open the file, VNLE-Chapter8-Begin-CaseStudy.mpp. The audit table has been set on the project. Review the data in the following order:

1. Select Tools, then Spelling to check for spelling errors. Are there any words spelled incorrectly?

2. Are there any task calendars set on any tasks? If there are any, remove them from the task by clicking the Task calendar field and selecting None.

3. There should be a milestone at the end of each summary group of tasks. Are there any missing? Change the milestone by selecting Yes in the Milestone drop-down list.

4. Are there any predecessors or successors missing or are there any predecessors or successors on summary tasks? If any are missing, what tasks have missing successors or predecessors? If some are missing, how would you fix it so that the tasks have the correct relationships?

5. Are there any task constraints? If so, remove them. To do so, change the task constraint to As Soon As Possible.

6. Are there any tasks missing resources being assigned to them? Which tasks are missing resources? How would you add the resources and allocate them correctly?

There is no result file for this case study. As a note, the file VNEL-Chapter8-CaseStudy-withoutAudit.mpp is also available on the CD but the audit table has not been applied to it if you would like to try your own audits on it.

Upon reviewing the schedule, Chris realizes that the current schedule ends on March 30 based on task relationships, estimated work effort, and no lag time. However, the event takes place in September. Next, Chris will look at adjusting and optimizing the schedule.

Reviewing the Schedule

A schedule review helps remove any glaring errors that could cause embarrassment or some false scheduling before you present the schedule to your team and management. Start your review by doing the following:

- Check for the most common errors such as misspelled words, unnecessary constraints, proper milestones, resources assigned appropriately, and task relationships (predecessors and successors) assigned appropriately.
- Use grouping, filtering, or an audit view to help review your schedule.

Once you have done this you can move on to other aspects of reviewing, such as revisiting the critical path or checking for overallocation.

Review Questions

1. What are at least five items you should check when reviewing your schedule?
2. What are the three most important tabs you should review on Tools, Options?
3. What are some of the methods you can use for reviewing your schedule?
4. How can a special audit view help you review your schedule?
5. Why is reviewing and correcting the schedule somewhat of an art?
6. How do you need to treat adding, removing, and changing tasks after your schedule is built?
7. How might you include reserve or contingency in your project?
8. Where do you enter PERT estimates in Project?

Reviewing Work Overload and the Critical Path

If you can find a path with no obstacles,
it probably doesn't lead anywhere.
—Frank A. Clark

Topics Covered in This Chapter

Understanding How Overallocation Happens

Ways to View Overallocation

Leveling Your Project Manually

Leveling Your Project Using Automated Leveling

Reviewing the Critical Path

One Last Look at Your Schedule

The Project Schedule Building Methodology So Far

Summary

Practice: Reviewing Overallocation and the Critical Path

Case Study: Leveling and the Critical Path

In the last chapter, I went over the relatively simple aspects of polishing your schedule, which included reviewing for some common errors and fixing the issues. We need an entire chapter to discuss the difficult aspects: fixing resource overallocation and reviewing the critical path. Adjusting these two elements in the schedule is what most people really want from a scheduling tool, even if they don't know exactly what the two terms mean. The first subject I cover in this chapter is overallocation, which means that the resources on the schedule have so much work assigned in the same time period that they can't get the work done unless they work overtime (and even doing that might not work). The project manager or scheduler must do something to the schedule to even their work out. Sometimes people don't like the idea of adjusting the schedule because the tasks or projects will not get done on the dates that management has mandated. They want to look the other way and hope it gets done on time. However, the purpose of scheduling is to figure out how to manage allocating the right resources, in the right amounts, for the right time frames so the work can get done. It's also important to understand that sometimes the way Project allocates resources it looks like some resources are overallocated when in reality they are not. In many cases, resources are working three projects at the same time and project managers schedule the resources at 100%. Because the project managers are ignoring the real workload of the resources, Project can't show that they are overallocated.

You read about the critical path in Chapter 5, "Sequencing the Work: Creating the Critical Path," when you learned about sequence the work with Project. You learned that you should build the schedule sequencing first, without regard to resources or entering estimates. You can view an initial critical path before the resources or estimates are entered, but adding resources to tasks can affect the critical path dramatically. If the duration increases or decreases, the critical path can change. In this chapter, I revisit the critical path to make sure you understand how it is important and why you want to make corrections for your final pass of the project schedule. You can find the definition of the critical path in any project management book. A simple definition is that the critical path is the sequence of the tasks through the project that have no slack (room to slip): If the duration of any tasks on the path changes it will affect the end date of the project. The definition includes understanding that some tasks can start later than originally scheduled yet can finish without affecting the scheduled beginning of successor tasks or the end date of the project because they have slack or float. I do not want to make this book a lesson in the critical path method technique for managing a schedule, but it's important that you understand how Project—by the way it is programmed—helps you use this technique to help you create the most efficient schedule.

Resource allocation and the critical path

See *Project Management for Mere Mortals* to help clarify and solidify the concept of resource overallocation, and specifically Chapter 9 about the critical path.

Understanding How Overallocation Happens

To understand how overallocation occurs, it helps to look at how Project assigns resources to tasks. The following example (Figure 9.1) shows a project with three tasks: Build, Document, and Test. The resource R1 has been assigned to each task at 100% units.

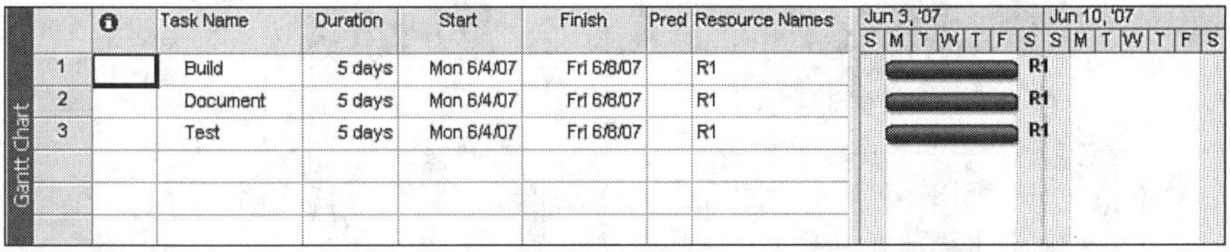

	ⓘ	Task Name	Duration	Start	Finish	Pred	Resource Names	Jun 3, '07 S M T W T F S	Jun 10, '07 S M T W T F S
1		Build	5 days	Mon 6/4/07	Fri 6/8/07		R1	R1	
2		Document	5 days	Mon 6/4/07	Fri 6/8/07		R1	R1	
3		Test	5 days	Mon 6/4/07	Fri 6/8/07		R1	R1	

Figure 9.1 *Three tasks with the same resource allocated*

Although it shows that R1 has been assigned to all three tasks at the same time in the Gantt view, it might not be apparent that the work can't get done. However, when you change to the Resource Usage view, it's very apparent because Project is assigning the work at 8 hours a day as shown in Figure 9.2.

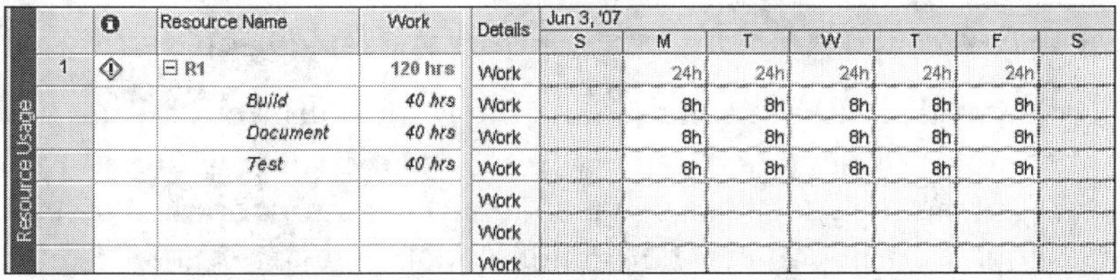

	ⓘ	Resource Name	Work	Details	Jun 3, '07 S	M	T	W	T	F	S
1	⟐	⊟ R1	120 hrs	Work		24h	24h	24h	24h	24h	
		Build	40 hrs	Work		8h	8h	8h	8h	8h	
		Document	40 hrs	Work		8h	8h	8h	8h	8h	
		Test	40 hrs	Work		8h	8h	8h	8h	8h	
				Work							
				Work							
				Work							

Figure 9.2 *Resource Usage view shows overallocation*

An icon appears in the Indicator field and when you hover the cursor over the indicator, it suggests that the resource needs to be leveled using a day-by-day setting. The resource name (Work field) and the rolled up day-by-day totals in the grid display in red to indicate an overallocation. To alleviate overallocation, you will want to distribute all task work as evenly as possible over the schedule for the resources assigned so they aren't trying to do too much work in a particular time frame; this activity is called leveling. Part of the trick is performing leveling as quickly and efficiently as possible.

In Figure 9.2, notice that the allocation of the resource work hours is set equally across each task. By default, Project allocates resources using a flat contour per day. If you double-click any of the tasks showing in the Resource Usage view, you will see the Assignment Information dialog box as shown in Figure 9.3. The Work contour field displays Flat as the default work contour and also shows the other kinds of contouring you can apply to a task.

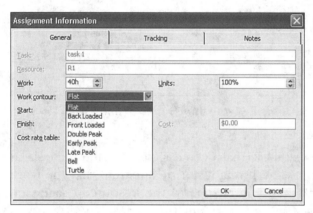

Figure 9.3 *Work contour as shown in Assignment Information dialog box*

Use work contouring rarely or for advanced scheduling

The work contour indicates how the work is distributed over time. Although it might be tempting to try and use some of the other contours to spread the allocation of a resource, the contour applied to a task should actually reflect the kind of work being done, rather than using it for distributing the work. Do not change the default contouring if you are new to using Project. To see what each of the contours does to a task, create a 5-day task and apply each contour to the task. As you can see, it distributes the work according to the work contour. For instance, the Bell Work contour will schedule 40 hours worth of work so little work is done at the beginning, most work is done in the middle of the task, then the work diminishes, just like a Bell curve. The Test task in Figure 9.4 shows the bell work contour.

	ⓘ	Resource Name	Work	Details	M	T	W	T	F	S	Jun 10, '07 S	M	T	W	T	F
1	◇	⊟ R1	120 hrs	Work	16.8h	17.6h	19.2h	22.4h	24h				8h	6.4h	3.2h	1.6h	0.8h
		Build	40 hrs	Work	8h	8h	8h	8h	8h								
		Document	40 hrs	Work	8h	8h	8h	8h	8h								
	⏸	Test	40 hrs	Work	0.8h	1.6h	3.2h	6.4h	8h				8h	6.4h	3.2h	1.6h	0.8h
				Work													
				Work													
				Work													

Figure 9.4   *Test task with bell work contour applied*

In this book, I explain overallocation and leveling using the default method of a flat contour. It is important to understand contouring because as you try to level out the work of resources or enter actual work progress, Project continues to use the default contour to calculate the planned or remaining work.

Many users of Project expect miracles from the automated leveling feature, hoping the tool itself will figure out how to make sure the resources can get the work done by the end date of the Project. Here's a typical scenario (I might be exaggerating, but it has happened to many of us in building a schedule): Your organization gives you the date by which you are supposed to finish the Project. Then you get a certain number of resources based on initial planning numbers. You create the detailed schedule and realize that you should have started months earlier, need to reduce the scope, or will have to work overtime to make the date. Rather than leveling or working through the issues, some project managers publish the schedule as it is and hope they can somehow make the date. The project probably won't get done by the mandated date, although if the estimates were fairly close and the number of resources doesn't increase, you just won't make the finish date. Then you and your team might complain about having too much work but you can't prove it because you didn't create a realistic schedule. Instead, you might consider being realistic, which means creating a real schedule, then discussing the trade-offs to get the work done based on the evidence of what is showing in the schedule.

Users of Project look to the tool for help in performing the leveling (smoothing out the work to make sure resources aren't overallocated). Many people expect Project to level the resources for them. It does some of the work, but Project doesn't really understand the work itself; it uses what you've input to make decisions and even with that, Project is limited to certain rules. Leveling is a difficult intellectual exercise. The schedule lets you analyze what you have, then you have to make the changes to allocate resources fairly and adjust the tasks to get the work done as close to the plan as possible.

With that in mind you could think of several ways of logically leveling resources' time, as shown earlier in Figure 9.2. R1 is supposed to do all the work and right now, during the same week. Logically, R1 cannot work all of the tasks at the same time. For instance, you really can't test until you build. Therefore, if you link the Test task so it is a successor of the Build task, leveling occurs, as shown in Figures 9.5 and 9.6.

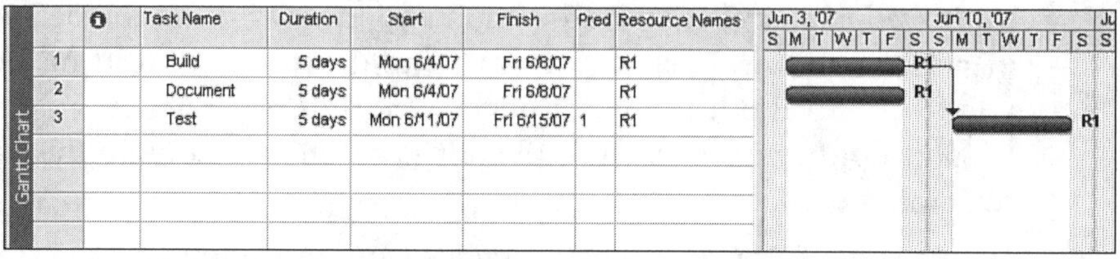

Figure 9.5 *Linking two tasks sequentially reallocates work*

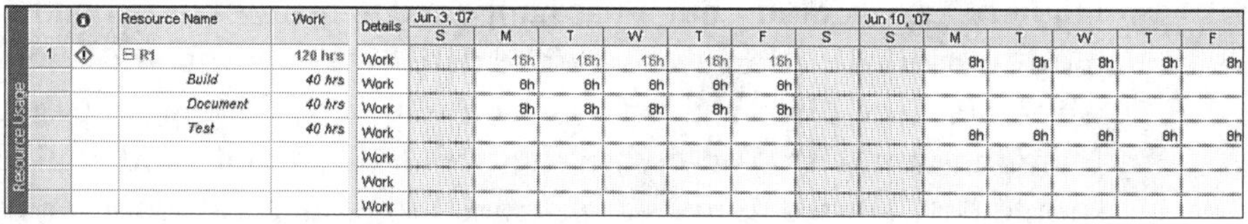

Figure 9.6 *Resource Usage demonstrates how a resource is leveled*

Based on this change, you realize R1 can document while building and testing. To do this, R1 can work part time on the documentation task while building and testing. So you allocate R1 at 50% at the task level as shown in Figure 9.7.

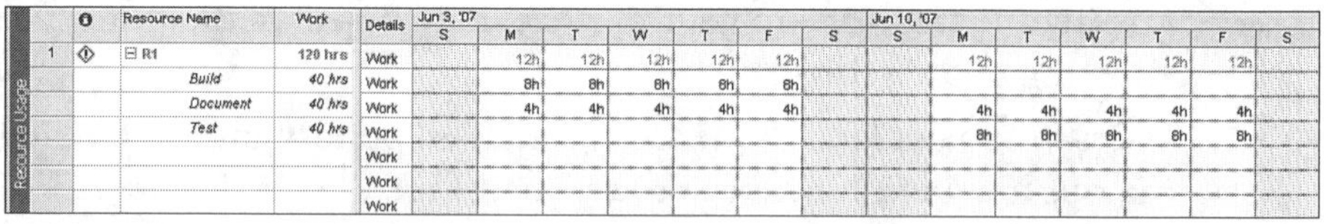

Figure 9.7 *Leveling of the Document task*

Now the resource work allocation is more reasonable but R1 still has too much work. You could choose to take a chance and leave the schedule as is because you had some conservative estimates that contained some contingency, or perhaps R1 agrees to work overtime. It's probably best if you continue to level. In this case, you decide to assign the resource at 70% for the first task, 30% for the second task, and 70% for the last task. Figures 9.8 and 9.9 show the result with the last 2 weeks of the Resource Usage view displaying.

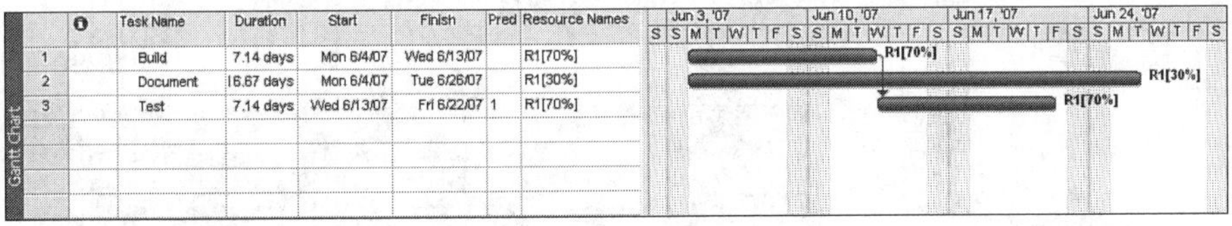

Figure 9.8   *Changing assigned units elongates the schedule*

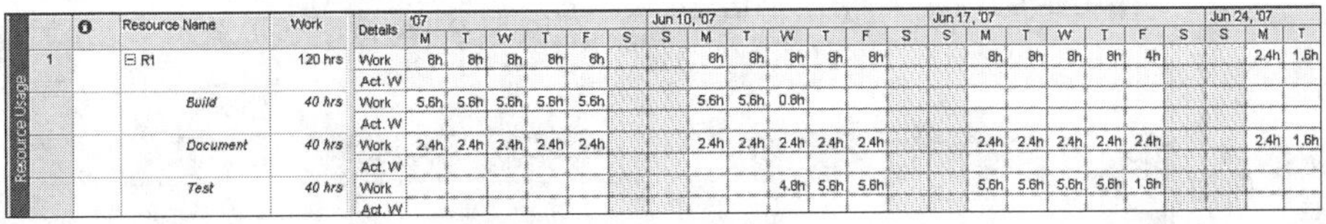

Figure 9.9   *Changing assigned units levels the resource*

This isn't bad. R1 can work 8 hours a day for 3 weeks. Most people get frustrated that Project continues to allocate the work at a flat contour, so in this case the task will be done on Tuesday. On Friday, June 22, total work is 4 hours; on Monday, June 25, 2.4 hours; and on June 26, 1.6 hours. In reality, the work can end on Friday if the work on June 25 and 26 is moved. You might decide to zero out the hours on Monday and Tuesday and move the remaining 4 hours to Friday. If you do not expect to do much more leveling or make many changes on your project, this might be okay. However, once you edit time on a day, Project will continue to leave whatever you enter in that day there, so if you are doing any leveling or continuing to build the schedule, leave it and use it as contingency. As a note, if this task is on the critical path or potentially could be, this is a place to gain 2 days. As R1 works and actual time is applied, if the work gets completed on Friday as planned, the schedule will show completion on Friday.

Then again, if you had to get all the work done within the 1 week originally shown, you really only have the option of adding a lot of resources. Figures 9.10 and 9.11 show a view of how many people you would have to assign each task to ensure no one was overallocated. Or you could assign each person to a task. The problem with the two examples is that it is a mathematical exercise rather than a thought process taking into account the nature and coordination of the work itself and the skills of the resources. For instance, perhaps the project should have two people building, an experienced tester performing the test, and a writer performing the Document task to ensure better quality and control. Testing really does usually have to follow building, so it doesn't make sense to set it up so you are doing them at the same time.

	❶	Task Name	Duration	Start	Finish	Pred	Resource Names
1		Build	4.9 days	Mon 6/4/07	Fri 6/8/07		R1[34%],R2[34%],R3[34%]
2		Document	4.9 days	Mon 6/4/07	Fri 6/8/07		R1[34%],R2[34%],R3[34%]
3		Test	4.9 days	Mon 6/4/07	Fri 6/8/07		R1[34%],R2[34%],R3[34%]

Figure 9.10   *More resources added*

	❶	Resource Name	Work	Details	Jun 3, '07 S	M	T	W	T	F	S
1	◇	⊟ R1	40 hrs	Work		8.17h	8.17h	8.17h	8.17h	7.37h	
		Build	13.33 hrs	Work		2.72h	2.72h	2.72h	2.72h	2.45h	
		Document	13.33 hrs	Work		2.72h	2.72h	2.72h	2.72h	2.45h	
		Test	13.33 hrs	Work		2.72h	2.72h	2.72h	2.72h	2.45h	
2	◇	⊟ R2	40 hrs	Work		8.17h	8.17h	8.17h	8.17h	7.37h	
		Build	13.33 hrs	Work		2.72h	2.72h	2.72h	2.72h	2.45h	
		Document	13.33 hrs	Work		2.72h	2.72h	2.72h	2.72h	2.45h	
		Test	13.33 hrs	Work		2.72h	2.72h	2.72h	2.72h	2.45h	
3	◇	⊟ R3	40 hrs	Work		8.17h	8.17h	8.17h	8.17h	7.37h	
		Build	13.33 hrs	Work		2.72h	2.72h	2.72h	2.72h	2.45h	
		Document	13.33 hrs	Work		2.72h	2.72h	2.72h	2.72h	2.45h	
		Test	13.33 hrs	Work		2.72h	2.72h	2.72h	2.72h	2.45h	

Figure 9.11   *Resource usage showing work distribution*

In the next sections, I describe how to view and analyze overallocation and provide some ideas on what to do about it.

Ways to Review Overallocation

There are several ways to review overallocation. We've looked at the Resource Usage view and there are some additional things that you can do with it to review the allocation of resources. I will illustrate some of the views using the Roofing project. Because we built the schedule so well in previous chapters, there really isn't anyone terribly overallocated, so I have changed the schedule to make sure some of the resources are overallocated.

In the Resource Usage view, you can add several pieces of information to help understand the overallocation. Figure 9.12 has several more fields to help analyze the overallocation. To see this view, on the right side of the separator bar, right-click anywhere in the grid. By default, the Overallocation and Remaining availability selections will show in the Detail styles list and you can select both of them by clicking each of them. (You can't add them at the same time, so you'll have to perform this action twice.) It is also useful to see the percent allocation field. To see that, you must right-click again in the grid, click Detail Styles and on the list in the left side of the Detail Styles dialog box, select Percent Allocation, click Show and then click OK.

	Resource Name	Work	Details	May 20, '07 S	M	T	W	T	F	May 27, '07 S	M	T	W	T	F
2	⊟ Wilson	130 hrs	Work		13.33h	16h	20.67h	10.67h	10.67h		10.67h	10.67h	10.67h	10.67h	2.67h
			Overalloc.		5.33h	8h	12.67h	2.67h	2.67h		2.67h	2.67h	2.67h	2.67h	
			% Alloc.		167%	200%	258%	133%	133%		133%	133%	133%	133%	33%
			Rem. Avail.		0h	0h	0h	0h	0h		0h	0h	0h	0h	5.33h
	Remove previous roofing	50 hrs	Work		13.33h	13.33h	10h								
			Overalloc.		5.33h	5.33h	2h								
			% Alloc.		167%	167%	125%								
			Rem. Avail.												
	Perform roofing	80 hrs	Work			2.67h	10.67h	10.67h	10.67h		10.67h	10.67h	10.67h	10.67h	2.67h
			Overalloc.			2.67h	2.67h	2.67h			2.67h	2.67h	2.67h	2.67h	
			% Alloc.			33%	133%	133%	139%		133%	133%	133%	133%	33%
			Rem. Avail.												
3	⊟ Jose	110 hrs	Work		8h	10.67h	16.67h	10.67h	10.67h		10.67h	10.67h	10.67h	10.67h	2.67h
			Overalloc.			2.67h	8.67h	2.67h	2.67h		2.67h	2.67h	2.67h	2.67h	
			% Alloc.		100%	133%	208%	133%	133%		133%	133%	133%	133%	33%
			Rem. Avail.		0h	0h	0h	0h	0h		0h	0h	0h	0h	5.33h
	Remove previous roofing	30 hrs	Work		8h	8h	6h								
			Overalloc.												
			% Alloc.		100%	100%	75%								
			Rem. Avail.												
	Perform roofing	80 hrs	Work			2.67h	10.67h	10.67h	10.67h		10.67h	10.67h	10.67h	10.67h	2.67h
			Overalloc.			2.67h	2.67h	2.67h			2.67h	2.67h	2.67h	2.67h	
			% Alloc.			33%	133%	133%	133%		133%	133%	133%	133%	33%
4	⊟ Lila	34 hrs	Work		8h	8h	8h								
			Overalloc.												
			% Alloc.		100%	100%	75%								
			Rem. Avail.		0h	0h	2h	8h	8h		8h	8h	8h	8h	8h

Figure 9.12 *Resource Usage showing Work, Overallocation, Percent Allocation, and Remaining availability*

You can also click the Zoom Out button and view the Resource Usage grid in a weekly view. In analyzing the view you would see that the Chief is also overallocated (although this is not showing in Figure 9.12). You would notice that his Maximum Units are 25% (2 hours each day), but on a Friday and a Monday he is working 6 hours and 4 hours, respectively. In reality, he might work 3 hours on one day, and 1 hour on another day. It's simply important he gets the work done within the time frame, and it's not really important if it shows he's overallocated here and there. In all, he can accomplish his work in the time frame provided. The Chief's overallocation is not really overallocation, but Project will warn you that it is based on the rules you set up (in this case, Maximum Units).

Another great method for analyzing overallocation is to view the Resource Graph. To do so, select View, and then click Resource Graph. On the left side of the separator bar is the resource. In Figure 9.13, you will see Wilson's allocation. You can right-click in the graph area on the right side of the separator bar and see various other kinds of charts you can select in this same graph style.

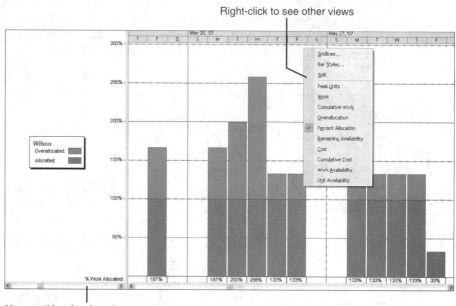

Figure 9.13 *Resource Graph for analyzing overallocation*

You can also analyze resource overallocation on a task-by-task basis via the Task Usage view. Figure 9.14 focuses the view on the two main tasks that had overallocated resources: Remove previous roofing and Perform roofing. You can see that Wilson is overallocated. The Perform roofing task has a lead because someone could start laying down new roofing on a side of the house once substantial removal of the old roofing occurs. Due to the amount of time Wilson is allocated, he can't do both. Because your aim is to ensure the resources do not work much over 8 hours a day, you might need to ask Lila to do more or obtain another resource. However, another resource might be difficult to find, and Lila is really a part-time worker. Maybe you just need to even the work out by adding a few more days to the schedule. All of these are alternatives you can use, depending on what your real driver for the project is.

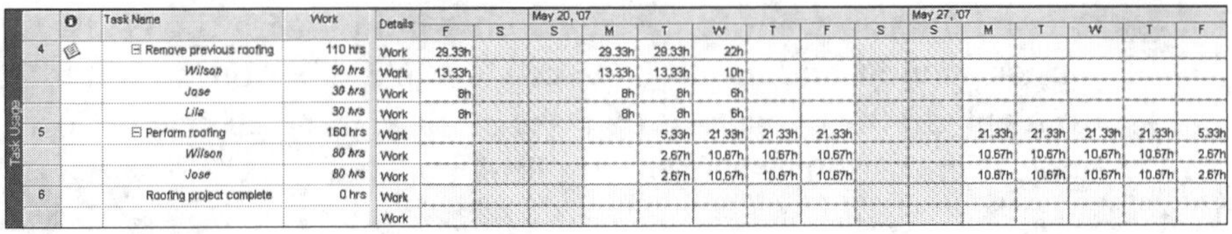

	❶	Task Name	Work	Details	May 20, '07 F	S	S	M	T	W	T	F	S	May 27, '07 S	M	T	W	T	F
4	📋	⊟ Remove previous roofing	110 hrs	Work	29.33h			29.33h	29.33h	22h									
		Wilson	50 hrs	Work	13.33h			13.33h	13.33h	10h									
		Jose	30 hrs	Work	8h			8h	8h	6h									
		Lila	30 hrs	Work	8h			8h	8h	6h									
5		⊟ Perform roofing	160 hrs	Work				5.33h	21.33h	21.33h	21.33h			21.33h	21.33h	21.33h	21.33h	5.33h	
		Wilson	80 hrs	Work				2.67h	10.67h	10.67h	10.67h			10.67h	10.67h	10.67h	10.67h	2.67h	
		Jose	80 hrs	Work				2.67h	10.67h	10.67h	10.67h			10.67h	10.67h	10.67h	10.67h	2.67h	
6		Roofing project complete	0 hrs	Work															
				Work															

Figure 9.14   *Task Usage to help resolve overallocations*

Consider what your scheduling driver is

While you are resolving overallocations, you need to consider what your scheduling drivers are to make decisions. You need to consider each resource's workload, skill set of the resources, whether you can get more resources, the importance of making the end date, and if resources can work some overtime. Just because you can reschedule to reduce overallocation, it might not be necessary.

You can include these views in a split screen view as well, with the Gantt Chart being on the top and one of the views at the bottom, although there's a certain amount of adjustments you have to make to the view. To display a view similar to Figure 9.15, you would highlight all the tasks in the Gantt Chart, and then scroll in the bottom window to see exactly how each resource was allocated on a day-by-day basis. If you use this method you often have to make some adjustments to the timescale grid in the usage view.

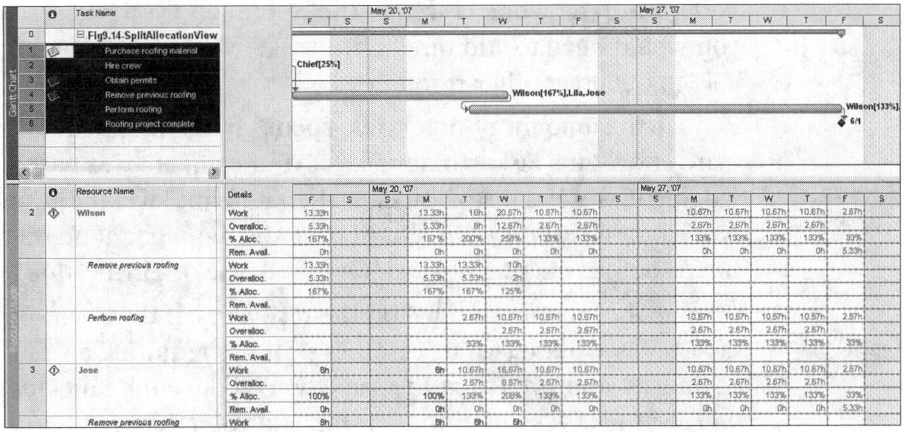

Figure 9.15   *Gantt chart with Resource Usage view in split window*

You might also want to use the split window with the Gantt Chart in the upper window and the Task Usage view in the bottom window. Don't forget to highlight the overallocated tasks in the Gantt chart view. Now let's take a look at the various ways you can level resources.

Leveling Your Project Manually

If your schedule is short you might consider leveling your schedule manually before using Project's automated leveling tool. If you have a long project and resources are overallocated, consider leveling in chunks: looking at phases or summary tasks first, then leveling across the entire project.

The following list describes the major ways you can level your project manually when resources are overallocated on tasks. In most cases, you would adjust the duration, units (amount of available time a resource is assigned), work, or sequencing of tasks to accomplish your leveling as described earlier in Figures 9.5 through 9.11.

- Link tasks with the same resource(s) sequentially. This solution was described earlier with the example of Figure 9.5. A problem with this solution is that you might be able to get the work done faster if the tasks can logically be accomplished simultaneously. In such a case, though, you would need different resources. If you are limited to a single resource, linking the tasks might be your best solution.

- Assign a different resource to one of the tasks. An issue with this solution might be that the other resource is not as qualified or might not understand the work as well as the resource(s) you had assigned and you would need to add time to the task. Of course, you might not be able to obtain another resource.

- Reduce the amount of time to be spent on the task. Reducing the estimate effort on a task can be risky. If your estimate was based on expert judgment or good historical data, then it might level the resources' work, but in reality you might not see the work get done on time since the resources might still have to work to the original estimate.

- Change the amount of units on the resources. If the resource is set at 80%, but is working on three other projects requiring a similar amount of time as your project at the same time, reduce the units more. You will see the task's duration increase, and you might not like it. This might be an accurate reflection of what needs to happen, and so the schedule's end date could move out, but odds are that if you don't change it, the resource won't get the work done anyway.

- Add resources to the task to help get it done faster. In theory, adding resources to a task will get the work done faster and in many cases it helps, so this sometimes seems to be the easy answer. However, project managers often don't have the luxury of adding more resources. If you can add resources, you would need to obtain permission to use them, and they would have to be qualified to do the work. There is often ramp-up and management time for additional resources that might also need to be added to the schedule. You would need to consider the nature of the work to decide if more resources will really help.

- Reduce the scope of the task's work. By reducing scope you will eliminate some portion of the deliverable and thus reduce the effort. You might be able to assign the resource at fewer units or move around the times you need the resources. This solution can be risky because when you reduce scope, you might not be delivering everything your client or sponsor expected.

- Reduce quality. By reducing quality, you could reduce some of the effort required to complete the task. For instance, maybe you could eliminate some review cycles. However, if quality is reduced, you might have to do rework later when the product of the project is delivered.

- Delay the start of tasks or resource's assignments on the task. Sometimes you just need to start the task a day or a week later so resources are available to do the work. Perhaps you can actually start the task at the end of the phase rather than at the beginning. Or maybe only one resource is overallocated. Perhaps you could delay the start of that resource's work by a day or two, even though the rest of the resources can start on the task as scheduled. This solution often works well on tasks that have slack. However, a delay not only changes the end date of the task; if it is on the critical path, it can delay the end date of the project. See the section "Leveling Your Project Using Automated Leveling" later in this chapter for more information about delaying a resource's start on a task. See the later discussion of critical path and slack to understand more about slack. Project's automated leveling function uses delay as one of its major adjustments to the schedule.

- Split a task. You might have a situation where a resource is scheduled to work on two tasks at the same time and is overloaded. However, you could split the first task so the resource can start working on it.

Then the resource can move to the second task, then return to the first task when done. This works especially well when Task 2 is on the critical path. However, splitting tasks might mean that the split task actually takes longer because of ramp-up time needed when returning to the task. This probably happens more often in real life and never gets reflected in the schedule. A split task is illustrated in Figure 9.16. Project's automated leveling function splits tasks as one of its major adjustments to the schedule when it levels.

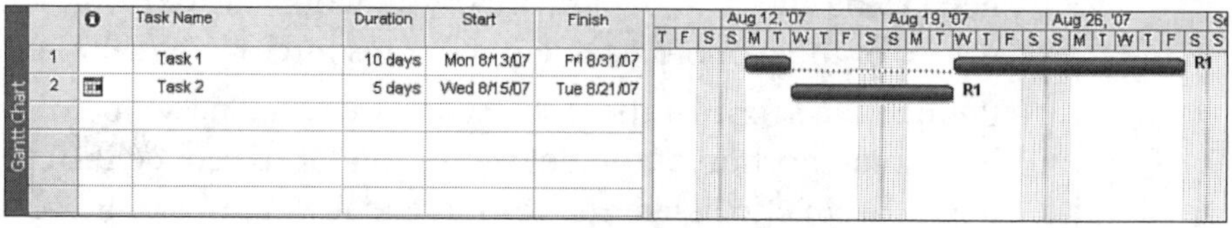

Figure 9.16   *Splitting a task can help eliminate overallocation*

To split a task, select Edit and then click Split Task. On the right side of the Gantt Chart, hover over the taskbar of the task you want to split, until you see the start date you want the split to start, as shown in Figure 9.17. Hold down your left mouse button and slide it until you see the start and end date for the second portion of the split that you want, and then release the mouse button. It takes some practice to get used to splitting a task, so you might need to practice it several times.

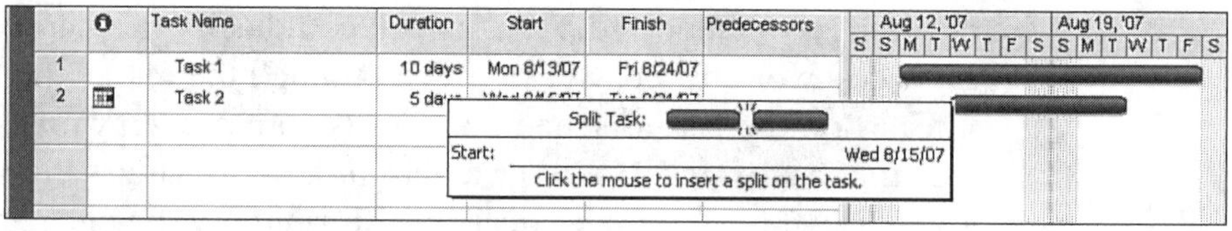

Figure 9.17   *Use the taskbar and mouse to split a task*

Sometimes none of these alternatives are needed. By reviewing allocation, you find out that you made a mistake and just need to correct the error. However, when your schedule is as good as you can make it and people are still overallocated, leveling makes you consider trade-offs. Trade-offs are the key in leveling resources as they allow you, your team, and your sponsors to consider the alternatives.

Leveling Your Project Using Automated Leveling

Hopefully it's clear that leveling is about understanding the true nature of the work tasks and the skill of the resources, which is something Project will never understand. So if you use automated leveling, remember that it is not making the decisions—you are. You therefore have to tell Project how you want to level. Out of the box, Project will only look at delaying tasks based on specific rules determined by how you created the schedule. Project will only make one of the following three adjustments in your schedule: split a task, delay a task, or delay the date a resource will start on a task. All of these adjustments can change the end date of the task. Some students want Project to do more than these three adjustments. You will have to do other kinds of leveling such as adding resources, changing the amount of units the resource can work, or reducing the scope of the task.

Automated leveling does not change the amount of work assigned to a task, the number of units a resource has been assigned, the actual resources assigned to a task, or the relationships assigned between tasks. Project affects only the length of the task and its start or end date. It bases its delays of resource start dates or splitting of tasks on the following decisions as it reviews the schedule:

- Are the resources on the task overallocated? If not, Project will not do anything with the task.
- Can the task be leveled according to the rules listed in the next section?
- What are the predecessor relationships that allow leveling?
- Does the task have slack, which makes it a good candidate for leveling?
- What leveling settings have been selected on tasks and resources (which you will see in the Resource Leveling dialog box shown in Figure 9.18 when you select Tools) and then click Level resources?

Let's take a quick look at leveling the roofing project. This example uses the roofing project from Chapter 7, "Using Project to Enter Cost Estimates," and it is as good as it can be after you performed a review. It shows that during the week of May 20, Wilson is scheduled to work 48 hours rather than 40 hours (as shown in Figure 9.19). You know you have an issue with Remove previous roofing and Perform roofing for Wilson. Rather than manually leveling, you want to see what Project can do. Using the settings in the Level

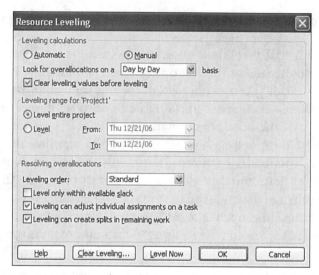

Figure 9.18   *Resource Leveling dialog box and choices available*

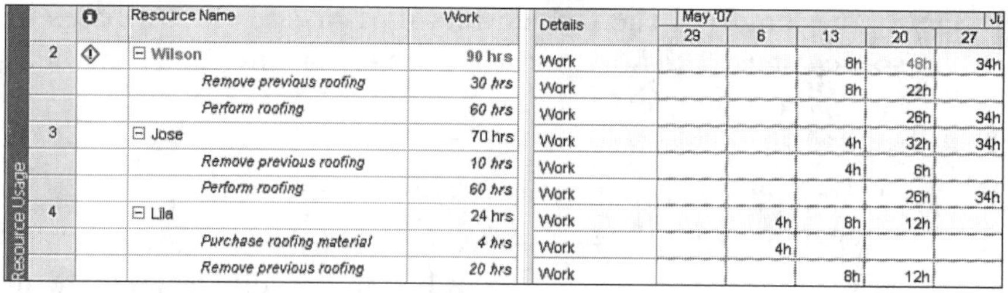

	ⓘ	Resource Name	Work	Details	May '07 29	6	13	20	27	Ju
2	◈	⊟ Wilson	90 hrs	Work				8h	48h	34h
		Remove previous roofing	30 hrs	Work				8h	22h	
		Perform roofing	60 hrs	Work					26h	34h
3		⊟ Jose	70 hrs	Work				4h	32h	34h
		Remove previous roofing	10 hrs	Work				4h	6h	
		Perform roofing	60 hrs	Work					26h	34h
4		⊟ Lila	24 hrs	Work			4h	8h	12h	
		Purchase roofing material	4 hrs	Work			4h			
		Remove previous roofing	20 hrs	Work				8h	12h	

Figure 9.19   *Wilson is overallocated one week*

Resources dialog box, you would select to level the tasks scheduled between 5/11 and 6/1 to focus on the two tasks only.

Without changing any leveling settings in the schedule or the Resource Leveling dialog box, select Level now in the Resource Leveling dialog box for the dates 5/18 thru 6/1 (the dates of the Remove previous roofing and Perform roofing projects).

Figure 9.20 shows that Project has changed the end date of the project from 6/1 to 6/4. Project also puts a delay on Wilson of 1 day (shown in Figure 9.20). To do this you would select the split window and select the Resource Schedule in the Task Form view in the lower window (again, as shown in Figure 9.20).

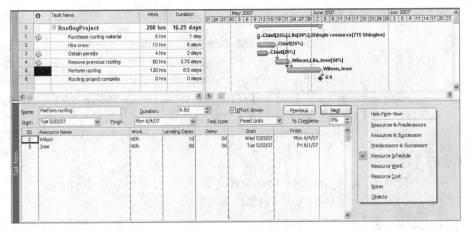

Figure 9.20 *Wilson's start date is delayed 1 day*

Figure 9.21 shows how Project evened out the work but added 2 hours during the week of June 3 (on Monday) for Wilson. You might think about leaving the leveled schedule as is and using Monday for contingency. Then you also might ask Jose to work a bit more on Friday to help get the work done if everything progresses as scheduled. If you feel you need the schedule completing on 6/1, you could add 2 hours to Jose's work on Friday and zero out Wilson's work on Monday. Remember to use caution in editing the Resource Usage view by entering Work directly as described previously.

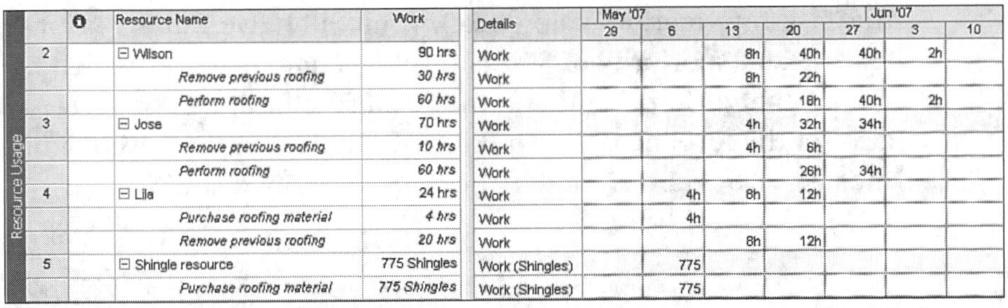

	❶	Resource Name	Work	Details	May '07					Jun '07	
					29	6	13	20	27	3	10
2		⊟ Wilson	90 hrs	Work				8h	40h	40h	2h
		Remove previous roofing	30 hrs	Work				8h	22h		
		Perform roofing	60 hrs	Work				18h	40h	2h	
3		⊟ Jose	70 hrs	Work				4h	32h	34h	
		Remove previous roofing	10 hrs	Work				4h	6h		
		Perform roofing	60 hrs	Work					26h	34h	
4		⊟ Lila	24 hrs	Work		4h	8h	12h			
		Purchase roofing material	4 hrs	Work		4h					
		Remove previous roofing	20 hrs	Work			8h	12h			
5		⊟ Shingle resource	775 Shingles	Work (Shingles)		775					
		Purchase roofing material	775 Shingles	Work (Shingles)		775					

Figure 9.21 *Resource Usage view showing Wilson's leveled assignment*

Now you can see how Project will level; there isn't some special magic. In fact, Project added 2 hours on Monday, which seems rather a waste, but it did even out the time. You can make some minor adjustments after the leveling to make your schedule make more sense.

Rules for Leveling

In this section I describe what settings you can choose in the Resource Leveling dialog box to set how resources will be leveled, but you also need to be aware of the settings in Project itself that might already be set that affect the selections you choose. I describe those settings in the next section. Some of the settings tell Project to not even attempt leveling the resources on the task. The next section then covers those Resource Leveling dialog box settings.

Project Settings

The Project settings that affect leveling include Priority of the task, Constraints on a task, and Actual start date.

Priority of the Task

You can set a priority on each task from 1 to 1,000 signifying its importance to your project or the resource assigned on it. A task priority of 1,000 cannot be automatically leveled. By default each task is assigned a priority of 500. If you have set a task to a priority level of 1,000, it will not be leveled. If you set a task at 1, it can be leveled (as long as it doesn't contain other items described later that indicate it can't be leveled). The Priority field is used only for resource leveling and will help make sure that tasks are leveled according to priority.

For instance, in the project of Build, Document, and Test, you could assign priorities to the tasks as shown in Figure 9.22. You can insert the Priority column to set the priority for each task (you can also set it on the General tab in the Task Information dialog box). You could give Build a priority of 1,000, leave Test at a priority of 500, and set Document at 200, which means Document is not as important and the resources on it can be leveled. You could also set the leveling order to Priority, Standard in the Leveling order field so the tasks would be leveled by priority (described later).

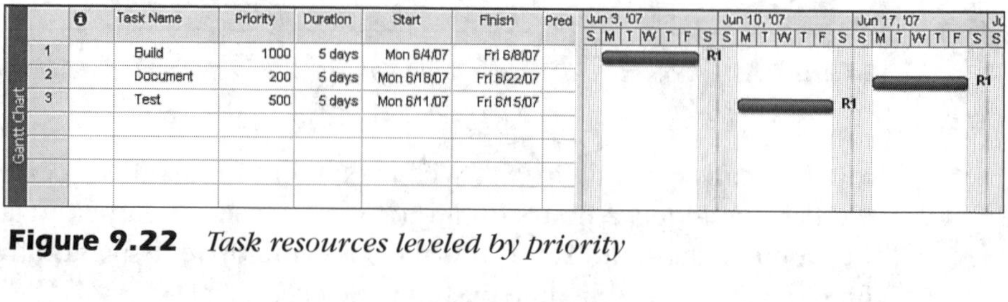

	ⓘ	Task Name	Priority	Duration	Start	Finish	Pred
1		Build	1000	5 days	Mon 6/4/07	Fri 6/8/07	
2		Document	200	5 days	Mon 6/18/07	Fri 6/22/07	
3		Test	500	5 days	Mon 6/11/07	Fri 6/15/07	

Figure 9.22   *Task resources leveled by priority*

Projects can also have priorities

You can also assign priorities to projects. If you build a master project and use a shared resource pool you can level between multiple projects. The same leveling rules will apply. However, projects with a higher priority (1,000 being the highest) take higher priority for resource work, so they will not allow leveling.

Constraints on a Task

Tasks with Must start on or Must finish on cannot be leveled. As late as possible also will not be leveled if you chose to schedule your project from a Start date (usually the default setting in Project, Project Information). Tasks with the As Soon As Possible constraint will not be leveled if you chose to schedule your project from a Finish date.

Actual Start Date

If an actual start date has been recorded in your schedule, the resources on the task will not be leveled unless you have the Leveling can create splits in remaining work check box selected in the Resource Leveling dialog box.

Leveling Settings

The selections that affect how resources are leveled are described as follows.

The Basis for Leveling

The basis for leveling choices are minute by minute, hour by hour, day by day, week by week, and month by month. This means that in making its decisions about overallocation and when it will delay (or split) a task, Project will look at how much the resource is overallocated based on what you select. Unless your project is a delicate project requiring minute-by-minute or hour-by-hour scheduling (e.g., taking a power plant offline for maintenance) you should use day by day (the default) or week by week. Week-by-week allocation might be enough: You have scheduled a task for the resource according to a certain number of units (say 50%), expecting a resource to get the work done within the week. The resource might be overallocated on 1 day by 4 hours (having to do two tasks on the same day), but you know he or she can finish the task in the following few days and still make the target date. You will not take the time to micromanage and even out these kinds of tasks.

Leveling Order

The three leveling orders are ID only, Standard, or Priority, Standard.

- **ID only**

   ID only means that when Project levels, it is going to delay the tasks based on the task number (see Figure 9.23 showing where the ID of the task is) first before considering other parameters and using the rules for leveling earlier, so the lower number tasks are considered more important (Task 1 is more important to not delay, as opposed to Task 3). Using ID for leveling assumes that the tasks at the beginning of the project cannot be delayed, as they need to get done prior to the ones at the end of the schedule. An example of leveling using this order is shown in Figure 9.23. Notice that the priority for each task is still on each task, but automated leveling did not use it because I selected the leveling order of ID only.

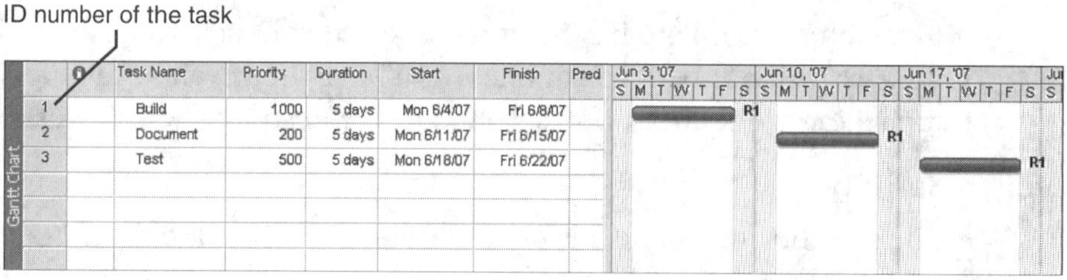

ID number of the task

Figure 9.23   *Task resources leveled by ID*

- **Standard**

   Standard is the default leveling selection. It means that when Project goes through its leveling decisions, it is going to level based on task predecessor relationships, amount of slack, and task starting dates within the project (a task starting later in the project is a better candidate for delay than one early in the project), as well as the rules for leveling discussed earlier. One of the reasons Project looks at slack is because there's a chance a task with slack can start later and not delay the start of the successor task and the project finish if there is enough slack. In Figure 9.24, Document and Test are successors to Build. The task priorities are the default 500, and Document and Test can start at the same time due to the original linking. Document is a 3-day task.

Because of slack, Document was leveled to occur last. If Document had been a 5-day task, it would have been leveled to occur prior to the Test task.

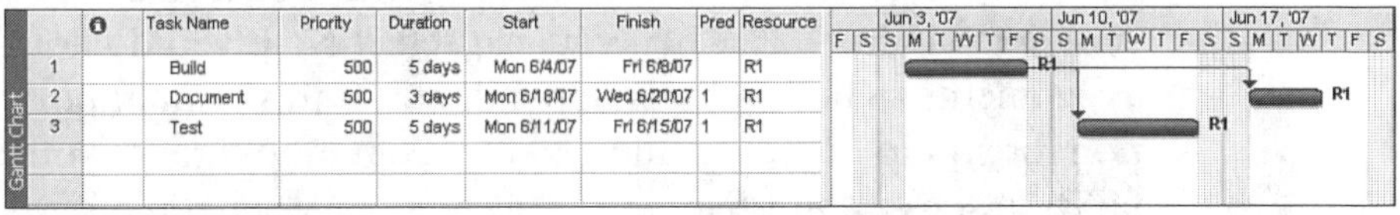

Figure 9.24   *Resources leveled using Standard order*

- **Priority, Standard**

  Priority, Standard means that Project looks first at priorities and then at the task predecessor relationships, slack (see preceding information on slack), dates, and constraints to determine whether and how tasks should be leveled. You saw an example of how leveling might occur for this kind of setting in Figure 9.22.

Other Settings

The rest of the settings need to be set to agree with the kind of leveling you want on your project prior to actually leveling. The rest of the settings are as follows:

- **Level only within available slack:** This check box is not checked by default. Projects have slack when you have a lot of tasks of varying lengths scheduled in parallel. This selection will cause Project to look at overallocated tasks that allow delay due to slack and will change those first without changing the end date of your project. There's a good chance you won't leverage much with this selection. But you might try leveling your schedule first with this selection on and see what happens. To understand more about slack, see "Review the Critical Path" later in the chapter.

- **Leveling can adjust individual assignments on a task:** This check box is selected by default. This selection allows leveling to adjust each resource on a task independently if it can. For instance, in Figure 9.20, Wilson and Jose are both working on the Perform roofing task, and leveling delayed Wilson's start date, but not Jose's. If this check box was not selected, Project could not have delayed Wilson's start.

This selection affects all tasks on your project the same way. On some tasks, you might want to allow resources to be leveled independently and on other tasks, you cannot allow it due to the nature of the work (e.g., the whole team must start and finish together). If this is so, you can insert the column Level assignments into your Gantt Chart as shown in Figure 9.25. Then you can select No if you do not want assignments to be leveled independently. If this is an important function for you to do, you could add that column to one of your auditing views, discussed in Chapter 8, "Polishing Your Schedule."

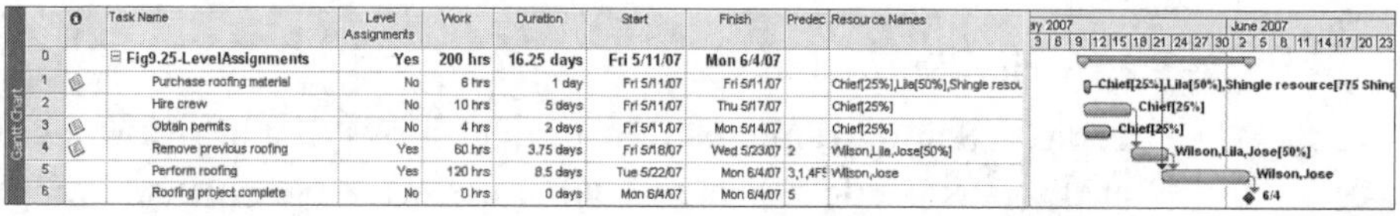

Figure 9.25 *Adding the Level assignments column to a Gantt Chart view to flag leveling rules for tasks*

- **Leveling can create splits in remaining work**. This selection is set by default. You can use this selection when you want to allow a task to be split to help the leveling process. In Figure 9.26, you can see how this setting affects leveling. I entered some actual work on the Document task and progressed the schedule (see more on progressing the schedule in Chapter 11, "Tracking Your Schedule"). Then I chose to level the schedule. Project's leveling actually split the Build task to start after the Document task because actual work has been entered on the Document task, but it split the Build task to start immediately after Documentation.

On some tasks it might be important not to split the remaining work. For instance, you might have a task such as pouring the foundation of a building, which should not be interrupted (you shouldn't pour some of it, then have your resources move to another task, then start up again 2 days later). If this is the case, you can insert the column Leveling can split as shown in Figure 9.26 and per task select if the task can be split.

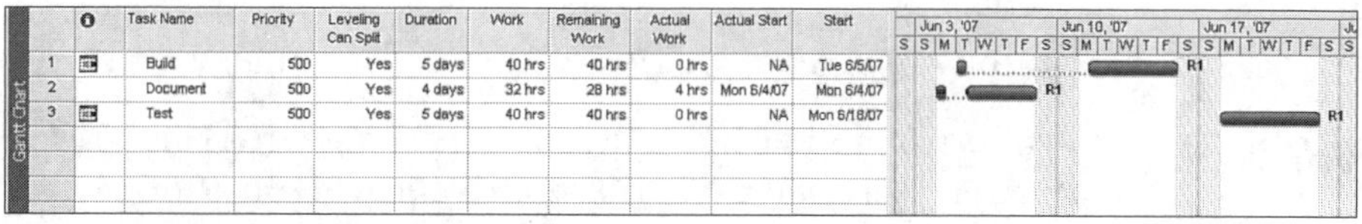

	0	Task Name	Priority	Leveling Can Split	Duration	Work	Remaining Work	Actual Work	Actual Start	Start
1		Build	500	Yes	5 days	40 hrs	40 hrs	0 hrs	NA	Tue 6/5/07
2		Document	500	Yes	4 days	32 hrs	28 hrs	4 hrs	Mon 6/4/07	Mon 6/4/07
3		Test	500	Yes	5 days	40 hrs	40 hrs	0 hrs	NA	Mon 6/18/07

Figure 9.26 *Leveling splits tasks*

Project Leveling Decisions

As you look at these rules and actually perform leveling, you will often find it frustrating that Project seems to make decisions you just can't abide by, such as putting tasks at the end of the schedule that shouldn't be there or splitting tasks for weeks before resuming the task again. Often the best way to perform leveling is to do it in parts, just like when you sequence your tasks. Level for a certain time frame or for certain tasks. Leveling can be extremely onerous in a very large project if you are leveling the entire project at once, so select only the time frames you want to level and you can figure out the issues easier than if you level the entire project at once (unless it is very small).

Also, Project seems frustrating when it can't level even though it's not doing so for a very good reason. For instance, in Figure 9.12, only the time frame in which the Remove and Perform roofing tasks were to be completed is selected. If you tried running the leveling, you would receive the message shown in Figure 9.27. If you are leveling the whole schedule and get dozens of these messages, it would be hard to understand what is going on. Project will go through all its decision making, and at some point if it can't resolve the overallocation using any of its rules, you might receive something similar. You can note the message, skip it, and level only what you can, or you might receive message after message telling you it can't resolve the overallocation until nothing is leveled. The real issue all along with the schedule was that you have a task that cannot be delayed.

Project can't resolve that. You will have to take the time to replace resources, add other resources, or change the units. In the end you will probably have to change the dates of the project unless you want to leave the resource overscheduled. If you need to leave a resource's units overscheduled, one of the solutions the message suggests is to increase the resource's availability. If you want to consider increasing the resource's availability, you can increase it for just a short amount of time by using the Available from and Available to fields on the General tab in the Resource Information dialog box. It increases the limits but only through the time frame when the resource is needed more. See Chapter 6, "Understanding Resources and Their Effects on Tasks," for more about the availability settings for a resource in the Resource Information dialog box.

Finish-to-finish relationships affect automatic leveling

Because leveling is looking at delaying tasks, note that Finish-to-Finish relationships are not good candidates for leveling. Because the two tasks are dependent on each other to finish at the same time, Project (and even you, if you level manually) probably won't be able to delay either task.

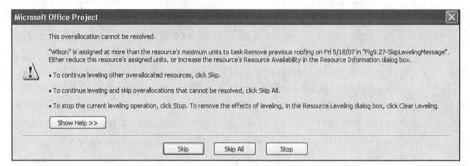

Figure 9.27   *Message indicating that automated leveling will be skipped*

While you are going through the leveling process, use the Leveling Gantt to see how leveling affects your project. To do so, follow these steps:

1. On the Gantt Chart, select View and then choose More Views.
2. Click Leveling Gantt and then click Apply. You will see a Gantt Chart that is ready to show you what happens once you level.
3. To proceed with the leveling process, select Tools and then click Level Resources (with all the rules and settings you want to apply to the leveling).
4. In the Resource Leveling dialog box, click Level Now. The Leveling Gantt will show where there is a leveling delay and the change of dates based on the leveling. At the same time, you could also be in the split window with Resource Schedule showing in the screen at the bottom (remember to right-click). The result of using the Leveling Gantt and split window is shown in Figure 9.28.

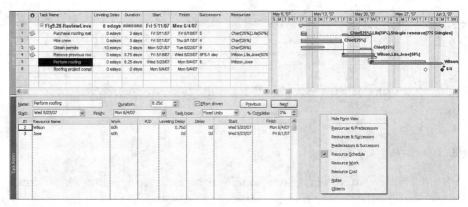

Figure 9.28 *Leveling Gantt showing how automated leveling affected the project and the split window showing leveling on the Perform roofing task*

Resource Leveling Flag

There is one more rule that can be set that is not apparent, but one you need to consider prior to leveling. You can set whether the resource can be leveled or not. By default, only work resources can be leveled, based on an expectation that material, cost, and budget resources (cost and budget resources being available for Project 2007 only) are not the kinds of resources you worry about being overallocated. However, there might be some work resources that cannot be leveled. For instance, in a construction project, perhaps you have a backhoe and you cannot obtain a second one, so the rules for leveling do not apply for its tasks. You can flag the resource as not being capable of being leveled. In Figure 9.29 you see that the Can level column has been inserted into the Resource Sheet.

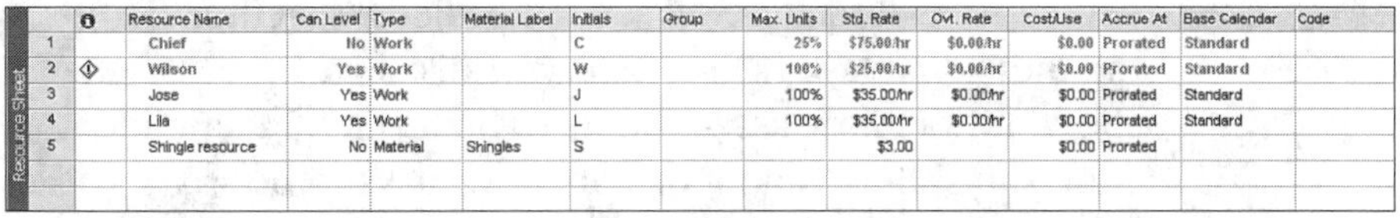

		Resource Name	Can Level	Type	Material Label	Initials	Group	Max. Units	Std. Rate	Ovt. Rate	Cost/Use	Accrue At	Base Calendar	Code
1		Chief	No	Work		C		25%	$75.00/hr	$0.00/hr	$0.00	Prorated	Standard	
2	⬦	Wilson	Yes	Work		W		100%	$25.00/hr	$0.00/hr	$0.00	Prorated	Standard	
3		Jose	Yes	Work		J		100%	$35.00/hr	$0.00/hr	$0.00	Prorated	Standard	
4		Lila	Yes	Work		L		100%	$35.00/hr	$0.00/hr	$0.00	Prorated	Standard	
5		Shingle resource	No	Material	Shingles	S			$3.00		$0.00	Prorated		

Figure 9.29 *Can level column inserted in Resource Sheet*

Using this setting, if the project is leveled with the defaults, compare Figure 9.30 to Figure 9.28. All the tasks that were leveled before that had the Chief on them are not leveled in Figure 9.30.

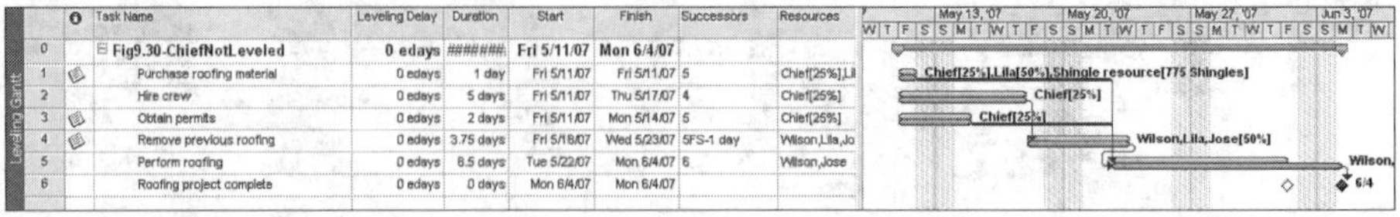

Figure 9.30 *Resource that cannot be leveled affects leveling*

Performing Leveling

Now that you've taken a look at the rules of leveling, the following section describes how you use automated leveling. Keep in mind that you should level particular areas of the project first, and then when you are happy with that leveling, you move on to other sections. For instance, level during the time frames of a particular phase for really large projects, or select just certain types of tasks. Also, once you level one project, if you are sharing resources or reviewing leveling in master projects, level in one project, and then add the other project to the equation.

This set of steps assumes that you are scheduling the project from a start date rather than a finish date (the Schedule from field is set in the Project Information dialog box). First, review the tasks that have Must Finish On, Must Start On, or As late As Possible constraints and any tasks that have an actual start date. This review ensures you are aware of the tasks that will not be leveled under any circumstances. Set the rules for leveling first and then perform the actions that allow you to level.

1. Set the rules for priority and leveling of the project, tasks, and resources first. Set each task's priority if you want base leveling on important versus less important tasks. Set Project priorities if you expect to eventually level several projects together. If appropriate, set the individual task flags to allow or disallow Level assignments (to allow or not allow assignments to be leveled independently) and Leveling can split (to allow or not allow tasks to be split). For each resource, set the flag if they can be leveled or not; if not, their assignment on any task will not be considered for leveling.

2. Select View, then click More Views. Then select Leveling Gantt and click Apply. This will show the Gantt Chart prior to leveling but prepares your view prior to the leveling process.

3. Then select Tools and click Level Resources.

4. It is sometimes a good idea to clear previous leveling first. In the resulting Level Resources dialog box, click Clear Leveling. Select entire project (unless you are leveling just some particular tasks). This ensures that you have cleared any leveling you might have already done if it was not appropriate. If you leveled previously and liked the results, don't clear the leveling. Clearing just particular tasks can also be useful if you think some of the leveling is something you want to keep and shouldn't be cleared.

5. Select Tools and click Level Resources again. In the resulting Level Resources dialog box, set the rules for leveling. Based on your desired rules, select the basis you want to level on (day by day, etc.), leveling order, and whether you want to allow splits, allow individual assignments, and level for tasks having slack only. Remember that these selections apply to the overall project, but any specific leveling selection on a task or resource will take precedence.

6. Because of the issues with how leveling surprises most people first using the function, I would suggest you always select Manual in the Resource Leveling dialog box.

7. Select the leveling range for the project. Select the entire project or click the Level option and select a From and To date. For a small project, you can choose to level the entire project, but for a large project you might choose first to level the time frame for a particular phase. After leveling, you can more easily see what was leveled.

8. You should have already set the leveling order according to this method for leveling, so when you are ready click Level Now. Notice any message (e.g., the one in Figure 9.27) so that you can consider manually leveling those tasks.

9. Review and analyze what happened in the Leveling Gantt.

10. Choose Clear Leveling if you are not pleased with the results and consider manually leveling as described earlier, or try different rules for leveling. You might need to go through several iterations to level your schedule. At points throughout your process, you might want to save versions of the schedule in case you want to revert back to one of your versions.

Reviewing the Critical Path

In Chapter 5, I described how you sequence your task activities via linking to build the critical path. Before Project or other scheduling tools, you would have to manually build the schedule's critical path by going through a process of estimating durations of tasks, manually creating the task relationships, then figuring out the early start and finish dates and late start and finish dates of the tasks. When you use Project, you don't have to actually calculate the early start and finish dates and late start and finish dates. Project does that for you based on your entering estimates and linking tasks. If at any point in building the schedule you do not link your tasks, you miss being able to see your critical path and benefit from analyzing and adjusting it. To revisit the critical path, take a look at Figure 9.31.

Figure 9.31   *Critical path example*

Let's say you have one resource on each of the tasks and you've been asked to complete the project by 7/20. To make this simple, the example is not taking into account resource units or work effort, although a real schedule would. The critical path is always the longest path of tasks through the schedule and is the shortest time that the project can be completed. If any task on that path changes, it would change the end date of the project (either an earlier or later finish). Although there are several long tasks in the example, such as Task B and Task F, if they are not on the longest path, then they have slack: The tasks could either start later or finish later and the finish date of the project would not be affected. As you already saw, based on your initial schedule-building effort, you are 5 days overdue. The critical path is not easily visible by default in the Gantt Chart of Project. You can set up a view to see the critical path task in red on the Gantt Chart to easily see it and you can use a table to indicate critical path information as shown in Figure 9.32. To set up a similar view for critical path analysis you would do the following:

1. Select Format and then click Gantt Chart Wizard. The selection called Gantt Chart Wizard allows you to show various kinds of additional colors and lines on the schedule. On the second screen of the wizard, click the Critical path option, finish stepping through the wizard, and format the chart. Although you can't see it in this book, the tasks on the critical path are shown in red. See Chapter 13, "Project Mysteries Resolved!" for more about using the wizard.

> **You can also use the Tracking Gantt view**
>
> You might also want to select View and then click Tracking Gantt to see the critical path. It's easier to click to get there, but it changes the look and feel of the Gantt Chart slightly, which you might not like.

2. Then to see the specific data about each task on the critical path, select Views, click Table and select Schedule from the drop-down list. This displays the Late start, Late finish, and Slack columns as shown in Figure 9.32.

Figure 9.32 *Gantt Chart Wizard applied and Table: Schedule showing critical path and slack*

Notice that Task B has a slack of 3 days, Task D has a slack of 6 days, and Task F has slack of 4 days. Notice the Late Start and Late Finish columns. Task B could actually start on 7/16 rather than the 7/11 date it is scheduled for now, and still complete on time. However, if the start or finish dates or durations change on Tasks A, C, or E, the project end date will change (signified by the milestone of Task G).

So what does reviewing the critical path have to do with polishing your schedule, the theme of this chapter and Chapter 8? After you've reviewed for common errors and resource overallocations, you want to review the critical path thoroughly to see if you can tighten your schedule or to see if there are any tasks that are so close to the critical path that you should build in some contingency for them. Although in this simple example you have no resources on these tasks, let's say you have only one resource on Task E. Task E is a great candidate to try and shorten, so you could add another resource to it and reduce the effort by half. When you do that, you would get a different view of the critical path, as shown in Figure 9.33.

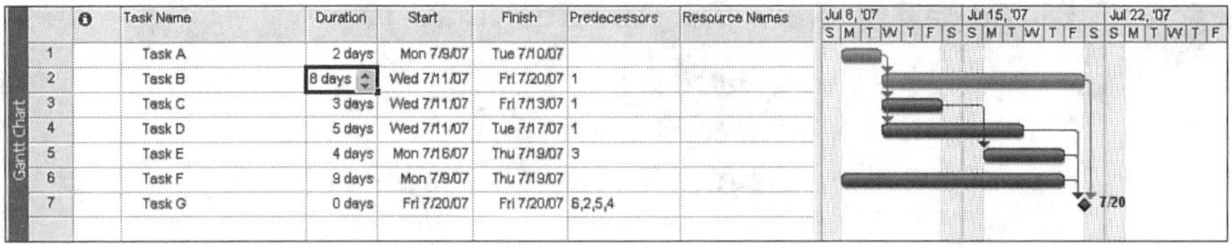

	ⓘ	Task Name	Duration	Start	Finish	Predecessors	Resource Names
1		Task A	2 days	Mon 7/9/07	Tue 7/10/07		
2		Task B	8 days	Wed 7/11/07	Fri 7/20/07	1	
3		Task C	3 days	Wed 7/11/07	Fri 7/13/07	1	
4		Task D	5 days	Wed 7/11/07	Tue 7/17/07	1	
5		Task E	4 days	Mon 7/16/07	Thu 7/19/07	3	
6		Task F	9 days	Mon 7/9/07	Thu 7/19/07		
7		Task G	0 days	Fri 7/20/07	Fri 7/20/07	6,2,5,4	

Figure 9.33 *The critical path adjusted*

Now you can see that the only tasks with slack are Tasks C, D, E, and F, and Task B is now on the critical path. You also met your due date of 7/20. If you wanted to try and beat your end date, you could continue to try and adjust the work on Task B if you need to: Can you add more resources or reduce scope on Task B? If so, and you bring Task B in, even for 1 day, then Tasks E and F will move to the critical path.

Formatting text to see the critical path

You can also format the text of the tasks that are in the critical path. For instance, you can make all critical path tasks red, or you can change their font to italic or bold. This can be very handy so you don't always have to look at the Gantt Chart throughout the tracking of your project. Formatting of text is described in Chapter 13.

This sample described shortening the critical path by adding a resource. However, there are many more techniques you can use to shorten the critical path. Consider the following possibilities for shortening tasks on the critical path:

- Add resources
- Reduce scope
- Assign a more knowledgeable resource who can do the task faster
- Break a critical task into smaller tasks that can be worked on simultaneously by different resources
- Reduce the time spent on the task (watch out for reduced quality)
- See if you can create more leads on tasks
- Reduce quality
- Revise task dependencies to allow more parallel scheduling. This technique is called fast tracking.

Of course, there is a risk to all of these techniques to reduce the critical path. You will need to justify why you would do each and be willing to take the risk the change might imply.

Hopefully, you can see that reviewing and shortening the critical path is a delicate matter. If Task E really required the one resource and could not have another resource added, you might have to live with your schedule and try and convince the sponsors of your project that they can't get the project before 7/25. Otherwise, the resource will be working 16-hour days to make the expected project end date. Understanding and adjusting the critical path is one of the most important elements of scheduling that you can work on.

Learn more about the concepts of the critical path

Chapter 9 of *Project Management for Mere Mortals* discusses the critical path. It is well worth your time to learn more about how you build and adjust the critical path to create the best schedule you can.

One Last Look at Your Schedule

While you built your schedule, there were some things you avoided. Hopefully, you didn't put any constraints on the schedule. If you have some constraints you need to include in your schedule, now's the time to add them. You could possibly remove deadline dates that might have made it difficult to review the critical path (e.g., if you put them on milestones). If you need to add leads and lags, you might have looked at doing so while visiting the critical path, but you might look at adding them just before you are ready to baseline. Review the costs and original budget and see if they sync up logically. If you are way over or under your budget after finishing your review and corrections, there might be something seriously wrong with the original budget or with the scope of your project. Print out the schedule and review it one last time with your team.

One last caveat: This isn't the last time you should review the schedule. You need to use the same techniques of reviewing for errors, overallocation, and the critical path once you start executing the project. As you start recording progress, and as you add, change, or remove tasks, you need to continue the review.

The Project Schedule Building Methodology So Far

Based on what you have learned, the following steps and sequence describe the best methods for building your schedule. The items emphasized in this chapter are indicated in italics. Because many organizations do not enter costs, I have also added an "optional" indicator in this list.

The steps for building a project schedule so far are as follows:

- ☑ If you are using a template, select the appropriate template (you will probably want to change it based on the input of your project team). If you are building a project from scratch, build a WBS with your team, then move to the next step.

- ☑ Set up your project calendar if you do not have one available. Make sure you reflect your company's hours in Tools, Options, Calendar, if different than the defaults.

- ☑ In the Project Information dialog box, set your project Start date and make sure your project calendar is assigned to the project.

- ☑ Start building (if your project is from scratch) or editing (if you are using a template) your task list. Make sure you indicate summary tasks and subtasks to help indicate the outline of your project schedule.

- ☑ Add milestone tasks to indicate significant events, deliverables, or approval points in your project.

- ☑ Enter deadline dates for appropriate tasks. This is a better way of indicating dates when tasks need to be completed rather than typing in a Finish date on a task.

☑ Add task calendars to tasks to indicate exceptions to the project calendar if needed. You will probably not need these kinds of calendars often.

☑ Review all tasks. Decide what kind of tasks they are for the schedule-building process. Change the Task type and Effort-driven fields if appropriate.

☑ Link all tasks in the schedule, determining if they are Finish-to-Start, Start-to-Start, Finish-to-Finish, or Start-to-Finish relationships. Link among phases or task groupings first, then link between phases or groupings. Use the Predecessor and Successor columns to help you see if all tasks are linked.

☑ Build the project team. Add all resources that might work on the project to the Resource Sheet for the project. If you are performing effort-based scheduling, enter the Maximum Units each resource can work on the project. You can use generic or real resources, but when you know who will do the work, you should replace generic resources with real resources.

☑ Assign the resources to each task. If you are performing effort-based scheduling, you might need to change the percentage of allocation a resource is assigned to individual tasks in some cases.

☑ Enter estimates to project tasks. For effort-based scheduling, enter two of the three variables in the Work formula: Work = Duration × Units.

☑ Review the schedule and enter leads and lags on tasks if appropriate.

☑ Review the critical path and adjust tasks if appropriate.

☑ [Optional] Set your cost default cost calculation methods: Have Project automatically calculate Actual Costs and decide on and set up your cost accrual method for the entire project.

☑ [Optional] Set up any other kinds of resources, such as material resources (set up cost and budget resources if you are using Project 2007) if you want to include costs other than labor or equipment work costs in your project.

☑ [Optional] Insert the Cost and Fixed Cost fields in the Gantt Chart view (or use the Table: Cost view). Enter rates on resources, enter Fixed Costs on tasks, or enter total budget on the project summary task line depending on how your organization has decided to enter cost.

☑ Check your schedule for logic and scheduling errors using a special audit view or reviewing the errors using methods described Chapter 8.

☑ *Review and adjust your schedule for workload issues and to tighten the critical path.*

Summary

After you have fixed the general errors of your schedule, you are ready to move on to the hard part of the schedule: overallocation of resources and ensuring the critical path is as tight as it can be. You will need to consider both, and changing one can change the other. For instance, if you reduce an overallocation, the duration of a task might increase, and the critical path might change or expand if the changed task was on the critical path in the first place. If you tighten the critical path by making someone work more (increasing their units), then that person might become overallocated due to other projects or tasks he or she might be on.

To review overallocation, use the Resource Usage and Task Usage views to see what issues you have. Consider whether you actually have issues; sometimes resources are showing as overallocated because they exceed their daily maximum units, but they could work on one task one day, and finish the other task the next day when they are not overallocated, so you don't want to worry about such situations. In fact, I recommend looking at overallocation on a week-by-week basis, not a day-by-day basis (unless you have tasks or a project so critical that it needs that kind of monitoring). If it looks like the resources can get their work done within the week, then don't worry about it. Once you do determine that a resource is overallocated, you can choose various ways to level out the resource's work, and you might choose a combination of manually leveling and using the automated leveling in Project. To level resources you can consider reducing the scope or quality of the task, adding more resources or replacing resources on the task, decreasing the units a resource is assigned on a task, or delaying or splitting the work on a task. If you use the automated leveling method in Project, you will need to think about setting the rules first: Do tasks have priorities? Do you want to level based on task ID, priorities, or first by relationships? Make sure you have your rules set, then run leveling. Make sure you are using the Leveling Gantt to easily see what changes, and clear your settings and leveling as needed. Leveling can be a long and arduous process, especially with a long schedule. Tackle it in sections and if you build the schedule first, with forethought about task relationships, decent estimates, and the real time resources you'll have to work on tasks, the leveling will be easier.

In reviewing the critical path, make sure all your task relationships make sense and you have predecessor and successor tasks for every task except summary tasks and tasks starting on the project start date or the last task. In the Gantt Chart, change the table to Schedule, use the Gantt Chart Wizard to review the critical path, and see if there are any tasks you can shorten with changes in scope, by adding resources, or by decreasing the estimates. By looking at overallocation and reviewing the critical path, you will do more for your schedule than any other activity. You should not publish your schedule without understanding the risks and possible contingencies for issues with both.

Practice: Reviewing Overallocation and the Critical Path

You have two opportunities to sharpen your reviewing skills in the following practices. You will review for overallocation and use leveling to help fix a problem, and you will review the critical path.

Practice 9.1

Review and Resolve Resource Overallocation

To start, use the project called HousePainting-Practice-Chapter9-Practice1.mpp on your CD. The house-painting project has been changed to make sure resources are overallocated for this practice.

1. Open HousePainting-Practice-Chapter9-Practice1.mpp. Select View and then click the Resource Sheet. Notice that each resource has a calendar showing Standard, which in this project means they are available to work for 8 hours a day. What are the Max. Units allowed for each resource? Which resource has been set to work only 2 hours per day?

2. Now select View, then click Resource Usage. Which resources are overallocated? Which resource is not overallocated? Note the tasks that are creating the overallocations for each resource.

3. Select View, Gantt Chart. Note the beginning and end dates of the two tasks on which the resources are overallocated. (The tasks are Scrape and Sand and Inspect and Rescrape and they are scheduled from May 9 through May 17.)

4. Select View, More views, Leveling Gantt, and then click Apply. If the Leveling Gantt Chart is not showing on the right, highlight the Scrape and Sand task and click Scroll to task (called Go to task in Project 2002 and Project 2003) or use the scroll bar on the right side of the chart so you see the leveling Gantt

bars. This is very important. Without using this Leveling Gantt view, it's hard to quickly see what happened to your tasks based on running the automated leveling.

5. Although you won't change any task priorities, let's review how you set them. Highlight the Leveling Delay column. Select Insert and click Column. In the Insert dialog box, select Priority and click OK. Note that the priority for all tasks is set at 500. If you wanted to set some rules around what task should be leveled first, you could set the priority for the tasks.

6. Level the tasks that have resources overallocated without setting any rules first. To do so, select Tools and then click Level resources. In the Level Resources dialog box, click the Level option and enter 5/9/07 in the From field and 5/17/07 in the To field. Make sure Standard is set in the Leveling order field. The dialog box should look like Figure 9.34.

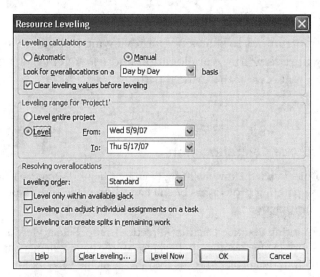

Figure 9.34   *Set up for the practice*

7. Once this is set up, click Level Now.

8. What is the warning message you received? What is the overallocation that cannot be resolved by leveling? Click Skip.

9. What happened? You should see a split in the Inspect and Rescrape task. Select View, Resource usage. Did this help level out resources? Did the overallocation get leveled completely?

10. Select File, Save. You can do leveling in increments, and once you are satisfied with a leveling situation, you can choose to save the file.

11. Although the resource Me is not fully leveled, you decide that you can deal with that overallocation. However, the resource Spouse is still overallocated for a few days. The first day that shows overallocation does not seem to be an issue. On Wednesday, May 9, it shows Spouse is working 2 hours, which is okay, but on Thursday and Friday, it shows Spouse working 4 hours each day. Spouse is overallocated by 2 hours each day. You realize that you allocated Spouse at 50% on the task, so you decide you should change the task to be allocated at 25%.

12. Select View, More Views, Leveling Gantt and then click Apply.

13. Select Window, Split. Click the Inspect and Rescrape task.

14. In the lower portion of the window, enter 25% instead of 50% for Spouse and click OK. What happened to the Leveling Gantt chart?

15. Remove the split window by selecting Window and then clicking Remove Split. Select View and click the Resource Usage view. Did it take care of the overallocation for Spouse?

16. Since the change in units merely moved the problem to the next week, try automated leveling again. Change to the Leveling Gantt view first. If it is not showing, select View, More Views, Leveling Gantt and click Apply.

17. The Scrape and Sand and Inspect and Rescrape are now set from 5/9 to 5/21. Select Tools, Level Resources and in the Level Resources dialog, select the Level radio button (note that it is still selected, which means settings are persistent, and you need to always review your leveling settings). Leave 5/9/07 in the *From* field, but enter 5/21/07 in the *To* field.

18. Click Level Now. What happened to the Leveling Gantt? What's the end date of the project now? Select View, Resource Usage. Is Spouse still overallocated?

If you want to see the result, see HousePainting-Practice-Chapter9-Practice1-Result.mpp on the CD.

Practice 9.2

Reviewing and Adjusting the Critical Path

To start, use the project called HousePainting-Practice-Chapter9-Practice2.mpp on your CD. The project has been changed from previous versions to create a more interesting critical path for this practice.

1. Open HousePainting-Practice-Chapter9-Practice2.mpp. Select Format and click Gantt Chart Wizard. The first dialog box of the Gantt Chart Wizard appears. This wizard lets you do various formatting for your project. You will choose to have it format the critical path, which displays all the critical path tasks in red. Click Next.

2. In the resulting dialog box, notice the list of Gantt Chart displays you can select, such as Standard, Critical path, and Baseline. Select the Critical path option and click Next.

3. On the next screen, you can choose what kind of information you would like on the bars. In this case, leave the default and click Next.

4. Click Next in the next dialog box, and on the next screen click Format It. On the final screen, click Exit Wizard.

5. What three tasks are not on the critical path? Next, you will review the slack and late start and finish dates of the tasks. Select View, click Table, and select Schedule from the list. What is the Late start date for the Inspect and Rescrape task? What other two tasks have Free Slack?

6. To tighten the schedule, you can look at all tasks on the critical path. Let's say you want to bring the date in by a week. You see that the scraping and sanding is the longest task. It's a very difficult task, but you realize you could really bring the schedule in if you can figure out how to make that shorter. You decide you will take the week off from work, so you will increase the units you work to 100% to allow you to work 8 hours a day. To do so, select Window, and then click Split.

7. Highlight the Scrape and Sand task. In the Units field in the bottom window for Me enter 100 and click OK. What did this do for your schedule? You should have saved more than 5 days and now you are feeling good, because you also have a lot of contingency. You could even get done early if your estimates are accurate. How did the Free slack change on the Inspect and rescrape task?

If you want to see the result, see HousePainting-Practice-Chapter8-Practice2-Result.mpp on the CD.

Case Study: Leveling and the Critical Path

At this point, in reviewing the schedule, Chris realizes she has plenty of lag time. She starts adjusting many of the tasks to make sure the work starts when it should, rather than too early. There are many tasks she starts now, including the first main tasks such as creating the project scope, communication plan and the marketing plan. But the design doesn't need to start until later. One of the best ways to do this is to look at each phase and the deadlines in each phase. The Create a Tradeshow Marketing Plan has a deadline of March 30. So all of the work can be started for that. Then Chris can create a milestone called "Start Detailed Tradeshow Plan" and put a constraint of Start No Earlier Than for 3/30 on it. Then change all the tasks that had a predecessor for the "Tradeshow Marketing Plan Complete" (which is task 17, and change them to 19.) So first, Chris adds start dates for each phase using constraints and re-adjusts the task relationships appropriately.

Then, Chris is ready to roll up her sleeves and work on the hard part: leveling overallocation and refining the critical path. She knows after this exercise, she can review the schedule with her team, and then go to June with the project's schedule baseline. This isn't all she's finalized in her project: She has worked on her risk, communication, and quality plans as well. She is feeling good because she's doing all the right things to manage a project and covering all her bases, but she knows when things get started, things can go wrong.

Open the file, VNLE-Chapter9-Begin-CaseStudy.mpp for this case study and perform the following review:

1. Review overallocations. To do so, select the Resource Usage view.

2. Scroll through the length of the project to review the overallocations from January 1, 2007 through 10/1/2007. You notice that the project manager, core team, and VP of Marketing are the only ones overallocated according to Project. Review the project manager's overallocation. As you review it, the only overallocation that really is a problem is the last week in the schedule: You are scheduled to work 10 hours each day—and that is expected—so you don't see anything to be a problem. Even Tuesday, January 9 is not a problem. You can work on the tasks throughout that week and it's still less than 40 hours.

   As you review the core team, at first you think there might be some issues, but when you review the Maximum Units available for the resource, you realize 600% units is plenty of time. In fact, for January 9, 2007, the schedule shows overallocation of 48 hours, but you really have enough resources.

   As for the VP of marketing, you have a few days that show overallocation, but again, the work can be done within the time frame needed. For the days where the VP is overallocated, you might need to warn him that he's going to get a lot of requests.

   You note that January 9 seems to be the day both you and the core team are busy due to some heavy planning during that time. You might consider an early warning to everyone that you are going to need a lot of work during that time frame.

3. Just to see what automated leveling will do to these tasks, you decide to run it. Change to the Leveling Gantt view, and run automated leveling. It changed the first phase of the project to end 2 days later, but the

project still ends on time. This might be a change you want to accept.

4. Now review the critical path. Use the Gantt Chart Wizard, or select the Tracking Gantt view. What's the critical path? It looks very unusual. Only the last few tasks are showing on the critical path. Chris scratches her head, then realizes that because of all the lag time she added to the schedule, only the last tasks are displayed. She can't tighten up the last phase of the project, as it's the event itself. Because she used the proper methodology in the first place, she doesn't see too many issues. She guesses she's lucky. She's knows her next project, which doesn't have as much lag time, won't have this luxury.

If you would like to see the result of the scenario practice, see VNLE-Chapter9-End-CaseStudy.mpp to review the effect of leveling and the critical path.

Reviewing Overallocation and the Critical Path

To continue the review of your project, you will look for overallocation and inspect the critical path for shortening it if possible, to get the project done on time or as soon as possible. Start your review by doing the following:

- Check for overallocation. Review each phase or summary tasks in the project using the Resource Graph or Resource Usage view. Use automated resource leveling or manual leveling and delay tasks, change resources, or change task relationships, among other techniques.

- Review and shorten the critical path to make your project target dates, or to achieve scheduling efficiencies.

Once you have reviewed overallocation and the critical path and have reviewed the project schedule with your team, you are ready to set the baseline.

Review Questions

1. What is work contouring?

2. What is leveling?

3. Does Project level resources automatically for you?

4. What are some ways you can view overallocation?

5. What are some various methods to level your project manually?

6. What are project settings that affect leveling?

7. What are the settings of leveling?

8. Can Project's automated leveling capability level all overallocation situations?

9. Can you perform automated leveling for the project but turn off leveling for resources? How?

10. Why would you clear leveling when you are performing automatic leveling?

11. What is the Gantt Chart Wizard?

12. What are some methods for reducing the duration of tasks on the critical path?

13. When you are done reviewing and correcting your schedule, what should you do?

Baselining: The Key to Tracking Your Schedule

Time is a dressmaker specializing in alterations.
—*Faith Baldwin*

Topics Covered in This Chapter

The quote at the top of this page is perfect for thinking about your project plan. No matter how fastidious you are, as soon as you start executing your project, something will change. The very essence of the human condition, even for projects, is that something will change or occur that we did not expect. Baselining records what you originally planned, so that you know how to react to change. Baselining is one of the most misunderstood functions in Project. This chapter might be one of the shortest in the book, but it is probably one of the most important.

As a project manager, you need to make sure you baseline your project plan, including the project schedule. In Chapter 8, "Polishing Your Schedule" and Chapter 9, "Reviewing Work Overload and the Critical Path," I discussed reviewing and setting your schedule to make it the best it can be, usually after you've completed your planning. For a small project, this planning might take hours or days. For a large project, the planning could take weeks, or maybe months. Baselining provides a snapshot so that you can compare changes during execution of the project to your estimates. Many people baseline to help with change control: If your plan hasn't been baselined, then when stakeholders request a change, you won't be able to effectively communicate the impact that change has on the timeline. Many project managers find baselining a double-edged sword: It also means that if the project takes a lot longer than planned, you and your team didn't do a very good job of planning, and it's obvious.

The best way to explain baselining is to return to some of the embedded formulas in Project. They are:

$$Work = Actual\ Work + Remaining\ Work$$

$$Duration = Actual\ Duration + Remaining\ Duration$$

When you start tracking your project during execution and enter actual work or duration, and it ends up being more or less than what you originally estimated, you lose the original estimate numbers. For instance, let's say your original Work estimate was 40 hours for Task 1. However, your team member tells you that he has worked 50 hours and has 10 more hours to work. Based on the formula, the Work field will increase to 60 hours. The only field that will have the original 40 hours is a baseline Work field. This chapter describes why you should baseline, how to baseline, and the kinds of reports and analysis you can perform because you baseline. Setting a baseline is the key to tracking, and without it, it is very hard to see where you should perform course corrections to achieve your project goals, which is one of the most important jobs of a project manager.

Read about baselines in *Project Management for Mere Mortals*

Read about the importance of baselining in Chapter 11 of *Project Management for Mere Mortals*.

What Is a Project Baseline?

A baseline is a snapshot in time of your project schedule. It captures estimate and date information in your Project file, which you can use to understand what is happening to your schedule as your project progresses during execution. Project is great for planning projects, but it has numerous features to help you track schedule progress. The tracking features help you see the ebb and flow of your work as input progression into your schedule. As you enter progress into the schedule, it can be confusing to see things change (especially the Work and Duration fields) when you know you originally entered particular estimate values and you see them change. You can't see that original estimate anywhere if you don't baseline. At one organization where I taught they did not know about baselining and had created a new field for all their projects called Estimate and entered their original estimates in that field.

Some organizations do not require baselining because they believe Project will intimidate their new project managers. However, if it is taught correctly and in a culture accepting of the idea that baselining helps you learn, most project managers will embrace it as a habit. Baselining becomes a great tool for project manager growth and for an organization to learn more about how it can improve estimating.

So what does baselining look like in Project? Let's take a look at the fields that Project captures for this snapshot in time. First, baselining does not keep all information about the original schedule; it captures Date, Work, Duration, and Cost fields about tasks, resources, or assignments. So if you change a task name, note, or the resource itself on a task, you will not have that information. Baseline fields already exist in Project, and you can insert more into the Project file, as shown in Figure 10.1.

	❶	Task Name	Baseline Cost	Cost	Baseline Work	Work	Baseline Duration	Duration	Baseline Start	Start	Baseline Finish	Finish
0		⊟ **RoofingProject**	$0.00	$10,890.00	0 hrs	200 hrs	0 days?	16.25 days	NA	Fri 5/11/07	NA	Mon 6/4/07
1		Hire crew	$0.00	$750.00	0 hrs	10 hrs	0 days?	5 days	NA	Fri 5/11/07	NA	Thu 5/17/07
2	📝	Obtain permits	$0.00	$425.00	0 hrs	4 hrs	0 days?	2 days	NA	Fri 5/11/07	NA	Mon 5/14/07
3	📝	Purchase roofing materia	$0.00	$4,115.00	0 hrs	6 hrs	0 days?	1 day	NA	Fri 5/11/07	NA	Fri 5/11/07
4	📝	Remove previous roofing	$0.00	$2,000.00	0 hrs	60 hrs	0 days?	3.75 days	NA	Fri 5/18/07	NA	Wed 5/23/07
5		Perform roofing	$0.00	$3,600.00	0 hrs	120 hrs	0 days?	7.5 days	NA	Tue 5/22/07	NA	Fri 6/1/07
6		Roofing project complete	$0.00	$0.00	0 hrs	0 hrs	0 days?	1 day	NA	Fri 6/1/07	NA	Mon 6/4/07

Figure 10.1 *Some baseline fields added to the Project file on the Gantt Chart*

In Figure 10.1, you see some of the typical fields that you might baseline for a task. For each task, resource, or assignment you have various kinds of baselines available as follows:

- For tasks you have Baseline Duration, Work, Costs, and Start and Finish dates; all of theses are shown in Figure 10.1.
- For resources, you have Baseline Work and Cost data, including work and cost distributed over time.
- For assignments (each resource on a task with work assigned to her or him) you have Work, Cost, and Start and Finish dates. In Task Usage or Resource Usage views you can also see Work and Costs distributed over time.

Take a look at the various baselines for tasks, resources, and assignments. To do so, select the Gantt Chart view and Insert a column and view all the kinds of baselines available for tasks by scrolling through the Column Definition dialog box as shown in Figure 10.2. Select the Resource Sheet and scroll through the baseline fields available for resources. Select the Task Usage sheet and select Format, and then click Detail style and scroll through the baseline fields available. Also, select Insert, then click Column to see the fields available there for the usage views. Baselines are available for assignments on the left and right side of the separator bars.

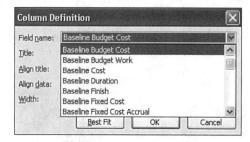

Figure 10.2 *Scroll through the task baseline fields available, including some of the new Project 2007 baseline fields, such as Baseline Budget Cost and Baseline Budget Work*

While scrolling, you might also have noticed that there are several baselines. In Figure 10.2, you see Baseline Cost. This is a field that captures the original baseline for cost of your project. If you make changes to your costs as your project is executing you can take a second snapshot and save the new information to the Baseline1 cost field (multiple baselines are available starting with Project 2003). Project provides you the capability to save an original baseline (all original baseline fields start with Baseline and have no number after them) and 10 other baselines (all fields have 1 through 10 after Baseline).

So why does Project provide 11 baselines? Multiple baselines allow organizations to have various ways to record changes in projects through time. I worked with one organization that saved two baselines. It used the original baseline to record the work, duration, and date data after initial planning. Then, when design was complete, the organization used Baseline1 to record the work, duration and data again. The organization was mature in understanding that a more definitive estimate occurs during the design effort, and it accepted that as part of its project management methodology. Other organizations use the various baselines to record changes over time for scope cost and time changes. Mature organizations have definitive approval procedures for changing the baselines.

Note that in Figure 10.1 there is no information other than a zero or NA in the baseline fields. The fields have no recorded values until you baseline. The next section discusses how you baseline, but after you baseline, you will see the same thing that is shown in Figure 10.3: The baseline fields display an exact copy of the values in the associated Cost, Work, Duration, Start, and Finish fields.

		Task Name	Baseline Cost	Cost	Baseline Work	Work	Baseline Duration	Duration	Baseline Start	Start	Baseline Finish	Finish
0		⊟ Fig10.1-RoofingProject	$0.00	$10,890.00	0 hrs	200 hrs	0 days?	16.25 days	NA	Fri 5/11/07	NA	Mon 6/4/07
1		Hire crew	$0.00	$750.00	0 hrs	10 hrs	0 days?	5 days	NA	Fri 5/11/07	NA	Thu 5/17/07
2		Obtain permits	$0.00	$425.00	0 hrs	4 hrs	0 days?	2 days	NA	Fri 5/11/07	NA	Mon 5/14/07
3		Purchase roofing materia	$0.00	$4,115.00	0 hrs	6 hrs	0 days?	1 day	NA	Fri 5/11/07	NA	Fri 5/11/07
4		Remove previous roofing	$0.00	$2,000.00	0 hrs	60 hrs	0 days?	3.75 days	NA	Fri 5/18/07	NA	Wed 5/23/07
5		Perform roofing	$0.00	$3,600.00	0 hrs	120 hrs	0 days?	7.5 days	NA	Tue 5/22/07	NA	Fri 6/1/07
6		Roofing project complete	$0.00	$0.00	0 hrs	0 hrs	0 days?	1 day	NA	Fri 6/1/07	NA	Mon 6/4/07

Figure 10.3 *Compare Figure 10.1 to 10.3: The act of baselining records snapshot data in baseline fields*

As you track or change your schedule, the baseline data remains constant. For instance, let's say the Chief has started hiring the crew and it is a worker's market: Lila and Jose, independent contractors the Chief has used in the past, have some great jobs already, and it is taking him some time to negotiate rates and dates with them. It has taken 12 hours so far, and he is estimating it will take 2 more hours to finalize their contracts. The information is entered in the project shown in Figure 10.4. If you entered 12 hours in the Actual work column, and 2 hours in Remaining Work, notice that the Work field increased to 14 hours, whereas the Baseline Work field stays at 10 hours. If you did not baseline, then you might not remember that the original estimate was 10 hours.

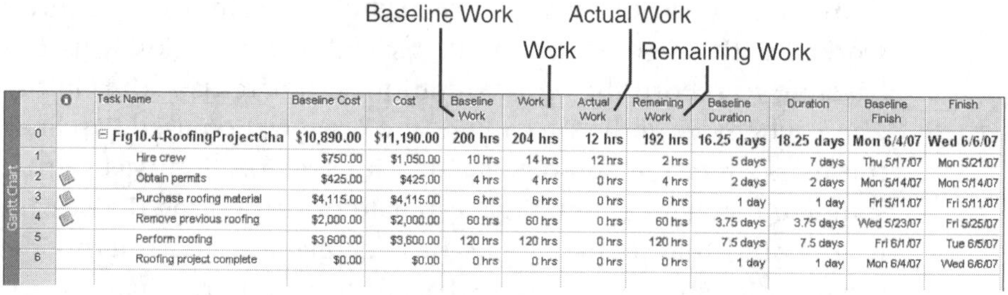

Figure 10.4 *Entering Actual Work changes the Work field and Baseline work shows the original estimate*

So, the formula,

$$Work = Actual\ Work + Remaining\ Work$$

is translated as 14 = 12 + 2 when real information is entered into the fields. You can also see how the Finish date of the project might change based on the changes to the project. The Tracking Gantt displays in Figure 10.5 and because the Hire crew task is taking longer than expected, the project might finish later than expected. The bar on the top of each task is the new task estimate based on the change, whereas the bottom bar is the baseline, which indicates the original estimate.

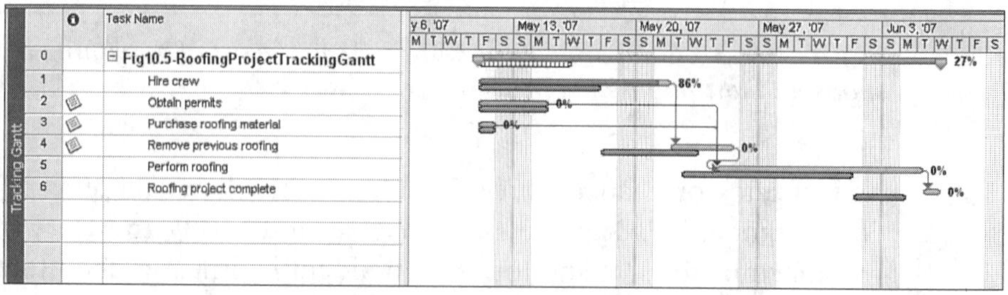

Figure 10.5 *Tracking Gantt indicates possible new dates of completion as compared to the original plan*

Using an Interim Plan

When you take a look at baselining, you might be curious about the option to save an interim plan. The interim plan was originally used to save baseline information over time in a project in versions prior to Project 2003 because there was only one baseline. The main reason for the interim plan is to save start and finish dates so you can compare them to the baseline or original schedule you created. You also have the capability of saving baseline information to interim plans to save versions of the baselines over the life of a project. An interim plan can be used to record date changes between phases. You have two options for saving an interim plan: saving start and finish dates or saving baselines. If you use an interim plan, you will need to add the fields into your Gantt Chart or whatever view you are using. Many organizations use the interim plan for recording phases or when there are changes in scope to a project. Although you can keep interim plans in mind if you need to record baseline information at various phases of a project, you could use baselines to do the same thing. This chapter focuses on baselining only as the most typical way of recording estimate and date changes to a project schedule.

Setting a Baseline

In this section I describe how you baseline and the various fields available in the Set Baseline dialog box. The act of baselining is easy, and although the results are not obvious, the benefits are tremendous. When you are satisfied with your project schedule—after it has been approved (if necessary in your organization) and prior to execution—do the following:

1. Select Tools, Tracking, and click Set Baseline (this is called Save baseline in Project 2002 and Project 2003). The Set Baseline dialog box appears, as shown in Figure 10.6.

2. Select the baseline you would like to record. If it is the initial baseline, select Baseline (with no number after the field) to record the original baseline as shown in Figure 10.6. Otherwise, select another baseline number.

3. To baseline, make sure the Set Baseline (or Save Baseline in Project 2002 and Project 2003) option is selected and make sure the Entire project option is selected to ensure the entire project is baselined. These are usually the default selections. Click OK.

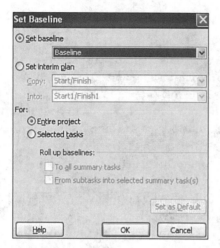

Figure 10.6   *Set Baseline dialog box with selection for various baselines*

4. Because it is hard to tell if the project was baselined, you might want to take a quick look at the baseline. To do so, select View, and then click Tracking Gantt. If the bar chart is not showing, click the first task, and click the Scroll to Task (called Go to Selected Task in versions prior to Project 2007) button or use the scroll bar at the bottom of the screen to see the bar chart as shown in Figure 10.7. The baseline is the lower gray bar. You should use the Tracking Gantt or other views to track your project once you have it baselined.

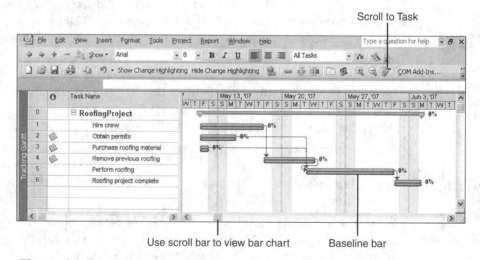

Figure 10.7   *View Tracking Gantt*

Baselining Tasks

You can select specific tasks in the Set Baseline dialog box as well as the entire project. For instance, you might create the entire schedule, but you are only in the planning phase of the project. You could baseline the tasks in the planning phase only and continue to work on the rest of the schedule. Another reason you might baseline a task or tasks is that you originally created and baselined the entire schedule and started executing the project. Then you realized you had forgotten some additional tasks. If you feel you can get them into the project without changing the scope significantly or your organization approves the scope change, you might add them to the schedule, and then baseline them to record their addition and make them part of the current baseline. To baseline just particular tasks, do the following:

1. Highlight the task or tasks you want to baseline.

2. Select Tools, Tracking, and click Set Baseline. The Set Baseline dialog box displays as shown in Figure 10.8.

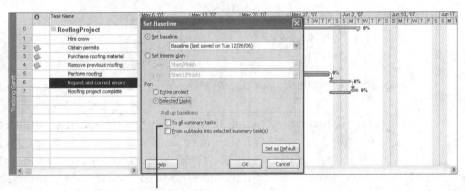

Roll up baseline selections

Figure 10.8   *Selecting a task to baseline*

3. Click the Selected tasks option. You have alternatives for how Project will calculate the new baselined task or tasks based on new selections available when you click Selected tasks. Notice the selections under Roll up baselines in Figure 10.8. You can choose to do one of the following:

- **Choose not to select rolling up the task:** This is set by default and neither of the check boxes under Roll up baselines in the Set Baseline dialog box are selected. If you choose not to select either of the check boxes, then you will not see the changed baseline information appear in summary tasks or the full project information. For example, you could baseline the roofing project and add the task called Inspect and correct errors. You could add the Chief to the task, which is estimated as 2 hours. If you do not select either of these options, notice the Project summary task in Figure 10.9. Although the task itself has been baselined, the total baseline shows the difference between the new task and the baselined task.

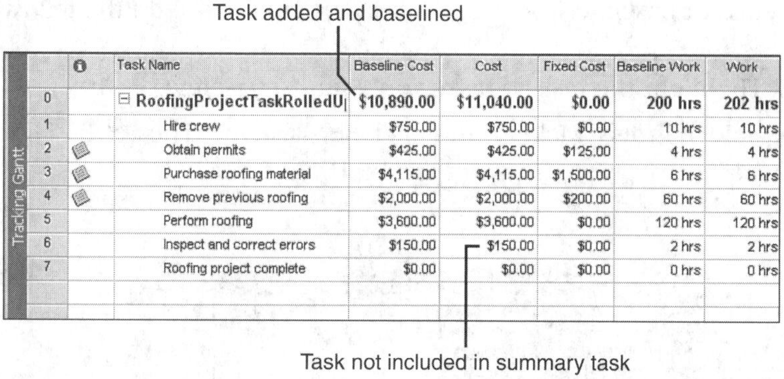

Task added and baselined

	0	Task Name	Baseline Cost	Cost	Fixed Cost	Baseline Work	Work
0		⊟ RoofingProjectTaskRolledU|	$10,890.00	$11,040.00	$0.00	200 hrs	202 hrs
1		Hire crew	$750.00	$750.00	$0.00	10 hrs	10 hrs
2		Obtain permits	$425.00	$425.00	$125.00	4 hrs	4 hrs
3		Purchase roofing material	$4,115.00	$4,115.00	$1,500.00	6 hrs	6 hrs
4		Remove previous roofing	$2,000.00	$2,000.00	$200.00	60 hrs	60 hrs
5		Perform roofing	$3,600.00	$3,600.00	$0.00	120 hrs	120 hrs
6		Inspect and correct errors	$150.00	$150.00	$0.00	2 hrs	2 hrs
7		Roofing project complete	$0.00	$0.00	$0.00	0 hrs	0 hrs

Task not included in summary task

Figure 10.9 *Additional baselined task not included in summary rollups*

- **To all summary tasks:** If you select this option, then the task will be included as part of all summary tasks it is a part of. As shown in Figure 10.10, you could select the To all summary tasks option, and then the Project summary task included the task. You would want to select this option in most cases, but in some cases, you might use the first selection (no roll up) if you want to emphasize that the change is not a part of the real project baseline.

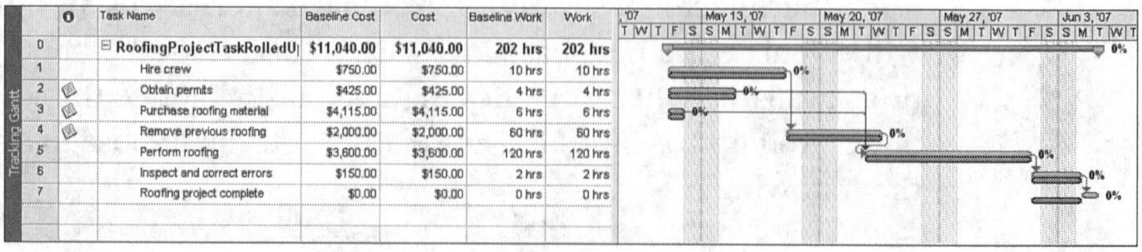

	0	Task Name	Baseline Cost	Cost	Baseline Work	Work
0		⊟ RoofingProjectTaskRolledU|	$11,040.00	$11,040.00	202 hrs	202 hrs
1		Hire crew	$750.00	$750.00	10 hrs	10 hrs
2		Obtain permits	$425.00	$425.00	4 hrs	4 hrs
3		Purchase roofing material	$4,115.00	$4,115.00	6 hrs	6 hrs
4		Remove previous roofing	$2,000.00	$2,000.00	60 hrs	60 hrs
5		Perform roofing	$3,600.00	$3,600.00	120 hrs	120 hrs
6		Inspect and correct errors	$150.00	$150.00	2 hrs	2 hrs
7		Roofing project complete	$0.00	$0.00	0 hrs	0 hrs

Figure 10.10 *Additional baselined task included in summary roll ups*

- **From subtasks into selected summary task(s):** If you select this option, then the baselined task information will be included as part of the summary task(s) you select but would not roll up to any summary tasks not selected. You might want to use this to indicate that the baseline of a phase or a set of summary tasks has changed, but recognize that is not part of the true project baseline.

4. After selecting whether you want to roll up the newly baselined task information or not, click OK.

Many organizations would prefer a process of approving changes to baselines, and then rebaselining the whole project rather than adding one task to the baseline. Others might allow individual tasks to be baselined separately, but it's important that you understand how rolling up the task change affects the entire baseline.

> **Review baselined tasks**
>
> Sometimes you might want to review larger projects that have not been baselined for a while. You might want to only baseline the new tasks. To do so, add Baseline Start or Baseline Finish to a view. If the value is N/A then the task hasn't been baselined and you could baseline the task. You could also switch to the Tracking Gantt view and see which tasks don't have baselines.

Clearing Baseline

Finally, you might have a need to clear the baseline and rebaseline now and then. An organization that has specific processes around baselining might not want you to clear baselines without approval, but sometimes you have good reasons to do so. For instance, you might have finished your schedule, you baseline it, and then a stakeholder points out that you were missing an important activity. If so, you would need to clear the baseline, fix the schedule and rebaseline. If you are well into executing your schedule, and you have captured actual progress and you want to rebaseline, it's probably better to save a version of the file so you know what is different, and then rebaseline. It would be better to just save another baseline (e.g., Baseline1) to keep the original data for the baseline. You might also decide to rebaseline only the tasks that change rather than the whole schedule. To clear the baseline, do the following:

1. Select Tools, click Tracking, then click Clear Baseline. The Clear Baseline dialog box appears.

2. By default, the Clear baseline plan option is selected. In the drop-down list next to the option, select the baseline you want to clear.

3. Choose to clear the baseline for the entire project or selected tasks next, then click OK. The Clear Baseline dialog box is displayed in Figure 10.11.

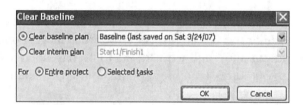

Figure 10.11   *The Clear Baseline dialog box and its selections*

The baseline will be cleared; if you rebaseline, any changes to the project schedule made up to then will be changed. Notice that this is where you can also clear the interim plan if you have been using one.

Baselines for Tracking and Variance Reports

Although there will be more about tracking and variance reporting in the next chapter, in this section I cover some of the ways you can view baseline information, track the changes in your plan using the baseline, and view variance reports that you cannot see without baselining.

You have several ways to view baseline information. In fact, once you have baselined and you are ready to track your schedule, it's a good idea to change to views that allow you to review the baseline information for analysis. A good view is the Tracking Gantt and a different table or the split window to view baseline information. If you are using Work as your main estimate, the Work table is an excellent way to view your project. If you have more than one resource on the project, you can view the split window Resource Work view as shown in Figure 10.12. To do so, take the following steps:

1. Select View, Tracking Gantt.

2. Select View, Table: Work.

3. Finally, select Window and click Split. Move the cursor to the lower window, and in the right gray area, right-click and select Resource work as shown in Figure 10.12.

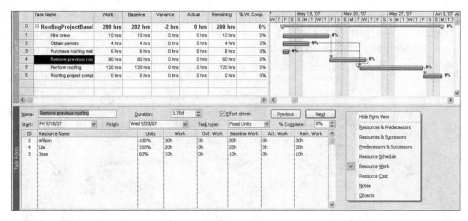

Figure 10.12   *One view for reviewing the baseline*

If you would like to view some of the various baseline data you can select View, Table, More tables, and then apply the Baseline table as shown in Figure 10.13. Doing this in the Gantt Chart can be very useful when you start making a lot of changes in your project schedule.

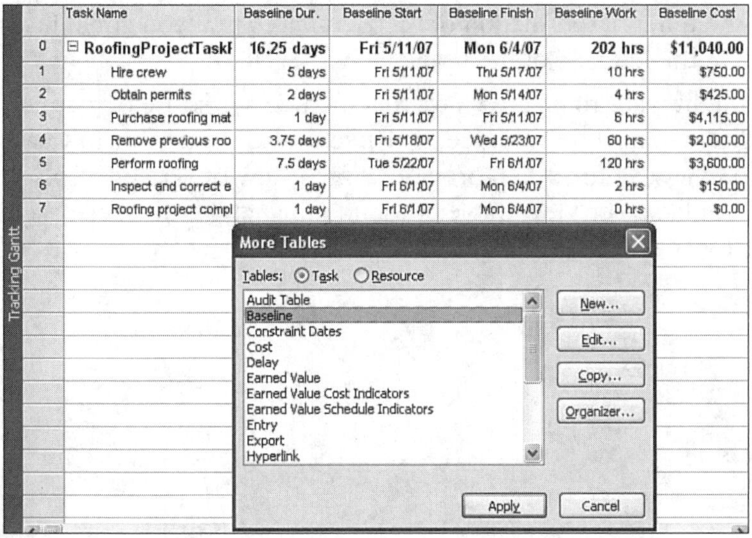

	Task Name	Baseline Dur.	Baseline Start	Baseline Finish	Baseline Work	Baseline Cost
0	⊟ RoofingProjectTaskF	16.25 days	Fri 5/11/07	Mon 6/4/07	202 hrs	$11,040.00
1	Hire crew	5 days	Fri 5/11/07	Thu 5/17/07	10 hrs	$750.00
2	Obtain permits	2 days	Fri 5/11/07	Mon 5/14/07	4 hrs	$425.00
3	Purchase roofing mat	1 day	Fri 5/11/07	Fri 5/11/07	6 hrs	$4,115.00
4	Remove previous roo	3.75 days	Fri 5/18/07	Wed 5/23/07	60 hrs	$2,000.00
5	Perform roofing	7.5 days	Tue 5/22/07	Fri 6/1/07	120 hrs	$3,600.00
6	Inspect and correct e	1 day	Fri 6/1/07	Mon 6/4/07	2 hrs	$150.00
7	Roofing project compl	1 day	Fri 6/1/07	Mon 6/4/07	0 hrs	$0.00

Figure 10.13   *Applying the baseline table*

If you are using more than one baseline, you will probably have to set up your own table and views to analyze the differences between the various baselines. You will want to add the various columns such as Baseline finish, Baseline finish1, and Baseline finish2. You have one view that provides a visual view of multiple baselines that you can see by selecting View, More views, and then applying the Multiple baselines Gantt as shown in Figure 10.14. The bars are hard to see, but it shows very thin Gantt bars for each task for the three baselines and in different colors.

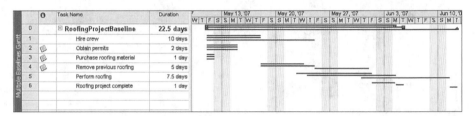

Figure 10.14 *Multiple baseline view*

For assignment views, you can also add baseline fields. As shown in Figure 10.15, you can add the Baseline work field to the right side of the Resource Usage view to see original estimating once actual progress starts to be applied. You can do this by selecting Format, Detail Styles. In the resulting Detail Styles dialog box, move the baseline field (in this case, Baseline Work) into the timephased section of the view. Note that you could insert baseline fields in the left side of the usage view as well.

You might want to create views that include a mixture of planned and baseline fields to analyze variance. Variance is discussed more in Chapter 11, but as a preview, Figure 10.16 provides a nice view of variance. To see this view, you would select View, Table: Variance to analyze changes based on actual progress.

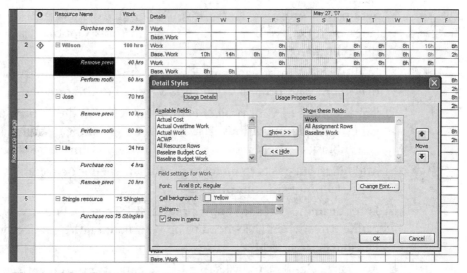

Figure 10.15　*Add Baseline fields to usage views*

Figure 10.16　*View variance table*

The Project Schedule Building Methodology So Far

Based on what you have learned, the following steps and sequence describe the best methods for building your schedule. The items emphasized in this chapter are indicated in italics. Because many organizations do not enter costs, I have also added an "optional" indicator in this list.

The steps for building a project schedule so far are as follows:

☑ If you are using a template, select the appropriate template (you will probably want to change it based on the input of your project team). If you are building a project from scratch, build a WBS with your team, then move to the next step.

☑ Set up your project calendar if you do not have one available. Make sure you reflect your company's hours in Tools, Options, Calendar, if different than the defaults.

☑ In the Project Information dialog box, set your project Start date and make sure your project calendar is assigned to the project.

☑ Start building (if your project is from scratch) or editing (if you are using a template) your task list. Make sure you indicate summary tasks and subtasks to help indicate the outline of your project schedule.

☑ Add milestone tasks to indicate significant events, deliverables, or approval points in your project.

☑ Enter deadline dates for appropriate tasks. This is a better way of indicating dates when tasks need to be completed rather than typing in a Finish date on a task.

☑ Add task calendars to tasks to indicate exceptions to the project calendar if needed. You will probably not need these kinds of calendars often.

☑ Review all tasks. Decide what kind of tasks they are for the schedule-building process. Change the Task type and Effort-driven fields if appropriate.

☑ Link all tasks in the schedule, determining if they are Finish-to-Start, Start-to-Start, Finish-to-Finish, or Start-to-Finish relationships. Link among phases or task groupings first, then link between phases or groupings. Use the Predecessor and Successor columns to help you see if all tasks are linked.

☑ Build the project team. Add all resources that might work on the project to the Resource Sheet for the project. If you are performing effort-based scheduling, enter the Maximum Units each resource can work on the project. You can use generic or real resources, but when you know who will do the work, you should replace generic resources with real resources.

☑ Assign the resources to each task. If you are performing effort-based scheduling, you might need to change the percentage of allocation a resource is assigned to individual tasks in some cases.

☑ Enter estimates to project tasks. For effort-based scheduling, enter two of the three variables in the Work formula: Work = Duration × Units.

☑ Review the schedule and enter leads and lags on tasks if appropriate.

☑ Review the critical path and adjust tasks if appropriate.

☑ [Optional] Set your cost default cost calculation methods: Have Project automatically calculate Actual Costs and decide on and set up your cost accrual method for the entire project.

☑ [Optional] Set up any other kinds of resources, such as material resources (set up cost and budget resources if you are using Project 2007) if you want to include costs other than labor or equipment work costs in your project.

☑ [Optional] Insert the Cost and Fixed Cost fields in the Gantt Chart view (or use the Table: Cost view). Enter rates on resources, enter Fixed Costs on tasks, or enter total budget on the project summary task line, depending on how your organization has decided to enter cost.

☑ Check your schedule for logic and scheduling errors using a special audit view or reviewing the errors using methods described in Chapter 8.

☑ Review and adjust your schedule for workload issues and to tighten the critical path.

☑ *Baseline your project schedule.*

Summary

When I first started using Project 2000 without really knowing much about how to use Project properly, I would always get a message asking if I would like to baseline the schedule every time I saved my project file. I found it annoying, and didn't understand the implications of baselining other than somehow it recorded my work in some fashion. I didn't realize baselining was part of the project file, nor that it would hold my original estimates at the time I baselined. Once I learned the proper way of building a project schedule and what baselining did, I was a convert to using it. Starting with Project 2002, the baselining message was eliminated, so now you need to know when you should baseline your project.

Baselining records the original thinking you or your project team had after working through the complete process of planning your project. Once you get the schedule approved (perhaps after planning or design), you should baseline. Change to the Tracking Gantt view and as you record actual progress, notice how you are doing based on your original estimates. If you are a confident project manager, understanding that no plan is set in stone, then you will appreciate that baselining will show you two important elements: what has changed from your original plan so you know what adjustments you need to make, and historical information so you can see where you can get better the next time you create your project estimates and the project schedule.

Insert baseline columns and baseline views and tables to look at original baseline information as you are tracking your schedule so you understand what the original estimate is and the implication for your schedule.

Practice: Baseline the House-Painting Project

In the following practices, you will practice setting a baseline and viewing how a change to the schedule shows the value of baselining.

Practice 10.1

Baseline

To start, use the project called HousePainting-Practice-Chapter10-Practice1.mpp on your CD. This is the roofing project that has been leveled and adjusted to make sure the project can be completed by the deadline.

1. Open HousePainting-Practice-Chapter10-Practice1.mpp.
2. Select Tools, Tracking, and then click Set baseline (or Save baseline in Project 2002 or Project 2003).
3. Leave the default settings, which means you will baseline the entire project for the original baseline and click OK.
4. Select View, Tracking Gantt.
5. If you want to see the result, see HousePainting-Practice-Chapter10-Practice1-Result.mpp on the CD.

Practice 10.2

Viewing Changes in the House Painting Project

This practice is a little different from previous exercises, as you are asked various questions about the project based on actual progress entered on the house-painting project. To start, open the project called HousePainting-Practice-Chapter10-Practice2.mpp on your CD and answer the following questions:

1. What was the baseline work on the Scrape and Sand task?
2. How many additional hours did Spouse and Me work from the baseline work assigned? To see this information, click the Scrape and Sand task and view the information in the split window.

3. Based on progress entered, will the project end according to the original baseline end date?

There is no resulting project. The answers are as follows:

1. 40 hours.
2. Spouse worked an additional 2 hours (Act Work of 12 hours minus Baseline Work of 10 hours) and Me worked an additional 12 hours (Act Work of 42 hours minus Baseline Work of 30 hours).
3. Yes, the end date has changed. It actually shows that the project will be completed 1 day early (6/21 rather than the original baseline of 6/22).

Case Study: Baselining the Schedule

Now you can baseline the VNLE schedule that you completed in Chapter 9. Chris made all the adjustments, reviewed all the overallocations that she determined are acceptable, and received stakeholder approval of the schedule. Now she's ready to baseline. As Chris, you can perform the simple action of baselining the VNLE schedule.

Open the file VNLE-Chapter10-Start-CaseStudy.mpp to work on this case study and baseline the schedule.

1. Baseline the schedule.
2. Switch to the Tracking Gantt view and review the baseline.

If you would like to see the result of the scenario practice, see VNLE-Chapter10-End-CaseStudy.mpp to review the baseline in the Tracking Gantt.

Baselining

When you are ready to move into executing your project, and based on approval and a thorough schedule review, you are ready to baseline. To do so follow these steps:

- Select Tools, Tracking, Set Baseline.
- Review the variance of your schedule after you have baselined for course correction when your schedule goes too far off-base.

To record your original estimates, baseline the schedule.

Review Questions

1. What is the project baseline?
2. Where is baseline information stored?
3. How many baselines are available in Project 2003 and Project 2007?
4. If you have not baselined, what do you see in the baseline fields?
5. How do you set the baseline?
6. What is a good view to see the baseline in the Gantt Chart?
7. When would you baseline a task in a project already baselined?
8. How do you clear the baseline? Why would you do so?
9. What are some ways you might view baseline information?

Tracking Your Schedule

There cannot be a crisis next week. My schedule is already full.
—*Henry Kissinger*

Topics Covered in This Chapter

Tracking is a loaded word in this chapter, as it means a lot of things. I am using the term *tracking* to describe the whole process of what you will do to review, update, and report on your schedule as you execute the work of your project. It includes monitoring, controlling, and reporting the progress of the project based on the baselined schedule. Tracking means that, as the project manager, you know what activities have to be performed to reach your milestones on time by reviewing them in the schedule. You capture status of the project schedule by entering actual progress information into the schedule based on accomplishments of the team. By reviewing the schedule based on expected progress (which you set when you baselined) and actual progress, you can then see if you are going to accomplish what you expected in the future. If not, you might make some adjustments and replan. During this tracking process, you create reports to help you analyze and tell others what is going on. By understanding alternatives, and with the help of others, you can make necessary adjustments on your project with your team and in the schedule. Tracking is an iterative process (just like planning) that should be performed at consistent intervals.

While planning, you might have had several meetings to gather information about the scope of the project, its activities, deliverables, estimates, and resources, until you and your stakeholders agreed on the best plan. It was an iterative process, the time of the meetings and process might not have been consistent. However, with tracking, you should have a time each day, week, few weeks, or month to gather and enter progress into your schedule. For instance, each week, you could ask your responsible team members, "What have you accomplished, and how much more do you have to finish the work?" Then, after they tell you something like, "I've worked 5 days and I have about 2 days left," you can enter the information into the schedule and see if this tracks with what you expected. By doing this, you have an indication of the future. If you do not perform this process, you might ask, "How are things going?" A team member might say, "Just fine," and you make assumptions that this means he or she will be done on time and the reporting of status is subjective. However, if the team member says he or she has 5 days left of work, and you see in the schedule that he or she is supposed to be done in 2 days, then you have a chance for corrective action. You might ask the team member to work extra time, maybe the task has slack and you can allow more time, or maybe with more discussion you decide you don't need to do some of the work you'd originally planned.

The following are the elements of tracking your project schedule:

- Decide on the kind of progress information you require to understand your schedule or budget status (e.g., Daily Actual Hours or % Complete). What you select should support the information you need based on if you are doing duration-based or effort-based scheduling. If you built your schedule based on work effort, you might want to capture daily hours, especially if you had the goal of trying to learn what it takes to complete work for historical purposes. If you built the schedule for duration-based scheduling, % Complete is probably good enough.

- Set up a regular time when you ask for progress. This can be done via e-mail, a meeting, or some other method, but it should be done at a regular interval. The data you gather gives you a point-in-time view of how much work has been accomplished on the task or deliverables of your plan. You should also find out how much work is left to get the most accurate status.

- Enter the progress data you receive into the schedule.

- Create reports for analysis to understand where you are based on the current progress.

- Communicate the project status with your team and management. Then, if necessary, you can make decisions to adjust the current path, or stay the course with the help of your team and management.

- Continue the process iteratively until the project is done. Often, this means weekly.

Read about tracking in *Project Management for Mere Mortals*

Read about tracking your project in Chapter 12 of *Project Management for Mere Mortals*. The chapter discusses in more depth obtaining status and analyzing variances to make better project decisions with your team.

Don't think of tracking as just the method you use, but also a way of revealing your project's progress. If all you need is to ask how much is done, without asking how much is left to complete the task, then you are wasting the greatest power of Project. You can do that in a spreadsheet and that might be all you need.

Why You Should Track

First, you might ask why you should track your project. You've got all your information into the project plan and schedule so you should just be able to execute the work, and everything will all work out, right? Most of us know better than that. Team members sometimes take longer to get the work done than planned due to competing priorities or inaccurate estimates. Sometimes clients ask for more, and it's hard to say no (although that should go under scope control). Sometimes materials or hardware you expected to be delivered for your project don't arrive on time. I once knew a project manager who said she always knew what needed to be done on her projects. It was in her head, and she knew how to keep it on track. She wasn't too bad at her job; however, no one else knew what was going on, and she had no objective information for management. When something did go wrong, it was hard to justify why.

The following provides a very short example of a project and how you can use Project to track and understand progress. Let's say you are gathering status once a week. The product of the project is a whitepaper that will help potential buyers understand the technical aspects of a new pharmaceutical product. Two authors (Author 1 and Author 2) and an editor perform the work. The project baseline is set as shown in Figure 11.1.

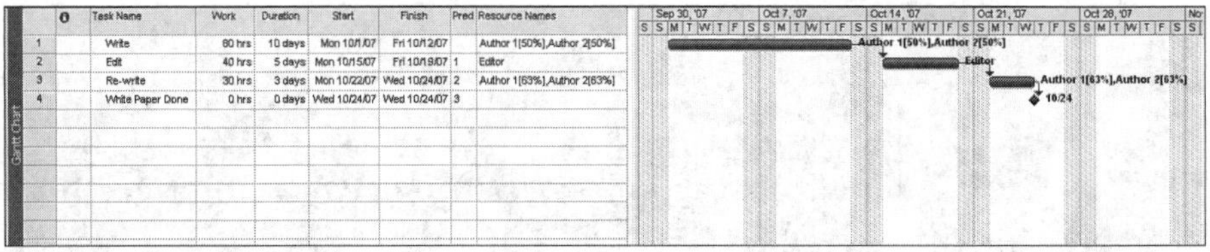

Figure 11.1   *Project set up for delivering a whitepaper*

The project starts as scheduled on October 1. The two authors have separate sections to write for the whitepaper and can work on the whitepaper about half of their available time. Your first status is on Monday, October 8. You capture the amount of work that has been completed as follows:

- Author 1 says she has completed 20 hours and now estimates that she has 30 hours left.

- Author 2 says he was told by his manager that he had to work on tweaking the product instead of writing the whitepaper so he only put 10 hours of time on the writing. He still thinks it will take 30 hours more, as originally estimated. He also says that he got the tweak completed and can move back to working on the project half of the time the coming week.

Based on the input, and your setting of the status date of October 5, you see that the schedule has changed as shown in Figure 11.2.

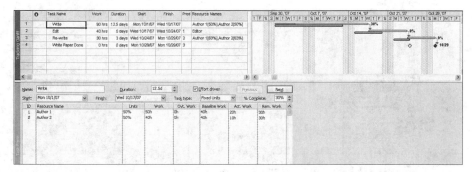

Figure 11.2 *Progressing the project indicates the project will end late*

You now know that your project is going to be 3 days late if everything stays the same. Now you have choices to discuss: Should you see if the authors could work more than half time to make up for their work to get back on track? Could you possibly shorten the edit or rewrite tasks? Could you accept everything as is and ask your sponsor if you can have 3 more days? Let's say you share the status with your sponsor, and after discussion, you decide to let it go. You both decide to see if the trend continues and to take measures during the third week if you need to catch up. You alert the authors' managers that you might be asking them to work overtime to perform the rewrite task if the project continues to look like it might be late.

Work continues and you are ready to take status for Week 2. On Monday, October 15, you ask for progress through the preceding Friday.

- Author 1 says she was able to get 20 additional hours done, but she still needs 15 hours to complete her section of the whitepaper.
- Author 2 was able to complete his work, which took him 30 hours last week, and he's handing in his section today.

You enter in the progress information as shown in Figure 11.3.

You use the Task Usage view to see how the work is scheduled for Author 1 for the coming week (October 14) as shown in Figure 11.4.

You review this with your sponsor and decide that you'd like to ask Author 1's manager if she could make up a few days by working full time on the task for a few days. The manager says yes. Also, you let the editor know that he can get started on Author 2's writing right away and will be able to start on Author 1's work at the end of the week. You also will continue to check status throughout the week to ensure the plan stays on course; as you do, things are looking up.

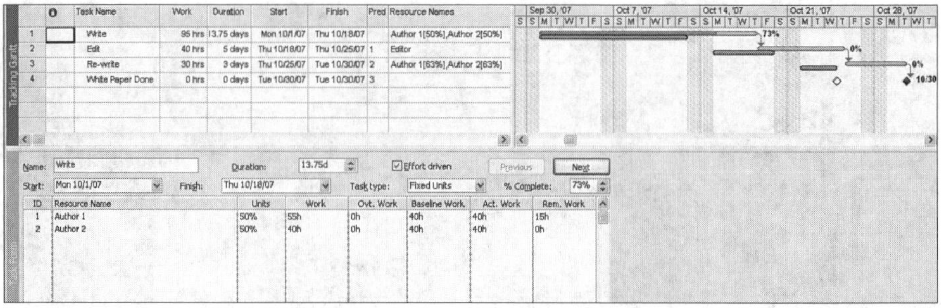

Figure 11.3   *Second week's status results*

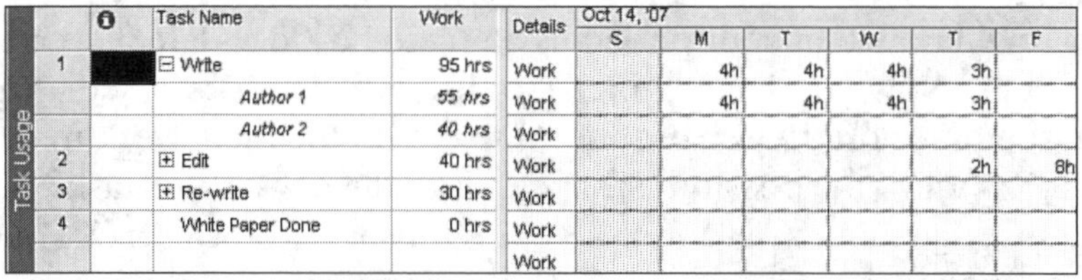

Figure 11.4   *Author 1 is scheduled for half time for Week 3*

You get status for the third week on Monday, October 22.

- Author 1 completed her writing task on Tuesday evening of the previous week and took 5 more hours than expected.

- The editor started the editing on Tuesday, October 16. He was able to complete the editing for Author 2 and turned over the edits to Author 2 for rewrite. He also started editing Author 1's work on Friday, but wasn't able to complete it and estimated 15 hours remaining for the coming week.

- Author 2 started the rewrite on Friday and made 4 hours' worth of progress accepting the edits.

The result of entering the information is shown in Figure 11.5. The team made up some time and the projected end date for the project is now only a few days from the original. Because you made adjustments early, you were able to give your project a chance to come in on time.

Now you can make your final plans to bring the project in as close to target as possible. You want to confirm that the editor will be able to complete the work on Monday and Tuesday and he says he can. You also ask Author 2 to complete his rewrite as early as possible. You ask Author 1 to work full time

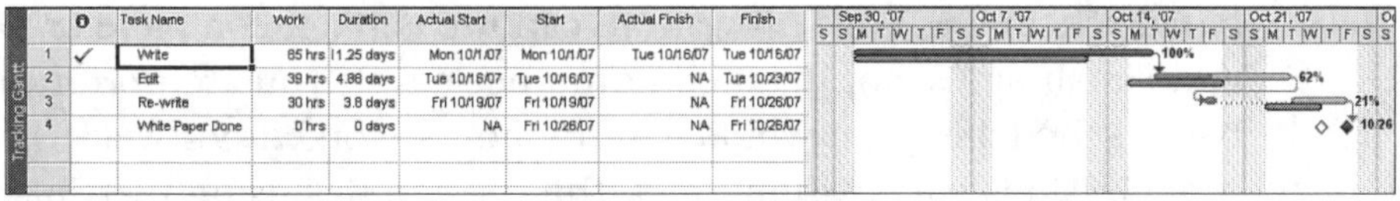

Figure 11.5 *Week 3 progress reflected in the project schedule*

on the rewrite until complete. You check with all of the resources every day to make sure they are on target, and you feel very positive. The team provides you their final progress information and when you get done, you are only 1 day behind the original target. Your final project input is shown in Figure 11.6. Your sponsor and team are satisfied after the rough start. If you absolutely had to bring it in on the target date, you could have possibly scheduled some overtime to do so, but your sponsor had said you could have a few days' leeway.

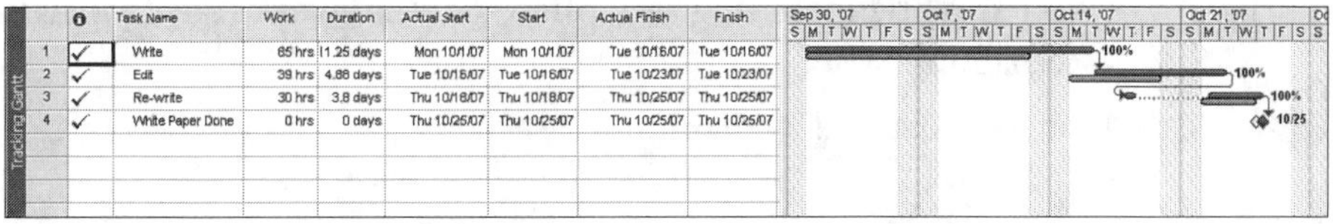

Figure 11.6 *Progress reflected in final project schedule*

In this example of effort-based schedule tracking, you asked how much work was done and how much remained each week. Finding the answers to how much is done, how much is remaining, and asking the questions at consistent intervals are the keys to good tracking. If you did not do this, not only is it hard to identify how far you are behind, but you might not be able to be very specific in analyzing and selecting the alternatives you want to take to get back on track. Consider that all the hard work in setting up the project schedule is rewarded when doing the tracking.

Fields for Tracking Progress

It's important to think about tracking your schedule while you are planning for it, because you need to know the kind of progress information you will be asking for during project execution. Knowing what data you want to capture will help you set up your schedule. If you are performing duration-based scheduling, you will want to capture Percent complete or Actual Start and Finish dates, not detailed hours per day. If you are performing effort-based scheduling, you would capture hours worked per week or day. Many organizations successfully track their schedules using the finish dates of tasks, others track the Percent complete, and others track day-by-day. The decision of how to track is based on what the organization needs to know.

Let's take a look at what you can track on your schedule and some interesting behaviors you might see based on the way you choose to track, once again revealing some of the mysteries of Project. The fields in the following list and shown in Figure 11.7 are most of the tracking fields you will use and are described in the sections that follow.

- % Complete and % Work Complete
- Actual Start and Actual Finish dates
- Actual Duration and Remaining Duration
- Actual Work, including timephased actual work (day-by-day hours) and Remaining Work
- Actual Cost and Remaining Cost

	Task Name	% Comp.	% Work Complete	Act. Start	Act. Finish	Act. Dur.	Rem. Dur.	Act. Work	Remaining Work	Act. Cost	Remaining Cost
1	Tracking Fields	0%	0%	NA	NA	0 days	1 day?	0 hrs	16 hrs	$0.00	$0.00

Figure 11.7   *Tracking fields in Project*

Recording status using Percent Complete and Actual Start and Finish dates is the least accurate method for assessing the status of a project, but is very effective in organizations that only need to understand task progress. Recording status using Actual Duration and Remaining Duration is more accurate, and capturing Actual Work and Remaining Work is the most accurate of all, especially if you capture it day-by-day. This third method is also the most time consuming for the project team. If your organization is not accustomed to tracking project status, it might represent a big culture shock to try to enforce hours per day and remaining work.

% Complete

This field is one of the most commonly used for tracking actual progress, but it is one of the most misunderstood. When you use this field, you are indicating the percentage of the task's duration that is complete. Many people confuse this field with Percent Work Complete, which is the assignment work as described later. Percent Complete is another of those fields that has a hidden formula connected to it and is based on duration:

Actual Duration/Duration × 100 = % Complete

The project schedule setup for Figure 11.8 illustrates how Percent Complete works. Notice that all of the actual fields' data are not filled in, and the project baseline is set (see Chapter 10, "Baselining: The Key to Tracking Your Schedule," to understand the importance of the baseline).

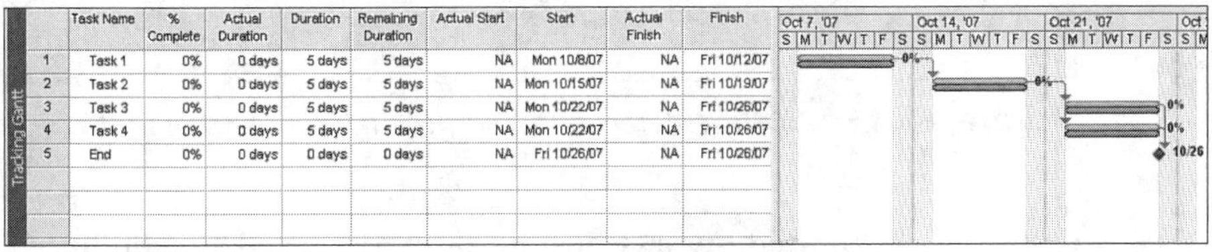

Figure 11.8 *Setup for Percent Complete*

When you enter 50% on Task 1, all of the actual fields are filled in based on the planned information as shown in Figure 11.9.

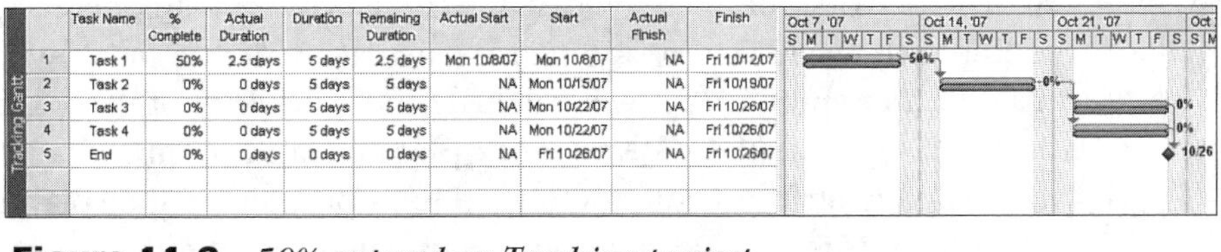

Figure 11.9 *50% entered on Tracking project*

If you enter 100% on Task 1 as shown in Figure 11.10, all of the actual fields are completed as originally planned. If you started on a different date, or the actual duration or work took any less or more than planned, then it will not be reflected by entering 100%.

	Task Name	% Complete	Actual Duration	Duration	Remaining Duration	Actual Start	Start	Actual Finish	Finish
1	Task 1	100%	5 days	5 days	0 days	Mon 10/8/07	Mon 10/8/07	Fri 10/12/07	Fri 10/12/07
2	Task 2	0%	0 days	5 days	5 days	NA	Mon 10/15/07	NA	Fri 10/19/07
3	Task 3	0%	0 days	5 days	5 days	NA	Mon 10/22/07	NA	Fri 10/26/07
4	Task 4	0%	0 days	5 days	5 days	NA	Mon 10/22/07	NA	Fri 10/26/07
5	End	0%	0 days	0 days	0 days	NA	Fri 10/26/07	NA	Fri 10/26/07

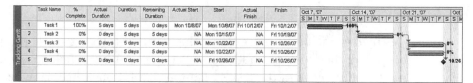

Figure 11.10 *100% entered on Tracking project*

However, if you actually started a day earlier than planned and you entered 100% and entered the actual date, your schedule will show that you have a chance to complete a day early based on the early start date as shown in Figure 11.11.

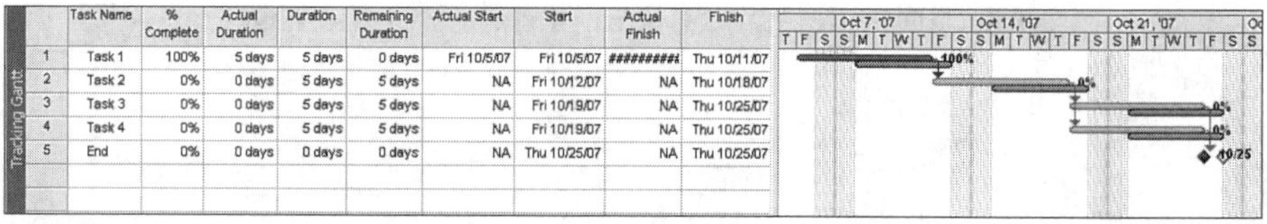

	Task Name	% Complete	Actual Duration	Duration	Remaining Duration	Actual Start	Start	Actual Finish	Finish
1	Task 1	100%	5 days	5 days	0 days	Fri 10/5/07	Fri 10/5/07	#########	Thu 10/11/07
2	Task 2	0%	0 days	5 days	5 days	NA	Fri 10/12/07	NA	Thu 10/18/07
3	Task 3	0%	0 days	5 days	5 days	NA	Fri 10/19/07	NA	Thu 10/25/07
4	Task 4	0%	0 days	5 days	5 days	NA	Fri 10/19/07	NA	Thu 10/25/07
5	End	0%	0 days	0 days	0 days	NA	Thu 10/25/07	NA	Thu 10/25/07

Figure 11.11 *100% entered and Actual Start date entered on Tracking project*

Entering % Complete works best on duration-based scheduling. If you enter it for effort-based schedules, you will not get information that is as accurate as you might have intended.

% Work Complete

The Percent complete field is for describing progress for all the work on the task. The % Work complete field, when there is more than one assignment on the task, will usually show a different calculation. If you have two resources on a task, and enter 50%, it will calculate the work for both resources as 50% complete. If Joe had 5 days of work planned, and Jennifer had 10 days of work planned and you enter 50%, then Joe's progress will display as 2.5 days and Jennifer as 5 days. Because people usually work at different rates, it's better to get status information separately for each resource, and you can enter the Percent Complete on the Task Usage or Resource Usage screen for each resource. Figure 11.12 illustrates % Work Complete for two different resources. Both R1 and R2 had the same amount of duration, but had different completion rates on the work. R1 completed 50% of the work, and R2 completed 25%. The Task Usage view shows that R1 completed 20 hours and R2 completed 10 hours. The total Percent Complete for the task is 38%.

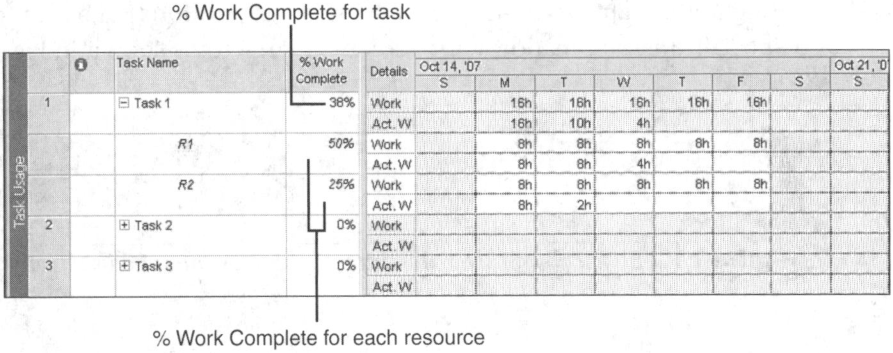

% Work Complete for task

% Work Complete for each resource

Figure 11.12   *% Work Complete versus % Complete*

What is Physical % Complete?

You might see a field called Physical % Complete and wonder if you should use that for tracking. If you are going to use the earned value technique for reporting your schedule status (see the section "Introducing Earned Value" later in this chapter for more information), then you might consider using this field. It uses whatever you enter in the field as Percent Complete and does not use the duration values to calculate. So if duration of the tasks is not an accurate reflection of the way you earn value for a task, you can use the Physical % Complete field.

Actual Start and Actual Finish Dates

These fields are the actual dates the task starts and ends. If you enter progress using Percent Complete, Actual Duration, or Actual Work without entering the Actual Start date, Project assumes and automatically enters the date you see in the Start field, which is the scheduled date for the task. When you enter the Actual Start 1 day later than the date scheduled, the dependent tasks will be moved out 1 day. If it's on the critical path, you will see that the project will be completed 1 day later. Of course, if you got started earlier, your task and dependent tasks will show that you could be done earlier than expected. Entering an Actual Finish date implies you are done with the task. Project will calculate the Actual Start date based on the expected duration as well. Enter Actual Finish only if the task is 100% complete.

Using Actual Start or Actual Finish dates is best for duration-based scheduling, especially in combination with Percent Complete, as shown in Figure 11.13.

	ⓘ	Task Name	Actual Duration	Duration	Baseline Duration	Actual Start	Start	Actual Finish	Finish	Oct 7, '07	Oct 14, '07	Oct 21, '07
1		Task 1	0 days	5 days	5 days	Wed 10/10/07	Wed 10/10/07	NA	Tue 10/16/07			
2		Task 2	0 days	5 days	5 days	NA	Wed 10/17/07	NA	Tue 10/23/07			

Figure 11.13 *Actual Start date entered changes the schedule flow*

Actual Duration

If you are performing duration-based scheduling, Actual Duration can be used in combination with Remaining Duration to describe the progress of tasks on the project. Let's take a look at a typical situation: You are 1 week into the project. You ask Maria how far along she is on her task that had a duration of 10 days. If she says "I'm about 75% done," what does that mean? If you were to enter that amount in Project, you'd get the calculation shown in Figure 11.14. So it looks like Mary has worked 7.5 days already, yet it's only been 5 days.

	ⓘ	% Complete	Task Name	Actual Duration	Baseline Duration	Duration	Remaining Duration	Oct 28, '07	Nov 4, '07	No
1		75%	Mary's Task	7.5 days	10 days	10 days	2.5 days			

Figure 11.14 *Entering 75% complete shows Mary has 2.5 days remaining on the task*

What she's probably trying to say is that she has taken 5 days, and she has 2.5 days' worth of work left. So it might be better to ask, "How long have you worked, and how much duration remaining do you have?" Mary might answer, "I've worked 5 days, and I have about 2.5 more days, I think." You would enter 5 days for Actual Duration and 2.5 days for Remaining Duration as shown in Figure 11.15. When you enter the Actual Duration and Remaining Duration values, Project calculates that the % Complete is actually 67%. The measurement of the task's progress is more accurate. It also shows that the task looks like it is getting done quicker than expected, so any dependent tasks could actually start sooner.

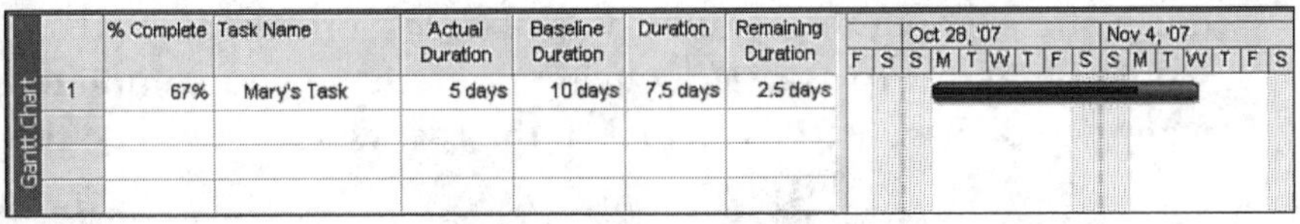
Gantt Chart
% Complete
Task Name
Actual Duration
Baseline Duration
Duration
Remaining Duration
Oct 28, '07
Nov 4, '07
F S S M T W T F S S M T W T F S
1
67%
Mary's Task
5 days
10 days
7.5 days
2.5 days

Figure 11.15 *Enter Actual Duration and Remaining Duration to increase accuracy of task progress status*

Another formula to keep in mind is this:

Actual Duration + Remaining Duration = Duration

Therefore, if you do not change the Remaining Duration field during tracking based on how much work your team members still have left to do, then the schedule's Duration field might not reflect what is really happening on the task. You want to get the most accurate information to predict the date the task will complete, so you might also want to include Actual Start date to help achieve greater accuracy.

Actual Work

If you are performing effort-based scheduling, there are a few ways to enter progress: day by day or per period hours. For both methods, you should ask for Remaining Work to obtain the most accurate progress information for forecasting task completion. An example might help to illustrate why it's better to obtain work status rather than % Complete for effort-based tracking. Let's say Maria has been scheduled to work on a task half her available time (20 hours per week) for 2 weeks. After the first week you ask her the task's status and she says, "I'm about 40% done." The result is shown in Figure 11.16.

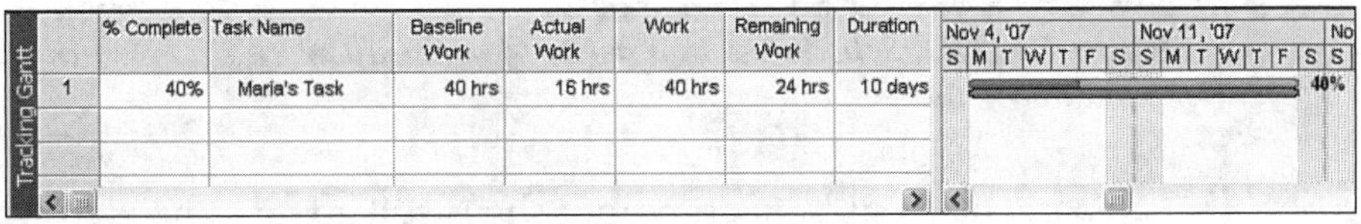
Tracking Gantt
% Complete
Task Name
Baseline Work
Actual Work
Work
Remaining Work
Duration
Nov 4, '07
Nov 11, '07
No
S M T W T F S S M T W T F S S
1
40%
Maria's Task
40 hrs
16 hrs
40 hrs
24 hrs
10 days
40%

Figure 11.16 *% Complete for effort-based scheduling*

What does this mean? She is actually 4 hours behind, because she should have completed 20 hours during the first week, not 16. Does her status mean she is going to get done a day later (Monday rather than Friday)? It would be better to ask, "How many hours have you completed, and how many do you have left?" Let's look at the two ways you can do this.

- **Actual hours per period:** If you simply need current work status and how much more there is, you can ask for totals per week (or some other period of time). In Maria's case, on the Friday of the first week, you might ask Maria, "How many hours did you work, and how many more do you think you have to complete the task?" If Maria says, "I've worked 16 hours, and I think it's going to take 30 more," you would enter that information and the schedule would look like Figure 11.17.

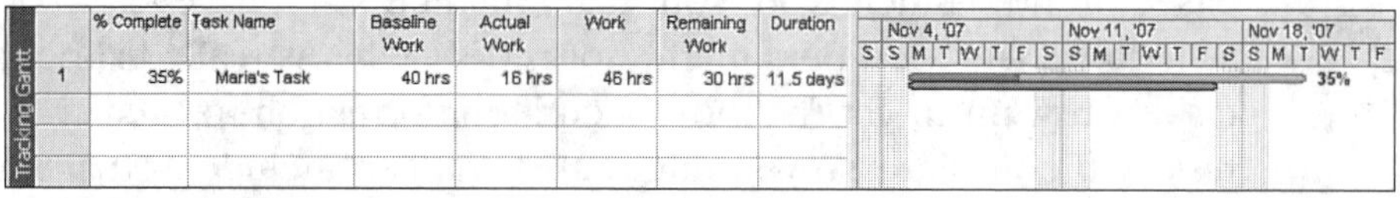
Tracking Gantt
% Complete
Task Name
Baseline Work
Actual Work
Work
Remaining Work
Duration
1
35%
Maria's Task
40 hrs
16 hrs
46 hrs
30 hrs
11.5 days
Nov 4, '07
Nov 11, '07
Nov 18, '07
S S M T W T F S S M T W T F S S M T W T F
35%

Figure 11.17 *Schedule when asking for Actual Work and Remaining Work*

If Maria continues to work at 50% of her time, the schedule has shown that she will be 2 days late in completing her work. At least now you have some idea of what will happen in the future at the present rate of completion. The next week you ask, she might say she's completed 20 more hours (you will need to add 20 hours to the Actual Work hours for a total of 36 hours), and has about 5 hours remaining. The schedule has changed as shown in Figure 11.18.

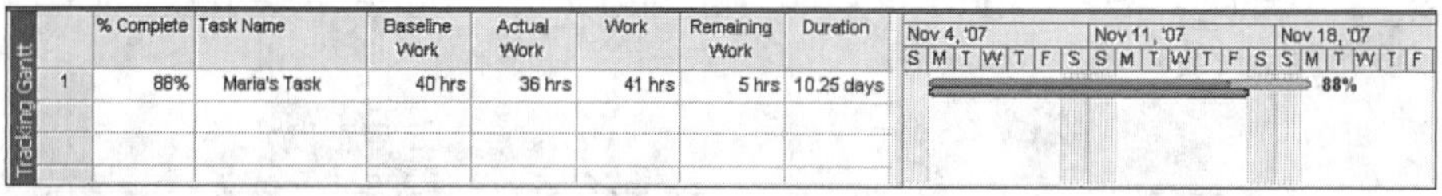
Tracking Gantt
% Complete
Task Name
Baseline Work
Actual Work
Work
Remaining Work
Duration
1
88%
Maria's Task
40 hrs
36 hrs
41 hrs
5 hrs
10.25 days
Nov 4, '07
Nov 11, '07
Nov 18, '07
S M T W T F S S M T W T F S S M T W T F
88%

Figure 11.18 *Schedule when asking for Actual Work and Remaining Work the following week*

Maria made up some time, but she is still going to need to work on Monday to finish the task. With this method you are accurately capturing the hours it is taking to complete the job. Once more, you might need to enter the Actual Start date if it is any different than the original planned date. If you enter Actual Work using this method, it assumes the Start date is the date the task starts.

- **Actual hours each day:** If you want to capture progress in the most accurate method, you could capture time day-by-day. This can be quite tedious. You would need to set up a method for your team to capture their time for you, as it would be hard for them to remember each day's work, and you might need help from someone else to enter the time into the schedule. You do not need to enter Start date with this method because you would actually enter the first day's hours of effort on the day it is reported. Let's set up a typical way in which this might work. You have created a method for capturing day-by-day time. A great method is for you to use the Resource Usage screen, which prints out each resource's tasks for the project within the time frames in which the work was expected to be completed. Maria would have the printed report she could use for entering her time each day as shown in Figure 11.19. You could also use an Excel spreadsheet.

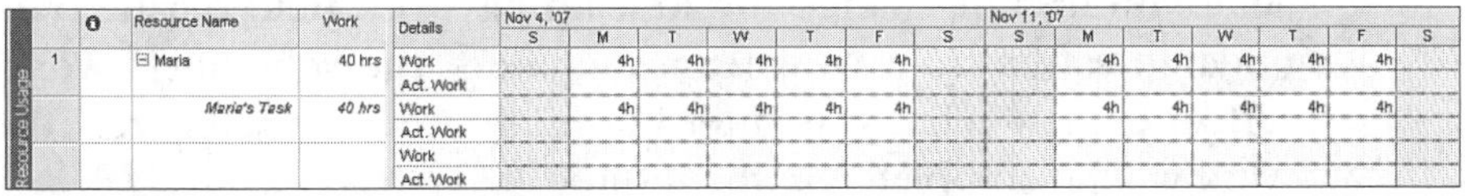

Figure 11.19   *Resource Usage screen for capturing time*

You might also remove the scheduled time information (the Work field in the grid on the right) if that might be distracting for the resources when filling in time. You would also want to request one more piece of information with this day-by-day process of capturing time: How many more hours are left to complete the task? Figure 11.20 is an example of the Resource Usage view if Maria has filled out her actual day-by-day hours.

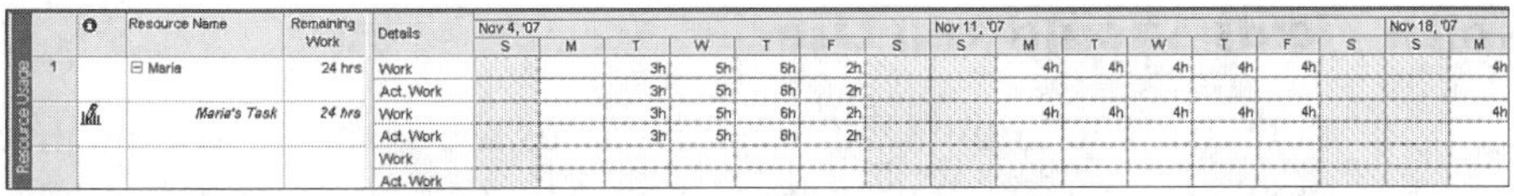

Figure 11.20   *Maria's time entered into the Resource Usage screen*

In the example you can see that Maria actually started on Tuesday, and put in hours toward the work each day. If she tells you she has 30 hours left, you could enter that in the Remaining Work field (the column could either be added to the Resource Usage sheet if needed), then the Gantt Chart for the project would look like Figure 11.21.

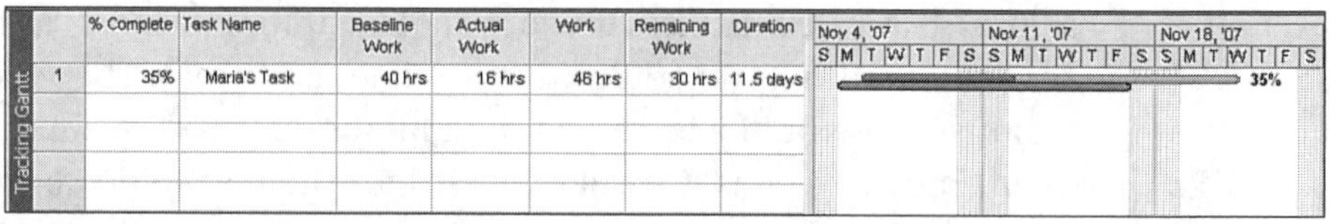

Figure 11.21 *Maria's Actual Work and Remaining Work entered*

Now you can make preparations for the task taking longer or ask Maria to try and get the work done earlier. Of course, this method is a lot of work; it is like filling out a timesheet. This method of tracking is fabulous for capturing historical data and will help project managers understand project effort for similar projects in the future.

With tracking for work effort, you have another formula to keep in mind:

$$\text{Actual Work} + \text{Remaining Work} = \text{Work}$$

So, if you do not change the Remaining Work field during tracking with updated status from your team members, the schedule's Work field will reflect exactly what you enter but might not accurately reflect when the work will be completed in the future.

Actual Costs

Capturing Actual Costs is split into two areas: costs of work resources who have rates associated with them and other costs, such as expenses. How you deal with costs might be different based on whether you chose duration-based or effort-based scheduling. The section "Tracking Costs" later in this chapter provides more information. If you do not include budget or costs in your schedule, then you don't have to worry about this field.

Which Fields Should You Use?

Now that you know what tracking fields are available, you might ask, "What should I use to track progress?" Table 11.1 lays out what you might use based on your need for varying degrees of accuracy. In all cases, this assumes you will baseline your schedule.

Table 11.1   *Tracking Method Selection*

Method of Scheduling	Setting up Schedule	Most Accurate Tracking	Less Accurate Tracking	Good, but Less Accurate
Duration-based	Use default Gantt Chart view. Use Fixed Duration task type Non-Effort-based Duration, link all tasks.	Actual Duration, Remaining Duration, and Actual Start date and Finish date.	% Complete and Actual Start and Actual Finish date.	Actual Start and Finish dates.
Effort-based	Use default Gantt Chart and add Work column to view. Use Split screen (Task Form) for entering more than one resource. Use Fixed Units, Effort-driven (default) task types. Link all tasks.	Actual Work in Resource Usage view (day-by-day) and Remaining Work.	Actual Work entered weekly (or other regular time frame) and Remaining Work plus Actual Start date.	% Complete and Actual Start and Finish date.

Although the previous section tells you the kind of data you should track, you should also consider how you report status. In the previous examples you know the date associated with the progress you entered, but the schedule just fills in the progress on the days on which it is expected the work would be performed (unless you entered day-by-day, which overrides the planned dates). For instance, when you enter 24 hours of Actual Work progress for a week for someone allocated on the task at 100%, Project will allocate the time of 8 hours each on Monday, Tuesday, and Wednesday. The next week you get progress and enter the next 24 hours, it will enter the time into the Thursday and Friday of the previous week if you do not set a status date and progress the time to indicate when the new time should really be added, so there is an additional consideration: the status date for the progress you are recording. Read the section "Using Status to Understand Your Project's Progress" later in this chapter to understand another step in tracking your schedule.

Tracking Costs

If you are tracking costs, you might want to review a few concepts from Chapter 7, "Using Project to Enter Cost Estimates." For instance, just like the Work field, the calculation for which is

$$\text{Work} = \text{Actual Work} + \text{Remaining Work}$$

costs have the same type of formula:

$$\text{Cost} = \text{Actual Cost} + \text{Remaining Cost}$$

The Cost field is calculated using several fields, and all of them can be used on the same task. To review, they are as follows:

- **Fixed Cost:** A Fixed Cost is a set amount applied to the task, not necessarily associated with resources. This field was used in versions prior to Project 2007 for indicating expenses or other kinds of costs independent of work resources on a task.

- **Cost Resource:** The Cost Resource is new in Project 2007 and allows you to enter a named cost resource when entering costs for a task (e.g., travel, lodging, courier services). In Project 2007 you might use this instead of Fixed Cost.

- **Work Resources:** When you enter rates for a resource, the hours they are scheduled to work on the task are multiplied by their standard rate and the Cost field is based on this calculation. You can also have a Per Use Cost associated with a Work Resource.

- **Material Resources:** The cost of the resource is estimated by assigning a unit of measure to the consumable resource (e.g., gas), assigning a rate to the unit, and assigning the resource to a task at the number of units the task will consume.

Project will calculate Actual Cost for the resource costs as you start tracking your project. By default, you cannot enter Actual Cost directly into the schedule. So if you add more work to a task and you have resources with rates on a task, the estimated cost will automatically be increased.

Project, by default, calculates Actual Cost based on Actual Work or Duration

Project automatically calculates Actual Cost based on a resource's rates multiplied by Actual Work on a project.

You cannot enter an amount into the Remaining Costs field

Just like the Work and Duration fields, it's important to consider if the task is done or not as to whether there are costs in the Remaining Costs field. If the task is done, and there is Remaining Work or Remaining Duration, you need to zero one of them out first because you cannot zero out the Remaining Costs field.

To track costs, you should select a view that shows Actual Costs and Remaining Costs, as well as Baseline Costs. You might need to insert the columns in another tracking view you decide to use for entering progress.

Set Up to Track Costs

Although described in Chapter 7, it's worth taking some time to revisit setup for tracking costs. If you didn't consider the setup while building your schedule, you will want to before tracking. The two tracking setups are whether Project calculates actual costs and the accrual method for resources and costs.

Project or Manual Actual Cost Calculation

By default, the Actual Costs are calculated if the Actual Costs are always calculated by Microsoft Office Project check box is selected in Tools, Options on the Calculation tab. This indicates that Project will calculate Actual Costs based on the planned costs originally calculated by Project. Figure 11.22 shows where the option is set.

Based on this setting, if you want to change the Actual Costs, you cannot do so until a task is marked as 100% complete. If you clear the check box as shown on Figure 11.22, you would have to enter Actual Costs because Project won't calculate them. Figure 11.23 illustrates leaving the default setting for Project to calculate Actual Costs for four different tasks. Each task is marked as 50% complete. You can compare the Cost field in the grid and it is the same.

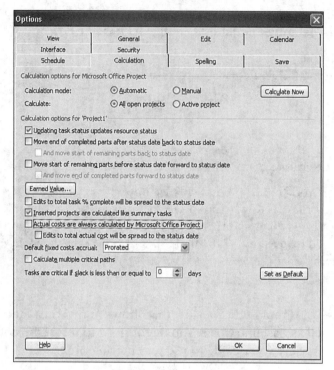

Figure 11.22 *Set Actual Cost behavior by choosing Tools, Options, Calculation*

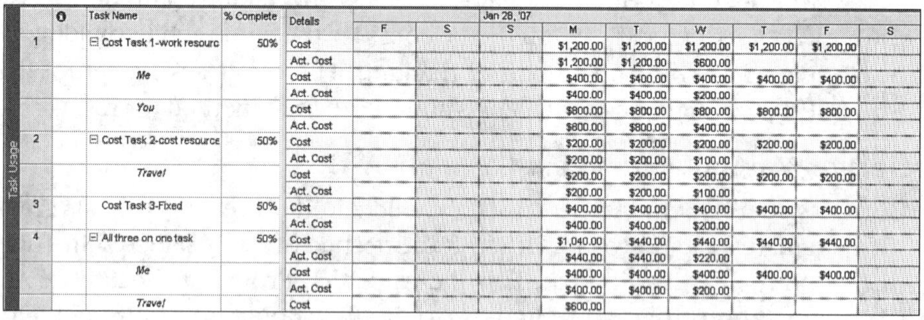

	①	Task Name	% Complete	Details	F	S	S	M	T	W	T	F	S
1		⊟ Cost Task 1-work resourc	50%	Cost				$1,200.00	$1,200.00	$1,200.00	$1,200.00	$1,200.00	
				Act. Cost				$1,200.00	$1,200.00	$600.00			
		Me		Cost				$400.00	$400.00	$400.00	$400.00	$400.00	
				Act. Cost				$400.00	$400.00	$200.00			
		You		Cost				$800.00	$800.00	$800.00	$800.00	$800.00	
				Act. Cost				$800.00	$800.00	$400.00			
2		⊟ Cost Task 2-cost resource	50%	Cost				$200.00	$200.00	$200.00	$200.00	$200.00	
				Act. Cost				$200.00	$200.00	$100.00			
		Travel		Cost				$200.00	$200.00	$200.00	$200.00	$200.00	
				Act. Cost				$200.00	$200.00	$100.00			
3		Cost Task 3-Fixed	50%	Cost				$400.00	$400.00	$400.00	$400.00	$400.00	
				Act. Cost				$400.00	$400.00	$200.00			
4		⊟ All three on one task	50%	Cost				$1,040.00	$440.00	$440.00	$440.00	$440.00	
				Act. Cost				$440.00	$440.00	$220.00			
		Me		Cost				$400.00	$400.00	$400.00	$400.00	$400.00	
				Act. Cost				$400.00	$400.00	$200.00			
		Travel		Cost				$600.00					

Figure 11.23 *Actual Costs are entered according to Cost estimates*

If you turn off the automatic Actual Cost calculation, you would get no entries in the Actual Cost fields (shown in Figure 11.23) and you would need to enter the costs yourself.

Accrual Method

The other setup item to consider is the accrual method for the resources and Fixed Costs. If you set up the accrual method, when Project calculates actual costs, it will enter them according to the accrual method of prorated, start, or end as shown in Figure 11.24 You might want some of your Actual Costs applied at the beginning or end of the task—based on when you pay the invoice—so set up the accrual method for tracking as well as for planning. Resource accrual methods are set up in the Resource Sheet, and if you select Fixed Costs you can set up the accrual method by using the field called Fixed Cost Accrual (and you can insert it in the Gantt Chart to set it).

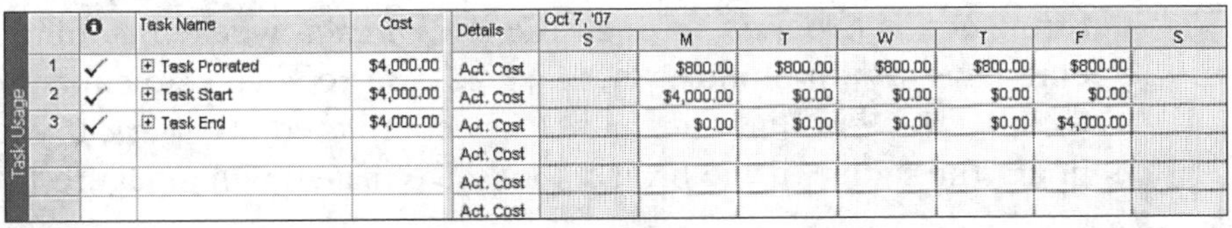

	❶	Task Name	Cost	Details	Oct 7, '07 S	M	T	W	T	F	S
1	✓	⊞ Task Prorated	$4,000.00	Act. Cost		$800.00	$800.00	$800.00	$800.00	$800.00	
2	✓	⊞ Task Start	$4,000.00	Act. Cost		$4,000.00	$0.00	$0.00	$0.00	$0.00	
3	✓	⊞ Task End	$4,000.00	Act. Cost		$0.00	$0.00	$0.00	$0.00	$4,000.00	
				Act. Cost							
				Act. Cost							
				Act. Cost							

Figure 11.24 *Accrual method records Actual Costs according to selected method*

Sometimes people want to show Actual Cost incurred at specific times in the schedule other than via an accrual method (maybe something like four equal payments). To show this, you have to complete the task first, then edit the Actual Cost, zero out where Project entered the Actual Cost, and enter the costs on the days you would like them to be recognized. For instance, Figure 11.25 shows a Fixed Cost being completed.

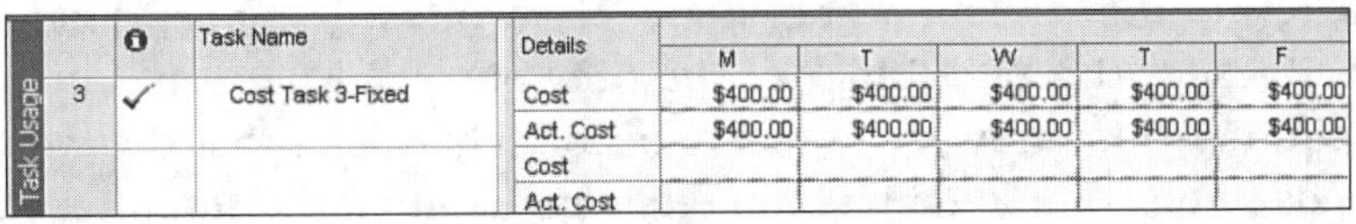

	❶	Task Name	Details	M	T	W	T	F
3	✓	Cost Task 3-Fixed	Cost	$400.00	$400.00	$400.00	$400.00	$400.00
			Act. Cost	$400.00	$400.00	$400.00	$400.00	$400.00
			Cost					
			Act. Cost					

Figure 11.25 *Actual Fixed Cost when 100% of task progress is recorded*

In this case, you paid the expense on Wednesday, and you want to indicate it in the schedule. As shown in Figure 11.26, after completion of the task, you would zero out all the other days, and enter the full Actual Cost on Wednesday.

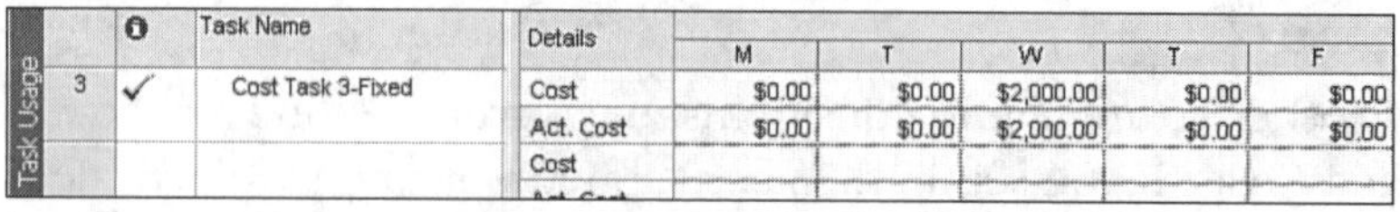

	❶	Task Name	Details		M	T	W	T	F
3	✓	Cost Task 3-Fixed	Cost		$0.00	$0.00	$2,000.00	$0.00	$0.00
			Act. Cost		$0.00	$0.00	$2,000.00	$0.00	$0.00
			Cost						

Figure 11.26   *Total Cost entered on day paid*

Using Status to Understand Your Project's Progress

Project has a capability to help you status your schedule as of any date you enter. Otherwise, status is based on the current date. To understand how the status date works, let's say you have a project that lasts 3 weeks. You are capturing actual progress through the end of each week, including the weekend. Let's say on Monday, October 22, you receive status for the week of October 14. You find out that R1 has completed 20 hours. If you enter 20 hours, the status for the project looks like that shown in Figure 11.27.

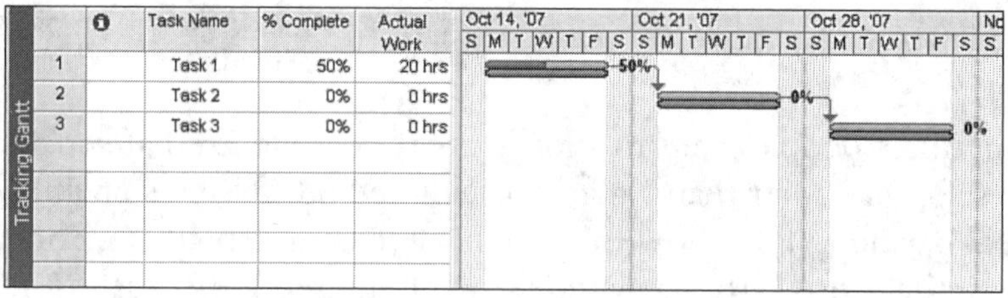

	❶	Task Name	% Complete	Actual Work
1		Task 1	50%	20 hrs
2		Task 2	0%	0 hrs
3		Task 3	0%	0 hrs

Figure 11.27   *Showing status without using the Status date*

Figure 11.27 is fine except for one thing: It is now Monday, October 22, and the rest of the 20 hours is not done. The work will not get done in the past (Wednesday through Friday of the previous week); it can only be done in the future. Somehow, you need to accurately reflect that the work that still needs to be completed will hopefully get done in the future. If you use the Status date and then progress the schedule, or perform a function that shows where the schedule work is based on the Status date, you get another view, shown in Figure 11.28.

Figure 11.28 represents an accurate view of the project: It moves out the timeline so you can see that the project is now late. So what is the status date, and how can you use it to accurately see where your schedule is as of that date? To see and enter the status date, select Project, then Project information. You will see a screen similar to Figure 11.29.

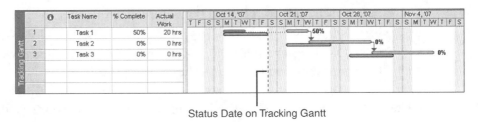

Status Date on Tracking Gantt

Figure 11.28 *Showing status using the Status date and progressing the schedule*

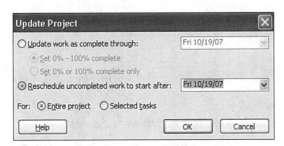

Status date field

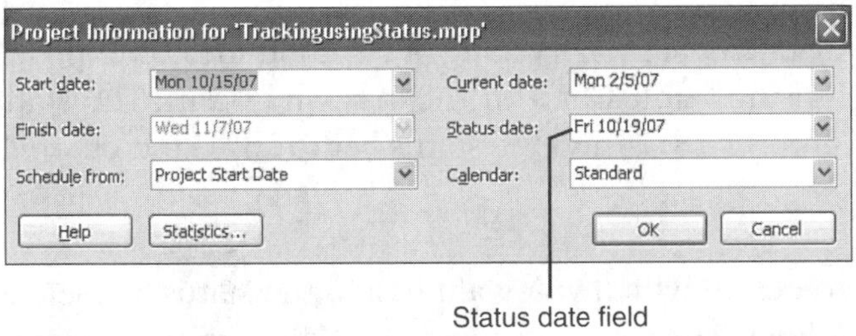

Figure 11.29 *Status date showing in the Project Information dialog box*

Then, when you are ready to progress your schedule, the Status date is set and you will do the following:

1. Select Tools, Tracking.
2. Select Update project. You will see a dialog box similar to that shown in Figure 11.30.

Figure 11.30 *Update Project dialog box for progressing the schedule*

3. Click the Reschedule uncompleted work to start after option. The Status date will no longer be unavailable. You are telling Project to move

out the schedule to reflect any incomplete work after the Status date. If you do not enter a Status date, Project uses the current date.

4. Click OK. The schedule will progress to show uncompleted work past the Status date you entered as shown in Figure 11.29.

This is the recommended method for accurately tracking your schedule. You could track your schedule using other methods, but this one will tell you the most about where you are and where you need to be.

Setting the Bar for Status Date

If you use the Status date for tracking, it's a good idea to expose the Status date gridline on the Gantt Chart or the Tracking Gantt. The status bar was exposed in Figure 11.28. To add the status bar to any Gantt chart view, do the following:

1. On the screen to which you want to add the status bar, select Format, then Gridlines. The Gridlines dialog box displays, as shown in Figure 11.31.

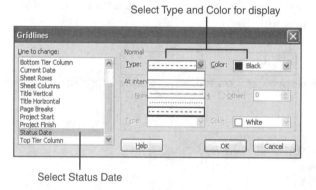

Figure 11.31 *Setting the status date bar to show on the Gantt Chart*

2. In the Line to change field, scroll down to Status date.

3. Select the type of line you want from the four possible lines from the drop-down list in the Type field.

4. Select the color of the line from the numerous available colors in the Color drop-down list. You will probably want to use a bold color, such as red, for the Status date gridline.

5. Click OK. The Status field will display for that view on that project from now on. You will have to set this up for other projects, unless you decide to create a custom status view for your project. Custom views for reporting are described later in this chapter.

> **Use Reschedule uncompleted work when capturing Actual Work or Duration and Remaining Work and Duration**
>
> Using the method just described is excellent for Effort-based scheduling. By asking how much you have done and how much is left, plus setting the Status date and rescheduling uncompleted work, you will get the most accurate view of your current schedule status. This works well for duration-based scheduling if you are capturing Actual Duration and Remaining Duration as well.

Methods for Entering Status

Now that you understand the actual data you can capture and status, in this section I describe various methods for entering actual progress. First, I want to introduce out-of-the-box methods to easily track your schedule. Then you can consider creating a customized data entry method.

Out-of-the-Box Methods

Out-of-the-box update methods are using the Task Update tool, using the Tracking Table, and using Tracking Gantt View.

Using the Task Update Tool

There is a nice tool on the Tools menu that allows you to easily update task information. It provides you quick access to the tracking fields if you are doing duration-based scheduling: the % Complete, Actual Duration, Remaining Duration, and Actual Start date, and Finish date fields. To use this tool, follow these steps:

1. Select Tools, Tracking. The dialog box shown in Figure 11.32 opens.

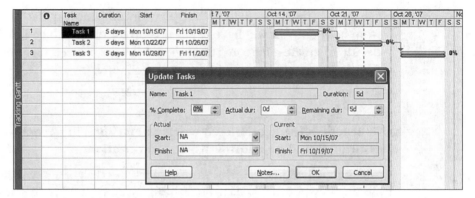

Figure 11.32 *Task Update tool for entering actual task progress data*

2. Enter the data you want to track according to the various methods listed later. Remember that Actual Start and Finish dates will override anything you enter in % Complete, Actual Duration, or Remaining Duration fields. If you enter an Actual Duration value of 5 days, with no Remaining Duration, but enter an Actual Start date of 10/16 and an Actual End date of 10/19, Project calculates the duration at 4 days, not 5. Project will change the Actual Duration to reflect it.

3. Press OK and the schedule will be updated.

The Task Update tool would be used primarily for duration-based scheduling because it lacks work information.

Using the Tracking Table and Tracking Gantt View

You can also use a handy tracking table with most of the fields I've discussed, and in combination with the Tracking Gantt view, it provides a terrific way to enter status. To create this tracking view, follow these steps:

1. Select View, Tracking Gantt.

2. In the Tracking view, select View, Table: Tracking. You will see a screen similar to Figure 11.33.

	Task Name	Act. Start	Act. Finish	% Comp.	Phys. % Comp.	Act. Dur.	Rem. Dur.	Act. Cost	Act. Work	
1	Task 1	NA	NA	0%	0%	0 days	5 days	$0.00	0 hrs	
2	Task 2	NA	NA	0%	0%	0 days	5 days	$0.00	0 hrs	
3	Task 3	NA	NA	0%	0%	0 days	5 days	$0.00	0 hrs	

Figure 11.33 *Tracking Gantt plus Tracking table*

3. Enter the data you have received to update the schedule. Because you have so many fields on the view from which to choose, establish your tracking method (effort-based or duration-based) to enter the data you need.

Notice that Remaining Work is not available

Also note that Remaining Work is not available in this tracking table. If you are performing effort-based tracking, you should either add the field or create a custom tracking table for yourself.

---

4. When you are done entering data, return to the kind of view you would like to use for reviewing your project schedule. To return to any view or table, select View, and then select the view in the drop-down list or select View, Table, and then select the kind of table information you want to review.

The Tracking Gantt and Tracking table suffice for many organizations as long as the people who are entering the actual task progress data understand how the fields are calculated.

Updating as Scheduled

You can easily update the project as scheduled using another out-of-the-box method best used for duration-based tracking. Figure 11.30 shows the Update Project dialog box where you can access this update method. To illustrate, a project has been set up for 3 weeks (shown in Figure 11.34). The project status date is 10/24. The Update as scheduled method will calculate the % Complete based on progress of the tasks as scheduled with the start and end dates.

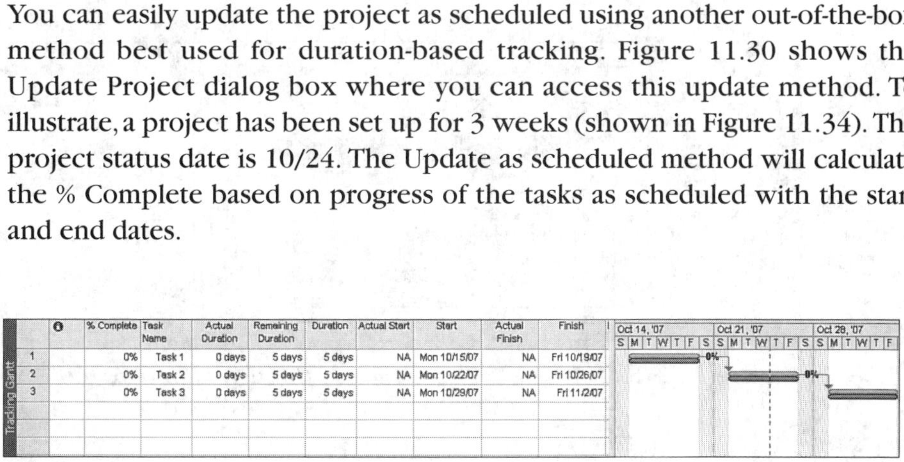

	0	% Complete	Task Name	Actual Duration	Remaining Duration	Duration	Actual Start	Start	Actual Finish	Finish
1		0%	Task 1	0 days	5 days	5 days	NA	Mon 10/15/07	NA	Fri 10/19/07
2		0%	Task 2	0 days	5 days	5 days	NA	Mon 10/22/07	NA	Fri 10/26/07
3		0%	Task 3	0 days	5 days	5 days	NA	Mon 10/29/07	NA	Fri 11/2/07

Figure 11.34 *Data entered for updating of project using Completion through tracking*

If you use the Status date of 10/24, the first submethod (Set 0%–100%) will assume the original Finish date and that Duration for the tasks is fulfilled, and Project updates the schedule according to Figure 11.35. Notice that Project set the completion for the first task at 100% because it should be done by 10/19 and it changed the % Complete value for Task 2 to 40%. As you can tell, this method assumes that the scheduled dates are the real dates for updating, but it gives credit for the work being done through the date shown.

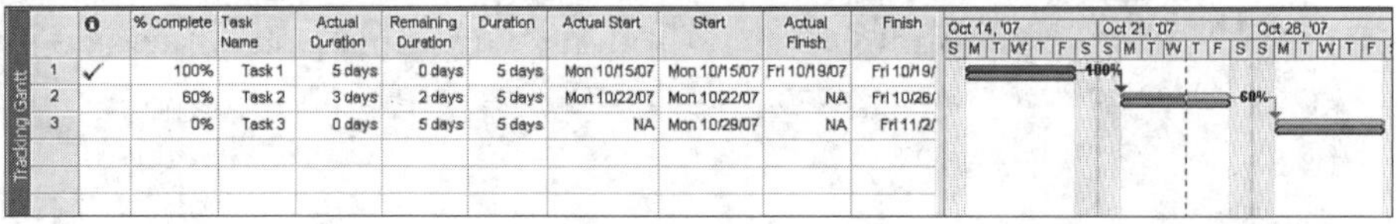

Figure 11.35 *Update Project set with completion through 10/24*

The second method (Set 0% or 100% complete only) works off a method of scheduling that some organizations use to indicate progress of all or none. Using the same project shown in Figure 11.34, the tracking method is Set 0% or 100% complete. This method means that either you have met the schedule finish date or not, so your tasks are either 100% complete based on the Status date (or Current date) or not at all complete. The project result using this tracking method is shown in Figure 11.36. This method gives you no credit for the second task.

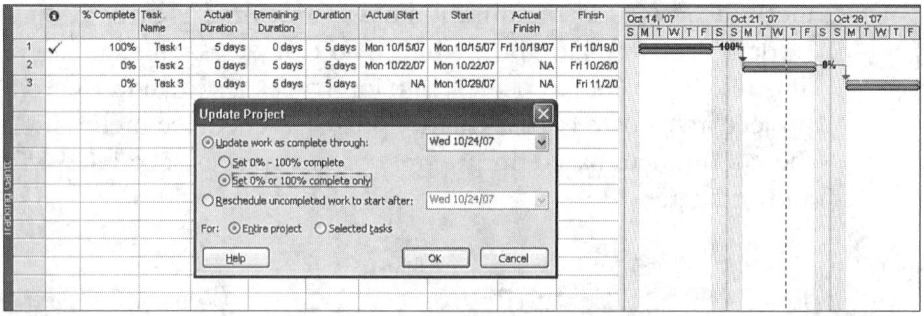

Figure 11.36 *The setup for completion through with 0 or 100% complete*

Using a Custom View or Report

The easiest way to enter tracking information might be building a custom view because you have unique needs or because you have only a few fields you want to ensure are updated. This is especially true for effort-based tracking, because no single view seems to have all the entry fields needed to track hours of effort. To understand how to build a custom view, see the section "Custom Reports" later in this chapter.

Duration-Based or Effort-Based Tracking

Now that you understand the project tracking data you can capture and where you can enter it, this section describes how you can enter the status data for duration- or effort-based tracking. Note that you might want to adapt the tracking methods described for your organization.

Duration-Based Status Tracking

For duration-based tracking use one of the methods described earlier for updating Project.

Done or Not Done

You might have set up a very simple duration-based schedule to track your activities, and all you want to track is if your tasks are done or not. If you have, here are the steps for tracking the schedule:

1. Set up the schedule as duration-based. You should either have one person per task, or you should set up the Task type as Fixed Duration, Non-effort driven. Use all the other methods for building the schedule properly. Don't forget to baseline your schedule.
2. When you are ready to track, select View, Tracking Gantt.

Use Actual Start and Finish Dates

To enter Start and Finish dates, follow these steps:

1. Obtain status data for each task you want to update. For each task to update, select the task, and then select Tools, Tracking, Update Tasks. A dialog box like the one shown previously in Figure 11.32 opens.

2. Based on the current date, if the task has started, enter the Start date in the Actual section of the dialog box. If the task is complete, enter the Finish date in the Actual area. If you enter the Actual Finish date, you do not need to enter the Start date unless it is different than the scheduled date showing in the Current area of the screen.

   If you would rather just indicate that the task is done, you can also enter 100 in the % Complete field, and Project will assume that the dates in the scheduled Start and Finish fields are correct and enter those dates into the Actual Start and Actual Finish dates once you apply the update.

3. Click OK when you have entered the information. When you use this method, always use the current date as your update method: You do not need to use a Status date if you do not want to, and you can just enter this information according to the date to which you are currently updating the project.

Use 0 or 100% Complete Based on Status Date

To use % Complete based on Status date, follow these steps:

1. Select Tools, Tracking, Update Project.

2. Leave the default option of Update work as complete through selected, and click Set 0% or 100% complete only.

3. Click OK. Project will assume the scheduled Start and Finish dates are accurate based on either the current date or the date you enter in the date field showing and will update each task on the schedule as either done or not.

Both of these methods are excellent for showing whether a task is complete or not with very little effort on your part. Many projects only require this level of tracking.

Using % Complete

If you would like to use % Complete based on a Status date or the Current date, you have a couple of options:

1. Select the task or tasks you would like to update.

2. Select Tools, Tracking, Update Project.

3. Leave the default settings (Update work as completely through and Set 0%–100% complete), but enter either the Current date or the Status date you would like to enter in the open date box.

4. Click OK. The schedule will assume the Start and Finish dates of the schedule are correct and update the progress of the tasks accordingly.

This is a second method:

1. For each task you need to update, select the task, and then select Tools, Tracking, Update tasks. A dialog box like the one shown previously in Figure 11.32 opens.

2. For each task, based on the status information you get from each team member, enter the Start date in the Actual section of the dialog box, then enter the % Complete value. If your team is done with the task, you can just enter 100% complete and the Actual Finish date (if different than the scheduled or Current Finish date).

3. Click OK. You could end here, but you might not have completed the update. If you received this status through a certain date (e.g., at the end of the week), you should progress your schedule.

4. Select Tools, Tracking, Update Project.

5. Select the Reschedule uncompleted work to start after option and enter the Status date through which the current information runs.

6. Click OK.

Be aware that with this method you are not getting all the information from the team: How much is left to do? This method works for many situations, but if you are looking for greater accuracy, you should consider the next method.

Actual Duration and Remaining Duration

The best method for getting duration-based status information is to obtain the Actual Start date, the Actual Duration, and Remaining Duration. Then you let Project calculate the % Complete value and your status on the project. To do this, follow these steps:

1. For each task you need to update, select the task, and then select Tools, Tracking, Update tasks. A dialog box like the one shown previously in Figure 11.32 opens.

2. For each task, based on the information you get from the team members about status, enter the Start date in the Actual section of the dialog box, and then enter Actual Duration and Remaining Duration. If your team is done with the task, you can just enter 100% complete and the Actual Finish date (if different than the scheduled or Current finish date).

3. Click OK. If you received this status through a certain date (e.g., at the end of the week), then you should progress your schedule.

4. Select Tools, Tracking, Update Project.

5. Select the Reschedule uncompleted work to start after option and enter the status date through which the current information runs.

6. Click OK.

You could also just enter the Status date and show the status gridline as described in the section "Using Status to Understand Your Project's Progress" earlier in this chapter.

Effort-Based Status Tracking

Effort-based status tracking is the most precise method of tracking because it treats capacity more discretely than duration. It is even more precise if you use day-by-day tracking. If you do decide to use day-by-day tracking, you really need to consider the effort it takes to capture the data versus the value to your organization. In fact, if your organization is interested in obtaining day-by-day effort on projects, you should really consider using Microsoft Office Project Server 2007. It has a method for project managers to obtain day-by-day data without having to enter it directly themselves. Behind the scenes, it is automating what I discuss next. To use effort-based status tracking, follow these steps:

1. Set up the schedule as effort-based. Use Fixed Units, Effort-driven, or Fixed Work. You need to also indicate the number of units the resource can work on the task. Use all the other methods for building the schedule properly including setting task dependencies through linking. Don't forget to baseline your schedule.

2. When you are ready to track, select View, Tracking Gantt. Then obtain status for each of your relevant tasks.

Actual Work Status Tracking (per Period)

The first method for tracking actual work status is to do it for a particular project per period. For instance, perhaps you obtain the actual work completed each week. Your team members will report on how many total hours they completed in the week and how many they have remaining. This method, once again, should also ask when the task was started to get a more accurate idea of the project's progress. To enter actual work for a particular time period, follow these steps:

1. Obtain the following data from each team member for the tasks in your schedule: Actual Work for the period and Remaining Work. Also, find out the date the task was started.

2. In the Tracking Gantt view, select View, Table, Tracking.

3. In this view, select Window and then click Split.

4. In the lower section of the screen, right-click in the gray area, and select Resource work as shown in Figure 11.37. This will provide you an area in which to easily enter the data. It also allows you to enter data if you have more than one resource on the task.

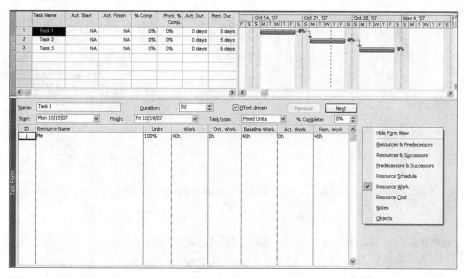

Figure 11.37 *Screen for entering Actual Work per period*

5. Enter the task start date in the Actual Start field (unless it is the same as the scheduled start date for the task), and then enter Actual Work and Remaining Work in the lower window of the screen.

6. Select Tools, Tracking, Update Project.

7. Select the Reschedule uncompleted work to start after option and enter the status date through which the current information runs.

8. Click OK.

Each week, you will need to capture the additional amount of time worked and increment the Actual Work field by that amount only. For instance, if Actual Work was 20 hours last week, and your resource reported he or she completed an additional 25 hours the following week, you would have to enter 45 hours in the Actual Work field and make sure the Remaining Work is accurate.

An alternative method for entering Actual Work is to set up a customized Resource Usage view, with Actual Work set up in the grid to the right and Remaining Work and Actual Start date in the area to the left as shown in Figure 11.38.

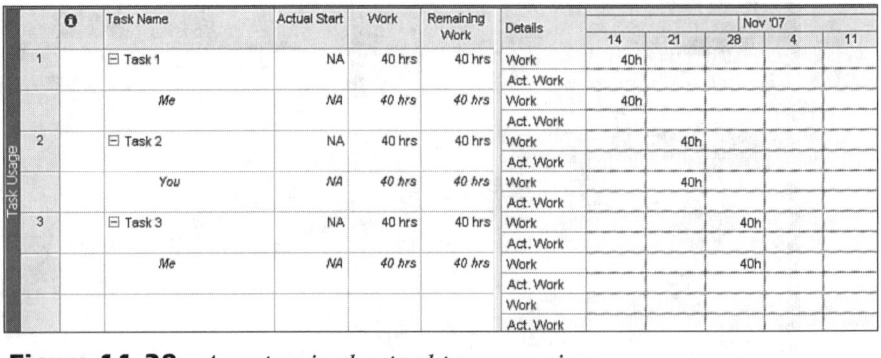

	❶	Task Name	Actual Start	Work	Remaining Work	Details		Nov '07			
							14	21	28	4	11
1		⊟ Task 1	NA	40 hrs	40 hrs	Work	40h				
						Act. Work					
		Me	NA	40 hrs	40 hrs	Work	40h				
						Act. Work					
2		⊟ Task 2	NA	40 hrs	40 hrs	Work		40h			
						Act. Work					
		You	NA	40 hrs	40 hrs	Work		40h			
						Act. Work					
3		⊟ Task 3	NA	40 hrs	40 hrs	Work			40h		
						Act. Work					
		Me	NA	40 hrs	40 hrs	Work			40h		
						Act. Work					
						Work					
						Act. Work					

Figure 11.38   *A customized actual progress view*

Actual Work Tracking Day-by-Day (Timephased)

The most precise method for tracking is day-by-day. This method of tracking gives you the start date and the hours each day, so you get a day-by-day progress of the work that people provide you. If you use this method, you will need to use the Resource Usage or Task Usage view to enter tracking data. The best way to get status is to have someone fill out a timesheet (perhaps an Excel spreadsheet), or send you the hours he or she worked on the task each day. If you can print out the Resource Usage view for each resource, that might be one of the best ways to capture data. It's extremely useful to get the data for a set period, for instance, each week. It is easier for team members to remember the time they worked for shorter periods (like a week), rather than a month if you are capturing day-by-day data.

1. Select View, then Resource Usage view. On the view, insert the Remaining Work column on the left side of the separator bar.

2. On the right side of the separator bar, in the gridline area, right-click. In the drop-down list, select Actual Work.

3. Enter time in the white area where you can enter time on the task or tasks for each resource as shown in Figure 11.39.

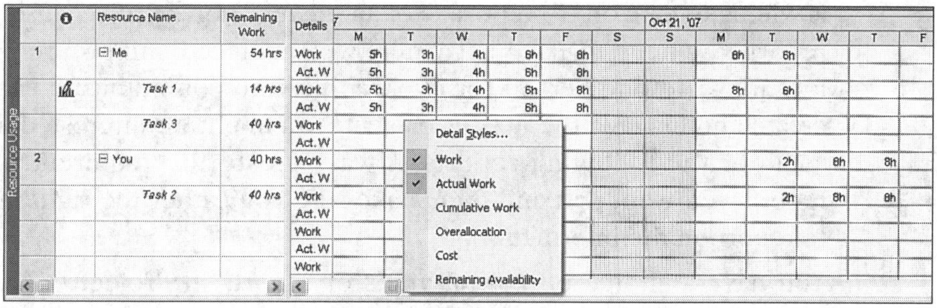

Figure 11.39   *The Resource Usage view for entering actual values*

4. As you can see, based on the time entered, Project has moved the work that didn't get done into the next week. It has automatically changed the project.

5. Select View, and then click Tracking view to see the change.

Because this can be time intensive, and if your organization is interested in using it, you could consider a method of obtaining the data in Excel, XML, or Access and import it to the Project schedule. You would need to put some development hours in doing so, but it would save a project manager or coordinator's time.

Reporting

Many people want to report to their executives using Project. However, Project was not designed for executive reporting: It's a detailed schedule and costs management tool. With Project 2007, you have a better capability for reporting with the new Visual Reports feature, but to report to executives, you sometimes need to consider another method for reporting. The schedule is a great foundation; if you use it properly, it really shows you where your issues are, and lets you make decisions about where you might need to compromise to get the work done. But it's not really for an executive to review in a detailed manner. I therefore introduce to you a couple of thoughts about how you would use Project to report to executives at the proper level. Also, if you are using Project within your organization and want to report on all of your projects, you can create a master project to show all your projects. But the effort to do so might be more than your organization is willing to take on. To report all of an organization's projects using a master report, you need to have extremely well-managed and secure project file locations and one person (or two people who communicate very well) to create and manage the master project. You might be interested in creating some of the following reports. Always create the requirements for the reports you want first and then make sure you gather the right information to report on the information.

You have a choice of several kinds of reports in Project (among others beyond the scope of this book):

- Progress reports
- Milestone reports
- Roll-Up reports
- Visual reports
- Standard Project reports
- Using filtering and grouping for reporting
- Custom reports

The following section introduces each report and how you might build it. Figure 11.40 presents a fairly detailed project with summary tasks, milestones, costs, and updated progress to illustrate the various reports.

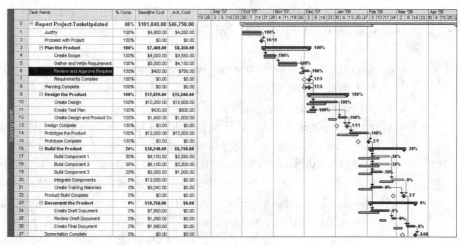

Figure 11.40   *Original project with details*

Progress Report

You might want to create a report to show progress made toward milestones. However, let's say you need to set up a report showing the high-level milestones and where you are currently as shown in Figure 11.41.

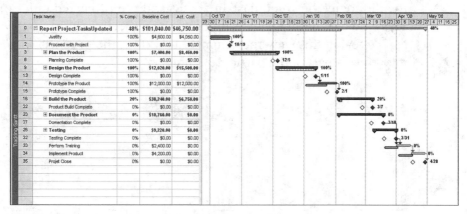

Figure 11.41   *High-level project report with milestones*

There are several things you would do to create this report and you can extrapolate the differences you might want to make for your own reports by adding columns besides % Complete or Cost columns. First, you would track the project regularly and you might do the following:

1. Change to the view to the Tracking Gantt. This way you will see baseline and actual progress.

2. Show only the Outline Level 1. Select Project from the menu bar, then click Outline. Click Show and select Outline Level 1. This assumes you have used summary tasks and perhaps a few other tasks on the same level as well as milestones to end each project. If you have any tasks that are not part of summary tasks, they will also show on the report.

3. Display important fields about the task such as % Complete or Actual Costs. To do this, you need to add the columns to the view by selecting Insert from the menu bar, then click Column to select the fields you want in the report.

The best way to be able to show this report again and again, without having to recreate it is to create a custom table and view. See the section "Custom Reports" later in this chapter for more information about how to do it.

Milestone Report

You could also create a milestone report to show expected milestones and the difference between baseline dates and the projected milestone dates. This would show all the milestones on the project, as shown in Figure 11.42. Notice that in this view, the summary task (Plan the product) shows when a milestone is part of the particular summary.

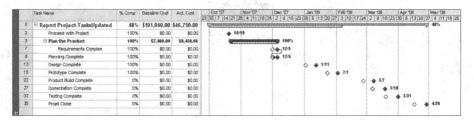

Figure 11.42 *Milestone report*

This report is created by selecting Tracking Gantt and using the Milestone filter. To select the Tracking Gantt, select View from the menu bar and select

Tracking Gantt. Then select Project, Filtered for, Milestones as shown in Figure 11.43. Note some of the other filters available. You can also build your own.

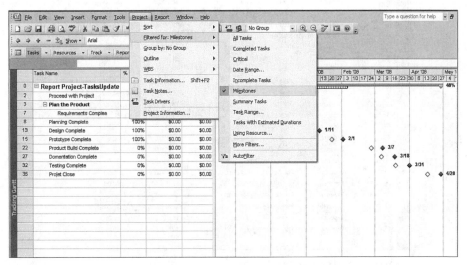

Figure 11.43 *Selecting filters*

You will need to build your schedule liberally with milestones to have an effective report.

Roll-Up Reports

You might like to show particular grouping of information rolled up. For instance, perhaps you need to understand all the tasks that are expenses and all that are capital for your project. If you create a custom field, and label each field according to its cost type, you can create a report you can send to the finance department as shown in Figure 11.44.

To create a roll-up report, see the section "Custom Reports" later in this chapter for specific instructions.

	ⓘ	Cost Type	Name	Baseline Cost	Actual Cost
			⊞ No Value	**$0.00**	**$0.00**
			⊟ **Capital**	**$49,060.00**	**$9,870.00**
17		Capital	Build Component 1	$8,100.00	$2,550.00
18		Capital	Build Component 2	$8,100.00	$3,200.00
19		Capital	Build Component 3	$5,000.00	$1,000.00
20		Capital	Integrate Components	$12,000.00	$0.00
24		Capital	Create Draft Document	$7,800.00	$3,120.00
25		Capital	Review Draft Document	$1,280.00	$0.00
26		Capital	Create Final Document	$1,680.00	$0.00
30		Capital	Perform fixes	$900.00	$0.00
34		Capital	Implement Product	$4,200.00	$0.00
			⊟ **Expense**	**$51,980.00**	**$40,000.00**
1	✓	Expense	Justify	$4,800.00	$4,050.00
4	✓	Expense	Create Scope	$4,000.00	$3,550.00
5	✓	Expense	Gather and Write Requirements	$3,000.00	$4,150.00
6	✓	Expense	Review and Approve Requiremen	$400.00	$750.00
10	✓	Expense	Create Design	$10,200.00	$13,600.00
11	✓	Expense	Create Test Plan	$420.00	$300.00
12	✓	Expense	Create Design and Product Docurr	$1,400.00	$1,600.00
14	✓	Expense	Prototype the Product	$12,000.00	$12,000.00
21	⊞	Expense	Create Training Materials	$5,040.00	$0.00
29		Expense	Perform Testing	$6,400.00	$0.00
31		Expense	Re-test	$1,920.00	$0.00
33		Expense	Perform Training	$2,400.00	$0.00

Figure 11.44   *Reporting by group*

Visual Reports

One of the best new features in Project 2007 is the Visual Reports. Because they are graphical, they might help you report to executives or management, and they might be useful for your own schedule analysis. Visual Reports uses the capability of Microsoft Office Excel's PivotTables (Excel 2003 or Excel 2007). If you also have Visio Professional 2007, you can create PivotDiagrams. In this book, I focus on Excel PivotTables. They allow you to look at data in charts as well as the tables of Excel. It is essentially taking table data and putting it in any kind of chart you prefer—such as pie charts, bars, or bubble graphs. While you are looking at the charts or tables, you can add fields to take a look at additional fields in the report.

You can learn more about using the PivotTable by using Excel help. To understand the available reports in Project, click Reports from the Project menu bar and click Visual Reports. You can save the data in an OLAP cube, which saves it separately in a file that you can use again and again. It is static data, so you would need to create the cube again to get the most current data. Figure 11.45 shows a nice visual report so you can quickly see the variance between what you estimated for Cost versus the Actual Cost for each task. Because the project was designed with summary tasks to represent the phases of the project, this report is filtered to just show the summary task and milestones. It does not show each and every task, so this might be very interesting for management to see trends or areas in projects where costs generally tend to go over budget or perhaps remain under budget.

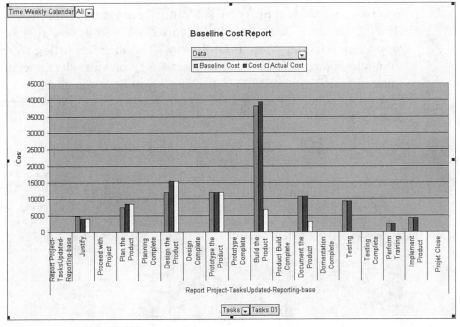

Figure 11.45   *Using a Visual Report*

You have several out-of-the-box reports available for Excel:

- Baseline Cost Report
- Baseline Work Report
- Budget Cost Report
- Budget Work Report
- Cash Flow Report
- Earned Value Over Time Report
- Resource Cost Summary Report
- Resource Remaining Work Report

- Resource Work Availability Report
- Resource Work Summary Report

When the reports display you can filter according to the fields available.

Standard Project Reports

You can also print reports by selecting Reports from the menu bar, then clicking Reports. In Project 2002 and 2003, you access this same set of reports by selecting View, then Reports. The main reporting categories are shown in Figure 11.46. From the categories, you can select specific reports, some of which are available in the views you have—such as Task Usage and Resource Usage views; they are simply translated to a printed reported as best they can be.

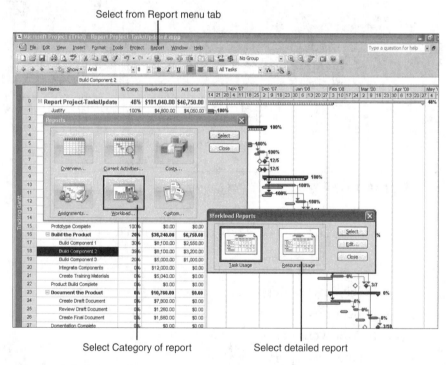

Figure 11.46   *Categories for selecting various reports*

Some project managers find these reports useful to review upcoming tasks and issues with resources rather than looking at the information in the schedule itself. Other project managers would rather just use Project views and tables interactively to get similar information. Take a look at these reports to see if any of them, either out of the box or with some customization, would be useful for you. To select a particular report, follow these steps:

1. Select Report (or View in Project 2002 or 2003), and then click Reports in the drop-down list. The Reports dialog box displays, as shown in Figure 11.46.

2. Select one of the categories showing. The particular category's report dialog box displays.

3. You can then click Select or Edit to set up for printing the report. Select allows you to show the report as is, and Edit allows you to customize it for printing.

4. If you elect to edit the report, you will see a dialog box and you can elect to change the format and filtering of the content of the data under the Definition, Details, and Sort tabs. Some of the items you can change are the name of the report, the kind of data (the kinds of fields to be displayed such as work, actual, etc.), the timescale (e.g., by day, weeks, months, etc.), filters (an example filter is work that is incomplete), and text format.

The report does not display well from the screen because it is formatted for printing.

Using Filtering and Grouping for Reporting

You can use filtering and grouping to report (as well as to analyze and track a schedule) in Project. These features are extremely powerful, enabling you to create a focused view of your project. Chapter 8, "Polishing Your Schedule," described how to use filtering and grouping for analyzing issues with your project and you might want to refer to it again to understand filters and groups. In this chapter I focus on using filters and groups for reporting and customizing your filters and groups.

Filtering

Filtering allows you to focus or report on whatever it is you want to analyze and filter out everything else. You can select one item to filter or if you select the AutoFilter capability, you can filter on several values within a particular field. For instance, you could filter for all tasks that are a milestone, as shown in Figure 11.42, or for a particular resource (to see only the tasks that particular resource is on). With AutoFiltering, however, you could select a field and filter for several values within the field. To filter so that you can focus on one item in your project, do the following:

1. Select Project, and then click Filtered for.
2. Choose to filter from the list showing, or select More Filters to see a longer list of possible filters already created for you.
3. In many cases, selecting the filter will filter out all other items and display the project with whatever you selected. However, if you elect to filter by a range you will be prompted by another dialog box asking you to provide the dates for the range of tasks you want to display.
4. To return to displaying all tasks, select Project, click Filtered for, and select All Tasks.

Many of these filters are available when you create a report (using either the standard Reports or Visual Reports), depending on the kind of report you are creating.

However, you can create custom filters, which might be useful for special reports, especially if you have created custom fields. In the example for Figure 11.47, a custom field called Cost Type was created. You could create a custom field for just showing the cost type of Expense, and be able to easily see and roll-up information on all tasks that will go to the finance department only for expenses.

To create a custom filter, do the following:

1. Select Project, click Filtered for:, and select More Filters from the dropdown list.
2. You will see the More Filters dialog box, as shown in Figure 11.47. Click the New button. Note that you could also highlight one of the filters in the list and click Copy to use one of the existing filters as an example.
3. Enter the new name of the filter in the Name field on top.
4. If this is a report you will use frequently, select the Show in menu check box.
5. Select the fields you would like to include in the filter report. Notice that you can add several fields and create and/or Boolean logic for the kinds of task, resource, or assignment data you want to see in your reports.

6. Select the test from the drop-down list, such as equals, does not equal, and so on, and then select the value on which you want the test performed.

7. When you are done, click OK. If you want to see the change immediately, click Apply. Otherwise, you can select the filter later.

It's a good idea to test the filter before finalizing it. If it's not exactly what you want, you can select Project, click Filtered for, and select More Filters. Then highlight your new filter and edit it.

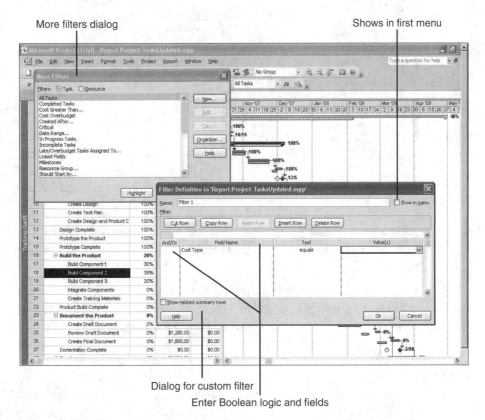

Figure 11.47   *Dialog boxes for creating custom filtering*

The new filter will appear in the drop-down list of the available default filters if you selected the Show in menu check box (as shown in Figure 11.48), or will be in the More Filters dialog box if you do not show it in the menu. You can also add the new filter for any custom tables or views you might create.

Custom filter

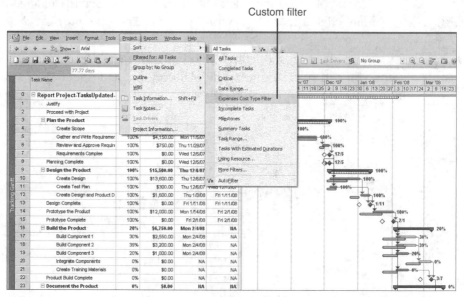

Figure 11.48 *Custom filter Expenses Filter showing in the drop-down list*

Although it might seem a bit of work, it's really worth your time to create custom filters for any frequent analysis or reporting you do on particular fields.

Consider using a combination of filtering and grouping to create special reports. For instance, perhaps you want to show all milestones by using filtering grouped by phase (if you created a custom field that you applied to each task).

Grouping

Grouping provides a reporting feature to see all items in your project categorized for comparison or overall views of the data. Grouping is also described in Chapter 8, but in this section I focus on customizing grouping for reporting. For instance, you can easily compare Expense task costs to Capital task costs using grouping, which you could not do with filtering. Grouping is based entirely on a flag or value; for instance, a task might be a Milestone or it's not (a flag). So when you elect to use grouping, it will show all the tasks that are not milestones in one group, called No value, and another group called Milestones. Or if you group tasks by Constraint type, it will show all the tasks within each of one of the eight constraint types (e.g., As Soon As Possible, or Must Finish On) if applicable. To group tasks, resources, or assignments in your project, do the following:

1. Select Project, and then click Group by.

2. Choose the grouping from the list showing, or select More Groups to see a longer list of possible groups. When you select the group, it will be immediately applied to your project.

3. To return to displaying the tasks without grouping, select Project, click Group by, and select No Group.

However, you can create custom groups, which might be useful for management reports, especially if you have created custom fields. For the example in Figure 11.49, the custom field called Cost Type was created with the values of Expense and Capital. Also, each resource was assigned to a resource group (either Mgmt or Team) so in the example you will see groups of No Value, Expenses, and Capital—and within each of the expense or capital groups, the resources group by Management and Team.

To create a custom group, do the following:

1. Select Project, click Group by, and select More groups from the drop-down list.

2. You will see the More Groups dialog box as shown in Figure 11.49. Click New. Note that you could also highlight one of the groups in the list and click Copy to use one of the existing groups as an example.

3. Enter the new name of the group in the Name field on top.

4. If this is a report you will use frequently, select the Show in menu check box.

5. Select the fields you would like to include in the grouping. Notice that you can add several fields for the kinds of task, resource, or assignment data you want to see in your reports.

6. You have some other selections on the screen, including selecting some formatting styles, such as the color of the grouping bars. By default, the main group will show as yellow and groups within that group will be shown in gray.

7. When you are done, click OK. If you want the new group to be applied, click Apply. Otherwise, you can select it later.

It's a good idea to test the grouping before finalizing it. If it's not exactly what you want, you can select Project, click Group by, select More Groups, highlight your new group, and edit it.

Select a new group or edit an existing one

Shows in menu

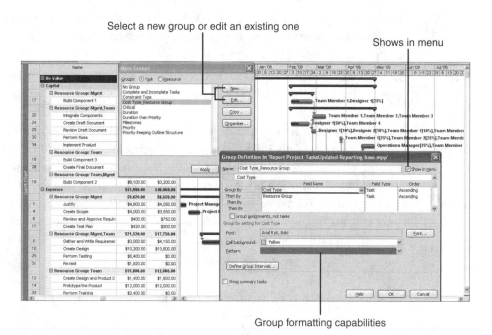

Group formatting capabilities

Figure 11.49 *Dialog boxes for creating custom grouping*

The new grouping will appear in the drop-down list of the available default groups if you selected the Show in menu check box or will be in the More Groups dialog box if you do not show it in the menu. You can also add the new groups for any custom tables or views you might create.

Although it might seem a bit of work, it's really worth your time to create custom groups for any frequent analysis or reporting you do on particular fields.

Do not edit existing filters or groups: Copy them, then edit

Generally, it is a good idea to leave Project's default groups or filters in place so that you have them as a template. Rather than selecting a current filter or group and using Edit to customize the group and filter for your use, it's better to copy it, create a new one, and then edit the new filter or group for your needs.

Custom Reports

To report effectively in Project, you might want to learn how to create custom reports—your own views—for you and your management team. You could build these custom views to show just the fields you want your project managers to use for entering actual progress or for reviewing costs. The following example will show how you create a custom report for management to understand progress based on the view you saw in Figure 11.42. You could create the view on the fly by adding columns and changing the timescale, but you would have to do this each time you wanted to create the report. Not only is this time consuming, but you might forget some of the actions you took to build the view. If you make a custom view, all you have to do is apply the view after you change the data each reporting period. You are building the interface screens to the project data you want.

To build a custom report, first define your requirements. In Figure 11.41, the requirements were to show original estimates of milestone dates and costs according to the status date. This report is called the Milestone-Cost Progress Report. You need to build the individual elements you want for it—the custom table, view, filter, and groups—as necessary. For instance, in this case, you would create a special table called the Milestone-Cost Progress Table. Then you would create the Milestone-Cost Progress Report via a custom view where you would set the timescale, status date gridline, and Gantt Chart layout for the right side of the report. If you needed to have special filters or groups, you could build those, and then apply them to the report. However, in this case, you will just need to apply the Milestone filter to the view for the report. To build a custom view, follow the steps outlined in the next section. The steps use the sample report as an example during these instructions.

Building a Custom Table

To build a custom view, first build a custom table:

1. Select View, click Table, and then select More Tables.

2. In the More Tables dialog box, click New if you want to start the table from scratch, or click Copy if you would like to start with an existing table as a model. The Table Definition dialog box displays similar to what is shown in Figure 11.50.

3. In the Name field, enter the new custom table name.

4. If you chose to copy a table, insert or remove fields as necessary. If you selected a new table, go to the Field name area and select each column you want to include in the table by clicking the drop-down list for each field. Note that you can change the formatting on each column if you want.

> **Copy table helps with formatting**
>
> You might want to choose to Copy a table, usually the Entry table for task views, or the Resource Entry for resource tables. If you do not, you will need to remember to add the fields such as ID, Indicator, or Name for the task table, and then format each column to a reasonable width, justification, and so on. It's usually easier to just start with a table that already has some of your fields and formatting requirements satisfied.

5. Choose whether you want to show the table in the menu by clicking Show in menu. If you think you might use this table for other views, you might do that, but because this table is being used for a view, you might choose not to show it in the menu.

6. Select any formatting as shown on the screen that you'd like to include.

7. When done, click OK. If you want to apply the new table to the current view, click Apply. Review it to make sure if the table is what you want. You might forget a column or want to adjust the column width for one of the fields. Select Edit in the More Tables dialog box to make the adjustments until you are satisfied.

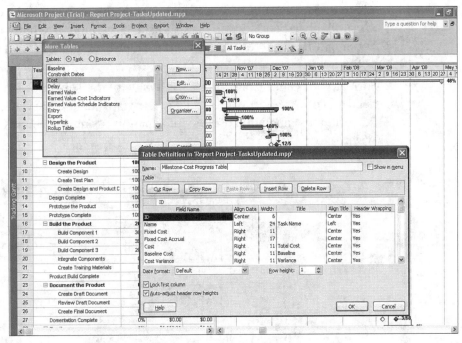

Figure 11.50   *Table Definition for creating a custom table*

Building a Custom View

Now that you have the table, you are ready to create a custom view for the new report. To do so, follow these steps:

1. Select View, and click More Views.

2. In the More Views dialog box, click New if you want to start the view from scratch, or click Copy if you would like to start with an existing table as a model. The View Definition dialog box, similar to Figure 11.51, opens.

3. In the Name field, enter the new custom view name. In the example, you see Milestone-Cost Program Report, as this will be the report.

4. Change the table, group, and filter selections. In this case, the Table will be the custom table previously created and will display in the drop-down list once applied and you have applied a custom filter of top level and milestones.

5. Choose whether you want to show the view in the menu by selecting the Show in menu dialog box. In the case of a view or report you will be using often, it is a good idea to select this check box.

6. When done, click OK. If you want to apply the new view, click Apply. It's probably a good idea to do so, to see if the table is what you want. You might forget a column or want to adjust the column width for one of the fields.

7. Format your Gantt Chart on the right side of the separator bar, as needed. For instance, you could add the status data grid (via Format, the Gridlines) and add baseline information (using the Gantt Chart Wizard).

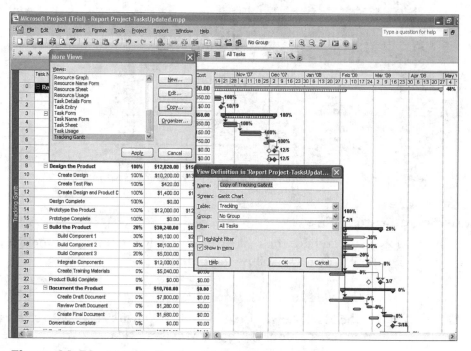

Figure 11.51   *View Definition for creating a custom view*

Once created, the view will display in the View drop-down list (select View from the menu bar), or in the view bar on the left side to select the view.

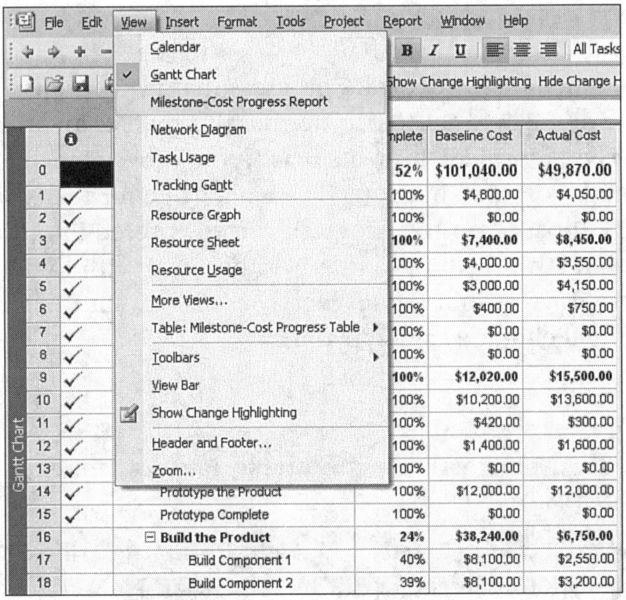

Figure 11.52   *Custom view in drop-down list*

Moving the View into the Organizer

The report is available any time you need to use it if you move the view and its related parts into Global.mpt by using the Organizer. If you do not move the custom view, table, group, or filter into Global.mpt, it will only be available in the project for which you created it.

To move your custom objects into the Organizer, follow these steps:

1. In the project in which you created the view, select Tools, and then click Organizer.

2. Click the Tables tab. Click the table in the right side and click Copy to move the table into the right side of the Organizer. Click the Views tab and do the same. Do the same thing for the custom filters and groups you want to move to the Global template.

3. Close the Organizer.

If others in the organization want to use the view, you can send them the project and they can repeat the steps to move the custom object into the Global template.

Introducing Earned Value

Earned value is a method of reporting progress that many project managers want to use, or eventually want to use, because it provides an objective way to provide status on a project. It posits that as you move along in a project, based on planned work and budget, you earn a value for the work accomplished per period based on the progress you've entered into the project. Earned value is an advanced topic that I do not deal with in detail in this book, but as you progress in using Project, you might want to take a deeper look into how the technique can help you.

> **Read about the earned value technique in *Project Management for Mere Mortals***
>
> Chapter 12 of *Project Management for Mere Mortals* describes the concepts and calculations of earned value in more detail. It's well worth your time to review the information in that chapter so you can see the underlying calculations occurring in the earned value reports that Project provides.

You might also look up earned value in Wikipedia for a nice discussion that includes charts, formulas, and comparisons about earned value management.

Based on the information entered using your schedule tracking method, Project will calculate the earned value of each task for you. For any project that has progress reported in it, you can easily create an Earned Value report. Select View, click Table, and then select More Tables. You will see several tables that provide earned value information.

Project calculates earned value at the summary task, task, and assignment levels and at timephased amounts. Project uses % Complete at the task level, and % Work complete at the assignment levels, which can sometimes show slightly different calculations in roll-ups. This might or might not be an issue for you. If you are just starting with earned value, this should not concern you, but if you have requirements for preciseness for earned value, you might consider some customization or earned value add-ins to increase your preciseness.

Earned value can be a very meaningful way to view progress and head off issues early. However, it's important to build a proper schedule. You will need to truly understand the scope of the project, make sure it's properly translated into the schedule via the WBS, and make sure you consistently enter accurate progress information to get the best results. If your organization decides to use earned value reporting, all project managers will need to build their projects using similar structures (e.g., effort-based scheduling, with phases as summary tasks) or you will not be analyzing projects the same way.

The following sections describe the earned value tables available in Project, and describe the earned value fields in the tables. Project has three earned value tables: Earned Value Table, Earned Value Cost Indicators Table, and Earned Value Budget Indicators Table. With the new Visual Reports feature in Project 2007, you also can use the Earned Value Over Time report that graphically charts the projection of earned value for a project. The earned value tables use the Status date (or today's date if you are not using the Status date) as the point-in-time indicator of where the baselined task costs and schedule should have been.

Earned Value Table

The Earned Value Table provides both schedule and cost variance information within one table. Fields on this report are as follows:

- Planned Value (PV) is the planned baselined costs.
- Earned Value (EV) is the work progress of % Complete multiplied by the baseline costs.
- Actual Cost (AC) is the cost of work completed on the task and project.
- Schedule Variance (SV) shows you how behind or ahead of schedule you are in terms of cost and is calculated as EV – PV.
- Cost Variance (CV) shows you how over or under budget your project is and is calculated as EV – AC.

In Figure 11.53, the SV and CV for the entire project are negative, which means you are behind schedule and over budget. However, if you look at the work completed for the Justify task, things were actually ahead of schedule and under budget initially. On this table, you have three more fields, which help you determine status.

- EAC (Estimate at Completion) provides you with what the cost will be at completion of the task or project based on the current performance. In Figure 11.53, the estimate is $108,040 for the project. The EAC calculation is (AC + BAC – EV)/CPI. CPI is explained with the Earned Value Cost Indicator field later.
- BAC (Budget at Completion) provides the total planned baselined cost for the task or project. If you were not using earned value and you added the Baseline Cost field, it would have the same amount showing in this field.
- VAC (Variance at Completion) is calculated as BAC – EAC. In the case of Figure 11.53, the VAC is negative $7,180.11, so the project is over budget. With this information, you can perhaps start thinking about reducing your scope, getting less costly resources, or getting approval to continue with a higher budget.

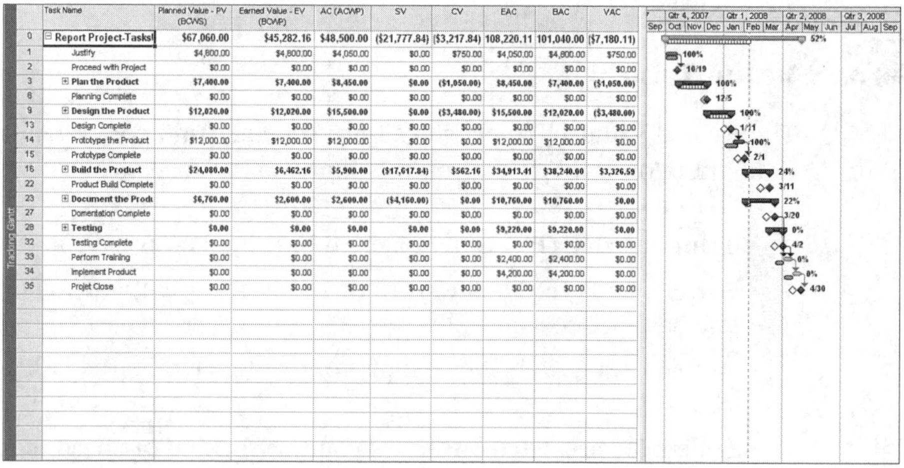

	Task Name	Planned Value - PV (BCWS)	Earned Value - EV (BCWP)	AC (ACWP)	SV	CV	EAC	BAC	VAC
0	Report Project-Tasks	$67,060.00	$45,282.16	$48,500.00	($21,777.84)	($3,217.84)	108,220.11	101,040.00	($7,180.11)
1	Justify	$4,800.00	$4,800.00	$4,050.00	$0.00	$750.00	$4,050.00	$4,800.00	$750.00
2	Proceed with Project	$0.00	$0.00	$0.00	$0.00	$0.00	$0.00	$0.00	$0.00
3	Plan the Product	$7,400.00	$7,400.00	$8,450.00	$0.00	($1,050.00)	$8,450.00	$7,400.00	($1,050.00)
8	Planning Complete	$0.00	$0.00	$0.00	$0.00	$0.00	$0.00	$0.00	$0.00
9	Design the Product	$12,020.00	$12,020.00	$15,500.00	$0.00	($3,480.00)	$15,500.00	$12,020.00	($3,480.00)
13	Design Complete	$0.00	$0.00	$0.00	$0.00	$0.00	$0.00	$0.00	$0.00
14	Prototype the Product	$12,000.00	$12,000.00	$12,000.00	$0.00	$0.00	$12,000.00	$12,000.00	$0.00
15	Prototype Complete	$0.00	$0.00	$0.00	$0.00	$0.00	$0.00	$0.00	$0.00
16	Build the Product	$24,080.00	$6,462.16	$5,900.00	($17,617.84)	$562.16	$34,913.41	$38,240.00	$3,326.59
22	Product Build Complete	$0.00	$0.00	$0.00	$0.00	$0.00	$0.00	$0.00	$0.00
23	Document the Prod	$6,760.00	$2,600.00	$2,600.00	($4,160.00)	$0.00	$10,760.00	$10,760.00	$0.00
27	Domentation Complete	$0.00	$0.00	$0.00	$0.00	$0.00	$0.00	$0.00	$0.00
28	Testing	$0.00	$0.00	$0.00	$0.00	$0.00	$9,220.00	$9,220.00	$0.00
32	Testing Complete	$0.00	$0.00	$0.00	$0.00	$0.00	$0.00	$0.00	$0.00
33	Perform Training	$0.00	$0.00	$0.00	$0.00	$0.00	$2,400.00	$2,400.00	$0.00
34	Implement Product	$0.00	$0.00	$0.00	$0.00	$0.00	$4,200.00	$4,200.00	$0.00
35	Projet Close	$0.00	$0.00	$0.00	$0.00	$0.00	$0.00	$0.00	$0.00

Figure 11.53 *Earned value tables*

BCWS, BCWP, and ACWP = PV, EV, and AC, respectively

You will see BCWS (budgeted cost of work scheduled), BCWP (budgeted cost of work performed), and ACWP (actual cost of work performed) as well as PV, EV, and AC in Project, as well as many publications about earned value. BCWS, BCWP, and ACWP were terms originally used in publications describing earned value techniques and are slowly being replaced by PC, EV, and AC in earned value management formulas for simplification.

Earned Value Cost Indicators Table

The Earned Value Cost Indicators table, shown in Figure 11.54, uses indicators to help you understand if the project is over or under budget for the period. This report focuses on costs. PV, EV, and CV were already defined, but the CV% and CPI are indicators that are very useful for seeing at a glance how the budget is looking on your project.

- CV% is the Cost Variance percentage. The formula is [EV - AC/EV] × 100, so this is the ratio of how much it should cost to how much it actually cost up to the point of the status date of the report.
- CPI (Cost Performance Index) is the ratio of budgeted cost to actual cost for the task or project and its formula is EV/AC. If the CPI is 1, you are right on budget. If it is less than 1 your project is over budget, and if it is greater than 1 you are under budget.
- TCPI (To Complete Performance Index) shows the ratio of work still needing to be completed to how much is still available to spend. The formula is (BAC - EV)/(BAC - AC). You can see if you are going to have extra money or run out of money on the task. If you have an amount over 1, you are likely going to run over your budget and you need to improve performance on the project (or get some leniency to continue in the direction in which you are going).

In Figure 11.54, CV% is -7% and the CPI is .93, indicating the project is over budget. The BAC, EAC, and VAC were defined earlier.

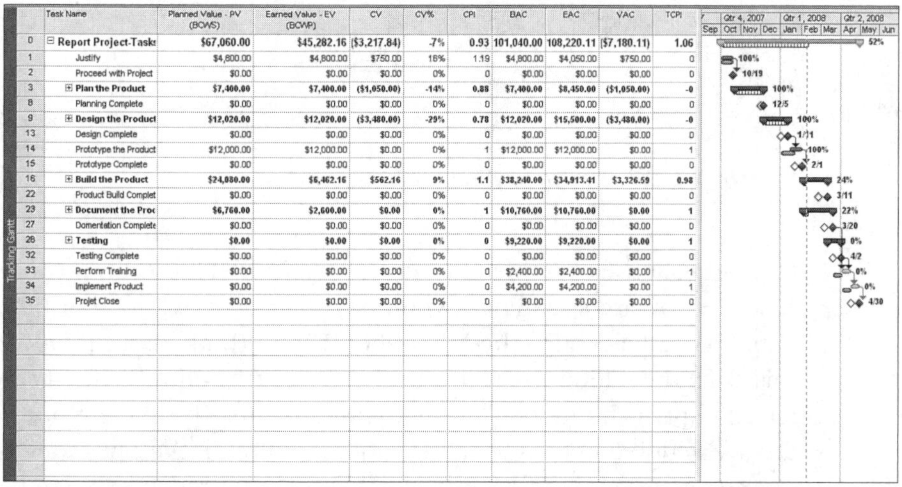

	Task Name	Planned Value - PV (BCWS)	Earned Value - EV (BCWP)	CV	CV%	CPI	BAC	EAC	VAC	TCPI
0	⊟ **Report Project-Tasks**	**$67,060.00**	**$45,282.16**	**($3,217.84)**	**-7%**	**0.93**	**101,040.00**	**108,220.11**	**($7,180.11)**	**1.06**
1	Justify	$4,800.00	$4,800.00	$750.00	16%	1.19	$4,800.00	$4,050.00	$750.00	0
2	Proceed with Project	$0.00	$0.00	$0.00	0%	0	$0.00	$0.00	$0.00	0
3	⊞ **Plan the Product**	**$7,400.00**	**$7,400.00**	**($1,050.00)**	**-14%**	**0.88**	**$7,400.00**	**$8,450.00**	**($1,050.00)**	**-0**
8	Planning Complete	$0.00	$0.00	$0.00	0%	0	$0.00	$0.00	$0.00	0
9	⊞ **Design the Product**	**$12,020.00**	**$12,020.00**	**($3,480.00)**	**-29%**	**0.78**	**$12,020.00**	**$15,500.00**	**($3,480.00)**	**-0**
13	Design Complete	$0.00	$0.00	$0.00	0%	0	$0.00	$0.00	$0.00	0
14	Prototype the Product	$12,000.00	$12,000.00	$0.00	0%	1	$12,000.00	$12,000.00	$0.00	1
15	Prototype Complete	$0.00	$0.00	$0.00	0%	0	$0.00	$0.00	$0.00	0
16	⊞ **Build the Product**	**$24,080.00**	**$6,462.16**	**$562.16**	**9%**	**1.1**	**$38,240.00**	**$34,913.41**	**$3,326.59**	**0.98**
22	Product Build Complet	$0.00	$0.00	$0.00	0%	0	$0.00	$0.00	$0.00	0
23	⊞ **Document the Proc**	**$6,760.00**	**$2,600.00**	**$0.00**	**0%**	**1**	**$10,760.00**	**$10,760.00**	**$0.00**	**1**
27	Domentation Complete	$0.00	$0.00	$0.00	0%	0	$0.00	$0.00	$0.00	0
28	⊞ **Testing**	**$0.00**	**$0.00**	**$0.00**	**0%**	**0**	**$9,220.00**	**$9,220.00**	**$0.00**	**1**
32	Testing Complete	$0.00	$0.00	$0.00	0%	0	$0.00	$0.00	$0.00	0
33	Perform Training	$0.00	$0.00	$0.00	0%	0	$2,400.00	$2,400.00	$0.00	1
34	Implement Product	$0.00	$0.00	$0.00	0%	0	$4,200.00	$4,200.00	$0.00	1
35	Projet Close	$0.00	$0.00	$0.00	0%	0	$0.00	$0.00	$0.00	0

Figure 11.54 *Earned Value Cost Indicators table*

Earned Value Schedule Indicators Table

The Earned Value Schedule Indicators table focuses on the schedule, but it also provides a cost value to the work progress you've performed up to the status date of the project. It provides ratio indicators to understand if the project is behind or ahead of schedule. Figure 11.55 shows two new fields not defined previously.

- SV% (Schedule Variance Percentage) helps you to quickly see how much over, under, or on target you are for the task or project. The formula for SV% is (SV/PV) × 100.

- SPI (Schedule Performance Indicator) provides an indication of how you are doing on the schedule, with the value of 1 meaning you are on schedule. The formula is EV/PV for SPI. If the SPI is over 1, your project is ahead of schedule, and if it is under 1, it is behind schedule.

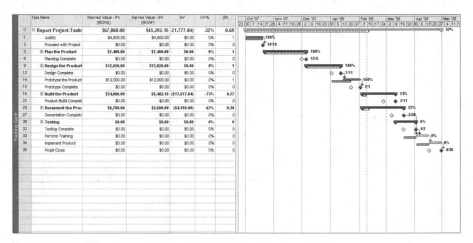

Figure 11.55   *Earned Value Schedule Indicators table*

In looking at the example in Figure 11.55, your SPI is .68, but your CPI is .93. It seems you are spending less money than planned, so your budget issues aren't as bad as your schedule issues. If you think about it, however, what this might be telling you is that because you are behind schedule, you simply haven't spent the money yet that was expected. People are not getting the tasks scheduled because they are still working on the ones they are behind on, so the costs on the project aren't being incurred as expected.

Earned Value Visual Report

With the new visual reports capability in Project 2007 you also have an earned value graph capability that is terrific for showing the earned value trend.

1. Select Reports, and then click Visual Reports.

2. On the All tab in the resulting Visual Reports – Create Report dialog box, select Earned value over time report and click View. You will see a report similar to the one shown in Figure 11.56 for projects in which you have started tracking. The chart will be created in the Excel Pivot-Table format, and you can also elect to show it in a table. You can save the data, and when you update the data, you can create the chart again.

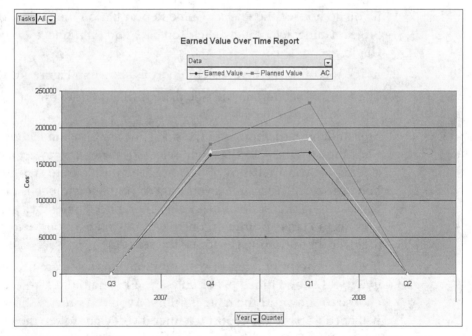

Figure 11.56 *Earned Value Over Time Report in Project 2007 Visual Reports*

Earned value reporting is made easy in Project with the tables and charts available, and many people are excited about the prospect of using them for earned value reporting. However, it is very hard, because the up-front process of defining scope well and building a structured WBS—and then getting accurate consistent data as the project progresses—takes a lot of time, effort, and commitment from an organization.

Printing in Project

Although we all use our computers more and more for creating, analyzing, and adjusting our documents, sometimes we just need that piece of paper to look at. If you need to print a report from Project, it helps if you use a printing wizard that was added in Project 2003 and continues in Project 2007. The wizard is in the Project Guide (the panel that shows up in the left side of the project when you open it for the first time unless you've turned it off) and you use it to step through the print setup. To use the Project Guide print guide, follow these steps:

1. If you do not see the Project Guide Report bar on the toolbar of the Project Guide, select View, click Toolbars, and then select Project Guide.

2. At the top of the screen, select Report as shown in Figure 11.57.

3. The fourth selection on the side pane is called Print current view as a report. Click that hyperlink.

4. A printing wizard appears in the side pane as shown in Figure 11.57. Click through the selections, and select Print preview to get a printable report you are happy with. You have four panes to step through. You can select the columns you want to print, how much is on one page, and the timescale to make a useful report. Sometimes the Gantt Chart is too large to print on one page and you might have to paste together the various pages to see the schedule.

5. If you have to print a report with multiple pages you are usually limited to 8-1/2 by 11-inch paper unless you have a plotter. You can choose to show just the table portion or you can preview how you will need to paste the report together if you want to see the entire Gantt Chart. You can do this by going to Print preview and selecting the preview multiple pages button as shown in Figure 11.58. Sometimes after viewing this, you might decide to change the timescale to make it smaller, or decide it's not worth printing out the Gantt Chart.

6. When you are ready to print the report, select Print.

Formatting selections

Report tab for Project Guide

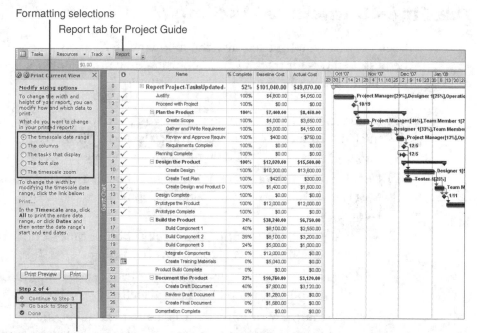

Go to next step for print formatting

Figure 11.57 *Project Guide panel for formatting report printing*

Multiple Pages printing preview button

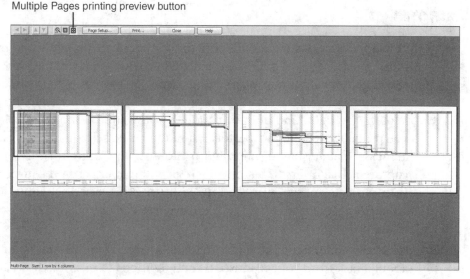

Figure 11.58 *Use the multiple pages print preview*

The Project Schedule Tracking Methodology

Based on what you have learned, the following steps and sequence describe the best methods for tracking and reporting on your schedule. The steps for tracking a project schedule so far are as follows:

- ☑ Build your project according to how you need to track. If you need to track by work effort, make sure you estimate by Work. Use the steps for the project schedule building methodology in the previous chapters.
- ☑ Decide what you want to track in your schedule (e.g., Duration, Work, Cost) and how you want to track (% Complete, Actual Work, Actual Duration).
- ☑ Set up standard times during the week (or other time period) to obtain task update information from your team.
- ☑ Obtain task progress information. Ask at least two questions: How much have you done, and how much is left?
- ☑ Use a custom view, or enter actual data in the tracking fields available in Project based on a duration-based or an effort-based scheduling setup.

Summary

Tracking and reporting are the two things that many people want Project for in the first place, not building the schedule. However, you have to build the schedule to track how you are doing according to plan. When you create the schedule, think about how you want to track and report to make sure you capture the right kind of information. If you want to report on % Complete, you probably need to just perform duration-based scheduling, so you can create tasks that are based on duration, rather than work effort. If you want to capture actual hours to historically review the hours each resource spent on your project, you will want to start with an effort-based schedule. Then you would capture either total weekly (or whatever period you choose) or day-by-day task effort.

Create or understand the views that allow you to capture status information about a task from your resources. You might create custom views and tables to help you track the kind of information you really want or just use the Tools, Tracking, Update Tasks tool.

Use the status date to indicate when you last updated progress in the schedule. The status date might be today's date, last week, or a couple of days ago when you actually gathered the actual information from your team. If you need to report to management about your schedule at any given time, create reports that display milestones or summary tasks. You can do this through filtering or grouping. You might use Visual Reports to display the difference between your baseline estimates and your actual progress.

The true power of Project is in capturing actual work during execution of the project, and then progressing the schedule to understand how current performance predicts how the project schedule and budget will end up if the current trend continues. By tracking status of your schedule, you can review areas that show poor performance and make corrections to head off a delay. Project doesn't track and make the adjustments for you, but it helps you see very clearly where the issues are.

Practice: Tracking and Reporting on Your Schedule

This practice will give you some experience with both tracking and reporting on your schedule.

Practice 11.1

Tracking Your Project

To start, use the project called HousePainting-Practice-Chapter11-Practice1.mpp on your CD. This is the house-painting project ready for tracking.

1. Open HousePainting-Practice-Chapter11-Practice1.mpp. You will enter progress information into the schedule.

2. Select View, and click Table: Tracking. You will see columns that provide an area in which you enter data.

3. Select Window and click Split Window. In the gray area on the lower right side, right-click and select the Resource Work task form. You will see Baseline work and other areas in which you can enter information in the split window. For this practice, enter actual date and hours worked, but you could enter day-by-day hours in the Resource Usage or Task Usage views if you wanted to.

4. On the Gather Materials task, enter a start date of 5/8/07. Then in the lower window, enter 4 in the Act. Work field and enter 0 in Rem. Work. Click OK.

5. Move to the Scrape and Sand task and highlight it. For Spouse, enter 12 in the Act. Work field and 0 in the Rem. Work field. For Me, enter 34 in Act. Work,

and 0 in Rem. Work in the lower window. Click OK. Note that you did not enter the Act. Start date, as the scheduled start date (5/10/07) was the date the task started.

6. Highlight the Inspect and Rescrape field. In the lower window, enter 8 in Act. Work, and 5 in Rem. Work for Me and enter 9 in Act. Work for Spouse (you won't change Rem. Work). Click OK.

7. Let's say this is as far as you've gotten and you are ready to check the status. Because you have the Tracking Gantt on, you can take a look and see that your schedule is slipping, but so far, you are not in any danger of missing your Deadline date of 5/25 on the Prepping task.

8. Select Project, and then click Project information. Enter 5/15/07 in the Status Date field (be careful; depending on when you are working on this book, you can easily enter the wrong date).

9. Select Tools, click Tracking, and then select Update Project. In the Update Project dialog box, select the Reschedule uncompleted work to start after option and click OK. What is the end date for the Prepping Complete task now? What's the end date for the project itself?

10. Now it is the next week. On the Inspect and Rescrape task, enter 13 and set Rem. Work at 0 for Me. Set Act. Work for Spouse at 12. Notice that you do not need to enter zero in the Rem. Work field. Click OK.

11. For Prepping Complete, because it is a milestone, enter 100%. You can either do this in the lower window or in the % Comp. field (not the Phys.% Comp. field).

12. On the Mask Windows task, enter Act. Start of 5/22. In the lower window enter Act. Work of 2 and Rem. Work of 10 for Child. For Me, enter 5 in Act. Work and 15 in Rem. Work.

13. Select Project, then click Project information. Enter 5/24 in the Status Date field.

14. Select Tools, click Tracking and then select Update Project. In the Update Project dialog box, select the Reschedule uncompleted work to start after option and click OK. What is the end date for the schedule now? Are you still going to make your deadline at the present rate?

15. If you want to see the result, see HousePainting-Practice-Chapter11-Practice1-Result.mpp on the CD.

Practice 11.2

Creating a Report for the Roofing Project

To start, use the project called HousePainting-Practice-Chapter11-Practice2.mpp on your CD. This is the roofing project that has status recorded and is ready for reporting.

1. Your spouse is worried about the house painting project. She believes the current trend suggests you are going to be late and a half-finished house will ruin the enjoyment of your vacation in July. You decide to create some reports to help analyze the situation. First, you will look at just the milestones, to focus on just dates at the end of each phase. Open HousePainting-Practice-Chapter11-Practice2.mpp.

2. Select Project, click Filtered for:, and select Milestones in the drop-down list. Take a look at the baseline milestone for the finish date and the current projected date. It looks like you have plenty of time for your deadline, but you have managed to move out a bit, and you might need to make some course correction now.

3. You decide to check a variance report to see where you fell behind the most. Select View, and click Table: Variance. You consider that it might be that your child is finding too many other things to do rather than help out, and you have to admit you didn't get started on the Mask Windows task when you should have. You decide to discuss this with your child, and vow to start the tasks on time from now on.

4. You also decide you are going to check status every few days and want an easy way to view progress to analyze the situation quickly. You decide to create a view that shows the Tracking Gantt and the variance table. Select View, click Table, and then select More Tables.

5. In the More Tables dialog box, make sure you have the Variance table highlighted and click Copy. The Table Definition dialog box displays.

6. Enter My Variance Table in the Name field. Click the Start field showing in the rows area, and click Insert row. Select % Complete to add a new column to the table. Click on the Finish Variance field and click Delete row. Click OK, and because you want to see what the table will look like, click Apply.

7. It looks good, so now you are ready to make sure you have a new view that has what you want. Select View and click More Views.

8. In the More Views dialog box, make sure the Tracking Gantt is highlighted and click Copy. The View Definition dialog box opens.

9. In the Name field, enter My Variance Report.

10. Make sure the Table field has My variance table entered. Make sure the Show in menu check box is selected.

11. When done, click OK, and then click Apply.

12. You also decide you want to see the Status date gridline. Select Format, and then click Gridlines. Highlight the Status date in the Line to change section. Select a line type in the Type drop-down list, and in the Color field, select Red. Click OK. The Status date will show up on the view.

13. Select View from the menu bar, and notice that this new view is now available for you to use any time. Don't forget that if you want to use it on other projects, you need to move it into the Global.mpt file by using the Organizer.

14. If you want to see the result, see HousePainting-Practice-Chapter11-Practice2-Result.mpp on the CD.

Case Study: Tracking the Schedule

On the VNLE project, as you remember, Chris set the baseline for the project after getting approval from the project stakeholders and her team. They decided the timeline and estimates were the best they could do for now, so Chris and her team started working on their tasks. Chris set up weekly status meetings with the team members. In the case of executives helping, she would stop by and ask how they were doing when they were working on their tasks. In the meetings, Chris asked each team member who was providing status two things: How many days have you worked and how many days do you have remaining? Chris obtained status throughout the Create trade show marketing plan phase and entered the actual progress. Things slipped a bit. During the execution of the Create detailed trade show plan phase, Chris obtained the status information shown in Table 11.2.

Open the file VNLE-Chapter11-Begin-CaseStudy.mpp to work on this scenario.

1. Under Create detailed trade show plan enter the durations shown in Table 11.2 in the Act. Dur. field of the Tracking Gantt view of the project. Where you see dashes, it means you do not need to enter the information because Project will do so for you.

Table 11.2 *Tracking Method Selection*

Task	Actual Duration	Remaining Duration	% Complete
Design booth sales approach	2	—	—
Create IT demo requirements	2	—	—
Design the trade show experience	4	0	—
Design marketing collateral	2	0	—
Design booth	2	0	—
Determine vendor partnership strategy	3	—	—
Determine target vendors	6	—	—
Review and revise demo requirements	2	—	—
Design demo	1	—	—
Obtain booth and demo design approval	—	—	100
Determine housing and travel requirements	2	—	—
Gather marketing materials and booth shipping requirements	1	—	—
Determine catering requirements	1	—	—
Determine trade show on-site requirements	2	0	—
Verify product inventory supports marketing plan	1	—	—
Detailed trade show plan complete	—	—	100

2. When you have finished entering the durations, you should have a file similar to VNLE-Chapter11-Middle-CaseStudy.mpp on your CD. For the next section you can select the file to work on or use the one you completed.

3. Set the Status Date. Select Project, Project information and set the Status Date to 6/22/2007.

4. Set up the Status Date gridline on the Tracking Gantt Chart. Select Format, click Gridlines, highlight the Status Date, and select a line type and color.

5. Select View, Table: Variance.

6. Select Project, Filtered for, and select Milestones in the drop-down list. Change the timescale in the view to week-by-week so that you can see the entire project in the Tracking Gantt Chart. Review the schedule. Are you in trouble for making the trade show? Why or why not?

Chris shares the milestone report with June. She's not exactly pleased with the delays and asks Chris to make sure things don't continue the way they have been going.

Tracking and Reporting

When you are ready to move into executing your project, obtain status from team members and enter progress data into your schedule. Select the method for entering the data, and what data you need to enter. To do so, follow these steps:

- Determine your schedule tracking method—Duration or Effort-Based.
- Select the view or table you will use to enter the data, and then enter the data regularly.
- Review the updates regularly via tracking views and reports.

Tracking and reporting your schedule helps you identify issues before they become a crisis so you can take action to get back on track.

Review Questions

1. Why should you track your schedule?

2. What are the major tracking fields?

3. What is the difference between % Complete and % Work complete?

4. Do you need to enter Actual Start and Actual Finish dates when tracking?

5. Why do you need to obtain progress data to enter in the Remaining Duration or Remaining Work fields when entering Actual Duration or Actual Work into the project?

6. What two method can you use when you are tracking work effort?

7. Which is the least detailed tracking method, duration-based or effort-based tracking?

8. Can you enter information into the Remaining Costs field?

9. Why can't you enter data into the Actual Cost field when tracking?

10. If you have a prorated accrual method, how will Project enter Actual Costs?

11. What is the Status Date?

12. What are methods for entering status data?

13. What are some duration-based status tracking techniques?

14. What are some effort-based status tracking techniques?

15. What are some of Project's reports?

16. What is earned value?

17. What earned value reports are available in Project?

18. What is one of the best ways to preview how Project will print your project schedule?

Closing Down Your Schedule: The End Is Only the Beginning

The beginnings and endings of all human undertakings are untidy.
—John Galsworth

Topics Covered in This Chapter

Closing Tasks and the Entire Schedule

Using What You Learned on Future Projects

The Project Schedule Closing Methodology

Summary

Practice: Closing the House Painting Project

Case Study: Closing the VNLE Project

Neglecting to close the schedule is as common as neglecting to close the project itself in many organizations. Closing the project means acquiring formal acceptance from the project sponsor or client, filing all project documents, conducting a lessons-learned session (where your project team discusses what went wrong and how they can make the project better), and tidying up the project schedule. In the heart of every true project manager is someone who wants to learn from the mistakes or successes of the current project and apply that learning to the next project. Having closing processes can inspire a project manager to get better.

Also, the term *closing* isn't limited to just the end of the project. It can be a process you go through at the end of every phase, summary task, or categorization of work according to how you structured your WBS. To a certain extent, while you track your schedule you are also closing out as you review each task and think about how the completion of the task contributes to the completion of a milestone or phase. As you review each phase, you might also find now and then that you did not completely zero out all of the remaining work for a task. At the end of your project, by going through processes to close your schedule, you have a chance to get better at the next project by noting forgotten tasks, resources who did not perform as well as you'd hoped, or issues that occurred within the project that you did not expect. By thinking about what you could have done to avoid them, you might be better prepared for the next project. Now if this is a personal, small, or informal project, you might not need to follow the rigor of closing down your project schedule, but consider a closing for your organization's formal processes.

You might want to add some tasks to your schedule to help ensure you follow closing processes. You'll want to include activities such as verification (where the deliverables are formally accepted), gather and file (archive) project documents, and perform a lessons learned or postmortem. Now and then, you might even include a lessons-learned meeting after certain phases of the project are complete so that you can include any of your team's insights and suggestions for improvement into activities for the next phase or phases of the project.

> **Read about closing projects and lessons learned in *Project Management for Mere Mortals***
>
> Read about lessons learned and other processes in Chapter 14 of *Project Management for Mere Mortals* to learn more about key project management closing processes that accompany schedule-closing processes.

Closing Tasks and the Entire Schedule

Closing the project schedule is simple. You review the tasks to see if all of the status information has been entered for each task, and you decide if you should complete the task or update the task to indicate there was more time spent on the task than indicated. If any of your costs were different than the baseline or there were additional costs, you would add them. Throughout the closing process you should also add notes to tasks to explain variances or issues. You also want to make sure all your milestones are complete and you need to manually mark them as 100% complete. Although the steps for closing are simple, making the time to think through closing is not always at the top of your priority list. Let's take a look at the Roofing Project as an example of the steps for closing.

It's easy to see if a task is completed because you will see a check mark next to it if you have a view with the Indicators column showing (e.g., the Gantt Chart view). In Figure 12.1, one of the tasks—Purchase roofing material—is showing 80% complete on its Gantt Chart bar, but it was completed. So Chief, who is reviewing the schedule for closeout, will simply need to go in and zero out the remaining work for the task. He also remembers that they had to purchase extra shingles, so he will note that on the task as well, especially because the task's costs will show a variance from the baseline cost estimate.

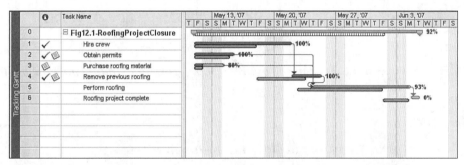

Figure 12.1   *Completed project needs to reflect closure in the schedule*

To review and update the task information, Chief uses the split window and selects Resource work in the Task Form view by right-clicking in the gray area to the side of the lower window pane. He notices he forgot to zero out Lila's remaining work. He does so and also records why they had to purchase 25 extra shingles. Some of the results of Chief's closing activities are shown in Figure 12.2.

On the Perform roofing task, the Chief will need to zero out some remaining work still showing for Wilson. He also had to purchase $200 of materials during the Perform roofing task, so he inserts the Actual Cost column, and adds $200 to the Actual Cost currently showing in the field. He adds a note on the tasks that describes the additional purchase. Finally, he opens the Roofing project complete task and sets it to 0%.

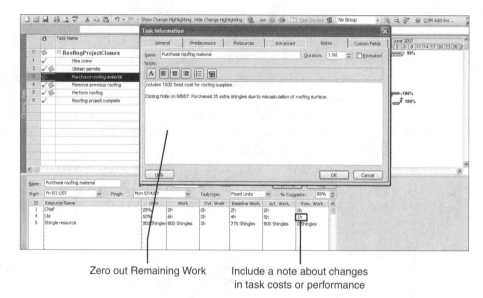

Zero out Remaining Work   Include a note about changes
in task costs or performance

Figure 12.2 *Zeroing out remaining work and adding notes help reflect a closed project*

You must manually set milestones at 100%

Although some people expect Project to automatically set milestones to 100% when all its predecessors are complete, it doesn't, so you have to manually set the milestone at 100%. Although summary tasks and the project summary task will roll up the completion of any subtasks, if one of them is a milestone, and you have not indicated the task is 100% complete, the summary or project summary task will not show as complete.

Once the Chief sets the milestones to 100% complete (on this project, there is just the project complete milestone, but you would usually have many more), then all of the check marks will be shown on every task, including the summary, and the entire schedule is shown as complete. At this point, the Chief might want to make a note on the project summary task that sums up the project as shown in Figure 12.3.

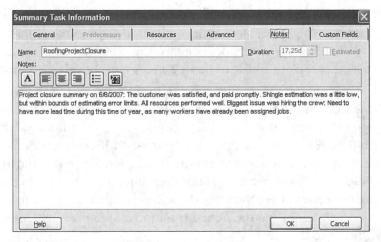

Figure 12.3 *Project summary task closure note included at end of project*

Finally, the Chief changes the view to a "closing" view, as shown in Figure 12.4, and stores the project .mpp file in the company's project archives. The closing view is a summary of all the project information that the roofing company likes to see at the end of a project. The view was created as a custom view as described in Chapter 11, "Tracking Your Schedule," and provides for a quick summary of what occurred. If anyone needs to review the project after closure, the custom view lets them quickly see the relevant information about the project.

		Task Name	Baseline Cost	Actual Cost	Cost Variance	Baseline Work	Actual Work	Work Variance	Duration Variance	Actual Duration	Duration Variance	'007	June 2007
0	✓	⊟ RoofingProjectClosure	$10,890.00	$11,150.00	$260.00	200 hrs	191 hrs	-9 hrs	1 day	17.25 days	1 day		100%
1	✓	Hire crew	$750.00	$1,050.00	$300.00	10 hrs	14 hrs	4 hrs	2 days	7 days	2 days		100%
2	✓	Obtain permits	$425.00	$500.00	$75.00	4 hrs	5 hrs	1 hr	0.5 days	2.5 days	0.5 days		100%
3	✓	Purchase roofing materia	$4,115.00	$4,225.00	$110.00	6 hrs	7 hrs	1 hr	0.25 days	1.25 days	0.25 days		100%
4	✓	Remove previous roofing	$2,000.00	$1,805.00	($195.00)	60 hrs	53 hrs	-7 hrs	-0.83 days	3.13 days	-0.83 days		100%
5	✓	Perform roofing	$3,600.00	$3,570.00	($30.00)	120 hrs	112 hrs	-8 hrs	-0.38 days	7.13 days	-0.38 days		100%
6	✓	Roofing project complete	$0.00	$0.00	$0.00	0 hrs	0 hrs	0 hrs	0 days	1 day	0 days		100%

Figure 12.4 *Custom project closing view to be archived*

Many of the steps the Chief already took could be performed during tracking, and probably should be. However, it is common to miss some items here and there, so making a purposeful review of your project is always worthwhile at the end. You should also leave your project in a view that allows you or others to easily inspect results once the project is closed.

The steps to close your project schedules are as follows:

1. Select View, and then click Tracking Gantt. Make sure you are using the Entry table or add the Indicators column to any view that does not display the field. The Indicators column shows check marks indicating that a task is complete and also shows if notes have been added to a task.

2. Select Window, and then click Split. In the gray area to the right of the Task form in the lower window, right-click and select Resource Work. Using this view allows you to quickly zero out remaining work for multiple resources and make milestones 100% complete because both fields are in the window. If you used duration for your estimates, you could still use this view by simply zeroing out work, but if you want to change any kind of remaining durations or add data to Actual Duration, you should add the Actual Duration and Remaining Duration columns to the view.

3. Review each task to make sure it has a check mark next to it. Highlight each task that does not have a check mark in the Indicators column and in the Resource work view of the Task form, enter zero in the Rem. Work field for each resource.

4. If there were any additional actual costs, insert the Actual Cost column in the top window and add the amount to the Actual Cost field. You should double-click the task, select the Notes tab, and enter the amount of the additional cost and why the additional cost was incurred.

5. Review all tasks for large variances or additional information you want to record. For each task, double-click the task, select the Notes tab, and enter information as to why the task exhibited such variance or a particular circumstance you want to describe.

6. Add any relevant columns or change the view to leave the project in a set view for display of future reviews.

7. Select File, and then click Save, storing the project in a place your organization uses for historical reference.

Steps 1 through 5 could be done during the tracking process. By remembering that you want to record this kind of information for closing during tracking, you can save time for the closing process later. However, at the end of a project or phase, you should still take the time to review your tasks for closing, even if it is just an hour or two. By finishing the project and writing notes on lessons learned, you will probably remember them better than thinking you will keep them in the back of your mind for next time.

Using What You Learned on Future Projects

There is one more item to consider that is connected to closing: creating or updating templates your organization might like to use for future projects. If you have created a project that is organized well or includes phases or the tasks you perform regularly that other project managers can use, you might want to make the project a template. For all intents and purposes, the roofing, house-painting, and even the VNLE project scenario for event planning can be thought of as a basis for templates. Although each project in an organization might have its unique activities, you can use the template as a base, and then change it according to the needs of your project. Although described in Chapter 3, "Building Your Schedule: Scoping Your Project," let's review how you create a template.

1. In the project file you want to save as a template, select File, Save As.
2. The Save As dialog box opens, and in the Save as type field, select Template from the drop-down list. Click Save.
3. In the Save As Template dialog box that opens, click on all of the fields displaying so that check marks display and click Save.
4. In the project you have open, you will notice that all the actual and baseline values were removed. Before you finish saving the template, you have some cleaning up to do. In previous chapters I warned you that a lot of the data you enter into any project is invisible unless the column for the data is showing in the view you have up. For instance, if you had added a custom field and had entered values for each task, those values would now be in this template, although the view you have might not show them. You also have notes that are not appropriate for the project. So you have some cleaning up to do if you want to use the project as a template. The following list describes some of these clean-up tasks.

   - Select Project, click Project Information, and review the fields in the resulting dialog box. Make sure that you reset any of the fields there, including ensuring NA is in the Status date and that the proper calendar for a template is attached. You might want to change the project Start date to a more current date, although anyone using the template will need to change the date when they change the template for their project anyway.

- Double-click each task that has a note showing in the Indicators column, and remove it if it is specific to the old project. Sometimes the notes are relevant for the templates, as they might describe the general activities that would be performed on the task. In the roofing project, the notes were all specific to the project, so you would remove them by double-clicking the task, selecting the Notes tab, and deleting all of the data (using the Backspace key or highlighting and deleting the words). Once done, click OK.

- If there are any constraints on the tasks as shown in the Indicators column, double-click the task, click the Advanced tab and select As soon as possible for the Constraint type. Click OK.

- To clean up resource data, select View, then click Resource Sheet. To make sure there is no hidden data about resources in the template, delete all of the resources on the Resource Sheet by clicking on the rows and pressing the Del key. You can always add the resources again if it is appropriate. Many organizations like to include generic resources that indicate the kind of skill set or position needed for each task, and you can add them at this point. You should not put actual resources on a template.

- To double check that the tasks are cleared of previous data, you might click through all of the tables (View, click Table, then select each of the main tables showing on the default list one by one) to check to make sure none of the fields contain improper data. For instance, the Hyperlink table will show you if anyone added hyperlinks on the tasks. Because the hyperlink probably would not be relevant to the tasks in a template, you would want to remove them there. You could also apply the Task-Audit-Table view provided on the CD in Chapter 8, "Polishing Your Schedule," to look through all the columns and make sure they are set properly or cleared out.

5. Finally, change the view to the view you want everyone to see when first opening the template. It could be a custom view you create for your organization to make sure that people update the project as you would like them to use it. For instance, you might add the Work column to the Entry table and the Gantt Chart view.

6. Select File and click Save. You can send the template to others who might need it. They should—on receiving it—open and save it, making

sure what they save is an .mpt file. When they select File, click New, and select On computer in the New Project in the left side pane, they will see the template in the Templates dialog box to use for their initial project creation. Figure 12.5 shows the closed Roofing Project as a template, once the preceding steps were followed. Notice that the template has durations and dates. You could remove the duration estimates (change the duration to 1 day), but you can also leave them so future projects have some base estimates.

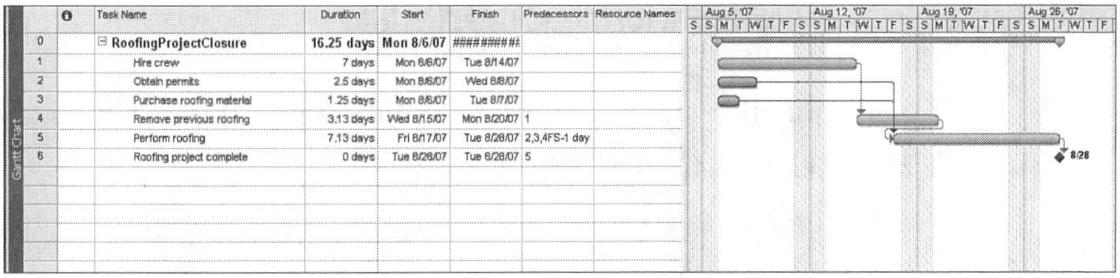

Figure 12.5 *The closed Roofing Project as a template*

Someone in an organization should be responsible for issuing and updating templates, although it is certainly okay for each individual to keep templates if your organization does not have the capability to support a centralized support area. However, if your organization wants to use templates to help manage schedules with uniform phases and tasks, it's a good idea to make sure one person or a small group consistently manages the process. It's not easy to keep the template updated, but it should be a consistent practice to do so.

As an example of the process for updating the templates, let's say Chief uses the template for the next roofing project. He realizes that the template is missing an activity that is always performed as part of the Remove previous roofing task. The way the task is now set up in the template hides the work because the crew that actually hauls away the old roofing material is not added to the task and is often not scheduled properly. Chief decides that right after the Remove previous roofing task, he will add a new task called Haul away old roofing. Chief talks to other roofing chiefs about the task, and they agree it should be added. The template administrator adds the new task to the template after the Remove previous roofing task and in parallel with Perform roofing.

Closing activities often identify the work and processes that can be added for other people to use so everyone gets better on an organization's projects. Once again, this process is probably not necessary if you are using Project for your personal projects, but it should be added to your organization's project management repertoire.

The Project Schedule Closing Methodology

Based on what we have learned, the following steps and sequence describe the best methods for closing your schedule:

☑ Zero out all remaining work or duration for all completed tasks.

☑ Make all milestones 100% complete.

☑ Add notes to tasks to indicate insights or lessons learned about task performance.

☑ Add additional Actual Costs as needed to completed tasks.

☑ Review the summary or project summary tasks for check marks next to them. If they do not have check marks, a subtask has not been closed properly.

☑ Create templates based on well-structured projects, and update existing templates based on lessons learned.

Summary

Although in small or personal projects, you might not need to formally follow the closing processes, you should in large, formal projects so that you can take the lessons you learned to future projects with you. Closing is a formal process of ensuring acceptance from your project sponsor, making sure you store your project files, and performing a lessons-learned session with your team to get suggestions on how you could improve the next project. The elements of closing should be reflected in your schedule. Don't forget that closing isn't just about the entire schedule. You can also follow the processes for each phase of your project. For formal acceptance, you should ensure you have approval tasks in your project. You should also have tasks in your schedule for organizing and storing project files and lessons learned.

There are also specific steps for closing tasks in your schedule. In your project schedule, zero out all remaining work, make sure all milestones show completion at 100%, add additional costs or necessary task information, and include notes on all tasks with significant variances or important information you want to save with the closed project file. You might add a note on the top-level project task that provides lessons learned for the project or the project schedule. Finally, take what you have learned to a template. If you have a project that would make a good template, save the project as a template and clean up the file as necessary for others to use. If you have learned of some more activities that would help improve an existing template, suggest the improvements to the other project managers using the template and get the new tasks added to the template.

Practice: Closing the House-Painting Project

Although short, the following exercise helps you practice closing a project.

Practice 12.1

Closing the House Painting Project

To start, use the project called HousePainting-Practice-Chapter12-Practice1.mpp on your CD. Some information has been entered as you've been tracking, but you are done with the project and need to close the schedule out completely.

1. Open the project called HousePainting-Practice-Chapter12-Practice1.mpp on your CD.

2. Notice that the Prime summary task is not complete. That's because the milestone, Priming Complete, has not been marked as 100% complete. Click the Priming Complete task and in the split window below, enter 100 in the % Complete field and click OK. Note that in this practice, you already have the split window showing, but if you were closing your own projects, you would want to use the split window and select the Resource Work view in the Task form to help you easily enter this information.

3. You notice that the Paint task is also not closed. This is probably just an oversight, as you know you finished the task. Click the Paint task. In the Task form of the split window, you see that Child still had 2 hours in remaining work. You are pretty sure the work that Child did was 5 hours, so enter 0 in Rem. Work, and click OK.

4. You hadn't entered the time for Inspect and Retouch, so you will do so now. For Me, enter 7 in the Act. Work field, and for Spouse enter 10 in the Act. Work field. You should not need to zero out remaining work.

5. Now, you need to indicate that the entire project is complete. Click Painting Complete and enter 100 in the % Complete field. By the way, notice that you did get the work done by the deadline, but it was pretty close. You saw a lot of delays, and it took longer than the original estimate for some of the tasks.

6. Because you are planning an interior painting project next year, you decide a lessons-learned session is in order. You talk to your family about what could have gone better for the project. Child mentions that it was very difficult to get motivated on masking the windows, but that Priming and Painting were tasks that weren't as onerous. Spouse says that it was just too hot to work on a few of those days in the latter part of June. You realized that after chatting with some coworkers, you probably could have used some time-saving paint devices for part of the work. Double-click the House painting project summary task (task zero), and click the Notes tab. Enter a few words about your lessons learned and click OK.

7. If you want to see the result of this closing process, see HousePainting-Practice-Chapter12-Practice1-Result.mpp on the CD.

Case Study: Closing the VNLE Project

Chris's team has completed the VNLE project. The team made it to the event, dealt with some mishaps here and there, and, exhausted but satisfied, traveled back home with a lot of prospects in front of them. Although at first Chris thought the project wasn't a success because Virtually Nostalgia did not get the best in show award, or as much booth traffic as expected, when she found out they received best new vendor, she knew they'd done something right. More than that, when her team got their bonuses, she was pleased. Maybe she had the makings of a project manager after all. Chris knows one thing she learned from the Project class she took. Always close out the schedule, and she takes the time to do so.

> **Read Chapter 13 of *Project Management for Mere Mortals***
>
> Chapter 13 of *Project Management for Mere Mortals* details the process the team went through in closing the VNLE project.

Open the file, VNLE-Chapter12-Begin-CaseStudy.mpp to work on this case study.

1. Complete all tasks that are still outstanding by zeroing out remaining work. Assume that all the work in Actual Work is correct and all you are doing is making sure any tasks still requiring completion are completed. Don't forget that you can do this easily by using the Resource Work view in the Task form using the Split Window feature.

   On the Lessons learned task, enter 10 hours and 0 remaining work for the core team and 2 hours and 0 remaining work for the project manager. On the task, enter the following in the notes column: "For future events, need to get someone on site earlier to have more time to deal with logistics issues."

2. Enter 100% for all milestones that have not been completed.

3. On the final task, enter a note that describes the success of the project: "Received Best New Vendor with 126 points. Need to check out Bye Gone Days to understand what made them successful to help us improve on the next event."

4. On the Verify and correct logistics task, add $500 to the Actual cost field and add a note that says, "Had to purchase wireless Internet connection at $500 for sales team."

5. Review your schedule and make sure all tasks have a check mark next to them.

After filing all the project documents and celebrating with the team, when Chris closed the project file for the last time, she felt the project was truly complete, and she knew she had a great start for her next project.

Closing the Schedule and Project

Along with filing your project documents and celebrating project completion with your team, don't forget to close the schedule, too. To do so follow these steps:

- Look for all tasks that are not complete and zero out remaining work.
- Include notes about variances and make sure milestones are also 100%.
- Use the project as a template if it's reusable.

Closing brings real completion to the project. Good project closing habits lead into better future projects.

Review Questions

1. What are some activities you should include in your schedule for closing?

2. What do you need to do to the schedule itself for closeout?

3. Where can you add information about lessons learned from your project?

4. What are some things you clean up when saving a project template from a completed project?

13

Project Mysteries Resolved!

*Always bear in mind that your own resolution
to succeed is more important than any other.*
—*Abraham Lincoln*

Topics Covered in This Chapter

Additional Tips and Tricks

Underlying Project Behavior Settings: The Options Dialog Box

Using the Methodology from This Book

Getting More Information

Summary

This chapter provides a few additional tips and tricks that might or might not have been discussed in other chapters of the book. It's organized so you can take a quick glance at the information and decide if you want to take a closer look. In this chapter, I also reiterate why you want to use the methodology in this book and lay out the steps. You could use the list as a checklist to make sure you are following the methodology for building, tracking, and closing a Project schedule. Just remember that the list, although sequential, can be used as you iterate through your project phases. You need to return to planning when you add or change tasks. The chapter also contains how to find more information on Project. Because Project is such a complex and versatile application, there are numerous sites on the Internet that provide great information for specific solutions in using the tool. Once you get the basics down and understand the major underlying formulas and behaviors of Project this book conveys, you might only need the Internet and the help files in Project for advanced topics. This chapter does not contain any practices but you could open any project file and try any of the tips and tricks you find in this chapter. This information is not critical to creating a project schedule, but it just might make you more efficient when working in Project.

Additional Tips and Tricks

Project has some capabilities that can help you use Project more efficiently or provide more visual elements in your Project file. You might scan this section and see if any of these features interest you. As usual, practice creates habit, so if you like any of these features, you might need to use them several times to become adept at using them.

Formatting Gantt Chart Bars

When you display the Gantt Chart, it contains default characteristics out of the box. You will see the bars (e.g., task, summary, and milestones), links, and resources. As you apply actual progress, you will also see a black bar to indicate that the progress has been applied. If you switch to the Tracking Gantt, you will see the critical path (in red), the baseline if you have set it, and the percentage complete for the work on the task. Usually, these are the only formats you need for your Gantt Chart bars, but now and then, you need something different. You can set the bars in three different ways to change the default bar style settings:

- Set individual bars via the Format bar function.
- Set all or particular bars in your project via Bar styles.
- Use the Gantt Chart Wizard (for quick and nonpersistent formatting needs).

Using these methods, you can set the beginning, middle, and end of the bar as shown in Figure 13.1.

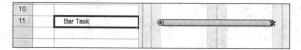

Figure 13.1   *The beginning and end of a bar chart using a customized format*

Setting Individual Chart Bars Using the Format Bar

You can set the shape, type, color and patterns for the start, middle, and end of individual bars in a project by highlighting a task, selecting Format, and then clicking Format bar. If you click on the various drop-down lists for each portion of a bar, you can select your preferences for formatting. You can style one bar or several bars by clicking all the rows whose bar styles you want to change. You can also right-click or double-click an individual bar in the Gantt Chart itself to get to the same Format Bar dialog box that allows you to change your formats.

Using Format, Bar Styles

Bar styles allows you to change the styles for one or all of the multiple bar types that might be in your schedule as shown in Figure 13.2. To format bar styles, select Format and then click Bar styles, or, in the chart area of a Gantt or Tracking Gantt view, double-click to open the Bar Styles dialog box immediately. You can also right-click to select from a list of options for formatting the Gantt Chart.

Bars are drawn in the order listed in the dialog box

The bars on a Gantt Chart are rendered in the order in which they appear in the bar styles table. For instance, the taskbar is rendered first, then the split bar, and the Progress bar is drawn next on top of the taskbar. Make sure you are careful about changing the order, or you might be surprised how bars are displayed in your charts.

Bars tab for selecting colors and patterns

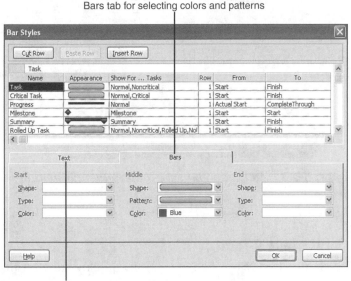

Text tab for displaying more text on the bar chart

Figure 13.2 *Bar styles allow you to change formats for several bars on your project at once*

The last four columns for each row in the table contain drop-down lists to make selections for displaying the bars. The lower portion of the dialog box has two tabs, one for Text and the other for Bars. The Bars tab allows you to select the shape, type, color, and pattern similar to the dialog box you use for the Format bar capability described earlier.

Add text on a bar chart for reports

Use the Text tab to add important information on the bar charts so you don't have to include the table grid in all reports. Figure 13.3 shows the Baseline duration added to the inside of the bars in the current project.

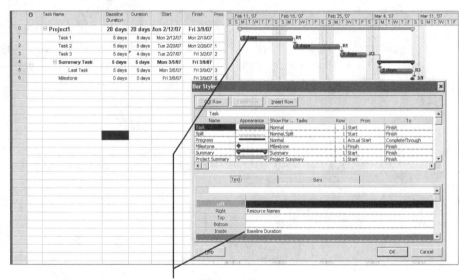

Baseline Duration included on inside of the bar.

Figure 13.3   *Add text to bars for additional information or to enhance reports*

Using the Gantt Chart Wizard

The Gantt Chart Wizard allows you to quickly show critical path tasks, the baseline, and other customized displays on any view using a Gantt Chart, although it is best used on the Gantt Chart view. While you are using the Gantt Chart view to build your project, you might use the Gantt Chart

Wizard to review critical path tasks. Or maybe you'd like to review the baseline on the Gantt Chart view as shown in Figure 13.4, rather than switching to the Tracking Gantt view.

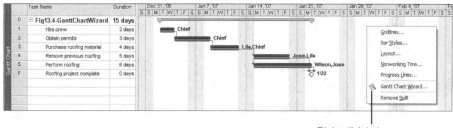

Right click in bar area to choose Gantt Chart Wizard

Figure 13.4 *Using the Gantt Chart Wizard to show the baseline on the Gantt Chart view*

To use the Gantt Chart Wizard, follow these steps:

1. In your project file, select Format and click Gantt Chart Wizard. You can also right-click in the bar chart area of a project file to see the drop-down list where you choose Gantt Chart Wizard, as shown in Figure 13.4. The introductory box of the Gantt Chart Wizard appears. Click Next.

2. In the next dialog box, select the Standard, Critical path, Baseline, Other, or Custom Gantt Chart options, based on what you want to do as described here and click Next.

    • Select the Standard option to return to the standard bar format display in the Gantt Chart view. After using the Gantt Chart Wizard, this is the best way to return to the default format.

    • Select the Critical path option to display the tasks that are on the critical path (in red).

    • Select the Baseline option to display the tasks and the baseline as shown in Figure 13.4.

    • Select the Other option if you want to select some custom bar formats provided out of the box. Click the drop-down list next to the button to implement other bar styles as shown in Figure 13.5.

• Select the Custom Gantt Chart option to select the different task types formats using the wizard. Project will step you through many more individual dialog boxes so you can format the critical path, baseline, regular, milestone, and summary tasks separately. After each dialog box comes up for each selection, yousee the dialog box described in Step 3.

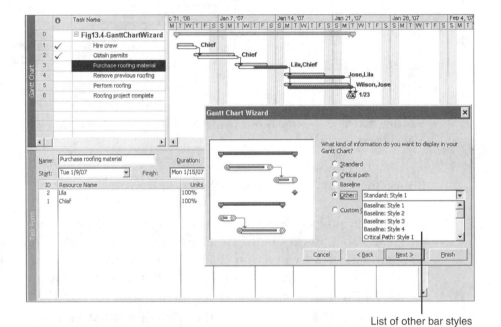

List of other bar styles

Figure 13.5   *Using the Gantt Chart Wizard to select other bar styles quickly*

3. On the next screen, you can select the kind of text you would like to show on the bars. You can choose to display both Resources and Dates, just Resources, just Dates, or no text (called None). A very useful selection called Custom task information allows you to select the custom text. You have a limited set of selections for the information you would like on the bars but it allows you to do more with the Gantt Chart.

The Custom task information button takes you to more dialog boxes that allow you to select the text you want on the left and right as well as the inside of a regular, summary, and milestone taskbar (although you couldn't really put any text inside of a milestone) as shown in

Figure 13.6. Use the inside of the bar carefully. If you have a progress line, text inside the bar will not display well. After you see the three additional dialog boxes for selecting text, Project takes you to Step 4.

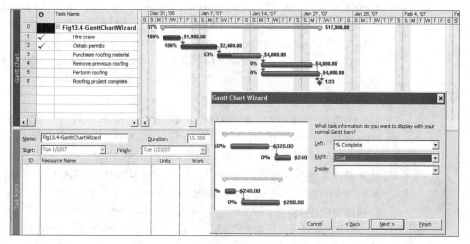

Figure 13.6 *Customize text and position of text using the Gantt Chart Wizard*

4. The next dialog box asks if you want to draw lines to show links between the tasks on the chart. Click Yes or No, and then click Next.

5. The final dialog box allows you to format the Gantt Chart according to all the options you selected previously. In this and previous dialog boxes, you could cancel or go back to previous selections if you want to change something. When you are ready to see your formatted bar chart, click Format It.

6. On the final screen, click Exit Wizard.

The Gantt Chart Wizard only applies to the view you are on

Because the Gantt Chart Wizard will only apply to the view you are on, you will need to re-create your choices for any other view unless you create and save a custom view in the Organizer for other projects.

Other Gantt Chart Formatting Capabilities

There are a couple of formatting capabilities you can use to display the Gantt Chart portion of a view more to your liking. A few are listed here.

- **Gridlines:** Select Format, and then click Gridlines to add or change gridlines to provide more visual cues for dates on the timescale of the Gantt chart (e.g., current, status, project start, or project finish date). You can also use this to highlight the rows or columns in the bar chart or the table area of a view. For instance, if you wanted to make the dividing gridlines between tasks black or fuchsia, you could.

- **Layout:** Select Format, and then click Layout to change the date format on the bars or change the height of the bars. Depending on which chart you click, you will get a different Layout dialog box. For instance, if you select this option on the Network Diagram view you will get different options than if you click on the Gantt Chart view. In fact, you will want to select Layout in the Network Diagram view if you are using the network diagram. There are some selections in its dialog box you will find useful.

> **Don't show links**
>
> You can use the Gantt Chart Wizard and create a nice view for people not familiar with Project. You could select not to show links to make a simpler visual of the work.

- **Nonworking time:** You might have noticed that the weekends show as gray, dotted columns in your Gantt Chart bar. You can even change what those look like. Right-click in the bar chart area and you will see a selection in the resulting list called Nonworking time. Select it and you can change the nonworking column display by choosing a different color or pattern. You can display the columns in front of the taskbars rather than behind them, which is the default. An example of this format is shown in Figure 13.7, where the columns showing Saturday and Sunday (nonworking days) have a different pattern and color than the default.

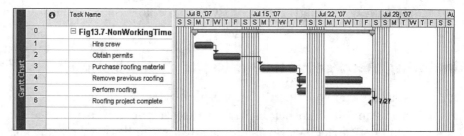

Figure 13.7 *Change Nonworking time display on the bar chart*

- **Timescale:** You can also change how the timescale shows for the bar chart by selecting Format, and then clicking Timescale. You will see a dialog box that allows you to select a multitude of different settings as shown in Figure 13.8. By default, Project only shows the Middle tier (Weeks) and a Bottom tier (Days). You can include a top tier that might show the months or years as well. You might find the Zoom In and Zoom Out buttons on the toolbar easier to use, although adjusting the timescale provides you more discrete formatting capabilities.

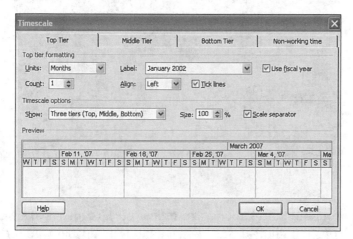

Figure 13.8 *Format the timescale for your project displays*

The main point of this section is that if you think you are limited to what Project has provided you for the bar styles or for formatting the Gantt Charts, you aren't. You can change colors, styles, sizes, start and end points, gridlines, layouts, and timescales. In fact, you could get carried away with formatting too many different styles and colors on your Gantt Chart, so take it easy with the options you have.

Formatting Text for Particular Kinds of Tasks

Not only can you change formats and styles in the bar charts on your Gantt charts and other visual displays in Project, you can also change the text, but don't get carried away using too many fonts and colors. For any task row, you can highlight it and select a different font, font style, size, color, and background color and pattern. To do so, highlight a task or tasks and select Format from the main menu, then click Font.

However, there is a wonderful feature for easily highlighting all of the same kinds of tasks. Just as the bar chart can display all critical tasks in red, you can also do the same in the text in the table for the view you are on. Although this book does not show color, Figure 13.9 shows the text for all critical tasks in red, all summary tasks in bold blue italics, and all milestones in bold, 11-point text.

	ⓘ	Task Name	Duration	Start	Finish	Predecessors	Resource Names
0		⊟ **Fig13.9-TextStyles**	**15 days**	**Mon 7/9/07**	**Fri 7/27/07**		
1		Hire crew	2 days	Mon 7/9/07	Tue 7/10/07		
2		Obtain permits	3 days	Wed 7/11/07	Fri 7/13/07	1	
3		Purchase roofing material	4 days	Mon 7/16/07	Thu 7/19/07	2	
4		⊟ *Summary Task*	*6 days*	*Fri 7/20/07*	*Fri 7/27/07*	*3*	
5		Remove previous roofing	5 days	Fri 7/20/07	Thu 7/26/07		
6		Perform roofing	6 days	Fri 7/20/07	Fri 7/27/07	3	
7		**Roofing project comp**	**0 days**	**Fri 7/27/07**	**Fri 7/27/07**	**6,5**	

Figure 13.9   *Text for certain kinds of tasks can be formatted in the table display*

Project is programmed to recognize milestones, regular tasks, summary tasks, and so on, so it's not surprising that it has this capability. To set the text formatting for particular tasks, select Format, and then click Text styles. A dialog box opens (see Figure 13.10). The drop-down list after the Item to change field shows you several of the kinds of tasks you can change all at once. Select the kind of task you want to change and choose your various font selections from the dialog box and click OK when done.

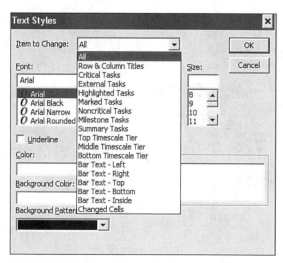

Figure 13.10 *Change the font, color, and background for all tasks of a certain kind in your project*

Project Guide

Next, consider the Project Guide and what it can do for you or your organization. Although the Project Guide is easy to overlook because it takes up so much room on the left side of your Project interface that you might remove it, you might find it useful. First, to remind you of what it is, when you open a project it usually shows up on the left side of the screen (by default) as shown in Figure 13.11.

To use the Project Guide, if its pane or toolbar are not showing, select View, click Toolbars, and then click Project Guide. To remove it, you can go through the same steps, but there is an icon on the Project Guide toolbar that lets you toggle it off, as shown in Figure 13.11.

The Project Guide lists each general step for building your project schedule and the order in which you should perform them. In fact, if you select the first step, Define the project, as shown in the Project Guide in Figure 13.11, it has you set your project start date, which this book tells you to do first as well. The second step is to set the calendar, another thing this book suggests at the beginning of creating a project. As further illustration of the Project Guide's use, Figure 13.12 illustrates how the Project Guide steps you through building a calendar with easy-to-use fields with drop-down selections. You might find the method for setting up the calendar in the Project Guide more

Toggle the Project Guide off and on

Go back and forth through panes   Tool bar for changing function for Project Guide

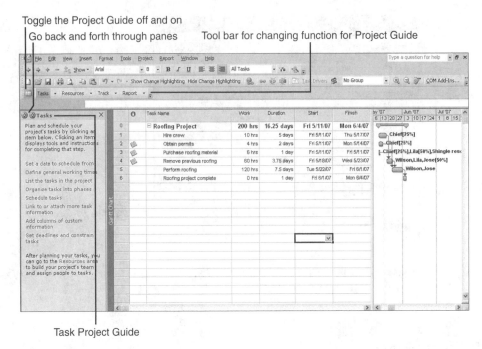

Task Project Guide

Figure 13.11 *The Project Guide displays by default at the left side of your view when you open a project*

intuitive than the standard way of using Tools, Change Working Time, which this book describes.

You can click through the four Project Guide panels—Tasks, Resources, Track, and Report—to see what Project recommends about developing your project for each function you should perform. Click on each of the panes and click on some of the steps showing in each pane. You will also see nice little hints (shown as light bulbs) now and then that provide you a bit more information about the function. You could click on each step and just review the hints for some nice tips and tricks from Project itself.

The following describes a few places in the Project Guide that you might find useful or that you might want to substitute for some of the more awkward functions available in Project.

Defining the Project Calendar

Under the Tasks pane of the Project Guide, select Define general working times. You will see a different pane for customizing a project calendar as shown in Figure 13.12.

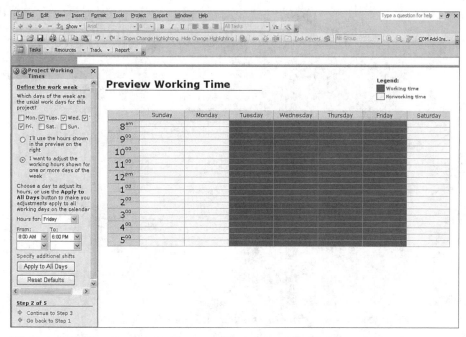

Figure 13.12 *Project Guide provides a wizard for setting your project calendar*

You might find this wizard much easier to use than when you select Tools, Change Working Time.

Tracking the Project

Remember the various methods for tracking your schedule? After reading Chapter 11, "Tracking Your Schedule," you might have gotten interested in creating a special view to update project progress. Well, in the Project Guide, you have a very handy wizard with some fields for tracking. To use the Project Guide's tracking views, select the Track panel of the Project Guide and click Prepare to track the progress of your project. You will see a display for tracking work percentage complete as shown in Figure 13.13.

You can click on the other methods of tracking, Actual Work done and Work Remaining (which provides a similar view to that shown in Figure 13.13 but which includes Actual Work and Remaining Work columns) and tracking of work done per time period, which displays a Task Usage view that allows you to enter hours for a task day by day.

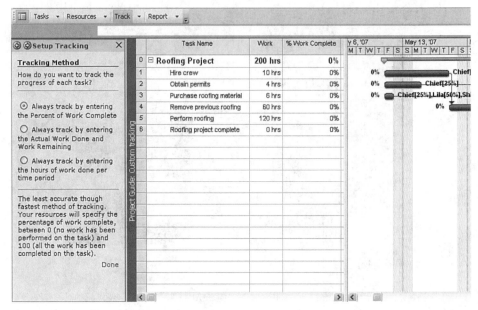

Figure 13.13 *Tracking view using the Project Guide*

Status for Progress Information

You might also find the pane for checking project progress very useful. In Chapter 11, you learned about how the status date and progressing your project made you aware of how far ahead or behind your schedule might be in comparison with the status date. If you select the Track panel of the Project Guide and click Check the progress of the project, you will receive a display similar that shown in Figure 13.14. By entering a status date, Project calculates if you are behind on particular tasks by showing an indicator in the task table in the Status indicator field.

Also at the bottom of the pane you will see some built-in filters and groupings to better review and analyze your project.

Reporting and Tracking

Although this pane is called Reporting, it does an excellent job of tracking your project schedule as well. In Chapter 11, you read about the various views and reports you can use to review your project schedule. Perhaps the most useful aspect of the Project Guide is this Report panel because it puts the various analysis techniques together in one place. The first selection under the Report tab, Select a view or report, allows you to select views,

Status Indicator

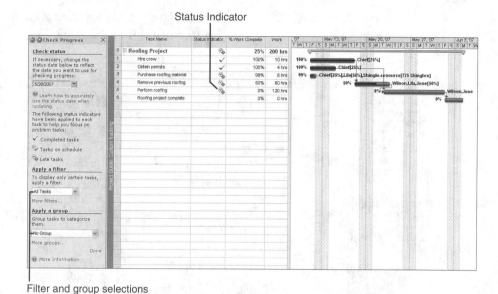

Filter and group selections

Figure 13.14 *Check progress using the Track pane of the Project Guide*

reports, or Visual Reports (Project 2007 only) in one place. This is a great way to become familiar with all the various ways you can look at your project data. The second selection, Change the content or order of information in a view, lets you select groups and filters in one place. In this chapter, you learned about changing bar styles. The third selection, Change the look or content of the Gantt Chart, provides a wizard to take you through the same kind of formatting selections for Gantt Chart taskbars.

See Chapter 11 for further discussion of the Print current view as a report selection. You can see how to obtain a more printable report by using the settings through this Project Guide step rather than using the Print selection in the File menu, which you are more familiar with using in other Microsoft applications.

For further analysis of the project, if you select Compare progress against baseline work, you will see a Tracking Gantt and a variance table put together, and you can select See the project's critical tasks to see the Gantt Chart with the critical path tasks highlighted. Take a look at Figure 13.15. Chapter 9, "Reviewing Work Overload and the Critical Path," described over-allocation and some various views you can use for analyzing it. In the Report pane of the Project Guide, the See how resources' time is allocated option provides a terrific split window view, showing where a resource might be overallocated. It shows the Resource Usage view on top and a Gantt Chart view for only the selected resource at the bottom of the pane.

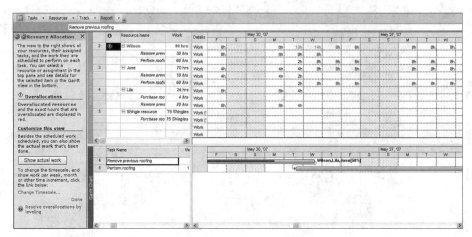

Figure 13.15 *View to help resolve overallocation in the Project Guide*

The final selection in the Reporting pane is Project costs. Click it and it will show Total Cost, Baseline, Variance, Actual, and Remaining fields in one view. This is a great way to quickly review how your budget is faring at various times during project tracking.

Hopefully, after just seeing some of these screens in this book, you are interested in exploring the Project Guide to not only explain important functions in Project but also guide you in the proper sequence of building a schedule.

You can customize the Project Guide

Some organizations include their particular project planning and tracking methods in the Project Guide. For instance, if you want people to build a project using specific phases, you can actually customize the Project Guide to take the user through a series of steps to make sure they add the phases and relevant tasks and data under each phase. If you would like to find out more about Project Guide customization, just type "Project Guide customization" in a search engine.

Toolbars

Toolbars are the various horizontal rows of icons—known as toolbar buttons—at the top of Project. Usually each row is a particular toolbar. The first row showing on the Project interface is the main menu bar. The second row is the Standard toolbar, and it contains the buttons for some of the most common functions you might use in Project. The third row is the Formatting toolbar, which helps you format text, for instance. You can sometimes have too many toolbars or sometimes not enough. Toolbars are accessed by clicking View, then clicking on Toolbars, as shown in Figure 13.16.

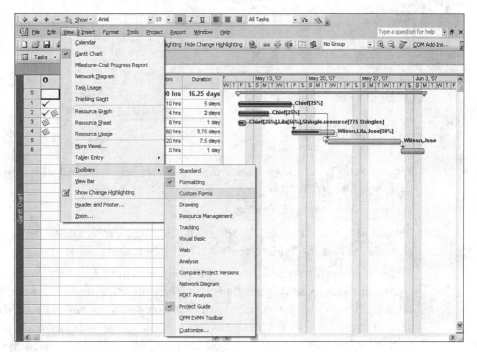

Figure 13.16 *Toolbars can be used to help you perform specific tasks*

Occasionally the function you want to perform in Project is accessed best from a particular toolbar. For instance, one of the toolbars, Custom forms, shows all the various entry forms that allow you to click a task or resource to easily enter information about them in a dialog box as shown in Figure 13.17.

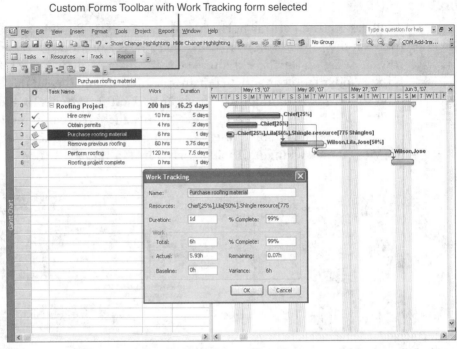

Custom Forms Toolbar with Work Tracking form selected

Figure 13.17 *Form for Work tracking allows you to quickly enter information for a task when tracking*

In your idle hours wondering about all the things Project does, you could click and add various toolbars to see what other functions are available to you.

There is one more quick tip about toolbars. There is a way to set how the two default toolbars display via selecting Tools, clicking Customize, and then clicking Toolbars. The resulting dialog box shows a tab called Options, as shown in Figure 13.18. Throughout this book, references are made to toolbar buttons, such as the Link or Scroll To Task buttons, which often make tasks easier in Project. Out of the box, not all of those buttons appear. To see all the buttons at once, you can select Show standard and Formatting toolbars on two rows to have quick access to those handy functions.

There is one more function that is useful to note in Figure 13.18. If you select Always show full menus and select an item in the main menu bar—such as Tools—you will see every function available under that menu option. Otherwise, you will get an abbreviated list, then a full list after a short pause. When learning Project, it's useful to make the selection show full menus so you see all options.

Show toolbars on two rows to find Project icons easier

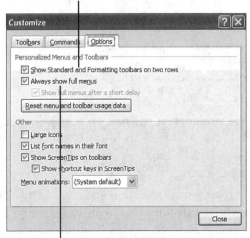

Show full drop down lists from the main menu bar

Figure 13.18 *Customize display of toolbars and drop-down lists from the main menu*

Hovering over Fields

You might find "Hovering over Fields" to be a strange title for a section, perhaps conjuring up thoughts of aliens in Roswell, New Mexico. But hovering your mouse is one of the best tips you will get for using Project. Although hovering to see tool tips is actually a common behavior in all Microsoft products, you will find it especially useful in Project. For instance, hovering over the name of a column field (as shown in Figure 13.19) you will see a hyperlink that you can click to get a definition of the field.

	❶	Task Name	Duration	Start	Finish	Predecess
0		⊟ **ProjectGuide**	.25 da Duration Help on Duration		Thu 5/31/07	
1	✓	Hire crew	4 days	Fri 5/11/07	Wed 5/16/07	
2	✓	Obtain permits	2.5 days	Fri 5/11/07	Tue 5/15/07	
3		Purchase roofing material	1.17 days	Fri 5/11/07	Mon 5/14/07	

Figure 13.19 *Placing mouse and hovering over a field provides help text about a field*

You can hover over buttons and bars on your Gantt Chart, as shown in Figure 13.20, to learn more about the information the simple text or bar represents. Using Project, and learning to use the hovering technique to learn more about fields, gives you one more skill to add to your resume.

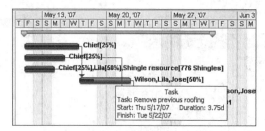

Figure 13.20 *Hovering over a bar provides information behind it*

Double-Clicking and Right-Clicking

If you put your cursor on a task or resource in the Gantt Chart view or Resource Sheet and then double-click, you will get the Task Information or Resource Information dialog box. This is much easier than clicking on the Task Information button in the Standard toolbar, or selecting it from the drop-down list that shows in the menu bar after selecting Project. If you double-click a Gantt bar, you will open the Format Bar dialog box. Try double-clicking various objects within Project to see if you can perform some functions more quickly. Once you find your favorites you won't go back to using the main menu bar.

Also, try right-clicking in various areas of Project. The selections you get when right-clicking depend on where you are. For instance, if you are in the Resource Usage view, and you right-click in the right grid area of the view, you get a list of fields you can add to the grid rather than just seeing the Work field there. If you are in the Gantt Chart view and right-click in the chart area, you get several options for changing formatting of the bar chart. Try right-clicking on various views wherever you have set your mouse in your Project interface to get a feel for the various shortcuts you have. Again, once you try right-clicking in some areas, you won't go back to other forms of accessing functions in Project.

Keyboard Shortcuts

Project also has many keyboard shortcuts that you might prefer using. Click Help in the menu bar, and then choose Microsoft Office Project Help. Type "keyboard shortcuts" in the Search area, and you will see a selection to take you to a list of shortcuts you might want to use.

Smart Tags (Preference Indicators)

Every now and then you might notice a strange little visual cue when you change data in the Work or Duration fields or the number of resources or their allocations on a task field. A little green triangle shows up in the upper left corner of the field being changed, and if you hover (see, those hovering skills come in handy again) over the triangle, you will see a warning sign symbol that lets you select a drop-down list to confirm that you wanted to do what you did. This particular function, also known in some circles as smart tags, allows you to think about what you are trying to do and lets you make another choice. For instance, in Figure 13.21, you'll see options to confirm what you were trying to do when you changed the duration, and you can elect to leave your choice as is or perform the operation you really intended.

Figure 13.21   *After changing Duration, a warning indicator allows you to confirm what you changed*

You can turn off having these indicators by selecting Tools, Options and selecting the Interface tab. The first section, called Show indicators and option buttons for, dictates if these smart tags show up on your screen. For instance, if you clear the Edits to work, units, or duration check box, you would not receive the smart tag shown in Figure 13.21.

Using Your Mouse to Change the Gantt Chart

You can use your mouse to change the bars, links, or other elements on a Gantt Chart. Many people are more visually oriented or inclined to use their mouse to perform functions rather than enter data in a table. So, as shown as best as possible in Figure 13.22, you could set your cursor on the bar for Task 1, then pull the mouse down and connect it to Task 2. You would see the line, and then a link, and when you connect to Task 2, you create a link between the two tasks. If you would rather indicate relationships by dragging the mouse between bars, you can. You could also increase the duration by simply pulling the end of the taskbar out further, or you could move the entire task to start and end on other dates without increasing or decreasing the Duration. Notice the pop-up box called Finish-to-Start link. Whenever you use the mouse to move objects around in Project, it will display an information pop-up.

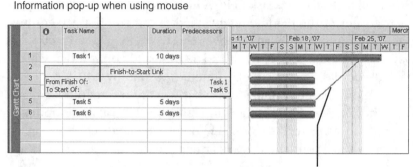

Information pop-up when using mouse

Link being drawn between tasks using the mouse

Figure 13.22 *You can manipulate Gantt Chart bars and other visual objects using your mouse*

Moving Columns in Tables Around if You Don't Like Their Order

If you don't like the order of columns showing in a view, you can move them around. If you click the column you want to move and hover over the top header of it, you will see a small icon that is a small point with four arrows. When you see that, you can hold down the left mouse button and drag and drop the column to wherever you would like. This is similar to behavior you see in some other Microsoft applications when you want to move an object from one location to another.

Creating Custom Fields Containing Values, Formulas, and Indicators

Although beyond the scope of this book, as it is an advanced function, you can create custom fields. The custom fields allow you to include your own or your organization's required data in a project file. For instance, perhaps you would like to indicate status on each task field in Project. You can indicate status by creating values to select from a drop-down list (On schedule, Behind, In trouble) or indicators such as red, green, or yellow status lights. You can also create formulas in fields that calculate a value based on formulas you create. Select Tools from the menu bar, and click Customize, then select Fields to open the Customize Fields dialog box. The Help button in the dialog box will provide more information if you think you might need this function.

Underlying Project Behavior Settings: The Options Dialog Box

In this book, you occasionally received directions to set some configurations by selecting Tools, and then clicking Options. For instance, there is a default configuration setting that has Project always calculate actual costs (rather than having you enter them manually) as discussed in Chapter 7, "Using Project to Enter Cost Estimates," and Chapter 11. The Options dialog box has tabs for several configuration settings that direct the behavior, interface, or way that data displays in Project. You really do not need to understand what the Options dialog box does to use Project. In fact, many people do not even know the dialog box exists and use Project successfully. However, the Options dialog box is too important to leave out of the book. Many people have "ah-ha" moments when they see what some of the settings are and how they affect how Project works. In this section I describe what some of the more important or interesting settings in the Options dialog box do, but not all of them. Remember that the options chosen in this dialog box affect how Project looks, but in almost all cases do not affect your data (although there are a few important exceptions that are described). If you are interested in any of the fields in the Options dialog box not described here, you can click the Help button.

Setting the Options for All Projects

First, you need to understand an important concept about the Options settings when you choose to change them. On some tabs, when you make a change to a setting and click OK, it will affect only the project you have open. On other tabs, if you click Set as Default as shown in Figure 13.23, and then click OK, it will change the setting for all future projects. If you made a change to a setting, and then clicked OK without selecting Set as Default, the change will apply only to the open project. Also, Set as Default does not apply to existing projects, only those you create from the time you made the change.

Options on Project templates override your default settings

If you use a template, the Options settings that are part of the template override what you might have chosen for your own settings. For instance, if you choose to set the default task type to Fixed Work by selecting Set as Default on the Schedule tab, all future projects you create from scratch will set task type to Fixed Work. However, if you use a template that has the Default task type as Fixed Duration, all new tasks you create in the schedule will be set to Fixed Duration. You can change that in the Schedule tab for that project, but it is likely that existing tasks in the schedule are Fixed Duration tasks.

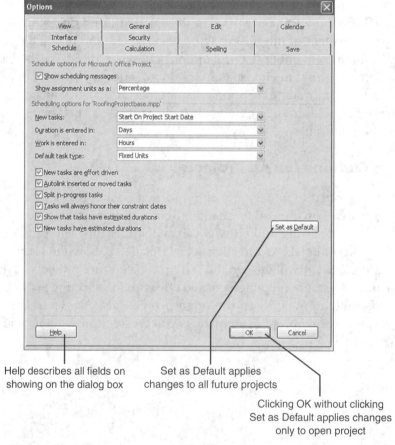

Help describes all fields on showing on the dialog box

Set as Default applies changes to all future projects

Clicking OK without clicking Set as Default applies changes only to open project

Figure 13.23 *Set as default sets the options for all future projects*

If you are in an organization, and you have settings you would like everyone to have in the Options dialog box, you might consider using templates as well. If you set up the templates with your organization's preferred Options settings, and everyone uses templates, you will always have the same settings. Otherwise, make sure you take screen shots of your preferred settings, and if someone changes something in his or her project and sees behavior he or she doesn't understand, you can always check his or her settings against the copy of the settings you have on file.

View Tab

The View tab, shown in Figure 13.24, sets some of the interface and data display items for your current open project. Ever wonder why the Gantt Chart

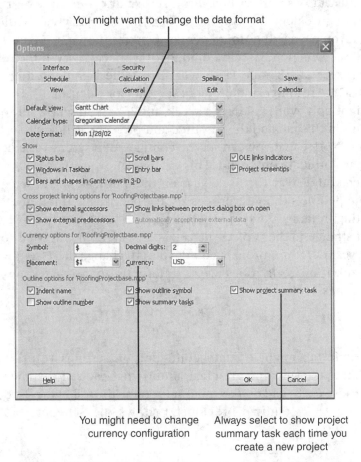

Figure 13.24 *The View tab sets interface and data displays*

view is the first one you see when you open Project? It's set right here. The first field on the screen is called Default view, and you can select any other views to show up by default for your current project. Notice that on this tab, there is no Set as default button. That means if you want something to be set for all projects, you have to open this tab and set it every time. One of the first things you should do when you create each project is to show the project summary task. That setting is in the bottom right corner of this screen.

You will probably want to leave most of the other configuration settings on the View tab as they are unless you need to use a different currency or you prefer another date format in all the date fields that will display for your project.

Calendar Tab

The Calendar tab can affect how Project displays your view on the Gantt Chart although calendars rule the underlying workday calculations. For instance, if you change the Hours per day field (as shown in Figure 13.25) to 6 you will see Duration based on 6 hours of work each day. If the resource's calendar is set to an 8-hour day, it will display the Duration differently, but will still use the resource and project calendars for calculations. Your organization might only work 6.5 days a week, and if so, you will want to change the settings in this tab and the resource and project calendars to reflect the same thing. Notice that you can set the configuration settings as a default for every future project you create. This tab also allows you to set your fiscal year. When you display the fiscal year on the timescale it can wreak havoc with some people's thought processes. People usually think of a calendar year starting in January when scheduling, so if you use a fiscal year, it can look a bit strange to the project managers. Be careful if you want to change the fiscal year here. You probably don't want to change these settings unless your organization really does work differently than what shows in the default settings.

Schedule Tab

The Schedule tab might contain configuration settings you do want to change, but make sure you are clear about what each of the changes will affect. Because each field on this tab is important, the following list describes each. Figure 13.23 (shown previously) shows the Schedule tab and its default selections.

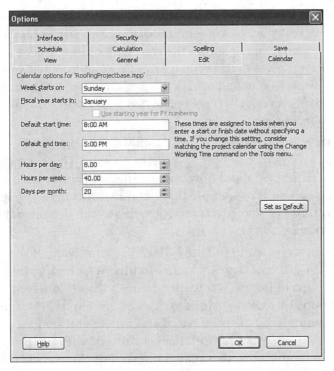

Figure 13.25 *Calendar tab affects how Duration is displayed*

- **Show scheduling messages:** This flag can be set to show messages
  that describe scheduling issues or not. You often get messages that
  warn you about these scheduling issues—such as the Fixed Duration
  task moving past its fixed duration date length or a task that isn't supposed to start because it has a constraint. If you clear this check box,
  you will not get those messages anymore. You should leave the defaults
  unless you get so proficient with Project that you understand the reasons for the messages and find them more annoying than helpful.

- **Show assignment units as a:** If you click on the drop-down list you
  can select Decimal or Percentage (the default). Your selection should
  be based on how people think. Are resources (especially people)
  assigned as a percentage (50% of their time) or as a decimal (.50 of
  their time)? Most people leave the default, but some people prefer decimals because they just don't think of people resources as being measured in percentages.

- **New tasks:** In the drop-down list you can select Start on project start date (the default) or Start on current date. When you enter a new task, the Start field by default shows the start date of the project. You might prefer for the task to start on the current date, although if you link the task to indicate some kind of task relationship, it won't matter. Either way, you really do need to consider when a task starts and not rely on Project to make the decision.

- **Duration is entered in:** In the drop-down list, your choices are Minutes, Hours, Days (the default), Weeks, or Months. This can provide you some real flexibility about how you are thinking about what Duration means. Of course, most people think of it in terms of days (e.g., a calendar day). You probably want to leave this as the default, unless you have good reason to change it.

- **Work is entered in:** In the drop-down list, your choices are Minutes, Hours (the default), Days, Weeks, or Months. Most people think of work in terms of hours (you work 8 hours a day), but there are some organizations that change Work to be measured in days because they consider work to be duration-based and can be any amount of hours in a day. This also makes the Work field consistent with the Duration field so that they see 1 day rather than 8 hours in the Work field. You should leave this if you are performing effort-based scheduling but might change it to Days if you are performing effort-based scheduling.

- **Default task type:** In the drop-down list, your choices are Fixed Duration, Fixed Units (the default), or Fixed Work. You might have very good reason for changing this setting. Your organization might decide it prefers Fixed Duration or Fixed Work as the task type and ask everyone to change the setting for their projects. This is a great way to achieve consistency in building and tracking project schedules.

The rest of the fields on the Schedule tab are check boxes that are selected by default.

- **New tasks are effort driven:** This is the companion setting to Default task type. You can elect to clear this check box if you would like to keep Project from calculating Fixed Unit or Fixed Duration tasks as shared, which reduces duration if more people are added to a task. This is a setting you might choose to change for your entire organization and all projects if you want to have duration-based scheduling as your standard.

- **Autolink inserted or moved tasks:** If you have linked all your tasks, you might have noticed that if you insert a task between two tasks, it automatically gets linked between the two tasks. That's because of this selection. You might want to clear this check box if you would rather new tasks not be linked, so you can make the decision about linking yourself. If you clear this check box, the task will start at the project start date or the current date, depending on what you selected as the default in New tasks.

- **Split in-progress tasks:** This allows you to see the taskbar and the work on tasks separated by a dotted line if work is for some reason not sequential on a task. For instance, if you are entering actual work for Monday and Tuesday, but have remaining work, then when you status or progress your task with a status date of the next Monday, you will see a dotted line in the task rather than a solid bar. If you clear this check box, you will no longer see a split like that for tasks that have started.

- **Tasks will always honor their constraint dates:** You might want to clear this check box if you would like Project to allow more flexible scheduling based on task relationships rather than constraint dates. For instance, you might have a Must Finish On constraint date of 5/15/07 on a Lay foundation task that is linked to a Prepare foundation task. However, as your project continues, you have more and more delays and the Prepare foundation task gets pushed out. At some point, the Prepare foundation end date goes past the date you must start the Lay foundation task to make the Must Finish On date. Project will actually make the Lay foundation date start before the completion of Prepare foundation, although it would be physically impossible for you to do that.

- **Show that tasks have estimated duration:** This removes the question mark after the "day" in the Duration field in a schedule. The question mark is used to indicate if the Duration is estimated or not. This is a matter of style. Some people like to use the question mark to indicate that the estimate is not final and then change it manually when the estimate is more solid. This way, project managers can iterate through the project solidifying estimates using the question mark as a visual cue to let them know if they have more work to do on estimates or not.

- **New tasks have estimated durations:** On every schedule you start you will see a question mark after the days in the Duration field if you do not enter a number directly into that field. If you clear this check box, the question mark will no longer appear when you add a new task (and if you have selected the check box for the previous field).

As you can tell, there is a lot to think about for the Schedule tab. After you use Project for a while, you might want to return to this tab and decide if you want to change the default settings.

Calculation Tab

Most of the selections on the Calculation tab, shown in Figure 13.26, are for advanced users who have used Project for a while or who understand their preferences in calculations well. Some project managers prefer taking off the default Automatic Calculation mode. As they build the schedule, they perform the calculations at specific points during schedule creation. With the Calculation mode set to Manual, you might enter Task 1 for 5 days and Task 2 for 5 days, and then link them. In manual mode, Task 2 will show as starting on the start date of the project, which is the same date as Task 1. As soon as you click Calculate now (or press Shift + F9) the task will move out to start after the end date of the predecessor task. This setting can be dangerous for people who do not understand its power, and remove the setting, calculate manually, and then find the schedule has changed dramatically from how they entered it. The Actual Costs are always calculated by Microsoft Office Project field was described in Chapter 7 and Chapter 11, and you might want to clear that check box if you want to enter actual costs manually.

Save Tab

This tab lets you set your preferences for saving files in Project. You might have reason to change some items on the Save tab. This tab houses the location in which your projects are stored by default (in the My Documents folder) when you save a project file unless you change it on each save. It also changes the location in which templates are stored. If your organization shares templates, and you keep them in a network location, you could change the location by highlighting the User templates field and clicking Modify.

Interface Tab

This tab sets some interface display items. For instance, if you just don't like the Project Guide, you can turn it off here. This is also where you can set up

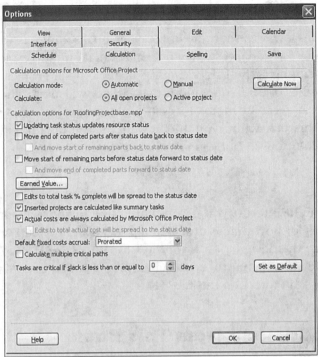

Figure 13.26 *The Calculation tab affects scheduling calculations in Project*

the customization as described in earlier in regards to the Project Guide. You can also turn smart tags off on this tab.

Security

Use the Help file to review the security items you can select if you are interested in the security settings on this tab. You usually do not need to change the defaults on this tab.

Spelling

This tab sets the rules for checking spelling in Project when you select Tools, and then click Spelling. You can check the rules out when you explore this tab, but you usually do not need to change the options.

General

This tab provides a way to set some of your personal settings as well as standard default rates for resources when they are added on the Resource Sheet. An interesting setting is the Undo levels, available only in Project 2007. You can set the number of Undo operations that Project will allow. The default is 20, which you can set to be more or less. If you decide to enter a default standard rate on this tab, when you add resources, the default rate will be assigned to each resource, but you can change the rate later.

Edit

The Edit tab might interest you if you would like to shorten some of the viewing options for how time is designated in fields in Project. For instance, you can change the designation from Days to D or Hr to H if you think it would be better to shorten those designations. You can even change the hyperlink colors in Project on this tab.

Using the Methodology from This Book

In each chapter of this book you saw a checklist for the Project schedule updating methodology. This section provides all of the steps for building, tracking, and closing in one place. You might want to use it as checklist, to follow the methodology as you first learn Project. It takes a lot of practice to get into the habit of building the project the right way. I still find myself trying to make tasks perform a certain way and shake my head after wasting time, when all I should have done was change the task type. Old habits die hard, but to minimize frustration, you'll want to use the best methods as often as possible.

Planning

The following are the steps involved in planning:

☑ If you are using a template, select the appropriate template (you will probably want to change it based on the input of your project team). If you are building a project from scratch, build a WBS with your team, then move to the next step.

☑ Set up your project calendar if you do not have one available. Make sure the hours per day setting in Tools, Options, Calendar tab reflects the same number of working hours as the project calendar.

☑ In the Project Information dialog box, set your project Start date and make sure your project calendar is assigned to the project.

☑ Start building (if your project is from scratch) or editing (if you are using a template) your task list. Make sure you indicate summary tasks and subtasks to help indicate the outline of your project schedule.

☑ Add milestone tasks to indicate significant events, deliverables, or approval points in your project.

☑ Enter deadline dates for appropriate tasks. This is a better way of indicating dates when tasks need to be completed, rather than typing in a Finish date on a task.

☑ Add task calendars to tasks to indicate exceptions to the project calendar if needed. You will probably not need these kinds of calendars often.

☑ Review all tasks. Decide what kind of tasks they are for the schedule building process. Change the Task type and Effort-driven fields if appropriate.

☑ Link all tasks in the schedule, determining if they are Finish-to-Start, Start-to-Start, Finish-to-Finish or Start-to-Finish relationships. Link tasks within phases or task groupings first, then link relevant subtasks between phases or groupings. Use the Predecessor and Successor columns to help you see if all tasks are linked.

☑ Build the project team. Add all resources that might work on the project to the Resource Sheet for the project. If you are performing Effort-based scheduling, enter the Maximum Units each resource can work on the project. You can use generic or real resources, but when you know who will do the work, you should replace generic resources with real resources.

☑ Assign the resources to each task. If you are performing Effort-based scheduling, you might need to change the percentage of allocation a resource is assigned to individual tasks in some cases.

☑ Enter estimates to project tasks. For Effort-based scheduling, enter two of the three variables in the Work formula: Work = Duration × Units.

☑ Review the schedule and enter leads and lags on tasks if appropriate.

☑ Review the critical path and adjust tasks if appropriate.

☑ [Optional] Set your Cost Default Cost calculation methods: Have Project automatically calculate Actual Costs and decide on and set up your cost accrual method for the entire project.

☑ [Optional] Set up any other kinds of resources, such as material resources (set up Cost and Budget resources if you are using Project 2007) if you want to include costs other than labor or equipment work costs in your project.

☑ [Optional] Insert the Cost and Fixed cost fields in the Gantt Chart view (or use the Table: Cost view). Enter Rates on resources, enter Fixed Costs on tasks, or enter Total Budget on the project summary task line depending on how your organization has decided to enter cost.

☑ Check your schedule for logic and scheduling errors using a special audit view or reviewing the errors using methods described in this chapter.

☑ Review and adjust your schedule for workload issues and to tighten the critical path.

☑ Baseline your project schedule.

Every time you add new tasks, you should look at this list to see if you are adding the tasks and analyzing the changes appropriately. You might be in trouble without knowing it if you add the tasks and forget to review the critical path and resource overallocations.

Tracking and Reporting

The following are the steps involved in tracking:

☑ Build your project according to how you need to track. If you need to track by work effort, make sure you estimate by work. Use the steps for the Project schedule building methodology in the previous chapters.

☑ Decide what you want to track in your schedule (e.g., Duration, Work, Cost) and how you want to track (% Complete, Actual Work, Actual Duration).

☑ Set up standard times during the week (or other time period) to obtain task update information from your team.

☑ Obtain task progress information. Ask at least two questions: How much have you done, and how much is left?

☑ Use a custom view, or enter actual data in the tracking fields available in Project based on a Duration-based or an Effort-based scheduling setup.

Make sure you obtain task progress regularly, iterating through the tracking process during each period you set up.

Closing

The following are the steps involved in closing:

☑ Zero out all remaining Work or Duration for all completed tasks.

☑ Make all milestones 100% complete.

☑ Add notes to tasks to indicate insights or lessons learned about task performance.

☑ Add additional Actual costs as needed to completed tasks.

☑ Review the summary or project summary tasks for check marks next to them. If they do not have check marks, then a subtask has not been closed properly.

☑ Create templates based on well-structured projects, and update existing templates based on lessons learned.

Getting More Information

There's been a lot written on Microsoft Project. There are a lot of people who make their living by helping others use the tool, because they clicked, double-clicked, right-clicked, added toolbars, and customized views enough times that they are experts. Luckily, the best of experts like to share their knowledge so they will be acknowledged as experts, and fortunately for you, a lot of people show off their expertise for free. Because of that, you can probably find solutions for most of your more complex requirements or answers to your questions.

Use a Search Engine

I can't say enough about using a search engine. You can usually type in a few words of your question and you can find it if you also include "Microsoft Project" in your query. For instance, you could type "Microsoft Project Earned Value" into a search engine, and the first several hits will take you to more detailed information, including a webcast that Microsoft provided in the past. People often tell me to go to the Microsoft site to find information, and I get lost in the myriad of links and hierarchies, whereas by using a search engine, I find the item I need immediately.

Join MPA: The Microsoft Project Association

You can join an association of other people interested in Microsoft Project. It is made up of novices and experts alike (as well as a lot of people somewhere in between), and if you have a good chapter in your part of the world, you will have frequent meetings where experts will share their knowledge and their skills. You will also receive a newsletter that has the most current news and great tips about Project. You can find how to join at www.mympa.org.

Go to Microsoft's Site About Project

Type "Microsoft Office Project" in a search engine, and you will find the home page for Microsoft Project. You can also user a browser to access http://office.microsoft.com/project.

Check out Microsoft Project Newsgroups

There are forums for discussing Project and you can enter "Microsoft Project Newsgroups" into a search engine or enter http://www.microsoft.com/technet/community/newsgroups/desktoppt/project.mspx in your browser (if you can actually type that all in without a mistake!). You might find others discussing what you wanted to know about.

Use the Project Help File or Project Guide

The Help available in Project is pretty good, so use it. Click Help from the main menu bar and select a help capability.

Summary

You have no practices in this chapter, but I suggest you try some of the tips and tricks on any Project file to get a feel for what's available to you. Hopefully, using some of the tips, you will become a bit more efficient in using Project. Also, don't forget that if you see some behaviors in the Project that seem different than when someone else was using it, you should check the settings in Tools, Options. You might find you have one different setting that causes Project to show data just a bit differently.

In this book, I attempted to tell you just what you need to know to build and track a Project schedule, and go to the heart of what's behind Project and its behaviors. I focused on how Project works and then stepped you through the things you really need to do to create a useful schedule. I didn't go into every little aspect of Project nor could I give you the wisdom of creating a WBS that is right for you and your organization. I also described the two options in for creating and tracking schedules: Effort-based or Duration-based. I described how you assign resources, using costs (or using a top-level budget), and using some of the out-of-the-box features to analyze and report on your schedule.

In fact, besides learning the proper methodology in the remainder of the book, the first and second chapters provided the foundation of what you need to know about Project. Whether it all made sense in that chapter might depend on the way you obtain context for learning any new tool; maybe you just need practice using a tool before the concepts make sense or maybe you've already used the tool, but now some of those strange quirks you've seen make sense. If you feel like Project has a mind of its own, hopefully this book revealed to you the "mind" of Project. Too many people initially feel like abandoning this fabulous tool, but once they know its behaviors, they feel like they actually do have the control they should have.

One last word about project management and using Project. Project is not enough to make you a project manager. I'm astounded by how many organizations decide that project management is the key to solving their project issues. They buy everyone a copy of Project, have them take a class on it, but forget to provide classes on project management. This tool in the hands of people who do not know the underlying foundation for project success can be dangerous. I have met Project experts who I would never have manage a project because they think that the schedule is the project, and if people would just do what it says, everything would be fine. Learn and practice the discipline of project management as a companion to using the tool (if you don't already have project management knowledge).

Don't become so enamored with the tool that it becomes your job (unless you are a project scheduler). Use the methodology and just what you need to know to create good schedules that help you become a better project manager. Project can help a project manager analyze progress today, see the alternatives for the future, and learn from the past, but your skills as a well-rounded project manager will help your project succeed far better than just knowing how to use Project.

Review Questions

1. What three methods can you use to format Gantt Chart bars?

2. What are some other format changes you can make to the Gantt Chart?

3. How would you change the text format for all milestone tasks?

4. What are the four Project Guide panels?

5. What are the two selections on the Project Guide that help you track you projects?

6. What are some selections in the Report panel of the Project Guide that can help you analyze and track your project?

7. How do you select another toolbar to show other functions available in Project?

8. What does hovering the cursor over fields or toolbar buttons do?

9. Can you use your mouse to manipulate taskbars on the Gantt Chart bars?

10. How do you get to the Options dialog box? What does the Options dialog box do?

11. Which Options tab allows you to show the project summary task?

12. What does the Autolink inserted or moved tasks check box on the Schedule tab do?

13. Where can you look for more information about Project?

Appendix:
Answers to Review Questions

Chapter 1

1. You would want to use Project rather than a spreadsheet or text file to manage your projects because you can easily create and represent task relationships, understand how the work changes when you add or delete resources from a task, review the critical path, optimize your schedule, and learn from past project schedules more easily.

2. The overall methodology for creating and maintaining a schedule in Project is as follows:
   - Create and enter the project scope
   - Define key task attributes
   - Define task relationships
   - Add resources and estimate their work
   - Estimate the cost of tasks and the project
   - Review the schedule
   - Optimize the schedule
   - Baseline
   - Track the schedule
   - Close down the schedule

3. The most important functions that facilitate project success are defining project scope and identifying stakeholders and their needs.

4. Risk management is a technique that you can use to identify risk contingencies or opportunity enhancements that you can incorporate into your schedule. Risk management itself is not part of the schedule-building process.

5. The five project processes that you could incorporate as project phases into your schedule are Initiating, Planning, Executing, Monitoring and Controlling, and Closing.

6. Effort-based scheduling is a way to show what will change in a schedule based on the number of people you place on the task, the amount of effort (work in hours), and how long the task might take over time.

7. Duration-based scheduling is based on identifying one person responsible for the task or tasks and their estimate of the length of time it will take to accomplish the work, rather than understanding and capturing the effort it takes to get the work done.

Chapter 2

1. Besides selecting a default view with a Project field available, the most direct way of exposing a field in Project is to select Insert from the menu bar and click Insert. You can then select the field from the resulting Column Definition dialog box that displays.

2. The three major categories of a project data structure are tasks, resources, and assignments.

3. The major fields in Project are Work, Duration, Cost, Start and Finish dates, Predecessor and Successors (task relationships), and Units (amount of a resource is available for assignment on a task).

4. You can see timephased data in Project in the Resource Usage and Task Usage views. You can use the Zoom in and Zoom out buttons to see how Project has scheduled a resource's assignment over a particular time span.

5. Although not a named designation in Project, current or estimate at completion is the first designation. The Work, Duration, and other fields assume the designation in its field name. The other three designations are part of the field names: Baseline, Remaining, and Actual.

6. The most important formula to understand in Project is this:

$$\text{Duration} \times \text{Units} = \text{Work}$$

7. A resource's availability is calculated based on the resource's calendar (designating the weeks of the month and hours per day the resource

can work) and the units available for assignment to a task (e.g., 100% or 50% units).

8. The View Bar is a vertical strip at the left of the Project interface that allows you to quickly select major views in Project.

9. The Task Form, an alternative view displaying each resource's work, unit, and other assignment information for a task, is displayed in the lower pane of the Gantt Chart view when you select Split Window. You can select other views for the lower pane if you want after the default Task Form displays.

10. You might want to use the Scroll to Task button if a task's Gantt bar in the Gantt Chart bar is not showing readily in the right portion of the screen, or if the timephased hours in the Resource Usage or Task Usage view are not showing. To use the button, you need to select the task, then click the button to see the bar or values for the task.

11. You would use the Tracking table when you want to enter progress information when you have started executing your project. When you are building your project or resource information for a project, you use the Entry table, which, by default, displays in the Gantt Chart and Resource Sheet views.

Chapter 3

1. A project charter provides you authorization to proceed with the work of your project and includes information about the project, such as its driver and purpose, high-level requirements, major dates, an esti- mated budget, and other important information.

2. A scope statement is a written document that describes the work of the project in detail. It might include the objectives of the project, deliverables, a high-level schedule, an estimated budget, a listing of project risks, a list of what is outside the scope of your project, and the kind of resources needed for the project.

3. A work breakdown structure (WBS) is a hierarchical representation of the deliverables of your project and their decomposed activities. It can be presented in outline or visual format.

4. You can create a work breakdown structure in Project. You can create a task outline that indicates the categories or phases of your project

usually created as summary tasks, and the activities under them as sub-tasks. You might have several levels in the WBS. It is best to create or review the WBS before entering it into Project directly.

5. Sometimes you see filenames such as Project1, Project2, and Project3 in your current Project session because you have started several new projects without saving them. When you close Project, it will ask you if you want to save the files.

6. The file format extension for a project file is .mpp and the extension for a template is .mpt.

7. You enter the project's start date in the Project Information dialog box (not in the Start field of the first task).

8. You associate a calendar to a project file so that you account for non-working days so that work will not be scheduled on those dates.

9. You do not have to create a project calendar for every project you create. You can use calendars that have been previously created by using the Organizer function in Project.

10. The project summary task is the zero line in a project file. It rolls up the details from all the tasks in the project

11. You create a subtask of a summary task by indenting a task under another task. You can use the Indent button on the toolbar.

12. You can insert almost any object in a note. When you display a task note, you can select the Object button and insert the object, or a shortcut for the object.

13. A project template allows you to use the knowledge and wisdom of project managers who performed similar projects before you. You can see the WBS they built and the tasks and sequences they used in their schedules to deliver their projects. You can adapt the templates to your own unique project by adding and removing tasks as necessary.

14. You can share templates with other people in your organization by sending them a project file that is a template. They can save the file as a template and use it over and over again.

Chapter 4

1. Methods for reviewing task information are as follows:
   - Click the Task information icon and the dialog box shows immediately
   - Double-click and the dialog box shows immediately
   - Right-click and select Task Information in the drop-down list
   - Click Project in the menu bar and select Task Information in the drop-down list
   - Set your cursor on the blue Gantt Chart bar, right-click, and select Task Information in the drop-down list

2. The Multiple Task Information dialog box allows you to change the task field values for several selected tasks all at once.

3. The main tabs on the Task Information dialog box that describe information about a task are General, Predecessors, Resources, Advanced, Notes, and Custom Fields.

4. Custom fields are additional fields that you can use to include your own information describing a task (or resource) in Project.

5. Milestones clearly signify a special event, deliverable, or approval point in a Project schedule, and help you gauge where you are when you start tracking your schedule.

6. A deadline date is a field that Project provides to help you indicate when a task should be complete. You enter a deadline date by double-clicking a task and in the Task Information dialog box, selecting the Advanced tab. You can then enter a date in the Deadline field. You can also insert the Deadline column into views.

7. The eight constraint types are As late as possible, As soon as possible, Finish no earlier than, Finish no later than, Must finish on, Must start on, Start no earlier than, and Start no later than. You should not enter constraints when building your schedule—as soon as possible is the default constraint and you should use that constraint type.

8. Task calendars help you override the working time established in project and resource calendars so that you can work special hours for certain tasks only.

9. If you receive a duration estimate from a manager and do not know how many resources are working on the task, you are building a duration-based calendar.

10. When you enter a duration estimate on a task and no resources are assigned, the Work field will show as zero (unless you have entered something into it). This is because of the formula Work = Duration × Units.

11. The three task types are Fixed Units, Fixed Duration, and Fixed Work.

12. If you have a 2-week fixed duration task, and your original estimate was 40 working hours with 50% of a resource working, the percentage of time the resource work's on the task will increase to 75% if you change your work estimate to 60 on the task.

13. The effort-driven designation indicates that the task's work is shared. If you add a resource to a task that already has a resource, the duration is decreased (unless the task is a Fixed Duration task type). If you remove a resource from a task that already has a resource, the duration is increased (unless the task is a Fixed Duration task).

Chapter 5

1. Methods for linking tasks are as follows:
   - Selecting the tasks and using the Link tasks button on the toolbar
   - Typing the predecessor's task ID in the Predecessors field on the Gantt Chart
   - Using the Predecessor's tab in the Task Information dialog box to enter the Task ID of the predecessor task
   - Using the split window to type in the predecessor's Task ID in the Predecessors field

2. Predecessors are tasks that should be worked on directly before another task and successors are tasks that should be worked on directly after another task.

3. The four task relationships are Finish-to-Start, Start-to-Start, Finish-to-Finish, and Start-to-Finish. Start-to-Finish is the least used type of task relationship.

4. To link tasks in a large schedule, you should link first among all the tasks in the summary task grouping. This way, you can work on chunks, rather than linking all the tasks together.

5. Some advantages of using the network diagram for sequencing tasks are that it is very visual and you can use your mouse to easily link tasks. A disadvantage of using the network diagram is that you cannot see many tasks on one page to easily link tasks.

6. You use a master project to link tasks from two different projects by inserting the two projects as subprojects in the master project. Then, after expanding the tasks in the subprojects, you can select a task in one project and link it (using any preferred linking method) to the dependent task in the other project.

7. A lead is when a successor task can start before the finish of the predecessor task. You might use a lead when you want a successor task's work to get a head start and not wait for the completion of the predecessor task.

8. A lag is when a successor task should be delayed after the finish of the predecessor task. You might use a lag to show a waiting period or delay between two tasks.

9. You should include the Successor column in your Gantt Chart when linking tasks to make sure all tasks are truly linked. When you methodically link tasks you might miss including successors and it's a good way to see if there are any tasks without successors.

10. The critical path is the longest sequence of tasks (determined by their durations) through the project schedule that define the end date of the project. Once you establish a critical path, it can change if any of your duration estimates on tasks that were not on the critical path increase significantly.

Chapter 6

1. You will enter resources for your project in the Resource Sheet. It is good practice to enter them there, rather than typing in the resources as you are assigning them to tasks.

2. Besides using the Multiple Resource Information dialog box to enter the same value for multiple selected resources, you can use the Fill Down capability. You can select a cell, select Edit from the menu bar, and click Fill, then click Down to copy the same value for the resources.

3. The two resource types are Work and Material and the new resource type in Project 2007 is Cost.

4. You change the resource calendar by selecting the resource and selecting the Resource Information button from the toolbar. Then you select the Working Time tab in the Resource Information dialog box (for Project 2002 or Project 2003) or the Change working time button on the General tab (for Project 2007).

5. You would create a custom field for resources when you want to include special information about a resource that is not provided programmatically by Project. You could create a special field, such as Employee type, and then sort and filter by it for reporting purposes.

6. The resource's calendar, Maximum Units, assigned on the Resource Sheet, and the amount of resource units assigned on a task affect a resource's availability. Also, the resource is assigned based on work contouring (evenly distributed over the time span of a task), and if the work is being shared with others.

7. Duration-based scheduling is a form of estimating and scheduling to schedule duration of a task without regard to the effort (work) or number of people assigned.

8. Effort-based scheduling is a form of estimating and scheduling that schedules the project using work estimates, units a resource is assigned to a task, and the duration of the task to indicate and manage the full effort of the task. It is a more discrete form of estimating and scheduling and is more accurate than duration-based scheduling.

9. You can assign resources to tasks by using the Assign resources button on the toolbar, or using the Resources tab in the Task Information dialog box. You could also use the split window and enter resources on the Task Form.

10. You would enter duration-based task estimates by entering the duration estimate in the Duration field, and assign a responsible resource to the task. You would most likely ensure the task type on the tasks in the schedule is Fixed Duration, Non-Effort-based.

11. You would enter effort-based task estimates by entering Work and Duration estimates in their respective fields for a task. You might also enter Duration and Units for each task, or Work and Units. You would most likely use the default Fixed Units, Effort-driven or Fixed Work tasks types on all your tasks.

12. You revisit leads and lags and the critical path when you add resources and estimates because the durations of tasks change and the critical path might have changed. You might also have a better opportunity to include leads on tasks.

13. A resource pool is a list of resources that can be shared across projects. Your organization might want to use this to help drive consistency and create efficiency so that everyone does not have to enter resources for each of their projects.

Chapter 7

1. The three cost estimating methods are top-down, bottom-up, and parametric.

2. Two Cost formulas are as follows:

   Cost = Actual Cost + Remaining Cost

   Resource Rate × Total hours on the task + Fixed Costs = Cost

3. You can stop Project from calculating Actual Costs automatically by selecting Tools on the menu bar, clicking Options, and clearing the Actual Costs are always calculated by Microsoft Office Project check box on the Calculation tab.

4. The three accrual methods in Project are Prorated, End, and Start.

5. Standard rates are used for calculating costs when a resource is assigned to a task and a rate has been entered for the resource; the rate is used times the hours the resource is assigned on the task to contribute to the total cost of the task.

6. Per use Costs is a Cost/Use Rate assigned to a resource. When the resource is assigned to a task, the rate is added to the task's cost.

7. A fixed cost is any nonresource expense on a task.

8. A cost resource in Project 2007 is a resource that can be added to a task to track cost items such as travel, lodging, and so on. A budget cost resource allows you to enter a cost resource on the project summary task to indicate the overall budget of the project.

9. Material costs are calculated by assigning a material resource with a rate in the Std. Rate field. The rate is used for each measurable unit

applied to the task via the Standard Rate for a material resource. The rate is multiplied by the number of units required for the task to calculate the material cost.

10. Some methods for viewing costs include using the Tables: Cost view, inserting the Cost column into the Gantt Chart, using the Split Window function to view the Resource Cost view in the lower window's Task Form, or selecting the Statistics button in the Project Information dialog box.

11. You can only enter the Budget Cost for your project on the Task Usage or Resource Usage views. You will need to insert the Budget Cost column, and you must enter the value in that field for the specific budget cost resource.

12. You can add different rates for one resource on the Cost tab of the Resource Information dialog box. The Cost Rate table allows you to enter five different rates for the resource.

13. You can compare the original project budget with the one that Project calculates by displaying the project summary task's Cost field, and comparing it to the budget you enter. You can enter the budget in the Fixed Cost field or enter the budget in the Budget Cost field using a Budget Cost resource.

Chapter 8

1. The items you should check when reviewing your schedule are Spelling and style, Project preferences (Tools > Options selections in Project), Project attributes, Task calendars, tasks and summary tasks (outlining), Milestones, Task relationships, Task types, Task constraints, Work and Duration, Resources and their attributes, Resource calendars, Costs, Critical path, and Workloads.

2. Three of the important tabs on Tools, Options are Schedule, Calculation, and Calendar.

3. Methods you can use to review your schedule are formatting text, sorting, grouping, filtering, adding columns or using different views or tables, using graphs and viewing or printing reports, reviewing the schedule manually, using Task drivers (Project 2007), Change highlighting (Project 2007) and multiple Undos (Project 2007), or using a special audit view.

4. A special audit view, which you can create by adding columns to a table, can help you quickly see and change errors in the schedule. By exposing all the key fields that might have issues, you can methodically review them.

5. Reviewing your schedule is an art because you need to understand the tolerances of your organization when dealing with overallocation or other scheduling issues you might need to change. Your schedule shows you the math, but because a project is a human endeavor, you must make decisions to change or not change your schedule based on knowledge of your organization and its preferences.

6. After your schedule is built you need to treat adding, removing, and changing tasks the same way as when you build the schedule. You need to consider the scope and how a task change might affect the scope. You need to enter resources and estimates for the new or changed tasks with the same consideration as when you build the schedule.

7. You might include reserve or contingency in your project by adding an extra percentage amount to tasks, adding extra days to the project, including extra costs in the Fixed Cost field, adding a line item for reserves, or using the PERT method for estimating tasks.

8. The PERT method is used to obtain the best, worst, and expected estimates for a task, and based on a formula, calculates the weighted average of the estimates that you can use for your estimate. You could also use the pessimistic estimate to help provide contingency as well. You enter PERT estimates by selecting View from the menu bar and clicking PERT analysis in the drop-down list. You can use the button on the toolbar to guide you through entering each kind of estimate (best, worst, and expected) for tasks.

Chapter 9

1. Work contouring indicates how the work is distributed over time. Resources are allocated by default using a flat contour.

2. Leveling is smoothing out the distribution of workload over time for overallocated resources.

3. Project has an automatic leveling function, and it can level many aspects of resource overallocation, but it is not a panacea.

4. You can view overallocation using the Resource Graph, the Resource Usage, and the Gantt Chart and the Task Usage views in a split window.

5. Some methods for leveling a project manually are linking tasks with the same resource(s) sequentially, assigning a different resource to the task, reducing the amount of time to be spent on the task, changing the amount of units on the resource(s), adding resources to the task, reducing the scope of the task's work, reducing the quality (which usually reduces the amount of work), delaying the start of tasks or the resource's assignment on the task, or splitting a task.

6. Project settings that can affect leveling are task priority, constraints, and actual start date.

7. Leveling settings are Leveling order (ID only, Standard, Priority/Standard), Level on within available slack, Leveling can adjust individual assignments on a task, and Leveling can create splits in remaining work.

8. Project's automatic leveling capability cannot level all overallocations if the task relationships do not allow a delay.

9. You can perform automated leveling for the project and turn off leveling for an individual resource by inserting the Can level column in the Resource Sheet and set it to No for a resource.

10. Clearing leveling helps remove any leveling that might not have been appropriate before you level again.

11. The Gantt Chart Wizard allows you to format the Gantt Chart bars so they show up in red on your Gantt Chart and you can easily review the critical path.

12. Ways to reduce the duration of tasks on the critical path are adding resources, reducing scope, assigning a more knowledgeable resource, breaking a critical task into smaller tasks that can be worked on simultaneously by different resources, reducing the time spent on the task, seeing if you can create some leads on tasks, reducing quality, and revising task dependencies to allow more parallel scheduling.

13. Once done reviewing and correcting your schedule, you should share it with your project team to ensure it still makes sense.

Chapter 10

1. The project baseline is a snapshot in time of your project schedule.

2. Baseline information is stored in the project file. Project has several baseline fields that can store the baseline values.

3. There are 11 baselines available in Project 2003 and Project 2007—the original baseline and 10 others.

4. If you have not baselined, depending on the nature of the field, you might see zeroes or NA in a baseline field.

5. You set the baseline by selecting Tools, Tracking, Set Baseline (called Save Baseline in Project 2002 and Project 2003).

6. The Tracking Gantt view is a good view to see the baseline in the Gantt Chart.

7. You might baseline a task in a project that was already baselined if you have forgotten a task and you started entering actual progress. You might also baseline a task if you have approval to add the task as part of additional project scope.

8. You clear the baseline by selecting Tools, Tracking, Clear Baseline. You might clear the baseline if you have baselined too soon and you need to change the schedule prior to execution.

9. You might view baseline information by using the Tracking Gantt, selecting Table: Work, displaying the Resource Work view in the Task Form in a split window, using the Baseline table, or selecting the Multiple Baselines view.

Chapter 11

1. You should track your schedule to identify delays and issues on your project and to have objective information to analyze and select alternatives for course correction.

2. The major tracking fields are % Complete, % Work Complete, Actual Start and Actual Finish dates, Actual Duration and Remaining Duration, Actual Work, including timephased actual work (day-by-day hours) and Remaining Work, Actual Cost, and Remaining Cost.

3. % Complete indicates progression on the entire task, whereas % Work Complete indicates progression on the individual assignments on the task.

4. Although you do not need to enter Actual Start and Actual Finish dates when tracking, it is a good idea. If you enter % Complete, Project assumes the scheduled Start and Finish dates are the actual dates, so if the actual dates are different than Start or Finish date, you should enter the Actual Start or Actual Finish dates.

5. You need to consider the Remaining Duration or Remaining Work fields when you enter task progress into the schedule because they tell you how much duration or work is estimated to complete the task. If you do not obtain remaining values, you and your team might be making assumptions that your project is on track when it might not be.

6. When you are tracking work effort you can use one of two methods: Actual Hours per Period or Actual Hours each Day.

7. Duration-based tracking is the least detailed and accurate method of tracking progress.

8. Project does not allow you to enter data into the Remaining Cost field.

9. You can't enter data into the Actual Cost field when tracking because, by default, Project has a setting that allows only Project to calculate Actual Cost. You can change the default by selecting Tools from the menu bar, then clicking Options. On the Calculation tab, you can clear the Actual costs are calculated if the Actual costs are always calculated by Microsoft Office Project check box.

10. If you have a prorated accrual method, Project will enter Actual Costs distributed evenly over the time period of the task as actual progress is entered.

11. The Status date is a date you can set to indicate the time frame of the data of the project progress. If your schedule's data should reflect updates only through a particular date, use the status date to indicate it. The current date is used as the Status date for progress if you do not enter a value in the Status date field.

12. Methods for entering status data are using the Task Update tool, using the Tracking table and Tracking Gantt view, updating as scheduling (using the Update Project dialog box), or using a custom view.

13. Some duration-based status tracking techniques are entering Actual Start and Actual Finish dates, entering 0 or 100% complete based on

Status date, entering % Complete, or entering Actual Duration and Remaining Duration.

14. Some effort-based status tracking techniques are Actual Work (per period) and daily Actual Work.

15. Some Project reports are Progress, Milestone, Roll-Up, Visual, Standard Project, custom, and using filtering and grouping.

16. Earned value is a method of reporting progress based on planned work and budget to indicate that value is earned for the work accomplished per period based on the progress you've entered into the project.

17. The earned value reports available in Project are Earned Value table, Earned Value Cost Indicators table, Earned Value Schedule Indicators table, and in Project 2007 only, the Earned Value over Time Report (a Visual Report).

18. The best way to preview how Project will print your project schedule is to use the Print current view as a report field option on the Report pane of the Project Guide. It will step you through formatting your report.

Chapter 12

1. Some activities you should include in your schedule for closing are acquiring formal acceptance, filing all of the project documents, conducting a lessons-learned session, and tidying up the project schedule.

2. To close your schedule, you need to zero out the Remaining Work or Duration for all tasks, change all milestones to 100%, and add notes to tasks describing variance or issues on tasks.

3. You can add information about lessons learned on the project summary task as a note.

4. Some things to look for when cleaning up a template based on a previous project are to ensure the data in the Project Information dialog box is updated, clean up notes, remove constraints, clean up resources on the Resource Sheet, and remove any of the hidden data that might still be in the template (e.g., hyperlinks).

Chapter 13

1. You can format Gantt Chart bars by setting individual bars via the Format bar, set all or particular bars in your project via Bar styles, and use the Gantt Chart Wizard (for quick and nonpersistent formatting needs).

2. You can change the gridlines, layout (date format or height of bars), the way the nonworking time displays, and the timescale in the Gantt Chart.

3. You would change the text format for all milestone tasks by selecting Format, and clicking Text styles. The drop-down list after the Item to change field will show Milestones, you would select it, and then you could change the format using options in the dialog box.

4. The four Project Guide panels are Tasks, Resources, Track, and Report.

5. The two selections on the Project Guide that help you track your project are Prepare to track the progress of your project from the Track panel and Check the progress of the project from the Track panel.

6. The Progress against baseline work, See the project's critical tasks, and See how resources' time is allocated selections help you analyze and track your schedule in the Report pane of the Project Guide.

7. You can show other functions available in Project in toolbars by selecting View from the menu bar, then clicking Toolbars.

8. Hovering the cursor over fields or toolbar buttons reveals hyperlinks or tool tips to provide more information about the field or button.

9. Yes, you can use the mouse to manipulate taskbars on the Gantt Chart bars. For instance, if you want to link two tasks, you can click the first task in the Gantt Chart, hold down your cursor, and drag it to the second taskbar.

10. You open the Options dialog box by selecting Tools from the menu bar, then clicking Options. The Options dialog box has many tabs that contain settings and flags that affect the behavior and display of Project.

11. The View tab of the Options dialog box allows you to show the project summary task when you select the Show project summary task check box.

12. The Autolink inserted or moved tasks check box on the Schedule tab either links a new task or moved tasks to the task before or after it

(when it is checked), or places the new or moved task to the beginning of the project unlinked (if the check box is not selected).

13. You can look for more information about Project by using a search engine and typing in keywords to find help, joining the Microsoft Project Association, linking to the home page of Microsoft Project, Project newsgroups, and the Project Help File or the Project Guide.

Glossary

accrual

Method you can set to indicate when Project should charge the planned cost and when the actual cost is booked. Project has three methods: Start, which charges and books the costs at the start of a task; Prorated, which charges and books the costs evenly over the length of the task; and End, which charges and books the costs at the completion of the task.

assignment

A particular resource added to perform work on a particular task. One resource can have multiple assignments. Assignment is one of three categories in the Project data structure besides resource and task. The Resource Usage and Task Usage views are assignment views that allow you to see detailed information about resources' assignments on tasks.

availability

Amount of time a resource is available to work during a particular time frame. Availability is based on several things: the resource's calendar, how much he or she can be assigned to a project (Maximum Units in the Resource Sheet), and how much he or she is assigned to a particular task. Once assigned to tasks, the resource's availability is reduced by the amount of work he or she is assigned.

baseline

A baseline provides a point in time for you to compare your plans against what is actually happening during project execution. The schedule baseline is a copy of the tasks that must be completed to execute the project on time. In Project, it is a snapshot of your schedule or particular tasks at a particular time. A baseline sets your original plan so that you can track progress when you start executing the plan.

bottom-up estimating

An estimating technique in which the smallest task of a project is estimated.

budget

The budget is an amount of money that covers the entire cost of the project. In Project you can use a budget resource to indicate the planned work or cost expenditures for a project.

budget resource

A designation for a resource to indicate a planned expenditure in your project schedule. Project has two kinds of budget resources: cost and work. Budget resources can only be assigned at the zero project summary task to indicate overall planned expenditures on the project.

calendar

Used to schedule the available time for work on a project. Project allows three kinds of calendars: project, resource, and task. The project calendar schedules tasks, the resource calendar defines the time a resource is available for work, and a task calendar can be attached to an individual task to override the project calendar to indicate work time for the task.

closing

The process of gaining formal acceptance of the product of your project, archiving project files, and conducting a lessons-learned session with the project team. In Project you will also zero out all remaining work in your schedule, and include notes on variances and other issues to keep in the project file.

constraint

In the broadest sense of a project, a constraint is anything that limits your project. In Project, constraint has a special meaning applied to dates. Constraints are specific dates applied to tasks to limit their start or finish. Project has eight particular constraints: As late as possible, As soon as possible, Start no earlier than, Finish no earlier than, Start no later than, Finish no later than, Must finish on, and Must start on.

contingency

Time or cost extras that can be included in your schedule to help take care of unforeseen issues on the project.

cost

Scheduled cost of any entity within Project, depending on what you are viewing. Task cost is the cost of the amount of resources and their rates multiplied by the work hours on a task (including overtime, cost resources, and fixed costs). Resource cost is the total amount of work on all tasks times the resource rates. The Cost field is the scheduled or projected cost, and can change as actual progress is entered into your schedule. The formula for cost is: Cost = Actual cost + Remaining cost.

cost resource

A new type of resource in Project 2007, which indicates a resource that can be added to a task to track items such as travel, lodging, and so on. The cost resource is not dependent on the amount of work or duration of a task like a work resource.

crashing

A schedule compression method that reduces the overall duration of a task for the least cost.

critical path

The critical path is the series of tasks with no delay that must be accomplished to meet the end date of the project. If the duration of any task on that path changes, the end data of the project will change. In Project, you create the critical path by sequencing all tasks in the order in which they should be completed using task relationships and linking.

custom field

Fields in Project that allow you display resource, task, or assignment data specific to you or your organization that are not already available in Project. Project contains Cost, Date, Duration, Finish, Flag, Number, Outline Code, Start, and Text custom fields that allow you to enter formulas, indicators, or values for your own or your organization's particular needs.

deadline

A field available in Project that allows you to indicate the date a task must be completed. Project displays a warning icon if the date will be missed. Use the Deadline date rather than typing in a Finish date or using a constraint on a task when building your schedule.

duration

The span of time on a task from the Start date to the Finish date, which includes only the time that is active (excluding weekends if weekends are not available to be scheduled). You cannot change the duration for a summary task, because it is the sum of its subtask's durations.

Keep these formulas for duration in mind:
Finish date – Start date = Duration
Actual duration + Remaining duration = Duration

duration-based scheduling

A form of estimating and scheduling task durations only, without regard to the effort (work) or number of people assigned.

earned value technique

The earned value technique is another way of measuring work performance and comparing it to what was planned. Earned value gives you the opportunity to look at both the variance of the schedule and cost variance in the same analysis. Project contains the following tables for viewing earned value information for your project: Earned Value table, Earned Value Cost Indicators table, Earned Value Schedule Indicators table, and in Project 2007 only, the Earned Value over Time report (a Visual Report).

effort-based scheduling

A form of estimating and scheduling work, resources, and duration so that the tasks address the full effort of the work. It is a more discrete form of estimating and scheduling and is generally more accurate than duration-based scheduling.

effort driven

A designation for tasks in Project indicating that a task's work can be shared among the assigned resources but the value of the work remains at its current value.

estimate

Expected amount of work or duration it will take to complete a task.

estimate to complete (ETC)

Remaining duration or work left to complete a task. This concept is very important as you track the progress of your project tasks during execution.

fast tracking

A schedule compression method that overlaps activities to shorten the overall duration of the project.

filter

A feature that allows you to display only the tasks or resources that apply to the kind of information you specify. For instance, in the Gantt Chart you can select to filter by tasks assigned to Joe, and only those tasks that Joe is assigned will display.

finish date

Date the task is scheduled or projected to complete. As actual progress is entered into the schedule, this date can change, based on the duration of the project. If you want to see the original estimated date for task completion, you need to baseline your schedule.

fixed cost

Any nonresource expense on a task. Project 2007 provides another way to indicate nonresource costs, called a cost resource.

fixed duration

A task type that affects how Project schedules the task to indicate that you want the task to complete within the duration you enter. The value you enter in the Duration field for the task will not change, whether you change the work or the number of resources working on the task based on the formula Work = Duration × Units (amount of a resource).

fixed units

A task type that affects how Project schedules the task to indicate that you want the amount of resource units on the task to remain what you enter if Work or Duration changes. The Units (percentage) value of a resource you enter when assigning the resource to a task does not change, whether you change the Work or the Duration based on the formula Work = Duration × Units (amount of a resource).

fixed work

A task type that affects how Project schedules the task to indicate that you want the task to complete using the work value you enter. The value you enter in the Work field for the task will not change, whether you change the Duration or the number of resources working on the task based on the formula Work = Duration × Units (amount of a resource).

Gantt Chart

The default Project interface for entering and reviewing project schedule data. The table on the left shows text task information, and the chart on the right shows the visual representation of the data in Gantt format.

generic resources

Resources that represent a position or skill. For instance, Business Analyst is a generic resource.

Global.mpt

A special file in Project that contains the default settings for views, tables, calendars, and other Project objects. You can move new settings for the objects to be shared by other Project files by using the Organizer.

grouping

A method to categorize tasks or resources with a particular characteristic. For instance, you could select to group all tasks that are milestones. Tasks that are not milestones would display as another group.

lag

A delay in the start of a successor task.

lead

Allows the successor task to start prior to the finish of its predecessor task. In Project, a lead is entered as a negative lag.

lessons learned

A fundamental process that you put into place when you want to improve your work and the work of your organization. In this technique you are looking for the processes, tools, and techniques that worked well on the project as well as the processes, tools, and techniques that need improvement.

leveling

A technique to smooth out an overallocated resource's workload. Project has an automated leveling feature that can delay or split tasks to reschedule a resource's work. For instance, you can perform manual leveling by reducing the scope or quality of the work (and reduce the time frame required), change linking, assign a different resource to the task, or change the percentage of time the resource can spend on the task.

linking tasks

In Project, the way you indicate a task relationship between tasks.

master project

A project with subprojects inserted in a master file.

material resources

A type of resource assigned to a task that can be consumed in completing the task. An example of a material resource is gas, which would be measured in liters.

maximum units

The total capacity of resource that is available to be assigned to tasks on a project. You can assign Maximum Units on the Resource Sheet of the project. As an example, if you indicate 50%, the resource is available to work half time. If the resource is available 500%, it indicates you have five resources available to work on the task.

milestone

Special events, deliverables, or approval points in a Project schedule that help you gauge where you are when you start tracking your schedule.

overallocation
>An indication that a resource is scheduled for more work in a day than he or she is available for based on his or her resource calendar and the maximum units allowed.

Organizer
>A feature in Project that allows you to share Project objects (e.g., default or custom views, tables, or calendars) with other Project files.

predecessor
>A task that is completed before another task.

project
>A project is a unique endeavor that has a beginning and an end.

project plan
>A project plan is a road map that provides the context for the project. In it you will document your thoughts and actions for every aspect of the planning you are about to undertake. You will also provide information on how you will execute the plan as well as how you monitor and control the plan.

priority
>In Project, a way to indicate if resources on a project or task can be leveled. Priority is set at 0 to 1,000 and the highest priority tasks or projects are leveled last or not at all.

project charter
>A document that provides you authorization to proceed with the work of your project and includes information about the project, such as its driver and purpose, high-level requirements, major dates, an estimated budget, and other important information.

remaining duration or work
>Amount of duration or work still required to complete the task. See estimate to complete.

reserve
>An amount of money that is set aside as part of the budget but is only used for specific types of situations.

resources
>People, equipment, supplies, materials, or other items that help ensure a task is completed.

resource calendar

Defines the hours and days available for a resource to perform work on project. The Standard calendar is assigned to each resource by default (Monday–Friday, 8 hours each day), but exceptions and other calendars (e.g., 10 × 4) could be assigned to the resource.

resource sharing

An .mpp file that contains resources entered on the Resource Sheet to be shared among many projects. The file that that is shared is called the resource pool. The resource pool is all the resources that can be assigned within the organization for project work in an enterprise environment .

Resource Sheet

A Project interface that allows entry and review of project resources and their attributes.

Resource Usage

A Project interface that allows you to see timephased data for each resource with the tasks they are assigned listed below.

risk management

Identification, analysis, and monitoring of risk throughout the project life cycle. Risk management is a technique that you can use to identify risk contingencies or opportunity enhancements that you can incorporate into your schedule.

schedule compression

A term used in project management to describe activities that you perform to reduce the duration of your project.

scheduling engine

The set of formulas, flags, and settings in Project that affect the behavior of your schedule.

scope

All the expected deliverables to fulfill the work of the project.

slack

The amount of delay or slip a task has before it affects a dependent task or is moved to the critical path to affect the project's finish date.

Split Window

In Project, a way to view different project information in the lower pane of a project interface. When you choose to split the window in the Gantt

Chart view, the bottom pane displayed is the Task Form, which provides more information about the task.

standard rate

Rate applied when a resource is assigned to a task, based on the number of hours (or other unit of time) estimated for the work.

start date

Scheduled date the task or project will start.

status date

The date set to indicate the time frame to reflect the actual values entered in Project. The current date is the status date if no date is entered in the Status date field.

successor

A task that is started after another task.

table

An interface in Project that exposes a set of columns to describe data about tasks or resources in a view.

task relationship

Also known as dependency; a dependency between two tasks to indicate the relationship of the finish and start dates based on the flow of work to be performed. The four task dependencies are Finish-to-Start (FS), Start-to-Start (SS), Finish-to-Finish (FF), and Start-to-Finish (SF).

task type

An attribute of a task that defines if the Work, Duration, or Units values are fixed to ensure no variability for the value entered based on the formula Work = Duration × Units.

Task Usage

A Project interface that allows you to see timephased data for each task in the Project schedule, with each assigned resource's timephased data displaying for each task.

template

A special project file (designated by the .mpt extension) that can be reused by other project managers. The template is accessed via the Templates dialog box in Project and can be opened and used repeatedly as a start for a project file. This is different than the Global.mpt file, which holds default and custom settings for project files.

timephased

Project work data distributed over time. You can review task, resource, or assignment data in Resource Usage or Task Usage views.

Tracking Gantt

A Project interface that includes a table of task data on the left side and on the right side graphically displays baseline, critical path, and percentage progression of tasks in the Gantt Chart.

units

Percentage or portion of a resource that is assigned to work on a task or is available for a project. The amount available is based on how much time in a day the resource is available or the quantity of the resource needed (for material resources). If the resource is assigned 100%, it is assigned full time.

variance analysis

A method that analyzes the planned activities against the completed activities that determines if there is any difference.

view

A term Project uses to describe the various interfaces allowing you to review data in Project's data structure.

WBS

See Work breakdown structure.

work

Effort to be performed on a task. This could be total labor on a task, or labor to be performed by a resource for his or her portion on the task.

Work breakdown structure

A hierarchical depiction of the deliverables or activities of the project that covers the total scope of the project's work.

work contour

The way that Project distributes assigned work over time. Contour shapes, for example, are flat, turtle, front-loaded, or back-loaded, among others.

Work formula

A formula that exists in Project: Work = Duration × Units (portion of a resource or resources). Although the formula cannot be disabled in Project, it is influenced by the task type and effort-driven designation you select.

work package

The lowest level of the work component in a branch of the work breakdown structure. The lowest level can include activities, costs, and milestones applied to it.

Index

Symbols

% complete field, 459-460
%Work complete, 460
24-hour calendars, 103

A

accrual methods
  costs, 307, 471
  setting, 326
Actual cost + Remaining cost = Cost, 46
actual cost of work performed (ACWP)
    field, 506
actual costs
  calculating, 307, 469
  editing, 335-337
  field, 466, 505
  setting up, 469-470
actual duration
  field, 462-463
  tracking, 481-482
Actual Duration + Remaining Duration =
    Duration, 463
Actual Duration + Remaining Duration =
    Work, 44-45
Actual finish date field, 461
actual start dates
  field, 461
  resources, leveling, 407
actual value, 40
actual work
  baselines, 436

tracking
  day-by-day, 484-485
  per period, 483-484
Actual work field, 463-466
  daily hours, 465-466
  data, entering
    day-by-day, 484-485
    per period, 483-484
  period hours, 464
Actual Work + Remaining Work =
    Work, 44, 466
actual work time, 16
ACWP (actual cost of work performed)
    field, 506
adding. *See also* setting
  baseline fields, 444
  blank rows, 59
  budgets
    accrual methods, 326
    Fixed costs, 322-323
    overtime costs, 325-326
    resources, 323-325
    work resources, 278-279
  columns, 79
    Resource Sheet view, 243
    views, 26
  constraints to schedules, 419
  contingencies, 380-381
  costs
    examples, 310-311
    labor, 308